RESEARCH IN EDUCATION

A Conceptual Introduction

Second Edition

RESEARCH IN EDUCATION

A Conceptual Introduction

James H. McMillan
Virginia Commonwealth University

Sally Schumacher
Virginia Commonwealth University

Second Edition

Scott, Foresman and Company
Glenview, Illinois   London, England

To Donald T. Campbell and Louis M. Smith

Acknowledgments

We are grateful to the Literary Executor of the late Sir Ronald A. Fisher, F. R. S., to Dr. Frank Yates, F. R. S., and the Longman Group Ltd., London, for permission to reprint from Tables III, IV, VII, and XXXII from their book *Statistical Tables for Biological, Agricultural and Medical Research* (6th Edition, 1974).

The list on pages 267 and 268 was compiled by Gilbert Sax from the following sources: Hyman, H. H. (1954), *Interviewing in social research*, p. 155, Chicago: The University of Chicago Press; Benney, M., Riesman, D., and Star, S. A. (1956), Age and sex in the interview, *The American Journal of Sociology*, 62(2), pp. 143–152; Sheatsley, P. B. (1951), An analysis of interviewer characteristics and their relationship to performance—Part III, *International Journal of Opinion and Attitude Research*, 5(2), pp. 191–220; Cantril, Hadley et al. (1944), *Gauging public opinion*, Princeton, N.J.: Princeton University Press, pp. 114–116; Robinson, D. & Rohde, S. (1946), Two experiments with an anti-Semitism poll, *Journal of Abnormal and Social Psychology*, 41(2), pp. 136–144; Katz D. (1942), Do interviewers bias polls?, *Public Opinion Quarterly*, 6(2), pp. 248–268.

Library of Congress Cataloging-in-Publication Data

McMillan, James H.
    Research in education: a conceptual introduction/James H.
McMillan, Sally Schumacher.—2nd ed.
        p.   cm.
    Bibliography: p.
    Includes index.
    ISBN 0-673-39792-0
    1. Education—Research.   2. Education—Research—Evaluation.
    3. Educational statistics.   I. Schumacher, Sally.   II. Title.
    LB1028.M365   1989
    370'.7'8—dc19
                                                    88-29099
                                                          CIP

ISBN 0-673-39792-0

PREFACE

The increasing use of research as a basis for knowledge about education and for influencing decisions, programs, and policy requires educators to possess research skills. To assist students in attaining skills in reading, conducting, and understanding research, *Research in Education*, Second Edition, presents a comprehensive and accurate, yet relatively nontechnical, introduction to the principles, concepts, and methods currently used in educational research.

Students enrolled in their first educational research course typically have two instructional needs, and this book is designed to meet both of those needs. Some students plan to take additional work in statistics, research design, qualitative methodologies, or evaluation. In addition to mastering the fundamental principles of research, these students also need to develop both an awareness of the breadth of educational research and a broad conceptual base for understanding more technical and advanced aspects of research. Other students, whose immediate career goals lie more in educational practice than in conducting research, need an emphasis on key research terms, practice in reading studies critically, a knowledge of the way design and procedures may affect empirical findings, and an understanding of applied and evaluation research. Because most students intend to use their research skills in practical situations, we explain the importance of basic research but emphasize applied and evaluation research.

■ Rationale ■

Educational research has been strongly influenced by the psychological research paradigm, with an emphasis on designing experiments, doing research with groups of students, testing hypotheses, measurement, and statistics. We believe that educational research is no longer dominated by this quantitative deductive approach and that qualitative methods also contribute significantly to our knowledge of education. Qualitative research, which operates from an inductive research paradigm, focuses on a particular event, person, process, institution, or concept in a case study design. Such studies are noted for their richness of contextual descriptions and inductive analysis to provide an understanding of the phenomenon investigated. Thus, we present a balanced emphasis on quantitative and qualitative designs and methodologies. Our experience has been that by presenting both quantitative and qualitative research and changing one's "lenses" to view education, students gain a deeper understanding, knowledge, and appreciation for each paradigm in educational research.

Although we note that educational research contains studies that combine both quantitative and qualitative approaches, we chose to emphasize the distinctions between the two approaches. Students first need to understand the logic of each approach before moving to more advanced designs that integrate quantitative and qualitative methods.

■ Organization of the Second Edition ■

Those of you familiar with the first edition will note that we have retained the basic organization of the book. You will also note some important additions and revisions and some reorganization of topics. These revisions were prompted by (1) increased articulation of certain qualitative designs and methods, (2) more recent statements of distinctions between quantitative and qualitative research paradigms, and (3) the encouragement of our colleagues to continue in the direction we began in 1984.

We have added new topics and done extensive revision in many chapters. New topics include a broader definition of scientific inquiry and characteristics of research, greater specification of qualitative methodologies in all general chapters, research synthesis and meta-analysis, qualitative design and purposeful sampling, measurement, correlational research, ethnographic interview, legal research, and guidelines for proposals. The changes are reflected in the increase in citations and replacement of over half of the references.

We have divided the second edition into five parts. In the general chapters of Part I, "Fundamental Principles of Educational Research," and Part V, "Communication of Research," we present separate, but parallel, discussions of quantitative and qualitative approaches. In Part II, "Quantitative Research Designs and Methods," and Part III, "Qualitative Research Designs and Methods," each approach is discussed more specifically. Part IV, "Evaluation Research Designs and Methods," presents the application of quantitative and qualitative methods in evaluation research.

More specifically, Part I, "Fundamental Principles of Educational Research," defines research as scientific and disciplined inquiry to produce knowledge. We briefly introduce quantitative and qualitative research and carefully delineate the functions of basic, applied, and evaluation research. We present an overview of research designs, techniques, and formats. Problem selection, formulation, and statement of both quantitative and qualitative problems are discussed and illustrated. The literature review chapter includes descriptions of current sources, techniques for manual and computer searches, guidelines for writing literature reviews in quantitative and qualitative research, and meta-analysis reviews. In designing research, we begin by noting principles that are important for all designs. We then discuss how quantitative and qualitative studies handle in different ways the issues of internal and external validity of designs.

Part II, "Quantitative Research Designs and Methods," begins with descriptive statistics and techniques to collect data with instruments. We present new material on the important topic of measurement and include a new chapter to emphasize descriptive, correlational, and predictive research. We discuss designs for experimental, quasi-experimental, single-subject and *ex post facto* research, and we introduce inferential statistics. The statistical chapters will help both the consumer of research and the researcher develop a conceptual understanding of basic statistical procedures.

Part III, "Qualitative Research Designs and Methods," presents two qualitative methodologies. Ethnographic research is described as using purposeful sampling, multimethod data collection strategies, and inductive data analysis. Analytical research, the study of the past events, includes concept analysis, historical and policy-making research, and legal research. We emphasize the search and criticism of sources. Each chapter concludes with the role of each form of qualitative research in education.

Parts IV and V return to a more general perspective of educational research. Part IV, "Evaluation Research Designs and Methods," describes the purposes and roles of evaluation research. An overview of four approaches to evaluation is followed by procedures to develop an evaluation design and criteria for judging evaluation proposals and reports. Part V, "Communication of Research," notes the various forms of research communication, research writing styles and formats. This part describes formats for quantitative and qualitative research proposals and explains typical criticisms of proposals.

■ Instructional Aids ■

In each chapter we have maintained a number of instructional aids to assist students: a list of key terms, sample self-instructional test items and application problems, and criteria for evaluating studies conducted by different methodologies. We believe the instructor, rather than the book, should determine course objectives and level of student competency. The book has been organized so that the instructor can emphasize general knowledge, certain methodologies, or specific skills, such as making an annotated bibliography on a topic, writing a critical literature review, developing a preliminary proposal with a problem statement and design, or conducting a small-scale study. We have used all four approaches to meet different student and programmatic needs.

A major instructional aid of this book is the use of excerpts from published studies in all chapters except 1 and 14. Excerpts were chosen to illustrate text explanations concisely; to represent different disciplines; and to be applicable to a variety of education practices, such as administration, supervision, instruction, special education, early childhood, counseling, adult education, and programs in noneducational agencies. The excerpts are especially helpful in introducing students gradually to the style and format of published articles.

■ Acknowledgments ■

Because this book resulted from a merging of our specializations as researchers and professors, there is no senior author. Each author contributed equally to the book. Many people contributed to this endeavor. We gratefully acknowledge the support of our colleagues, mentors, and friends, all of whom are too numerous to name. We especially thank our master degree and doctoral candidates who challenged us to be more explicit and the reviewers whose ideas, criticisms, and suggestions helped fashion the book. The reviewers for the first edition were H. Parker Blount, Georgia State University; Alice Boberg, University of Calgary; David J. Cowden, Western Michigan University; Jane A. Goldman, University of Connecticut; Harry Hsu, University of Pittsburgh; Sylvia T. Johnson, Howard University; Stephen Olejnick, University of Florida; and Robert J. Yonker, Bowling Green State University. The reviewers for the second edition were Gerald W. Bracey, Cherry Creek Schools, Colorado; Jane A. Goldman, University of Connecticut; Harry Hsu, University of Pittsburgh; and Herman W. Meyers, University of Vermont.

We recognize that much of the instructional organization of this edition is relatively new. We appreciate comments and suggestions from colleagues and students as we gather material for the third edition.

We sincerely appreciate the guidance and support of our editor, Christopher Jennison, our associate project editor, Roberta Casey, and others at Scott, Foresman. Sue Goins and Merrill Rippley were our capable typists for the text. Janet Dooley did the typing for the Instructor's Manual for both editions. Finally, our families, Mrs. F. X. Schumacher, Donald F. X. and Marcia Schumacher, and Janice McMillan, have provided continued encouragement for this exciting, if at times difficult, undertaking.

James H. McMillan
Sally Schumacher

BRIEF CONTENTS

CONTENTS

CHAPTER 5   INTRODUCTION TO DESIGNING RESEARCH   *157*

PART IV
EVALUATION RESEARCH DESIGNS
AND METHODS   471

CHAPTER 13   EVALUATION RESEARCH   472

RESEARCH IN EDUCATION

A Conceptual Introduction

Second Edition

PART I

FUNDAMENTAL PRINCIPLES
OF EDUCATIONAL RESEARCH

What is research? Educators unfamiliar with scientific methods frequently ask this question. They may also ask: Why is research considered more useful in making decisions than experience or the advice of others? How does research influence educational practices? What kinds of studies are done in education? Is there a simple way to understand a research article?

Chapters 1 and 2 answer these questions by providing an introduction to the field of educational research, an overview of designs and methodologies, and the format of quantitative and qualitative research journal articles. This introduction will familiarize the reader with basic terminology and fundamental concepts of research.

All research begins with a problem statement and usually involves a literature review. Chapters 3 and 4 help one to recognize and state a research problem. How is a problem stated in order to be useful in planning a study? What should a problem statement convey to a reader? How are problem statements evaluated? Why is a literature review important? What are the sources for a literature review? How does one conduct a manual or a computer search of the literature? How is a literature review evaluated?

We present the fundamentals of planning quantitative and qualitative studies in Chapter 5. How are subjects selected? What are the potential biases and limitations researchers need to know about before conducting a study or when reading research? How are instruments selected? What about instrument validity and reliability? How does choice of an instrument affect the results? What kind of designs do qualitative studies use? How is a qualitative study conducted? How do qualitative researchers establish accuracy and credibility during the research process? How do qualitative researchers minimize bias?

Together, these five chapters present basic principles of research that are necessary for a student to understand when conducting, reading, and analyzing different types of research and methodologies. Subsequent parts will discuss in greater detail the procedures for specific methodologies.

CHAPTER 1

INTRODUCTION TO THE FIELD OF EDUCATIONAL RESEARCH

■ KEY TERMS ■

replication
research synthesis
science
theory
scientific inquiry
scientific method
research
research methods
disciplined inquiry
objectivity
verification
explanation
empirical
data

deductive reasoning
inductive reasoning
hypothetic-deductive
    approach
empirico-inductive
    approach
quantitative research
qualitative research
generalizability
basic research
scientific law
applied research
evaluation research

Educational research has gradually affected most of our ideas about education and the practices we use to achieve our objectives in education. Yet many excellent teachers and administrators know little about educational research and assume that research has had no effect on their daily activities. Practitioners may also assume that research cannot be useful in program planning and development.

Educational research is scientific and disciplined inquiry using quantitative and qualitative approaches. Educators and others use basic, applied, and evaluation research for different purposes. This chapter introduces you to the field of educational research, including its contributions and limitations, by describing how research results are used to improve educational practices. Most important, we introduce the language and logic of research used in reading and conducting studies.

■ SOURCES OF KNOWLEDGE ABOUT EDUCATION ■

Educators are constantly trying to understand educational processes and must make professional decisions that have immediate and long-range effects on others: students, teachers, parents, and, ultimately, our communities and nation. How do educators acquire an understanding to make decisions? Furthermore, noneducational groups, such as state legislatures, the United States Congress, and the federal courts, have increasingly mandated changes in education. How do noneducators acquire their views of education and obtain their information about schools and instruction?

Sources of Knowledge

Information for understanding education and for making educational decisions comes from many sources. Most of us tend to rely on several sources, including personal experience, expert opinion, tradition, intuition, common sense, and beliefs about what is right or wrong. Each of these sources is legitimate in some situations and yet, in other situations, each source may be inadequate as the only basis for making decisions. The past experience of others or personal experience may be inappropriate for new problems. Experts or authorities may be distant from the realities and complexities of a particular situation. Tradition is useful as long as it is not based on a notion of an idealized past. Intuition may be subject to bias. Logic can be based on false premises. In a nation or community of cultural pluralism, determining what is "right" may be difficult.

Another source of information, research, has been used increasingly in order to make decisions. Because research systematically describes or measures reality, it is a better source of knowledge than one's own experience, beliefs, or intuition alone. Some studies are abstract and provide general information about a common educational practice. This type of research influences the way one thinks about education. Some studies provide detailed information about a specific practice at a particular site, such as a school, a classroom, or a program. This type of research can be used immediately in planning, developing, improving, or adopting a specific practice for widespread usage.

Development of Knowledge to Improve Educational Practices

Why has research become a valuable source of information and knowledge in education? First, research and scientific knowledge have been important in other fields for many years. Research in agriculture and in medicine has led to increased food production and improved health practices. Educators and policy-makers expected similar effects if educational research increased and the results were widely disseminated. In 1968 fewer than 2,000 persons were engaged in full-time

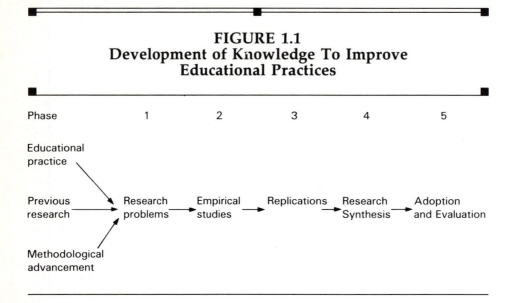

FIGURE 1.1
Development of Knowledge To Improve
Educational Practices

educational research supported by public and private funds. In the same year, 15,000 researchers investigated agricultural productivity and 60,000 persons worked in research and development in the health sciences. The Department of Education, the National Science Foundation, the National Foundation for the Arts and Humanities, and other private and public agencies provide funding for educational research. These monies are not as extensive as those provided for medical research or in other fields; however, educational research continues to be valued and supported in other ways.

Second, educational research makes contributions to knowledge about education and educational practices. The impact of educational research on schools and policymakers seeking to improve educational practices may be seen as a process (Walberg, 1986). Figure 1.1 shows five phases of the process to develop educational knowledge to improve practices. These phases are: 1) identification of research problems, 2) empirical studies, 3) replications, 4) research synthesis and reviews, and 5) practitioner adoption and evaluation.

Research problems (Phase 1) begin with an identification of valued outcomes. Practical fields, like education, are concerned with valued outcomes such as learning. Research questions and problems come from the following sources: common observation, practical wisdom, policy controversies, prior research, and new methodological techniques applied in the study of education. Researchers conduct empirical studies (Phase 2), and then they attempt **replications**[1] (Phase 3) with different subjects and in a variety of settings and circumstances. Exact replication studies by subsequent investigators, although often attempted and highly desired, are rare in education. **Research synthesis** and reviews (Phase 4) systematically evaluate and statistically or narratively summarize comparable

[1]Terms printed in **boldface** type are defined in the Glossary.

studies. Such an analysis helps to organize and make sense of the overall findings of prior research. Thus, the preponderance of evidence from many careful studies, rather than a few exact replications of the original research, builds a research-based knowledge in education. Practitioners and policymakers can reasonably accept the implications of research findings that are consistent, "that are effective considering total costs, and that are without harmful side effects" (Walberg, 1986, p. 215). Continuing local evaluation (Phase 5) is still needed.

Third, reviews of recent research identified some notable findings that have definite policy and practical implications (Walberg, Schiller, & Haertel, 1979). For example, 87 to 100 percent of selected studies on psychological incentives and engagement in learning indicate that teacher cues to students, teacher reinforcement of students, teacher engagement of a class in a lesson, and individual student engagement in a lesson have positive effects on student achievement. Whereas, only 6 to 14 percent of the studies of favoritism, disorganization, apathy, cliqueness, and friction in the social-psychological classroom climate indicate positive effects on achievement. Studies on lecture versus discussion suggest different effects on different outcomes. Sixty-eight percent of the studies showed positive effects on achievement; 100 percent of the studies showed positive effects on retention; and 86 percent of the studies showed positive effects on attitudes. It is likely that these findings will be confirmed by more comprehensive and explicit research synthesis techniques that are now being developed (See Chapter 4).[2]

Narrative reviews of research, a different type of research review, can suggest major generalizations as hypotheses for future empirical studies. For example, Miskel and Cosgrove (1985) reviewed over sixty qualitative and quantitative studies on leader succession in school settings and identified fourteen generalizations which have been partially verified. Some of these are:

— The reasons for administrator succession create different levels of instability in school organizations.
— The composition of the administrator selection committees and the methods they use relate to the amount of change that accompany succession events.
— Administrators chosen from outside the school or district produce more change and instability in schools than those selected from inside.
— Superintendent successions have greater educational effects than principal successions.
— When the perceptions of leader behavior are widely shared, successions in schools occur with fewer negative disruptions.
— Inside and outside successors possess different orientations toward their careers, professional personnel, educational programs, and needed changes.
— Outsiders and insiders are given different mandates for changing schools.
— Community factors limit the amount of influence that new leaders have in initiating school changes.

[2]See J. Walberg, (1986), "Synthesis of research on teaching," in M. Wittrock (Ed.), *Handbook of research on teaching, Third edition*, (pp. 214–229), for a summary of the results from a number of research syntheses conducted in the 1980s.

Other research reviews identify areas of needed research. A leading scholar in teaching and learning, Lee S. Shulman (1987), suggests that there are at least four major sources for the teaching knowledge base of classroom teachers. These include: (1) scholarship in content disciplines, (2) the materials and settings of the institutionalized educational process (for example, curricula, textbooks, school organizations and finance, and structure of the teaching profession), (3) research on schooling, social organizations, human learning, teaching and development, and the other social and cultural phenomena that affect what teachers can do, and (4) the wisdom of practice itself. The wisdom of practice itself, the maxims that guide and provide reflective rationalization for the practices of able teachers, is the least codified area of educational knowledge. Shulman's general views might also apply to administrators, school counselors, librarians, reading specialists, and other professionals involved in education.

Furthermore, many educators who are not full-time researchers read research and conduct studies to plan and develop new programs, to improve educational practices, to assess learning, and to allocate resources to meet changing conditions and needs in their own settings. Increasingly, reliable information has become a necessity in a complex technical society. Research provides valid information and knowledge about education in order to make decisions. The research process suggests principles to guide educators in wise decision-making.

■ RESEARCH AS SCIENTIFIC AND ■ DISCIPLINED INQUIRY

Research is a relatively new activity in the history of education, just as free public schools for all children is a relatively recent notion in the history of mankind. Yet, in the early centuries before reading and writing were common, individuals developed knowledge of the world around them through personal experiences and observations of others' experiences. They then passed their knowledge to the next generation in the form of storytelling. They conveyed their collective wisdom as a series of detailed descriptions of individuals and events in particular situations and contexts. No one expected these stories to predict one's future actions, because actions depended on perceptions and feelings about a situation. Life was tenuous and hazardous in those times. Stories, however, provided an understanding, a repertoire of wisdom from which a person could *extrapolate* or *extend* known experience into an unknown area so as to arrive at a useful conjecture or image of the future.

Knowledge was also developed in another manner—human activities were measured with numbers. The early units of measure and scales had very practical purposes: to measure in a consistent, reliable manner the length of a day, the distance one walked, or the amount of space in an area. By having the same units of measure stand for the same meaning, one did not need to know the descriptive contextual details of the measured activity. A mile was a mile whether it was on flat soft sand or a rocky terrain. A foot was twelve inches whether it measured the height of a person, the length of an animal's skin, or the interior of a hut. If these measurements were reliable, one could measure segments of those natural laws which caused events to be orderly and predictable.

There are different kinds of knowledge needed about education and many types of research conducted in education to develop this knowledge. Educational research has been called scientific inquiry and disciplined inquiry (social science). Both views are included in our definition of research and the characteristics of research in education.

Scientific Inquiry

The ultimate aim of **science** is the generation and verification of theory. A **theory** predicts and explains natural phenomena. Instead of explaining each and every separate behavior of adolescents, for example, the scientist seeks general explanations which link together different behaviors. Similarly, instead of trying to explain adolescents' methods of solving mathematic problems, the scientist seeks general explanations of all kinds in problem-solving.

A noted scholar, Fred N. Kerlinger (1986), defines theory as a set of interrelated constructs and propositions that specify relations among variables to explain and predict phenomena. This definition indicates three things about a general theory. First, a theory is a set of propositions consisting of defined constructs. Second, a theory states the interrelations among a set of variables. Third, theory explains phenomena. By explaining which variables relate to which other variables and how they relate, a scientist can predict from certain variables to certain other variables. If one can predict from variable A (test anxiety, for example) to variable B (test performance), then one can deduce the possibility of "control" through intervention with, say, instruction on test-taking skills.

Much valuable social science research is *not* specifically theory-oriented. Instead, this research concentrates on the shorter-range goals of finding specific relations. The most useful and valued relations, however, are those that are most generalized, those that are tied to other relations of a theory. Specific relations (such as test anxiety relating to test performance), although interesting and important, are less widely applicable than if one found the relations in a "network of interrelated variables that are parts of a theory" (Kerlinger, 1986, p. 10). Modest, limited, and specific aims are good, but theory formulation and verification are better because they are more general and explanatory.

Theory generation and verification are central to scientific inquiry. A theory, to be useful in the development of scientific knowledge, must meet certain criteria. First, a theory should provide a simple explanation of the observed relations relevant to a particular problem. Second, a theory should be consistent with both the observed relations and an already established body of knowledge. A theoretical statement is the most efficient and probable account of the evidence accumulated through prior research. Third, a theory is considered a tentative explanation and should provide means for verification and revision. Fourth, a theory should stimulate further research in areas which need investigation. Careful analysis of a theory and its empirical support can suggest relations to be studied in subsequent research.

A scientist values the empirical approach for "its manner of exposing to falsification, in every conceivable way, the system to be tested" (Popper, 1959, p. 42). The purpose is not to promote false knowledge, but to select that which is most accurate and reliable by exposing competing theories to empirical testing. Scientific inquiry, thus, contrasts sharply to other ways of arriving at valid and trustworthy knowledge.

Scientific inquiry is the search for knowledge by using recognized methods in data collection, analysis, and interpretation. The term "scientific" refers to an approach and is not synonymous with science. Science is a body of established knowledge, whereas "scientific" refers to the way the knowledge was generated. The scientific method is usually a sequential research process. The typical steps in the **scientific method** are:

1. Define a problem.
2. State the hypothesis to be tested.
3. Collect and analyze data.
4. Interpret the results and draw conclusions about the problem.

Scientific inquiry is simply an approach to developing valid and trustworthy knowledge.

Research Defined

Briefly defined, **research** is a systematic process of collecting and logically analyzing information (data) for some purpose. This definition is general because there are many methods available to investigate a problem or question. Educational research is not limited to the approaches used in the physical and natural sciences, nor should the word "research" be used indiscriminately to describe what is actually casual observation and speculation. **Research methods** (sometimes called "methodology") are the ways one collects and analyzes data. These methods were developed for acquiring knowledge by reliable and trustworthy procedures. Data collection may be done with measurement techniques, extensive interviews and observations, or a collection of documents.

Research methodology is systematic and purposeful. Procedures are not haphazard activities; they are planned to yield data on a particular research problem. In a broader context, methodology refers to a design whereby the researcher selects data collection and analysis procedures to investigate a specific research problem. It is possible to have a design that provides no valid or reliable data on the problem, but the deliberate choice of a design increases the likelihood that the data will yield information on the research question.

Educational Research as
Disciplined Inquiry

When we speak of research in education, we refer to a family of methods which share the characteristics of disciplined inquiry. **Disciplined inquiry,** unlike opinion and belief, "is conducted and reported in such a way that the argument can be examined painstakingly. The report does not depend for its appeal on the eloquence of the writer or any surface plausibility" (Cronbach & Supples, 1969, p. 15). "Disciplined" does not refer to ritualization and narrow forms of investigation nor necessarily following well-established, formal procedures. Some of the most excellent inquiry is speculative in its initial stages, trying out combinations of ideas and procedures or restlessly casting about for ideas. Cronbach and Supples (1969, pp. 15–16) further suggest:

> Whatever the character of a study, if it is disciplined the investigator has anticipated the traditional questions that are pertinent. He institutes control at each step of information collection and reasoning to avoid the sources of error to which these questions refer. If the errors cannot be eliminated, he takes them into account by discussing the margin for error in his conclusions. Thus, the report of a disciplined inquiry has a texture that displays the raw materials entering the argument and the logical processes by which they were compressed and rearranged to make the conclusion credible.

L. S. Shulman (1981) notes that educational researchers debate about appropriate research methods to study education for several reasons. First, educational inquiry demands the selection of a particular set of measured observations or facts from infinite possibilities. After all, educational institutions and practices are abundant in the American society. Just as in a court of law where legal adversaries may disagree profoundly about the relevance of a piece of evidence or the correctness of the verdict drawn from reasoning with the evidence, so it is in a disciplined inquiry in education. There is often lack of consensus about the data or evidence and/or the chains of reasoning.

Second, disciplined inquiry not only refers to a systematic investigation, it also refers to the disciplines themselves. Disciplines such as psychology, sociology, history, political science, anthropology, and others serve as sources for principles of research and for the canons of evidence (data) used by the investigator. Research principles are different in the different disciplines.

Third, the major reason why research methodology is an exciting area in education is that education is not itself a science or a discipline. Education is a field of inquiry where the phenomena, events, people, processes, and institutions constitute the raw materials for inquiries of many kinds. The perspectives and research methods of many disciplines can be brought to bear on the questions arising from education and inherent in education.

The Characteristics of Educational Research

The following characteristics are common to many types of research conducted in education: objective, precise, verifiable, explanatory, empirical, logical, and probabilistic. Taken together, these seven characteristics describe the nature of research.

1. *Objectivity.* Objectivity is both a procedure and a characteristic. To the lay person, objectivity means unbiased, open-minded, not subjective. As a procedure, **objectivity** refers to data collection and analysis procedures from which only one meaning or interpretation can be made. Standardized tests in education are objective, for example, because several people, given the instructions, can score the same test and get the same score. Objectivity in qualitative (nonstatistical) research means explicitness in the way the data were collected, categorized, reconstructed, and interpreted. Objectivity thus refers to the quality of the data produced by the procedures for collecting and analyzing data and not the researcher's personal characteristics (Scriven, 1972).

The importance of objectivity is broader and pervades the entire research process. Exact descriptions of research procedures allow other researchers to replicate a study. This is done more easily in a controlled laboratory situation with measurements made by machines of high reliability and precision. Educational research is seldom conducted in a laboratory, and it involves the study of human beings. Although objectivity is important in all research, it is more difficult in research on humans.

2. *Precision.* Research uses a technical language. Technical research language is employed not to confuse the reader but to convey exact meanings. The concepts of classroom atmosphere, leadership, creativity, or student engagement have precise meanings in research that may differ from conventional meanings. Such expressions as *validity* and *reliability* in measurement, *research design, random sample,* and *statistical significance* convey technical procedures. The most precise expression in quantitative research is a mathematical equation or statistical finding. Precision in qualitative research is achieved through words rather than numbers. Precision is expressed by extensive and detailed descriptions in order to convey subtle connotations and meanings. Precise language describes the study accurately so that the study may be replicated or extended and the results may be used correctly.

Precision in research also refers to precise measurement. In studies which use instruments such as tests, rating scales, observation schedules, or closed-response questionnaires and interviews, precise measurement is crucial. Precise measurement in these studies refers to instrument validity and reliability.

3. *Verification.* To develop knowledge, a single study attempts to be designed and presented in such a manner to allow **verification**—the results can be confirmed or revised in subsequent research. Results can be verified in different ways, depending on the purpose of the original study. If the research tests a theory, then further testing with other groups or in other settings could confirm or revise the theory. If the study is a qualitative exploratory research to propose the-

ory, then the proposed theory could be verified with designs using quantitative approaches. Some qualitative studies, however, provide descriptive understandings about relatively unique situations, and these insights or understandings are extended, but not replicated, in subsequent research of other situations or historical eras for revision or confirmation. Qualitative research is not verified in the same manner as quantitative research.

The characteristic of verification or extension also refers to sharing the results of the study. Research is a social enterprise, and its information is presented to the professional community for public scrutiny. Through this process, researchers develop a body of knowledge and identify new research questions.

4. *Parsimonious explanation.* Research attempts to explain relationships among phenomena and to reduce the **explanation** to simple statements. The theory "frustration leads to aggression" is an explanation that predicts, and it can be tested for verification. The generalization "the cumulative effect of complex events, rather than a single leader, causes wars" is an explanation that can be investigated further. The ultimate aim of research is thus to reduce complex realities to simple explanations.

5. *Empiricism.* Research is characterized by a strong empirical attitude and approach. The word *empirical* has lay and technical meanings. The lay meaning of *empirical* is that which is guided by practical experience, not by research. This pragmatic perspective states that if it works, it is right; regardless of the reasons, it must be right because it works. To the researcher, **empirical** means guided by evidence obtained from systematic research methods rather than by opinions or authorities. Empiricism and an empirical attitude require a temporary suspension of personal experience and beliefs. Critical elements in research are evidence and logical interpretations based on the evidence.

To a researcher, evidence is **data,** meaning it is results obtained from research from which interpretations or conclusions are drawn. In a general sense, the terms *data, sources,* and *evidence* are used synonymously, meaning information obtained by research methods. Test scores and computer printouts, observation notes and interview records, historical documents and judicial rulings are all called data. Researchers may say, "the data indicate that children with low reading ability tend to achieve less in school." By this they mean that the relationship between some type of reading ability scores and school achievement indicators warrant making this interpretation.

6. *Logical reasoning.* All research requires logical reasoning. Reasoning is a thinking process, using prescribed rules of logic, in which one proceeds from a general statement to the specific conclusion (deduction) or, the reverse, from specific statements to a generalization (induction). For example, one might reason deductively by saying:

Example: A — All living organisms breathe.
　　　　　　B — Breathing organisms die.
　　　　　　C — Dogs are breathing organisms.
　　　　　　D — Dogs die.

In **deductive reasoning,** if the premises (A, B, and C) are correct, then the conclusion (D) is automatically correct. The conclusion of a deductive logical syllogism can never extend beyond the content of the premises. Totally "new" conclusions would not occur because the premises are not challenged empirically. Deductive logic, however, can identify new relationships within existing knowledge.

One might reason inductively by saying:

Example: 1 — Every dog which died in the last 5 years was overweight.
          2 — Therefore, every dog dies from being overweight.

Note that in **inductive reasoning,** a researcher reaches a conclusion (2) by observing particular cases (1—every dog in the last 5 years) and generalizing from the cases to the whole class (2—every dog). It is necessary to observe all cases in the class (dogs) to draw an inductive logical conclusion. In practice, this is usually not possible and one generally must use imperfect induction based on incomplete observation. The conclusions are, thus, limited to the particular class or cases observed (group). It is important to note that neither system of logical reasoning is totally satisfactory, but when both are integrated into a research process, they make a single study more effective.

Deductive and inductive reasoning also characterize research approaches. Deductions from theory identify hypotheses, which, when tested, provide data to confirm, reject, or modify the theory. This approach, from the top down, is called the **hypothetic-deductive approach** and is typical of quantitative experimental studies which investigate hypotheses deduced from theories. Leading scholars of hypothetic-deductive methods (Campbell, 1982; Cronbach, 1975) recognize the limitations of this approach to produce "new" knowledge. The **empirico-inductive approach** builds "abstractions from the particulars that have been gathered" (Bogdan & Biklen, 1982, p. 29). Theory developed this way emerges from the bottom up and is called "grounded theory" (Glaser & Strauss, 1967). The researcher reconstructs a picture that takes shape as he or she collects and examines the parts. The process of data analysis is like a funnel: things are open at the beginning and become more directed and specific at the end as limited generalizations are slowly induced. This empirico-inductive approach is typical of qualitative studies (ethnographic and historical), especially discovery-oriented or exploratory studies, to suggest a "working hypothesis" (Cronbach, 1975, pp. 124–125) for future research or an understanding of the particular cases examined.[3]

7. *Probabilistic thinking.* One misconception of research is that the results are absolute and that conclusions are true beyond a shadow of a doubt. This is not the situation. As noted by a leading educational researcher, "Behavioral science and research does not offer certainty. (Neither does natural science!) It does not even offer relative certainty. All it offers is probabilistic knowledge. If A is done, then B

---

[3]Qualitative researchers (ethnographic and historical) debate whether the resulting generalizations are propositional statements or naturalistic generalizations. See R. E. Stake (1978), Y. S. Lincoln & E. G. Guba (1985, pp. 112–124), and J. Goetz & M. LeCompte (1984).

will probably occur" (Kerlinger, 1979, p. 28). The previous statements "frustration leads to aggression" and "the cumulative effect of complex events, rather than a single leader, causes wars" are technically incorrect. More accurate statements would be: "frustration *probably* leads to aggression" and "the cumulative effect of complex events, rather than a single leader, *tends* to cause wars." One way of defining research might be to say that it is a method of reducing uncertainty. Research can never tell us that something is so certain that no doubt exists. It can, however, say something like this: the odds are 70 to 30 that it is true.

Probabilistic thinking is central to research. All scientific and applied disciplines are probabilistic. The behavioral and social sciences have more uncertainty than the physical sciences. Both quantitative and qualitative research statements have an implicit or explicit probabilistic meaning. Researchers thus often write that their results "tend to indicate" or "are suggestive."

The Research Process

The research process typically involves several phases. These phases are not always sequential nor are they an orderly step-by-step process. Research is more an interactive process between the researcher and the logic of the problem, design, and interpretations. Below is a summary of the process with variations noted.

1. *Selection of a general problem.* The problem defines the area of education in which research will be conducted, such as instruction, administration, adult education, or special education.
2. *Review the literature on the problem.* The most important literature is prior research and theory, but other literature may be useful. In some studies, an exhaustive literature review is done before one collects data. In other studies, the literature review is tentative and preliminary before data collection and then expanded as data are collected.
3. *Select the specific research problem, question, or hypothesis.* This requires the investigator to decide a design and methodology, specifically whether quantitative or qualitative methods will be used. If qualitative methods are to be used, the research problem or questions are a preliminary guide and will become more specific as the research progresses.
4. *Collect data.* Ethical and legal concerns regarding data collection and analysis must also be resolved.
5. *Analyze and present or display data.*
6. *Interpret the findings and state conclusions or generalizations regarding the problem.* Decisions about the reporting format appropriate for the purpose of the study and the intended audiences or readers are made.

The process may be relatively short or it may take several years and longer.

The research process is essentially one of reflective inquiry. Each decision made by the researcher is reported explicitly, often with a rationale for the choice. It is an exciting intellectual process with different skills used in the various phases.

■ QUANTITATIVE AND QUALITATIVE ■ RESEARCH APPROACHES

The terms "quantitative" and "qualitative" are used frequently to identify different approaches to research. While there has been much debate recently about the two approaches,[4] it is helpful to introduce the terms on two levels of discourse. At one level quantitative and qualitative refer to distinctions about the nature of knowledge: how one understands the world and the ultimate purpose of the research. On another level of discourse, the terms refer to research methods—how data are collected and analyzed—and the type of generalizations derived from the data.

Traditionally, both quantitative and qualitative research studies are conducted in education. The most obvious distinction to a reader between quantitative and qualitative research is the form of data presentation. **Quantitative research** presents statistical results represented with numbers; **qualitative research** presents facts in a narration with words. The distinctions, however, are more than in the form of data presentation. Purists suggest that quantitative and qualitative research methods are based on different assumptions about the world, the research purpose, research methods, prototypical studies, the research role, and the importance of context in the study. These distinctions are noted briefly below.

1. *Assumptions about the world.* Quantitative research is usually based on what is called a "logical positivist" philosophy which assumes there are social facts with a *single objective reality,* separated from the feelings and beliefs of individuals. Qualitative research is based more on what is called a "naturalistic-phenomenological" philosophy which assumes that *multiple realities* are socially constructed through individual and collective definitions of the situation.

2. *Research purpose.* Quantitative research seeks to establish relationships and explain *causes* of changes in measured social facts. Qualitative research is more concerned with *understanding* the social phenomenon from the participants' perspectives. This occurs through the researcher's participation in the life of those actors in a research role or through historical empathy with participants in past social events.

3. *Research methods and process.* In quantitative studies there is an established set of procedures and steps that guide the researcher. In qualitative studies, there is greater flexibility in both the methods and the research process. Typically, a qualitative researcher uses an *emergent design* and makes decisions about the data collection strategies during the study. In contrast, quantitative researchers choose methods as part of a *preestablished design* before data collection.

4. *Prototypical studies.* The quantitative researcher employs *experimental* or *correlational* designs to reduce error, bias, and extraneous variables. The prototypical qualitative study of ongoing events is an *ethnography,* which helps readers understand the multiple constructions of reality (definitions of the situation by

---

[4]See, for example, Rist (1977), Shulman (1981), J. L. Smith (1983), Bednarz (1985), Allender (1986), J. L. Smith & L. Heshusius (1986), and Firestone (1987).

the persons studied). The prototypical study of past events is *historical research* using analytical research techniques to reconstruct and understand the multiple realities of past events. Whereas quantitative research seeks to control for bias through design, qualitative research seeks to take into account subjectivity in data analysis and interpretation.

5. *Researcher role.* The ideal quantitative researcher is *detached* from the study to avoid bias. Qualitative researchers become *"immersed"* in the situation, present or past, and the phenomenon being studied. For example, ethnographers assume interactive social roles in which they record observations and interviews with participants in a range of contexts. Qualitative scholars emphasize the importance of data collected by a skilled, prepared *person* in contrast to an *instrument*. Historians acquire a historical sensitivity to the period being examined. Qualitative research is marked by "disciplined subjectivity" (Erickson, 1973), self-examination, criticism of the quality of the data obtained, and the problems encountered.

6. *Importance of the context in the study.* Most quantitative research attempts to establish *universal context-free generalizations.* The qualitative researcher believes that human actions are strongly influenced by the settings in which they occur. Further, as Wilson (1977) states, "those who work within this tradition [qualitative] assert that the social scientist cannot understand human behavior without understanding the framework within which the subjects interpret their thoughts, feelings, and actions" (p. 249). This framework or context is acquired by the ethnographer and the historian during data collection and analysis. Qualitative research develops *context-bound generalizations.*

Many of these distinctions between quantitative and qualitative research are not absolute when one conducts research or one reads a completed study. Experienced researchers can and do combine both quantitative and qualitative research methods in a single study in order to investigate a particular research problem. The distinctions, however, are useful devices in an introduction to research for describing and understanding research methods, a goal of this textbook. These distinctions are further introduced in Chapters 2 and 5 and explained in detail in Part II, Quantitative Research Designs and Methods, and Part III, Qualitative Research Designs and Methods.

■ THE FUNCTIONS OF RESEARCH ■

Research advances knowledge and improves practice. This simple statement raises many questions. What does it mean to advance knowledge—that is, develop a scientific body of knowledge? How can scientific knowledge, often characterized as impractical, improve educational practice? These questions are not new to researchers, readers, or users of research. They are perhaps more relevant and pressing today because of the increased use of research results. Some misconceptions of the functions of research have led to unwarranted criticism of research efforts and scientific knowledge.

Consider some of the possible uses of research in educational situations. Suppose a needs assessment study found that many students in a school were reading below grade level and few students were achieving high scores on a standardized test. Should this school use its limited resources for a gifted program or for a remedial program? Suppose an administrator reads that underachieving children who received "massive rewards" scored higher in mathematics than the control group. Does this mean that the administrator should ask the teacher to use a positive reinforcement program with each underachieving child? Suppose a guidance counselor reads a scientific study verifying the theory that frustration leads to aggression. Does this theory suggest an explanation as to why a high school student who lost a part-time job, scored poorly on college entrance exams, and was removed from the track team for academic ineligibility was sent to the office for fighting? Does this theory, verified by one study, tell the counselor what to do in this situation?

A useful way to understand how research advances knowledge and improves practice is to examine the functions or usage of different types of research. We classify the functions of research as *basic, applied,* and *evaluation.* Basic research, sometimes called pure or fundamental research, and applied research are familiar terms in education, and distinctions have been noted by educational researchers and scholars (Kerlinger, 1979, and Cook & Campbell, 1979). Evaluation research has more recently been recognized as a type of research that differs in important ways from basic and applied research (Worthen & Sanders, 1973, and Campbell, 1982). The differences between basic, applied, and evaluation research are essentially in the functions, especially the degree to which they facilitate decision-making.[5]

The distinctions between basic, applied, and evaluation research are sufficiently elaborated to identify the differences in the research topic, purpose, level of discourse and generalizability of explanations, and intended use of the study (Table 1.1). **Generalizability** is the extent to which the findings of one study can be used as knowledge about other populations and situations—that is, to predict. Understanding the functions of basic, applied, and evaluation research aids in conducting, reading, and using research. Most studies are designed and judged adequate as one type of research and less adequate as other types of research. Rarely is a single study equally adequate as basic, applied, and evaluation research.

First, we need to define *field, discipline,* and *science.* Field, in this discussion, is an area of research, knowledge, and practice that is more than a single academic

[5]The authors recognize that the distinctions between basic, applied, and evaluation research as presented here are probably oversimplified and overemphasized for illustrative purposes. Some researchers view evaluation as a variant of applied research despite twenty years of elaboration by distinguished scholars, researchers, and evaluators. Evaluation research is conceptually similar to action research except action research is limited to classroom problems and is frequently conducted by the teacher.

TABLE 1.1
Functions of Types of Research

Basic	Applied	Evaluation
Topic of Research: Physical, behavioral, and social sciences	Applied field: medicine, engineering, education	Practice in a given site(s)
Purpose: 1. Test theories, scientific laws, basic principles	1. Test the usefulness of scientific theories within a given field	1. Assess the merit of specific practice
2. Determine empirical relationships among phenomena and analytical generalizations[a]	2. Determine empirical relationships and analytical generalizations within a given field	2. Assess the worth of a specific practice
Level of Discourse/ Generalizability: Abstract, related to, science	General, related to a given field	1. Concrete, specific to a particular practice 2. Apply to specific practice at given site(s)
Intended Use: 1. Add to scientific knowledge of basic laws and principles	1. Add to research-based knowledge in a given field	1. Add to research-based knowledge about a specific practice
2. Advance further inquiry and methodology	2. Advance research and methodology in a given field	2. Advance research and methodology of a specific practice
		3. Aid in decision-making at a given site(s)

[a]I. I. Mitroff and R. H. Kilmann (1978) suggest four types of scientists and methodological approaches: analytical scientist, conceptual theorist, conceptual humanist, and particular humanist.

discipline, as is medicine or education. "Discipline" refers to a method of organizing academic knowledge. Disciplines are usually classified as the physical, behavioral, and social sciences. Physical science is the study of the natural universe; behavioral science is the study of an organism; and social science is the study of human social systems. Although scholars and scientists debate whether a particular discipline is a science, they generally agree it is the research topic that distinguishes physical, behavioral, and social science.

Basic Research

Kerlinger states that "**basic research** is research done to test theory . . . with little or no thought of applications of the results of the research to practical problems" (1979, p. 283). Basic research, which is concerned exclusively with knowing, explaining, and predicting natural and social phenomena, starts with a theory, a basic principle, or a generalization. A proposition such as "if we frustrate children, then they probably will be aggressive toward others" states and explains a relationship. An analytical generalization also explains relationships, but these relationships are among past events. The generalization "wars are caused by social, economic, and political movements occurring before the military action" is thus an explanation and a theory. A theory may or may not have empirical support. If a theory has been supported consistently by research, then it may be called a law. A **scientific law** is a statement that has a theoretical base and considerable empirical support. A scientific law such as gravity (Homans, 1967) is generalizable—that is, it explains many individual cases.

Abstractness is important to any theory in basic research. As Kerlinger notes, "general laws, general statements of relations, are necessarily abstract because they must apply to many specific cases" (1979, p. 12). Without such abstractness, there would be no science. For example, the abstract statement "reinforcement leads to retention of learning" is valuable because it covers many manifestations of reinforcement and retention. Abstractness, part of the power of science, is always remote from everyday concerns and warm human relations. The results of basic research are related to previous research and knowledge within the science.

One often hears that the purpose of science is to improve mankind or human society; however, to confuse social and scientific purposes may erode objectivity, and more important, the scientist's commitment to objectivity. Basic research has never been designed for solving human and social problems, making decisions, and taking action. The scientist is preoccupied with developing knowledge and is not expected nor required to spell out the practical implications of a study. To do this requires a leap from an abstract level of discourse to a concrete and specific level. This usually cannot be done within a single study.

The effects of basic research are felt indirectly only over considerable periods of time[6] because new knowledge challenges fixed sets of beliefs and dogma. Trends in theoretical thinking and a series of studies, such as those conducted by Piaget and his colleagues in the cognitive development of children, have the greatest probability of an impact. Basic research influences indirectly the ways people think and perceive, an impact that may or may not lead to action.

Thus, the purpose of basic research is first to add to our knowledge of basic principles and scientific laws. Second, basic research advances further scientific

---

[6]Establishing knowledge is a slow process, whether the knowledge is nomothetic or idiographic (Maslow, 1966). "Nomothetic" means law-making; "idiographic" means to describe things individually. Disciplines can be characterized as nomothetic (physics, economics) or as idiographic (anthropology, history). Both types of knowledge are important, but different.

inquiry and methodology and, indirectly, the methodology of applied research. Basic research may have a more overt influence on applied research by identifying theories to be tested in a field of application, such as medicine or education. Using basic research methodology, researchers may test organizational theories in educational settings to develop theories of educational administration; or they may test theories of learning, cognitive development, creativity, and others in instructional programs. Basic research methodologies, especially measurement and statistics, are used or adapted to applied and evaluation research.

Applied Research

Applied research is conducted in a field of common practice and is concerned with the application and development of research-based knowledge about that practice. Medicine, engineering, social work, and education are applied fields that use scientific knowledge but are not themselves science. "Applied research (as opposed to basic research) is . . . aimed at producing knowledge relevant to providing a solution (generalizable) to a *general* problem" (Worthen & Sanders, 1973, p. 23). In other words, applied studies focus on research problems common to a given field.

Applied research tests the usefulness of scientific theories and determines empirical and analytical relationships within a given field. A scientist, for example, might investigate and try to understand human intelligence in its many manifestations, including schooling. An educational researcher might determine the relationship of intelligence to achievement or analyze federal court rulings on the instructional use of certain books. Implications of such studies are stated in general terms and not as specific recommendations for immediate action.

Applied research, like basic research, is abstract and general, using the language common to those in the field. Many educational studies on achievement, teaching, learning, exceptional children, and the like use terms that have a special meaning within the profession. The generalizability of applied research is usually limited to the delineated field. Educational research thus focuses on knowledge about *educational* theories and practices rather than on *universal* knowledge.

Education, as an applied field of common practices, is not yet recognized as a science. Similar to the established social sciences and disciplines, the generation and verification of theories to develop scientific knowledge about education is highly valued. In early periods of developing a discipline from an applied field, however, initial efforts are usually directed more toward establishing empirical facts. In later periods, facts from separate studies can be synthesized and ultimately integrated into theories. Educational research, in general, has focused on establishing empirical facts and frameworks (Clifford, 1973). The development of new research methodologies, especially research synthesis, may enable researchers to identify those educational theoretical frameworks which have substantial empirical evidence (Walberg, 1986).

Applied research adds to the research-based knowledge in the given field. The effects of applied research are felt indirectly over a period of time. When a series of studies are presented, published, and critiqued for a considerable time, this knowledge influences the way practitioners think and perceive a common problem. Applied studies stimulate further research and suggest new theories of practice and of science and can stimulate basic research and methodological development. An example is the development of more appropriate statistics to study phenomena that relate to school achievement (Kerlinger, 1979). The need to measure learning at different ages has stimulated basic research in the measurement of child and adult intelligence.

Evaluation Research

Evaluation research focuses on a particular practice at a given site(s). The practice may be a program, a product, or a process, but the site is crucial. **Evaluation research** assesses the merit and worth of a particular practice in terms of the values operating at the site(s). Evaluation determines whether the practice works—that is, does it do what is intended at the site? Evaluation also determines whether the practice is worth the costs of development, implementation, or widespread adoption. Costs may be those of materials, time and space, staff skills and morale, and community concerns.

Formal evaluation can be conducted by a researcher in a given field or by a practitioner at the site. Evaluation research, which is as rigorous as other types of research, generally requires specialized training in several methodologies and disciplines as well as skills in interpersonal relations and communication. Many comprehensive evaluations contain both quantitative and qualitative data from a series of studies conducted at different implementation phases of the practice.

An evaluation study is communicated in concrete language which is specific to the practice and meaningful to the participant. The findings should have "site-specific interpretability" (Campbell, 1982). Because evaluation aids in immediate decision-making, the findings usually have limited generalizability. An innovative ecology curriculum in Surrytown Public Schools, including the materials, staff, and students, will probably not survive the decade and is of little interest to schools with other environmental problems and instructional resources. Both applied and evaluation research may study practices common to many education settings, but the evaluation focuses first on the implementation at a given site.

Evaluation research can add to our knowledge about a specific practice and can stimulate further research and methodological development to study practices. Evaluation studies often identify variables or suggest hypotheses for other evaluation and applied research. Qualitative, holistic analysis of the site context has emphasized the importance of certain methodologies. Assessment of achievement has encouraged measurement in education that was not attempted previously, such as the attributes of pupils aged two to five years and exceptional children with special needs. A series of evaluation studies on the particular practice at diverse sites, such as Head Start classrooms, or upon organization change processes (Rosenblum & Louis, 1981) can add to the existing knowledge in the applied field.

Basic, applied, and evaluation research differ primarily because of different purposes, functions, and questions of investigation. Basic research, which tests theories and explains empirical and analytical relations in the physical, behavioral, and social sciences, is used to establish scientific laws. Applied research tests the usefulness of scientific theories in the field of application and investigates practical relationships common to the given field. Neither basic nor applied research is designed to produce direct solutions to a specific problem at a given site. After a considerable period of time, both types of research can influence indirectly the way scientists, researchers, and practitioners think about and perceive their respective problems. Evaluation research assesses the merit and worth of a particular practice at a given site(s) against one or more scales of values. Unlike basic and applied research, evaluation provides information for immediate use as a practice is developed, implemented, and institutionalized.[7]

■ EDUCATION AS A FIELD OF INQUIRY ■
AND PRACTICE

Education is an area of interdisciplinary research that tests scientific theories, determines empirical and analytical relations, and assesses the worth of educational practices. Educational practice centers on instruction and learning and includes practices that influence instruction, such as curriculum development, innovations, administration, supervision, and staff development. Research-based knowledge reflects this duality of education as a field of both inquiry and practice.

Interdisciplinary Field of Inquiry

Education is an interdisciplinary field of inquiry that has borrowed concepts and theories from psychology, sociology, anthropology, political science, economics, and other disciplines. Theories using concepts like intelligence, role, norm, status, power, authority, cost effectiveness, self-concept, human development, diffusion, culture, and the like have been tested in educational practices, and new educational concepts have emerged. When economic analysis was applied to education, for example, the concept of profit was modified to cost-benefit, implying that not all educational outcomes could be stated as monetary values.

Educational research has also borrowed methodologies developed originally in the disciplines of the behavioral and social sciences. Psychology, especially measurement, traditionally has dominated educational research and continues to

---

[7]See J. B. Cousins and K. A. Leithwood (1986), Current empirical research on evaluation utilization, *Review of Educational Research, 56*(3), 331–364, for factors which influence evaluation utilization.

exert a strong influence. Researchers have more recently valued methodologies used in other social sciences, such as sociological survey research, anthropological participant-observation, historical and legal research, and economic analysis. Some of these approaches are applied directly to education, while other approaches are modified to investigate an educational problem. Such modifications, however, can rarely violate those disciplines from which the methods were drawn.

The use of different concepts and methodologies from various disciplines enriches and extends research-based knowledge in education. Researchers can study almost any single topic with a variety of methods. The topic of science education can, for example, be studied by a survey of curriculum needs at a site, an experiment comparing student achievement with different materials, an observation study of classroom interaction, a historical study of science textbooks, an ethnographic study of the instructional processes in specific science classrooms or a legal study of the teaching of evolution in a science curriculum. Each of these approaches adds to our knowledge about science education.

In an interdisciplinary field, all research methodologies are valued for their potential usefulness in developing knowledge. Researchers may feel that one methodology is better than another, but this is misleading because each methodology has its own limitations. Different methodologies and designs provide different kinds of knowledge about educational practices.

Limitations of Educational Research

Knowledge acquired through research is limited by the nature of both educational practice and research. Educational research is constrained by ethical and legal considerations in conducting research on human beings, the public nature of education, the complexity of educational practices, and methodological limitations. Each of these four constraints ultimately influences our knowledge about education.

1. *Human Subjects.* Educational research focuses primarily on human beings. The researcher is ethically responsible for protecting the rights and welfare of the subjects while conducting a study. Researchers must protect subjects from physical and mental discomfort, harm, and danger. Many studies require informed consent from the subjects, parents, or institution, and there are laws to protect the confidentiality of the data and the privacy of the individual.[8] Researchers have followed many of these ethical principles informally for years. These principles (see Chapter 5) often impose limitations on the kinds of studies that can be conducted in valid and objective ways in education. Physical and mental discomfort

---

[8]The three laws, all passed in 1974, are the Family Education Rights and Privacy Act, the National Research Act, and the Privacy Act. Although there is consensus about the intent of these laws, there is much variation in the interpretation and implementation of the regulations. A researcher abides by the procedures of the agency for whom data is collected.

of subjects may affect the length of testing periods, the replication of studies, the types of treatments, and ultimately the research questions investigated.

2. *Public Institution.* Education is a public enterprise influenced by the external environment. Although many practices seem to undergo no drastic change, the institutions change. An elementary school can change its entire faculty and school population every six years. The community surrounding a school can change drastically when industry or an ethnic group establishes itself in the area. Legislative mandates and judicial orders have changed the structure of schools and added or deleted programs. Because schools exist for educational purposes, not for research purposes, studies cannot unduly interfere with educational processes. Longitudinal and replication studies on a changing clientele and institution are difficult to conduct. It is often said that we do not know ultimately the effects of schooling because these effects may occur years later outside an educational setting.

The public nature of education also influences the kinds of research questions investigated. Most studies make the subjects and other groups aware of the research topic. Some topics may be too controversial for a conservative community or too divisive for a staff. Some studies are not conducted because of possible subsequent issues that may be detrimental to maintaining an educational organization.

3. *Complexity of Research Problems.* A third factor that limits educational research is the complexity of the research problems. The human beings involved—students, teachers, administrators, parents, the collective community—are complex living organisms, and they actively select the environmental stimuli to which they respond. Furthermore, different individuals process the stimuli differently. Educational research has demonstrated the complexities of individual differences and that responses to stimuli may be predictable and unpredictable. The educational researcher thus deals simultaneously with many variables, often ambiguous ones, in a single study.

In addition, there is a growing awareness among social scientists that individuals cannot be studied meaningfully outside the context of real life. Behavior is determined by both individual and situational characteristics, and to study individuals without regard to situations is incomplete. Thus, educational researchers not only must contend with individual differences among people, they must also consider a myriad of situational elements.

4. *Methodological Difficulties.* A fourth factor that limits quantitative educational research is methodological difficulties. Educational research measures complex human characteristics, thinking, and problem-solving skills. The measurement of achievement, intelligence, leadership styles, group interaction, or readiness skills involves conceptual definitions and issues of validity and reliability. Some educational research has been possible only as valid and reliable instruments were developed. Other research has been delayed by a lack of valid instruments.

Qualitative research also has methodological difficulties, especially those inherent in the researcher's decisions involving which data collection and data analysis methods to use to assure valid findings. Qualitative research is sometimes criticized from the conventional viewpoint for the lack of reliable and generalizable findings and the tendency to focus on the unique elements of education rather than the common elements.

The Importance of Educational Research

Despite these difficulties, educational research has made considerable gains in knowledge. Some educational research, especially the measurement of intelligence and achievement, has a long tradition of resolving methodological problems. Other methodologies have been used more recently in education, and the resulting knowledge is accumulating. The importance of educational research is demonstrated in part by the increase in the number of educational research journals. Our society and educational leaders have used research increasingly to aid in policy- and decision-making.

Information derived from authority, philosophy, tradition, or personal experience is less likely to be objective and reality-based. In a technological society valid information is necessary for educational decisions. Research-based information is more likely to define the problem carefully and to reflect the complexity of educational processes. If one plans to improve education, the first step is to have valid information and knowledge about education.

In many ways research influences the roles of educators and the institutions in which they work. Educators frequently are unaware that they have used the results of educational research or have performed some part of a research process in their professional lives. The activities enumerated below illustrate the more common uses of educational research in educational programs and institutions. It is not an exhaustive list.

1. Acquire a new or different perspective about education or an educational process which generates ideas on how to approach a practical problem.
2. Use research results to aid in policy- and decision-making and to justify decisions between alternatives.
3. Recognize a much-heralded "innovation" as similar to that which was done twenty or forty years ago.
4. Adopt those programs identified from a research literature review which have a greater likelihood of producing desirable effects.
5. Determine the next step of program development from a formal local evaluation report.
6. Read published research studies critically.
7. Separate educational claims by authorities and position papers of organized groups from those based on research.
8. Identify an instructional or educational need systematically rather than intuitively.
9. Test an assumption or a hypothesis deduced from a theory or a claim to provide more reliable knowledge and implications for educational practice.

10. Intelligently interpret standardized test results of students in a program.
11. Administer standardized group or individual tests in such a manner as to increase the validity and reliability of the data.
12. Respond to requests to participate in a research project.

With a conceptual understanding of research, practitioners can read, conduct small scale studies, and take an active role in research projects. With further training and experience, practitioners can design and conduct studies for the advancement of knowledge and the improvement of educational practice.

■ SUMMARY ■

This chapter has discussed the development of educational knowledge, scientific and disciplined inquiry, characteristics of research in education, and the functions of basic, applied, and evaluation research, and it has described education as a field of interdisciplinary inquiry and practice. The major ideas in the chapter are summarized below.

1. Research provides a better source for knowledge and decision-making than personal experience, beliefs, tradition, logic, or intuition alone.
2. The process to develop reliable educational knowledge involves identification of research problems, empirical studies, replications, research synthesis and review, and practitioner adoption and evaluation.
3. Science aims at the generation and verification of theory, a set of interrelated constructs and propositions that specifies relations among variables to explain and predict phenomena.
4. A theory should provide a simple explanation of observed relations, account for accumulated evidence, provide for verification, and stimulate further research.
5. Research is a systematic process of collecting and logically analyzing data for some purpose.
6. Educational research is disciplined inquiry in which different disciplines provide different principles of research by which to collect and reason from data.
7. Characteristics of research in education include: objective, precise, verifiable, explanatory, empirical, logical, and probabilistic.
8. Quantitative and qualitative research, both of which are conducted in education, differ in the assumptions about the world, research purpose, research methods and process, prototypical studies, researcher role, and the importance of the context in the study.
9. Basic research tests theories and explains empirical and analytical relations in physical, behavioral, and social sciences.
10. Applied research tests the usefulness of scientific theories in the field of

application and investigates relationships and analytical generalizations common to the given field.

11. Neither basic nor applied research is designed to provide direct solutions to a specific problem at a given site. Both basic and applied research can influence indirectly, after a considerable period of time, the way scientists, researchers, and practitioners think about and perceive their respective problems.

12. Evaluation research assesses the merit and worth of a particular practice at a given site or sites against one or more scales of values.

13. Education is an interdisciplinary field of inquiry—that is, researchers borrow concepts, theories, and methodologies from disciplines and apply these to education.

14. Educational knowledge is constrained by ethical and legal considerations, the public nature of education, the complexity of educational practices, and methodological limitations.

■ SELF-INSTRUCTIONAL REVIEW EXERCISES ■

Sample answers are in the back of the book.

Test Items

1. Knowledge based on systematic collection and analysis of data is
   a. a belief.
   b. research.
   c. personal experience.
   d. tradition.

2. A theory, generated and verified by research, is useful because it
   a. provides a simple explanation of observed relations.
   b. accounts for accumulated evidence.
   c. is general enough to cover many individual cases and manifestations.
   d. All of the above are correct.

3. Research
   a. is the use of systematic, explicit methods and logical reasoning which can be examined critically.
   b. is limited to measurement and statistical approaches.
   c. depends on the researcher's personal characteristics.
   d. is characterized as being unquestionable or absolute, beyond a shadow of a doubt.

4. Quantitative and qualitative research are similar in
   a. the researcher role.
   b. the prototypical studies.
   c. assumptions about the world.
   d. empirical data emphases.

Statements 5 through 10 are functions of different types of research. Match each of the functions with the type of research. There may be more than one response per question.

5. tests theories and explains relations in physical, behavioral
   and social sciences

6. assesses the merit and worth of
   a particular practice at a given
   site

7. tests the usefulness of scientific
   theories in a given field

8. establishes an accepted body of
   research-based knowledge in a
   given field

9. establishes an accepted body of
   scientific knowledge

10. develops knowledge, furthers
    research and methodology

a. basic research
b. applied research
c. evaluation research

11. The most general abstract knowledge is derived from
    a. evaluation research on a practice.
    b. applied research in a given field.
    c. basic research in a physical, behavioral, and social science.
    d. educational research.

12. An explanation—that is, a statement of relations of some particular
    though broad phenomena—is *not*
    a. theory.
    b. a scientific law.
    c. an analytical generalization.
    d. an expert's opinion.

13. Educational research is *not* limited by
    a. ethical and legal constraints in conducting research.
    b. dependence on one methodology.
    c. methodological difficulties.
    d. complexities of practices of human subjects.

Application Problems

The following are examples of research results. How could these results be used?
Choose one of the following responses and illustrate it. There is not a single correct answer. For feedback, you can compare your answers with the sample
answers in the back of the book.

    a. to influence the way the reader thinks or perceives a problem
    b. to generate decision-making leading to action
    c. to generate a new research question or problem

1. A teacher reads a research study reporting that children from broken
   homes are more likely to exhibit deviant behavior in schools than are children from intact homes.
2. A study reports that a test measuring reading comprehension in grades 1
   through 4 has been validated on students in grades 1 and 2 but not grades
   3 and 4.
3. An educational historian notes that a well-known study of the organization of public schools from 1900 to 1950 stops short of the 1954 Supreme
   Court ruling on "separate but equal."
4. A principal reads a survey of the parents of his school pupils suggesting
   that these parents do not understand the new report card and grading
   system.
5. A curriculum developer field-tested a pilot module of a strategy to help
   Adult Basic Education teachers teach a reading strategy. The results of a
   representative sample of the teachers in the state suggested that the module be revised to include a rationale for the strategy, a clear specification of
   the type of student who would benefit from the strategy, and alternative
   techniques to respond to student difficulties.
6. Previous research indicated that school systems were tightly structured organizations with hierarchical authority. A professor of administration
   recalled that several superintendents and principals saw many elements of
   autonomous behavior by principals and teachers at school level even
   though no empirical studies had reported this.

CHAPTER 2

RESEARCH DESIGNS, DATA COLLECTION TECHNIQUES, AND RESEARCH REPORTS

■ **KEY TERMS** ■

research design
experimental design
nonexperimental design
true experimental design
random assignment
quasi-experimental
single-subject design
descriptive design
correlational design
correlation
survey research
ex post facto design
qualitative design
case study design
ethnographic study
analytical
concept analysis
historical analysis

legal analysis
quantitative technique
structured observations
standardized interviews
questionnaires
tests
unobtrusive measurement
nonreactive
qualitative technique
ethnographic observation
ethnographic interview
documents
abstract
research problem
hypothesis
methodology
references

This chapter completes our overview of the field of educational research. Its goals are to introduce terminology related to the way research is designed and data are gathered and to acquaint you with the organization of published research reports. We will cover each of the designs and techniques in greater detail in later chapters. Our experience in teaching research is that while it takes time to learn new terms and concepts, it is best to become acquainted with these terms and concepts as early as possible. As they are reviewed in the context of actual studies and explained in greater detail later in the book, you will gain a more complete understanding and retention.

■ RESEARCH DESIGNS ■

We have examined the way that research can be viewed as scientific inquiry and disciplined inquiry, that approaches to research can be primarily quantitative or qualitative, and that research can be categorized as basic, applied, or evaluation. Another way to think about research is based on the research design of the study. **Research design** refers to the plan and structure of the investigation used to obtain evidence to answer research questions. The design describes the procedures for conducting the study, including when, from whom, and under what conditions the data will be obtained. In other words, design indicates how the research is set up: what happens to the subjects and what methods of data collection are used.

The purpose of a research design is to provide the most valid, accurate answers possible to research questions. Since there are many types of research questions and many types of designs, it is important to match the design with the question. Research design is a very important part of an investigation, since certain limitations and cautions in interpreting the results are related to each design, and also because the research design determines how the data should be analyzed.

To help you understand designs better we have classified them into four major types: *experimental, nonexperimental, ex post facto,* and *qualitative.* We will introduce the most common designs in each category, and we will discuss them in greater detail in later chapters.

Table 2.1 lists the major types of research designs. Each type communicates something different about the nature of the study. It should be noted that these categories are independent of the classification of research as scientific or disciplined inquiry or as basic, applied, or evaluation; that is, basic research can be experimental or nonexperimental, and applied research can be single-subject or correlational. (Certain trends will, however, be identified—much basic research, for example, uses true experimental designs, whereas most applied and evaluation research uses other types of experimental designs, nonexperimental designs, or *ex post facto* designs.)

Experimental Designs

An important characteristic of designs is to distinguish between experimental and nonexperimental types. In an **experimental design** the researcher manipulates what the subjects will experience. In other words, the investigator has some control over what will happen to the subjects by systematically imposing or withholding specified conditions. Typically, the researcher then makes comparisons between subjects who have had and others who have not had the imposed conditions. Experimental designs also have a particular purpose in mind: to investigate cause-and-effect relationships between manipulated conditions and

TABLE 2.1
Major Types of Research Designs

Experimental	Nonexperimental	*Ex Post Facto*	Qualitative
True Experimental	Descriptive		Ethnographic
Quasi-Experimental	Correlational		Analytical
Single Subject	Survey		Concept Analysis
			Historical Analysis
			Legal Analysis

measured outcomes. In a **nonexperimental design** there is no manipulation of conditions. Rather, the investigator makes observations or obtains measures from subjects to describe something that has occurred. Also, nonexperimental designs generally are not intended to show cause-and-effect relationships.

There are many different types of experimental designs. Here we will describe the three most common types. Chapter 9 will present these designs, and others, in greater detail.

True Experimental. The unique characteristic of a **true experimental design** is random assignment of subjects to different groups. With **random assignment,** every subject used in the study has an equal chance of being in each group. This procedure, when carried out with a large enough sample, helps ensure that there are no major differences between subjects in each group before experimental treatment begins. This enables the researcher to conclude that the results are not due to differences in the subjects before receiving each treatment.

The physical and biological sciences frequently use true experimental designs because they provide the most powerful approach for determining the effect of one factor on another. In these disciplines it is also relatively easy to meet the conditions of random assignment and manipulation. If a group of farmers wants to determine which of two fertilizers causes the best growth, they can divide large plots of land into smaller sections and randomly give some sections fertilizer A and the others fertilizer B. As long as the same amount of rain and sun and the same insect problems and other factors affect each section—which would probably be the case—the farmers can determine which fertilizer is best. In the social sciences, however, and especially in education, it is often difficult to meet these conditions. True experiments are especially difficult to employ in applied research, in which researchers should maintain naturally occurring conditions. Excerpt 2.1 summarizes an example of a study that was a true experiment.

EXCERPT 2.1
True Experimental Design

This study was conducted to determine whether the provision of contextual aids would help students reduce inter-sentence interference. Forty-two fourth and fifth grade children attending school in a predominantly middle class suburban community participated in the experiment. Twenty-one children within each grade were randomly assigned in equal numbers to the context and no-context conditions of the experiment.

Source: Adapted from Levin, J. R., Ghatala, E. S., & Truman, D. L. (1979). Reducing inter-sentence interference via contextual aids. *American Educational Research Journal. 16* (3), 249–256.

Quasi-Experimental.   A design that approximates the true experimental type is called **quasi-experimental.** The purpose of the method is the same—to determine cause and effect—and there is direct manipulation of conditions. However, there is no random assignment of subjects. A common situation for implementing quasi-experimental designs involves several classes or schools that can be used to determine the effect of curricular materials or teaching methods. The classes are "intact," already organized for an instructional purpose. The classes are not assigned randomly and have different teachers. It is possible, however, to give an experimental treatment to some of the classes and treat other classes as controls. Excerpt 2.2 illustrates quasi-experimental research.

Single-Subject Designs.   Research in education has been influenced heavily by a tradition in which groups of subjects, rather than individuals, are studied. The reason for studying groups is that intra-individual differences and measurement error can be assessed by using an average score for the whole group. In many situations, however, it is impossible or inconvenient to study entire groups of subjects. Furthermore, the researcher may be interested in one or two subjects, not large groups of subjects. **Single-subject designs** offer an alternative by specifying methods that can be used with a single individual or just a few subjects and still allow reasonable cause-and-effect conclusions.

Similar to quasi-experimental, there is direct manipulation but no random assignment. Suppose, for example, you are interested in the effectiveness of a new behavior modification program on controlling unruly behavior. There are three students in your class with whom you want to try the program, so a group design is inappropriate. Conceptualizing the problem as a single-subject design, you would first record the behavior of one of the students to assure yourself that the behavior is stable and consistent before implementing the new program. You then continue recording behavior after the new program has been implemented.

EXCERPT 2.2
Quasi-experimental Research Design

This experiment studied the effect of humor and humorous examples upon the comprehension and retention of lecture material. The study was a quasi-experiment in which intact classes of university students viewed either a serious lecture or one of three versions of a humorous lecture. To determine whether there were existing differences between classes, scores on tests given prior to the experiment were compared. It was observed that any existing differences were not significant. A test of comprehension and retention was given immediately after the lecture and again six weeks later. Results indicated that immediate comprehension was not facilitated by the use of humorous examples, but retention six weeks later was higher for students who viewed the humorous examples.

Source: Adapted from Kaplan, R. M., & Pascoe, G. C. (1977). Humorous lectures and humorous examples: Some effects upon comprehension and retention. *Journal of Educational Psychology. 69*, 61–65.

If you see a change in behavior that coincides with the implementation of the new method, and other causes could not be identified, then you may be able to infer that the new program caused the change in behavior.

Nonexperimental Designs

As we have already indicated, nonexperimental designs describe something that has occurred or examines relationships between things without suggesting direct cause-and-effect relationships. (It should be noted that in some situations nonexperimental designs are used to investigate tentative or exploratory cause-and-effect relationships.) Let's look at three types of nonexperimental designs: descriptive, correlational, and survey.

Descriptive.   Research using a **descriptive design** simply describes an existing phenomenon by using numbers to characterize individuals or a group. It assesses the nature of existing conditions. The purpose of most descriptive research is limited to characterizing something as it is, though some descriptive research suggests tentative causal relationships. There is no manipulation of treatments or subjects; the researcher measures things as they are. The following questions could be answered by means of descriptive designs: How many times during a school day does Ms. Jones use negative reinforcement with her pupils? What are the pupils' attitudes toward school discipline? What is the self-concept of the school's fourth graders? What is the reading achievement level of different ethnic groups in the school? Excerpt 2.3 illustrates a descriptive design.

EXCERPT 2.3
Descriptive Design

Two hundred thirty-six fifth and sixth grade children were asked to indicate the degree to which eight causes influenced the success or failure they experienced on a test. The children tended to attribute success to the teacher's good explanation of the material, to good home conditions, to easy subject matter, to high interest, and to the ease of the test. Failure was attributed to insufficient preparation, low ability, lack of effort, difficulty of the subject matter, and difficulty of the test. Girls, more than boys, tended to attribute their outcome to preparation and home condition. Boys, more than girls, believed that they have higher ability when successful.

Source: Adapted from Bar-Tal, D., & Darom, E. (1979). Pupils' attributions of success and failure. *Child Development. 50,* 264–267.

Correlational.   Correlational designs are technically a form of descriptive designs, but because they are used extensively in education they are classified as a distinct type of research. **Correlational design** is concerned with assessing relationships between two or more phenomena. This type of study usually involves a statistical measure of the degree of relationship, called **correlation.** The relationship that is measured is a statement about the degree of association between the variables of interest. A *positive correlation* means that high values of one variable are associated with high values on a second variable. The relationship between height and weight, between IQ scores and achievement test scores, and between self-concept and grades are examples of positive correlation. A *negative correlation* or relationship means that high values of variables are associated with low value of a second variable. Examples of negative correlations include those between exercise and heart failure, between successful test performance and feelings of incompetence, and between absence from school and school achievement. Excerpt 2.4 is an example of research using a correlational design.

Survey.   In **survey research** the investigator selects a sample of subjects and administers a questionnaire or conducts interviews to collect data. Surveys are used frequently in educational research to describe attitudes, beliefs, opinions, and other types of information. Usually the research is designed so that information about a large number of people (population) can be obtained by the responses of a smaller group of subjects selected from the large group (sample). Surveys are used for a wide variety of purposes. They can describe the frequency of demographic characteristics or traits held, explore relationships between dif-

EXCERPT 2.4
Correlational Design

This article isolates correlates of departmental quality at the masters and doctoral level in regional colleges and universities. The 45 departments in the sample represent 14 public institutions in two states and include departments in biology, chemistry, education, history, and mathematics. In addition to simple correlation, the analysis is based on multivariate linear regression. Departmental quality is found to be correlated with individual and combined measures of faculty (scholarly productivity, grantsmanship, age and tenure status, geographical origin of highest degree, and teaching workload), students (number and ability), program (proportion of institutional degree programs at the advanced graduate level and curricular concentration), and facilities (library size). The findings suggest that the factors associated with graduate departmental quality are more multidimensional in regional colleges and universities than in highly ranked research universities.

Source: From "Correlates of Departmental Quality in Regional Colleges and Universities" by Clifton F. Conrad and Robert T. Blackburn, *American Educational Research Journal*, Summer 1985, Vol. 22, No. 2, pp. 279–295. Copyright © 1985, American Educational Research Association, Washington, DC. Reprinted by permission.

ferent factors, or delineate the reasons for particular practices. There is a specified sequence of steps that is followed in survey research, as detailed in Chapter 8.

Ex Post Facto Designs

An *ex post facto* **design** is used to explore possible causal relationships among variables that cannot be manipulated by the researcher. The investigator compares two or more samples that are comparable except for a specified factor. The possible causes are studied after they have occurred. Rather than manipulating what *will* happen to subjects, as in experimental designs, the research focuses on what has happened differently for comparable groups of subjects, then explores if the subjects in each group are different in some way. For example, an important question concerning day care for children is the relative effect the type of day care program may have on school readiness. Some day care programs are more "academic" than others. Since it would be very difficult to manipulate experimentally the type of day care a child attends, an *ex post facto* design would be appropriate. The investigator would identify two groups of children who have similar backgrounds but who have attended different types of day care. The subjects would be given a school readiness test to see if those who attended a highly academically oriented day care facility differ from children who attended a less academically oriented day care.

Qualitative Research Designs

As previously indicated in Chapter 1, the term "qualitative" can refer to a philosophy or a methodology. In this chapter we introduce common qualitative methodologies, focusing first on qualitative designs and then on qualitative data collection techniques.

Qualitative designs are less structured than quantitative ones. In a **qualitative design** the specific procedures are identified *during* the research rather than specified ahead of time. Each step is dependent on prior information. Traditional qualitative research is also distinguished by using a **case study design,** in which a single "case" is studied in depth. This could be an individual, one group of students, a school, a program, or a concept. The purpose is to understand the person(s) or phenomena. Since qualitative designs investigate behavior as it occurs naturally in noncontrived situations, there is no manipulation of conditions or experience. In this sense qualitative designs are nonexperimental. Finally, the data consist of words in the form of rich verbal descriptions, rather than numbers.

Ethnographic Designs.   In an **ethnographic study** the researcher relies on observation, interviewing, and document analysis, or a combination of these, to provide an in-depth understanding of what is studied. Typically the researcher is at a selected site for a lengthy time period in order to understand fully the subjects and phenomena being studied.

An ethnographic study begins with a planning phase, in which general research questions, the kind of site, and types of participants needed are identified. The ethnographer then establishes rapport and trust with the participants. Once fully acclimated, the investigator chooses appropriate data collection strategies and collects the data. An ethnographic interview is illustrated in Excerpt 2.5. Note the emphasis on obtaining a rich description of mental retardation from the perspective of a mentally retarded adult.

Analytical Designs.   Qualitative research that is termed **"analytical"** investigates problems through an analysis of documents. The researcher identifies, studies, and then synthesizes the data to provide an understanding of events that may or may not have been directly observable. Usually these events have occurred in the past, thus documents are the source of data. The purpose of the study is to understand a past event, person, or movement by a thorough and detailed description and analysis. The researcher interprets these facts to provide explanations of the past and clarifies the collective educational meanings that may be underlying current practices and issues.

Examples of analytical research include concept analysis, historical analysis, and legal analysis. **Concept analysis** is the study of educational concepts such as "open education," "ability grouping," or "leadership" to describe the meaning and appropriate use of the concept. **Historical analysis** involves a systematic collection and criticism of documents that describe past events. The analysis examines

EXCERPT 2.5
Ethnographic Study

In the pages that follow we present the edited transcripts of some of the discussions we have had over the past year with a 26-year-old man we will call Ed Murphy. (For methodology, see Bogdan, 1974, and Bogdan & Taylor, 1975.) Ed has been labeled mentally retarded by his family, school teachers, and others in his life. At the age of 15 he was placed in a state institution for the retarded. His institutional records, as do many professionals with whom he has come into contact, describe him as "a good boy, but easily confused; mental retardation-cultural-familial type." Ed currently works as a janitor in a large urban nursing home and lives in a boarding house with four other men who, like himself, are former residents of state institutions.

AN INSIDER'S VIEW

When I was born the doctors didn't give me six months to live. My mother told them that she could keep me alive, but they didn't believe it. It took a hell of a lot of work, but she showed with love and determination that she could be the mother to a handicapped child. I don't know for a fact what I had, but they thought it was severe retardation and cerebral palsy. They thought I would never walk. I still have seizures. Maybe that has something to do with it too.

My first memory is about my grandmother. She was a fine lady. I went to visit her right before she died. I knew she was sick, but I didn't realize that I would never see her again. I was special in my grandmother's eyes. My mother told me that she had a wish—it was that I would walk. I did walk, but it wasn't until the age of four. . . .

I remember elementary school; my mind used to drift a lot. When I was at school, concentrating was almost impossible. I was so much into my own thoughts—my daydreams—I wasn't really in class. I would think of the cowboy movies—the rest of the kids would be in class and I would be on the battlefield someplace. The nuns would yell at me to snap out of it, but they were nice. That was my major problem all through school—that I daydreamed. I think all people do that. It wasn't related to retardation. I think a lot of kids do that and are diagnosed as retarded, but it has nothing to do with retardation at all. It really has to do with how people deal with the people around them and their situation. I don't think I was bored. I think all the kids were competing to be the honor students, but I was never interested in that. I was in my own world—I was happy. I wouldn't recommend it to someone, but daydreaming can be a good thing. I kind of stood in the background—I kind of knew that I was different—I knew that I had a problem, but when you're young you don't think of it as a problem. A lot of people are like I was. The problem is getting labeled as being something. After that you're not really a person. It's like a sty in your eye—it's noticeable. Like that teacher and the way she looked at me. In the fifth grade—in the fifth grade my classmates thought I was different, and my teacher knew I was different. One day she looked at me and she was on the phone to the office. Her conversation was like this, "When are you going to transfer him?" This was the phone in the room. I was there. She looked at me and knew I was knowledgeable about what she was saying. Her negative picture of me stood out like a sore thumb. . . .

I remember the psychiatrist well. He was short and middle-aged and had a foreign accent. The first few minutes he asked me how I felt and I replied, "Pretty good." Then I fell right into his trap. He asked if I thought people hated me and I said "Yes." I started getting hypernervous. By then he had the hook in the fish, and there was no two ways about it. He realized I was nervous and ended the interview. He was friendly and he fed me the bait. The thing was that it ended so fast. After I got out I realized that I had screwed up. I cried. I was upset. He came on like he wanted honest answers but being honest in that situation doesn't get you any place but the State School.

When the psychiatrist interviewed me he had my records in front of him—so he already knew I was mentally retarded. It's the same with everyone. If you are considered mentally retarded there is no way you can win. There is no way they give you a favorable report. They put horses out of misery quicker than they do people. It's a real blow to you being sent to the State School.

I remember the day they took me and my sister. We knew where we were going, but we didn't know anything specific about it. It was scary.

CONCLUSION

Ed's story stands by itself as a rich source of understanding. We will resist the temptation to analyze it and reflect on what it tells us about Ed. Our position is that at times and to a much greater extent than we do now, we must listen to people who have been labeled retarded with the idea of finding out about ourselves, our society, and the nature of the label (Becker, 1966).

There are specifics that can be learned from stories such as Ed's (for discussion, see Allport, 1942; Becker, 1966; Bogdan, 1974). For example, his story clearly illustrates that mental retardation is a demeaning concept that leads to a number of penalties for those so labeled. These penalties include lowered self-image and limited social and economic opportunity. Also, his story shows the profound effect of early prognosis on how people are treated and on the way that they think about themselves. It clearly demonstrates how segregated living environments and facilities such as state schools severely limit basic socialization for skills that are needed to participate in the larger society. His story also illustrates how being institutionalized is a function of a variety of social and economic contingencies—family difficulties, lack of alternatives—more than the nature of the person's disability or treatment needs. It also touches on the difficulties faced by people who are "protected." We can more accurately assess the resentment and the restrictions this protection imposes. We can also see the profound effects of simple words of praise and rejection on the person's self-concept. Ed's story points to how some people who work "with" the so-called "retarded" develop joking styles that minimize the real and normal problems and conflicts that the labeled is attempting to deal with and how the object of them feels about this. Although his story mentions all these specifics, there are two general points that we should remember.

The first point is simple but is seldom taken into account in conducting research or planning programs. People who are labeled retarded have their own understandings about themselves, their situation, and their experiences. These understandings are often different from those of the professionals. For example, although cure and treatment might dominate the official views of state schools and rehabilitation centers and programs, boredom, manipulation, coercion, and embarrassment often constitute the client's view. . . .

The second area that his story points to has to do with the lack of alternative ways that those who are "different" have to conceptualize their situation.

---

causes and trends and often relates the past to current events. An example of historical analysis is illustrated in Excerpt 2.6. **Legal analysis** focuses on selected law and court decisions to better understand the "law" and legal issues. This could include a review of judicial interpretations as illustrated in specific court cases or the analysis of a series of cases to identify legal principles as they apply to educational law.

■ DATA COLLECTION TECHNIQUES ■

Another way to classify research besides research design (experimental, nonexperimental, *ex post facto,* and qualitative) is to examine the technique used in the study to collect the data. That is, how did the researcher obtain the data? There are basically six ways to collect data: observation, questionnaire, interview, documents, tests, and unobtrusive measures. All research uses a variation of one or more of these, depending on strengths and limitations of each and other considerations. The techniques can be further classified as either quantitative or qualitative, as indicated in Table 2.2. One fundamental difference is that quantitative approaches use numbers to describe phenomena, while qualitative techniques use narrative descriptions. (Some studies that use qualitative data collection techniques, however, use numbers to summarize the findings). While most of the techniques can be used with any of the research designs, research design is closely related to technique. Virtually all experimental designs use quantitative techniques and most case study designs use qualitative techniques. Following you will find an introduction to each technique, with more detail in later chapters.

Quantitative Techniques

There is an historically strong tradition in educational research to use numbers and measurement. The approach emphasizes *a priori* categories to collect data in the form of numbers. The goal is to collect data to provide statistical descriptions, relationships, and explanations. **Quantitative techniques** are used with experimental, descriptive, and correlational designs as a way to summarize a large

---

EXCERPT 2.6
Historical Analysis

This study traces the ideas of the sex education movement in the United States toward the end of the nineteenth century and early twentieth century. The author sought to estimate the extent to which sex education was taught in schools and the aims and depths of anxiety of sex educators. The concept of morality, changes in ideology, attitudes and behaviors regarding sex and its implications during those years are discussed.

Source: Adapted from Strong, B. (1972). Ideas of early sex education movements in America, 1890–1920. *History of Education Quarterly. 13*, 129–161.

number of observations and to indicate numerically the amount of error in collecting and reporting the data.

Structured Observations.   All research requires some kind of observation about people, things, or processes. What we are concerned with in **structured observations,** however, is a particular kind of data-gathering, one in which the researcher directly observes, visually and auditorially, some phenomenon and then systematically records the resulting observations. The observer has predetermined specific categories of behavior that will be recorded; what he or she will observe is determined before the research is conducted. Usually, behavioral units are identified and a systematic process of recording is used to check or count specific behaviors. For example, the observer may record how many times students ask questions, the type of question asked, or how long the teacher took to respond to each question.

Standardized Interviews.   In an interview there is direct verbal interaction between the interviewer and the subject. A **standardized interview** is an oral, in-person administration of a standard set of questions that are prepared in advance. The questions are usually structured or semi-structured. When asked a structured question the subject selects the response from alternatives provided by the interviewer. Semi-structured questions are phrased to allow unique responses for each subject. Regardless of the type of question, the responses are coded, tabulated, and summarized numerically.

Questionnaires.   **Questionnaires** encompass a variety of instruments in which the subject responds to written questions to elicit reactions, beliefs, and attitudes. The researcher chooses or constructs a set of appropriate questions and asks the subjects to answer them, usually in a form that asks the subject to check the re-

TABLE 2.2
Techniques to Collect Data

Quantitative	Qualitative
Types:	
Structured Observations	Ethnographic Observation
Standardized Interviews	Ethnographic Interview
Tests	
Questionnaires	Documents
Unobtrusive Measures	
Characteristics:	
instrument used in data collection	data collected without an instrument
data appear as numbers	data appear as words
a priori decision in data presentation	not *a priori* decision on data presentation; depends on data collected
data takes one form—response as determined by instrument	data may take many forms—field notes, documents, interview notes, or tapes
data are tabulated and described statistically	tabulation limited to help identify patterns; used to support qualitative meanings
meaning is derived from statistical procedures employed	meaning is derived from qualitative strategies employed

sponse (yes, no, maybe). This is a very common technique for collecting data in educational research, and most survey research uses questionnaires. Questionnaires are not necessarily easier than other techniques and should be employed carefully.

Tests.   The term **"tests"** refers to the use of test scores as data. This technique involves subject response to either written or oral questions to measure knowledge, ability, aptitude, or some other trait. A numerical value is obtained as a result of each subject's answers to a standard set of questions. The instrument is used as a way to describe or measure a characteristic of the subject.

Unobtrusive Measures.   Most of the techniques that have been summarized are *intrusive;* the respondents or subjects realize they are being measured or assessed. In **unobtrusive measurement,** on the other hand, the subjects are unaware of being participants in the study. Unobtrusive techniques are **nonreactive.** Nothing out of the ordinary, like an observer or questionnaire, is introduced into a situation. This technique thus has the advantage of eliminating sources of bias that are present when respondents realize they are subjects in a research study.

Qualitative Techniques

As indicated earlier, **qualitative techniques** collect data in the form of words rather than numbers. There is an in-depth verbal description of phenomena. While there are different qualitative techniques that can be used to provide verbal descriptions, the goal of each is to capture the richness and complexity of behavior that occurs in natural settings from the participants' perspective. Once collected, the data are analyzed inductively to generate findings.

Ethnographic Observation.   **Ethnographic observation** has the distinctive feature of observing phenomena in naturally occurring situations over an extended period of time and writing extensive field notes to describe what happened. The researcher does not collect data to answer a specific hypothesis; rather, explanations are induced from the notes. Since the context of the observations is important, the observer is careful to document his or her role in the situation and what effect that may have on the findings. This type of observation is one in which many anthropologists engage to describe and analyze culture. It should be pointed out that some researchers use the term "ethnographic" to refer more generally to our definition of qualitative research.

Ethnographic Interview.   An **ethnographic interview** is often characterized as an unstructured or in-depth interview. The interviewer may use a general interview guide but not a set of specific questions worded precisely the same for every interviewee. Rather, there may be a few general questions, with considerable latitude to pursue a wide range of topics. The interviewee can shape the content of the interview by focusing on topics of importance or interest. In fact, the interviewer usually encourages the person to talk in detail about areas of interest. Often the researcher will tape the interviews and transcribe the tapes to analyze common themes or results. (See Excerpt 2.5.)

Documents.   **Documents** are records of past events that are written or printed; they may be letters, diaries, tax records and receipts, maps, journals, newspapers, court records, official minutes, regulations, laws, and the like. Historical, legal, and some policy-making studies are examples of research that depend on documents as the source of data. Much of the researcher's time is spent in locating documents with specialized bibliographies and indexes and in analyzing the sources. The documents are usually preserved in archives, manuscript collection repositories, or libraries. Rigorous techniques of criticism are applied to the documents to ascertain the traces of past events. The researcher interprets these facts to provide explanations of the past and clarifies the collective educational meanings that may be underlying current practices and issues.

■ HOW TO READ RESEARCH ■

Research is reported in a variety of ways, most commonly as a published article or as a paper delivered at a conference. The purpose of the report is to indicate clearly what the researcher has done, why it was done, and what it means. To do this effectively, researchers use a more or less standard format. This format is similar to the process of conceptualizing and conducting the research. Since the process of doing research is different for quantitative as compared to qualitative approaches, there are differences in the reporting formats used by each approach. Thus we will review the basic formats for reporting research for each approach separately.

How to Read Quantitative Research: A Nonexperimental Example

Although there is no universal pattern in the format of conducting or reporting quantitative research, most studies adhere to the sequence of scientific inquiry. There is variation in terms used, but the sequence indicated below is almost always adhered to:

1. Abstract
2. Introduction
3. Statement of research problem
4. Review of literature
5. Statement of research hypotheses or questions
6. Methodology
   a. subjects
   b. instruments
   c. procedure
7. Results
8. Discussion, implications, conclusions
9. References

In writing a research report, the writer begins with the introduction and continues sequentially to the conclusion. In planning to conduct research, the researchers begin by formulating a research problem. Excerpt 2.7 illustrates each of the steps listed above in a quantitative research article.

Abstract.   The **abstract** is a paragraph that summarizes the journal article. It follows the authors' names and is usually italicized or printed in type that is smaller than the type of the article itself. Most abstracts contain a statement of the purpose of the study, a brief description of the subjects and what they did during the study, and a summary of important results. The abstract is useful because it provides a quick overview of the research, and after studying it, the reader usually will know whether to read the article itself.

Introduction.   The introduction is usually limited to the first paragraph of the article. The purpose of the introduction is to put the study in context. This is often accomplished by quoting previous research in the general topic, citing leading researchers in the area, or developing the historical context of the study. The introduction acts as a lead-in to a statement of the more specific purpose of the study.

Research Problem.   The first step in planning a quantitative study is to formulate a research problem. The **research problem** is a clear and succinct statement that indicates the purpose of the study. Researchers begin with a general idea of what they intend to study, such as the relationship of self-concept to achievement, and then they refine this general goal to a concise sentence that indicates more specifically what is being investigated—for example, what is the relationship between fourth graders' self-concept of ability in mathematics and their achievement in math as indicated by standardized test scores?

The statement of the research problem can be found in one of several locations in articles. It can be the last sentence of the introduction, or it may follow the review of literature and come just before the methods section. In our illustrative article, the problem is stated after the review of literature and just before the hypotheses.

Review of Literature.   After researchers formulate a research problem they conduct a search for studies that are related to the problem. The review summarizes and analyzes previous research and shows how the present study is related to this research. The length of the review can vary, but it should be selective and should concentrate on the way the present study will contribute to existing knowledge. As in the example, it should be long enough to demonstrate to the reader that the researcher has a sound understanding of the relationship between what has been done and what will be done. There is usually no separate heading to identify the review of literature, but it is always located before the methods section.

Research Hypothesis or Question.   Following the literature review researchers state the hypothesis, hypotheses, or question(s). Based on information from the review, researchers write a **hypothesis** that indicates what they predict will happen in the study. A hypothesis can be tested empirically, and it provides focus for the research. For some research it is inappropriate to make a prediction of results, and in some studies a research question rather than a hypothesis is indicated. Whether it is a question or a hypothesis, the sentence should contain objectively defined terms and state relationships in a clear, concise manner, as does the hypothesis in our example.

Methodology.   In the methods or **methodology** section, the researcher indicates the subjects, instruments, and procedures used in the study. Ideally, this section contains enough information so that other researchers could replicate the study. There is usually a subheading for each part of the methods section.

In the *subjects* subsection (sometimes referred to as the *sample* or *participants*), the researcher describes the characteristics of the individuals from whom information is gathered. There is an indication of the number of subjects and the way they were selected for the study.

The instruments subsection describes the techniques used to gather information. There is an indication of the validity and reliability for each measuring device to show that the techniques are appropriate for the study. Sometimes examples of items are included to help the reader understand the nature of the instrument.

The *procedure* subsection is used to explain how the study was conducted. The authors describe when the information was collected, where, and by whom. They describe what was done to the subjects and the manner in which the data were collected. It is important to provide a full description of the procedures. There needs to be sufficient information so that the reader would know how to proceed in replicating the study. The procedures may also affect the ways subjects respond. Readers thus need to examine the procedures carefully in interpreting the results.

Results.   A summary of the analyses of the data collected is reported in the *results* or *findings* section. This section may appear confusing to the beginning researcher because statistical symbols and conventions are used in presenting the results. The results are usually indicated in tables and graphs within the text of the article. The results should be presented objectively without interpretation or discussion, summarizing what was found. (Sometimes interpretation will follow the results in this section.) Since the results section contains crucial information in the article, the reader must be able to understand and evaluate the material. This is important in order to avoid uncritical acceptance of the conclusions.

Discussion, Implications, and Conclusions.   In this section the researchers indicate how the results are related to the research problem or hypothesis. It is a nontechnical interpretation of whether the results support a hypothesis or answer a research question. If the study is exploratory or contains unexpected findings, the researchers explain why they believe they obtained these results. The explanation should include an analysis of any deficiencies in the methodology utilized and an indication of other research that may explain why certain results were obtained. This section is also used to indicate implications of the study for future research and practical applications and to give overall conclusions. This section is identified by several different labels. The most common words are *discussion, conclusion,* or *summary.*

References.   **References** and reference notes that are cited in the article follow the discussion. The style of the notation will vary. The journal in which our model article is published uses 1974 APA (American Psychological Association) format, which has been revised.

Guidelines for Evaluating Quantitative Research

There is no agreed-upon method or approach in reading research articles. Some readers begin with the conclusion, and others follow the written sequence. Our experience suggests that a reader should begin with the abstract, then scan the introduction, research problem, and conclusion sections. If, after reading these sections, the reader is still interested in the article, he or she should start at the beginning and read the entire article more carefully. Whenever reading research, one should keep in mind the practical or meaningful significance of the study. Research is significant if there are no serious weaknesses in the design and the differences obtained between groups or individuals are large enough to suggest changes in theory or practice.

Other questions should be kept in mind in reading research. While you need to become acquainted with these considerations now, a full understanding and application of the questions is expected only after further study of each topic. The following questions, organized according to each major section of a research article, constitute a guideline for evaluating quantitative research.[1]

Research Problems

1. How clearly and succinctly is the problem stated?
2. Is it sufficiently delimited so as to be amenable to investigation? At the same time, does it have sufficient practical value (to educators, students, parents) to warrant study?
3. Possibly with the exception of some descriptive research, is it stated in such a way that it expresses the relationship of the two or more variables?
4. Does it have a rationale? Has the problem been studied before? If so, should this problem be studied again? Is the study likely to provide additional knowledge?
5. Will the findings give rise to further hypotheses, thereby increasing the probability of adding to existing knowledge?

[1]Excerpts from *Educational Research: Readings in Focus,* Second Edition, by Irvin J. Lehmann and William A. Mehrens. Copyright © 1979 by Holt, Rinehart and Winston, Inc., reprinted by permission of the publisher.

EXCERPT 2.7
Example of a Quantitative
Research Report

COGNITIVE DEVELOPMENT AND COGNITIVE STYLE AS FACTORS IN MATHEMATICS ACHIEVEMENT

Sheila Vaidya and Norman Chansky *Temple University*

The purpose of the study was to provide a theoretical framework for the learning of mathematics from Piaget's theory about the development of the number concept and Witkin's theory of field dependence-independence. The relationship between operativity on Piagetian tasks of number, classification, seriation, field dependence-independence, and mathematics achievement on concepts, computations, and applications was investigated. Results were analyzed separately within each grade for the total mathematics achievement test score, as well as for the three subtests consisting of mathematics concepts, computations, and applications. In all grades, field independence was related to high mathematics achievement, especially for the concepts and applications subtests. High operativity was found to be related to high achievement in mathematics concepts only in the second grade. The educational implications of the findings are discussed.

INTRODUCTION

Piaget (1965) has shown how a child constructs the number concept through a progressive organization of the logic of classification and seriation. The natural development of the logic of classification and seriation, which integrates the psychological development of the number concept, suggests, according to Piaget (1975), that the natural organization of children's mathematical ideas has relevance for mathematics education.

RESEARCH PROBLEM

The present study examined how the learning of mathematics as determined by performance on mathematics achievement tests among second, third-, and fourth-grade children may be related to their cognitive development and their cognitive styles. Thus, operativity was determined on Piagetian number, classification, and seriation tasks. Individual differences in field dependence-independence were investigated for subjects at the same level of operativity to determine relationships with mathematics achievement in second-, third-, and fourth-grades.

REVIEW OF LITERATURE

While exploring the significance of Piaget's ideas for mathematics education, some investigators (Dimitrovsky & Almy, 1975; Omotoso, 1976; Brill, Weiserbs, & Reid, Note 1) have found that among elementary school children, there is a significant and positive relationship between performance on the Piagetian tasks of number, classification, seriation, and mathematics learned in school as determined by performance on mathematics achievement tests. Since performance on the Piagetian tasks is determined by the cognitive developmental level of the child, it is important to consider the effect of cognitive developmental aspects in the learning of mathematics among elementary school children.

In addition to cognitive development, individual differences in cognitive styles among children, specifically in field dependence-independence (Witkin, Moore, Goodenough, and Cox, 1977) are also likely to affect mathematics achievement. A field-independent cognitive style is characterized by an analytic approach to a situation, consisting of the ability to overcome an embedding context while transcending the salient features. In contrast, a field-dependent cognitive style is global. It is determined by the prevailing field or context of a situation. Field independence is likely to influence mathematics achievement because of the assumption that the analytic ability required in field dependence and mathematics achievement tests involves perceptual disembedding and developing problem-solving strategies that depend on reorganizing and restructuring information (Bien, 1974). Researching the field dependence-independence variable in mathematics achievement, Bien (1974) and Buriel (1978) both found higher mathematics achievement among field-independent subjects.

Although the separate effects of cognitive developmental level and field dependence-independence with reference to mathematics achievement have been investigated, the effects of both cognitive developmental level and individual differences in field dependence-independence among subjects at the same level of cognitive development have not been investigated with respect to the learning of the various aspects of mathematics, such as concepts, computations, and applications.

RESEARCH HYPOTHESIS

It was hypothesized that high-operational children would obtain higher scores on mathematics achievement tests than low-operational children and that field-independent children would obtain higher scores on mathematics achievement tests than field-dependent children. Further, subjects who were both high operational and field independent were expected to obtain higher scores on the mathematics achievement test than the other three groups of subjects (high operational-field dependent, low operational-field independent, low operational-field dependent). Thus, an Operativity x Cognitive Style interaction was hypothesized.

METHOD

Subjects. The sample consisted of 102 subjects randomly selected from the second, third, and fourth grades of a suburban Philadelphia school. The school is predominantly (94%) Anglo-American. There were 34 subjects (17 males and 17 females) from each grade. The mean ages of the subjects in the second, third, and fourth grades were 7.38, 8.02, and 9.06 years, respectively.

INSTRUMENTS

Conservation Test Battery. This test was adapted from the conservation tests used by Lunzer (1970) and by Wilkinson and Lunzer (Note 2). The testing procedure incorporated a standardized form of administration, although it retained the depth yielded by the clinical interview method typically used by Piaget. The forms of the test designed by Lunzer and Wilkinson were taken from Inhelder and Piaget (1964) and Piaget (1965). Lunzer and Wilkinson made some alterations to facilitate test administration and to provide uniformity in the testing procedure.

The battery specified exact and detailed procedures for each test. The conservation of number, seriation, and classification tests were composed of subtests, with more than one item in each subtest. Detailed instructions were provided for the scoring of each subtest.

Children's Embedded Figures Test (CEFT). Developed especially for use with children in the age group of 5–10 years, this test is a modification of the original Embedded Figures Test (Witkin, Oltman, Raskin, & Karp, 1971). The test consists of 25 chromatic test items in which a small figure is embedded within a larger geometric design. A standardized procedure of administration was followed. The subject was instructed to find the figure (a tent for the first 11 items and a house for the remaining 14 items). Responses were scored as 0 or 1. Subjects were given a score of 1 only if they correctly located the figure within the geometric design on their first attempt. The test score was the total number of figures correctly located. The maximum possible score on this test is 25, with higher scores indicating greater field independence.

Stanford Achievement Test (SAT). Learning of mathematics was determined from the measure of mathematics achievement taken from the Mathematics section of the SAT, which was administered to all children at the beginning of the school year as part of the school's regularly scheduled assessment testing. The Mathematics section of the SAT consists of three subtests that measure three aspects of mathematics achievement, namely, mathematics concepts, computations, and applications. Children were tested with batteries appropriate to their grade level. The number of correct items on each subtest determines the subject's raw score. The interpretation of the raw scores is based on norms obtained from over 275,000 students drawn from 43 states in the United States. Based on the norms, raw scores are converted to standard scores and percentile ranks.

PROCEDURE

Number conservation, classification, and seriation tasks from the Conservation Test Battery (Wilkinson & Lunzer, Note 2) were administered individually to each child to determine the level of operativity on those tasks. The CEFT (Witkin et al., 1971) was also administered individually to each child to determine field dependence-independence. The test order was counterbalanced. There was no uneven distribution of subjects on operativity or field dependence-independence due to the order of test administration. Mathematics achievement test scores on the SAT Primary Levels I, II, and III for the second-, third-, and fourth-grade levels, respectively, were obtained from the school records.

Subjects were classified as *high operational* or *low operational*. A Guttman (1950) scaling analysis of the battery indicated that the test battery was not reproducible or scalable (index of reproducibility = .87; index of scalability = .32). Hence, to be classified as high operational, subjects were required to be operational on 7 out of the 10 conservation tasks (70%) in the battery, with the additional requirement that at least 3 of these 7 tasks should be among the 5 top-ranked tasks according to difficulty. Subjects who did not meet these criteria were classified as low operational. Subjects whose scores were at or above their grade-median CEFT were classified as field independent; those whose scores were below, were classified as *field dependent*. The grade medians were 9.00, 10.00, and 13.00 for Grades 2, 3, and 4, respectively.

RESULTS

A separate analysis was performed for each grade. A preliminary analysis of the data within each grade indicated no significant sex differences on operativity, cognitive style, and mathematics achievement. Hence, the sex variable was not incorporated in the analysis. A 2 x 2 (Operativity x Cognitive Style) analysis of variance (ANOVA) with the total mathematics raw score as the dependent variable was performed for each grade. In addition, a 2 x 2 multivariate analysis of variance (MANOVA), with the three subtest raw scores of concepts, computations, and applications as the dependent variables, was performed at each grade level. Finally, a combined analysis of all grades was also performed by obtaining a common scale score on the total mathematics achievement test (Madden, Gardner, Rudman, Karlsen, & Merwin, 1975) for all subjects. A 3 x 2 x 2 (Grade Level x Operativity x Cognitive Style) ANOVA was performed, with the scaled score as the dependent variable.

Analyses of the total mathematics raw scores indicated a significant main effect for operativity, $F(1, 30) = 19.80$, $p < .01$, in only the second grade. High-operational subjects obtained higher scores than low-operational subjects. There was a significant main effect for cognitive style in all three grades: in the second grade, $F(1, 30) = 11.51$, $p < .01$; in the third grade, $F(1, 30) = 10.63$, $p < .01$; and in the fourth grade, $F(1, 30) = 7.80$, $p < .01$. In each grade, field-independent subjects obtained higher scores than field-dependent subjects. The means are presented in Tables 1 and 2. No significant interactions were found at any grade level.

Table 1

Raw Score Means on the Total Mathematics Test for Operativity and Cognitive Style in Each Grade

	Grade		
Variable	**2**	**3**	**4**
High operational	50.73	73.32	72.49
Low operational	42.78	67.91	66.82
Field independent	49.69	77.66	74.49
Field dependent	48.83	63.57	62.82

Since the total mathematics score combines the scores on the three subtests, all of which are intercorrelated, a MANOVA was performed at each grade level. The effects were generally reliable across grades and within subtest scores. Analyses of the three subtest raw scores indicated a significant main effect for operativity in the second grade only, $F(3, 30) = 15.35$, $p < .01$, and for cognitive style at all grade levels: in the second grade, $F(3, 30) = 4.81$, $p < .01$; in the third grade, $F(3, 30) = 5.59$, $p < .01$; and in the fourth grade, $F(3, 30) = 3.66$, $p < .01$. Univariate F ratios demonstrated that in the second and fourth grades, the significant effect was due to the concepts subtest: in the second grade, $F(1, 30) = 15.35$, $p < .01$; in the

Table 2

Raw Score Means and ns for the 2 x 2 (Operativity x Cognitive Style) Analysis at Each Grade Level

Grade	High operational, field independent	Low operational, field independent	High operational field dependent	Low operational, field dependent
2				
M	54.18	45.20	47.29	40.37
SD	2.01	2.56	2.09	2.24
n	11	5	7	11
3				
M	77.50	77.83	69.14	58.00
SD	4.53	3.85	4.88	4.83
n	12	6	7	9
4				
M	74.23	74.75	66.75	58.89
SD	3.44	4.85	5.44	4.44
n	13	4	8	9

fourth grade, $F(1, 30) = 8.93$, $p < .01$. In the third grade, it was due to the effect of computations and applications subtests: for computations, $F(1, 30) = 7.84$, $p < .01$; for applications, $F(1, 30) = 13.26$, $p < .01$. Again, no interactions were found to be significant.

The previously mentioned analyses were performed on the raw scores. The scaled score is alleged to provide an index of a developmental trend in achievement. Analyses of the scaled scores resulted in significant main effects for operativity, $F(1, 90) = 10.50$, $p < .01$; for cognitive style, $F(1, 90) = 93.34$, $p < .01$; and for grade level, $F(2, 90) = 93.34$, $p < .01$. No interactions were significant. Post hoc analyses using the Scheffé procedure revealed significant grade effects. As expected, there was a progressive increase in the means across the three grades. In the second, third, and fourth grades, the means were 123.50, 136.97, and 152, respectively. When the intraclass correlations were computed for the three significant main effects, they were found to be .75 for grade level, .11 for cognitive style, and .04 for operativity. Thus, grade level, a correlate of many developmental trends, accounts for the largest percentage of the variance in mathematics achievement. Cognitive style and operativity variables follow but are of lesser importance.

That the cognitive-development and cognitive-style variables are unrelated is also clear. They were only slightly correlated with one another. The phi coefficients were .30 in Grade 2, .23 in Grade 3, and .30 in Grade 4.

DISCUSSION, IMPLICATIONS, CONCLUSIONS

Results of the present investigation indicate that operativity is significantly related to mathematics achievement at the second-grade level, whereas a field-independent cognitive style is related to mathematics achievement at all grade levels, specifically to the concepts subtest at the third-grade level. Thus, the abilities involved in high operativity (i.e., the understanding of the logic of number, classification, and seriation on Piagetian tasks and the disembedding ability in field independence) are both important for determining mathematics achievement at the second-grade level. However, in Grades 3 and 4, cognitive style is more important than operativity in determining mathematics achievement.

The results have important educational implications. The significant relationship between a field-independent cognitive style and mathematics achievement at all three grades does emphasize the importance of gearing instruction to the cognitive style of the individual learner. Witkin et al. (1977) suggest that a matching of teacher and student cognitive styles is more likely to result in effective teaching and a greater interpersonal relationship between the teacher and the student than would a mismatching of cognitive styles.

Teachers may be able to gear instruction to individual cognitive styles if they know how cognitive styles affect the learning of mathematics. Bien (1974) has shown that when field-dependent subjects were presented with a structure by circling the relevant information in a word-problem-solving task, there was no significant difference in the performance of field-dependent and field-independent subjects, thus indicating that field-dependent subjects are more successful at solving mathematics problems when they are provided with an external structure. The subjects used in Bien's study were from the fourth grade.

The effects of the external structure on field independence and other factors contributing to the gearing of instruction to cognitive styles need to be researched. The developmental implications of the findings are not clear, since operativity was not related to mathematics achievement beyond the second grade.

Reference Notes

[1]Brill, M., Weiserbs, B., & Reid, D. K. *The relations among seriation, class inclusion and academic achievement in emotionally disturbed and learning disabled children.* Paper presented at the eighth annual Symposium of the Jean Piaget Society, Philadelphia, May 1978.

[2]Wilkinson, J. E., & Lunzer, E. A. *The developing individual in a changing world.* Paper presented at the biennial meeting of the International Society for the Study of Human Development, August 1973.

References

Bien, E. C. The relationship of cognitive style and structure of arithmetic materials to performance in fourth grade arithmetic (Doctoral dissertation, University of Pennsylvania, 1974). *Dissertation Abstracts International,* 1974, *35,* 2040–2041. (University Microfilms No. 74-22,809)

Buriel, R. Relationship of three field-dependence measures to the reading and mathematics achievement of Anglo-American and Mexican-American children. *Journal of Educational Psychology,* 1978, *70,* 167–174.

Dimitrovsky, L., & Almy, M. Early conservation as a predictor of arithmetic achievement. *Journal of Psychology,* 1975, *91,* 65–70.

Guttman, L. The basis for scalogram analysis. In S. A. Stouffer (Ed.), *Measurement and prediction.* Princeton, N.J.: Princeton University Press, 1950.

Inhelder, B., & Piaget, J. *Early growth of logic in the child.* New York: Norton, 1964.

Lunzer, E. A. Construction of a standardized battery of Piagetian tests to assess the development of effective intelligence. *Research in Education,* 1970, *3,* 53–72.

Madden, R., Gardner, E. F., Rudman, H. C., Karlsen, B., & Merwin, J. C. *Stanford Achievement Test (Tech. Data Report).* New York: Harcourt Brace Jovanovich, 1975.

Omotoso, H. M. Piaget's cognitive tasks as factors in the acquisition of mathematics among Nigerian children. *West African Journal of Educational and Vocational Measurement,* 1976, *3,* 17–24.

Piaget, J. *The child's conception of number.* New York: Norton, 1965.

Piaget, J. Comments on mathematical education. *Contemporary Education,* 1975, *47,* 5–10.

Witkin, H. A., Moore, C. A., Goodenough, D. R., & Cox, P. W. Field dependent and field independent cognitive styles and their educational implications. *Review of Educational Research,* 1977, *47,* 1–64.

Witkin, H. A., Oltman, P. K., Raskin, E., & Karp, S. A. *Manual for the Embedded Figures Tests.* Palo Alto, Calif.: Consulting Psychologists Press, 1971.

This research is a part of the first author's dissertation submitted in partial fulfillment of the requirements for the PhD degree at Temple University.

The authors acknowledge the contributions of Patricia Minuchin, Daniel Rosenthal, and David Fitzgerald as committee members. This work has benefited from the learned comments of James J. Roberge. The authors also wish to thank the principal, teachers, and students at the Jenkintown Grade School for their assistance in data collection.

Requests for reprints should be sent to Sheila Vaidya, who is now at Drexel University, Nesbitt College, Philadelphia, Pennsylvania 19104.

Source: From Vaidya, S. and Chansky, N., "Cognitive Development and Cognitive Style as Factors in Mathematics Achievement." *Journal of Educational Psychology*, 72, 326–330, 1980. Copyright © 1980 by the American Psychological Association. Reprinted by permission of the publisher and author.

Review of Literature

1. How adequately has the literature been surveyed?
2. Does the review present pertinent material or is it just filler?
3. Were primary or secondary sources used? Were secondary sources relied on too heavily?
4. Does the review critically evaluate previous findings and studies, or is it only a summary of what is known without pointing out any possible deficiencies or alternative explanations?
5. Does the review support the need for studying the problem?
6. Does the review establish a theoretical framework for the problem?

Hypotheses or Questions

1. Are any assumptions advanced with respect to the hypotheses or questions? If so, are they explicit (they should be), or are they implicit?
2. Are hypotheses consistent with theory and known facts? Are they testable? Do they provide a suggested answer to the problem?
3. Are all terms adequately defined in operational fashion?

Methodology

1. Are the procedures, design, and instruments employed to gather the data described with sufficient clarity so as to permit another researcher to replicate the study?
2. Is the population described fully? Did the researcher use the total population or did he or she sample from it? If a sample is used, is it representative of the population from which it was selected? Note: The manner of sampling is very important.
3. Is evidence presented about the validity and reliability of instruments?
4. Was a pretest used? Was there a pilot study? If so, why? What were the results? Was the problem or question or procedure changed as a result of the

pretest or pilot study, and if so, was this modification justifiable or desirable?
5. Are there any obvious weaknesses in the overall design of the study?

Results

1. Are statistical techniques needed to analyze the data? If so, were the most appropriate and meaningful statistical techniques employed?
2. Have the results been presented adequately?

Discussion, Implications, Conclusions

1. Are the conclusions and generalizations consistent with the findings? What are the implications of the findings? Has the researcher overgeneralized his or her findings?
2. Does the researcher discuss the limitations of the study?
3. Are there any extraneous factors that might have affected the findings? Have they been considered by the researchers?
4. Are the conclusions presented consistent with theory or known facts?
5. Have the conclusions (both those relevant to the original hypothesis and any serendipitous findings) been presented adequately and discussed?

How to Read Qualitative Research: An Ethnographic Example

There is greater diversity in the formats used to report qualitative research than in the formats typical of quantitative studies. This is because of the many types of qualitative studies, and the fact that until recently there has not been much educational qualitative research reported. While there is not a single mode for representing qualitative research, many of the published reports will have the major sections presented below. In contrast to quantitative studies, however, these sections may not be identified clearly or are identified by descriptive terms related to the topic.

Introduction.   The introduction provides a general background of the study, indicating the potential importance of the research. It summarizes the general intentions of the investigator, along with a general statement of the research problem or purpose. For a journal article, usually only one of many research foci are reported. The introduction includes a preliminary literature review to present possible conceptual frameworks that will be useful in understanding the data and results. The review justifies the need for a descriptive case study. The introduction may also indicate the structure of the rest of the report.

EXCERPT 2.8
Example of a Qualitative Research Report

CAN ELEMENTARY SCHOOLTEACHING BE A CAREER?: A SEARCH FOR NEW WAYS OF UNDERSTANDING WOMEN'S WORK

Sari Knopp Biklen *Syracuse University*

INTRODUCTION

Is the prevailing notion of career sufficient? To examine this question, we first look at how literature and society construct meaning for the concept of career. We then compare this perspective with those of a particular group, women who teach elementary school. We show, through the informants' life stories, how the traditional external concept is inadequate to organize these women's lives. Finally, we suggest what elements a revised concept of career must include.[1]

Recent work in both education and gender scholarship make this a particularly appropriate time to examine these concerns. Scholarly as well as federal concern with the quality of education has marshalled national attention to schools and particularly to teachers.[2] Little of this focus on teachers, however, has revealed how gender issues intersect with educational concerns.[3] Since elementary schoolteaching is considered an occupation for women, this omission is stunning.

Demographic analysts suggest that expanding opportunities for women have contributed to the drain of bright women from the field.[4] The public wonders whether the lack of upwardly mobile applicants to teach creates a mediocre teaching force. Concomitantly, public disdain exists for those who want to spend the day with young children. Policy-makers turn their attention, therefore, to figuring out how to attract bright, creative recruits into teaching, certainly an important problem.

Careers: Traditional Definitions. In spite of changes in the work force, the opening of fields that were previously more resistant to women, and the addition of women in professional and upper management positions, the structure of career is based on the ways in which men have been able to live their lives, free from primary responsibility for the family. One begins work, that is, after college or graduate school, or advanced medical or scientific training, and works continually, moving upward in graduated stages. From this perspective, a career is "a pre-established total pattern of organized professional activity, with upward movement through recognized preparatory stages, and advancement based on merit and bearing honor."[5] This view emphasizes the coherence of the career and the goal orientation of the career occupant.[6] One can therefore study the structure of individual careers, such as the medical, the legal, and the academic.[7]

Two elements are paramount. First is upward movement.[8] This view presents careers as trajectories, measurable in the public sphere. The professional career is defined by the nature of participation in the wage-labor system and by the status that accrues from that participation.[9] Looked at in this way, teaching is at least a "semi-professional," at best a fringe profession.[10]

The second element is career commitment. By commitment is meant dedication to one's work. Personal or family life is supposed to be fit around the demands of work. Career commitment has two major aspects, both of which relate to time. The first aspect is long-term commitment. Here, career commitment refers to the decision to undertake a career in the first place. Hence, if a woman decides to become a teacher rather than a principal, she is said to have lowered her career commitment.[11] Associated with this aspect of career commitment is the question of the length of time a woman expects to work. Mason measured teachers' career commitment, for example, by asking them where they planned to be in five years.[12]

The second aspect of career commitment relates to the short-term use of time for work. One common yardstick for differentiating occupations from professional careers, for example, is the career's tendency to spill over the 9-to-5 time slot. Doctors are a case in point:

Central to the status of a profession is a field's ability to induce members to do their job no matter how long it takes and no matter what other demands are made on their lives. These requirements are stringent in medicine, where lives may be at stake in the physician's decision about how high a priority should be given to finishing a job.[13]

Our notion of the professional career includes a heavy work load and a large time commitment.[14] Women in professional careers must accept this view in order to succeed: "To the extent that male work values dominate, women who wish to succeed must accept male definitions and expectations about work commitments."[15] The implications of this view for women are direct. For women to put career commitment over family commitments, to set their professional priorities straight, so to speak, they must act against social norms.[16]

Two key elements of the external understanding of the career, then, are upward movements and career commitment.[17] We will examine the work perspectives of a group of elementary schoolteachers to depict an alternative view. First, however, we examine literature on teachers' work lives.

Teachers and Careers. Teaching has been described both as "careerless"[18] and as an occupation of "lateral careers."[19] Movement between schools can signify a lateral career change. Teachers may, for example, consider a transfer to a school in a higher socioeconomic neighborhood a promotion. The label of "careerless" refers to the structure of the teaching occupation; namely, to the impossibility of promotion within teaching. Advancement means becoming an administrator and leaving teaching. Additionally, teaching is structured to accommodate the in-and-out patterns of women's employment; that is, "To persist in teaching is, in a sense, to be 'passed over' for higher position or marriage."[20] In this view, a lifetime commitment to teaching evidences failure rather than success.

Elementary schoolteachers' low career commitment has been widely noted and correlated primarily with gender.[21] This literature reflects a notion that normative expectations about women's roles carry over into the occupational setting. Teaching becomes an extension of the female role.

More recent research on women and work, undertaken from the new scholarship-on-women perspective, has questioned this approach,[22] suggesting that the ways in which we have examined women's working lives has been inadequate and misleading because it is based on stereotypical assumptions about women.[23] In this view, we are hindered in thinking clearly about the work women do because of our immersion in a sociology of occupations which takes the lives of men as the norm.[24]

Scholars working from this perspective have looked at the issue of work commitment somewhat differently. They have examined factors in the workplace which may account for women's differing experience.[25] They have argued that power rather than gender influences behavior,[26] and discussed work commitment in a different frame.[27] They have criticized the models sociologists have brought to the study of men's and women's work.[28] Some have analyzed media advice to working women.[29] This study can be seen in this context of the new scholarship on women.

METHODOLOGY

Methods and Participants. The issues discussed in this paper are part of a larger study that focused on how a group of elementary schoolteachers looked upon their work, what they valued and criticized about their occupation, and how they negotiated their work interests with sex role and family expectations.[30] The investigator relied upon the qualitative methods of participant observation and in-depth interviewing.[31] The inductive nature of these methodological approaches and the emphasis on participant perspectives causes researchers in this mode to search for the ways that those being studied make sense out of their experiences. Qualitative researchers assume that people act on the basis of their interpretations of experience. Hence, they are interested in what subjects experience and how they interpret these experiences.[32]

Observations and interviews were conducted in schools over an eight-month period in one primary setting and a subsidiary one. Both schools were located in a middle-sized city in the American Northeast. The primary setting, Vista City Elementary,[33] had a student population of 800, and an outstanding academic reputation. When the local newspaper published achievement test results each spring, Vista City Elementary always boasted the highest scores. The data reported in this paper come from this primary setting.

All but two of the classroom teachers at Vista City were women. They ranged in age from their mid-twenties to their late fifties. They were single, married, and divorced. Most of the single women had worked continuously at teaching, though two had tried other kinds of jobs for a short period, hoping for more recognition. Those who were married had families and children who were important in their lives. Among the married women, as well, there was some variety in their long-term patterns. Some of the married teachers had husbands who wanted traditional families and had conservative values about women's roles. Some of the older teachers had conservative fathers who had forbidden them as young adults to enter the labor market. Still others had taken only six weeks out for the births of their children, or had stayed home for a few years before returning to work. In one case, a teacher never finished her undergraduate education until her children went to school.

There was a range of interest and involvement in women's issues as well. Two of the teachers were active in the local National Organization for Women. Others expressed some interest in factors that facilitated women's working or that promoted women's advancement. None of the single women who were interviewed expressed any interest in women's issues; although some of the married women did, they assumed primary responsibility for the home as well as their classrooms. They could not be described as rebels against social norms.

Characterized as their lives were by "interrupted careers" and by deference to their husbands' social values, it is difficult to understand how one could argue that these women had a sense of their work as teaching careers. Yet, I will suggest that the traditional way of evaluating career or work commitment—as continuous upward movement through occupational stages—fails to do justice to the views of these women. In this next section, we move to the internalized structuring of career as we examine how the teachers described their work.

Teachers Describe Their Work. During the first several months of interviewing and observing, teachers would often say, in response to a question asking them to describe their work experiences, "I have always worked." In the early stages of my research, I would then form a mental picture of a person who had worked continuously in a full-time position and had a career goal clearly in sight. I would settle back in my seat waiting to hear the details, thinking to myself, "I'm on to something. This certainly contradicts what I've read about women's in-and-out employment patterns." As the women described their work histories to me, however, they almost always described a discontinuous pattern of childraising, part-time work, and finally, full-time re-entry into the employment market. Most surprisingly, they would end their stories reiterating that they had always worked.

Kate Bridges was one of the teachers who described herself as having always worked, but who portrayed her actual work history in this discontinuous pattern. She described her feelings about her occupation: "I have felt passionately about teaching for 20 years." She may have felt passionately about it but she had not, exactly, been teaching for 20 years.

She recalled "teaching fairly consistently since 1960–61," but she was "in and out" with babies. "I'd come home for a year and I'd say: 'Mother in the home forever.' And then all of a sudden I was back teaching again." She had a variety of teaching assignments:

I started out in the public schools in San Francisco, I taught there for two years in an inner-city kind of school and I loved that. And then when the babies came along I was looking for part-time work and I worked with disturbed kids. It seemed ideal because I had a friend with children the same ages and we were both teachers. We decided to start a nursery school and then she got pregnant again and left it to me. And I had it for two years and just loved it. There it was, my own school.

She moved to Chicago in connection with her husband's work and taught teachers part-time in a college education department. At that point, her teaching had "gotten increasingly almost full-time and you know any part-time job is a full-time-and-a-half one anyway." Her last move was to Vista City, again for her husband's work. She stayed "mostly" at home for about seven years, though she had worked part-time at a drug rehabilitation center developing its educational program. Then she felt she must return to teaching. She got a full-time teaching position at an elementary school. She described her determination at that time: "I'm going to start my teaching career and if I don't accept this job now, God knows if I will ever get my foot in the door."[34] As the above comment indicates, Kate formally acknowledged that the beginning of her teaching career started when she began to teach full-time in an elementary school. Her conflicts arose from her perception, however, that she had been interested in, involved with, and thinking about teaching for 20 years. As she saw it, she had remained committed to teaching because of her internal occupational consistency. She had always thought of herself as a teacher.

Kate had worked hard for 20 years, and some of this work involved teaching children in schools. She had not always been able, then, to translate her passion for teaching into an occupational reality. While she always considered herself a teacher, she had not always physically engaged in full-time teaching. And this is the crux of the issue. As Kate and her colleagues saw it, bearing and caring for children of one's own did not necessarily reflect upon one's career commitment.

Again, these teachers were not women who would violate acceptable social norms. They were in the mainstream. At the same time, however, they valued their work identities as teachers and did not want to have to choose between work and family. The career pattern Kate reveals is one defined by internal consistency about one's occupation rather than continuing external employment.[35]

Teachers and Their Husbands. Husbands had a major impact on the ways in which married teachers made decisions about work. Some women, like Kate, spoke to their husbands directly about their occupational intentions. Other women had husbands who resisted their wives' occupational interest. The cases of three women whose desire to work full-time outside the home compelled them to develop strategies to overcome their husbands' resistance reveal the tactics they developed to enable them to return to the labor market. Their situations are valuable to study because on the surface these women appear the most complacent with women's roles.

Sylvia Richardson, in her fifties, had taught seventh graders for five years prior to taking a nine-year hiatus to raise her children, "and wait until my youngest was solidly in school." She had since been teaching for nine years. Her husband had not wanted her to return to work because he liked having her at home. "We're not for this women's lib thing," she said. As her urge to return to the classroom strengthened, she decided that, to gain flexibility, she would become a substitute teacher. At this time, one of her old teaching friends gave her a little advice: "Listen," said the friend, "Don't go and sub in the seventh grade because the kids are really different from when you were there." Sylvia decided that, "If seventh and eighth graders were really violent, and if it was going to be just a terribly difficult situation for me every day, then I'd better pick a group that wasn't going to be this demanding." Then her husband would not be able to say to her, "We don't need this aggravation. Come on home." What enabled her to change from subbing, which her husband did not classify as a full-time position, to full-time teaching, was her availability. As she began subbing every day, her husband finally relented on the full-time teaching position. "At least we'll know where to find you," he told her.

Sylvia Richardson employed a strategy in order to re-enter teaching. She chose a grade level that would be less "difficult" than junior high so that she could leave her work problems behind her when she came home. Sylvia represents an interesting example of how women may strategize to accomplish their goals when they do not want to challenge social norms.

While Sylvia used every opportunity to dissociate herself from feminism, she shared, at the same time, feminist appraisals of the damage to self-esteem that may be the toll of full-time housework. As she put it, "It's really hard for someone to just stay home and take care of a child and do all the housework because you feel terrible about yourself. But, on the other hand, the family needs attending to."[36] While the strategy that Sylvia Richardson chose seemed to have reaped benefits for her, the costs others had to pay were higher.

Take the case of Jessica Bonwit. She had also stopped working in schools when her three children were born, though she ran a family day-care program during this period. But, "something went click after six years," and she knew that she had to get back to teaching in a school. Her husband, however, did not share in the work. Jessica promised her husband that his life would not alter as far as his home commitments were concerned. As she said, "He didn't mind so much when I went back to work, because his life didn't change at all from before I was working to when I went back to work, but he also knew that I had a real professional interest in teaching and also that I was really happy doing it."[37]

Jessica's price for her full-time work was to carry both home and school responsibilities. She resented her husband's selfishness: "I love my husband, but sometimes I don't like him very much." Her teaching was so important to her that, at least for the time, she was willing to carry this burden. The impact of her choice will only emerge in the future.

Carrie Amundsen had never worked before she had children, but, like the other two women, she, too, had to develop a strategy in order to join the work force as a full-time employee. Although Carrie was in her fifties, she had only been teaching for 10 years. Her husband had never wanted her to work. In fact, she confided, she almost did not marry him because of his views on working women. She referred to him as "the original male chauvinist pig." She had to find a way to ease herself into the work market. She said, "Here's how I did it."

"Actually," she began, "I wasn't even planning to go back to work. I had never gotten my bachelor's degree, so I went and took a course in math at the university." She reportedly had no goal in mind except "enrichment," but she had "loved" the course and "ended up taking some more courses." When she had taken as much math as she could, she "somehow made some connections" between her own children's experiences in school learning how to read and the special struggles some other children had. Further, there were particular reasons for these struggles. Her interest sparked. When she finished her undergraduate degree, she got a master's degree in special education.

By this time, she had gained experience in schools and wanted to put it to good use. In the city where she lived, a specialist in her area was starting a program and asked her if she would work in it. She told him, "My husband will never let me work full-time." Her future employer responded, "Let me worry about your husband." So she and the faculty member "worked out a deal" where she would say to her husband that she would just try it out for one year. "It worked," and she "loved" teaching. At the end of that year she "weaseled" her way into first one year and then another.

These three teachers chose tactics to maneuver their way into teaching without having to do an ideological battle with their husbands or to rebel against social norms. On their own time tables they translated their mental commitment into occupational reality. While away from their positions in institutions of schooling, the women often ran home day-care centers, they stayed in touch with their colleagues and discussed classroom life, they planned to return to work, and they sometimes strategized to overcome their husbands' resistance to their working.

Externally, then, the lives of these women represent the interrupted career pattern. Internally, however, they thought of themselves as teachers, whether or not they were in the job market, and they made choices that kept them close to children or to educational concerns. While they did not, in some ways, challenge the boundaries of their lives, they exhibited a coherence in their attitude toward their work.

External Structure and Internal Concepts. Clearly, this is a different way of thinking about coherence in one's working life. We have been accustomed to thinking about coherence in work life in terms of continual upward movement. These women, on the other hand, said, through their lives, that they wanted to have children and family life as well as be teachers.

They questioned why breaks for child-rearing were equated with lack of job commitment when they had always thought of themselves as teachers. The external structure and their internal conceptualization conflicted.

Career commitment is, as we have said, however, inseparable from upward mobility in the traditional concept of career. Again, many of the teachers studied brought a different perspective to these issues. As we have seen, the teachers focused on children and this focus determined to a large part their work orientation.

The most committed teachers at Vista City Elementary School brought a high level of idealism to their work. These expectations caused them to work hard to accomplish their goals. It contributed to their reputations as excellent teachers. At the same time, the work setting brought frustrations because it did not match their conceptions of how they wanted to work. Some of these teachers focused more determinedly on their classroom work, isolating them from other adults in the building. Not all teachers reflected this pattern, however, for some brought their idealism to other aspects of the job, such as committee work. In neither case, however, did teachers' high commitment or idealism further their careers. Few opportunities for advancement are available. The structure of the occupation was determined. Idealism caused teachers to focus on the quality of work and work setting.

Since administrative opportunities are limited, few teachers face the situation of deciding what to do when opportunity knocks. Those who are faced with such a decision, however, reveal the idealism about teaching that other teachers often exhibited in their daily work. When Barbara Timmitts was first offered the position of instructional specialist, for example, she turned it down. She felt that she had not taught long enough to do the job well. She took it the second time it was offered, not because she was certain that she would do excellently at it, but because she wanted the job and was fearful it would not be offered a third time.

If we examine how Barbara Timmitts thinks about her job offer, we notice that her major concern was whether or not she would perform well, rather than how the position might serve her career advancement. It is this kind of work orientation that I define as idealistic, because it reflects a person's ideal concept of how a job ought to be done. The teachers focused on the content of the occupation, rather than on their work as a link to other occupational choices. Quality of performance overrode career value. These teachers often thought of how they served the occupation rather than of how the occupation could serve them.

Christine Bart did not have an administrative position. Although she chaired the first-grade team, she received no extra remuneration for it. Like Barbara, however, she played a strong role among teachers both at the school and on district-wide committees. Like Barbara, her sense of idealism shaped the commitments she undertook. When I asked Christine about her leadership goals, she said that she thought she would not be interested in being a school principal. From her view, principals seemed powerless. Caught between parents' demands and central administration regulations, their hands were tied.

Bart was not sure that what administrators do is effective. She shared the view of many teachers at Vista City—that one cannot be effective or productive as an administrator and that those positions waste valuable talent. She saw Barbara Timmitts as a case in point: "My priority is in here with these kids. You look at someone like Barbara Timmitts. Barbara Timmetts is about the best teacher in this school and she was promoted to pushing a cart around the halls. She walks around with requisition slips and a pencil in her hand. Now what is that?" Children are the core of the work.

Amelia Dickenson had directed the gifted program before she was transferred out of the administrative position back into the classroom. When I asked her what it was like being back in the classroom full-time, she replied, "It's really great; I just love it! You really feel like you're accomplishing something."[38]

Teachers' commitment to their work and their attempt to execute their jobs close to their ideal conception of it, were revealed in daily work as well. While teachers often complained about the small number of breaks they had during the day, many teachers gave up their breaks in service to their teaching. Roberta Blake, for example, said that she had no free periods during the day, not even lunch. She explained that she believes in mainstreaming, so instead of having her class of special education students go out in a group to "the specials" (art, music, and gym), she sends them out a few at a time with different typical classes. Her beliefs, then, cause more work for her. As she put it, "After all, that's why this class is here— to be mainstreamed."

Kate Bridges rarely went to the teachers' room to eat her lunch. It was not just that the smoke bothered her. She decided, rather, that returning papers to her pupils in the afternoon, that they completed in the morning, improved educational results. "I have so many papers that have accumulated over the morning. Why not correct a paper and give instant feedback? If you could pass back the paper and have the kids working on it as soon as they return from lunch—I mean, the mileage on it is infinitely more. It is taking it out of your skin, though. So I'm sitting here eating a sandwich and correcting these papers and I also know it's better education (and I'm not having to correct that set of papers at night)." Kate saw her choice as a "tradeoff," however, because remaining in her room isolated her from collegial relationships.

The sixth grade team also gave up the opportunity to take a break during the day. They had asked the administration to schedule all their students' "specials" at 8:15 (school started at 8 o'clock) so that they could spend the rest of the day with their students. Because their students "switched" classes for different subjects, team members said that they did not have "a lot of time with the students." Apparently they wanted as much time with their students as they could get.

Sandra Miller gave up her lunchtimes and every afternoon for a month to do her "levels testing" because she wanted to give the tests to her pupils in the way she thought students ought to be tested,—"when there was nobody else around." That way she would also not have to cut her reading groups to give the tests.

At Vista City Elementary, these "breaks" amounted to little time. Teachers got three "free" periods a week while their students went to art, music, or gym classes. From the perspective of these teachers, the day was not structured so as to maximize the education of their students. Teachers reported that they felt able to reach their goals only when they sacrificed some of their own planning time. This sacrifice did not mean that teachers wanted to be without breaks, but in the balance of things, they preferred to create optimal teaching conditions.

Sacrificing time was not the only way in which teachers attempted to live closely to their ideal of good teaching. Their idealism was expressed in many other ways. One teacher had taken a tutoring job the previous summer because she wanted the particular experience she would gain, even though the pay was terrible. She summed up her views with, "And I really learned a lot." Jessica Bonwit turned down a teaching assignment, when she came back from teaching after time home with her children, because it was not close enough to her minimum requirements for a good teaching situation. She did not mean a situation that would be easy for her, she said, but one that would enable her to work at even a near distance to her image of a good educational situation.

A teaching assistant gave up the tenure she had gained in the district because the special child with whom she worked was being transferred to another district. She had not wanted the child to be transferred because it was the middle of the year. Her attempts to postpone the move until the next year had been unsuccessful. She could have remained in the district while the child got a new aide in the new district, but she could not face jeopardizing all the progress her student had made that year. It was most important to her to finish the work she had begun. Even though the school to which she was going had no program for the child, she was determined to continue to make mainstreaming a successful experience for him: "We're going to make this work. Even if they don't have a program there, we'll make it successful. No matter what, we will make a good program for Jacob there."

These teachers focused their energies on the content of the work, not on its use to them for upward mobility. Hence, their major frustrations came, not when their hopes for advancement were crushed, but rather when they were forced to make compromises which they felt endangered their educational vision.[39]

The Vista City teachers carried their occupational ideals into the workplace. These ideals centered on the content of the work rather than on its career-ladder potential. This idealism is symbolized, perhaps, by the language one teacher used to describe her first teaching position: It was a "marriage" between her and the children; it is this kind of relationship that many teachers sought.

The teachers' idealism about their work also affected their aspirations about how worthwhile it would be to be an administrator. The teachers at Vista City Elementary were particularly critical of those in the central offices, whether of the personnel who planned the staff development sessions or of the special education administration, who were criticized for being out of touch with the school staffs and incapable of handling difficult problems. From the perspective of these teachers, it was usually mediocre teachers who became principals and central office staff. Since the hassles and demands were also great there, they could see little reason to hanker after these positions.

They did have goals—of being what they called "great teachers." A great teacher had a school or district-wide reputation for excellence. Style did not determine one's reputation. Some were more or less strict, more or less interested in, say, learning centers. They were the teachers whose classes the parents hoped their children would be placed in because in these classes most children learned, were stimulated, and were happy.

Those with reputations as great teachers were able to wield more power and strengthen their autonomy. These were great benefits. Formally, for example, they were elected to faculty council and nominated to serve on district-wide committees. Informally, the principal solicited their views and gave them greater leeway to organize their classrooms and curricula. But foremost stood the reputation and the personal satisfaction it generated. As the teachers saw it, to be a great teacher meant "something." They were not sure that being a great administrator carried an equivalent weight.

CONCLUSION

Conclusion. The perspectives that Vista City teachers brought to their work reveal the inadequacy of current conceptualizations of career. To substantively include women, the concept of career must describe the patterns of women's lives as well as those of men's. To do this, data must be generated from both women's as well as men's experiences, not from the lives of men applied to women. As the study of these teachers' lives suggest, we cannot have a career model which describes only those women who combine great ambition with a willingness to challenge social norms.

To revise our conceptualization, we need to approach the working lives of women freed from the confines of the concept of the male career. As the life stories presented here suggest, parent roles must be conceptualized as compatible, not competitive, with work roles. Parenting is not the opposite of career commitment. Or, to put it another way, when women choose to bear and nurture children, they do not thus signify a lack of career commitment. If we need to account for why some women hesitate to leave their children, we might rather consider the structural effects of the social neglect of child care options and the stigma accorded to day-care.

A revised concept of career must reflect an alternative concept of success, one that does not equate success in life with success at work. Critics of current perspectives in the sociology of occupations have rightly noted that employing a gender model for women (in which work and family concerns are discussed) and a job model for men (in which only issues from the work setting are relevant) leads to social inequity.[40] If careers are essentially masculine, then women who have children may never be taken seriously in their work. We must hold varied models rather than a narrowly defined concept of career paths in mind. That we think of the bearing and nurturing of children as a detour reveals the limitations of the concept's applicability to contemporary society. Even women in higher status professions than teaching, who slow down the pace of their careers to have children, are considered to take their work "less seriously" than those whose careers are not interrupted. The term "career interruption" suggests deviance from the ideal pattern which is molded around "the clockwork of male careers."[41] In this view, women occupy career niches but do not shape career paths. A generic career model must, at its base, account for the lives of both men and women equally well.

Notes

[1]Earlier versions of this paper were presented at the 10th Research on Women and Education Conference. CSU/Long Beach, California, November 1984, and at the A.E.R.A. annual meeting, Chicago, April 1985. The research reported here was conducted under a grant from the National Institute of Education. The views expressed here, however, are my own. I would like to thank Sally Gregory Kohlstedt, Douglas Biklen, Charol Shakeshaft and the anonymous reviewers at *Issues in Education* for their helpful comments on earlier drafts.

[2]*See,* for example, The National Commission on Excellence in Education, *A Nation At Risk: The Imperative for Educational Reform* (Washington: U.S. Department of Education, 1983); Ernest Boyer, *High School: A Report on Secondary Education in America* (Princeton, NJ: Carnegie Foundation for the Advancement of Teaching, 1983); and John Goodlad, *A Place Called School: Prospects for the Future* (New York: McGraw-Hill, 1983).

[3]Mary Kay Tetreault and Patricia Schmuck, "Equity As An Elective: An Analysis of Selected Educational Reform Reports and Issues of Gender," *Issues in Education* 3 (1985): 45–67.

[4]Philip Schlecty and V. Vance, "Recruitment, Selection and Retention: The Shape of the Teaching Force" (Paper delivered at invitational conference "Research on Teaching: Implications for Practice," Warrentown, VA, February 1982).

[5]Burton Bledstein, *The Culture of Professionalism* (New York: Norton, 1976), 172. *See,* also, Harold Walensky, "The Professionalization of Everyone," *American Journal of Sociology* 70 (1964): 137–158.

[6]An alternative use of the concept has been the employment of career to describe change in people's lives. In this use it refers to the various positions, stages, and ways of thinking people pass through in the course of their lives. It emphasizes the participant's perspectives on life. *See* Everett Hughes, "Institutional Office and the Person," *American Journal of Sociology* 43 (1937): 404–413.

[7]Oswald Hall, "Stages of A Medical Career," *American Journal of Sociology* 26 (1948): 524–538; Dan Lortie, "Laymen to Lawmen: Law Schools, Careers and Professional Socialization," *Harvard Educational Review* 29 (1959): 352–369; and L. Wilson, *The Academic Man* (New York: Oxford University Press, 1942).

[8]Dan Lortie, *School-teacher* (Chicago: University of Chicago, 1975).

[9]*See,* for example, M. Blaxall and B. Reagan, eds., *Women and the Workplace: The Implications of Occupational Segregation,* special issue of *SIGNS* 1, pt. 2 (1976); and M. S. Larson, *The Rise of Professionalism* (Berkeley: University of California, 1977).

[10]Amitai Etzioni, ed., *The Semi-Professions and Their Organization* (New York: Free Press, 1969); and Blanche Geer, "Teaching," *International Encyclopedia of the Social Sciences* 15 (1968): 560–5.

[11]*See* Veronica Nieva and Barbara Gulick, *Women and Work* (New York: Praeger, 1981).

[12]W. S. Mason, *The Beginning Teacher: Status and Career Orientations* (Washington DC: Government Printing Office, 1961).

[13]B. G. Bourne and N. J. Wilker, "Commitment and the Cultural Mandate: Women in Medicine," in *Women and Work,* eds. Rachel Kahn-Hut, Arlene Kaplan Daniels and Richard Colvard (New York: Oxford University Press, 1982): 111–122.

[14]Mary Frank Fox and Sharlene Hesse-Biber, *Women at Work* (Palo Alto, CA: Mayfield, 1984).

[15]Kahn-Hut, Daniels and Colvard, *Women and Work,* 2.

[16]Rose Coser and Gerald Rokoff, "Women in the Occupational World: Social Disruption and Conflict," *Social Problems* 18 (1970): 534–554.

[17]It is important to remember that these are not rigid categories. The movement upward, for example, is not the same for all professions. Think of doctors, who once having achieved their professional status and position, practice in the same town for the rest of their lives. They may do emergency room work to break the routine or expand their practices, but if they are not connected with a university hospital, becoming a department chair is not a career goal. And, while some university professors would want to advance to a deanship, others consider the scholar's role at odds with the administrator's, and would not more deign to take the position than they would to write for *Parade.*

[18]Lortie, *School-teacher.*

[19]Howard S. Becker, "The Career of the Chicago Public School Teacher," *American Journal of Sociology* 57 (1952).

[20]Lortie, *School-teacher, 89.*

[21]*See* W. S. Mason, R. J. Dressel, and R. K. Bain, "Sex Role and the Career Orientations of Beginning Teachers," *Harvard Educational Reviews* 29 (1959): 370–383; Robert Dreeben, *The Nature of Teaching* (Glenview, IL: Scott, Foresman, 1970); Blanche Geer, "Occupational Commitment and The Teaching Profession," *The School Review* 74 (1966); Oswald Hall, "The Social Structure of the Teaching Profession," in *Struggle for Power in Education,* eds. F. W. Lutz and J. J. Azzarelli (New York: Center for Applied Research in Education, 1966), 35–48; Dan Lortie, *School-teacher;* J. D. Grambs, "The Roles of the Teacher," in *The Teacher's Role in American Society,* ed. T. Stiles, 14th Yearbook of the John Dewey Society, New York; R. L. Simpson and I. H. Simpson, "Women and Bureaucracy in the Semi-Professions," in *The Semi-Professions and Their Organization,* 196–255; and M. G. Sobel, "Commitment to Work," in *Working Mothers,* eds. L. W. Hoffman and F. I. Nye (San Francisco: Jossey-Bass, 1975): 63–80.

[22]Sari Knopp Biklen and Charol Shakeshaft, "The New Scholarship on Women," in *Handbook for Achieving Sex Equity in Schools,* ed. Susan Klein (Baltimore: Johns Hopkins Press, 1985), and Catharine Stimpson, "The New Scholarship about Women: The State of the Art," *Annals of Scholarship* 2 (1980): 2–14.

[23]*See* Kahn-Hut, Daniels, and Colvard, *Women and Work;* Cynthia F. Epstein, "Sex Role Stereotyping, Occupations and Social Exchange," *Women's Studies* 3 (1976): 185–194; Rosabeth M. Kanter, "The Impact of Hierarchical Structures on the Work Behavior of Women and Men," *Social Problems* 23 (1976): 415–430; Judith Long Laws, "Work Aspirations of Women: False Leads and New Starts," *Signs* 1:3, pt. 2 (1976): 33–49; and Coser and Rokoff, "Women in the Occupational World."

[24]*See* Joan Acker, "Issues in the Sociological Study of Women's Work," in *Women Working,* eds. A. H. Stromberg and S. Harkness (Palo Alto, CA: Mayfield, 1978): 134–161. More studies are appearing which examine how women in teaching construct experience. *See,* for example, Dee Spencer-Hall, *Teachers as Persons: Case Studies of the Lives of Women Teachers* (Final report to N.I.E., July 1982);

Margaret Nelson, "From the One-Room Schoolhouse to the Graded School: Teaching in Vermont, 1910–1950," *Frontiers* 7 (1983): 14–20; Richard Quantz, "Teachers as Women: An Ethnohistory of the 1930s" (Paper delivered at the annual meeting of the American Educational Research Association, New York, March 1982); Polly Kaufman, *Women Teachers on the Frontier* (New Haven, CT: Yale University Press, 1984); Boston Women Teachers Group, "A Study of the Effect of Teaching on Teachers" (Paper delivered at the American Educational Research Association's annual meeting, Boston, 1980); and Michael Apple, "Work, Gender and Teaching," *Teachers College Record* 84 (1983): 611–628.

[25]Judith Agassi, "The Quality of Women's Working LIfe," in *The Quality of Working Life,* eds. L. Davis and A. Cherns, vol. 1 (New York: New York Free Press, 1975), 280–298; Sobel, "Commitment to Work;" Fox and Hess-Biber, "Women at Work;" and Nieva and Gulick, "Women and Work."

[26]Kanter, "The Impact of Hierarchical Structures."

[27]*See,* for example, Constantina Safilios-Rothschild, "Towards the Conceptualization and Measurement of Work Commitment," *Human Relations* 24 (1971): 489–493, and Sobel, "Commitment to Work."

[28]R. L. Feldberg and E. R. Glenn, "Male and Female: Job Versus Gender Models in the Sociology of Work," *Social Problems* (1979): 524–538.

[29]Nona Glazer, "Overworking the Working Woman: The Double Day in a Mass Magazine," *Women's Studies International Quarterly* 3 (1980): 79–93.

[30]Sari Knopp Biklen, *Teaching as an Occupation for Women: A Case Study on an Elementary School* (Final Report to N.I.E. under Grant no. NIE–G–81–007).

[31]Robert Bogdan and Sari Knopp Biklen, *Qualitative Research for Education* (Boston: Allyn and Bacon, 1982). *See,* also, Judith P. Goetz and Margaret Lecompte, *Ethnography and Qualitative Design in Educational Research* (Orlando, FL: Academic Press, 1984).

[32]Ibid.

[33]The names of the schools and the teachers have been changed to protect their promised anonymity.

[34]To accept this position, she had to refuse to go with her husband to Europe on his sabbatical. This caused some temporary marital discord.

[35]Kate's pattern was reflected in the lives of other married teachers at Vista City Elementary. Jessica Bonwit, for example, left full-time teaching for a six-year period while her three children were very young. During this period, however, she did not stop working. She started a home day-care program for six to eight children. Christine Bart described her work history as "continuous" though "not always in permanent jobs."

[36]I suggest that this example is typical of many teachers' solutions to problems. They often sought the individual resolution rather than a change in the status quo.

[37]Perhaps, Jessica was prepared in some way for a marriage of this type. Her own upbringing did not emphasize her worth in a world of men: *I was raised in an Italian family where the boys were valued much more highly than the girls. So with my brother, they always listened to him with both ears. But, with me, they only listened with one ear. It was like, "What were you saying?" So, I got in the habit of talking things over with myself.*

[38]Even the principal explained her reluctance to consider applying for a superintendency on this basis. It would take her too far away from her children.

[39]At the same time, teachers who were untenured were fearful about the insecurity of their positions. As untenured, Jessica Bonwit said on the last day of school when she was unsure whether she would be able to return the following year, "The job status situation is so disheartening for me. I just think it is devastating to teachers not to know where they are going to be next year. It's a terrible way to treat us." The occupational structure was disheartening.

[40]Feldberg and Glenn, "Male and Female."

[41]Arlie Hochschild, "Inside the Clockwork of Male Careers," in *Women and the Power to Change,* ed. Florence Howe (New York: McGraw-Hill, 1971): 47–80.

Methodology.   The methodology section describes the design of the study, including the selection and description of the site, the role of the researcher, initial entry for observation, the time and length of the study, the number of participants and how they were selected, and data collection and analysis strategies. This information is needed to evaluate the soundness of the procedures. The amount of detail contained in this section will vary, depending on the type of research report. In relatively short published articles the methodology may be part of the introduction.

Findings and Interpretations.   In this section the researcher presents the data that were gathered, usually in the form of lengthy narratives, and analyzes the data. This should be done in sufficient detail to allow the reader to judge the accuracy of the analysis. The data are used to illustrate and substantiate the researcher's interpretations. Analysis is often intermixed with presentation of data. The data are usually quotes by participants. It is important to indicate the purpose of data analysis and to describe what has been learned by synthesizing the information. Because the presentation is in narrative form, frequently there are a number of descriptive subtitles connoting different findings.

Conclusions.   The conclusion usually includes a restatement of the initial focus of the study and how the data results and analyses impinge on that focus. Implications of the results can be elaborated, as well as implications for further research.

Guidelines for Evaluating Qualitative Research

To understand qualitative research it is necessary to read the entire report. This is how you are able to identify with the investigators and understand how they have come to their conclusions. The process by which this occurs is important, and to understand this process it is necessary to read from beginning to end. Similar to quantitative studies, there are certain questions that should be asked about the report to judge its quality.

Introduction

1. Is the focus, purpose, or topic of the study stated clearly?
2. Are there situations or problems that lead to the focus of the study? Is there a rationale for the study? Is it clear that the study is important?
3. Is there background research and theory to help refine the research questions?
4. Does the introduction contain an overview of the design?
5. Is the literature review pertinent to the focus of the research? Is the literature analyzed as well as described?

Methodology

1. Are the particular site(s) described to identify its uniqueness or typicality?
2. How was initial entry into the field established?
3. How was the researcher's presence in the field explained to others? What was the role of the researcher?
4. Who was observed? How long were they observed? How much time was spent collecting data?
5. Does the researcher report any limitations to access of pertinent data?
6. Are the data representative of naturally occurring behavior?
7. Are limitations of the design acknowledged?

Findings and Interpretations

1. Are the perspectives of the different participants clearly presented? Are participants' words or comments quoted?
2. Is contextual information for participants' statements provided?
3. Are multiple perspectives presented?
4. Are the results well documented? Are assertions and interpretations illustrated by results?
5. Is it clear what the researcher believes the data indicated? Are personal beliefs kept separate from the data?
6. Are the interpretations reasonable? Were researcher preconceptions and biases acknowledged?

Conclusions

1. Are the conclusions logically consistent with the findings?
2. Are limitations of the research design and focus indicated?
3. Are implications of the findings indicated?

■ SUMMARY ■

This chapter has provided an overview of common terminology of types of research with reference to their design, the techniques used to collect data, and the standard format of published articles. The major points in this chapter are:

1. Research design is the general plan of the study, including when, from whom, and how data are collected.
2. In experimental research design the practitioner studies cause-and-effect relationships by manipulating a factor and seeing how that factor relates to the outcome of the study.
3. True experimental research design is characterized by randomization of subjects to groups, control over factors that might disrupt the study, and decisions as to which treatment is given each group.

4. Quasi-experimental research design investigates causation despite nonrandom assignment and a lack of complete control.
5. Single-subject research design investigates the causal relationship between a factor and the behavior of a single individual.
6. "Nonexperimental" is a generic term that refers to research in which there is no direct control over causation. Nonexperimental research designs can be classified as descriptives correlational or *ex post facto* designs which study cause-and-effect relationships that have occurred in the past.
7. Correlational research is a type of descriptive study that investigates the relationship between two or more variables.
8. Techniques to gather information include quantitative and qualitative approaches. Quantitative techniques, like questionnaires and tests, use numbers as data, while qualitative techniques, like ethnography, use narrative descriptions.
9. Qualitative research designs are emergent and use a case study approach to better understand phenomena.
10. The format of quantitative studies follows a well-established sequence with similar sections. In qualitative studies the format will vary but will usually include an introduction and literature review, methodology, findings and interpretation, and conclusions.

■ SELF-INSTRUCTIONAL REVIEW EXERCISES ■

Sample answers are in the back of the book.

Test Items

1. True experimental designs contain all of the following characteristics except
   a. a control or comparison group.
   b. random assignment of subjects.
   c. manipulation of extraneous variables.
   d. manipulation of subjects.

2. Quasi-experimental designs differs from true experimental designs in
   a. degree of control.
   b. use of comparison or control group.
   c. random assignment.
   d. Both a and c are correct.

3. In nonexperimental research designs the investigator can do all of the following *except*
   a. make inferences from a sample to a population.
   b. describe existing conditions.
   c. establish cause-and-effect relationships.
   d. predict one phenomenon from another.

4. Historical research is
   a. basic research.
   b. applied research.
   c. analytic research.
   d. *ex post facto* research.

5. In correlational research the investigator is studying
   a. the existing conditions in a descriptive manner.
   b. cause-and-effect relationships.
   c. the same event at two points in time.
   d. the degree of relationship between two phenomena.

6. Structured observations are in the same category as
   a. applied research.
   b. descriptive research.
   c. evaluation research.
   d. none of the above.

7. Qualitative data collection techniques are distinguished from quantitative techniques by
   a. the research design used.
   b. the function of the research.
   c. using words rather than numbers.
   d. providing more meaningful results.

8. Ethnographic research is characterized by
   a. intense one-to-one relationships.
   b. copious field notes.
   c. clearly defined hypotheses.
   d. unobtrusive observations.

9. The abstract of an article contains
   a. a full description of the subjects.
   b. recommendations for further study.
   c. the purpose of the study.
   d. Both a and c are correct.

10. The methodology section of a quantitative research article contains
    a. subjects, materials, instruments.
    b. participants, instruments, procedure.
    c. subjects, instruments, data analyses.
    d. participants, subjects, procedures.

11. The hypotheses in quantitative research should follow the
    a. research problem.
    b. review of literature.
    c. introduction.
    d. abstract.

12. The purpose of the methodology section of qualitative studies is to
    a. provide a general background for the study.
    b. summarize the design of the study.
    c. show how researcher interpretations will be made.
    d. present the focus of the study.

Application Problems

1. Classify each study described below with respect to its research design: experimental, nonexperimental, *ex post facto*, or qualitative.
    a. a pilot investigation of the validity of the Back Stroke Test to identify problem swimmers
    b. a comparison of the effect of two reading programs on fourth-grade classes in Kalamazoo
    c. an investigation of the structure of attitudes of college students
    d. the effect of extrinsic rewards on the motivation of randomly assigned children to play groups
    e. a survey of principals' attitudes toward collective bargaining
    f. a study of the relative effectiveness of different counseling techniques used by counselors over the last five years
    g. an investigation of the difference in attendance between two high schools with different leadership styles
    h. a posttest-only study of the effect of humorously written review sentences on comprehension for two groups of children
    i. a study of the meaning of merit pay to teachers

2. Read a quantitative research article and identify the sentences that correspond to the standard sections named below.
    a. abstract
    b. introduction
    c. statement of research problem
    d. review of literature
    e. statement of research hypotheses
    f. subjects
    g. instruments
    h. procedures
    i. results
    j. discussion, implications, conclusions

3. Describe the research in problem 2 with respect to research design and technique.

4. Read a qualitative research article and identify the major sections:
    a. introduction
    b. methodology
    c. results and interpretations
    d. conclusions

CHAPTER 3

RESEARCH PROBLEMS: STATEMENTS, QUESTIONS, AND HYPOTHESES

■ KEY TERMS ■

research problem
significance of the problem

Quantitative:
  construct
  variable
  categorical variable
  continuous/measured variable
  dependent variable
  independent variable
  manipulated/experimental variable
  predictor variable
  criterion variable
  operational definition
  hypothesis

Qualitative:
  case
  qualitative observations
  narrative descriptions
  concept
  phenomenology
  grounded theory
  foreshadowed problems

This chapter presents the first and perhaps most difficult aspect of research: formulating a clear, concise, and manageable research problem. The research problem statement is crucial because it communicates to others the focus and importance of the problem, the educational context and scope, and the framework for reporting the results. To state a formal research problem requires considerable preliminary work and selecting the logic, such as deductive or inductive reasoning, for the problem.

   This chapter also discusses common sources used to generate research problems and criteria for the significance of research problems. Quantitative problem formulations use deductive reasoning to select the constructs, variables, and operational definitions, which are instruments. Qualitative problems require inductive reasoning. Qualitative problems are reformulated as the researcher builds from observations of social situations of current or past events of a selected case and later relates them to broader phenomena. We also cite criteria for judging the adequacy of the problem statement.

■ THE NATURE OF RESEARCH PROBLEMS ■

Researchers can ask many questions about educational theories and practices. Consider the following range of questions:

What is the present status of a group's opinions or performance?

What are the effects of a specific practice, innovation, or policy?

How do past historical events, court rulings, or policies influence current educational issues?

How does Mrs. Kay teach biology to lower achieving students?

What are the theoretical assumptions that guide daily practices and long-range planning?

Why is Ellen quiet during small group reading and disruptive when students choose their learning centers and their activities?

What is the best way to conduct one's work?

Questions comprise the initial step in research.

Some questions, although important to an individual or a group, may not connote research problems as stated. The noun "problem" has conventional and technical meanings. In the conventional sense, a problem is a set of conditions needing discussion, a decision, a solution, or information. A **research problem** implies the possibility of empirical investigation—that is, of data collection and analysis.

Explanations of how to do something, vague propositions, and value questions are not research problems *per se*. Questions like, "How can we achieve equality or opportunity?" or "How can we prevent student dropout?" are how-to-do-it questions. Such propositions as "Democratic institutions are a natural manifestation of the American culture" are too vague or broad to be researchable. Value questions ask which of two or more things are good or bad, desirable or undesirable, better or worse, should or should not be done. Value questions, as stated, cannot be investigated empirically. Although how-to-do-it questions, vague propositions, and value questions are meaningful to administrators, parents, teachers, philosophers, and political leaders, these questions, as stated, are beyond research. In the process of asking such questions, however, a researchable problem may emerge.

A research problem, in contrast with a practical problem, is formally stated to indicate a need for empirical investigation. Quantitative research problems may be phrased as questions or hypotheses. Let us look at some examples. "What are the attitudes of the parents toward a school's student retention policy?" "Is there a difference in Levinson's adult developmental periods between age cohorts of male and female graduate students?" "There is a positive relationship between preschool attendance and social maturity in elementary students—that is, A relates to B." "Does academic aptitude, self-concept, and level of aspiration influence academic achievement—that is, do A, B, and C relate to D?" Each of these statements implies data collections and analysis.

Qualitative research problems are phrased as research statements or questions, but *never* as hypotheses. A research hypothesis implies deductive reasoning; qualitative research uses primarily inductive reasoning to suggest an understanding of a particular situation or historical period. Qualitative problems usually are phrased more broadly than quantitative problems by using terms such as "how," "what," and "why." Qualitative problems state the situation or context in such a way as to limit the problem. A qualitative problem might be a study of one specific situation, a person, one state, or a historical period. Some examples of ethnographic research questions are "How does Mrs. Jackson, an elementary teacher, assist Joan, a student teacher, during her student teaching?", or "What does being a 'single parent' mean to Mr. Strong who has two young children to rear—how does being a single parent affect his parenting role and other aspects of his life?"

Qualitative studies also examine the past through historical or legal documents. These research questions are typically phrased in the past tense. For example, "When and why were teachers first required to be certified by the state of Vermont, how have the requirements for teacher certification changed since then, and why were these changes made?" Qualitative research problems may be phrased as research statements such as "The purpose of this study is to examine and analyze the legal grounds upheld by federal and state courts in cases involving student disruption from 1952 to 1988 to provide a judicial definition of the term 'student disruption'."

Sources of Problems

Problems are identified initially as general topics. After much preliminary work, the general topic is focused as a specific research problem. Where does one begin to find even general topics? The most common sources are casual observations, deductions from theory, review of the literature, current social issues, practical situations, and personal experiences and insights. Let us examine the kinds of studies these sources might suggest.

Casual observations are rich sources of questions and hunches. Decisions are frequently based on the probable effects of practices on pupils, staff, or the community, without empirical data. Research questions can be suggested by observations of certain relationships for which no satisfactory explanation exists; routine ways of doing things that are based on authority or tradition lacking research evidence; or innovations and technological changes that need long-term confirmation. Such studies may solve a practical problem, propose a new theory, or identify variables not yet in the literature.

Deductions from theory can suggest research problems. Theories are general principles whose applicability to specific educational problems are unknown until tested empirically. The validity and scope of organizational and many other theories might be tested under educational conditions. Such studies could verify the usefulness of a theory for explaining educational occurrences.

Related literature may suggest a need to replicate a study with or without variation. Repeating a study may increase the generalizability and validity of the previous findings. In many instances, it is impossible to randomize the subjects, which limits the *generalizability* of the findings. As experiments are repeated at different times and in different settings, with similar results, however, researchers can have more confidence in the findings. Citing related literature enables qualitative studies to *extend the empirical understandings* to other situations.

Current social and political issues in American society often result in educational research. The women's movement raised questions about sex equity in general and in sex stereotyping of educational materials and practices. The civil rights movement led to research on the education of minority children and the effects of desegregation on racial attitudes, race relations, self-concept, achievement, and the like.

Practical situations, because information is needed by decision-makers at a given site, may suggest evaluation studies. Although a research problem is not stated as a value question, the information it engenders is used to make value-based decisions. Questions for such research may focus on educational needs; information for program planning, development, and implementations; or the effectiveness of a practice.

Personal experience and insights may suggest research problems that should be examined more in depth through qualitative methodologies. For example, a teacher who has worked with exceptional children can recognize more readily the meanings in a situation involving exceptional children than an ethnographer who has had no prior contact with exceptional children. A historian who has served as a department chairperson could more easily empathize with a historical figure who was the president of a university. The ability to empathize and to recognize the subtle meanings in a situation is important in most qualitative research.

Illustrative Topics

Educational research includes a broad array of topics about practices, the application of knowledge from social science, and methodological advancement. Within each topic reside many specific research questions with implications for educational theory, knowledge, and practice. Although the following list is not exhaustive, it demonstrates the breadth of the field of educational research and the potential range of research problems.

1. Use of instructional materials—textbooks, audio-visual aids, computers, and calculators.
2. Instructional techniques or teaching methods in social studies, vocational education, mathematics, science, language arts, and other curricula.
3. Perceptions of and attitudes toward educational policies, programs, and materials.
4. Child and adult development.
5. Grouping procedures, retention, and promotion.
6. Selection of students for special programs: special education, remediation, gifted and talented, and advanced placement.
7. Unique or innovative curriculums, programs, or policies at a given site.
8. Training programs like in-service training seminars, workshops, and continuing education.
9. Acquisition of knowledge, skills, and attitudes.
10. Sociometry, peer pressure, and social groups.
11. Alternative programs like Adult Basic Education, General Education Diploma, and advanced placement.
12. Follow-up of graduates.
13. Policy-making and decision-making in education.
14. Demographic profiles of students, teachers, and administrators.
15. Policy-making organizations that influence education, like the executive, judicial, and legislative branches of government, and special interest groups.
16. Specialized programs: guidance, extracurricular, library, enrichment, intervention and early childhood.
17. History of a program, policy, or institution.
18. Teacher evaluation: pre-service, tenured, and nontenured.
19. Student self-esteem; teacher and administrator morale.
20. Out-of-school activities like television viewing, reading, leisure time activities, employment, and family and social activities.
21. Roles of administrators—directors, superintendents, principals, supervisors, team leaders, chairpersons.
22. Legal liability of teachers, administrators, and institutions.
23. Vocational and career socialization.
24. Theories, like cognitive development, moral development, learning, information processing, creativity, and group dynamics.
25. Educational policies, such as minimum competency testing, integration, and reorganization.
26. Educational measurement, such as development of instruments and the validity and reliability of instruments.

Formal Problem Statements

Researchers use formal problem statements to guide their research. The statements introduce the reader to the importance of the problem, place the problem in an educational context, and provide the framework for reporting the results.

The problem statement orients the reader to the significance of the study and the research questions or hypotheses to follow.

The Focus, Educational Context, and Importance of the Problem.   In any well-written problem statement, the reader is not kept in suspense but is told directly and immediately the general focus, educational context, and importance of the problem. For example, the first paragraphs in "Attitudes, Self-Esteem, and Learning in Formal and Informal Schools" (Groobman, Forward, & Peterson, 1976) tell that what little research exists comparing formal and informal schools tends to assess traditional academic achievement. The researchers suggest that it is more important to investigate nonperformance factors that theoretically differentiate between formal and informal schools. Both the title and the introduction tell the reader that the educational context is formal and informal schools; the focus is on both performance and nonperformance factors—attitudes, self-esteem, and learning; it is a comparison study; and the importance is theoretical, with a research question different from those in previous investigations.

A different focus, educational context, and importance of the problem are stated in "The High School as a Social Service Agency: Historical Perspectives on Current Policy Issues": "The purpose of this essay is to examine historically the expansion of social services to youth through American public secondary education . . . . [to] shed light on the difficult choices policy-makers face today" (Tyack, 1979, p. 45). Within the first two paragraphs of the study the reader is told that the educational context is American public secondary education; that the concept examined is social services expansion; that the study is historical, encompassing the years 1890 to 1975; and that an understanding of the reasons such programs were added in the first place may help policymakers decide which educational functions and services to cut for balanced budgets.

A Framework for Results and Conclusions.   The problem statement also provides the framework for reporting the conclusions. Unlike the research design, where researchers state what methods they will use to complete the study, the problem statement merely indicates what is probably necessary to conduct the study and explains that the findings will present this information. Excerpt 3.1 exemplifies the framework for the findings of a study. This study reports the relative importance of Havighurst's developmental tasks for adults. The framework for reporting the findings is a comparison of the importance of the developmental tasks by three variables: gender, income level, and age group. Notice that the importance of the study is threefold. The conclusions will relate the findings to prior research on adult developmental tasks and literature regarding gender differences and draw implications for programs.

Qualitative problem statements also provide the framework for reporting the findings and interpretations. Excerpt 3.2 illustrates the framework for a historical study of California vocational guidance programs from 1910–30. Interpretations of this study will relate the findings to prior research on the role of schools in society, the impact of vocational guidance on students' occupational choices, and guidance program implementation.

EXCERPT 3.1
Quantitative Problem Statement

Although widely accepted by social scientists and educators as reflective of stages of development and as basis for planned learning experiences, there exist only a few empirical studies of Havighurst's adult development tasks concerned with the relative differences between men and women, income levels, and age groups. It has been suggested, though not substantiated, that the tasks are outdated, biased in favor of middle class adults. If true, this could seriously hamper the potential use of developmental tasks as a source for program development in adult education. Thus, the purpose of this study is to compare by gender, income levels, and age groups the relative importance of Havighurst's developmental tasks.

Source: From Merriam, S., & Mullins, L., "Havighurst's adult developmental tasks: A study of their importance relative to income, age, and sex," *Adult Education*, 31(2), 124, 1981. Reprinted by permission of the American Association for Adult and Continuing Education.

The introductory paragraphs of a study are difficult to write; they must convey much information succinctly. Researchers frequently rewrite the paragraphs as they formulate the significance of the study and research questions. They may even write the final paragraphs after the study is completed. Researchers, however, begin with a problem statement to guide their activities.

■ PROBLEM FORMULATION IN ■
QUANTITATIVE RESEARCH

Asking questions about a topic related to education is the starting point for defining a research problem, but educational research topics are not problem statements *per se*. A problem statement is more specific than a topic and limits the scope of the research problem.

A researcher starts with a general topic and narrows the topic to a problem. For example, the topic of educational policy-making might focus on school board policies. This is still a broad topic and may be narrowed to certain policies, such as fiscal, student, or personnel. The topic can be focused even more: Is the researcher interested in the antecedents to policies, the process of policy-making, or the consequences of policies? Is it the effects of policies, and if so, effects on whom? From one general topic, a number of questions could thus be generated: What influences school board formulations of policies? What was the intent of the teacher evaluation policy and how were the procedures implemented? What effect does teacher evaluation have on teacher morale? What effect does teacher evaluation have on administrator attitudes and behavior? What are the opinions

---

EXCERPT 3.2
Qualitative Problem Statement

By the end of the 1920s, few educators disputed the idea that helping young people in their choice of occupation was a primary responsibility of secondary education. Although implementation varied from one place to another, high schools across the nation—especially those in large urban school districts—had begun to experiment with new procedures to counsel youth in their vocational choices and to guide them into appropriate occupations. But how did it all turn out? What impact did guidance have on secondary education? And how did it influence young people in their choice of occupations? Did it make any difference at all?

These questions have in recent years become the subject of considerable historiographical debate. . . . Thus, while we have learned a great deal in recent years about the ideas that leading educators and social reformers entertained and advocated, we still know relatively little about how guidance programs were implemented and how they operated once they were put in place.

This essay addresses these issues of practice by examining the origins and development of vocational guidance in California between 1910 and 1930. Concerned that the transition from school to work had become problematic under modern industrial conditions, California educators shared with school officials across the country the belief that guidance would rationalize the relationship between school and work and by 1930 had succeeded in making at least a modicum of guidance a common feature in high schools across the state. There is little evidence, however, that guidance had much direct impact on the way young people in California made vocational choices. In fact, by the end of the 1920s guidance no longer had much contact with the labor market at all but instead focused almost exclusively on meeting the institutional needs of the school—helping students fill out course schedules, dealing with special and problem cases, and administering mental tests.

Source: From "Choosing a Vocation: The Origins and Transformation of Vocational Guidance in California, 1910–1930" by Harvey Kantor, *History of Education Quarterly*, Vol. 26, No. 3, 1986. Reprinted by permission of the author.

of administrators, parents, and teachers toward our present teacher evaluation policy? How frequently in the last five years has the teacher evaluation policy in a school system led to changed teacher behavior, nonrenewal of contract, denial of tenure, or proceedings resulting in a court case?

Suppose the topic of interest was instruction. Again, a researcher could ask similar questions: What kind of instruction? Is the focus on antecedents, the process, or the consequences? Is the focus on specific ages, or students with certain characteristics? A topic like the use of hand calculators in mathematics instruction might generate the question, "Is there a difference among comparable students in the use of hand calculators in mathematics computation?" Notice that the question fails to specify how frequently hand calculators are used, how mathematics computation is determined, or which students other than they are similar. This problem would be more precise if it were stated: "Among comparable fourth grade students, is there a difference in the mathematics computation scores of the SRA Achievement Test between those students who had used hand calculators in mathematics for a semester and those who had not?"

To make the study manageable, researchers narrow their topics to a particular problem. If a problem is too general the results are difficult to interpret. Several activities can help focus a topic as a problem. Reading secondary literature may clarify the problem and narrow it to possible questions and variables. Talking with those who might use the study can clarify their needs and questions. Brainstorming with others who have research training, experience, or specialized knowledge of the problem area is beneficial. Ultimately, the researcher has to make decisions about the selection of variables, the population, and the *logic for the problem*. Initial problem statements are usually reworked and reworded many times as each word is scrutinized for the exact meaning and the logical reasoning to be employed in the research. The deductive logic of quantitative problems is illustrated in Figure 3.1. We explain each term and its various meanings in Figure 3.1 in the next section.

The Deductive Logic of Constructs, Variables, and Operational Definitions

To formulate a problem, the researcher selects an abstract construct and then reasons if the selected variables are logically deduced from the construct. The next step is to select the observations which are reasoned to relate to the variables by deduction. The observations are then operationally defined by a researcher-chosen instrument to measure the phenomenon. The three-step deductive reasoning from abstract constructs to less abstract variables to a set of observations is schematically represented in Figure 3.1 and is explained in more detail below. In other words, the researcher must make a number of decisions to propose a predetermined design *before* data are collected.

Constructs.   In research, higher level concepts are called constructs. Constructs express the idea behind a set of particulars. A construct is often derived from a theory. The construct *anxiety*, for example, is derived from personality theory. A **construct** is a complex abstraction that is not directly observable. Examples of constructs are motivation, intelligence, thinking, anxiety, aggression, self-concept, achievement, and aptitude. What is observable is the behavior presumed to be a consequence of the hypothesized construct. Another way to define a construct is to say that we create constructs by combining concepts in meaningful patterns. Such concepts as visual perception, sight-sound discrimination, audio acuity, and left-to-right orientation are meaningfully combined to suggest the construction *reading readiness*. The construct *creativity* is generally

FIGURE 3.1
Deductive Logic in Quantitative Research: Constructs, Variables and Observations

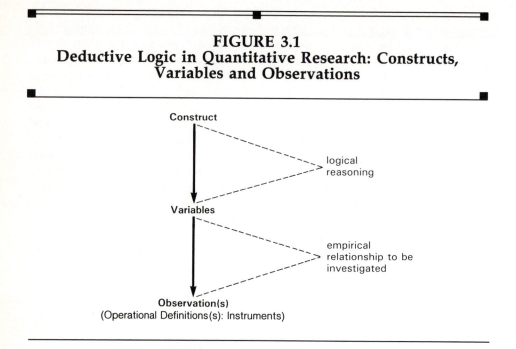

recognized to consist of flexibility, originality, elaboration, and other concepts. Constructs change their meaning or are discarded as theories are developed or empirical evidence is accumulated.

Because constructs are intangible entities and not directly observable, researchers use indicators as a way of measuring or classifying most of the particulars of the construct. These indicators are called variables. As noted above, there may be more than one variable for a construct and more than one type of observation for a variable. The researcher deductively chooses the most valid indicators.

Variables.   In Figure 3.1, a **variable** is an event, category, behavior, or an attribute that expresses a construct and has different values, depending on how it is used in a particular study. There are several types of variables. A variable used to categorize subjects, objects, or entities into two or more categories is a **categorical variable.** The simplest type of categorical variable has only two classes; it is a dichotomous variable. Male-female, married-single, and pass-fail are dichotomous variables. Categorical variables can have more than two classes, such as income level, educational level, nationality, or religious affiliation. A **continuous or measured variable** is one in which the property or attribute of an object, subject, or entity is measured numerically and can assume an infinite number of values within a range. Weight, height, and age are common examples of continuous variables. In education, typical measured variables are achievement, verbal ability, aptitude, attitudes, and specific skills.

Quantitative research investigates the relationship between categorical or measured variables. Some variables are antecedents to other variables. Researchers may know this from previous studies, or they may hypothesize from a theory that one variable is an antecedent to another. They may, for example, say that academic achievement is preceded by intelligence. It is assumed that to achieve in school, a child needs to have some degree of intelligence. The variable *intelligence* is an antecedent to the variable *achievement*. To some extent, achievement is a consequence of intelligence; it is dependent upon an individual's degree of intelligence. The variable which is a consequence of some phenomenon is the focus of the study; it must be a measured variable. The antecedent variable may be either categorical or measured. Each variable should be a separate and distinct phenomenon. Educational research investigates many factors as variables: classroom variables such as teaching styles, interaction pattern, cognitive level of questions; environmental variables such as parental educational level, social class, family structure; and personal variables such as age, sex, intelligence, motivation, or self-concept.

In experimental research, we often call the variable that is the consequence of or is dependent upon antecedent variables the **dependent variable.** A variable that is antecedent to or precedes the dependent variable is called the **independent, manipulated, or experimental variable,** i.e., the variable that is manipulated or changed by the researcher to investigate the effect on a dependent variable. The effect of the manipulation is observed on the dependent variable. It is called a dependent variable because its value depends upon and varies with the value of the independent variable. Suppose a researcher wanted to see the effect of the timing of a review on social studies achievement. The research manipulates the timing of the review—immediate and delayed—and then measures the effects on social studies achievement. After the relationship has been established empirically, the researcher can predict from the independent variable to the dependent variable. The most frequently used experimental variables in education are instructional or teaching methods.

In non-experimental research such as descriptive, correlational, and survey studies, the variables are not directly or actively manipulated by the researcher. In descriptive research and some survey research, there may be only one variable of interest. Studies which describe the reading achievement level of second graders or surveys of parental attitudes toward various school policies contain only one variable of interest.

In some correlational research, the antecedent variable is called the **predictor variable** and the predicted variable is the **criterion variable.** In a study which examines the relationship of scores on the Scholastic Aptitude Test to success in college, the predictor variable is the SAT scores and the criterion variable is college success. In other correlation studies, there is no obvious antecedent variable. An example is a study of the relationship of self-concept and achievement. The researcher is not interested in which variable precedes the other variable, but, instead, he or she is interested in the strength and direction of the relationship between the variables. Some researchers will use the terminology "independent" and "dependent" variable with correlational or other non-experimental research when it is clear that the independent variable precedes or is antecedent to the dependent variable.

A variable may be independent in one study and dependent in another study; a variable also may be a predictor or a criterion variable in other research. Whether the variable functions as a independent or dependent variable, or as a predictor or criterion variable, or as the only variable in a study depends on the purpose and the logic of the study. The problem statement is phrased to indicate how the variables will function in the proposed study.

Observations: Operational Definitions.   "Observation(s)" in Figure 3.1 refers to the data collection method which the researcher deductively reasons is related to the variable of interest. In quantitative research, "observation" usually refers to an instrument which can measure relationships between variables as indicated by prior validity and reliability studies of the instrument.

Each variable in a quantitative study must be defined operationally and subsequently categorized, measured, or manipulated. There are two kinds of definitions: constitutive and operational. A constitutive definition, similar to that found in a dictionary, defines a term by using other terms. A dictionary may define *anxiety* as "apprehension or vague fear" or *intelligence* as "mental acuity" and "the ability to think abstractly." These definitions are insufficient for researchers. Notice that for *intelligence* common synonyms are part of the constitutive definition. Researchers use operational definitions. An **operational definition** assigns meaning to a variable by specifying the activities or operations necessary to measure, categorize, or manipulate the variable. Operational definitions tell the researcher and reader what is necessary for answering the question or testing the hypothesis.

To use an extreme example, the hypothesis "Intelligence relates positively to achievement" can be defined operationally by specifying how the researcher will measure the two variables. The variable "intelligence" is measured by the scores on X intelligence test, or, stated another way, intelligence is what X intelligence test measures in the study. Achievement may be defined operationally by citing a standardized test, a teacher-made achievement test, grades, or other assessment methods. Variables frequently can be defined operationally in several ways and some operations may be more valid for a research problem than others. The operational definition for a variable is often not as valid as a researcher desires. To conduct research, however, one must define each variable operationally.

Specific research questions and hypotheses may operationalize the variables. For example, the hypothesis, "There is a positive relationship between self-esteem and creativity," may be stated operationally by saying: "There is a positive relationship between the scores on the Coopersmith Self-Esteem Scale and the scores on the Torrance Test of Creative Thinking." Such a statement indicates that the researcher has chosen these operational procedures as the most valid measures for the two variables.

Problem Formulation

A useful procedure for transforming a general topic or question into a manageable problem is to identify the population, the variables, and the logic of the problem. Suppose a supervisor is interested in different ways to organize a program for elementary students found to be talented and gifted and to learn its effect on student creativity. Talented and gifted programs have been organized in several ways: as special programs in which students remain together for a comprehensive program; as pullout programs in which students attend regular classes except for two hours' daily instruction by selected teachers; and as enrichment programs in which students complete enrichment activities as an extension of their regular instruction. The question becomes: "Is there a difference in creativity (the dependent variable) between talented and gifted elementary students (the population) who participate in a special program, a pullout program, or an enrichment program (three levels of one independent variable)?" This question is narrowed to the degree that it identifies the population and the two variables. The logic of the question is clear because the independent and dependent variables can be identified.

Suppose a question was phrased: "Does mainstreaming do any good?" As phrased, the question has neither a population nor variables. A researcher might decide that the real interest lies in changes in the attitudes of nonhandicapped children toward handicapped children. Attitude becomes the dependent variable, and nonhandicapped children is a partial identification of the population. The researcher decides that probably the age group most likely to experience a change in attitudes is high school students rather than younger children, who may be just forming attitudes. High school students comprise the designated population. The researcher decides, furthermore, that "mainstreaming" is too vague, and the independent variable should be six weeks' participation in a mainstreamed class. Now the research problem is phrased: "Is there a difference between high school students' (the population) attitudes toward handicapped students (the dependent variable) who participated in a six weeks' mainstreamed class and the attitude of those who did not (the independent variable)?" Notice that the question fails to mention change, the primary focus of the study. The question is thus rephrased: "Is there a difference between the pre- and post-attitudes toward handicapped students (dependent variable) between high school students (the population) who participated in a six weeks' mainstreamed class and those who did not (the independent variable)?" Now the question is focused and the logic of the problem explicit.

Some problems have a defined population and variables, but one cannot distinguish the independent from the dependent variable. If a researcher is interested in self-esteem and academic achievement, which is the dependent variable? Is the problem investigating whether achievement relates to positive self-esteem (the dependent variable) or is the problem whether self-esteem relates positively to achievement (the dependent variable)? The difficulty here lies in the nature of the variables. In these problems, categorical and measured variables are used, but not manipulated or experimental variables. The problem can be phrased: "Among sixth-grade students, is there a difference between low self-esteem and high self-esteem students and their academic achievement?" The population is sixth-grade students, and the variables are self-esteem and academic achievement. Neither variable is manipulated, since the subjects already have these attributes—that is, self-esteem and achievement. Neither variable is labeled as independent or dependent because one cannot determine which is antecedent to the other. A study can, however, ascertain whether a relationship exists with an *ex post facto* design or a correlational study.

Descriptive studies, such as a status study or survey research, may have only one variable. The Annual Gallup Poll, for example, describes the opinions of American citizens on public education. American citizens are the population and the single variable is their opinions on education. Similar research problems with only one variable are: "What are the attitudes of a school staff toward the new student retention policy?" or "What are the opinions of the students' parents on teaching a unit on sex education in eighth-grade Health?"

By identifying the major construct, variables, and population, the researcher clarifies the focus and logic of a problem. This process is not easy and, as mentioned previously, it is not done without preliminary work. Reading literature, brainstorming with others, and talking with experienced researchers can help in stating a problem. With the idea now clearly in mind, the researcher can write a formal problem statement. A formal problem statement may be phrased as statements of research purpose, specific research questions, or as research hypotheses, depending on the purpose of the study and the selected design. Each of these ways of stating specific research problems is explained below.

Statements of Research Purposes

Studies frequently contain statements of purposes or objectives that imply questions. Excerpt 3.1 stated, "The purpose of this study is to compare by gender, income levels, and age groups the relative importance of Havighurst's developmental tasks" (Merriam & Mullins, 1981, p. 124). Implied in the statement of purpose is the question: Is there a difference by gender, income level, and age group on the importance of Havighurst's developmental tasks? The researchers explain Havighurst's adult developmental tasks and define the three variables. Gender, of course, refers to male or female; income level was categorized as low (less than $8,000 per year), middle (between $8,000 and $19,000 per year), and upper (over $20,000 per year). Age was defined as young (18–34 years), middle aged (35–59 years), and older (over 60 years). Readers may argue that an annual income of $20,000 is not upper income or that ages 18 to 34 is not young in the conventional sense. These terms, however, are not used in the conventional sense but are categorical variables defined for the purpose of this study (operational definitions).

The logic of the statement of research purpose suggests the design for the study. Refer again to the statement, "The purpose of this study is to compare by gender, income levels, and age groups the relative importance of Havighurst's developmental tasks." The first step is to analyze the specific problem to decide what is required in order to investigate the problem. Three research activities are indicated: the terms "Havighurst's developmental tasks" for young adulthood, middle age, and older adults suggests an instrument with the tasks listed; "relative importance" suggests that a group of people will rank-order the importance of the tasks; and "to compare" suggests that groups of people who differ by gender, income level, and age are necessary for comparisons. To conduct the study the researchers would thus have to construct a rating scale listing the tasks; determine the sample size for three comparisons—that is, by gender, income level, and age group as defined in the study; select the sample; collect the data; and use the appropriate statistical test for analysis of the rankings.

Specific Research Questions

Quantitative studies may state the research problem in question form. The question format is often preferred because it is simple and direct. Psychologically, it orients the researcher to the immediate task: to develop a design to answer the question. Research questions may be descriptive questions, relationship questions, or difference questions.

Descriptive Research Questions.   Descriptive research questions typically ask "what is" and imply a survey research design. These terms, however, are not always used in the wording of the research questions. For example, a research question may be "What is the achievement level of our fourth-grade students on the SRA Achievement Battery?". Evaluation research often investigates the perceptions of groups concerned with a practice, such as "What are the administrators' opinions of a program?", "What are the attitudes of our students toward the mainstreamed children?", "Which of the alternative bus routes do our pupils' parents prefer?", or "What does the staff perceive as our most important instructional needs?".

Relationship Questions.   Relationship questions ask, "What is the relationship between two or more variables?" and imply a correlational design. This does not mean that the exact words "What is the relationship between variable A and variable B?" always appear in the statement. As an example, "Does self-concept relate to achievement?" asks a question about the relationship between one variable (self-concept) and another variable (achievement). Studies that determine the best predictors for a variable, such as predictors of college success, imply relationship questions between the possible predictor variables like Scholastic Aptitude Test scores, high school grade point average, recommendations, and extracurricular activities and the dependent variable, college success. Excerpt 3.3 illustrates a problem statement that implies a relationship question between selected long-range predictors and children's social adjustment. The problem statement suggests the design for the study.

EXCERPT 3.3
Relationship Questions

The objectives of the present inquiry were: (a) to identify long-range correlates or predictors of social adjustment and (b) to determine the multiple correlation between a best set of these correlates or predictors and the social adjustment of children after 6 or 9 years had elapsed. The subjects were children who were first evaluated in third or sixth grade and for whom social adjustment was assessed 6 or 9 years later.

Source: Feldhusen, J. F., Roeser, T. D., & Thurston, J. R. (1977). Prediction of social adjustment over a period of 6 or 9 years. *Journal of Special Education. 11*(1), 31.

Difference Questions.   Difference questions typically ask "Is there a difference between two groups or two or more treatments?". They are used when the study compares two or more observations. Stating the question as "Is there a difference?" rather than "Is there a relationship?" between two or more observations clarifies the underlying logic of the study. Questions such as "Is there a difference between pretest and posttest scores?" are more useful than those phrased, "Is there a relationship between pretest and posttest scores?". Let's apply these types of questions to the statement from Excerpt 3.1, "The purpose of this study is to compare by gender, income levels, and age groups the relative importance of Havighurst's developmental tasks." This statement implies three research questions: "Is there a difference between rank order of the tasks by gender?", "Is there a difference between rank order of the tasks by income level?", and "Is there a difference in rank order of the tasks by age group?". Comparisons can be made between two or more data sets which may be pre- and posttest scores using one group or posttest scores only with two or more groups.

If the researchers firmly believe that, in addition to predicting a difference between two or more observations, they can predict the direction in which the difference lies, then the direction is stated in the research question. The question, "Is there a difference in pretest and posttest scores?" may thus be stated: "Is there greater mastery of reading comprehension on the posttest than on the pretest?" Excerpt 3.4 illustrates directional research questions with three comparisons. The retention of students receiving no review is compared with the retention of students using the original lesson study guide, students using a summary version audiotape, and students using a compressed speech version.

Research questions are not statistical questions stated for data analysis. Statistical questions may be phrased: "Is there a statistically significant difference between A and B observations?" or "Is there a statistically significant relationship

---

EXCERPT 3.4
Difference Questions

1. Would students using the original lesson study guide in review of a previously mastered AT lesson demonstrate better retention than students receiving no review?
2. Would students using a summary version of the original lesson audiotape in review of a previously mastered AT lesson demonstrate better retention than students receiving no review?
3. Would students using a compressed speech version of the original lesson audiotape demonstrate better retention of a previously mastered AT lesson than students receiving no review?

Source: From Smith, H. G., "Investigation of Several Techniques for Reviewing Audio-Tutorial Instruction," *Educational Communication and Technology Journal, 27*(3), 196, Fall 1979. Copyright © 1979 by AECT. Reprinted by permission of the Association for Educational Communication and Technology.

---

between A variable and B variable?" Statistical questions are stated in the methodology section of a study. Research questions are stated in the introduction of a study and suggest the design.

Research Hypotheses

A research **hypothesis** is a tentative statement of the expected relationship between two or more variables. The statement describes, in other words, the predicted results. Problem statements and hypotheses are similar in substance, except that hypotheses are declarative statements, more specific than problem statements, clearly testable, and indicative of the expected results. For the research problem, "Is there a relationship between review and retention?" the hypothesis might be: "There is a positive relationship between review and retention." Empirical testing is feasible to the extent that each variable can be manipulated, categorized, or measured. If a variable cannot be manipulated, categorized, or measured, there is no quantitative method of analysis for testing the hypothesis.

Three examples of hypotheses are: "The greater the perceived differences between adults as learners and pre-adults as learners, the greater the overall differences in teaching behaviors" (Beder & Darkenwald, 1982, p. 144); "Low reading students in a remedial reading course will achieve higher reading comprehension than comparable students in an English literature course"; and

"Democratic leadership style produces greater faculty satisfaction than authoritarian leadership style." Although the word *relationship* is not used in every hypothesis, relation expressions such as *will achieve, produces, is a function of,* and *effects* connect the variables.

A hypothesis implies an if-then logic (Kerlinger, 1979). Most hypotheses can be put into an if-then form to indicate the relationship between variables. In each of the three examples above, the hypothesis has an independent and a dependent variable: If perceived differences, then greater differences in teaching behavior; if a remedial course, then higher reading comprehension; and if democratic leadership style, then faculty satisfaction. The logic is similar for hypotheses with more than two variables.

A hypothesis is a conjectural explanation of phenomena that is accepted or rejected by empirical evidence. In the above examples, the perceived difference between adults as learners and pre-adults as learners explains the differences in teaching behaviors; a remedial reading course explains higher achievement; and democratic leadership style accounts for faculty satisfaction.

Hypotheses are especially important in correlational and experimental research which investigate relations between variables. To be useful in research, a hypothesis should meet several standards:

1. *The hypothesis should state the expected relationship or difference between two or more variables.* A statement such as "if teacher feedback, then student science achievement" implies a relationship but it is not a hypothesis. The directional hypothesis might state: "Teacher feedback will relate positively to student science achievement" or "There is a positive relationship between teacher feedback and student science achievement."

In experimental research where an experimental treatment such as the use of microcomputers in mathematics is administered to one group of subjects but not to another group, researchers typically hypothesize directional differences. For example: "Fifth-grade students who receive microcomputer-assisted instruction will have higher math achievement than comparable students who did not receive microcomputer-assisted instruction."

2. *A hypothesis should be testable.* A testable hypothesis is verifiable; one can draw conclusions from empirical observations that indicate whether the relationship is supported or not supported. The researcher can determine if the hypothesized consequences did or did not occur. To be testable, a hypothesis must include related variables that can be measured or categorized by some objective procedure. For example, because one can classify first-grade students as having attended preschool or not, a hypothesis might state: "Children who attend preschool will have higher scores on a scale of social maturity than children who do not attend preschool." If a variable cannot be measured or categorized, there is no method to make the necessary statistical comparisons.

3. *A hypothesis should offer a tentative explanation based on theory or previous research.* A well-grounded hypothesis indicates there is sufficient research or theory for considering the hypothesis important enough to test. A research hypothesis usually is stated after a literature review; the researcher has knowledge of the previous work. A hypothesis generally does not disagree with the pre-

ponderance of prior evidence but, if tested, it could extend our knowledge on the research problem. If the hypothesis is theoretically grounded in social science, it is possible for the results of the study to contribute to the theory under examination. In many areas of education, however, there is little conclusive evidence and only some educational research and theory serve as a basis for the research hypothesis.

4. *A hypothesis should be concise and lucid.* A hypothesis in its simplest form should have a clear logical coherence and order of arrangement. Brief statements aid both the reader and the researcher in interpreting the results. A general rule is to state only one relationship per hypothesis similar to Excerpt 3.4, which stated three separate questions for one study. Although a researcher may have one general broad hypothesis, it is better to rephrase the broad statement into more specific hypotheses for clarity.

■ PROBLEM FORMULATION IN ■ QUALITATIVE RESEARCH

Problem formulation in qualitative research begins with selecting a general topic and a methodology (ethnographic research or an analysis of historical/legal documents). The topic and methodology are interrelated and are selected interactively rather than in separate research steps. For example, an early research decision is whether to examine ongoing events or past events. A study of current phenomena requires that the researcher have access to a site or a group of people who have some shared social experience, such as working in the same school system, participating in a special project or a class, and the like. A study of past events requires archival collections of primary documents which are available and accessible to the researcher. These considerations begin to shape and influence the selection of a general topic.

The researcher begins by narrowing a general topic to a more definitive topic. Suppose a researcher is interested in the teaching of reading and writing. There are several theoretical orientations to literacy, such as decoding, skills, and whole language. The researcher is interested in the whole language approach and his/her personal observations and experience has led the researcher to expect that a *whole language* classroom operates differently from the *phonics* or *skills* classroom. For example, there would be no spelling books, no sets of reading texts with controlled readability, and no writing assignments. Instead, children's writing would be integrated in a children's literature reading program with "whole meaningful texts" as instructional materials rather than "isolated words, sounds, or vocabulary-controlled 'stories'" (Edelsky, Draper, & Smith, 1983, p. 259). The researcher begins to wonder, "How does a teacher get children to read and to write regularly to meet expectations in this unusual situation?"

As another example, suppose a researcher noticed that testing in the public schools had increased in the last decade, and she or he had heard criticism that teachers, administrators, and counselors use testing to segregate children and promote social control through "tracking" and ability grouping. The researcher, however, is interested in whether the past can provide an understanding in how testing was used originally: were tests accepted as a scientific vehicle for separating students by intelligence or were tests found to be unreliable measures for Mexican and black children (Rafferty, 1988)? The broad topic of testing in public schools is now a more definitive topic of intelligence testing and its scientific properties when applied to the public schools for grouping or "tracking" children.

Most qualitative research interests come from personal experiences and a long interest in a topic developed from accidents of current biography and personal history. These accidents, which Riemer (1977) calls "opportunistic research," give the researcher physical and/or psychological access to present or past social settings. Such access becomes the starting point for meaningful qualitative research only when it is accompanied by some degree of interest or concern. Examples of current biography are a job, a change in an intimate relationship, or an enjoyed activity. Personal history refers to some prior experience, such as the researcher developing an interest in working married professional women and how they manage their changing lives because of changes in her own personal and professional lives. In other words, research problems lie in many personal situations and experiences and general reading which need only to be recognized as potential research problems. Further thinking, puzzling, and awareness of qualitative research traditions enable a researcher to select the logic for the problem.

The Inductive Logic of Observations, Descriptions, and Concepts

Qualitative research, in contrast to quantitative research, employs primarily *inductive reasoning.* The "problem" is most clearly stated after much data collection and analysis. The researcher obtains many observations of a present or past situation which form detailed descriptions of people's perceptions and social realities, and then generates from these descriptions an understanding or a theory to explain the phenomenon. Inductive reasoning allows one to *explore* and *discover* with an emerging research design rather than test deductions from theories in a predetermined design.

Inductive logic in qualitative research also *builds* the findings from the data by analyzing and presenting data in increasingly abstract and synthesized forms. Narrative descriptions are built through inductive reasoning from an analysis of qualitative observations. Concepts are generated by inductive logic from the narrative descriptions. Qualitative research uses an emergent design where each research decision depends upon prior data collection. The problem formulation begins with selecting a particular case for an in-depth study. The inductive process of qualitative research is illustrated in Figure 3.2. We explain each term and its various meanings in Figure 3.2 in the next section. The research problem is reformulated through inductive reasoning.

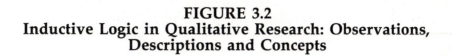

FIGURE 3.2
Inductive Logic in Qualitative Research: Observations, Descriptions and Concepts

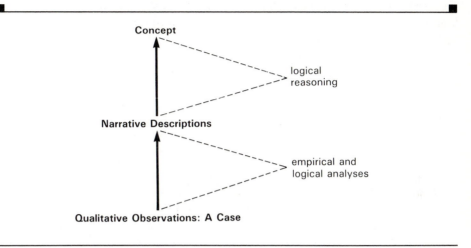

Qualitative Observations: A Case. In Figure 3.2, the qualitative observations are of a selected case. A **case** is a particular situation selected by the researcher in which some phenomenon will be described by participants' meanings of events and processes. The researcher selects a particular case of a problem and a qualitative methodology (ethnographic observation, ethnographic interview, or analysis of documents). For example, in a study of "Hookin' 'Em In at the Start of School in a 'Whole Language' Classroom" (Edelsky, Draper, & Smith, 1983), the case selected was that of a sixth-grade classroom whose teacher who had a *whole language* view of literacy. In an oral history study (also called "ethnographic interview") the case selected was a group of women teachers who worked in the small city of Hamilton, Ohio, who might provide insights into the failure of teacher unionization attempts in the 1930s (Quantz, 1985). The case chosen for a study of the origins of the high school extracurriculum was that of Chicago, 1880 to 1915 (Gutowski, 1988), to be examined from historical documents of the Chicago school system, school newspapers, student annuals and club productions (such as *Ohio, Echo, Harrison Tech High Annuals, Red and White, Lane Tech Yearbook, Quill*), journals of the times (such as *School Review, NEA*), and the *Chicago Tribune*. The selected case limits the research problem to a particular context—one sixth-grade classroom, one school system in the 1930s, high school extracurricula in one school system from 1880 to 1915.

Researchers select a particular case, rather than a variable, through which they gain an understanding of a broader phenomenon. The broader phenomenon in each of the examples cited above were the teaching of writing, teacher unionization, and the high school extracurricula program.

In Figure 3.2, **qualitative observations,** obtained over a lengthy time, are recorded as field notes of ethnographic observations, transcripts of ethnographic interviews, or researcher notes of historical documents. Each field note, transcript, or historical note contains the date of occurrence and the context, such as the social scene, situation, and participants. Initial observations may lead to observations of other people, sites, and archive collections as the researcher discovers more aspects about the selected case. In other words, "case" does not refer to one person or one archival collection or one locale but the social situation examined. Data collection strategies are adjusted to obtain a holistic view of the phenomena and then to study certain aspects in depth. In Excerpt 3.5 the selected case was one group of women teachers in a particular locale, Hamilton, Ohio. The researcher chose to study a phenomenon in depth with a case study design rather than an experimental, nonexperimental, or *ex post facto* design.

Narrative Descriptions.   In Figure 3.2, **narrative descriptions** are detailed narrations of people, incidents, and processes. The entire descriptive narration is completed after data collection because of the discovery-orientation of the research. To inductively generate a descriptive narration, certain kinds of data must be in the field notes, transcripts, or notes of historical/legal documents.

Descriptive narrations, sometimes called "rich" or "thick" description told in "loving detail," contain at least four elements: people, incidents, participants' language, and participants' "meanings." First, participants are described as individuals who have different personal histories and display different physical, emotional, and intellectual characteristics in various situations. Second, incidents form a narration about the social scenes, similar to telling a story. Third, descriptions emphasize the participants' language, not that of the researcher. Participants' names for incidents, locations, objects, special events and processes are noted. Language refers to many forms of communication such as verbal and non-verbal expression, drawings, cartoons, symbols, and the like. In "Spelling 'Mississippi': Recontextualizing a Literacy-Related Speech Event" (Gilmore, 1983), the language of black students in a school in a low-income Philadelphia neighborhood was called "sub-rosa literacy." Sub-rosa literacy was the informal language of classroom "talkers," of notes passed by "tellers" to their friends in a class, and of "doin' steps" in the school playground, one of which was the street rhyme of "Mississippi" accompanied by choreography and rhythm. Fourth, descriptions emphasize participant "meanings." Participant "meanings" are people's views of reality or how they perceive their world. Participant meanings are conveyed when a person states "why" or "because" an event happened.

Concepts.   In Figure 3.2, a **concept** is an abstraction from observed phenomena; it is a word that states the commonalities among those observed events and situations and distinguishes the phenomena from other events and situations. Concepts are used in place of descriptive phrases. For example, the concept of a

EXCERPT 3.5
Selected Case for Qualitative Observations

If unionization failed, it is because real people made choices concerning their own very personal worlds. Attention to the larger forces of history provide a framework of understanding, but without a depiction of the finer detail of the participants' subjective realities, we fail fully to understand the dynamics of history . . . . [which] . . . often involved real women living in their own subjective, but equally real, worlds.

This paper is an oral history. Its goal is to describe the shared subjective reality of one group of women teachers during the 1930s and to compare that reality with some assumptions historians make about unionization. Based primarily on oral interviews and influenced by ethnohistory, the paper presents a group definition of schools and life in a small midwestern city during the Great Depression.[6] As such it brings an anthropological perspective to historical study. By attempting to discover the cultural definitions of participants in an historical situation, it investigates the subjective side of history. This paper is less interested in portraying the way things really were than in exploring the way participants perceived them to be. As a case study, it lays no claim to a generalizable truth. It should not be understood as presenting anything but a piece in the mosaic. Resulting from a study of Hamilton, Ohio, it should not be used to try to explain Enid, Oklahoma; Riverside, California; or any other small city. On the other hand, any historical analysis that lays claim to a general explanation of the unionization movement of teachers during the 1930s and fails to consider the teachers' subjective realities, such as found in Hamilton, will be laying false claim to universality.

Source: From "The Complex Visions of Female Teachers and the Failure of Unionization in the 1930s: An Oral History" by Richard A. Quantz, *History of Education Quarterly*, Vol. 25, No. 4, 1985. Reprinted by permission of the author.

whole language classroom in "Hookin' 'Em In at the Start of School in a "Whole Language" Classroom" (Edelsky, Draper, & Smith, 1983) is described in such detail that one could not confuse it with a *phonic* or *skills* classroom. H. Wolcott's (1973) description of *The Man in the Principal's Office* is so comprehensive that one would not think of the principal as a central office administrator nor as a teacher.

Social science concepts are generated from the patterns and themes in the descriptive narration and the original data. Inductive analysis develops the abstract concept from the particulars (observations) which have been gathered and categorized in the narration. Concepts, however, are more than the accumulation of data regarding people, incidents, participant language and participant "meanings." The researcher induces subtle connotations of a concept. Thus, the concept of *whole language classroom* is complex, including four "implicit teacher rules," six teacher roles, and eight different "cueing devices" (Edelsky, Draper & Smith, 1983).

Concepts are used in several ways in qualitative research, depending on the purpose of the study: to further an understanding of the concept or to generate formal grounded theory. **Phenomenology** is an analysis of qualitative data to provide an understanding of a concept from participants' perspectives and views of social realities. The researcher constructs a picture that takes shape as he or she collects data and examines the parts. The subtle meanings of the concept can be understood more clearly by the readers. For example, a study explained the subtle meanings of teacher unionization failure with teachers' descriptions of their relationship to schools. Teachers described this relationship in terms of "four metaphors: the subordinate authority figure, the school as family, the natural female avocation, and the dual-self" (Quantz, 1985, p. 442). Only one teacher did not use these metaphors.

Another purpose of qualitative research is that of the development of grounded theory (Glaser & Strauss, 1967). The researcher reflects on the findings for their meaning about humans in general, not just the educational event or process. **Grounded theory,** a sophisticated analysis, links participant perceptions to more general social science theories.

Problem Reformulations

Qualitative research problems are reformulated several times *after* the researcher has begun data collection. In contrast, quantitative research problems are stated *before* data collection. The research problem is stated initially in planning for the study, reformulated during beginning data collection, and reformulated as necessary throughout data collection. The continuing reformulation of the research problem reflects an emergent design. Reformulations of a research problem relates to changing data collection strategies to acquire the "totality" of the phenomena and then to study some aspect in greater depth. The specific research problem emerges and is condensed toward the end of data collection. The condensed version of the research problem in most publications often is not the exact same problem statement which initiated the research.

Foreshadowed Problems.   Qualitative researchers begin with **foreshadowed problems** (Malinowski, 1922), anticipated research problems which will be reformulated during data collection. The statement of foreshadowed problems depends to some extent on prior knowledge of the events and processes at a site, of the people to be interviewed, or archival collection documents. Thus, foreshadowed problems are not directly derived from an exhaustive literature review as in quantitative research, but rather from initial researcher experiences gained from planning the study. A preliminary literature review, however, aids the researcher in the phrasing of foreshadowed problems.

Foreshadowed problems are usually phrased as broad, general questions. Questions focus on the "what," "how," and "why" of the situation. The "what" refers to who, when, where, and which social scenes happened? The "how" refers to processes examined and what influenced these processes. The "why" refers to participant "meanings," their explanations for the incidents and social scenes observed. Each of these questions are purposefully broad for the logic of discovery and an emergent design.

Foreshadowed problems are reformulated frequently during the early phases of data collection. Ethnographers may switch from observations to interviewing; interviewers may adjust the questions to illicit descriptions of topics not originally planned; historical and legal researchers often scan documents to decide what is important to glean from the written records.

An ethnographic study of a *whole language* classroom illustrates this process (see Excerpt 3.6). The foreshadowed problem based on preliminary knowledge was "How does this teacher get children to meet her unusual expectations? . . . What are the norms here for reading and writing? How does the teacher get students to expect to write? How are certain procedures established (e.g., journal and book writing)? What student-teacher relationships are in evidence?" (Edelsky, Draper, & Smith, 1983, p. 261–262). Although the researchers expected to see a gradual change, it was evident that students were already becoming what the teacher desired during the first school day. The researchers changed their plans and interviewed children on the second school day. This led to a reformulation of the problem: "What is happening here?" The final reformulation and condensed problem statement became "how it [how teachers get classroom life to become what they want it to be] happens in a classroom with an effective teacher who has a whole language view of literacy" (Edelsky, Draper, & Smith, 1983, p. 260).

Condensed Problem Statement.   Condensed problem statements may be written any time during or after data collection. The condensed problem statement is usually the major research question which focuses the entire study. The title, literature review, and discussion often use abstract terms of qualitative scholars; however, the research problem may or may not be phrased in descriptive terms. For example, in "Individualism and Community: Ritual Discourse in a Parochial High School," the research problem is "Such continuing ties [to St. Anne's School] are not formed only of good intentions; they must be reaffirmed through repeated concrete experiences that are deemed 'good' and 'worthwhile.' What brought about attachment to St. Anne's, when the school restricted students' freedom of movement through a closed campus, restricted their choice of courses, and added financial burdens to many students' families?" (Lesko, 1986, p. 26). The title of "Individualism and Community. . ." refers to concepts found in anthropology and sociology.

Statements of Qualitative Research Purposes and Questions

Qualitative research contains statements of research purposes and questions which imply the inductive logic for the problem. The statement of research purpose is the final condensed version of the initial problem statement. Specific research questions may be stated or implied. Statements of purpose imply the

---

EXCERPT 3.6
Problem Reformulations and Emergent Design

What confronted the sixth grade students in our research, however, were the expectations of one of a small minority of teachers who work from a *whole language* view of literacy. Karen Smith (hereafter referred to as KS), the sixth grade teacher and one of the authors, used no workbooks or skillsheets.[4] In visits to this classroom during the previous year, the other co-authors, Carole Edelsky and Kelly Draper, saw constant evidence that KS's knowledge and her "theories of language learning" played a significant role in her curriculum decisions and in the obvious literacy development that ordinarily would not have been expected for a classroom in an inner city school such as Laurel.[5]. . .
Preliminary knowledge from planning the research

The phenomenon we were attempting to explore was how, at the beginning of the year, teachers "coerce" children (following McDermott 1977)[6] so that classroom life becomes what they want it to be. However, we were interested in more than just how that happens in any classroom, but how it happens in a classroom with an effective teacher who has a *whole language* view of literacy. . . .
Final condensed problem statement

Our main data collection was through participant observation of teacher-student interaction all day every day for the first two weeks of school and then three days per week for the next three weeks.[7] Video and audio tape recordings, made periodically, were used to confirm and modify the focus for further observations. We made field notes during classroom observations and videotape viewings. Students were interviewed during the first and third weeks. We also interviewed KS prior to the beginning of school and during the fourth week. We returned in December and again in January to verify if the kinds of interaction observed in September were still occurring.
Data collection strategies

No researcher looks at everything. Decisions about what to look at are based, in part, on the researchers' prior knowledge. In addition to knowledge of research findings, we began with considerable prior knowledge of this teacher. Both the data collection and analysis were informed by this prior knowledge; one cannot unknow what one knows.
Preliminary knowledge from planning the research

We began with the question: How does this teacher get children to meet her unusual expectations? Our initial observations were guided by an assortment of questions: What are the norms here for reading and writing? How does the teacher get students to expect to write? How are certain procedures established (e.g., journal and book writing)? What student-teacher relationships are in evidence?
Foreshadowed Problems

We expected to see gradual change occurring over the first few weeks of school, with some students wavering in accepting KS's uncommon demands, some adapting to the new concept of school and literacy almost immediately, and others taking considerable time to adjust. However, during the first day of school it was evident that the students already were becoming what the teacher wanted them to be. By that afternoon, they were cleaning up without being asked, helping one another, and taking responsibility for making decisions and completing assignments. Here were children in a relatively new environment almost immediately performing like "natives."[8]

Initial expectations and first day of data collection

Quickly we realized that we had made an erroneous assumption regarding gradual adaptation. Our original plan had called for student interviews following the first week of school, but these indications that our object of interest was rushing by prompted us to interview some children on the second day of school. These students had recognized that this class was different; they reported the absence of traditional classroom skills practices, spelling books, sets of textbooks, and subject designation. But they were unable to verbalize what KS expected or how they knew what to do. They said they had "known all along" this new school year was going to be "hard" but filled with "fun" projects (constructing a haunted house and putting on plays for the whole school were eagerly anticipated). Nevertheless, despite conducting science experiments, participating in discussions, rehearsing reading performances they would later give for first graders, and so on, they thought that so far they had not done any "work."

Changed data collection strategies and data summary

After the second day of school we began looking for unstated rules (tacit understandings) as explanations for how the students knew when to do exactly as the teacher said and when to follow the general idea of her statement and act prudently. To our original question (How does this teacher, with her theory of literacy, get students to meet her demands?), we now had added a second: What's happening here? The process of addressing (juggling) both questions was cyclical, requiring a shifting focus from broad to narrow and back again. In viewing the videotapes, it was evident that addressing both questions was necessary to account for what we were observing: a teacher who managed to get things going her way very quickly, but who certainly did not match the description of an effective teacher at the beginning of the year, as found in the literature on effective schools.

First reformulation of research problem

Source: From "Hookin' 'Em In at the Start of School in a 'Whole Language' Classroom" by Carole Edelsky, Kelly Draper, and Karen Smith. Reproduced by permission of the American Anthropological Association from *Anthropology & Education Quarterly* 14:4, 1983. Not for further reproduction.

chosen methodology: ethnographic observation, ethnographic interview or analysis of archival records.

Ethnographic Problem Statements and Questions.   Ethnographic problems focus on current phenomena for which data can be obtained through interacting with the participants in a selected social situation. Excerpt 3.7 illustrates a problem statement and research questions for a study of seatwork in first-grade classrooms. The purpose is "to describe . . . how well this arrangement [seatwork] works for different achievement groups" (Anderson, Brubaker, Alleman-Brooks, & Duffy, 1985, p. 123). The researchers were interested in the use of seatwork for two goals: managerial (such as when students engage in a task without needing the teacher's attention for a predictable time and do not create distractions) and instructional (when students learn new skills, solidify concepts or develop independent work skills). To study the phenomenon of classroom seatwork, the researchers observed six first-grade classrooms in four Title I schools for seven months and periodically held "informal conversations" about what pupils were thinking and learning with twenty-three target students selected from the teacher-assigned highest and lowest reading groups. The logic of the problem statement implies the research design.

Historical Problem Statements and Questions.   Historical research problems focus on past events and require access to documents in historical archives. Research problems are often generated when archival documents are made available to scholars. Excerpt 3.8 illustrates a historical study which focused on a published doctoral dissertation by Horace Mann Bond, who became an administrator, teacher, and president of several black universities during his lifetime. The Bond Papers archive provided the documents to examine briefly "the personal and historiographical circumstances surrounding the book's publication" (Urban, 1987, p. 365). The logic of the statement of purpose implies five research questions which focused on Bond's personal circumstances, historiographical circumstances, Reconstruction history, educational history, and black history.

Legal Problem Statements and Questions.   Legal problems focus on past court decisions and require access to a legal library. Research problems are often initiated by cases which modify a legal principle or establish a legal principle. The study in Excerpt 3.9, for example, examined "the courts' use of the irreparable harm standard when schools seek to enjoin teacher strikes" (Colton & Graber, 1980). A series of questions was asked of each legal case selected for examination. The study notes the limitations of the problem scope. The study does not examine the pros and cons of collective bargaining, teachers' right to strike, the efficacy of injunction, and causes of strikes.

EXCERPT 3.7
Ethnographic Problem Statement and Research Questions

Teachers have developed strategies for coping with the complexities of their job and for providing equitable treatment of all students. One common strategy, revealed in studies of time use in elementary schools, is creating time for working with small groups by having other students work independently. In many classrooms, students spend up to 70% of their instructional time doing independent seatwork assignments (Fisher et al., 1978). . . . Seatwork can fulfill both managerial and instructional goals. . . .

When these goals are met, what is the immediate result? That is, what student responses occur when seatwork is "working" for both students and teacher? How can a teacher know when goals have been met? Progress toward managerial goals is relatively easy to assess on the spot: Students refrain from interrupting the teacher as he or she works with other students, and classroom noise and activity are not disruptive. Assessing progress toward instructional goals of seatwork is more difficult, however, because student thought processes are at the heart of these instructional goals. How does a teacher know that a student correctly practiced a procedure or meaningfully used a concept when the teacher was not present? . . .

Given the difficulty for teachers of gathering information about thought processes while students are doing seatwork and given the amount of time that students spend in the activity, we wanted to know whether and how managerial and instructional goals were realized for students doing seatwork.

■ THE SIGNIFICANCE OF PROBLEM SELECTION ■

The **significance of the problem** is the rationale for a study. It tells the reader why the study is important and indicates the reasons for the researcher's choice of a particular problem. Because research requires knowledge, skills, planning, time, and fiscal resources, the problem to be investigated should be important. In other words, the study should have a potential payoff.

A research problem is significant when it is related to developing educational theory, knowledge, or practice. The significance of a study increases when there are several reasons for the inquiry. The significance may be based on one or more of the following criteria: whether it provides knowledge about an enduring practice, tests a theory, is generalizable, extends our understanding of a broader

---

EXCERPT 3.8
Historical Problem Statement and Research Questions

The recent opening of the Horace Mann Bond Papers to scholars, along with publication of an article on Bond's early career which used those papers, should spark renewed interest in the work of this noted teacher, scholar, and educational administrator. Visitors to the Bond Papers, housed at the University of Massachusetts at Amherst, will find a wealth of unpublished and published material relating to many notable events in the educational history of the twentieth century. Bond's interests were broad, encompassing both humanistic and social scientific approaches to the educational and social problems of blacks. He wrote noted critiques of the mental testing movement at several stages of his long career, did historical research for the plaintiffs in the *Brown v. Topeka* school desegregation suit, and traveled extensively to Africa and studied its civilizations in the later stages of his career.[1]

One of Bond's greatest contributions to scholarship is the topic of this essay: his doctoral dissertation which was published in 1939 under the title *Negro Education in Alabama: A Study in Cotton and Steel.* The merits of Bond's book were noted almost immediately after its publication. . . .

The continuing importance of Bond's work is demonstrated by numerous citations of it in recent and contemporary works in history, educational history, and black history. The fact that the book remains available today in a paperback edition is still more testimony to its significance. It is easy to see that the work cannot be called neglected; however, it seems to be more cited than understood and appreciated.[3] This essay seeks to entice contemporary readers to return to study of the work itself. In pursuit of that objective, it looks briefly at the personal and historiographical circumstances surrounding the book's publication. Then it discusses the content of the work in relation to subsequent historical studies in Reconstruction history and educational history. Finally, it attempts to place the book in the larger stream of work in black history.

Source: From "Horace Mann Bond's *Negro education in Alabama*" by Wayne J. Urban, *History of Education Quarterly*, Vol. 27, No. 3, Fall 1987. Reprinted by permission of Wayne J. Urban.

---

phenomenon, advances methodology, is related to a current issue, evaluates a specific practice at a given site, or is an exploratory study.

Knowledge of an Enduring Practice

The study may provide knowledge about an enduring educational practice. Previous research on the practice may have been done, but this particular research problem has not been investigated. The practice being studied is common to many schools but not necessarily found in every school. The study adds knowledge about an enduring common practice.

EXCERPT 3.9
Legal Problem Statement and Research Questions

The study reported here focuses upon the courts' use of the irreparable harm standard when schools seek to enjoin teacher strikes. Is the standard applied? Why or why not? If it is applied, what evidence of harm is adduced? How do the courts distinguish harm and inconvenience, on the one hand, from *irreparable* harm, on the other? How do plaintiffs demonstrate to the courts that irreparable harm is present or imminent, particularly if schools are being operated and parents are being advised to send their children? How do teacher defendants argue that strikes do not create irreparable harm, where such argument seems to run directly counter to teachers' claims about the importance of schooling and teaching? How do trial court judges respond to the intricacies of social science evidence about the effects of schooling in general and the effects of the absence of such schooling during a strike? How do judges respond to pressures exerted by teachers, by the board and by community spokespersons? How do they interpret the often-ambiguous guidance set forth in statutes and case law? Such questions are at the heart of the inquiry whose results are reported here.

At the outset, it may be useful to identify some areas which this research report does *not* address. It does not concern itself with the pros and cons of collective relationships between public employers and employees, between school boards and teachers. It does not analyze the complex and emotion-laden issue concerning the right of teachers to engage in strikes. It does not explore the causes or effects of strikes. Even the efficacy of injunctions is not of direct concern. This study focuses on the views and assessments of the parties to the injunctive process itself—the boards, the teachers and the courts. Our own views are held in abeyance insofar as possible.

Source: Colton, D. L., & Graber, E. E. (1980). *Enjoining teacher strikes: The irreparable harm standard* (Grant No. NIE-G-78-0149). Washington, DC: National Institute of Education, 2.

An example of a study of an enduring practice that may not be common to all schools is "The Influence of Categories of Cumulative Folder Information on Teacher Referrals of Low-achieving Children for Special Education Services" (Giesbrecht & Routh, 1979). Early in each academic year in elementary schools, referrals of low-achieving children for special services are usually requested from teachers. Very little is known, however, about what influences a teacher's referral. This study investigated three categories of influence typically found in a cumulative folder: previous teacher's comments on the child's behavior, the race attributed to the child, and the educational level ascribed to the child's parents.

Another example of an enduring practice is that of testing. As noted in Excerpt 3.10 much research has been done toward explaining the motivational and situational variables of testing. This study investigated the variable of evaluation apprehension on intelligence test performance of disadvantaged minority group children.

EXCERPT 3.10
Knowledge About an Enduring Practice

A number of research endeavors have been directed toward explicating motivational and situational parameters which allow testing situations to yield a valid assessment of children's cognitive abilities. The use of familiar examiners (Thomas, Hertzig, Dryman, & Fernandez, 1971), positive pretest interactions between examiner and child (Jacobson, Berger, Bergman, Millham, & Greeson, 1971), and testing location (Seitz, Abelson, Levine, & Zigler, 1975) have demonstrated that a motivational explanation for the poor performance of economically disadvantaged minority children is plausible.

While research has demonstrated that disadvantaged children dislike evaluation (Labov, 1970; Zigler, Abelson, & Seitz, 1973) and the testing milieu (Bee, Streissguth, Van Egeven, Leckie, & Nyman, 1970; Johnson, 1974; Labov, 1970), little research has independently assessed the motivational effects of evaluation apprehension on the intelligence test performance of disadvantaged minority group children.

Source: From "A Further Examination of Motivational Influences on Disadvantaged Minority Group Children's Intelligence Test Performance" by Wayne C. Piersel, Gene H. Brody, and Thomas R. Kratochwill, *Child Development,* 1977, 48, 1142–1145. Copyright © 1977 by the Society for Research in Child Development, Inc. Reprinted by permission of The University of Chicago Press.

Theory Testing

The study may test an existing theory with a verification design. The focus may be on social science theories of child or adult development, social interaction, organizational development, conflict, personality, and the like. Educational theories in curriculum development, instruction, diffusion of innovations, learning, and the like are examples of what is typically studied in this category. By testing a theory in different situations or on different populations, the researcher may modify or verify it.

Generalizability

The study may be designed for the results to be generalizable to different populations or practices. A study may replicate or include other variables not investigated in previous research. For example, several naturalistic studies, a short-term experiment in first-grade reading instruction, and an experimental field study in fourth-grade mathematics indicated that when teachers practice what they have been taught as good teaching behavior, students achieve more. "The Effects of Instructing Teachers About Good Teaching on the Mathematics

Achievement of Fourth Grade Students" (Ebmeier & Good, 1979) expanded this inquiry by adding the variables of student aptitude and teacher style in testing for instructional effects.

Extensions of Understanding

Many qualitative studies conducted in the phenomenological tradition provide an extension of understanding rather than generalizability. By describing a selected case of a social situation in detail, these studies give an understanding of the phenomena observed. An understanding of the phenomena provides an image of the future or a configuration of reasonable expectations which might be useful in similar situations.

Methodological Advancement

The study may increase the validity and reliability of an instrument or use a methodology different from that of previous studies. Much of the research on educational measurement investigates questions related to testing, such as testing procedures, the order of the items on an instrument, the item format or response set, or the information processes of the respondent. Other studies may develop a statistical or methodological technique and elaborate its usefulness for research. "The Attachment of a Retarded Child to an Inanimate Object: Translation into Clinical Utility," for example, is a study that "describes the attachment of a moderately retarded boy to coat hangers and the utility of the clinical observations to understand personality development in retarded children" (Haslett et al., 1977, p. 54). The study is important for theory development and methodological advancement.

Current Issues

The study may focus on a social issue of immediate concern. As mentioned previously, such organized political movements as women's rights and civil rights generated educational research. Public recognition of social problems has frequently led to an assessment of their educational effects. The increasing phenomenon of single-parent families, for example, raised questions about the impact of single parenting on student self-concept and achievement. Studies on the effects of extensive television watching on students and the use of calculators and minicomputers in educational programs originated from social concern about a highly technological society. Excerpt 3.11 investigates the effects of the form and the source of sex-typed labels on the initiative performance of young children.

EXCERPT 3.11
Social Issue

In attempting to explain the acquisition of sex-typed behaviors, Kohlberg (1966) and Mischel (1970) have both suggested that labeling an activity as sex appropriate or as sex inappropriate will affect children's performance on that activity. This suggestion has been confirmed by a number of experimental studies using children in the age range 3–12 years (Helper & Quinlivan 1973; Liebert, McCall, & Hanratty, 1971; Montemayor, 1974; Stein, Pohly, & Mueller, 1971; Thompson, 1975). However, it is likely that the impact of sex-typed labels is moderated by a number of variables. The present study was designed to investigate two potentially moderating variables, namely, the form of the sex-typed label and the source of the sex-typed label.

Source: From "Effects of Sex-typed Labels and Their Source on the Imitative Performance of Young Children" by David G. White, *Child Development,* 1978, 49, 1266–1269. Copyright © 1978 by the Society for Research in Child Development, Inc. Reprinted by permission of The University of Chicago Press.

Evaluation of a Specific Practice at a Given Site

The study may evaluate a specific practice for decision-makers at a given site or for external groups. As noted in Chapter 1, evaluation research determines merit: Does the practice work and how can it be improved at the site? It also determines the worth of a practice: Is the practice effective? Is it worth the costs? Do we want to expand its usage? Does it meet our needs? Evaluation research supplies information for immediate use in site decision-making. While the study is not concerned initially with generalizability or theory development, the study may have implications for developing such knowledge. Research problems in evaluation studies are stated in specific and concrete language meaningful to the site decision-makers and audiences for the report.

Exploratory Research

Exploratory research is usually conducted in new areas of research. Such studies may be quantitative or qualitative. For example, a study might field test a direct-coded testing method to determine if the method can be used by sixth-grade students and if it discriminates against any particular student group. Qualitative exploratory studies often examine phenomena which have not been studied previously. Most of the excerpts of qualitative research in this chapter are illustrations of exploratory research. Some exploratory studies develop theory.

■ STANDARDS OF ADEQUACY FOR ■ PROBLEM STATEMENTS

The following questions evaluate research problems by focusing on the three elements discussed in this chapter: the statement of the general research problem, the significance of the problem, and the specific research purpose, question, or hypothesis.

General Research Problem

1. Does the statement of the general research problem imply the possibility of empirical investigation?
2. Does the problem statement restrict the scope of the study?
3. Does the problem statement give the educational context in which the problem lies?

Significance of Problem

Is the significance of the problem discussed in terms of one or more of the following criteria?

— develops knowledge of an enduring practice
— develops theory
— generalizable—that is, expands knowledge or theory
— provides extension of understandings
— advances methodology
— is related to a current social or political issue
— evaluates a specific practice at a given site
— is exploratory research

Specific Research Question or Hypothesis

Quantitative:

1. Does the specific research purpose, question, or hypothesis state concisely what is to be determined?
2. Does the level of specificity indicate that the question or hypothesis is researchable? Or do the variables seem amenable to operational definitions?
3. Is the deductive logic of a research question, or the hypothesis with variables, precise? Are the independent and dependent variables identified?
4. Does the research question or hypothesis indicate the framework for reporting the results?

Qualitative:

1. Do the foreshadowed problems or the condensed problem statement indicate the particular case of some phenomena to be examined?
2. Is the qualitative methodology appropriate for description of present or past events?
3. Is the inductive logic of the research reasonably explicit?
4. Does the research purpose (understanding of a social situation or grounded theory) indicate the framework for reporting the findings?

Other Criteria for Standards of Adequacy

Before conducting a study, the researcher, a possible funding agency, review committees, and other groups also evaluate the problem according to other criteria. These criteria concern the ability of the researcher to conduct the study and the feasibility of the research design. Typical questions asked are:

1. Is the problem one in which the researcher has a vital interest and a topic in which the researcher has both knowledge and experience?
2. Are the problem and the design feasible in terms of measurement, access to the case, sample, or population, permission to use documented data, time frame for completion, financial resources, and the like?
3. Does the researcher have the skills to conduct the proposed research and to analyze and interpret the results?
4. Does the proposed research insure the protection of human subjects from physical or mental discomfort or harm? Is the right of informed consent of subjects provided? Will ethical research practices be followed?

■ SUMMARY ■

The following statements summarize the major aspects of research problem statements, problem formulation in quantitative and qualitative research, significance of a problem, and standards of adequacy for a problem statement.

1. A research problem implies the possibility of empirical investigation.
2. Sources for research problems are casual observations, theory, literature, current issues, practical situations, and personal insights.
3. Educational research includes a broad array of topics concerned with practices, the application of knowledge from the social sciences, and methodological advancement.
4. A research problem statement specifies the focus, educational context, importance, and the framework for reporting the findings.

5. In quantitative research, deductive logic is employed in selecting the construct, variables, and operational definitions.
6. A construct is a complex abstraction that is not directly observable.
7. A variable is an event, category, behavior, or attribute that expresses a construct and has different values, depending on how it is used in a particular study.
8. Variables may be categorical or continuous. A variable may be a dependent, independent, manipulated, experimental, predictor, or criterion variable in different designs.
9. An operational definition assigns meaning to a variable by specifying the activities or operations necessary to measure, categorize, or manipulate the variable.
10. To formulate a quantitative problem, a researcher decides the variables, the population and the deductive logic of the design.
11. Deductive logic is employed in research problems with descriptive questions (survey), relationship questions, difference questions, or a hypothesis.
12. A research hypothesis should state the expected relationship or difference between two or more variables, be testable, and offer a tentative explanation based on theory or previous research.
13. In qualitative research the general topic, the case, and the methodology are interrelated and selected interactively rather than in separate research steps.
14. A case is a particular situation selected by the researcher in which some phenomena will be described by participants' meanings of events and processes.
15. A qualitative study employs inductive logic to build observations to form a descriptive narration and to build a concept from that narration.
16. Qualitative observations, obtained over a lengthy time, are recorded as notes of ethnographic observations, transcripts of ethnographic interviews, or researcher notes of historical documents.
17. Qualitative descriptions are detailed narrations of people, incidents, and processes which emphasize participants' meanings.
18. A concept is an abstraction which states the commonalities among observed situations and distinguishes phenomena from other situations.
19. Concepts are used in qualitative research to provide an understanding of a situation from the perspectives of the participants or to suggest grounded theory.
20. Qualitative research problems are reformulated several times during data collection, while quantitative research problems are stated before data collection.
21. A research problem is significant if it provides knowledge about an enduring practice, tests theory, increases generalizability or extends empirical understandings, advances methodology, focuses on a current issue, evaluates a specific practice, or is an exploratory study.

22. Problem statements are judged by criteria for statement of a research problem, the problem significance, the specific research questions or hypotheses, and the appropriate logic and feasibility.

■ SELF-INSTRUCTIONAL REVIEW EXERCISES ■

Sample answers are in the back of the book.

Test Items

1. Which of the following statements is phrased as a research problem? The purpose of this study is to determine
   a. whether the promotion policy should be changed.
   b. the truth of the proposition that American education has encouraged a social class system in the United States.
   c. how students can overcome test anxiety.
   d. whether there is a difference in the mean gain scores in reading achievement between comparable students taught word attack skills and those taught comprehension skills.

2. The statement of the research problem provides
   a. the educational context of the study.
   b. the framework for reporting the results.
   c. the importance of the study.
   d. All of the above are correct.

3. Quantitative problem formulation requires
   a. the use of deductive logic for the problem.
   b. selection of a construct, variables, and operational definitions.
   c. selection of a population and/or sample.
   d. All of the above are correct.

4. Quantitative research questions may be phrased to indicate
   a. a descriptive study of current status of a group.
   b. a relationship study predicting the influence of one variable on another variable.
   c. a comparative study between two or more data sets.
   d. All of the above are correct.

5. A statement of the expected relationship or difference between two or more variables is called a
   a. concept.   c. definition.
   b. hypothesis.   d. construct.

6. Which is an *incorrect* statement regarding a research hypothesis? A research hypothesis
    a. is supported or not supported.
    b. relates variables that can be measured, manipulated, or categorized.
    c. is more specific than the problem statement.
    d. is the same as a statistical hypothesis.

7. Which of the following is *not* an operational definition?
    a. ratings of art drawings by three professors of art education
    b. IOWA Tests of Basic Skills
    c. divergent thinking of problem-solving skills
    d. classification of students in a graduate research course by whether or not they have had a statistical course

8. Which of the following criteria for a good research hypothesis is violated most in the following hypothesis: Students in an exploratory vocational educational program will make more contributions to society than those not enrolled in the program.
    a. A hypothesis is concise.
    b. A hypothesis is worthy of testing.
    c. A hypothesis can be stated operationally.
    d. A hypothesis is logically precise.

9. Qualitative problem formulation requires
    a. selection of a case and a particular methodology.
    b. use of inductive logic to build from qualitative observations a descriptive narration.
    c. physical and/or psychological access to social situations in the past or present.
    d. All of the above are correct.

10. A case in qualitative research refers to
    a. one person for an in-depth study.
    b. one archival collection or legal library.
    c. a particular situation selected by the researcher through which an understanding of some broader phenomena might be acquired.
    d. a variable.

11. Qualitative research may
    a. test a theory.
    b. provide an understanding of a concept from participants' meanings of social situations or suggest grounded theory.
    c. be derived from an exhaustive literature review.
    d. view individuals as subjects who can be replaced in a study.

12. Qualitative problems
    a. are reformulated several times after data collection has begun.
    b. are usually stated as broad foreshadowed problems which will be condensed later.
    c. focus on "what," "who," and "why" of social situations.
    d. All of the above are correct.

13. Which does *not* suggest significance for a research problem?
    a. evaluation of a specific practice at a given site.
    b. expansion of generalizability of prior research or extension of understandings in exploratory research.
    c. a focus which is unrelated to prior research or broader phenomena.
    d. a current issue.

Application Problems

Answer the questions for each research problem.

1. The following are examples of research topics. Indicate the decisions necessary in order to conduct the study, and restate each as a useful research question.
   a. effects of different ways of learning social studies
   b. effects of cooperative versus competitive instruction on attitudes toward learning
   c. opinions of parents toward education
   d. family characteristics and school attendance
   e. validity of WISC for school performance

2. Write a directional hypothesis for the following problem statement, and identify the type of variables in the hypothesis. "Low-achieving students frequently respond positively to behavior modification programs. Is there any relationship between the type of reward (tangible or intangible) and the amount of learning?"

3. State a hypothesis based on each of the research questions listed below:
   a. What is the effect of individualized and structured social studies on high school students?
   b. Is there any difference in students' engagement in tasks when a teacher uses a positive introduction and when a teacher uses a neutral introduction to tasks?
   c. Does nonpromotion of elementary pupils improve their personal adjustment?
   d. Do middle school children produce more narratives when taught in an academic teacher's class or when taught in a cognitive-development teacher's class?
   e. Do teachers' perceptions of job stress differ among teachers of mildly retarded, moderately retarded, and nonretarded children?

4. State the most likely independent and dependent variables for each research title listed below or state that no variables are identified.
   a. "Liberal Grading Improves Faculty Evaluations But Not Student Performance"
   b. "Classroom Behavior in Elementary School Children: Perceptions of Principals"
   c. "Relationship of Teacher Cognitive Styles to Pupils' Academic Achievement Gains"
   d. "Ideas of Early Sex Education Movements in America, 1890–1920"
   e. "Reducing Inter-Sentence Interference via Contextual Aids?"
   f. "Effect of Two School-Based Intervention Programs on Depressive Symptoms of Preadolescents"

5. Which research titles listed above also clearly identify the subjects?

6. In the following qualitative problem statements, identify the case to be studied.
   a. This study describes and analyzes how women faculty members at an urban university perceive their professional and personal lives and how they integrate their lives.
   b. School board records of a suburban school system were analyzed for the ideologies articulated by various school board members to legitimize system-wide curriculum policies from 1920 to 1980.
   c. The research problem is to describe how Miss Sue, a first year elementary school teacher, learns a professional role with students, faculty, administrators, and parents, and how she develops "meaning" for teacher professionalism.
   d. This study focuses on the courts' interpretations of academic freedom when applied to cases involving public school personnel and the legal grounds for their interpretations from 1950 to 1985.
   e. The research problem is to describe and analyze a faculty social system in the implementation of an innovative middle school program to propose grounded theoretical concepts.

CHAPTER 4

LITERATURE REVIEW

■ KEY TERMS ■

literature review	preliminary literature search
related literature	exhaustive search
secondary sources	database
primary sources	thesaurus
report literature	meta-analysis

Literature reviews, if conducted carefully and presented well, add much to an understanding of the selected problem and help place the results of a study in a historical perspective. Without reviews of the literature, it would be difficult to build a body of accepted knowledge on an educational topic.

This chapter explains the purposes and steps to locate, search, and criticize the literature. It also describes sources for secondary literature and reference services for primary literature. A quantitative literature review follows specific guidelines in the presentation and criticism of the literature to provide an understanding of the existing knowledge of the problem and a rationale for the research questions. Qualitative researchers present literature discussions and integrate criticism of the literature in the text of a study. Later in the chapter you will find a discussion of meta-analysis, a statistical methodology used to synthesize the results of prior research; this review process is described and assessed. Finally, we suggest some standards for evaluating traditional narrative literature reviews.

■ FUNCTIONS OF A REVIEW OF RELATED ■ LITERATURE

An interpretative review of the literature is exactly that—a summary and synthesis of relevant literature on a research problem. A **literature review** is usually a critique of the status of knowledge on a carefully defined educational topic. The literature review enables a reader to gain further insights from the purpose and the results of a study.

Literature for a review includes many types of sources: professional journals, reports, scholarly books and monographs, government documents, and dissertations. It may include empirical research, theoretical discussions, reviews of the status of knowledge, philosophical papers, and methodological treatises.[1]

Related literature is that which is obviously relevant to the problem, such as previous research investigating the same variables or a similar question; references to the theory and the empirical testing of the theory; and studies of similar practices. Thoroughly researched topics in education usually have sufficient studies pertinent to the research topic. Excerpt 4.1 is an example of a literature review of directly related studies, which are studies that investigated a similar problem.

New or little-researched topics usually require a review of any literature related in some essential way to the problem to provide the conceptual framework and a rationale for the study. Related literature may be found outside the field of education such as in sociological research on small-group interaction, political studies of voter behavior, or psychological research on cognitive processes. Related literature may also be in an educational context that is different from that of the research problem. Excerpt 4.2 contains an example of a literature review that relates three broad topics to the research problem.

A review of the literature serves several purposes in research. Knowledge from the literature is used in stating the significance of the problem, developing the research design, relating the results of the study to previous knowledge, and suggesting further research. A review of the literature enables a researcher to:

1. *Define and limit the problem.* Most studies that add to educational knowledge investigate only one aspect of the larger topic. The researcher initially becomes familiar with the major works in that topic and the possible breadth of the topic. The research problem is eventually limited to a subtopic within a larger body of previous theory, knowledge, or practice and stated in the appropriate terms.

2. *Place the study in a historical and associational perspective.* To add to the knowledge in any subfield, researchers analyze the way their studies will relate to existing knowledge. A researcher may thus state that the research of A, B, and C has added a certain amount to knowledge; the work of D and E has further added to our knowledge; and this study extends our knowledge by investigating the stated question.

3. *Avoid unintentional and unnecessary replication.* A thorough search of the literature enables the researcher to avoid unintentional replication and to select a different research problem. The researcher, however, may deliberately replicate a study for verification. A research topic that has been investigated with similar methods that failed to produce significant results

[1]We gratefully acknowledge the assistance of K. A. Cutler, Social Science Reference Librarian, and the Reference Services of the James Branch Cabell Library of Virginia Commonwealth University in the preparation of this chapter.

EXCERPT 4.1
Relevant Literature: Directly Related

Interaction between adults and children has been examined in both family and preschool settings but few studies have reported comparisons of mothers and preschool teachers either in terms of their attitudes or their behavior. Although Elardo and Caldwell (1973) reported a high level of agreement between parents and preschool teachers on a set of objectives, the technique used in their study may not have been sensitive to differences because the respondents were allowed to rate every objective as "very important." Cabler (1974) reported that principals and teachers of kindergarten children assigned higher priority to the development of such "personal" characteristics as self-concept and emotional maturity, while parents placed higher priority on "intellectual" development. More recently, Winetsky (1978) found that preschool teachers preferred that children be involved in self-directed activities, while mothers of preschool children showed a greater preference for teacher-directed activities. The mother-teacher differences revealed by Winetsky's questionnaire study are consistent with observed behavioral differences between mothers and day care workers interacting with 18-month-old infants: Mothers were more restrictive and verbally directive than were child care workers (Rubenstein & Howes, 1978). The study reported here presents additional evidence for differences between mothers and preschool teachers in the ways in which they interact with young children.[1]

Source: From "Some Contrasts Between Mothers and Preschool Teachers in Interaction with 4-year-old Children" by Robert D. Hess, et al., *American Educational Research Journal*, Summer 1979, Vol. 16, No. 3, pp. 307–316. Copyright © 1979, American Educational Research Association, Washington, DC. Reprinted by permission.

indicates a need to revise the problem or the research design. Evaluation studies may seem to duplicate prior research, but this duplication is necessary if the study is designed for site decision-making.

4. *Select promising methods and measures.* As researchers sort out the knowledge on a subject, they assess the research methods that have established that knowledge. Previous investigations provide a rationale and insight for the research design. Analysis of measures, sampling, and methods of prior research may lead to a more sophisticated design, the selection of a valid instrument, a more appropriate data analysis procedure, or a different methodology for studying the problem.

5. *Relate the findings to previous knowledge and suggest further research.* The results of a study are contrasted with those of previous research in order to state how the study added additional knowledge. If the study yielded nonsignificant results, the researcher's insights may relate to the research problem or to the design. Most researchers suggest directions for further research based on insights gained from conducting the study and the literature review.

EXCERPT 4.2
Relevant Literature: Broad Review

RELATED RESEARCH

It appears that previous researchers have not studied differences in the ways teachers teach adults as opposed to pre-adults. However, despite the lack of empirical inquiry on the subject, the professional literature is replete with exhortations not to teach adults as if they were children and with prescriptive principles concerning how to teach adults or facilitate adult learning. The most coherent and influential formulation of such principles is that advanced by Knowles, in which he contrasts "andragogical" or learner-centered methods with "pedagogical" or teacher-centered methods, arguing that the former are especially appropriate for adult education (8).

The prescriptive literature rests on at least three reasonably cogent foundations: informed professional opinion; philosophical assumptions associated with humanistic psychology and progressive education; and a growing body of research and theory on adult learning, development, and socialization. This latter body of knowledge is particularly germane to the present research, for it provides empirical support for the proposition that the learning needs, interests, and capacities of adults differ from those of pre-adults. If adults differ from pre-adults in ways that have implications for learning, then it is probable that they differ also in ways that are significant for teaching.

Research on adult development and socialization appears to be particularly pertinent to understanding differences between adults and pre-adults related to teaching and learning. Brim (1) and others (10) have argued, for example, that adults, compared with pre-adults, are more often the initiators of their own socialization (learning) experiences, exert more control over socialization processes and outcomes, and have more power and autonomy in relation to socializing agents such as teachers. Psychosocial development in adulthood builds extensively on prior knowledge and experience and tends to be oriented to immediate and concrete life tasks and opportunities (1) (9) (10).

A few studies, mostly on college students, have compared adults and pre-adults on specific characteristics presumably related to teaching and learning (2) (7) (12). The findings suggest that adults are more task-oriented, motivated, and psychologically mature than pre-adults and that they tend to have more positive attitudes toward education and clearer educational goals. Cross (3) has also suggested some salient differences.

The evidence that adults differ from pre-adults in ways that are likely to affect the behavior of teachers seems compelling. What is lacking in the literature are 1) efforts to identify specific teaching behaviors that might be expected to vary with student age status, and 2) conceptually grounded propositions that specify the conditions and circumstances likely to influence the magnitude of differences in teaching behavior.

Source: From Beder, H. W. & Darkenwald, C. G., "Differences between teaching adults and pre-adults: Some propositions and findings," *Adult Education*, 32(3), 142, 1982. Reprinted by permission of the American Association for Adult and Continuing Education.

■ SOURCES FOR A LITERATURE REVIEW ■

Although a literature review emphasizes primary sources, secondary sources are also useful. **Secondary sources** are syntheses of previous literature, both theoretical and empirical. Examples of secondary sources are monographs and articles found in encyclopedias and journals that assess the status of knowledge on a subject by summarizing original research. A secondary source may be a textbook in the field that combines many primary sources into a single unifying framework. Secondary sources are useful because they provide a quick overview of research developments on the topic. These sources eliminate much technical information about each primary source, but they cite extensive references.

Primary sources are the original research studies or writings by a theorist or researcher. Primary sources contain the full text of a research report or a theory and thus are more detailed and technical. Examples of primary sources are empirical studies published in journals or placed in information retrieval systems, scholarly monographs, research reports, and dissertations.

Primary and secondary sources provide different information. A secondary source gives an overview of the field, a general knowledge of what has been done on the topic, and a context for placing current primary sources into a framework. The essence of a literature review, however, is the primary sources. Primary sources provide detailed information of current research, theories, and methodologies used to investigate the problem.

To access both secondary and primary sources, a reviewer uses preliminary sources. Preliminary sources locate books, articles, reports, and other documents which are secondary or primary sources in a literature review. Most preliminary sources are either indexes which give the author, title, and place of publication or abstracts which give a brief summary of each publication cited with the bibliographic information. Preliminary sources are usually organized by subject but may contain other types of indexes.

Four formats may be used to access sources for a literature review: 1) print, such as a published index or the card catalog; 2) microtext, like rollfiche and microfiche; 3) on-line computer; and 4) CD ROM similar to a CD disk or a floppy microcomputer disk. Most libraries have more than one format to assure a "back-up" system. A student should check with a reference librarian regarding which formats access which types of sources. For our example, we will use a computer literature search which requires the reviewer to be knowledgeable of three or four formats to access the literature.

Reviewing the Literature

A review of the literature is usually carried out in sequential steps. Researchers often return to a supposedly completed step, however, as they gain understanding of the topic or if the problem is restated. Steps in reviewing the literature include the following:

1. *Analyze the problem statement.* The problem statement contains concepts or variables that indicate the topic of the literature search, such as mildly retarded children, reading instruction, or administrator evaluation.
2. *Search and read secondary sources.* Reading several secondary sources provides a brief overview of the topic and helps a researcher define the problem in more precise terms.
3. *Select the appropriate index for a reference service or database.* For most problems, a researcher selects two or three indexes to locate the most important primary literature. The number of indexes used depends on the purpose and scope of the review.
4. *Transform the problem statement into search language.* The problem statement is analyzed and the concepts or variables are first cross-referenced manually with a thesaurus or index for a specific reference service or database to identify those terms most likely to locate the desired literature. These key words are called "descriptors" or "terms." They constitute the language used in a manual or computer search.
5. *Conduct a manual and/or computer search.* Most reviewers initially use a manual search but may ultimately conduct a computer search. They then make a bibliography of the most relevant sources.
6. *Read the pertinent primary sources.* A reviewer writes a brief analysis of each primary source that is relevant to the problem on note cards that contain the bibliographic citation.
7. *Organize notes.* Empirical studies may be classified several ways, such as historical, by similar insights about the problem, or by methodology. The reviewer then organizes the note cards by ideas.
8. *Write the review.* The review cites only those studies, theories, and practices relevant to the problem statement, and it will differ somewhat with the type of study such as basic, applied, or evaluation research, hypothesis-testing or exploratory research, or quantitative or qualitative studies.

The most important sources for review of the secondary and primary literature for an educational problem are described briefly below. Selected sources for reviews of secondary literature are listed in Table 4.1. Techniques for a manual and/or computer search are described later in the chapter.

Sources for Reviews of Secondary Literature

Reviews of primary literature, which are called "secondary literature," are written by recognized authorities when sufficient work has been done for a critical assessment of the status of knowledge. The topics for a review are usually selected by a committee of researchers and scholars who are aware of current issues and research. Because continued work on a topic may not warrant a thorough review for a number of subsequent years, some reviews, although in a sense dated, provide useful information.

Several well-known publications are sources for reviews of literature by scholars in education. Table 4.1 cites a number of general secondary sources. For a more comprehensive annotated guide to print and nonprint primary and secondary sources, see M. L. Woodbury (1982), *A Guide to Sources of Educational Information* (2nd ed.). It contains annotations of more than 700 sources with directions for the location and use of these sources.

Review of Educational Research.   This journal, which is published quarterly by the American Educational Research Association, provides reviews of original research only. Each issue contains four or more critical essays with extensive bibliographies. Topics reviewed recently include educational administrators' mid-career socialization, the role of wait time in higher cognitive learning, reading disability research, and strategies for sequencing information.

Review of Research in Education.   This series has been published annually since 1973 by the American Educational Research Association. Each volume contains chapters organized by major topics, such as learning and instruction, administration and policy, and research methodologies. Recent reviews include "Changing Conceptions of Intelligence," "Changing Conceptions and Practices of Public School Administration," "Cognitive Styles: Some Conceptual, Methodological and Applied Issues," and "Sociology of Education: A Focus on Education as an Institution."

NSSE Yearbooks.   The yearbooks of the National Society for the Study of Education provide general overviews by recognized authorities on selected educational topics. Each annual volume comprises two books, each about a different topic in education. Although the bibliographies are not as exhaustive as in the *Reviews of Educational Research* or *Review of Research in Education,* an entire book provides a comprehensive perspective on a topic. Recent yearbook titles are *Academic Work and Educational Excellence: Raising Student Productivity, The Contributions of the Social Sciences to Educational Policy and Practice, Microcomputers and Education,* and *The Teaching of Writing.*

Encyclopedia of Educational Research (5th ed., 1982).   Published by the American Educational Research Association, this new edition, the first in thirteen years, is a four-volume critical synthesis of educational research. In it distinguished experts interpret findings and their implications for educational policy on all levels. The 256 articles, with extensive bibliographies, represent a comprehensive analysis of the field of educational research, including such topics as counseling, medical, and psychological services; curriculum areas and instructional techniques; human development and measured characteristics of learners; education in national and international development; education of exceptional persons; teachers and teaching; organization and administration; and influences on educational policies.

TABLE 4.1
Selected Sources for Reviews of Secondary Literature

**General
references**
Review of Educational Research (1931– , journal)
Review of Research in Education (1973– , annual)
Yearbook of the National Society for the Study of Education (1902– , annual)
Encyclopedia of Educational Research, 5th ed. (1982)
Books in Print

**Specialized
references**
Handbook of Research on Teaching, Third Ed. (1986)
Handbook of Research on Educational Administration (1987)
Encyclopedia of Educational Evaluation (1975–)
Yearbook of Adult and Continuing Education (1976–)
Yearbook of Special Education (1976–)
Annual Reviews of Psychology (1950–)
Evaluation Studies Review Annual (1975–)
Other specialized references

Specialized Annuals, Yearbooks, and Encyclopedias.   Specialized handbooks, encyclopedias, yearbooks, and annuals provide a comprehensive overview and a scholarly analysis of selected topics. The *Handbook of Research on Teaching, Third Edition* (1986) is the first definitive guide in twelve years to what is known about teachers, teaching, and the learning process. The thirty-five articles, each by a leading scholar, provide an in-depth survey of theory and research, identify emerging concepts and models of programs and policies, assess the significance of the research, and examine unresolved issues. New chapters in the third edition are "Teachers' Thought Processes," "Student Thought Processes," and "Teaching of Learning Strategies." The articles, which contain extensive bibliographies, are organized in five broad topics: theory and methods of research on teaching, the social and institutional context of teaching, research on teaching and teachers, adapting teaching to differences among learners, and research on the teaching of subjects and grade levels. The *Handbook of Research on Educational Administration* (1987), the first definitive guide to research findings and conclusions in educational administration, evaluates the major areas of inquiry prevalent during the last thirty years. The thirty-three articles, each by a leading authority, provide summaries and critical reviews of past work and identify promising concepts and competing views with different research paradigms. The articles are organized around five themes: the administrator, organizations, economics and finance, politics and policy, and special topics such as evaluation, law, and research methods.

The *Encyclopedia of Educational Evaluation* (1975) contains 1,443 articles organized by eleven evaluation-related topics, such as models, functions and targets, planning and design, and the social context of evaluation. Bibliographies are limited to no more than five references. The *Yearbook of Adult and Continuing Education*, published annually, provides general and specific essays primarily on post-secondary education. A recent edition has fifty articles categorized by adult education, adult basic education, continuing professional education, career education, community education, and alternative issues. The *Yearbook of Special Education*, published annually, presents brief articles and essays for the field of special education. A recent edition contained over sixty articles on current issues, implementing federal mandates, various exceptionalities and the roles of professionals. The *Annual Reviews of Psychology* usually have several chapters on aspects of psychology relevant to education, such as tests and measures, developmental psychology, and instructional methodology. Extensive bibliographies accompany each chapter. The *Evaluation Studies Review Annual* contains about fifty articles organized by broad topics. Articles are theoretical and contain current methodological statements and program research from several fields, including education.

Other Specialized References.   Other handbooks and encyclopedias, primarily from social science disciplines, may serve as secondary sources for literature reviews. Specialized references, for example, are in anthropology, social psychology, aging, applied psychology, applied sociology, child psychology, developmental psychology, adolescent children, nonverbal behavior research, small group research, organization management, industrial and organizational psychology, political science, and public administration.

Books in Print.   The subject index to *Books in Print* cites current scholarly monographs and other published books. Several associations and research centers produce monograph series, such as the American Educational Research Association's Monograph Series on Curriculum Evaluation (1970) and the Center for the Study of Evaluation's Monograph Series in Evaluation (1978).

Sources for a Primary Literature Review

Primary sources are empirical studies, research reports, government documents, and scholarly monographs. Indexes identify primary sources which are published or on microtext. An index gives the location of the source, and an abstract helps the reviewer decide which sources are relevant. Selected sources for a review of primary literature are listed in Table 4.2.

TABLE 4.2
Selected Sources for Review
of Primary Literature

Educational journals	*Current Index to Journals in Education* (1969–)
Report literature	*Resources in Education* (1969–)
General and educational periodicals, yearbooks, and monographs	*Educational Index* (1929–)
Published tests in education and psychology	*Mental Measurements Yearbooks* (periodically)
	Test Critiques (1984–1986)
Abstracts and indexes in specialized areas	*Psychological Abstracts* (1927–)
	Sociological Abstracts (1954–)
	Child Development Abstracts and Bibliography (1927–)
	Exceptional Child Education Resources (1969–)
	Research Related to Children (1950–)
	Resources in Vocational Education (1967–)
	Business Education Index (1940–)
	Completed Research in Health, Physical Education, and Recreation, Including International Sources (1959–)
	Physical Education Index (1978–)
	State Education Journal Index (1963–)
	Educational Administration Abstracts (1966–)
Government documents	*Monthly Catalogue of U.S. Government Publications* (1895–)
	Digest of Educational Statistics (1962–)
	American Statistics Index (1973–)
Dissertations and theses	*Dissertation Abstracts International* (1938–)
	Comprehensive Dissertation Index (1861–)
Citation indexes	*Science Citation Index* (1961–)
	Social Science Citation Index (1973–)
Research in progress or recently completed	Smithsonian Science Information Exchange (1973–)

Current Index to Journals in Education (CIJE).   Since 1969, *CIJE* has been published monthly and cumulated semiannually by the Educational Resources Information Center (ERIC). Its primary coverage is educational journals and periodicals, providing abstracts from over 780 publications. It is the most thorough indexing and abstracting service for educational periodicals, but it also includes educationally relevant articles published in such periodicals as the *Personnel Journal, Journal of Family Counseling,* and *Urban Affairs Quarterly.*

Resources in Education (RIE).   *RIE,* a monthly and cumulative semiannual publication furnished since 1969 by ERIC, indexes and abstracts more than 1,000 documents per issue. The Educational Resources Information Center was initiated by the U.S. Office of Education to provide a retrieval system of current research findings to teachers, administrators, researchers, and the public. ERIC consists of a central office and sixteen clearinghouses. Each clearinghouse catalogs, abstracts, and indexes documents in its subject. In addition, each clearinghouse publishes its own newsletters, bibliographies, and interpretative studies. Names of some of the clearinghouses are Elementary and Early Childhood Education, Counseling and Personnel Service, Educational Management, Handicapped and Gifted Children, Reading and Communication Skills, and Urban Education.

   RIE reviews what it calls **report literature**—documents other than journals. This includes speeches and presentations made at professional meetings, monographs, final reports of federally funded research, state education department documents, final reports of school district projects, and the like. Most of these reports are not published in full text in periodicals, but their research findings may be summarized a few years after the report is completed. Other reference services generally do not abstract report literature. Before 1966, therefore, report literature was not retrievable: it was not preserved or indexed. Most documents indexed in the *RIE* are in the ERIC Document Microfiche Collection. Universities, state departments of education, and many public school systems own the microfiche collection. For many educational problems, a search through *CIJE* and *RIE* is adequate for locating most of the recent relevant sources.

Educational Index.   The *Educational Index* primarily references educational periodicals, yearbooks, and monographs printed in English. It is published for ten months a year and indexes more than 300 journals related to education. *CIJE* is the preferred reference because it includes both an indexing system and annotation of educational periodical literature. If an exhaustive search is required, the *Educational Index* is useful because it provides coverage from 1929. Most reviewers use *CIJE* from 1969 to date and, for enduring topics, the *Educational Index.*

Literature on Measurement.   The major reference on standardized tests in education and psychology is *The Mental Measurements Yearbooks,* published periodically since 1938. *The Ninth Mental Measurements Yearbook (MMY),* 1985, contains descriptive information and critical reviews on 1,409 tests; 70 percent have been newly published since the *Eighth MMY* (1978), 17 percent are tests which have been revised since being listed in previous *MMYs,* and the remainder are tests which are widely used. Although the majority of the tests are personality, vocational, and intelligence tests, the *MMY* also includes tests in school achievement and most school subjects. Information provided about each test includes descriptive data on form, parts, norms, manuals, scoring services, prices, and time limits, and critical reviews which are usually written by two independent reviewers. The reviews are intended to be "frankly critical" in evaluating the test's strengths and weaknesses with a detailed analysis of the psychometric properties to enable test users to select and compare competing tests for specific applications. Six indexes are aids for effective use of the *MMY*. The *MMY*s are useful for selecting a test for a research design and choosing sources of information on test construction.

Test Critiques, Volumes I–V (1984–1986), is oriented to users in the field to serve as a desk reference handbook for testing practitioners. Each "critique" is written by one reviewer and provides information about the practical applications, technical aspects, and a summary of the instrument from a specialist's viewpoint. *Test Critiques* is useful as a practical guide to using a test once it has been selected. Other sources for measurement literature are cited in Chapter 5.

Abstracts and Indexes in Subjects Related to Education.   The sources discussed above have very broad coverage for most educational research problems. A number of abstracts and indexes have more narrow coverage by focusing on a single subject related to education. If a research problem is limited to a specific topic, a thorough search would include using the more specialized reference.

Psychological Abstracts, published monthly by the American Psychological Association since 1927, indexes and abstracts more than 950 journals, technical reports, monographs, and other scientific documents in psychology and related disciplines. *Psychological Abstracts* usually provides more thorough coverage than *CIJE* in educational problems related to some psychological topic, such as human development, counseling, exceptional children, attitudes, or learning.

Sociological Abstracts, which is similar to *Psychological Abstracts,* has been published five times a year since 1954. Because the subject index uses single terms, the reviewer must check the abstract in order to determine the article's relevance.

Child Development Abstracts and Bibliography cites articles from several disciplines and applied fields, including education. Since 1927 this quarterly publication has included author index, subject index, and abstracts.

Exceptional Child Education Resources (ECER), published since 1969, uses a format similar to that of *CIJE.* Of the 200 journals covered here, many are not listed in *CIJE.*

Research Related to Children, a series of bulletins published by the ERIC Clearinghouse on Elementary and Early Childhood Education since 1950, provides descriptions of research in process as well as recently completed research. Each bulletin contains subject, investigator, and institutional indexes along with project descriptions.

Resources in Vocational Education, formerly *Abstracts of Instructional and Research Materials in Vocational and Technical Education* (AIM/ARM) has been published six times a year since 1967. It provides subject and author indexes, projects in progress, and summaries of research, instructional materials, and curriculum projects.

Business Education Index, published annually since 1940, is a combined subject-author index. It covers articles from about forty periodicals.

Completed Research in Health, Physical Education and Recreation Including International Sources, published since 1959, covers the research and articles from 168 periodicals and includes theses and dissertations. It is the best abstracting service in physical education and provides a detailed subject index.

The *Physical Education Index* (1978–), published quarterly, provides a subject index on educational topics and specific sports. It also indexes sports medicine.

State Education Journal Index, published twice a year since 1963, is a subject and bibliographic index on articles in about 100 state education journals. These journals cover a broad range of topics and are useful primarily for such state educational issues as federal aid, collective bargaining, and teacher certification.

Educational Administration Abstracts, published since 1966, abstracts articles from about 100 journals. The reference classifies abstracts into forty-two subjects and provides an author and journal index but not a subject index.

Government Documents Indexes.   The *Monthly Catalogue of United States Government Publications* indexes books, pamphlets, maps, and periodicals of all types—over 15,000 per year. Congressional, departmental, and bureau publications are organized alphabetically by department and bureau with monthly and cumulative author, title, and subject indexes and series/report numbers. Two indexes to educational statistics compiled by the federal government are the *Digest of Educational Statistics* and the *American Statistics Index.* The *Digest of Educational Statistics,* published annually by the National Center for Education Statistics, contains demographic statistics and some longitudinal analyses. A recent edition provided statistics on enrollment, organizational patterns, staffing, student retention rates, educational finances, and educational achievement at all levels of education and in federally funded programs. The *American Statistics Index,* published monthly as an annual index and abstract service, cites publications of departments or agencies other than the Department of Education. For example, information on vocational education, employment and specialized training programs, welfare recipients with children in school, and drug abuse may be collected by Departments of Agriculture, Commerce, Health and Welfare, and Justice.[2]

Dissertations and Theses.   Because most dissertations and theses are original unpublished research, the *Dissertation Abstracts International* and *Comprehensive Dissertation Index* are used to locate relevant studies. The *Comprehensive Dissertation Index* provides a subject and author index for every dissertation and thesis for an advanced degree in education accepted by United States and Canadian universities. *Dissertation Abstracts International* abstracts dissertations accepted by

[2]Specialized indexes for legal research and other indexes for nonstatistical government publications commonly used in policy research are cited in Chapter 12.

more than 375 institutions in the United States and Canada. Presently, Section A abstracts dissertations in the humanities and social sciences, including education, and Section B abstracts dissertations in engineering and the sciences, including psychology.

Citation Indexes.   Citation indexes enable a researcher to determine the impact of a key study or theory on the works of other scholars and researchers. This is particularly important if the first work was controversial, began a subfield, or initiated a series of studies. The *Science Citation Index (SCI)* and *Social Science Citation Index (SSCI)* provide the bibliographic information for all the references that cited the earlier work. SCI indexes citations in science, medicine, agriculture, technology, and the behavioral sciences, including psychology. *SSCI* indexes citations in social, behavioral, and related sciences, including education and psychology.

Smithsonian Science Information Exchange (SSIE, 1973 to date). The SSIE is a clearinghouse for work in progress. Because there is a time lag between completion of a study and its publication, the SSIE enables a reviewer to locate research in progress or research recently completed but not yet in the literature. All fields of the social, behavioral, biological, and medical sciences and the summaries of about 80 percent of federally funded research are indexed and abstracted. To use this service, a reviewer must either request the information through a computer search or write Smithsonian Science Information Exchange, Suite 300, 1730 M Street, N.W., Washington, DC 20036.

■   THE SEARCH FOR THE LITERATURE   ■

The search is merely one step in a literature review. The search locates the literature that is relevant to the problem statement. Neither a manual nor a computer search is a "fishing expedition": both the reference service and the key terms are selected in such a way as to yield the most complete list of pertinent literature. After obtaining a bibliography of relevant literature, the next step is to read the abstracts and select the most relevant studies for full text reading.

The logical process for conducting a literature review is the same whether one does a manual or a computer-assisted search. Steps 1 through 5 of the process apply to both manual and computer-assisted searches. However, because computer searches are available through most university libraries and state departments of education, some professional associations and school systems, and commercial retrieval services,[3] reviewers need to have an understanding of the steps for a computer search. Beginning reviewers should follow steps 1 through 5 manually, adopt step 6 for a hand-written bibliography, and complete step 7.

---

[3]See E. Pugh & W. T. Brandhorst (1981), *Directory of ERIC search services,* Washington, D.C.: Educational Resources Information Center, National Institute of Education.

The Advantages of a Computer Search

Computer searches may be provided without direct charges to the user or may cost from thirty to a hundred dollars or more, depending on the type of search. Reviewers should consult a trained search analyst or reference librarian before conducting a computer search, because computerized information retrieval systems are changing rapidly. Following is a list of the advantages of this type of search.

1. *Identification of references with three or more descriptors.* A computer search quickly identifies only those references that contain all the essential descriptors for a research problem. See Figure 4.4.
2. *Search of multiple databases.* A researcher can look through multiple databases (see list below) quickly when executing a broad literature search on a complex problem.
3. *Selective limitation of the search.* Searches of databases such as ERIC can be selectively limited if the database codes each source by educational levels, age level descriptors, publication/document type, or target audiences.[4]
4. *Literature with current educational terminology.* With the aid of a search analyst, a reviewer can locate sources that use informal but current jargon—words not yet elevated to the status of a descriptor or term.
5. *Printout provided.* The computer supplies either the bibliographic citation or the citation with the abstract, which aids the reviewer in selecting sources.
6. *Time efficiency.* Literature searches have become more complex. Although "education" has the connotations of school systems and higher education, educational programs and related activities may be found in medical institutions, court systems, and industry. Research indexes and informational retrieval systems have increased. Computer searches, if carefully planned, are productive and efficient.

The most frequently used educational research databases available for computer searches[5] are:

ERIC (1966)
Exceptional Children Educational Resources (1966–)
PsycINFO [*Psychological Abstracts*] (1967–)
Books in Print (1979–)
Social SCISEARCH and Backfiles [*Social Science Citation Indexes*] (1972–)
GPO Monthly Catalogue [*Monthly Catalogue of U.S. Government Documents*] (1976–)
Public Affairs Information Service [PAIS] (1972–)

---

[4]Each of these "searchable fields" is defined and should be used with the code given in a current *Thesaurus of ERIC Descriptors*.

[5]The dates given are for the BRS (January, 1986). Most services offer the same year for the database; however, DIALOG offers *Books in Print* from 1900 to the present.

Legal Resources Index [LAWS] (1980–)
Sociological Abstracts (1963–)
Family Resources [NCFR] (1970–)
Ageline [AARP] (1978–)
National Rehabilitation Information Center [NRIC] (1950–)
National Institute of Mental Health Database [MCMH] (1969–)
Resources in Vocational Education (1978–)
Sport Database (1949–)
Bilingual Education Database (1978–)
Dissertation Abstracts Online (1861–)
National Newspaper Index (1979–)

A typical literature search encompasses the last ten years: however, some exhaustive searches encompass more than ten years. A useful procedure is to search *CIJE* and *RIE* from the present back to 1969, search *CIJE* and *Educational Index* from 1966 to 1968, and then search *Educational Index* from 1965 back as far as necessary for the review. Specialized indexes and abstract services in addition to the general education indexes may be necessary to locate primary sources.

Steps for Conducting a Manual or Computer Search

A computer search requires the reviewer to analyze the problem, determine the type of search, select the reference services (indexes, databases) and conduct the search. Many universities provide computer searchers for the ERIC database and have access to one of the three major information retrieval systems: DIALOG Information Retrieval Service, Bibliographic Retrieval Service (BRS), or Systems Data Corporation (SDC). Among the three information retrieval systems, over 200 different databases can be searched. Although there is considerable overlap among high usage databases, they may not all be available locally. The reviewer can find out from the search analyst which databases are available and the search procedure recommended: a manual search, an on-line computer search by the reviewer, or a computer search by the analyst.

The following are general steps for a search. Specific terms and directions given to a computer may differ with each database. A preliminary manual search will enable the reviewer to complete the steps more quickly than if the literature search is done totally with the computer. Most computer search forms require the following: the search topic, the key terms with synonyms and related terms, the years to be searched, and the language selection (English only or any other language). Additional directions or commands may be added for the search depending on the scope (broad or narrow) of the search.

1. *Analyze the Research Problem.* The researcher states the problem specifically and analyzes it. For example, the question "What are the effects of high school remedial mathematics programs on student computational skills?" describes the research problem in a few words and focuses the search on the terms "remedial mathematics program," "high school," and "computational skills." A problem stated as "What are the effects of remedial programs on achievement?" is too im-

precise to describe the problem or to do a search. Reading secondary sources can help focus and narrow the research problem.

2. *Determine the Type of Search.* Searches are made for several reasons: as a preliminary search to select a research problem; as an exhaustive review for a thesis, dissertation, or major research study; and as an update for a previous literature review. A **preliminary search** to select a research problem needs only ten or twenty of the most recent references for each descriptor or descriptor combination in one or two reference services. Because the problem is not yet narrowed, the researcher uses broad descriptors and few combinations. The broad scope is limited by the number of years searched and number of databases. An **exhaustive search** of the literature is done for a narrowly focused problem for ten or more years and uses the most relevant reference services. For example, the search for "teacher attitudes toward merit pay" is limited to the three concepts: "teachers," "attitudes," and "merit pay." An exhaustive search will require a computer search. The scope may be narrowed by the type of teacher, specific aspects of merit pay, publication type, or educational level of the merit pay system. A search may be used to update a literature review prepared by the reviewer or one found in a secondary source. Updating a literature review is done by selecting those descriptors used in the initial search and requesting the citations since the first search.

3. *Select the Reference Service (Database).* The problem is transformed into the key terms, which are usually the variables and population in the research question or hypotheses. By analyzing the problem statement, the researcher can select the most appropriate reference services. The *CIJE, RIE, Exceptional Child Education Resources,* and *Psychological Abstracts,* for example, will probably cover literature for a problem centering on handicapped children. Literature for a research problem on computer-assisted instruction may be found only in *CIJE* and *RIE.* If the problem is the effects of computer-assisted instruction on the cognitive processes of children, *Psychological Abstracts* may be useful. If the problem is the administration of computer-assisted instruction, then *Educational Administration Abstracts* will be useful. A research problem on teacher evaluation may be found in *CIJE, RIE, Educational Administration Abstracts,* and *State Education Journal Index.* By selecting the reference service, the reviewer is choosing the **database,** and, consequently, the sources which are indexed by a particular reference service. Although there is much overlap in the databases indexed by different reference services, some sources will be unique to each reference service. In addition, different reference services provide additional aids to the reviewer, such as annotations, abstracts, or different "searchable fields" to limit a broad or narrow search. These key words or phrases are then located in the thesaurus for the selected reference service. We will use the ERIC database in our example.

The *CIJE* contains a Subject Index, Author Index, and Main Entry Section. The EJ numbers locate the reference in the Main Entry Section, which provides the full bibliographic citation, major and minor descriptors for the citation, and an annotation. An annotation is a brief (usually one sentence) summary of the article rather than a 100– or 200–word abstract. Figure 4.1 is an example of a Main Entry Section of *CIJE.* After finding the entry in *CIJE,* the next step is to locate the article in the periodical section of the library or through interlibrary loan.

FIGURE 4.1
CIJE Main Entry Section

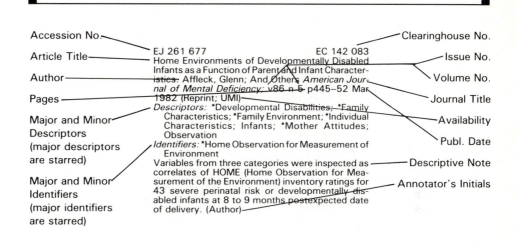

Accession No.

Article Title

Author

Pages

Major and Minor Descriptors (major descriptors are starred)

Major and Minor Identifiers (major identifiers are starred)

Clearinghouse No.

Issue No.

Volume No.

Journal Title

Availability

Publ. Date

Descriptive Note

Annotator's Initials

EJ 261 677   EC 142 083
Home Environments of Developmentally Disabled
Infants as a Function of Parent and Infant Characteristics. Affleck, Glenn; And Others *American Journal of Mental Deficiency;* v86 n 5 p445–52 Mar
1982 (Reprint; UMI)
Descriptors: *Developmental Disabilities; *Family
    Characteristics; *Family Environment; *Individual
    Characteristics; Infants; *Mother Attitudes;
    Observation
Identifiers: *Home Observation for Measurement of
    Environment
Variables from three categories were inspected as
correlates of HOME (Home Observation for Measurement of the Environment) inventory ratings for
43 severe perinatal risk or developmentally disabled infants at 8 to 9 months postexpected date
of delivery. (Author)

Source: Sample entry from *Current Index to Journals in Education.*

RIE provides several indexes (subject, author, institution, and publication type) to the abstracts called "Document Resume." Using any of these indexes, a reviewer obtains an ED number to locate the reference in the Document Resume section. Each entry in the Document Resume section contains the complete reference, an abstract, and other useful information. Figure 4.2 illustrates an *RIE* Document Resume. If the document is important to the researcher's problem, the reviewer uses the ED number to locate the document in an ERIC Document Microfiche Collection.

An abstract in *RIE* and other services, such as *Psychological Abstracts* or *Child Development Abstracts and Bibliography,* provides more detail than the annotations in *CIJE, Exceptional Child Education Resources,* or only a citation. As a rule, abstracts provide enough information to decide which literature is related to the problem.

4. *Select the Descriptors and Terms.* The scope of the search affects which descriptors are chosen from the *Thesaurus of ERIC Descriptors.* A **thesaurus** is a publication that lists and cross-references key terms or descriptors used in an index for a reference service (database) such as ERIC or *Psychological Abstracts.* Figure 4.3 is a sample entry for the *Thesaurus of ERIC Descriptors.*

Suppose a reviewer is interested in locating information on administrator opinions about social studies curricula, especially whether administrators think social studies should be interdisciplinary or should emphasize history, and whether they believe social problems and current events should be emphasized in a social studies curriculum. The reviewer is particularly interested in principals' attitudes. The key words in the problem statement, however, are only "adminis-

FIGURE 4.2
RIE Document Resume

ERIC Accession Number—Identification number sequentially assigned to documents as they are processed.

Author(s).

Title.

Organization where document originated.

Date published.

Contract or grant number.

Publication Type—Categories indicating the form or organization of the document, as contrasted to its subject matter. The category name is followed by the category code.

ERIC Document Reproduction Service (EDRS) Availability—"MF" means microfiche; "PC" means hard copy reproduced paper copy. When described as "Document Not Available from EDRS," alternate sources are cited above. Prices are subject to change. For latest price code schedule, see section on "How to Order ERIC Documents," in the most recent issue of RIE.

Alternate source for obtaining document.

ED 211 651　　　　　　UD 022 045
Colton, David L.　Berg, William M.
Budgeting for Desegregation in Large Cities. Final Report.
Washington Univ., St. Louis, Mo. Center for the Study of Law in Education.
Spons Agency—National Inst. of Education (ED), Washington, D.C.
Pub Date—Jan 81
Grant—NIE-G-79-0106
Note—286p.
Pub Type—Reports-Evaluative (142) — Reports-Research (143)
EDRS Price - MF01/PC12 Plus Postage
Descriptors—Board of Education Role, *Desegregation Plans, Educational Finance, Elementary Secondary Education, Facility Planning, *Finance Reform, Financial Policy, Government Role, *Government School Relationship, Magnet Schools, *Policy Formation, School Closing, School Community Relationship, *School Funds, *Urban Schools
　　This paper presents the results of an exploratory study of the process of mobilizing and allocating resources for desegregation in large cities. Examined were the effects of budgetary constraints on school desegregation and desegregation impact on educational finance. Four urban school districts were selected for site reports. Section one of this study reviews the literature pertinent to the conceptualization of the research questions. Section two reviews and discusses methodological aspects of the study. Section three describes the findings in the school districts selected for study. A concluding section presents summary observations about relationships between budgets and desegregation. Presented in the site reports are: (1) an historical overview and assessment of current financial status; (2) issues related to school closing and facilities plans; (3) issues related to the funding of magnet schools, staff development, multicultural curricula, and other programs related to desegregation; and (4) funding needs in the areas of transportation, safety and security, and school-community relations. This paper suggests that the broader political, economic, and legal ramifications of desegregation need to be considered in finance reform and policy formation. Also emphasized is the importance of communication among school boards, State and Federal legislatures, and individual school officials in the development of financial policies related to school desegregation. (Author/ML)

Clearinghouse Accession Number.

Sponsoring Agency—agency responsible for initiating, funding, and managing the research project.

Report Number—assigned by originator.

Descriptive Note (pagination first).

Descriptors—subject terms found in the *Thesaurus of ERIC Descriptors* that characterize substantive content. Only the major terms, preceded by an asterisk, are printed in the subject index.

Language of Document—documents written entirely in English are not designated, although "English" is carried in their computerized records.

Identifiers—additional identifying terms not found in the *Thesaurus*. Only the major terms, preceded by an asterisk, are printed in the subject index.

Informative abstract

Abstractor's initials

Source: Sample entry from *Resources in Education*, 1982, 17(5), 201.

FIGURE 4.3
ERIC Descriptors and Terms

Descriptor —

Computers   *Jul. 1966*
CIJE: 2680   RIE: 2492   GC: 910

Postings Note
(number of times term
was used in indexing
CIJE and RIE)

Scope Note
(usage definition) — SN   Devices that solve problems by accepting information, performing prescribed operations on it, and supplying the results obtained — usually consist of units for input, output, storage, control, and arithmetic or logical operations (note: use a more specific term if possible)

Descriptor
Group Code

Computer Output Microfilm
Computer Science
Computer Science Education
Computer Simulation
Computer Software
Computer Software Reviews
Computer Uses in Education
Cybernetics
Databases
Data Processing
Electromechanical Aids
Electronic Publishing
Expert Systems
Information Systems
Information Technology
Input Output
Instrumentation
Man Machine Systems
Online Vendors
Optical Data Disks
Optical Disks
Programming
Programming Languages
Technological Advancement
Telecommunications
Time Sharing
Videotex

Used for — UF   Computer Technology

Narrower Term — NT   Analog Computers
Computer Storage Devices
Digital Computers
Display Systems
Input Output Devices
Microcomputers
Minicomputers
Online Systems

Broader Term — BT   Electronic Equipment

Related Term — RT   Artificial Intelligence
Automation
Calculators
Computer Assisted Instruction
Computer Assisted Testing
Computer Graphics
Computer Literacy
Computer Managed Instruction
Computer Networks
Computer Oriented Programs

Source: Sample entry from *Thesaurus of ERIC Descriptors.*

trator," "opinions," and "social studies curricula." The reviewer selects descriptors that most closely fit each word, chooses related terms (RT) for an exhaustive search, narrow terms (NT) for a very specific search, and broad terms (BT) for literature that treats the term as part of a subclass. The *Thesaurus* has no descriptor for "social studies curricula," but "social studies" is a narrow term (NT), a subclass of the descriptor "curriculum." The descriptor "social studies" has the narrow term "civics" and the broad terms "curriculum" and "social science." To obtain the literature for a broad search, the reviewer would select the list of descriptors as illustrated in Table 4.3.

Because the references obtained using the BT descriptors fail to discuss principals' attitudes except when aggregated with all administrators, or they fail to focus on curriculum issues of an interdisciplinary approach and the integration of

TABLE 4.3
Selected Descriptors for a Broad Search

Problem:

Administrators	Opinions toward	Social Studies Curricula
BT Terms:		
Administration (BT)	*Attitudes* (BT)	*Curriculum* (BT)

current events and social problems in a social studies curricula, the reviewer must conduct a narrower search. The reviewer, using the *Thesaurus,* now selects the narrow or related terms as illustrated in Table 4.4. Notice that there is one term for "principal" but two possible terms for "administrator attitudes": administrator attitudes (NT) and administrator characteristics (RT). For social studies curriculum, there are eight possible terms. Two of these, current events (RT) and social problems (RT) are related conceptually to the research problem. There is, however, no entry for "interdisciplinary," but by combining the remaining five RT terms in a single search, one might locate such literature. To combine the five RT terms, a reviewer would have to use a computer search.

5. *Conduct the Literature Search.* At this point, a reviewer can either do the search manually or direct a computer search. If done manually, the reviewer takes the selected key words and uses the indexes to construct a bibliography. The reviewer would code his or her bibliography (see step 6) by degree of potential usefulness of each citation and proceed to step 7.

Directing an on-line computer search takes planning. The reviewer has already listed from the *Thesaurus* the descriptors, broad terms, narrow terms, and the number of citations (posting note) for each major descriptor in the ERIC database. The reviewer then determines the order in which the descriptors are entered into the computer, most important to least important, and makes a search plan. Once a reviewer is on-line in the search, it is costly to take time to decide the order of the searches and how descriptors—BT terms, NT terms, and RT terms—will be combined.

Descriptors are combined using *and* or *or.* The *or* connectors tend to increase the number of citations for a broad search whereas the *and* connectors tend to reduce the number of citations for a narrow search because all descriptors must be present in each citation. The first search is with combinations of descriptors that precisely fit the problem. The results will show how much work has been done on the topic[6] and whether there is sufficient literature on target. If there is insufficient literature, more searches are necessary in order to obtain the related literature.

---

[6]The *Thesaurus* posting note is the number of references containing the descriptor and is accurate at the time of publication. The computer will give a current update.

TABLE 4.4
Selected Descriptors for a Narrow Search

BT Terms:

Administrator (BT)	*Attitude* (BT)	*Curriculum* (BT)

NT Terms:

Principal (NT)	*Administrator Attitudes* (NT)	*Social Studies* (NT)

RT Terms:

	SN Attitudes, Opinions or Views held by Administrators	*Civics* (NT)
		Anthropology (RT)
		Economics (RT)
		Geography (RT)
		History (RT)
	UF Administrator Opinions	*Political Science* (RT)
		Current events (RT)
	Administrator Characteristics (RT)	*Social problems* (RT)

Let us take a hypothetical example to demonstrate the use of some computer commands. Suppose the problem is "using instructional films in elementary education with Spanish-speaking students." Figure 4.4 indicates how a reviewer combines descriptors for both broad and narrow searches. In Figure 4.4, A, B, and C represent the three major descriptors for the topic. E contains citations common to A and B or literature on instructional films in elementary education. G contains citations that have all three concepts: instructional films, elementary education, and Spanish-speaking persons.

The first search obtains the references for G, which combines all three concepts (A and B and C), and should produce a limited number of references, but these will be on target. In research topics in which there has been much work done, a narrow search is sufficient, but for topics on which little has been done, a broader search is necessary. The next searches might call for references with only two concepts, such as D (A and C), F (B and C), or E (A and B). These broader searches will produce references that may not be exactly on target but are related to the problem. The next relevant citations would be produced by D (Search 2) since "instructional films" and "Spanish-speaking" are more important key terms to the research problem than elementary education. If the information is insufficient, Search 3 for F will contain all references to Spanish-speaking persons and elementary education and Search 4 for E will contain all citations about instructional films for elementary education regardless of the language spoken. Searches

FIGURE 4.4
Combining Descriptors

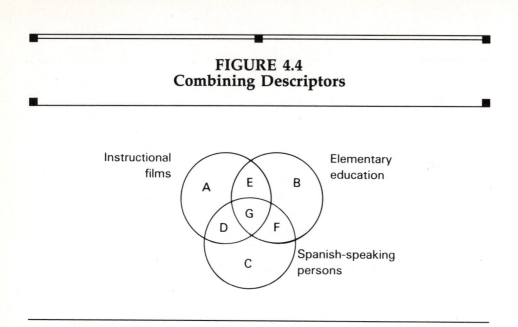

3 and 4 will not find the most pertinent literature but the sources may be related to the problem. In planning a search, the reviewer decides which key terms are most important in the problem. Because of the ERIC indexing procedures, both narrow and broad terms must be used for an exhaustive search.

A researcher can further limit the scope of a search by asking for the most recent references, using only major descriptors, or using non-subject descriptors. The researcher can obtain the most recent references by requesting a specific number, such as twenty-five of the most current references from *CIJE*. Then he or she can give a date command by the years to be searched, such as 1985–1990. Each reference in the ERIC database is assigned up to six Major Descriptors to cover its main focus. Minor Descriptors are used to indicate less important aspects of the topic or non-subject features such as educational level or research methods. To obtain only references in which the key terms have been classified as Major Descriptors, the descriptors are entered on-line followed by "/DE*" or "MAJ." This command usually reduces the citations by about 50 percent. A third command to limit the number of references is to use the Minor Descriptors, some of which are optional classifications. This will severely limit the number of citations. Because not all citations may have been assigned the type of Minor Descriptor involved in the search, some relevant literature may be omitted. Publication type, however, is assigned to every document in the ERIC database.

6. *Analyze the Printout.* The printout of a computer search can provide three levels of information with each reference, depending on the option selected by the reviewer. The first option provides the title and accession number (the EJ and/or ED number). The second option includes the complete bibliographic citation, the EJ and/or ED number and the descriptors for each reference. At present,

the cost of this option is $.05 per citation. The third option includes all of the above plus the abstract. The third option is the most useful in selecting sources and, at present, costs $.10 per abstract.

The reviewer then reads the abstracts for each reference on the printout in order to determine the relevance of the source to the problem. Most reviewers code or rank-order each citation by degree of potential usefulness. A typical code might be 3 to indicate *on target and most important,* 2 to indicate *related literature and may be useful,* and 1 to indicate *irrelevant and unnecessary.*

7. *Locate the References.* The majority of references will probably be in professional journals, although for some topics monographs, dissertations, and reports may be relevant. To locate references, one should spend time learning how a library is organized—which references are in bound volumes, on microfiche or microfilm, or in special collections—and the procedure to obtain these within the library. Reviewers frequently obtain copies of references which are pertinent to the problem and may need rechecking. Most libraries have copy machines and equipment to copy microtext on regular-sized paper.

References not available locally may be obtained through interlibrary loan or by obtaining a microfilm or a photostatic copy from the reference service or another library for a charge. Some reference services such as *Psychological Abstracts* provide the author's address. Using a directory of membership for the American Psychological Association and American Educational Research Association, one can obtain the address and write the author for a reprint of an article or paper.

Abstracting and
Organizing the References

The reviewer now reads, abstracts, and classifies each source, reading the most relevant and recent literature first. These articles and reports are more likely to benefit from previous research and literature reviews. From this reading the reviewer can gain a reasonable understanding of the problem and decide upon a method of classifying the references.

Abstracting an article or report on an index card, usually a four- by six-inch size, requires several steps. The abstract and summary is read first to determine whether it contains any information to justify reading the entire article or report. If the source is sufficiently related to the problem, then it is skimmed for the main points and the pertinent sections are selected for more careful reading for the purpose of abstracting. The exact bibliographic citation is recorded on the index card if it has not already been done. If the final review must follow a particular bibliographic style, the reference is recorded in that form. If not, the American Psychological Association style is frequently used.

As noted in Chapter 2, most research articles and reports follow a standard format that reduces the reading time and facilitates notetaking: abstract; introduction with the problem statement, significance, and a brief literature review;

specific research statement, question, or hypothesis; research procedures; results; and summary with discussion or implications. This format is generally followed in abstracting information on note cards.

Many research articles are only from three to six pages long and can be read quickly. Research reports, dissertations, and monographs are usually much longer. For the lengthy references, the reviewer skims the entire source and only reads those parts relevant to the problem.

Because one cannot tell which references are the most important for the writing of a literature review until after all sources are read, notetaking is kept very brief. If the notes prove insufficient for the literature review, the reviewer can reread the source. Phrases and abbreviations are used, although crucial points may be quoted, with the page numbers on which they may be found. All basic points, however—the problem, procedures, findings, and implications—are noted. In addition, reviewers write their critical reactions to and assessment of the study and its relationship to the problem. Any promising research techniques or problems revealed by the study that limit its usefulness for the literature review are noted. The reviewer's comments are important for generating ideas for criticism of the literature in the review.

Sources that present a theory, describe a program, or summarize opinions and recommendations are abstracted in a different manner. Only the main propositions of the theory, the unique aspects of the program, or the major position of the opinion articles are noted. Quotations are very selective and are taken more for illustrative purposes than documentation. A literature review consists not of a series of quotes but of the reviewer's synthesis and interpretation of the existing knowledge of the problem.

Finally, the reviewer develops a classification system appropriate for the way the literature provides insights about the problem and for the rationale of the study. The classification system for each literature review differs with the significance of the problem and the reviewer's criticism of the literature. A study, for example, that investigates the effects of desegregation might categorize the sources by different effects studied: student achievement, student self-concept, student racial attitudes, school-community relations, teacher-administrator relations, and the like. If the study uses a design or methodology different from that of prior research on the same problem, the references might be categorized by research procedures. If the study asks a question different from the one asked by previous research, the studies might be categorized by research questions. Opinions and theories should have categories distinct from those of empirical studies. Once the classification system is developed, each note card is coded, usually in the upper right-hand corner.

Classifying the references is the first step in organizing the review. The amount of research in any category can be determined quickly. Comparisons and contrasts in methodologies or findings can be synthesized by grouping similar studies. Usually the classification system becomes the subtopics in the written literature review.

■ PRESENTATION OF THE LITERATURE REVIEW ■ IN QUANTITATIVE RESEARCH

Searching the literature provides the researcher with many kinds of information, not all of which is written in the literature review. Only those articles and studies relevant to the study are cited. The literature review demonstrates that the researcher has an understanding of the topic and knowledge of the recent developments in the field. The review should clearly indicate how the selected literature relates to the objectives of the study. The problem statement precedes the literature review, and the research question or hypothesis follows the review. The significance of the study may precede or follow the review.

Organization of the Literature Review

A literature review is organized by sections: introduction, critical review, and summary. The introduction states the purpose or scope of the review. The purpose may be a preliminary review in order to state a problem or develop a proposal, or it may be an exhaustive review in order to analyze and critique the research-based knowledge on the topic.

The essence of the review is the criticism of the literature. The reviewer must organize the literature review logically as it relates to the selection and significance of the problem. Summarizing one study after another does not make for an informative literature review. Studies are classified, compared, and contrasted in terms of the way they contribute or fail to contribute to knowledge, including criticism of designs and methodologies used to obtain that knowledge.

The summary of the literature review states the status of knowledge on the topic and identifies gaps in it. The gaps in knowledge may be due to methodological difficulties, the lack of studies on the problem, or inconclusive results from studies on the problem. The summary provides the rationale for the specific research statement, question, or hypothesis.

Criticism of the Literature

Criticism in a literature review serves to illuminate, to discuss both the strengths and limitations of the knowledge of the problem. The criticism of the literature may be organized several ways: a) historically, by dates of publication; b) by variables or treatments; c) by research designs and methods; d) by the most general literature, or by that which is least related to the problem, and ending with the most closely related references; or e) by a combination of all of these.

Let us look more closely at Excerpt 4.2, which takes the reader from the *most general literature to the most relevant literature.* The study tests a series of hypotheses that say if teachers of adults and pre-adults have instructional autonomy, and if they believe that these different groups should be taught differently, the teachers will exhibit a greater overall difference in teaching behavior between adults and pre-adults. The review first presents the general professional principles that in teaching adults, "androgogical methods" are better than pedagogical methods. The foundations for this prescriptive literature are noted: professional opinion, philosophical assumptions, and research and theory on adult learning, development, and socialization. The literature review then discusses the empirical bases: studies that relate adult development and socialization to teaching and studies that compare specific learning characteristics of adults and pre-adults. The major study (Brim) is discussed in detail, while others are merely cited. The consistent findings of several comparable studies are reported, but one study that challenges these findings is also cited. The literature review ends with a statement of what is lacking in these studies: "efforts to identify specific teaching behaviors that might be expected to vary with student age status" (p. 143) and propositions specifying those conditions that influence the difference in teaching behavior. The review provides both the conceptual and empirical rationale for the research hypotheses.

Studies that are better designed than previous research emphasize *methodological criticisms of that research*. In Excerpt 4.3, R. Vasta and R. F. Sarmiento (1979) investigated the effects of grades on students' study behavior, attendance, and course evaluations in an experimental design. The literature review notes that the "literally hundreds" of studies on this topic have identified the "biasing" influence of student rating of instruction, especially on grading. The criticism rests on the correlational nature of most previous research, which led to inconclusive knowledge and plausible alternative hypotheses. The literature review thus states a rationale for a design in a natural setting that maintains experimental control sufficient to examine grade effects independent of subject variables, such as student study habits, aptitude, and perceptions of the quality of instruction.

A literature review may also be organized by the *variables or experimental treatments* in the study. The hypothesis, for example, in H. G. Smith, "Investigation of Several Techniques for Reviewing Audio-Tutorial Instruction" (1979) was that students using an audio-tutorial review retained more than students using only a study guide. Subjects were randomly assigned to one of four groups: review with study guide only, review with summary audiotape, review with compressed speech audiotape, and no review. The literature review first summarized the research, which indicated that forgetting increases with time and that reviewing previously learned material enhances the ability to recall. The study thus has three review groups and one group with no review. Research on the nature of the review suggested that readings (group one) and listening to a summary (group two) enhanced recall. Finally, while no studies of the use of accelerated speech in reviewing material were found, there was extensive literature suggesting that accelerated speech recording increased original learning (group three). The literature review from both on target and related literature provided an empirical rationale for the design and for the research hypotheses.

For each topic or idea introduced in the review, the researcher explains how it relates to the study. The writer cannot assume that the reader will make the con-

EXCERPT 4.3
Literature Review: Methodological Criticism

Beginning with Remmers' pioneering work (e.g., Remmers, 1930; Remmers, Hadley, & Long, 1932), the factors affecting students' ratings of instruction have been the subject of literally hundreds of research investigations. One important focus of much of this research has been the identification of "biasing" influences on student objectivity—that is, variables which alter students' ratings of presumably unrelated aspects of the instructional process (e.g., evaluations of textbook clarity affected by sex of the instructor). Perhaps the area receiving the most attention in this regard has been the relationship between students' grades and their ratings of the quality of instruction. Yet Feldman's (1976) recent extensive review of the literature offers only inconclusive support for the role of grades as a source of student bias:

Currently available evidence cannot be taken as definitely establishing a bias in teacher evaluation due to the grades students receive . . . but neither is it presently possible to rule out such bias. (p. 69)

One recurring difficulty in establishing the grade-evaluation relationship has been the correlation nature of most previous research. For example, it frequently has been reported that students receiving higher grades evaluate the quality of instruction more favorably than those receiving lower grades (e.g., Doyle & Whitely, 1974; Gessner, 1973; Kennedy, 1975). Although suggestive, such data do not clearly establish that the receipt of the grade had any effect on the student's evaluation of the course instruction. A plausible alternative hypothesis would be that the amount of effort expended for a particular course, or even the student's previous abilities or aptitude in the area, influence their perceptions of the quality of instruction (as well as, of course, their grade). This problem has been addressed previously (e.g., Costin, Greenough, & Menges, 1971), but it never has been adequately resolved.

Source: Vasta, R., & Sarmiento, R. F. (1979). Liberal grading improves evaluations but not performance. *Journal of Educational Psychology. 71*(2), 207.

nection. If the researcher cannot demonstrate how a particular study or theory relates to his or her study, then the reference is omitted. It may be interesting information, but it fails to further the understanding of the topic or provide a rationale for the study.

■ LITERATURE REVIEWS IN QUALITATIVE ■ RESEARCH

Ethnographic, historical, and legal researchers conduct preliminary literature reviews to propose a study. Unlike in many quantitative studies, these researchers locate and criticize most of the literature for the study during data collection and analysis. They do a continuing literature review because the exact research focus and questions evolve as the research progresses. Thus, by the completion of a study, these researchers have done an extensive literature review. The approach to reviewing the literature merely reflects the discovery-orientation and inductive analysis which is typical of qualitative research.

Preliminary Literature Review

In an ethnographic study to propose grounded theory (Glaser & Strauss, 1967), the preliminary literature review represents possible conceptual frameworks for phrasing foreshadowed problems (see Chapter 11). The literature review frequently cites broad areas of scholarly thinking, such as sociological, psychological, anthropological, political and others, with representative scholars, and it illustrates why certain concepts may become relevant in data collection and analysis. The preliminary literature review makes explicit the initial frameworks the ethnographer begins with to focus the observations and interviewing. (See Excerpts 11.1 and 11.2 in Chapter 11; see Excerpt 2.6 in Chapter 2.)

The literature review differs in ethnographic research with a phenomenological purpose, which is to describe and analyze naturalistic social scenes or a process without suggesting grounded theory. The literature review in these studies justifies the need for an in-depth descriptive study using an ethnographic approach. For example, prior research was conducted with quantitative procedures and did not examine the phenomena in descriptive depth as a human collective process or event. Or, prior qualitative research, for example, studied classes in secondary schools but elementary classes had not yet been examined. Frequently, as in Excerpt 4.4, there are unique or unusual events which have not been studied systematically at all. Excerpt 4.4, as the title indicates, is an insider's view of mental retardation which provides an understanding of retardation. The researchers point out that the meaning of the term "mental retardation" depends on those who use the term. The literature review suggests that the social construction of the term "mental retardation," originally a clinical label, has other connotations. The researchers used ethnographic interviews of a 26-year-old man who had been labeled "retarded" by his family, teachers, professionals, and a state institution for the retarded. The person's words reveal how his understanding of himself and his situation differed from that of those who labeled him. Mental retardation, as a concept, is more than a clinical label.

Historical and legal researchers also conduct preliminary literature reviews. The researcher contrasts the proposed focus and questions with prior research to justify a need for the study. For example, prior research did not examine certain school policies regarding minority groups (see Excerpt 12.1 in Chapter 12). Historians frequently contrast their work with prior research by citing access to "new" documents or archives made available to only the historian or to the scholarly community. The literature review may also cite current policies and the need to examine the past for an understanding of current debates. Excerpt 4.5 illustrates this use of the literature by citing the U.S. Justice Department investigation of standards of high schools and reactions by national associations, and linking

```
┌─────────────────────────────────────────────────────────┐
│                      EXCERPT 4.4                         │
│           An Ethnographic Literature Review              │
└─────────────────────────────────────────────────────────┘
```

If one wishes to understand the term *holy water,* one should not study the properties of the water, but rather the assumptions and beliefs of the people who use it. That is, holy water derives its meaning from those who attribute a special essence to it (Szasz, 1974).

Similarly, the meaning of the term *mental retardation* depends on those who use it to describe the cognitive states of other people. As some have argued, mental retardation is a social construction or a concept that exists in the minds of the "judges" rather than in the minds of the "judged" (Blatt, 1970; Braginsky and Braginsky, 1971; Dexter, 1964; Hurley, 1969; Mercer, 1973). A mentally retarded person is one who has been labeled as such according to rather arbitrarily created and applied criteria.

Retardate and other such clinical labels suggest generalizations about the nature of men and women to whom that term has been applied (Goffman, 1963). We assume that the mentally retarded possess common characteristics that allow them to be unambiguously distinguished from all others. We explain their behavior by special theories. It is as though humanity can be divided into two groups, the "normal" and the "retarded."

To be labeled retarded is to have a wide range of imperfections imputed to you. One imperfection is the inability to analyze your life and your current situation. Another is the inability to express yourself—to know and say who you are and what you wish to become.

Source: From "The Judged, Not the Judges: An Insider's View of Mental Retardation" by Robert Bogdan and Steven Taylor, *American Psychologist,* January 1976. Copyright © 1976 by the American Psychological Association. Reprinted by permission of the publisher and authors.

these current events to the broader historical issue of defining the nature and function of secondary education in the United States. The present study extends previous research to "discover how educational policy, student choices, and curriculum interacted during a period of severe economic and educational crisis" (Mirel & Angus, 1986, p. 102). Legal researchers often trace a legal principle as it is applied to new areas of educational law. The principle of liability, for example, may have been investigated in private organizations and certain areas of public school law but not in school athletics.

Continuous Review and Criticism of the Literature

Qualitative researchers continue to read broadly in the literature as they collect data. The literature does *not* provide the ethnographer with preconceived ideas, but it enables the researcher to understand the context of the site and social scenes observed. Relevant literature may provide analogies to the observed social scenes, a scholarly language to synthesize descriptions, or general analytical

---

EXCERPT 4.5
Literature Review in Historical Research

INTRODUCTION

In September 1985, the U.S. Justice Department announced that it was investigating whether high schools throughout the nation "had engaged in an 'offensive' form of discrimination by lowering academic standards to make it easier for minority students to graduate" [by] . . . fewer tracks, fewer electives, and more rigorous standards in American high schools. While supporters of curricular uniformity and higher standards see these moves as a cure for both racial discrimination and declining educational quality, some educators have labeled the "quest for excellence" itself as a new form of discrimination against minorities, one that portends dire consequences for American schools and society. In recent months . . . reports maintain that requiring more academic coursework from such students will only hasten their decision to drop out of school, thereby accelerating the already staggering dropout rates for minorities.[1]

This debate is the latest incarnation of a century-long struggle to define the nature and function of secondary education in the United States. Over the years, the contexts of that argument have remained essentially the same: whether to have a uniform or diversified curriculum, whether to emphasize cultural and intellectual education, vocational training, or custodial care, and concern about what kind of curriculum would reduce dropout rates. Educational historians have devoted considerable attention to these arguments, but they have dealt with them as ideological struggles whose impact on students and schools is more assumed than demonstrated.[2] These analyses spark a good deal of theoretical debate but offer few concrete answers to the questions educators and policy-makers are asking today: What is the relationship between curriculum reform and the youth labor market? Does curriculum reform precede or follow enrollment growth? To what extent and in what ways has the high school curriculum been "diluted"? Has curriculum reform contributed to racial and ethnic discrimination?

This paper is an effort to consider these questions by looking directly at the Detroit Public Schools between 1928 and 1940, a period of unequalled high school enrollment increase and substantial curriculum change. In an earlier article, we speculated that curriculum changes in Detroit during the Great Depression signified a major shift in the nature and the function of the high school: the turn from a vocational to a custodial emphasis. We also argued that the Detroit reforms had national significance in terms of educational policy-making, providing a prototype for the Life Adjustment Movement.[3] Here our analysis of Depression era curriculum changes in Detroit focuses on the interaction of economic and educational forces in this trendsetting school district during a watershed era in educational history. Our purpose is to discover how educational policy, student choices, and curriculum interacted during a period of severe economic and educational crisis.

Source: From "The Rising Tide of Custodialism: Enrollment Increases and Curriculum Reform in Detroit, 1928–1940" by Jeffrey E. Mirel and David L. Angus, *Issues in Education*, Vol. IV, No. 2, Fall 1986. Copyright © 1986 by the American Educational Research Association. Reprinted by permission.

schemes to analyze data. The literature helps the ethnographer to look at social scenes from many general perspectives and to understand the complexities to illuminate more subtle meanings.

The historian also reads broadly to acquire the necessary historical context of the era studied. The historical context includes general knowledge of social customs, institutions, political movements (international, national, and regional), education, recreation, economic cycles, technological changes, and the like. Knowledge of the general historical context of the event, person (biography), or institution examined allows the historian to understand and interpret the past event or people from the participants' perspectives rather than the historian's modern perspective.

Alternative Presentations of Literature

Literature in qualitative studies is presented as a) separate discussions and b) integration within the text. Prior research is presented as a separate discussion in the introduction to illustrate the importance of the study in extending our knowledge, and, possibly, to relate the topic to current discussions or policies (see Excerpt 4.4). A more detailed discussion is presented in the concluding interpretations of the study (see Excerpt 11.6 in Chapter 11). Seldom is an entire section of a journal article or an entire chapter of a report called a "Literature Review" because the traditional format of qualitative research is that of a narrative. Some journals impose this format on articles because of the typical readers. A comparison of Excerpts 2.5 and 2.8 in Chapter 2 illustrates some of these distinctions.

Most of the literature is integrated in the text with explanatory footnotes. One can easily see the use of explanatory footnotes differs in Excerpts 2.5 and 2.6 in Chapter 2. The typical style manual used by historians, legal researchers, and many ethnographers allows for explanatory footnotes rather than just text citations. (See Excerpt 4.5, which contains nine references in the first three explanatory footnotes of the excerpt. The 18-page article that contains this excerpt has 31 explanatory footnotes.) Thus, the qualitative researcher can cite, extend, or contrast each fact and interpretation with the exact document or reference. The footnotes and the bibliography, which includes background reading for ethnographic and historical context, reflect the extensive literature review for a qualitative study.

■   RESEARCH SYNTHESIS AND META-ANALYSIS   ■ LITERATURE REVIEWS

A traditional literature review is an interpretative narrative summary and critique of literature related to a problem. **Meta-analysis** is a review procedure which uses statistical techniques to synthesize the results of prior independently conducted studies. It is sometimes referred to as a "rigorous research review," a "systematic research synthesis," an "integrative research review," or simply meta-analysis. Noted researcher G. V. Glass (1976) defined meta-analysis in the following manner:

> *Primary analysis* is the original analysis of data in a research study. . . . *Secondary analysis* is the reanalysis of data for the purpose of answering the original research question with better statistical techniques, or answering new questions with old data. . . . Meta-analysis refers to the analysis of analyses. I use it to refer to the statistical analysis of a large collection of analysis results from individual studies for the purpose of integrating the findings. It connotes a rigorous alternative to . . . narrative discussions of research studies which typify our attempts to make sense of the rapidly expanding research literature (p. 3).

The synthesis of past results is central to almost any research project and is crucial in the development of a knowledge base in the disciplines and applied fields. Statisticians have long noted that in many fields of application the treatment effects are small and therefore difficult to detect in a single study. A natural question is whether the aggregate of studies might not have statistical and practical significance even though no single study does.

A key concept in any synthesis is the notion of *pattern.* The distinction between primary analysis and secondary analysis may be analogous to the distinction between taking observations at ground level and taking observations from the air. As one rises in an airplane, the precision achieved at ground level lessens and is replaced by a greater recognition of patterns. Thus, the pattern of skyscrapers that is indiscernible when driving into a large city becomes more evident from a higher elevation vantage point (Hedges & Olkin, 1986). Second, the conclusions based on a meta-analysis can be stronger than those of the component studies because pooling of data generally increases statistical power of the effect size.[7]

The Research Process

The steps to conduct integrative research reviews are similar to the tasks of original research.[8] Cooper (1984) characterized rigorous research synthesis as five phases: problem formulation, data collection, data evaluation, analysis and interpretation, and public presentation. Each phase of the review involves methodological issues and requires subjective decisions that can lead to procedural variations and can profoundly affect the outcome of the research review. Obviously the validity of the conclusions of research or research reviews depends

---

[7]Effect size (ES) in principle is the difference on a criterion measure between an experimental and a control group divided by the control group's standard deviation.

[8]Methodological treatises range from descriptions of the entire research process to highly technical discussions of the various statistical procedures. For the research process, see G. B. Jackson (1980), Methods for integrative reviews, *Review of Educational Research, 9*(3), 438–460; R. J. Light & D. B. Pillemer (1984), *Summing up: The science of reviewing research;* and H. Cooper (1984), *The integrative research review: A systematic approach.*

on the decisions made in each phase. Each of these phases will be summarized below from the viewpoint of aiding a reader to evaluate a research synthesis.

Problem Formulation.   To formulate a research synthesis problem, the reviewer must decide what questions or hypotheses to address and what evidence should be included in the review. Meta-analysis procedures are primarily applicable to integrative research reviews and are seldom applied to theoretical or methodological reviews.

The researcher asks "what operations are relevant to the concepts that concern the review?" To decide which operations or measures "fit" the concept being investigated, the reviewer examines the research design of each study and extracts information on a coding sheet. The coding sheet includes the reference, information on subjects, the operations for the independent and dependent variables, and the study outcomes with other additional information such as a third variable, interactions, number of variables used in the design or analysis, and information from the narrative review. Details of a study are necessary in order to make certain methodological decisions later. Figure 4.5 is a sample coding sheet. Coding sheets will vary with the hypothesis selected.

Data Collection.   This phase involves the specification of procedures to be used in finding relevant reviews. Whereas the primary researcher samples individuals, the reviewer, in a sense, retrieves researchers. In reality, reviewers are not trying to draw representative samples of studies from the literature, but they are attempting to retrieve an *entire* population of studies. This goal is rarely achieved, but it is more feasible in a review than in primary research. The reviewer hopes the review will cover "all previous research" on the problem. Three channels are used to locate studies: informal channels, primary channels, and secondary channels. *Informal channels* are 1) personal research of the reviewer, 2) the "invisible college" of scientists working on similar problems within a discipline who separately interact with a central researcher, and 3) attendance at professional meetings. Using these sources alone can easily introduce bias into data collection. *Primary channels* are 1) a reviewer's personal libraries or journals he or she regularly follows and 2) the ancestry approach. The ancestry approach involves tracking the research cited in already obtained relevant literature. Relying on only primary channels can introduce the bias of publication as the sole criterion for scientific merit, especially when published research is probably biased toward statistically significant findings.

Secondary channels—information retrieval systems and indexing/abstracting services—are the backbone of any systematic comprehensive literature review. A single indexing/abstracting service probably cannot provide an exhaustive bibliography on many topics because 1) services focus on disciplines and many research problems are interdisciplinary; 2) it takes one to two years for a published report to be indexed; and 3) a clearer conceptual understanding of the research problem can emerge from key terms of different services.

To minimize bias in data collection, a reviewer should use more than one major abstracting service, informal communications, and the bibliographies of past re-

FIGURE 4.5
Sample Coding Form

Author(s)_____

Title_____

Journal_____Year_____ Vol._____ Pgs._____

Source of Reference_____

1.   Group 1   Group 2

    Sex: Mn = _____ Fn = _____   Sex: Mn = _____ Fn = _____

    Age_____   Age_____

    Location_____   Location_____

    Other restrictions_____   Other restrictions_____

2.   Ethnic Group   Ethnic Group

    Mean_____ ad_____   Mean_____ ad_____

       Test_____   df error_____

       Test value_____   df effect_____

       p-level_____   effect size_____

    Direction of results_____

3.   Social class_____   Social class_____

    Standardized_____ Informal_____   Standardized_____ Informal_____

    How measured: How measured:

       Occupation_____   Occupation_____

       Salary_____   Salary_____

       Soc. status_____   Soc. status_____

    Mean_____ ad_____   Mean_____ ad_____

       Test_____   df error_____

       Test value_____   df effect_____

       p-level_____   effect size_____

    Direction of results_____

4.   Dependent measures

TAT (a-Ach)_____   Other_____

French's Test of Insight_____   _____

Ca. Popula. Inventory_____   _____

Source: Coding sheet for studies of ethnic group and social class differences in need for achievement. In H. Cooper (1984), *The integrative research review: A systematic approach* (pp. 33–34).

searchers or reviews. Reviewers should be explicit about how studies were gathered, providing information on sources, years, key words used in the search, and they should present whatever indices of potential retrieval bias is known to them. Reviewers should summarize the sample characteristics of individuals used in the separate studies.

Data Evaluation.   The data evaluation phase involves specifications of decisions about what retrieved evidence should be included in the review. Both primary researchers and research reviewers examine their data sets for wild values, errors in recording, and other unreliable measurements. In addition, the research reviewer should discard data because of questionable research design validity. In other words, the reviewer makes either a discrete decision—whether to include or exclude the data in the review—or a continuous decision—whether to weigh studies dependent on their relative degree of trustworthiness. Most social scientists agree that methodological quality should be the primary criterion for inclusion.

To minimize threats to the design validity of a research synthesis, the reviewer should:

1. Let only conceptual judgments influence the decision to include or exclude studies from a review.
2. State and justify explicitly the weighing scheme if studies are to be weighted differently.
3. Specify each design and method threat which relate to the results of the meta-analysis.
4. Use multiple coders and report intercoder agreement.
5. State explicitly the conventions used when incomplete or erroneous primary research reports were encountered.

Data Analysis and Interpretation.   In contrast to primary researchers, research reviewers interpret data using rules of inference which build on standard statistical techniques but are not the same. Analysis and interpretation methods are frequently idiosyncratic to the particular reviewer. This leads to criticisms of subjectivity and a concern that a variety of methods have been introduced into the reviewing process. Further, quantitative reviewing is based on certain premises. The basic premise is that a series of studies was selected that address an identical conceptual hypothesis. A reviewer should not attempt to combine studies quantitatively at a conceptual level broader than readers find useful.

Methods for data analysis range from simple vote counting methods (see example in Chapter 1) to sophisticated statistical techniques to obtain indices of the effect size.[9] Either the results or the raw data of each component study can be integrated. Reviewers should make explicit their assumptions regarding their inferences and conclusions and be careful to distinguish between study- and review-generated evidence.

Public Presentation.   The presentation of a research synthesis involves decisions about what information should be included in the final report. Two primary threats to validity are the omission of details on how the review was conducted and the omission of evidence about variables and moderators of relations that other inquirers may find (or will be) important to the hypothesis. Slavin (1984) suggests that the effect size for each study be included and the coding of studies on various criteria should be presented.

A Developing Methodology

Meta-analysis techniques are criticized similar to traditional narrative reviews. Traditional reviews can be susceptible to the reviewer's biases in deciding which studies are sufficiently "methodologically adequate" to be included or reviewed. Criticisms of meta-analysis have centered on the issue of "combining apples and oranges." Critics suggest that by combining the results of different studies, especially different types of designs, concepts, and their operations, one runs the risk of producing results which make neither conceptual nor statistical sense. Researchers continue to differ on whether meta-analyses should be conducted only for those studies selected as "the best evidence" (Slavin, 1986) or should include all studies, regardless of research design (Joyce, 1987). Re-analysis of meta-analytical studies has produced debatable conclusions.[10] Further, because of methodological variations, the conclusions of a series of meta-analyses on the same topic, such as the effects of teacher questioning levels on student achievement, can be quite different.[11] Meta-analysis emphasizes the main effects, when the interactions often are most important. Because there is nothing inherent in the

[9]For meta-analytic statistical procedures, see G. V. Glass, B. McGaw, & M. L. Smith (1981), *Meta-analysis in social research*; R. Rosenthal (1984), *Meta-analytic procedures for social science research*; J. E. Hunter, F. L. Schmidt, & G. B. Jackson (1982), *Meta-analysis: Cumulating research findings across studies*; and L. V. Hedges & I. Olkin (1985), *Statistical methods for meta-analysis.*

[10]See R. E. Slavin (1984), Meta-analysis in education: How has it been used?, *Educational Researcher, 13*(8), 6–15.

[11]G. E. Samson, B. Strykowski, T. Weinstein, & H. J. Walberg (1987), The effects of teacher questioning levels on student achievement: A quantitative synthesis, *Journal of Educational Research, 80*(5), 290–295.

procedures which makes misleading conclusions either inevitable or impossible, there is a growing consensus that meta-analysis can be a useful tool in research reviews, *if properly used.*

An inherent danger is that research syntheses may discourage further research in the synthesized area. For example, in the area of mainstreaming, only a few studies have used random assignment to special or regular classes. It would be tragic if the publication of a meta-analysis on this topic ended this line of inquiry. Meta-analysis should be recognized as a legitimate supplement to traditional narrative reviews rather than as a replacement.

■ STANDARDS OF ADEQUACY ■

A narrative literature review is judged adequate by three criteria: its selection of the sources, its criticism of the literature, and its summary and overall interpretation of the literature on the problem. Below are questions that aid a reader in determining the quality of the literature review.

Selection of the Literature

1. Is the purpose of the review (preliminary or exhaustive) indicated?
2. Are the parameters of the review reasonable?
   a. Why were certain bodies of literature included in the search and others excluded from it?
   b. Which years were included in the search?
3. Are primary sources emphasized in the review and secondary sources, if cited, used selectively?
4. Are recent developments in the problem emphasized in the review?
5. Is the literature selected relevant to the problem?
6. Are complete bibliographic data provided for each reference?

Criticism of the Literature

1. Is the review organized by topics or ideas, not by author?
2. Is the review organized logically?
3. Are major studies or theories discussed in detail and minor studies with similar limitations or results discussed as a group?
4. Is there adequate criticism of the design and methodology of important studies so that the reader can draw his or her own conclusions?
5. Are studies compared and contrasted and conflicting or inconclusive results noted?
6. Is the relevance of each reference to the problem explicit?

Summary and Interpretation

1. Does the summary provide an overall interpretation and understanding of our knowledge of the problem?
2. Do the implications provide theoretical or empirical justification for the specific research questions or hypotheses to follow?
3. Do the methodological implications provide a rationale for the design to follow?

A literature review is judged adequate in the context of the proposal or the completed study. The problem, the significance of the study, and the specific research question or hypothesis influence the type of literature review. A literature review is not judged by its length nor by the number of references included. The quality of the literature review is judged according to whether it furthers the understanding of the status of knowledge of the problem and provides a rationale for the study.

■ SUMMARY ■

The following statements summarize the reasons for conducting a literature review, the process of reviewing the literature, and the literature reviews in quantitative research, qualitative studies, and meta-analysis.

1. Literature includes theoretical discussions, reviews of the status of knowledge by authorities, philosophical papers, descriptions and evaluations of current practices, and empirical research.
2. Sources for the literature review are journals, reports, monographs, government documents, and dissertations.
3. Reviewing the literature enables the researcher to define and limit the problems, place the study in historical and associational perspective, avoid unnecessary replication, select promising methods and measures, relate the findings to previous knowledge, and suggest further research.
4. The selected literature should be relevant to the problem, either on target or related.
5. Primary sources are valued more highly in a literature review; secondary sources, however, provide useful information.
6. The process of reviewing the literature is as follows: analyze the problem statement, read secondary sources, select the appropriate indexes, transform the problem into search language, conduct a manual and/or computer search, read pertinent primary sources, organize notes, and write the review.
7. Secondary sources are syntheses of the research-based knowledge on a topic and are usually articles in general and specialized educational journals, annuals, yearbooks, handbooks, encyclopedias, or books.

8. Primary sources are the original studies or writings by a theorist or participant, which are found by using indexes to journals, educational documents, government documents, and dissertations.

9. Steps in conducting a search are: analyze the research problem, determine the type of search, select the reference services (databases), select the descriptors and key terms, conduct the search, code the bibliography or printout for relevant sources, and locate the references.

10. A computer search is cost effective when the problem is stated precisely and includes three or more key terms, and when the reviewer has determined the appropriate databases and years to be searched.

11. The reviewer reads each source that is most likely to be relevant, abstracts and makes commentary notes, and organizes the notes in a classification system.

12. In quantitative research, the literature review is organized logically by ideas and provides an understanding of our knowledge of the problem and a rationale for the research question or hypothesis.

13. Criticism of the literature indicates the strengths and limitations of our knowledge in terms of lack of studies on the problem, inconclusive results from studies on the same problem, or methodological difficulties.

14. In qualitative research, preliminary literature reviews suggest the need for the study, but the search and criticism of the literature is continuous during data collection and analysis. Literature is presented in introductory discussions and integrated in the text with extensive explanatory footnotes.

15. Meta-analysis is a research procedure which uses statistical techniques to synthesize the results of prior independently conducted studies.

■ SELF-INSTRUCTIONAL REVIEW EXERCISES ■

Sample answers are in the back of the book.

Test Items

1. Which of the following is the major advantage of conducting a literature review?
   a. encourages unnecessary duplication of research
   b. identifies variables and promising instruments
   c. places a study in a historical and associational perspective
   d. provides the research design

2. The review of the literature should be based as much as possible on which sources?
   a. preliminary
   b. secondary
   c. primary
   d. abstracts

Match the following descriptor statement with its source.

3. subsequent citations of a study
4. articles in educational research and professional journals
5. report literature in the ERIC system
6. statistical data of government agencies
7. status of knowledge on selected topics
8. research in progress
9. description and review of commercially published tests

a. *Current Index to Journals in Education*
b. *Resources in Education*
c. *Mental Measurements Yearbooks*
d. Encyclopedias, handbooks, annuals
e. none of the above

10. Which is the major method for locating sources?
    a. one's personal library or journal
    b. reference services
    c. tracking research cited in relevant literature (ancestry approach)
    d. attendance at professional meetings

11. Which of the following is the most useful in determining whether a source will probably be relevant to the problem?
    a. key word or descriptor   c. abstract
    b. annotation   d. database

12. An exhaustive search is done for which of the following purposes?
    a. for a major study   c. to develop a proposal
    b. to define and limit a problem d. to make a minor educational decision

13. A computer search is time efficient if the reviewer:
    a. has analyzed the problem statement.
    b. knows the databases, years, and key words for a search.
    c. can selectively limit the search.
    d. has decided the purpose of the literature search.
    e. All of the above are correct.

Match items 14 through 17 with the step in a computer search.

14. self-concept, self-esteem, remedial education, remedial program, elementary school children
15. *CIJE, Exceptional Child Education Abstracts,* and *Psychological Abstracts*

a. define research problem
b. state specific purpose of computer search
c. select database(s)
d. select descriptors

16. review relevant research articles for the past ten years
17. academic self-concept of elementary students in remedial programs

18. The literature review section in a completed quantitative study should *not* do which of the following?
    a. include all the references read by the reviewer
    b. provide criticism of the designs and methodologies used to develop knowledge of the problem
    c. show an understanding of the status of knowledge of the problem
    d. form an empirical or theoretical rationale, or both, for the research question or hypothesis

19. Meta-analytical literature reviews
    a. are narrative syntheses of prior research.
    b. can be applied in every literature review.
    c. statistically analyze the results of prior selected research to produce the effect size of a treatment.
    d. require few researcher decisions in the review process.

Application Problems

1. A supervisor wants to locate mathematics curriculum guidelines and evaluation studies of mathematics programs formulated under Title I of the Elementary and Secondary Education Act and those most recently done through Chapter I (in the current terminology). Which database and type of computer search would be most efficient?

2. Below is a problem statement and the key words for each concept. The key words are listed in order of importance to a literature search.

   How do teacher questioning techniques effect fourth-grade students' learning in social studies?

A. questioning techniques	G. recall
B. questioning	H. social studies
C. questioning behavior	I. history
D. questions	J. upper elementary
E. achievement	K. elementary education
F. skills	

   a. Direct a narrow computer search to obtain pertinent literature using *and* to join the key words from A through K which most closely match the research question.
   b. Direct a more thorough computer search using *or* to join the different key terms for the same concept, and *and* to connect the key words A through K.

3. A reviewer has classified his or her relevant sources in the following manner:
    a. evaluations of behavior modification programs: effects on instructional approach, teacher questioning style
    b. descriptions of behavior modification programs and management implications
    c. evaluations of behavior modification programs and management implications
    d. theories of stimulus-response learning
    e. studies of operant conditioning on animals

    Organize these in order for a literature review on the problem of "evaluation of instruction, student behavior, and learning in a behavior modification program."

CHAPTER 5

INTRODUCTION TO DESIGNING RESEARCH

■ KEY TERMS ■

research design
validity
internal validity

external validity
informed consent

Quantitative:

plausible rival hypotheses
subjects
sample
population
probability sampling
availability sampling
random sampling
simple random sampling
systematic sampling
stratified random sampling
proportional sampling
nonproportional sampling
cluster sampling
test validity
test reliability
internal validity

history
selection
statistical regression
pretest
testing
instrumentation
mortality
maturation
diffusion of treatment
experimenter bias
contamination
external validity
population external validity
ecological external validity
Hawthorne effect
construct validity

Qualitative:

emergent design
interactive techniques
non-interactive techniques
case study design
purposeful sampling
comprehensive sampling
maximum variation sampling
network selection
  (snowball sampling)

data collection and
  analyses strategies
credibility
interobserver reliability
extension of understandings
comparability
translatability

The purpose of this chapter is to introduce the fundamental principles of designing a study. The goal of research is to collect information that will investigate a research problem or question. This goal is attained only if the research is conceived and executed in such a manner that the data collected are accurate and directly relevant to the question posed. There are many ways to collect information, and the researcher must be aware of certain problems that may arise and must plan the data collection methods to minimize the problems. To demonstrate to readers of research that the appropriate steps have been taken to assure accurate information, most studies address different factors that contribute to the quality of the information collected.

In quantitative research, designing research involves choosing subjects, data collection techniques (such as questionnaires, observations, or interviews), and procedures for gathering the data. Together, these components of data collection comprise the methods part of the study.

For qualitative research, designing research includes selecting the site, purposeful sampling, and the strategies used for data collection and analysis. The logic used in designing qualitative research is different from what is used to design quantitative research. The essential elements of designing each type of research will be discussed in this chapter, with an emphasis on important principles for conceptualizing and planning a study. We will discuss each of these components, first for quantitative and then for qualitative research, with attention to principles in each component that enhance the quality of the research. We also discuss important ethical and legal considerations in planning and conducting research.

■ THE PURPOSE OF RESEARCH DESIGN ■

Research design[1] is a term that refers to a plan for selecting subjects, research sites, and data collection procedures to answer the research question(s). The design shows which individuals will be studied, and when, where, and under which circumstances they will be studied. The goal of a sound research design is to provide results that are judged to be credible. Credibility refers to the extent to which the results approximate reality and are judged to be trustworthy and reasonable. Credibility is enhanced when the research design takes into account potential sources of bias that may distort the findings. Bias is a form of systematic error, a factor that influences the results and undermines the quality of the research. The goal of a good research design, then, is to provide a credible answer to a question, and bias reduces the credibility of the results. By carefully designing the study the

---

[1]The term *research design* is often used to refer to specific types of designs, called "pre-experimental," "experimental," and "quasi-experimental" designs by Campbell and Stanley, 1963. This book's emphasis is on relating the fundamentals of error control to all aspects of collecting information, including but not limited to the designs of Campbell and Stanley. The principles discussed are important for descriptive research as well as for studies that infer causal relationships.

researcher can eliminate or at least reduce sources of error or bias. Not every potential source of bias can be controlled completely in research, but there are principles for planning research to minimize such influences.

In the context of research design, the term **validity** means the degree to which scientific explanations of phenomena match the realities of the world. Validity refers to the truth or falsity of propositions generated by research. Explanations about observed phenomena approximate what is reality or truth, and the degree to which the explanations are accurate comprises the **internal validity** of the research. Internal validity expresses the extent to which what is observed, measured, and analyzed matches reality. **External validity** refers to the generalizability of the results, the extent to which the results and conclusions can be generalized to other people and settings. In some studies, such as most applied research, there is a clear intent to generalize to other people and other settings, while in other studies generalization beyond the people, time, and context of the research is not intended or possible. Both internal and external validity are important concepts to understand in designing research. We will examine each in greater depth for quantitative and qualitative designs.

■ DESIGNING QUANTITATIVE RESEARCH ■

In designing or reading quantitative research it is necessary to consider who will be assessed (subjects), what they will be assessed by (instruments), how they will be assessed (procedures for data collection), and, for experimental designs, how experimental treatments are administered. Then it is important to ask: Is there anything that occurred that could provide an explanation of the results by means of a rival hypothesis? "Rival" is used in the sense that it is in addition to the stated hypothesis or intent of the research. (A rival hypothesis to the study of whether smoking causes lung cancer, for example, is that diet may contribute to the cause of lung cancer.) This question represents the search for bias. Campbell and Stanley (1963) refer to such explanations as **plausible rival hypotheses.** The search for plausible rival hypotheses is essential to ensure the quality of the research. Consider, for example, the questions below. Each addresses a possible source of error that could lead to a plausible rival hypothesis that would explain results.

1. Are the instruments used reliable and valid?
2. Does the researcher have an existing bias about the subjects or about the topic researched?
3. Are the subjects aware that they are being studied?
4. Are the subjects responding honestly?
5. Did both groups receive the treatments as described?
6. Does the sex of the interviewer make a difference?
7. Did very many subjects drop out before the end of the study?
8. Did the time of day the research was done affect the results?

Several techniques are used to reduce error in quantitative research, including randomization of subjects, holding conditions or factors constant, building conditions or factors into the design as independent variables, and making statistical adjustments (Wiersma, 1986). Randomization is desirable in either selecting subjects from a larger population, or in assigning subjects to groups to investigate the effect of one variable on another. Random selection, which is discussed in greater detail later in the chapter, allows the researcher to generalize the results beyond the immediate group studied. Random assignment helps control error associated with characteristics of subjects in different groups.

If the researcher believes that the conditions of data collection might affect the results and there is a reasonable opportunity for variation in the conditions to occur, the researcher can design the study to ensure that all conditions are as similar as possible. For example, in an observational study of the relationship between teacher behavior and student attention to the material, the time of day the observer records data and the subject matter of the lesson (mornings versus afternoons, or math versus history) could make a difference in student attention. One way to control this threat of bias, then, is to make sure that all the observations are done at the same time of day during lessons on the same topic. In this example, the researcher could also control these potential influences by making them independent variables. This could be achieved by assigning observers to each subject of interest and have each topic observed in both the morning and afternoon. Now the researcher can assess the effect of time of day and subject rather than simply controlling for it. Statistical adjustments can be made to equalize the influence a factor could have on the results. For instance, the researcher could control for the effect of previous student achievement in order to isolate the relationship of class size to present achievement.

In quantitative studies control of possible extraneous variables is essential, although educational research rarely exhibits the degree of control evident in studies of physical phenomena or psychology. Thus, the researcher must search constantly for factors (extraneous variables) that might influence the results or conclusions of the study. For quantitative research the concept of internal validity describes the efficacy with which extraneous variables have been controlled. The concern is with the way the procedures, sampling of subjects, and instruments affect the extent to which extraneous variables are present to complicate the interpretation of the findings. A study high in internal validity successfully controls all or most extraneous variables so that the researcher can be confident that, for instance, X caused changes in Y. Studies low in internal validity are difficult to interpret since it is impossible to tell whether the results were due to the independent variable or to some extraneous variable that was uncontrolled or unaccounted for. It is important for researchers to be aware of common factors that may be extraneous and to conceptualize and read research with these factors in mind. Since complete control of extraneous variables in educational research is difficult, if not impossible, all threats to internal validity that cannot be prevented should be accounted for in interpreting the results.

Subjects: Populations and Samples

One of the first steps in designing quantitative research is to choose the subjects. **Subjects** (abbreviated as *S*) are the individuals who participate in the study; it is from them that data are collected. As a group, subjects are usually referred to as the **sample.** The sample consists of individuals selected from a larger group of persons, called the **population.** In some studies the sample and population are the same (there is no larger group from which subjects have been selected), but the purpose of many studies is to generalize results to a large group of individuals. In these studies it is usually unnecessary to use all individuals in the population as subjects. Rather, a sample is selected from the population to provide subjects. This saves time and money, and provides valid results for the population if the sampling is done correctly. This is referred to as **probability sampling,** in which subjects are drawn from a larger population in such a way that the probability of selecting each member of the population is known.

In many educational studies, particularly experimental and quasi-experimental investigations, probability samples are not required or appropriate, or it may be impossible or unfeasible to select subjects from a larger group. Rather, **availability sampling** is used. In fact this form of sampling is the most common type in educational research. Availability sampling (also called convenience sampling) involves using whatever subjects are available to the researcher. This may, for example, be a class of students or a group of subjects gathered for a meeting. There are many circumstances that bring people together in situations that are efficiently and inexpensively tapped for research. However, there are two major limitations with availability sampling. First, the sample is not representative of a larger population, so generalizing is more restricted. The generalizability of the findings will be limited to the characteristics of the subjects. This does not suggest that the findings are not useful; it simply means that greater caution is necessary in generalizing the results. Often researchers will describe the subjects carefully to show that although they were not selected randomly from a larger population, the characteristics of the subjects appear representative of much of the population.

A second limitation is that an available sample may be biased. This is particularly true for *volunteer samples,* in which subjects volunteer to participate in the research. Studies indicate that volunteers differ from nonvolunteers in important ways. Rosenthal and Rosnow (1975) conclude that, in general, volunteers tend to be better educated, of higher social class, more intelligent, more sociable, more unconventional, less authoritarian, less conforming, more altruistic, and more extroverted than nonvolunteers. These characteristics could obviously affect the results to lead to conclusions that would be different if a probability sample was used. For example, suppose a researcher wanted to survey students on their attitudes toward the college they attended. Letters are sent to the graduated class of 500; 25 agree to come back to campus for interviews. Is it reasonable to conclude that the attitude of these 25 volunteer students are representative of the class?

TABLE 5.1
Randomly Assorted Digits

46614	20002	17918
16249	(052)17	54102
91530	62481	(053)74
62800	62660	20186
(100)89	96488	59058
47361	73443	11859
45690	71058	53634
50423	53342	71710
89292	32114	83942
23410	41943	33278
59844	81871	18710
98795	87894	(005)10
86085	(031)64	26333
37390	60137	93842
28420	10704	89412

Selecting Probability Samples.   There are several methods of sampling that can be used to draw representative, or unbiased, samples from a population.[2] A biased sample either over- or underestimates a population variable. The best way to choose a sample that is unbiased is to use **random sampling.** Sample selection is considered random if every member of the population has an equal chance of being chosen to be in the sample. In **simple random sampling,** subjects are selected from the population so that all members have the same probability of being selected. The most common type of simple random sampling is selecting names from a hat. A better way to conduct simple random sampling is to use a table of random numbers, which is a set of randomly assorted digits. (A table of random numbers is illustrated in Appendix B.) Suppose, for example, that a researcher had a population of 100 third graders and wanted to select 20 by simple random sampling. First, each third grader in the population is assigned a number from 001 to 100. Second, the researcher randomly selects a starting point in a table of random numbers. Then he or she reads all three-digit numbers, moving either across rows or down columns. Third, the researcher follows the three-digit rows

---

[2]See R. M. Jaeger (1984), *Sampling in education and the social sciences,* New York: Longman, for a more detailed discussion of how to select probability samples.

EXCERPT 5.1
Simple Random Sampling

The population of skilled readers from which the subjects for each of the 3 experiments were selected consisted of 400 elementary education majors in their junior year at Illinois State University.

For each of the 3 experiments, 50 subjects were randomly selected without replacement from the population. (That is, no subject was used in more than one experiment.)

Source: Lazerson, B. H. (1974–1975). The influence of highly variable spelling upon the reading performance of skilled readers of modern English. *Reading Research Quarterly. 10*, 583–615.

---

or columns while selecting twenty three-digit numbers between 000 and 100. Table 5.1 contains an example of simple random sampling. Five of the twenty subjects chosen to be included in the sample are circled, beginning with the top left and moving down each column.

A third, and perhaps best, method of drawing a random sample is to use a computer program that will do the sampling. There is no need to be sophisticated in the use of computers to do this type of sampling. In Excerpt 5.1 the researchers state that they used simple random sampling.

Systematic sampling is similar to simple random sampling except that the researcher randomly picks a number and then systematically selects subjects from a list of names beginning with the subject assigned the chosen number. If, for example, the number 5 is selected and there is a need to draw a ten percent sample, every tenth subject is selected—5, 15, 25, 35, and so on. Obviously, this approach can be used only when the subjects in the population can be listed sequentially, but it is easier than simple random sampling, especially with a large population. Systematic sampling should not be used if there is any possibility that the list of names is not in random order. (If, for example, the names are arranged in a cyclical pattern that coincides with the sampling interval, the resultant sample will be biased.)

A variation of simple random sampling is called **stratified random sampling.** In this procedure, the population is divided into subgroups, or strata, on the basis of a variable chosen by the researcher, such as gender, age, or level of education. Once the population has been divided, samples are drawn randomly from each subgroup. The number of subjects drawn is either proportional or nonproportional. **Proportional sampling** is based on the percentage of subjects in the population that is present in each strata. Thus, if forty percent of the subjects in the population is represented in the first stratum, then forty percent of the final sample should be from that stratum. In **nonproportional** (or disproportionate)

sampling, the researcher selects the same number of subjects to be in each stratum of the sample. Whether proportional or nonproportional, stratified random sampling is often more efficient than simple random sampling because a smaller number of subjects will need to be used. Dividing the population into subgroups also allows the researcher to compare subgroup results.

In Excerpt 5.2, for example, the researchers have stratified the teacher population on the basis of grade level and scores on the EFT (Embedded Figures Test) and the student population by classroom. The sampling is diagramed in Figure 5.1. To assure that the final sample has a sufficient number of subjects in each group, nonproportional sampling is used.

Cluster sampling is similar to stratified sampling in that groups of individuals are selected from the population and subjects are drawn from these groups. In cluster sampling, however, the researcher identifies convenient, naturally occurring group units, such as neighborhoods, schools, districts, or regions, not individual subjects, and then randomly selects some of these units for the study. Once the units have been selected, individuals are randomly selected from each one. Cluster sampling thus involves two stages, and because only the clusters have to be chosen in the first stage the researcher is saved the cost of individual selection from the full population. Cluster sampling usually results in a less representative sample of the population than either simple or stratified random sampling, and it is used most often in cases when it is infeasible or impractical to obtain a list of all members of the population.

Sample Size.   The number of subjects in a study is called the sample size, represented by the letter n. The researcher must determine the size of the sample that will provide sufficient data to answer the research question. The general rule in determining sample size is to use the largest sample possible, since the larger the sample the more representative it will be of the population. In situations in which a random sample is selected, however, a sample size that is only a small percentage of the population can approximate the characteristics of the population satisfactorily. Rowntree (1941) illustrates this point in a study of the percentage of income that was spent on rent by five categories of working-class families in England. Data were collected for the entire population and compared with the data that would have been reported by different sizes of random samples. As indicated in Table 5.2, there was little difference between a sample size of two percent (one in fifty) and ten percent (one in ten).

The determination of sample size should take into consideration several factors—the type of research, research hypotheses, financial constraints, the importance of the results, the number of variables studied, the methods of data collection, and the degree of accuracy needed. The impact of these factors is summarized below:[3]

---

[3]For a discussion of more systematic procedures for estimating the number of subjects needed, depending on the research design of the study, see H. C. Kraemer and S. Thielman (1987), *How many subjects? Statistical power analysis in research*, Newbury Park, CA: Sage Publications, Inc.

EXCERPT 5.2
Stratified Random Sampling

PARTICIPANTS

Thirty-six female elementary school teachers were randomly selected from a volunteer pool in a southern school district. The sample consisted of 18 second-grade teachers and 18 fifth-grade teachers and was restricted to female teachers, since there were few male teachers in the school district at the primary level. Based on the EFT scores, 9 teachers at each grade level were randomly selected from those who were field independent, and 9 others were selected from those who were field dependent. There were 12 students (6 males and 6 females) who were selected randomly from each teacher's classroom for purposes of testing. The second-grade children ranged in age from 7 years to 7 years 11 months, whereas the fifth-grade children ranged in age from 10 years to 10 years 11 months.

Source: Saracho, O. N., & Dayton, C. M. (1980). Relationship of teachers' cognitive styles to pupils' academic achievement gains. *Journal of Educational Psychology. 72,* 544–549.

1. *The type of research.* Correlational research should have a minimum of thirty subjects, and in research comparing groups there should be at least fifteen subjects in each group (some highly controlled experiments will contain as few as eight to ten subjects in each group).
2. *Research hypotheses.* If the researcher expects to find small differences or slight relationships, it is desirable to have as large a sample as possible. The effect of coaching courses on standardized test scores, for example, produces relatively small but perhaps important practical differences. This effect would be generally undetectable in studies with small numbers of subjects.
3. *Financial constraints.* Obviously, the cost of conducting a study will limit the number of subjects included in the sample. It is best to estimate these costs before beginning the study.
4. *Importance of results.* In exploratory research a smaller sample size is acceptable because the researcher is willing to tolerate a larger margin of error in the results. In research that will result in the placement of children in programs, or in the expenditure of a large amount of money, it is imperative for the researcher to attain a sample large enough so that error is minimized.
5. *Number of variables studied.* A larger sample is needed for studies that have many independent or dependent variables, or for studies in which many uncontrollable variables are present.
6. *Methods of data collection.* If methods of collecting information are not highly accurate or consistent, a larger sample will be needed to offset the error inherent in the data collection.

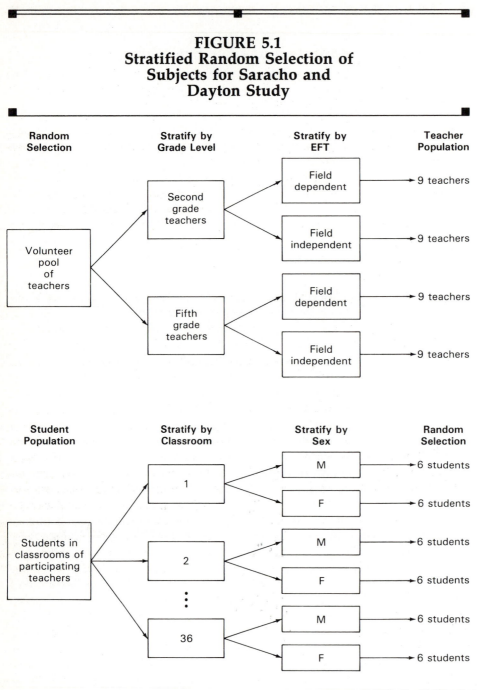

**FIGURE 5.1
Stratified Random Selection of
Subjects for Saracho and
Dayton Study**

TABLE 5.2
Percentage of Income Spent on Rent

Income Class	Number of Families	Population Data	Sample Size			
			1 in 10	1 in 20	1 in 30	1 in 50
A	1748	26.5	26.6	25.9	28.3	27.1
B	2477	22.7	22.9	23.5	22.3	22.6
C	2514	19.8	18.1	17.2	17.2	18.0
D	1676	15.8	16.0	14.4	17.1	16.9
E	3740	11.3	11.0	10.1	11.2	11.5

Source: Table from *Poverty and Progress: A Second Social Survey of York* by B. S. Rowntree. Reprinted by permission of The Joseph Rowntree Charitable Trust.

7. *Accuracy needed.* The accuracy of the results (the degree of confidence that can be placed in a statement that the sample data is the same as the population) is greater as the sample size increases. As the study by Rountree demonstrates, however, a point of diminishing returns is reached as the sample size increases to a certain percentage of the population.
8. *Size of the population.* As the size of the population increases, the researcher can take a progressively smaller percentage of subjects from the population.

Data Collection Techniques

Research involves gathering information about the variables in the study. The researcher chooses among a wide range of techniques and approaches for collecting data from the subjects. Each method has advantages and disadvantages, and the specific approach adopted should be the best method for answering the research question. Here are few common methods of gathering quantitative information:

1. Questionnaires
2. Standardized Interviews
3. Tests
4. Standardized Observations
5. Inventories
6. Rating scales
7. Unobtrusive measures

These methods will be discussed in greater detail in later chapters. At this point, however, it is important to understand some basic principles of measurement that are common for all methods, since knowledge of these principles is used both to choose instruments and to evaluate the adequacy of data collection reported in research studies.

Test Validity and Reliability.   **Test validity** is the extent to which inferences made on the basis of scores from an instrument are appropriate, meaningful, and useful. Validity is a judgment of the appropriateness of a measure for specific inferences or decisions that result from the scores that are generated. In other words, validity is a situation-specific concept: validity is dependent on the purpose, population, and situational factors in which measurement takes place. A test, questionnaire, or other measure can therefore be valid in one situation and invalid in another.

This has important implications for designing and evaluating research, since the findings are directly related to the measure selected. The investigator who is designing research should first clearly define the inferences or decisions that will be made from the results. Then an instrument should be selected that provides good evidence that making such inferences or decisions is valid. The evidence typically takes one of three forms: content, criterion-related, or construct (these are covered in greater detail in Chapter 7).

The evidence is reported in texts that summarize and critique measures, such as the *Mental Measurement Yearbooks,* in manuals that describe technical information about the measure, and in research articles in which the measure is used. In evaluating research the reader should look for statements that refer to validity and then evaluate the evidence provided in relation to the inference or decision made in the article. For instance, if normative data are to be used from a standardized instrument, the norms should have been generated from a population that is similar to the subjects in the study. In general, it is important to keep in mind that instruments are valid for some groups and in some situations, and invalid for other subjects or in other situations.

Test reliability refers to the consistency of measurement, the extent to which the results are similar over different forms of the same instrument or occasions of data collection. The goal of developing reliable measures is to minimize the influence of chance or other variables unrelated to the intent of the measure. If an instrument is unreliable, the information attained is ambiguous, inconsistent, and useless. It is therefore important for researchers to select and develop data-gathering procedures that will be high in reliability.

The specific methods for estimating and reporting reliability are very precise and are explained in detail in Chapter 7. Designers and readers of research should interpret reliability in much the same way as validity, looking for evidence that sufficient reliability of each measure is documented. Also, many studies fail to support a hypothesis because there is significant error in measuring the variables. Thus, with more reliable measures the hypothesis might be supported.

In reading the instruments section of a study or in designing data collection, there are a few things to keep in mind:

1. Are the instruments valid and reliable for the subjects of the particular research?
2. Are the characteristics of the subjects used to establish validity and reliability similar to the characteristics of the subjects in the study? If not, is it reasonable to use the instruments?
3. Are the instruments used the best ones? Are there others that are more valid and reliable?
4. Why did the researcher choose these instruments?
5. Are the instruments described well enough or referenced to allow another researcher to replicate the research?

Excerpt 5.3 is from the instruments section of a study. The extent of the description provided is about what is expected in reporting most types of research.

Sources for Locating Existing Instruments.   A general rule of advice in conducting research is to choose an instrument that has established the types of reliability and validity the researcher needs. Although reliability and validity are the most important considerations in selecting an instrument, there are other considerations like purchasing costs, availability, simplicity of administration and scoring, copyright limitations, level of difficulty, and appropriateness of norms.

While it is often difficult to find an instrument that will meet all criteria a researcher might have, there are thousands of instruments that have been developed, and it is probable that one is available that can be used intact or modified to meet a specific purpose. The easiest way to locate existing instruments is to use sources that summarize information on a number of instruments. The sources in the following list are widely used and accessible in most university libraries.[4]

Mitchell, J. V., Jr., ed. *Mental Measurements Yearbook.* Contains reviews of hundreds of tests in a number of categories, including achievement, character and personality, and intelligence (earlier editions edited by Oscar Buros).

Buros, O. K., ed. *Tests in Print* I and II; Mitchell, J. V., Jr., ed. *Tests in Print* III. Provides a summary of tests reviewed in all preceding mental measurement yearbooks.

Hoepfner, R., et al. *CSE Test Evaluations.* CSE stands for Center for the Study of Evaluation at the University of California at Los Angeles. This is a series of handbooks that summarize information on tests of higher order cognitive, affective, and interpersonal skills, as well as on achievement tests designed for use at different grade levels.

---

[4]An excellent and more detailed description of these sources, as well as of others, can be found in Appendix A, "Resources for the Development and Selection of Measuring Instruments," of K. D. Hopkins & J. C. Stanley (1981), *Educational and Psychological Measurement and Evaluation* (6th ed.), Englewood, NJ: Prentice-Hall.

**EXCERPT 5.3
Instruments Section**

DESCRIPTION OF INSTRUMENTS

Self-esteem. The Self-Esteem Inventory developed by Coopersmith (1959, 1967) was used to assess self-esteem. This instrument is operationally defined as a measure of "the evaluation which the individual makes and customarily maintains with regard to himself; it expresses an attitude of approval or disapproval, and indicates the extent to which the individual believes himself to be capable, significant, successful and worthy" (Coopersmith, 1967, pp. 4–5). The inventory consists of 58 short statements requiring a "like me" or "unlike me" response. Eight items, which constitute a lie scale, were not used in this study. Items are scored in a positive self-esteem direction, with all items responded to in the keyed direction worth two points. The inventory assesses children's self-esteem attitudes in four areas; peers, parents, school, and self. Reliability coefficients of .88 to .96 (test-retest) have been reported by Coopersmith (1967), and .81 (internal consistency) by Spatz and Johnston (1973). This measure was developed with fifth- and sixth-grade students. For purposes of this investigation, only total scores on the Self-Esteem Inventory were used.

Source: "Description of Instruments" from "Self-Esteem and Classroom Behavior in Elementary School Children" by William M. Reynolds, *Psychology in the Schools,* 17, 273–277, 1980. Reprinted by permission of the author.

Johnson, O. G. *Tests and Measurements in Child Development: Handbook II,* Volumes I and II. These volumes include a description of about 900 unpublished tests in child development.

Chun, K., et al. *Measures for Psychological Assessment: A Guide to 3,000 Original Sources and Their Applications.* A list of tests used in research reported in 26 different journals.

Comrey, A. L., et al. *A Sourcebook of Mental Health Measures.* This reference describes about 1,100 instruments related to mental health, including juvenile delinquency, personality, and alcoholism.

Borich, G. D., & Madden, S. K. *Evaluating Classroom Instruction—A Sourcebook of Instruments.* Contains instruments that can be used in the classroom.

Sweetland, R. C., & Keyser, D. J., eds., *Tests: A Comprehensive Reference for Assessments in Psychology, Education, and Business,* 2nd edition. Describes over 3,100 published tests.

Keyser, D. J., & Sweetland, R. C., eds., *Test Critiques, Volumes I–V.* Provides reviews of published tests, including a description and practical applications/uses.

Robinson, J. P., & Shaver, P. R. *Measures of Social Psychological Attitudes.* Describes hundreds of attitude instruments used in psychological and sociological research.

Simon, A., & Boyer, E. G. *Mirrors for Behavior II: An Anthology of Observation Instruments.* A description of many observation scales that can be used in the classroom.

Walker, D. K. *Socioemotional Measures for Pre-school and Kindergarten Children: A Handbook.* Categorizes instruments for use with young children in attitudes, personality, self-concept, and social skills.

Goodwin, W. L., & Driscoll, L. *Handbook for Measurement and Evaluation in Early Childhood Education.* A comprehensive review of affective, cognitive, and psychomotor measures for young children.

Sax, G. Selecting, Evaluating, and Using Standardized Tests, *Principles of Educational Psychological Measurement and Evaluation.* An excellent discussion of what to look for when choosing instruments; there is also a list of additional sources that describe existing instruments.

Developing Instruments.   Although there are many instruments available to educational researchers, there are occasions when researchers have to develop their own instruments. The most common situation that requires a locally developed measure is evaluation research for a specific setting. Unless the research will have an important direct impact on programs or individuals, it is unusual for the researcher to establish reliability and validity (as summarized in Chapter 7) prior to conducting the study. A more common approach is to develop an instrument that seems reasonable and to gather pilot data on it to revise the instrument. While it is probably not necessary to establish sophisticated estimates of reliability and validity, it is still possible for the instrument to be of such inferior quality that the results attained are uninterpretable. Thus, it is important for a researcher to follow a few basic steps if faced with a situation that requires the development of an instrument:

1. Become acquainted with common approaches to measure the trait or behavior of interest. There are many existing sources that summarize approaches for measuring such things as achievement, attitudes, interests, personality, and self-concept.
2. Write out specific objectives for your instrument, with one objective for each trait or behavior of interest.
3. After reading about the area and discussions with others about what approach would best measure the trait, brainstorm several items for each objective.
4. Ask professionals who are knowledgeable in the assessed area to review the items: Are they clear? Unbiased? Concise? Is the meaning the same for all readers?

5. Revise as necessary and find a small sample of individuals that is similar to those that will be used in the actual study and administer the instrument to them. This could be referred to as a "pilot test" of the instrument. Check for clarity, ambiguity in sentences, time for completion, directions, and any problems that may have been experienced.

6. Check for an adequate distribution of scores for each item in the instrument. If all the responses to an item are the same, it is difficult to know if the question is inadequate or if the trait actually lacks variability. As long as the responses result in a spread of scores, the chances are good that the item is an adequate measure of the trait.

7. Revise, delete, and add items where necessary, depending on feedback from the sample subjects in the pilot test.

Procedures

In quantitative studies the researcher plans the procedures that will be used to collect data, and, in the case of experimental research, the nature and administration of the experimental treatment. The researcher decides where the data will be collected (such as in a school, city, or laboratory setting), when the data will be collected (time of day and year), how the data will be collected (by whom and in what form), and, if necessary, specifics of the experimental treatment. Any procedures used to control bias (such as counterbalancing the order of instruments to control subject fatigue or boredom or being sure observers are unaware of which group is receiving the treatment and which is the control) are planned and implemented as part of the procedures. In reporting the study the researcher should present the procedures in sufficient detail to permit another researcher to replicate the study.

Internal Validity of Design

Internal validity, which we defined as the extent of control over extraneous variables, is strongest when the study's design (subjects, instruments, and procedures) effectively controls possible sources of error so that those sources are not reasonably related to the study's results. The sources of error for quantitative studies are thought of as "threats," because each source may invalidate the study's findings.

Several categories or types of threats to internal validity are pertinent to most quantitative studies. Each of these threats, as they are called, is described below with examples. These categories are taken from Campbell and Stanley (1963) and Cook and Campbell (1979).

History.   In the context of internal validity, **history** refers to incidents or events affecting the results that occur during the research. This is a threat to any research that is conducted across points in time, and it becomes more serious as the time between measures increases. Historical events are usually uncontrollable, especially those that occur outside the context of the study. A researcher might, for example, be interested in the way a film series changes attitudes of students toward communism. The researcher gives the students a pretest, administers the films over three weeks, then gives a posttest to see whether change has occurred. Alas, during the three weeks of films, Russia invades Afghanistan! The viewing of the films is confounded by this event. The researcher cannot know whether any differences obtained resulted from the films or from what happened in Afghanistan.

Events can also occur within groups of subjects. A researcher might, for example, be experimenting with two classes to determine which of two methods of teaching spelling is best. In the middle of one of the lessons, however, the lights go out; the students' work is disrupted and they lose concentration. The failure of this class to score well might be due as much to the distraction as to the method of teaching. Events affecting research that occur within the context of the study are called threats due to local history, and such problems pose a threat to any type of research.

Selection.   It is often desirable to form groups of subjects in order to study an independent variable of interest. If there is a systematic difference between the groups, however, it is possible that the results may be due to these existing differences. The threat of **selection** exists whenever groups of subjects cannot be assigned randomly, and although there are several approaches that help control this problem in cases where randomization is undesirable or impossible (matching, testing subjects more than once [repeated measures], adjusting posttest scores on the basis of initially measured group characteristics [analysis of covariance], and giving each group every treatment [counterbalancing], the researcher should always be concerned with this important threat.

Consider, for example, a teacher who wants to investigate whether the mastery or discovery approach is best for teaching adjectives and adverbs. The teacher secures the cooperation of another class in order to conduct a study. The two teachers flip a coin to decide which will use the discovery approach and which will use the mastery approach. The teachers assess achievement by giving each group a pretest and a posttest to determine growth in knowledge. It happens, however, that the average IQ score of the mastery group is 115 and of the discovery group 95. Here selection is a major problem, since we would expect the higher IQ group to achieve more than the lower IQ group under almost any condition. If uncontrolled and unaccounted for in some way, then such a threat to internal validity could render the study useless. The teacher would falsely conclude that the mastery learning method is more effective when its apparent success is really due to initial differences in ability.

As discussed previously, selection is also related to the manner in which the researcher chooses a sample. A common problem in research, for example, is using volunteers for the sample. The volunteer group may be more motivated or motivated for special reasons, and hence they would respond differently to the treatment or questions from the way a nonvolunteer group would respond.

Statistical Regression.   **Statistical regression** occurs because there is less than perfect correlation between two measures (or variables). Students who score very high or very low on a test the first time they take it, for example, tend to regress or score closer to the mean of the group the second time they take the test.

To illustrate this concept, think of Figure 5.2 as representing the same test taken twice by two students in a class in which the average score is 100. George's score on the first test is 150 and Sam's is 40. On the second test, we can expect George's score to be lower and Sam's score to be higher, even if their true abilities remain the same.

Regression is a problem whenever the researcher purposely chooses groups on the basis of extremely high or low scores. A school district may, for example, want to implement a special program to improve the self-concept of children who score low on a self-concept inventory. An assessment of the impact of the program could examine self-concept scores after the program (in a posttest), but the researcher would have to keep in mind that even if there is no program effect whatsoever, the initially low scores (on a pretest) would improve to some degree because of statistical regression. Similarly, it is usually difficult to find positive changes in programs for gifted children since, because of regression, posttest scores will tend to be slightly lower on average.

Testing.   Whenever research utilizes a pretest (some form of measurement that precedes a treatment or experience), it is possible that the test itself will have an impact on the subjects. Taking a **pretest** could, for example, provide the subject with practice on the type of questions asked, or familiarize the subject with the material tested. This kind of **testing** effect is commonly found in experiments measuring achievement over a short period of time. Testing can also be a serious threat to internal validity in research on attitudes or values. If an attitude questionnaire is used as a pretest, simply reading the questions might stimulate the subject to think about the topic and even change attitudes. A researcher might, for instance, be interested in evaluating the effect of a series of films on changes in students' attitudes toward physically handicapped children. The researcher gives a pretest, shows the films, then gives a posttest to find out whether changes have occurred. Any observed changes, however, might be caused by the pretest. The items in the questionnaire could have been enough to change the attitudes.

Instrumentation.   A threat to internal validity that is related to testing is called instrumentation. **Instrumentation** refers to the way changes in the instruments used to collect data might affect the results. This threat is particularly serious in observational research, when the observers may become fatigued or bored or change in some other way so as to affect the recording of data. Instrumentation is a reliability problem. If there is evidence that the measures are accurate in each instance, instrumentation is probably not a threat to internal validity. Testing is a change in the subject resulting from taking the test, while instrumentation is a change in the subject resulting from the testing itself.

FIGURE 5.2
Illustration of Statistical Regression

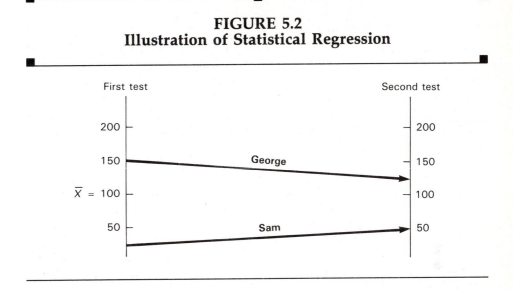

Mortality.   **Mortality,** also called subject *attrition*, occurs in a study when subjects systematically drop out or are lost during the investigation. This is a threat to many longitudinal studies that last over several weeks or months. A study, for example, of the effect of a program to assist low-achieving ninth graders conducted between the ninth and the twelfth grades would have apparent success if the lowest achieving students dropped out of school before twelfth grade and were not even included in the posttest analyses. For most nonexperimental and short duration research, mortality is no problem unless the treatment is especially demanding and systematically causes low performing subjects to drop out. In studies that have differential loss of subjects from different groups because of selection bias or the nature of the treatments, mortality is a serious threat to internal validity. Mortality is the same problem as selection, but it happens after the study is already set up and under way.

Maturation.   **Maturation** refers to changes in the subjects of a study over time. Subjects develop and change as a part of growing older, and in interpreting research that occurs over an extended period of time, such changes should be considered. Some changes, such as getting hungry, tired, or discouraged, can occur in a relatively short time, and are also considered maturational threats to internal validity. Suppose a researcher is investigating the attitudes of fourth graders toward reading, mathematics, and science. The researcher has developed an instrument for each subject and gives the instruments to all subjects in the same order. It takes the subjects a half hour to finish the reading instrument and another half hour to complete the mathematics questions. How will they respond to the science instrument? They will probably be tired, bored, and inattentive, and maturation would thus be a major problem in using their responses to the science items as an indication of their attitude toward science. Other examples are students who become more knowledgeable because of experience, or first graders who learn to dribble a basketball not because of an effective teacher but because they are maturing physically.

Diffusion of Treatment.   In experimental designs a treatment is given to one group, and the control or alternative condition group never comes in contact with the experimental treatment. If, for instance, a psychologist is studying cheating behavior and manipulates the incentive to cheat as the independent variable, one group might receive a high incentive for cheating and the other group a low incentive, but neither group would be aware of the treatment the other group was receiving. If, however, a teacher decided to test this notion with a class of students and told half the students they would receive a high incentive and the other half that they would, at the same time, receive a low incentive, then each group knows the conditions of the other. In such circumstances the treatments are diffused throughout all subjects, and it is possible that both treatments could affect either group. **Diffusion of treatment** may result in resentment or rivalry of one group, especially if the group members perceive that they have an inferior treatment or activity.

Experimenter Bias.   **Experimenter bias,** or **contamination,** refers to deliberate and unintentional effects that the experimenter has on the subjects. This type of bias is reflected in differential treatment of subjects, such as using a different voice tone, being more reassuring to one group than to others, reinforcing different behaviors, displaying different attitudes, selectively observing different subject responses, and any other demeanor that influences either the subjects' behavior or the evaluation of the behavior by the researcher. Experimenter bias also occurs if the characteristics of the experimenter, such as clothing, age, sex, educational level, and race affect subjects' responses. If, for example, an experimenter is carrying out a study on the difference in behavior with students of so-called master teachers as compared to behavior with students of so-called beginning teachers, and if we use observers to record behavior with students of both types of teachers, we need to be careful that the observers do not know which teachers have been classified as master or beginning. If the observers were aware of which group the students were in (master or beginning teacher) this knowledge may influence what the observers notice in the classrooms. In most research that involves the use of experimenters or observers as a part of the study it is best to keep these persons unaware of the specifics of the research. They need to have only enough information to carry out the research objectively and to collect the information.

Statistical Conclusion.   In most educational research, statistics are used as a basis for making conclusions about presumed effects and relationships. There are several principles of statistics that, if violated, can affect the inferences made from results as well as subsequent conclusions of the research. Cook and Campbell (1979) list several threats in this category that are beyond the scope of this book. Researchers need, however, to understand that the use of impressive sounding and looking statistics does not guarantee valid results. The best approach is to consult statisticians familiar with these threats.

External Validity of Design

External validity refers to the generalizability of the results. For quantitative designs there are two general categories of external validity that need to be considered in evaluating research findings: population external validity and ecological external validity.

Population External Validity.   The subjects used in an investigation have certain characteristics and can be described with respect to such variables as age, race, sex, and ability. Strictly speaking, the results of a study can be generalized only to other people who have the same, or at least similar, characteristics as those used in the experiment. The extent to which the results can be generalized to other people is referred to as **population external validity.** Consider the prevailing situation in much psychological research. Because of time, money, and other constraints, psychologists often use college students as subjects in research. The results of such research, then, are limited in generalizability to other college students, and not to all college students if the subjects are students from a large, prestigious university. In other words, what might be true for certain college students may not be true for sixth-grade students. Similarly, research conducted with elementary students should not be generalized to secondary students, nor that done with males generalized to females, nor that done with Mexican Americans generalized to blacks, and so forth. A treatment might be effective with one type of student and be ineffective with another. If subjects are volunteers for research, the findings may be limited to characteristics of the volunteers.

Ecological External Validity.   **Ecological validity** refers to the conditions of the research and the extent to which generalizing the results is limited to similar conditions. The conditions of the research include such factors as the nature of the independent and dependent variables, physical surroundings, time of day or year, pretest or posttest sensitization, and effects caused by the presence of an experimenter or treatment. Included in these factors is the well-known **Hawthorne effect,** the tendency for people to act differently simply because they realize they are subjects in research. (It is called the Hawthorne effect because the original study was conducted at the Western Electric Hawthorne Plant in Chicago. Although recent research has questioned the validity of the original study, the label "Hawthorne effect" endures.) Subjects may, under this condition, become anxious, fake responses in order to look good, or react in many other ways because of their knowledge of aspects of the research. A new treatment that is given to people can also disrupt the normal routine, and this novelty or disruption can limit generalizability.

EXCERPT 5.4
External Validity

DISCUSSION

Since only one teacher and the students from one classroom participated, and since the study focused only on language arts curriculum, the results of this study have to be accepted tentatively until replications are conducted. The congruence of the results with existing theory and previous research does provide some corroboration of their validity. . . .

While the results of this study and the previous research indicate a pragmatic superiority of cooperative over competitive and individualized learning structures, it does not follow that all individualization or competition should be dropped. What is needed is a series of studies which demonstrate the specific conditions under which each type of learning structure is effective and useful in achieving desired educational outcomes.

Source: Johnson, D. T., Johnson, R. T., Johnson, J., & Anderson, D. (1976). Effects of cooperative versus individualized instruction on student prosocial behavior, attitudes toward learning, and achievement. *Journal of Educational Psychology. 68,* 446–452.

Consider once again the psychologist in a university setting. Psychological experiments are often conducted in a small room in which the subject is alone. This procedure is desirable for controlling threats to internal validity, but it tends to restrict the degree of possible generalization, since the way subjects respond in an artificial setting may not be the same as in naturally occurring conditions. A related limitation is the extent to which a treatment is a representative instance of the underlying construct that is hypothesized to exist. This type of external validity is termed by Cook and Campbell (1979) **construct validity.** It refers to the adequacy with which we understand and communicate the complexity of the so-called treatment package, particularly those components of it that will allow the observed effect to be replicated as another test of the underlying construct. A specific behavior modification program, for example, might be employed as a method of using a principle of behaviorism (shaping, intermittent reinforcement, satiation, and so on), but for purposes of generalization, the consumer must analyze the adequacy with which the construct is represented by the program and whether there are peculiarities in the treatment that would make replication difficult. This problem occurs extensively in research that investigates the impact of a new curriculum or set of materials. The results may be impressive, but unless there is evidence that a generalizable construct has been used, and that the treatment is clear and easily understood, the external validity will be limited.

It is possible to be so strict with respect to external validity that practically all research is useful only in specific cases. While it is necessary to consider the external validity of studies, we need to be reasonable, not strict, in interpreting the results. It is common, for example, for researchers to cite, in the discussion or conclusion sections of the article, the limitations of generalizing their results. Excerpt 5.4 is a good example of researchers addressing the problem of external validity by limiting the generalizations that should be made.

■ DESIGNING QUALITATIVE RESEARCH ■

Qualitative research, similar to quantitative studies, requires a plan for selecting sites and participants and for data collection. The plan, unlike those in quantitative research, is referred to as an **emergent design,** in which each incremental research decision is dependent on prior information. The emergent design may, in reality, seem circular, as processes of purposeful sampling, data collection, and partial data analysis are simultaneous and interactive rather than discrete sequential steps. Qualitative researchers are just as concerned about design validity as are quantitative researchers, but the methods used to establish internal and external validity differ.[5]

There are many variations of qualitative research. Some studies use quantitative and qualitative methods to study a single problem. These are called methodological mixes (Patton, 1980) or methodological triangulation (Denzin, 1978). Other studies use qualitative methods to supply "additional findings" which compliment quantitative data. Traditionally, however, a qualitative method is chosen because the researcher is in a discovery orientation. The qualitative researcher views reality as multi-layered, interactive, and a shared social experience that can be studied from the participants' perspectives with either **interactive techniques** (ethnographic observation or ethnographic interview) or **non-interactive techniques** (use of historical documents). Each of these qualitative techniques is discussed in more detail in Chapter 11 (Ethnographic Research) and Chapter 12 (Analytic Research: Historical, Legal, and Policy Studies). In this chapter we introduce qualitative design, especially the logic and terminology appropriate for qualitative research. Within qualitative research, there is also much variation in how one conducts such a study.

---

[5]See R. C. Bogdan & S. K. Biklen (1982), *Qualitative research for education;* B. G. Glaser & A. L. Strauss (1967), *The discovery of grounded theory;* J. P. Goetz & M. D. LeCompte (1984), *Ethnography and qualitative design in educational research;* S. J. Taylor & R. C. Bogdan (1984), *Qualitative research methods: The search for meanings;* Y. S. Lincoln & E. G. Guba (1985), *Naturalistic inquiry;* L. M. Smith (1979), An evolving logic of participant observation in L. S. Shulman (Ed.), *Review of research in education* (Vol. 6) and (1981) Ethnography in *Encyclopedia of educational research* (5th ed.). Internal and external criticism of sources is discussed in Chapter 12.

Case Study Design

All researchers make decisions about which and how many people will be studied, and how, when, and where they will be studied. These are the questions which guide the qualitative researcher in 1) selecting the site and observing people, times, and places or 2) selecting the historical period and obtaining the primary documents. Most anthropologists, for example, begin the research process by identifying a group—a tribe, a village, an urban scene—that suggests some personal, empirical, or conceptual research problem. After obtaining access to the group, they decide who to study in the field while generating the specific research questions and determining relevant conceptual frameworks. Classical qualitative researchers resolve the sampling problem by studying groups in their entirety that have a natural socio-cultural boundary and face-to-face interaction, either in the present or the past.

Current qualitative researchers also investigate small, distinct groups such as all the participants in an innovative school, all the students in a selected classroom, one principal's role for an academic year, or one historical figure or institution. These are typically single-site studies or single historical periods using a few archive collections. Some qualitative researchers choose multiple sites with subsets of larger groups (Cusick, 1973) or comparative historical periods using multiple document collections. Ethnographers report the number of participants, the sampling criteria, the size of the subset selected and characteristics of the larger group. Historians report the selection criteria and the type and number of documents for each historical period. Multi-site studies, which usually involve more than two researchers, are considered a modified or hybrid methodological approach and are beyond the purpose of this chapter.[6]

Traditional qualitative research uses a **case study design,** meaning that the unit of analysis is the one phenomenon which the researcher selects to understand in depth regardless of the number of sites, participants, or documents for a study. The "one" may be, for example, one principal, one group of students in a teacher's class, one school, one program, one process, or one concept. The unit of analysis is related to the research foci. Sometimes the focus is on different groups in a program such as demographic groups (male/female or black/white) or programmatic groups (dropouts/graduates or those who do well/those who do poorly), but the purpose is to *understand* one phenomenon: the educational entity or process. Sometimes the focus is on different individuals or groups within a historical period in which primary documents (diaries, letters, official records) record their interactions in the past. Subunits of separate individuals or groups are not viewed as statistically comparative nor as mutually exclusive, but as different groups who are likely to be informative about the research foci. The single

---

[6]See R. E. Herriott & W. A. Firestone (1983), Multisite qualitative policy research: Optimizing description and generalizability, *Educational Researcher, 12*(3), 14–19, and M. B. Miles & A. M. Huberman (1984), *Qualitative data analysis: A sourcebook of new methods.*

EXCERPT 5.5
Case Study Design

THE RESEARCH

The present article is the outcome of research carried out by the author on a specific bilingual teacher's strategies and her thinking about these strategies in a Latin American history class. The research, lasting for a year and a half (September, 1984–February, 1985), was divided into classroom observations, interviews with students, and a series of interviews with the teacher conducted in school and at her home. The school, situated in a city in the northeastern United States, included a class (the focus of this research) in Latin American history for incoming Hispanic students. The class was for students in grades 9 and 11, and was coeducational. The medium of instruction was Spanish, and while the principal textbook was in Spanish, other resource books in Spanish and English were also included.

Source: From "*Echar Pa'lante*, Moving Onward: The Dilemmas and Strategies of a Bilingual Teacher" by Martha Montero-Sieburth and Marla Perez, *Anthropology & Education Quarterly*, Vol. 18, No. 3, September, 1987. Reprinted by permission of the American Anthropological Association.

---

unit of analysis and its subunits influences what the researcher can say empirically at the completion of the study about the research foci.

The case study design in Excerpt 5.5 focused on one teacher, Mrs. S., a Puerto Rican in her late thirties, and her Latin American class of fluctuating membership. The research purpose was to describe and analyze "a specific bilingual teacher's strategies and her thinking about these strategies in the Latin American history class" (Montero-Sieburth & Perez, 1987, p. 181).

Qualitative researchers view selection and sampling processes as dynamic, *ad hoc,* and phasic rather than static or *a priori* parameters of populations for a research design. Choosing selection and sampling procedures depends on the initial phrasing of the research problem and the subsequent subunits for observation and analysis. Typically the qualitative researcher defines the individuals or groups for which the initial research problem is appropriate, the context or site that is potentially associated with the question, and the time period to which the question may be relevant. The site or context, the activities, and time period are the boundaries which influence the selection process. The qualitative researcher then seeks access to the selected site or archive. Once research permission and entry for data collection is assured, the researcher refines the research foci through "first days in the field" (Geer, 1964) or by scanning the documents to gather information for purposeful sampling decisions. Now let's look at site selection and purposeful sampling for qualitative research.

Site Selection and Purposeful Sampling

Ethnographic studies are usually conducted at a single site. Although selection procedures may resemble some principles of probability, they do not require, desire, or depend on such guidelines. Probability sampling procedures such as simple random or stratified sampling may be inappropriate when 1) generalizability of the findings is not an objective; 2) only one or two subunits of a population are relevant to the research problem; 3) the researchers have no access to the whole group from which they wish to sample; or 4) statistical sampling is precluded because of logistical and ethical reasons.

Site Selection. A clear definition of the criteria for site selection is essential. The criteria is related to and appropriate for the research problem and purpose. If the research purpose is to study a little-known or singular phenomenon to propose theoretical constructs for later verification or to describe and explain in detail complex microprocesses, then a single site, a single individual or a small group can be used. For researchers studying special institutions, groups, or processes, the purpose is to generate findings which provide an *understanding* for, not generalized to, other institutions, other groups, or processes to infer similarities and differences. If the initial problem is phrased to describe and analyze teachers' decision-making regarding learning activities (Parker & Gehrke, 1986), students' perspectives and strategies regarding classroom management (Allen, 1986), or elementary teachers' concept of career (Biklen, 1985), then it should be likely that these viewpoints or actions are present and can be studied at the selected site.

Purposeful sampling. **Purposeful sampling,** in contrast to probabilistic sampling, is a "strategy when one wants to . . . come to understand something about certain select cases without needing [or desiring] to generalize to all such cases" (Patton, 1980, p. 100). Researchers use purposeful sampling to increase the utility of information obtained from small samples.[7] Purposeful sampling requires that information be obtained or known in the early data collection phase about variations among the subunits before the sample is chosen. The researcher initially searches for information-rich key informants, groups, places, or events from which to select subunits for more in-depth study. In other words, these samples are chosen because they are likely to be knowledgeable and informative about the phenomena the researcher is investigating. Types of purposeful sampling are comprehensive selection, maximum variation sampling, network selection, and other variations.

1. Researchers prefer **comprehensive sampling,** in which every participant, group, setting, event or other relevant information is examined. Each subunit is manageable in size and so heterogeneous that one does not want to lose possible variation. For example, a study of mainstreaming autistic children in one school division would probably have to observe all autistic children. A study of high school student interns in an external learning program (see Excerpt 5.6) examined

---

[7]Goetz & LeCompte (1984) prefer the term "criterion-based selection."

EXCERPT 5.6
Comprehensive Selection

. . . by discovering certain features of a work environment and setting them against a broader ethnographic portrait, we can generate case studies of learning at work that may be compared with one another.

These concepts arise from a three-year study of student interns in 35 different sites used by one external learning program in a major American city. Among the work places we observed and compared were a hospital speech clinic and a community newspaper, an animal shelter and a curriculum development firm, a food cooperative and a labor union. We also studied two legislators' offices and three museums. At the outset, our purpose was to develop a conceptual framework for the study of educational encounters in environments outside of schools. While we understood that high school interns are hardly representative of full-time workers, we wanted to find out how newcomers in work organizations learn. . . . From an educational perspective, our central problem was to discover and analyze the social process by which the newcomer to the workplace (in this case, the intern) was more or less systematically introduced into the definition, distribution, and use of that knowledge.

Source: From "Learning at Work: Case Studies in Non-School Education" by David Thornton Moore, *Anthropology & Education Quarterly*, Vol. 17, No. 3, September 1986. Reprinted by permission of the American Anthropological Association.

all thirty-five different sites. Each work setting was so heterogeneous—a hospital speech clinic, a community newspaper, a labor union, two legislative offices, an animal shelter, and the like—that comprehensive selection was necessary.
Other examples of comprehensive sampling are historians who reconstruct a biography of one person, legal researchers who analyze a single landmark case such as the 1954 school desegregation decision, and policy researchers who analyze the role of the Secretary of Education and trends in national educational policy. Because groups are rarely sufficiently small and resources are seldom plentiful, researchers use other sampling strategies.

2. **Maximum variation sampling** or quota selection is a strategy to "represent" subunits of the major unit of analysis, the research problem. The researcher may divide the population of elementary school teachers into three categories by number of years service and select key informants in each category to investigate career development (see Excerpt 2.6 in Chapter 2). This is *not* a representative sample because the qualitative researcher is merely using this strategy to enable the findings to describe in detail different meanings of teacher career development for individuals with different years of service.

3. **Network selection,** also called **snowball sampling,** is a "strategy in which each successive participant or group is named by a preceding group or individual" (Goetz & LeCompte, 1984, p. 79). Participant referrals are the basis for choosing a

sample. The researcher develops a profile of the attributes or particular trait sought and asks each participant to suggest others who fit the profile or have the attribute. The strategy may be used in situations where the individuals sought do not form a naturally bounded group but are scattered throughout populations. Network selection (snowball sampling) is frequently used in in-depth interview studies rather than participant observation research.

Snowball sampling is used in ethnographic interviews by anthropologists, oral history by historians, and life history case studies by sociologists. Historians interview famous people to obtain details by participants about historical events. Life histories by sociologists or psychologists provide insights in basic human processes such as aging.

4. Other purposeful sampling strategies which may be used for certain research and evaluation studies are extreme-case selection, typical-case selection, unique-case selection, reputational-case selection, and critical-case selection. Each of these is defined below.

> *Extreme-case selection* requires first the identification of typical or average cases and then the selection of the extreme cases. For example, a comparative case analysis of a very large school and a very small school (Barker & Gump, 1964) meant that the researchers determined the mean size of public high schools from public records and then found schools of the appropriate size.

> *Typical-case selection* requires the researcher to develop a profile of characteristics of an average case and then find an example of the case. Wolcott (1973) sought a typical elementary-school principal for an institutional role analysis and thus eliminated women, persons who were too old or too young, single males, and other individuals atypical of a profile developed from a national survey.

> *Unique-case selection* focuses on the unusual or rare case of some dimension which historical events frequently provide, such as the implementation of new federal policy mandates.

> *Reputational-case selection* occurs when knowledgeable experts recommend individuals or groups to a researcher, such as teachers who are considered "competent" by their principal or "effective schools" identified by state officials.

> *Critical-case selection* requires the identification of critical cases, those which can make points quite dramatically or are, for some reason, considered particularly important such as the "ideal or typical" case, the "real test" case, or politically sensitive case. Critical-case sampling permits *logical* generalizations and maximum application of information to other cases because if it is true of this one case, it is likely to be true of all other cases.

The specification of the site selection criteria and the purposeful sampling technique chosen are decided from prior information and are reported in the study to reduce threats to design validity. In addition, the persons or groups who actually participated in the study are reported in a manner to protect confidentiality of data. Historical and legal researchers specify the public archives and private collections used and frequently refer to each document or court case in explanatory footnotes. In this manner, researchers using non-interactive techniques to study the past reduce threats to design validity.

Phases of Data Collection and Analyses Strategies

Qualitative phases of data collection and analyses are interactive research processes which occur in overlapping cycles. These are not called procedures, but **data collection and analyses strategies,** techniques which are flexible and dependent on each prior strategy and the data obtained from that strategy. The research phases are relatively similar for ethnographic observation, ethnographic interviews and historical methodologies. Figure 5.3 illustrates five research phases: Phase 1 is Planning; Phases 2, 3, and 4 are Beginning, Basic, and Closing Data Collection; and Phase 5 is Completion. The five research phases, explained below, demonstrate the interactive processes of sampling and selecting, data recording, analysis and display, and tentative interpretations during the data collection period. Concerns for internal and external design validity influence data collection strategies.

Phase 1: Planning.   To plan a qualitative study, researchers analyze the problem statement and the anticipated research questions which focus the data collection efforts. They then describe the kind of setting or sites, the type of interviewees, or the historical documents which would seem logically to yield information about the problem. This description becomes the guideline for purposeful sampling and selection. In Phase 1, a researcher locates and gains permission to use the site, a network of persons, or an archive of documents.

Phase 2: Beginning Data Collection.   This phase includes the first days in the field in which the ethnographer establishes rapport, trust, and reciprocal relations (Wax, 1971) with the individuals and groups to be observed. The researcher obtains data primarily to become oriented to the field and to gain a sense of the "totality" of the setting for purposeful sampling.

The ethnographic interviewer in Phase 2 interviews the first few persons in a network and begins the snowball sampling technique. Simultaneously the interviewer polishes the interviewing and recording procedures. Adjustments are made in the interviewer's techniques of establishing rapport and trust and the order and phrasing of questions/statements during the interviews.

The historical and legal researcher in Phase 2 previews the appropriate collection(s) of preserved documents which may or may not be cataloged. If they are not cataloged, this must be done. Additional documents may have to be located and previewed in other public archives and private collections.

Early in the study, the qualitative researcher, regardless of the data collection technique, develops a way to organize, code, and retrieve collected data for formal data analysis (Phase 5). Transcripts of field notes or interviews and the investigator's records of documents are often thousands of typed pages.

FIGURE 5.3
Phases of Qualitative Research

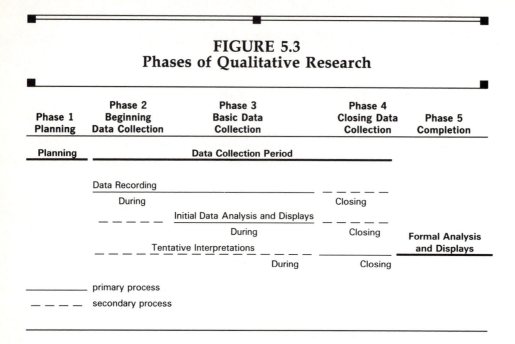

Phase 1 Planning	Phase 2 Beginning Data Collection	Phase 3 Basic Data Collection	Phase 4 Closing Data Collection	Phase 5 Completion

Planning   Data Collection Period

Data Recording

During   Closing

Initial Data Analysis and Displays

During   Closing

Tentative Interpretations   **Formal Analysis and Displays**

During   Closing

———————— primary process

— — — — secondary process

Phase 3: Basic Data Collection.   The researcher no longer is caught up in adjustments to the newness of the field setting, the archive and its method of cataloging documents, or the idiosyncracies of interviewees. In the basic data collection phase, the observer begins to "hear," to "see," and to "read" what is going on, rather than just listening, looking around, or scanning documents. The researcher continues to make choices of data collection sources and strategies.

Tentative data analysis begins as the researcher mentally processes many ideas and facts while collecting data. Initial working conceptualizations and descriptions are transformed and summarized. As initial patterns emerge, the researcher identifies ideas and facts which need corroboration in the closing phase.

Phase 4: Closing Data Collection.   Data collection draws to a close as the researcher "leaves the field," leaves the archive, or conducts the last interview. In qualitative research, there is no *a priori* date for the end of data collection as one might have in quantitative studies such as when a percent of completed instruments are returned. Ending data collection is related to the research problem and the depth and richness of the data collected. In Phase 4, the researcher gives more attention to possible interpretations and verification of the emergent findings with key informants, the remaining interviews, or documents. As Glaser and Strauss (1967) note:

> The continual intermeshing of data collection and analysis has direct bearing on how the research is brought to a close . . . . He believes in his own knowledgeability . . . not because of an arbitrary judgment but because he has taken very special pains

to discover what he thinks he may know, every step of the way from the beginning of his investigation until its publishable conclusions . . . . He has been living with partial analyses for many months, testing them each step of the way, until he has built his theory [interpretations]. What is more, if he has participated [or empathized] in the social life of his subject, then he has been living by his analyses, testing them not only by observation and interview [and reading] but also by daily living (pp. 224–225).

The researcher senses that further data collection will not yield any more data relevant to the research problem.

Phase 5: Completion.   Completion of the active data collection phase blends into formal data analysis and the construction of meaningful ways to present the data. Data analysis begins with a construction of "the facts" as found in the researcher-recorded data. The researcher reconstructs initial displays, time charts, network diagrams, frequency lists, process figures and others—to try to synthesize a holistic sense of the "totality," the relationship of the parts to the whole. The researcher asks a range of questions of the recorded data as he or she slowly *induces* conceptual themes and possible interpretations. Data analysis and display are essential before the researcher can draw final context-bound generalizations.

Credibility

Research is considered valid, credible, and trustworthy to the extent that the canons of reliability and validity are addressed when the inquiry is designed and conducted and the findings interpreted. When qualitative investigators have addressed the threats to reliability and validity explained below, their work is usually regarded as credible by other qualitative researchers. The term **credibility** in qualitative studies refers to the use of appropriate definitions of research criteria—reliability, internal and external validity—in qualitative inquiry.

Reliability and validity are important aspects of design shared by quantitative and qualitative researchers.[8] Some factors confounding the reliability of experimental designs are inapplicable to qualitative studies and others have special definitions. Quantitative and qualitative definitions of reliability and validity differ because each approach has unique conceptions of what constitutes "data." Quantitative researchers use numbers and measurement to document consistencies in behavior, and they use definitions of validity and reliability that relate to instrumentation employed to show consistency. Qualitative researchers, however, assume that the meaningfulness of human actions depends on the contexts or situations in which these actions, feelings, and perceptions occur. Thus, quali-

---

[8]This section draws primarily from D. Bednarz (1985), Quantity and quality in evaluation research: A divergent view, *Evaluation and Program Planning, 8,* 289–306, and J. P. Goetz and M. D. LeCompte (1984), *Ethnography and qualitative design,* pp. 208–233, who discuss ethnographic methods in terms of research criteria traditionally associated with quantitative studies. When appropriate, we have broadened the discussion to include ethnographic interview and historical research.

tative researchers study the ways participants in a social scene establish a shared sense of social reality which will vary somewhat with each social scene or context. Most qualitative research is discovery-oriented, enabling the researcher to understand the emerging logic in social situations from the participants' perspectives. A teacher, for example, interacts one way with a group of disruptive students in a first-grade classroom and interacts another way with a parent in the principle's office, because the teacher uses a different logic and language in each social scene. In discussing qualitative reliability and validity, we make references to characteristics of qualitative inquiry found in Chapters 11 and 12: an emphasis on context, eclectic approaches to theory development, and use of corroborative data analysis.

Constraints on Qualitative Reliability.   Reliability in quantitative research refers to the consistency of the observations obtained through the instrument employed in the study; reliability in qualitative research refers to the consistency of the researcher's interactive style, data recording, data analysis, and interpretation of the participant meanings in the data. Reliability, therefore, is immensely difficult to researchers interested in a naturalistic event or unique phenomena, present or past. The qualitative process is personalistic; no investigator observes, interviews, or studies documents exactly like another. Reliability issues are handled by the researcher during all phases of the research to obtain consistency in the description of the naturalistic event and its meanings for the participants.

Qualitative researchers share a common intellectual heritage from apprenticeship research training. They frequently assume that their audiences have a methodological knowledge similar to that found in quantitative training. The tradition of a lengthy, descriptive, and perhaps "artful" presentation of results has led to the use of shorthand descriptors in qualitative designs and methods which are misleading to a novice.[9] Because most qualitative research is categorized as ethnographic observation, ethnographic interview, or historical, the multimethod nature of the methodology is often ignored. A range of techniques may be used in any single study to supplement and corroborate findings, including the use of mechanically sophisticated methods of recording, transcribing, and analyzing. The failure to provide sufficient design specificity has created reliability threats to the research.[10]

External Reliability.   In quantitative research, the researcher demonstrates reliability with the instrument used in the study. In qualitative research, however, reliability issues are handled by the researcher-person throughout the entire research process: design planning, data collection, and formal data analysis. The

---

[9]The increase in methodological papers and studies published since 1980 suggests qualitative research concepts for the methods applied to education are still developing. For different emphases and terminology to establish credibility, see Y. S. Lincoln and E. G. Guba (1985).

[10]As Pelto and Pelto (1978) noted, the discrepancy in findings between two anthropological studies (Lewis, 1951; Redfield, 1930) of the same Mexican village is a consequence of different research designs—different research question, methods, time period, groups, and scientific assumptions in the study of belief systems and social structure. Similar instances occur in historical research which has spawned historiography, the study of changing interpretations of the past.

uniqueness or complexity of the phenomena and the individualistic and persona-listic nature of the qualitative process make approaching external reliability more difficult than in the quantitative modes of inquiry. External reliability is the extent to which independent researchers could discover the same phenomena in the same or similar situation. Some claim that no qualitative study can be reliable; however, the development, refinement, and validation of qualitative research findings may *not* require replication of events. Further, human behavior is never static and no study is replicated exactly, regardless of the methods and designs chosen.

Ethnographers enhance external reliability of their data by making explicit five aspects of the design: researcher role, informant selection, social context, data collection and analysis strategies, and analytical constructs and premises.

> *Researcher role.* The importance of the researcher's social relationship with the participants requires that studies identify the researcher's role and status within the group. Historians frequently cite personal or professional experiences which enable them to empathize with a historical figure or event.

> *Informant selection.* Informant selection, as a threat to reliability, is usually handled by careful description of the informants and the decision process used in their selection. Replicability requires a researcher to contact individuals similar to those who were informants in the prior study.

> *Social context.* Social contexts influence the content of the data. Contexts, either in a study of the past or the present, are described physically, socially, interpersonally, and functionally.

> *Data collection and analysis strategies.* Descriptions of data collection and analysis techniques are precise: the varieties of observational and interviewing methods, and how data were recorded and under what circumstances. Simply asserting that formal data analysis was done carefully is insufficient for establishing reliability and validity. The researcher must provide retrospective accounts of how data were synthesized[11] and identify the *general* strategies of data analysis and interpretation.

> *Analytical premises.* The primary safeguard against unreliability is making explicit the conceptual framework which informs the study and from which findings can be integrated or contrasted.

In Excerpt 5.7, a study of impression management in kindergarten classrooms, the social context and the analytical premises drawn from impression management theory (also called self-presentation theory) are explicit.

Internal Reliability. Internal reliability in a qualitative design addresses whether, within a single study, multiple observers agree. This issue is especially critical when a research team uses qualitative methods to study a problem at several sites or in several networks. Techniques often used to establish quantitative

---

[11]See M. B. Miles & A. M. Huberman, *Qualitative data analysis* (1984), for a thorough concurrent record of data analysis techniques used in a multi-site study.

EXCERPT 5.7
Qualitative External Reliability

Erving Goffman (1963) has referred to children as "communication delinquents" because often they violate the rules of adult interaction. This study represents an initial exploration into the dynamics of that delinquency as evidenced in two kindergarten peer cultures. It is believed that the "impression management" orientation taken by Goffman and others (e.g., Schlenker, 1985; Tedeschi, 1981) offers a conceptual vehicle for improving understandings of children's social behavior and development. The study applies a small portion of Goffman's rich conceptual perspective to the study of children's social interactions in classroom contexts. The effort is exploratory in nature and is a systematic analysis of the communications of five- and six-year-old children in two kindergarten classrooms. The goals of the analysis were to discover if children's face-to-face interactions with peers included "facework" components as described by Goffman (1967, 1971) and, if so, in what forms these components were expressed.

Based largely on the work of Cooley (1902), Mead (1934), and Goffman (1959), a growing research literature has emerged in the area of impression management theory (also called self-presentation theory). . . . Hence, people's views of themselves are strongly affected by how they believe they are being perceived and evaluated by others. Since the impressions of others affect feelings of self-worth, individuals are highly motivated to attempt to control or "manage" the impressions others may be forming (Goffman, 1959; Leary, 1983).

Source: From "Impression Management in Kindergarten Classrooms: An Analysis of Children's Face-Work in Peer Interactions" by J. Amos Hatch, *Anthropology & Education Quarterly*, Vol. 18, No. 2, June, 1987. Reprinted by permission of the American Anthropological Association.

---

reliability such as rating or coding of data by numbers are seldom done in qualitative research. Rather, the agreement sought among qualitative researchers is **interobserver reliability,** agreement on the description or composition of events rather than on the frequency of occurrence of events.

Qualitative researchers commonly use a *combination* of several of five possible strategies to reduce threats to internal reliability: low-inference descriptors, multiple researchers, participant researchers, peer examination, and mechanically recorded data.

> *Low-inference descriptors.* Verbatim accounts of conversations and transcripts, direct quotes from documents, and concrete, precise descriptions from field notes are the hallmarks of qualitative research and the principle method for establishing internal validity. Negative cases or discrepant data are also reported.

Multiple researchers. The use of multiple researchers is one method to minimize threats to internal validity. Qualitative research based on a team approach, however, is done infrequently, and most involve only two researchers.[12]

Participant researcher. Many researchers obtain the aid of an informant to corroborate what has been observed and recorded, interpretations of participant meanings, and explanations of overall processes.

Peer examination. Peer examination is the corroboration of findings by researchers in similar settings through any of three ways: integration of descriptions and conclusions from other qualitative studies in a study, integration of findings from concurrent studies at multi-sites, and publication of the results which allows for peer review.

Mechanically recorded data. Tape recorders, photographs, and videotapes may increase internal reliability, if different researchers proceed in the same manner (same camera angles, identical segments of behavior recorded).

Excerpt 5.8 illustrates the use of low-inference descriptors in the field notes, especially the use of verbatim accounts of conversations and precise descriptions of actions by participants of this learning scene.

Internal Validity of Design. Design validity refers to aspects of internal and external validity in qualitative research: the degree to which scientific explanations of phenomena match the realities of the world. Design validity addresses two questions. First, do researchers actually observe what they think they observe (internal validity)? Second, to what extent are the abstract generalizations and constructs generated, refined, or extended by other researchers applicable across groups (external validity)? As indicated above, reliability is a serious threat to much qualitative research. Validity, however, may be its major strength.

The claim of high internal validity of ethnography rests on the data collection and analysis techniques. Some strategies which increase internal validity are:

Lengthy data collection period. The lengthy data collection period provides opportunities for continual data analysis, comparison, and corroboration to refine constructs and to ensure the match between research-based categories and participant reality.

Participants' language. Informant interviews, phrased closely to the participants' language, are less abstract than many instruments used in other designs. Historians use the language of the era studied.

---

[12]The use of more than one researcher is handled in different ways: 1) extensive prior training and discussion during fieldwork to reach agreement on meaning (Becker, et al., 1961, 1968), 2) short-term observations for confirmation at different sites (Stake & Easley, 1978), and 3) more commonly, each field observer is independently responsible for a research site.

EXCERPT 5.8
Qualitative Internal Reliability

In the basement workroom of a custom furniture shop, Jacob, the master cabinetmaker, instructed Mike, one of his apprentices, to assemble two drawers for a chest after reminding him to tuck his long hair up under his hat. As Mike began to lay the pieces out on a workbench, Jacob said, "I suggest you do it on the floor," but Mike stayed at the bench. The apprentice started by putting several pieces together and trying to hold them steady as he balanced and aligned them. Like a house of cards, everything tumbled apart—twice. Jacob came around behind him to watch, and Mike said, "I've been trying to figure out how to clamp this so it will stay together." Jacob did two things at once: He turned the drawer so it rested on its bottom, saying, "Have everything ready to go; fit it together first"; and he put the pieces together very quickly, showing Mike where to clamp them. As Mike turned the clamps, Jacob cautioned him, "Not too tight. There's such a thing as a mechanic's feel where it's just right." Then he walked off to resume the sanding job he had been working on. When Mike completed another segment of the drawer, he called to Jacob, "Is this right?" Jacob looked over and said, "You've got to measure now." He watched as Mike extended the tape measure along the drawer sides. "Say it out loud," he commanded. Mike called out, "33⅛, 33¼." Jacob challenged the second reading and measured it himself, discovering that Mike was right. He said, "Okay," then turned to direct Peter, another apprentice, to check to see that all the holes were filled in another drawer. Mike began on the second piece.

This scene represents one brief segment of activity that occurred about 12 weeks into an 18-week placement for one student in a big-city experiential education program. As presented here, it also represents a chunk of raw data for a particular form of educational ethnography.

Source: From "Learning at Work: Case Studies in Non-School Education" by David Thornton Moore, *Anthropology & Education Quarterly*, Vol. 17, No. 3, September 1986. Reprinted by permission of the American Anthropological Association.

Field research. Participant observation is conducted in natural settings that reflect the reality of life experience more accurately than do contrived or laboratory settings. Historical and legal documents are records of events which occurred in natural situations.

Disciplined subjectivity. Researcher self-monitoring, called "disciplined subjectivity" (Erickson, 1973), submits all phases of the research process to continuous and rigorous questioning and reevaluation.

For qualitative studies, internal validity relates to the degree to which the generalizations and conceptual categories have *mutual meanings* between the participants and the researcher. Some threats to internal validity for experimental research are not considered threats in qualitative research; other threats can be equally troublesome for qualitative research, including history and maturation, observer effects, selection, mortality, and plausible alternative explanations. These threats, however, are defined and handled differently in qualitative research.

1. *History and Maturation.* Qualitative researchers, especially historians, assume history affects the nature of the data collected and that events rarely remain constant. In fact, studies of educational change processes consider history not a threat to internal validity but a research focus to investigate. The research task is to document baseline data of the phenomena under study from the participants' perspectives and supplementary sources. Change may be progressive, cyclic, or irrational, but the sources and the nature of change are described to indicate which elements remained the same and which elements changed. Whereas history affects the general social scene, maturation, a normative process, affects the progressive development in well-defined stages of individuals. Qualitative researchers view maturational stages as varying according to cultural norms or historical periods. The researcher is less concerned about what people are doing at some developmental stage than with how "appropriate behavior" is specified in a setting or an era and how individuals relate to these norms.

2. *Observer Effects.* Qualitative researchers handle observer effects in several ways. Data obtained from informants and participants is valid even though it represents a particular view or may be influenced by the researcher. Such data are problematic only if the data are claimed to be representative beyond the context. Many sources of invalidity can be minimized if the researcher spends enough time in the field, conducts a number of ethnographic interviews, or thoroughly searches several archives to obtain data from several perspectives and types of sources. Extended time in data collection allows the researcher to corroborate data and to code sources likely to produce artificial, contrived, or bias information. Participant reaction, independent corroboration, and confirmation—done at all stages of the research process—is probably the most effective technique to identify observer effect or researcher bias.

3. *Selection.* Selection becomes a problem when the complexity of the phenomena or the number of participants necessitates purposeful sampling. The researcher must describe the total possible documents, subgroups, events, settings, persons in a social network, and how purposeful sampling was done to determine whether the findings represent only certain groups or situations.

4. *Mortality.* Qualitative researchers view loss of subjects as a normal event and do not replace subjects, as do quantitative experimental researchers, because human informants and participants are not interchangeable. Mortality is handled in ways similar to history and maturation. Growth and attribution can serve as the focus of a study and, thus, baseline data is important to study the effects.

5. *Alternative Explanations.* Qualitative designs mandate retrospectively, delineating all plausible or rival explanations for the interpretations. Elimination of alternative explanations requires 1) an effective data retrieval system and 2) systematic use of corroboratory and alternative sources of data to obtain instances of data which negate findings or fail to substantiate the interpretations. To delineate

alternative explanations, qualitative researchers search for sources of bias or contamination *during* data collection and analysis and do not postpone this activity until after they finally leave the site or archive.

External Validity of Design.   Statistical generalization in many quantitative studies is related to probability sampling. Qualitative researchers, however, define external validity differently. Most qualitative studies use a case study design in which the single case is not treated as a probability sample of the larger universe. In other words, the researcher does not aim at generalization of results but the **extension of the understandings,** detailed descriptions of the events and people studied which enable others to understand similar situations and extend these understandings in subsequent research. Knowledge is not produced by replications but the preponderance of evidence found in separate case studies over a period of time. Threats to external validity for a qualitative study are those effects which limit its usefulness: comparability and translatability.

Comparability refers to the degree to which the research components— including the site(s), participant characteristics, the documents used, the unit of analysis, and concepts generated—are adequately described and defined so that researchers may use the study to extend understandings to other studies focusing on similar topics. **Translatability** refers to the degree to which the researcher uses theoretical frameworks and research strategies that are understood by other researchers in the same or related disciplines. Thus the meaning of the findings can be extended. The lack of comparability or translatability reduces the usefulness of a study to a systematic but idiosyncratic investigation, a limitation to its relevance for future inquiry.

To establish comparability and translatability, qualitative researchers should report the extent of typicality of the phenomenon (Wolcott, 1973), that is, the degree to which it may be compared or contrasted along relevant dimensions with other phenomena. For example, how typical or atypical were the urban secondary students investigated by Cusick (1973) or the principal in Wolcott's study (1973)? Once the typicality is established, a basis for extension of understandings is evident and the findings may be translated for applicability across sites and disciplines.[13] Four aspects affect meaningful cross-group extensions or cross-era extensions: selection effects, setting effects, history effects, and construct effects.

1. *Selection Effects.* The qualitative researcher's "virtual obsession" with describing the distinct characteristics of groups and periods studied demonstrates an appreciation of the importance of this information for extension purposes. Both qualitative and quantitative attributes of groups and sites are essential. These can include socio-economic status, educational attainment, age group, racial or ethnic composition, time decades, and contextual features of the location, the group, or the individual. Excerpt 5.9 describes the typicality of a Jewish elementary school on relevant dimensions.

---

[13]Increasing the number of sites in a case study design does not assure comparability; in most multi-site studies, sites are nonprobabilistic samples.

EXCERPT 5.9
Qualitative External Validity:
Comparability and Translatability

The particular school chosen for study was an elementary school operated under the auspices of a conservative Jewish synagogue.[3] This type of Jewish school was desired because it is statistically typical of a large percentage of Jewish schools in America (Lang 1968). As was the case with this school, the largest percentage of students attending Jewish schools nationally (44.4 percent) were enrolled in 2 to 5 day a week afternoon schools (Rockowitz and Lang 1976). Also, the largest number of Jewish schools appear to fall within the range of 100 to 299 students, as did this school with its approximately 250 students (Rockowitz and Lang 1976). Finally, the greatest number of conservative congregations who had such schools had a membership size of 100 to 249 families (Friedman 1979), as was the case in this study in which the congregation had approximately 200 families registered as members. The school met two afternoons (1½ hours each) and one Sunday morning (2½ hours) each week, although one of the afternoon sessions was optional. The curriculum in general conformed with the standard curriculum of the afternoon school.

Source: From "Explaining Jewish Student Failure" by David Schoen, *Anthropology & Education Quarterly*, Vol. 13, No. 4, Winter, 1982. Reprinted by permission of the American Anthropological Association.

2. *Setting Effects.* The qualitative researcher, except the historian, affects the group, individuals, or site simply by studying it. Concepts generated may be invalid for other situations because they are a function of the interaction of the context and the researcher or the dynamics of the research method. One resolution is to conduct an inside-outside study with corroboration between the participant and the observer (Montero-Sieburth & Perez, 1987; Smith & Geoffrey, 1968; Whyte, 1955).

3. *History Effects.* Cross-group comparisons of constructs may be limited because of unique historical experiences of groups and cultures. To assume that all group experiences are ethnocentric also may be erroneous. The researcher must state clearly both the common and contrastive dimensions of the salient features of the phenomena studied—degree of literacy or nonliteracy, technological versus non-technological society, rural versus urban, or constitutional or dictatorship form of government.

4. *Construct Effects.* Because a major outcome of qualitative research is the generation and refinement through cross-group and cross-era extension of constructs, qualitative researchers must be concerned with construct validity. Presentation of idiosyncratic explanations hinder across-group and cross-era examinations. When discrepancies are presented, qualitative researchers report the

attributes of the group, time period, settings (Smith & Keith, 1971; Wolcott, 1973). This alerts other researchers in their use of the findings.

The purpose of much qualitative research, however, is primarily descriptive and not limited only to theoretical studies. The choice to focus on narrative and analytic description relates partially to the status of knowledge regarding the phenomenon studied. Thus, the concluding paragraph of a study of a bilingual teacher's thinking and strategies (Montero-Seiburth & Perez, 1987) states:

> These strategies carry her [Mrs. S.'s] implicit, developing perspective on educational processes as they pertain to minority students. An investigation of such perspectives, evolving out of the comparable experiences of teachers in this country [U.S.], is a dire necessity in the field of educational thought. Such an investigation would, in its turn, lead ideally to a kind of understanding of bilingual education that is more sophisticated, more attentive to the nuances and the diversities of minority communities—above all, more informed by the *realities* of their experience—than is the case at present (p. 189).

When qualitative researchers have addressed the threats to reliability and validity noted above, their work is usually regarded as credible by other qualitative investigators. Many threats to design are handled by planning and conducting studies based on the appropriate criteria used to judge research quality.

■ ETHICAL AND LEGAL CONSIDERATIONS[14] ■

Since most educational research deals with human beings, it is necessary to understand the ethical and legal responsibilities of conducting research. Often researchers face situations in which the potential costs of using questionable methods must be balanced by the benefits of conducting the study. Questionable methods came about because of the nature of the research questions and methodology designed to provide valid results. The costs include injury or psychological difficulties, such as anxiety, shame, loss of self-esteem, and affronts to human dignity, or they may involve legal infringement on human rights. Such costs, if a potential result of the research, must be weighed against benefits such as gains for the research participants like increased self-understanding, satisfaction in helping, and knowledge of research methods, as well as more obvious benefits to theory and knowledge of human behavior.

It is ultimately the responsibility of each researcher to weigh these considerations and make the best professional judgment possible. To do this, it is necessary for the researcher to be fully aware of ethical and legal principles that should be addressed. We present these principles with discussion of implications.

---

[14]A more detailed analysis of ethical and legal considerations is summarized in P. Reynolds (1982), *Ethics and Social Research* (Englewood Cliffs, NJ: Prentice-Hall). While this discussion emphasizes issues that are of concern for both quantitative and qualitative researchers, it should be noted that there are additional ethical considerations for ethnographic field research (see Cassell & Wax, 1980).

Ethics of Research

Ethics generally are considered to deal with beliefs about what is right or wrong, proper or improper, good or bad. Naturally, there is some degree of disagreement about how to define what is ethically correct in research. But it is a very important question, one of increasing concern for private citizens, researchers, and legislators. Many professional and governmental groups have studied ethical issues in depth and have published guidelines for planning and conducting research in such a way as to protect the rights and welfare of the subjects. Most relevant for educational research is the recently published set of ethical principles published by the American Psychological Association (1983). The principles of most concern to educators are discussed below.

1. The primary investigator of a study is responsible for the ethical standards adhered to.
2. The investigator should inform the subjects of all aspects of the research that might influence willingness to participate, and answer all inquiries of subjects on features that may have adverse effects or consequences.
3. The investigator should be as open and honest with the subjects as possible. This usually involves a full disclosure of the purpose of the research, but there are circumstances in which either withholding information about the research or deceiving the subjects may be justified. Withholding information means that the participants are informed about only part of the purpose of the research. This may be done in studies where full disclosure would seriously affect the validity of the results. For example, in research on students' racial attitudes, it may be sufficient to inform students that the research is investigating attitudes towards others.

   A more volatile issue involves research in which, to put it bluntly, the researcher deliberately lies to the subjects. A good example is the classic study on teacher expectations by Rosenthal and Jacobson (1966). The researchers informed the teachers that certain students had been identified as "bloomers" on a test designed to predict intellectual gain. In fact, the "test" was a measure of intelligence, and the students were identified at random. In this design it was necessary to tell the teachers an untruth. Is such deception justified? After all, in this case the students would only benefit from the misinformation, and the results did have very important implications.

   From one perspective, the deception may be justified on the basis of the contribution of the findings. On the other hand, it is an affront to human dignity and self-respect and may encourage mistrust and cynicism toward researchers. It seems to us that deception should be used only in cases where (1) the significance of the potential results is greater than the detrimental effects of lying; (2) deception is the only valid way to carry out the study; and (3) appropriate debriefing, in which the researcher informs the participants of the nature of and reason for the deception following the completion of the study, is used. Deception does not mean that the subjects should not have a choice as to whether to participate at all in the study.

4. Subjects must be protected from physical and mental discomfort, harm, and danger. If any of these risks is possible, the researcher must inform the subjects of these risks.

5. Most studies require the investigator to secure informed consent from the subjects before they participate in the research. **Informed consent** is achieved by providing subjects with an explanation of the research, an opportunity to terminate their participation at any time with no penalty, and full disclosure of any risks associated with the study. Consent is usually obtained by asking subjects (or parents of minors) to sign a form that indicates understanding of the research and consent to participate. Almost all data-gathering in public schools that requires student participation beyond normal testing requires parental as well as school district and principal permission.

   Informed consent implies that the subjects have a choice about whether to participate. Yet there are many circumstances when it seems acceptable that the subjects never know that they have been participants. Sometimes it is impractical or impossible to locate subjects; sometimes knowledge of participation may invalidate the results. Some educational research is quite unobtrusive and has no risks for the subjects (such as the use of test data of students over the past ten years in order to chart achievement trends). Still, the researcher infringes on what many believe is the ethical right of participants to make their own decision about participation. In general, the more the research inconveniences subjects or creates the potential for harm, the more severe the ethical question in using them as subjects without their consent.

   Certainly people should never be coerced into participating. Coercion is enacted in different degrees. At one extreme, teachers can insist that their student participate or employers can "strongly suggest" that their employees cooperate as subjects. Less obvious subtle persuasion is exerted by convincing subjects that they are "benefiting" science, a program, or an institution. The researcher may indicate freedom of choice to participate or not participate, but the implicit message, "you're letting us down if you don't participate," may also be clear, resulting in partial coercion. In other cases, subjects are simply bribed. Where does freedom of choice end and coercion begin? It is often difficult to know, but it is the responsibility of the researcher to be aware of the power of subtle coercion and to clearly maintain the freedom of the potential participant to decide whether or not to be a subject in the research.

6. Information obtained about the subjects must be held confidential unless otherwise agreed upon, in advance, through informed consent (see Legal Constraints). This means that no one has access to individual data or the names of the participants except the researcher(s) and that the subjects know before they participate who will see the data. Confidentiality is assured by making certain that the data cannot be linked to individual

Legal Constraints

Most of the legal constraints placed on researchers since 1974 have focused on protecting the rights and the welfare of the subjects. These requirements are generally consistent with the ethical principles summarized above, and are in a constant state of reinterpretation and change by the courts.

The Family Educational Rights and Privacy Act of 1974, known as the Buckley Amendment, allows individuals to gain access to information pertaining to them, such as test scores, teacher comments, and recommendations. The act also provides that written permission of consent is legally necessary with data that identifies students by name. The consent must indicate the information that will be disclosed, the purpose of the disclosure, and to whom it will be disclosed. Exceptions to this requirement are granted for research using school records in which the results are of "legitimate educational interest," and when only group data are reported. It should be noted that data gathered in a study can usually be subpoenaed by the courts, even if confidentiality has been promised to the participants by the researcher.

The National Research Act of 1974 requires review of proposed research by an appropriate group in an institution (school division or university) to protect the rights and welfare of the subjects. While most research involving human subjects must be reviewed by such a group, there are some exceptions, such as research using test data that results from normal testing programs, or analyzing existing public data, records or documents without identifying individuals (see the January 26, 1981, *Federal Register*, published by the Department of Health and Human Services, for a complete listing of exemptions). It is advisable to have an authorized group, rather than an individual, review the research prior to conducting the study.

■ SUMMARY ■

This chapter introduced the fundamental characteristics of designing quantitative and qualitative research. In quantitative research we focused particular attention on selecting subjects and instruments and on variables that should be considered in designing and interpreting the research. Emergent design refers to the site selection, purposeful sampling strategies, and selection of data collection and analysis strategies which meet research criteria appropriate for qualitative studies. The following principles summarize the discussion.

1. Research design refers to the way a study is planned and conducted.
2. The purpose of a good research design is to enhance the credibility of the results by taking into account potential sources of bias or error.
3. Internally valid research approximates reality.
4. External validity refers to the generalizability of the results.
5. Randomization, holding factors constant, and statistical adjudgments can be employed in quantitative studies to mitigate plausible rival hypotheses.

subjects by name. This can be accomplished in several ways, includ
collecting the data anonymously; 2) using a system to link names
that can be destroyed; 3) using a third party to link names to data ar
give the results to the researcher without the names; 4) asking sub
use aliases or numbers; and 5) reporting only group, not individ
sults. Boruch and Cecil (1979) provide details of many di
procedures for assuring confidentiality.

7. For research conducted through an institution, such as a unive
   school system, approval for conducting the research should be
   from the institution before collecting any data.

8. The investigator has a responsibility to consider potential misint
   tions and misuses of the research and should make every e
   communicate results so that misunderstanding is minimized.

9. The investigator has the responsibility of recognizing when poten
   efits have been withheld from a control group. In such situati
   significance of the potential findings should be greater than the
   harm to some subjects. For example, a new program that purpo
   hance achievement of learning disabled children may be withh
   some L. D. children on the belief that an experiment is necessary
   ment the effectiveness of the program. In the process the cont
   may have benefited are denied participation in the program.

10. The investigator should provide subjects with the opportunity t
    the results of the study in which they are participating.

Some research, such as studies of the effects of drugs, obviously has
danger that must be considered carefully by the investigator. Much ed
research may not seem to involve any ethical problems, but the inve
view may be biased, and it is best to be conservative and seek the advic
proval of others. Most universities and funding agencies have committe
review of research in order to help ensure ethical safeguards. One of the
ing difficulties faced by educational researchers is securing coopera
administrators, teachers, and parents. This difficulty is lessened by re
who are aware of ethical principles and adhere to them.

There is also an interesting, if not frustrating, interaction between b
cal, on the one hand, and designing the research to provide the
objective data. It is relatively easy, for example, to observe behavior un
ly, and the subjects might never know they were in an experiment. A
previously noted, the Hawthorne effect can reduce the validity of the
maximize both internal and external validity, therefore, it seems best
jects are unaware that they are being studied. Suppose, for instance, a
planted a confederate in a class in order to unobtrusively record the att
havior of college students. Does the researcher have an obligation
students that their behavior is being recorded? If the students are awa
observed, will this awareness change their behavior and invalidate t
Situations like this present ethical dilemmas, and the researcher must
criteria listed above in order to determine the best course of action.

6. Probability sampling is used to be able to generalize to a larger population.
7. Probability sampling is done through simple random sampling, systematic sampling, or stratified random sampling.
8. The size of the sample should be as large as possible without reaching a point at which additional subjects contribute little or no new information.
9. In order to have acceptable reliability and validity for the subjects used in the study, instruments should be chosen carefully. Validity is an estimate of the appropriateness of the use of scores and reliability is an indication of the consistency of the assessment.
10. Researchers should try to locate existing instruments before developing their own.
11. Threats to the internal validity of quantitative studies include selection, history, statistical regression, testing, instrumentation, mortality, maturation, diffusion of treatment, experimenter bias, and statistical conclusion.
12. Threats to the external validity of quantitative studies are classified as population characteristics or ecological conditions.
13. Qualitative research uses an emergent design.
14. Most qualitative research uses a case study design in which one phenomena is selected for the investigation.
15. Qualitative studies use purposeful sampling, such as comprehensive selection, maximum variation sampling, or network sampling, rather than probability sampling.
16. Qualitative research includes five distinct phases: planning, beginning data collection, basic data collection, closing data collection, and completion.
17. Internal and external reliability are important to judge qualitative research.
18. The internal validity of qualitative research depends on data collection and analysis techniques.
19. In general, qualitative research has stronger internal validity and weaker reliability than quantitative research. However, external validity is often not the intent of many qualitative studies.
20. The procedures section of a study should show how the information was collected in detail sufficient to allow other researchers to replicate or extend the study.
21. Researchers should be aware of ethical responsibilities and legal constraints that accompany the gathering and reporting of information.

■ SELF-INSTRUCTIONAL REVIEW EXERCISES ■

Sample answers are in the back of the book.

Test Items

1. The purpose of research design is to
   a. select the instruments for a study.
   b. provide a valid, credible answer to a problem.

    c. determine the best type of statistical analysis.

    d. balance internal and external validity.

2. Bias in research

    a. answers research questions.

    b. provides control of extraneous variables.

    c. is error that affects the results.

    d. is always controlled.

3. Control of bias in quantitative research is provided by

    a. randomization of subjects.

    b. holding conditions constant.

    c. using factors as independent variables.

    d. All of the above.

4. Internal validity in quantitative research design is an assessment of

    a. the control of extraneous variables.

    b. the generalizability of the results.

    c. how well a test measures what it was intended to measure.

    d. the accuracy of the test.

5. If an unplanned event occurs while an experiment is being conducted and affects the results, _____ is a threat to the interpretation of the results.

    a. maturation   c. testing

    b. regression   d. history

6. Researchers assign subjects to groups randomly primarily to control for

    a. selection.   c. regression.

    b. maturation.   d. mortality.

7. Diffusion of treatment results when

    a. treatments are given to all subjects.

    b. one group knows about and is influenced by treatments other groups are receiving.

    c. the researcher effectively pretests the treatment.

    d. one group resents another.

8. External validity for quantitative research refers to

    a. the generalizability of the results.

    b. how well the research was done.

    c. the characteristics of the subjects.

    d. the use of research results in only the setting in which the experiment was done.

9. A sample in quantitative research is all of the following except for

    a. the group selected by the researcher.

    b. the group of subjects studied.

c. the group to whom the researcher intends to generalize results.

d. the group selected from a population.

10. A random sample
    a. must be as large as possible.
    b. is one in which every subject has an equal chance of being selected.
    c. is the same as randomization.
    d. is both b and c.

11. Stratified random sampling
    a. uses existing physical conditions in order to form groups.
    b. takes random samples from each subgroup.
    c. is less efficient than simple random sampling.
    d. needs more subjects than simple random sampling.

12. The degree to which the scores from a test are meaningful and appropriate is called
    a. validity.
    b. reliability.
    c. accuracy.
    d. stability.

13. The reliability of a test is an estimate of
    a. consistency.
    b. generalizability.
    c. what kind of error exists in the test.
    d. Both a and c are correct.

14. In the procedures section of most quantitative studies, there is an indication of
    a. where, when, and how the data were collected.
    b. who participated in the study.
    c. how the data were analyzed.
    d. Both a and b are correct.

15. Probability samples are
    a. usually proportional.
    b. used primarily in experimental research.
    c. drawn from a larger population.
    d. about the same as volunteer samples.

16. Qualitative research is best used for
    a. understanding a single phenomenon in depth.
    b. assessing cause and effect relationships.
    c. assessing the attitudes of students toward math.
    d. Both a and c are correct.

17. Qualitative designs typically use which of the following types of sampling?
    a. stratified
    b. simple random
    c. systematic
    d. purposeful

18. Which of the following correctly describes the phases of qualitative research?
    a. identifying the research problem, data collection, data analysis, completion
    b. planning, beginning data collection, basic data collection, closing data collection, completion
    c. identifying the research hypothesis, data collection, data analysis, conclusions
    d. planning, identifying the problem, data collection, completion

19. In qualitative design the term reliability refers to
    a. consistency of measurement.
    b. accuracy of measurement.
    c. consistency of data collection and analyses strategies.
    d. the replicability of the research.

20. Each of the following is used to enhance external reliability in qualitative research design *except:*
    a. reliability of instruments
    b. description of the social context
    c. description of the researcher role
    d. statement of the analytical premises

21. Internal reliability in qualitative research design refers to
    a. how closely the results approximate reality.
    b. information selection.
    c. accuracy of measures.
    d. interobserver reliability.

22. For qualitative studies, design validity refers to
    a. consistency of assessments.
    b. how well explanations of phenomena approximate realities of the world.
    c. the nature of field research.
    d. control of observer effects.

23. Informed consent is
    a. required for all research.
    b. providing subjects with a choice to be involved in research.
    c. the same as debriefing subjects.
    d. a procedure to allow subjects to see the results of the study.

Application Problems

1. For each case described on the next pages, list potential threats to internal and external validity.

a. Two researchers designed a study to investigate whether physical education performance is affected by being in a class with students of the same sex only or in a class with both sexes. A college instructor is found to cooperate with the researchers. Three sections of the same tennis class are offered, an all-male section, an all-female section, and a mixed section. The researchers control the instructor variable by using the same person as the instructor, informing the instructor about the study and emphasizing to the instructor the need to keep instructional activities the same for each section. One section is offered in the morning, one at noon, and one in the afternoon. Students sign up for the course by using the same procedure as for all courses, though there is a footnote about the gender composition in the schedule of courses. A pretest is given to control for existing differences in the groups.

b. In this study the effect of day care on children's prosocial behavior is examined. A group of volunteer parents agree to participate in the study (the investigators pay part of the day care fees). Children are assigned randomly from the pool of volunteers either to attend a day care of their choice or not to attend. Observers measure the degree of prosocial behavior before and after attending day care for nine months by observing the children on a playground.

c. A superintendent wishes to get some idea of whether or not a bond issue will pass in a forthcoming election. Records listing real estate taxpayers are obtained from the county office. From this list a random sample of ten percent of 3,000 persons is called by phone two weeks before election day and asked whether they intend to vote yes or no.

d. The Green County School Board decided that it wanted a status assessment of the ninth graders' attitudes toward science. A questionnaire was designed and distributed in January to all ninth-grade science teachers. Each teacher was told to give the questionnaire within six weeks, calculate mean scores for each question, and return the questionnaires and results to the district office. The instructors were told to take only one class period for the questionnaires in order to minimize interference with the course. Sixty percent of the questionnaires were returned.

PART II

QUANTITATIVE RESEARCH DESIGNS AND METHODS

Part II presents in greater detail the designs and methods of quantitative research. We begin by reviewing descriptive statistical concepts and procedures that are essential to understanding quantitative studies. We also review in some detail test validity and reliability, sources to use to evaluate instruments, and different ways of collecting quantitative data. These principles are useful in answering questions like: How can researchers summarize large amounts of data? Why is variability of results important? How can relationships be measured? What are the types of evidence researchers use to make valid inferences from subjects' responses? How do researchers establish reliability? What are the advantages and disadvantages of questionnaires compared to interviews? How are questionnaires designed? How is observational research or survey research conducted?

The next two chapters summarize the essentials of quantitative research designs. Chapter 7 considers descriptive, correlational, and predictive designs and Chapter 8 covers experimental, single subject, and *ex post facto* designs. How are relationships interpreted? What distinguishes experimental from non-experimental designs? How is a predictive study different from a simple relationship? What are the possible extraneous variables for the various experimental designs? How is causality inferred from single subject designs? What are the steps in conducting an *ex post facto* study? How is a survey conducted?

The last chapter in this part is a conceptual introduction to inferential statistics. The intent is to provide an understanding of the logic of probability as applied to testing hypotheses and questions. Basic terminology and statistical procedures are presented to enable a reader to interpret results sections of quantitative research and a researcher to select appropriate statistical procedures, based on the design of the study.

CHAPTER 6

DESCRIPTIVE STATISTICS

■ KEY TERMS ■

statistics
descriptive statistics
inferential statistics
measurement scales
nominal scales
ordinal scales
interval scales
ratio scales
frequency distribution
histogram
frequency polygon
measures of central tendency
mean
median
mode
normal distribution

skewed
positively skewed
negatively skewed
measure of variability
range
standard deviation
percentile rank
variance
standard scores
z-scores
scatter plot
positive relationship
negative relationship
correlation coefficient
intercorrelation matrix

This chapter explains some common statistical procedures that are used to describe instrument reliability and validity and report data in a quantitative study. The procedures represent parsimonious ways to summarize and organize information that has been collected. The most frequently used descriptive statistical procedures (those that describe phenomena) are presented, including frequency distributions, measures of central tendency, measures of variability, and measures of relationship. The reasons for using each procedure are discussed, with examples from published articles to illustrate how results are reported.

■ INTRODUCTION TO DESCRIPTIVE STATISTICS ■

Quantitative research relies heavily on numbers in reporting results, sampling, and in providing estimates of instrument reliability and validity. The numbers are usually accompanied by unrecognized strange words and even stranger symbols and are manipulated by something called "statistics." Like magic, statistics lead to conclusions. Often, readers of research simply prefer to skip over anything related to statistics. In the words of a prominent specialist in educational measurement: "For most educators, mere contemplation of the term 'statistics' conjures up images akin to bubonic plague and the abolition of tenure" (Popham, 1981, p. 66).

Even though some statisticians may like the image just described, in truth the fundamental concepts and principles of statistics are readily comprehensible. Skill in mathematics is not a prerequisite to an understanding of statistics, and there is no need to memorize complex formulas. In fact, learning about statistics can be fun, especially considering the great new words learned that are perfect for impressing friends and family!

More seriously, there are important reasons for all educators to gain a functional command of statistical principles:

1. To understand and critique professional articles (for example, were appropriate statistical tools used?).
2. To improve evaluation of student learning.
3. To conduct, even in modest and informal ways, research studies (for example, how should the results be analyzed?).
4. To understand evaluations of programs, personnel, and policies.
5. To help become better equipped as a citizen and consumer, making decisions based on quantitative data or arguments.
6. To upgrade the education profession by providing standard skills to communicate, debate, and discuss research that has implications for educational practice.

Types of Statistics

Statistics are methods of organizing and analyzing quantitative data. These methods are tools designed to help the researcher organize and interpret numbers derived from measuring a trait or variable. The mere presence of statistical procedures does not assure quality in the research. While the contribution of some results does depend on applying the correct statistical procedure, the quality of the research depends most on proper conceptualization, design, subject selection, instruments, and procedures. Statistics is an international language that only manipulates numbers. Statistics and numbers do not interpret themselves, and the meaning of the statistics is derived from the research design. Of course, the improper use of statistics invalidates the research, but the interpretation of statistical results is dependent on carefully designing and conducting the study—that is, it is heavily dependent on producing high quality quantitative data.

There are two broad categories of statistical techniques: descriptive and inferential. **Descriptive statistics** transform a set of numbers or observations into indices that describe or characterize the data. Descriptive statistics (sometimes referred to as *summary statistics*) are thus used to summarize, organize, and reduce large numbers of observations. Usually the reduction results in a few numbers, derived from mathematical formulas to represent all observations in each group of interest. Descriptive statistics portray and focus on *what is* with respect to the data, for example: "What is the average reading grade level of the fifth graders in the school?" "How many teachers found the in-service valuable?" "What percentage of students want to go to college?" and "What is the relationship between socioeconomic status of children and the effectiveness of token reinforcers?" The use of descriptive statistics is the most fundamental way to summarize data, and it is indispensable in interpreting the results of quantitative research.

Inferential statistics, on the other hand, are used to make inferences or predictions about the similarity of a sample to the population from which the sample is drawn. Since many research questions require the estimation of population characteristics from an available sample of subjects or behavior, inferential statistics are commonly used in reporting results. Chapter 10 discusses in greater detail the function and types of inferential statistics. Inferential statistics are dependent on descriptive statistics. Without a complete understanding of descriptive statistics, therefore, inferential statistics make very little sense.

There are many types of descriptive statistics that researchers may choose in characterizing a set of data. The choice usually depends on two factors: the type of measurement scale employed and the purpose of the research. The measurement scale is usually noted and, as indicated in the next section, there are descriptive statistical techniques that correspond to each scale. The purpose of the research, or research problem, actually depends on a knowledge of different statistical techniques, since each technique offers information for answering particular kinds of questions. Hence, each of the common descriptive techniques is presented here, with examples of the research problems it addresses.

Scales of Measurement

Measurement in education usually involves assigning numbers to things in order to differentiate one thing from another. Unlike measurement of physical phenomena, however, such as weight, density, or length, researchers can use numbers in different ways for investigating problems. These different ways are based on four properties of numbers. The four properties are: numbers can be distinct from one another (for example, 10 is different from 13; 0 is different from −5); numbers are relative to one another (for example, 13 is larger than 10; −3 less than 0); numbers can be related to each other in identified units (for example, 10 is five units of 2 greater than 5); and numbers can be related proportionately (for example, 10 is twice as large as 5; 25 is to 5 as 30 is to 6) (Hopkins & Glass, 1978). These properties, in turn, determine what psychometricians refer to as **measurement scales.** There are four *measurement scales:* nominal, ordinal, interval, and ratio.

Nominal Scales.   The first and most primitive level of measurement is called the **nominal,** or categorical, or classificatory **scale.** The word *nominal* implies *name,* which describes what this scale accomplishes—a naming of categories of people, events, or other phenomena. Common examples of nominal levels include differentiating on the basis of eye color, sex, political party affiliation, and type of reading group. The groups are simply names to differentiate them, there is no order implied (one group does not come before or after another), and there is no indication of the way the groups differ from each other. Often researchers assign numbers to the different groups (for example, yes = 1, no = 2, maybe = 3), but this is only for convenient coding of the groups in analyzing the data. Nominal data result in categorical variables.

Ordinal Scales.   The second type of measurement scale is called **ordinal,** and, as the name implies, measurement of this type assumes that values of the variable can be rank-ordered from highest to lowest. Each value can thus be related to others as being equal to, greater than, or less than. Examples of ordinal measurement include ranking class members by means of grade point average, ranking ideas from most important to least important, use of percentile ranks on achievement tests, and ordering scales of measurement from most primitive to highly refined. Ordinal scales generally result in continuous variables, in which the scores are derived from a theoretically infinite number of values between two points. It is also possible, however, to use continuous scores to make categories (such as when a researcher divides self-concept scores into high, medium, and low groups).

Interval Scales.   **Interval scales** share characteristics of ordinal scales and, in addition, indicate equal intervals between each number. Interval scales give meaning to the difference between numbers by providing a constant unit of measurement. The difference or interval between 5 and 6 is the same as the difference between 18 and 19. Percentile scores associated with the normal curve, for example, are not interval because the distance between percentile points varies depending on the percentiles that are compared. There is a greater difference between extreme percentiles (for example, 2nd and 3rd or 95th and 96th) than percentiles near the middle of the distribution. Examples of interval scales include Fahrenheit and Centigrade temperature and most standardized achievement test scores.

Ratio Scales.   **Ratio scales** represent the most refined type of measurement. Ratio scales are ordinal and interval, and in addition, the numbers can be compared by ratios: that is, a number can be compared meaningfully by saying it is twice or three times another number, or one-half or one-fourth of a number. Such observations as distance attained, strength expressed as weight lifted, or times in the mile run are ratio scale measurements. Most measurement in education, however, is not expressed as a ratio. Educators think in terms of *less than* or *greater than,* not multiples (for example, a student is more cooperative or less cooperative, not twice as cooperative or half as cooperative).

While it is not always easy to identify the scale of measurement of some variables, it is important to distinguish between nominal and higher levels. The use of many of the more common statistical procedures, such as the mean and variance, usually requires an interval or ratio scale of measurement, although an ordinal scale is sometimes acceptable. The choice of other, more advanced statistical procedures depends on whether the data are nominal or in the higher levels. If, for

FIGURE 6.1
Scales of Measurement

Scale		Characteristics	Examples
REFINED ↑	**RATIO**	Numbers represent equal units from absolute zero. Observations can be compared as ratios or percentages.	Distance, time, weight, Kelvin (absolute) temperature
	INTERVAL	Numbers represent equal units (intervals). Intervals between observations can be compared.	Year (A.D.), °F, °C
PRIMITIVE ↓	**ORDINAL**	Numbers indicate rank order of observations.	Percentile norms, social class
NOMINAL		Numbers represent categories. Numbers do not reflect differences in magnitude. Numbers serve to distinguish groups.	Sex, nationality, clinical diagnosis, college major

Source: From *Basic Statistics for the Behavioral Sciences* by Kenneth D. Hopkins and Gene V. Glass. Copyright © 1978 by Prentice-Hall, Inc. Reprinted by permission of Prentice-Hall, Inc., Englewood Cliffs, NJ.

example, a researcher wants to compare minority and nonminority students on the basis of their choices of careers, the data are nominal and certain statistical procedures would be appropriate for analyzing the data. If, on the other hand, these same students were being compared on achievement or attitudes toward school, a different set of statistical procedures would be appropriate because the scale of the achievement and attitude data is ordinal or interval. These differences will be discussed further in Chapter 10.

Figure 6.1 summarizes the characteristics and provides further examples of the four scales of measurement.

■ GRAPHIC PORTRAYALS OF DATA ■

When data are collected the observations must be organized so that the researcher can easily and correctly interpret the results. This section presents three common methods to pictorially represent group data.

TABLE 6.1
Unorganized Examination Scores
of Fifty Students

47	37	41	50	45
39	49	44	43	40
42	43	42	46	40
44	45	47	45	45
36	45	46	48	44
42	48	40	43	37
46	45	45	44	42
43	43	42	43	41
44	45	42	44	36
44	38	44	46	42

TABLE 6.2
Interval Frequency Distribution
of Scores in Table 6.1

Class Interval	Frequency (f)
48–50	4
45–47	14
42–44	21
39–41	6
36–38	5
	n =50

Frequency Distribution:
A Picture of a Group

In most studies there are many different scores, and if these scores are arrayed (arranged) without regard to their values, as in Table 6.1, it is difficult to make sense out of the data. The simplest organization of the scores would be to list them from

TABLE 6.3
Frequency Distribution of
Scores in Table 6.1

Scores in Rank Order	Tallies	Frequency (f)
50	1	1
49	1	1
48	11	2
47	11	2
46	1111	4
45	1111 111	8
44	1111 111	8
43	1111 1	6
42	1111 11	7
41	11	2
40	111	3
39	1	1
38	1	1
37	11	2
36	11	2
		n = 50

highest to lowest and create what is called a rank-order distribution. The rank-order distribution is transformed to a **frequency distribution** by indicating the number of times each score was attained, as indicated in Table 6.3.

It is also common to combine scores into class intervals and tally the number of scores in each interval, as indicated in Table 6.2. Intervals are especially useful for data in which few of the numbers are the same (such as ranking of states on median income).

Frequency distributions are very useful for answering many important questions. They indicate quickly the most and least frequently occurring scores; the general shape of the distribution (for example, clusters of scores at certain places or scores spread out evenly) and whether any scores are isolated from the others. In Excerpt 6.1 a frequency distribution is reported in a journal article to provide for the reader a general description of the results.

EXCERPT 6.1
Frequency Distribution

Some selected demographic characteristics of research participants are presented in Table 1. The respondents included 144 females (41.26%) and 205 males (58.74%), with the largest percentage of the sample (49.58%) falling within the 41 to 54 age range. Over 90% and 96%, respectively, report that they are heterosexual and Caucasian. There appears to be a concentration of research participants from the Northeast (45.27%), followed by the Central States (22.69%), with the least number of respondents from the Northwest (5.16%).

TABLE 1. Frequency and Percent of Selected Demographic Characteristics of Research Participants (N = 350)

Characteristics	N	%
Sex		
Female	144	41.26
Male	205	58.74
Age		
Under 25	0	0
25–40	91	26.00
41–54	175	49.58
55–65	70	20.06
Over 65	15	4.30
Sexual Orientation		
Bisexual	4	1.14
Homosexual	17	4.86
Heterosexual	321	91.70
Ethnicity		
Afro-American	4	1.15
Spanish American	1	.28
American Indian	1	.28
Asian	1	.28
Caucasian	337	96.28
Other	4	1.15
Geographic Region		
Northeast	158	45.27
Southeast	47	13.47
Central States	79	22.69
Northwest	18	5.16
Southwest	46	13.18

Source: From Alpert, J. L., Kaufman, J., and Gottsegen, G. B., "Prejudice and Discrimination Within the School Psychology Profession: Survey Results from the Committee on Prejudice and Discrimination," *Journal of School Psychology,* 19, 21–28, 1981. Reprinted by permission of Human Sciences Press.

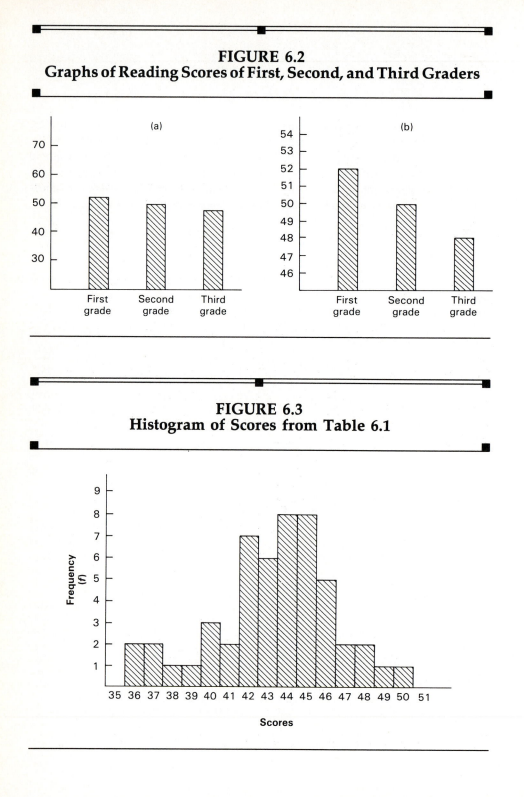

FIGURE 6.2
Graphs of Reading Scores of First, Second, and Third Graders

FIGURE 6.3
Histogram of Scores from Table 6.1

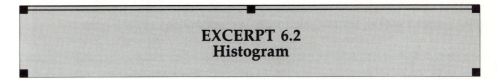

A histogram of the distribution of word recognition scores is presented in Figure 1. Subjects were divided into two groups. Those who learned the sounds in fewer than 10 trials are represented in white, those who took 10 or more trials, in black. From this figure, it is clear that there is very little overlap between the two groups of subjects. Those with large printed word repertoires learned the sounds easily. Those with small repertoires did not.

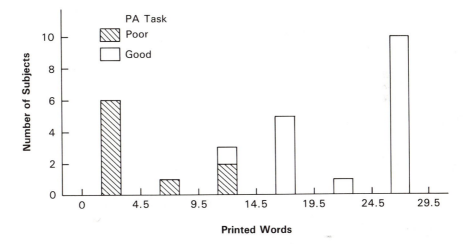

Figure 1. Distribution of good and poor sound learners on the printed-word identification task in Experiment 1. (PA = paired-associate learning.)

Source: From Ehri, L. C., & Wilce, L. S., "The mnemonic value of orthography among beginning readers," *Journal of Educational Psychology, 71,* 26–40. Copyright © 1979 by the American Psychological Association. Reprinted by permission of Linnea Carlson Ehri.

Histograms

Frequency data are often effectively displayed pictorially. One type of illustration uses columns or bars in a two-dimensional graph to represent the frequency of occurrence of each score or interval. This way of presenting a frequency distribution is called a **histogram.** The vertical dimension on the graph lists the frequencies of the scores, and the horizontal dimension rank-orders the scores from lowest to highest. The bars are drawn in the graph to correspond with the results. In our example, the data from Tables 6.1 and 6.2 are presented as a histogram in Figure 6.3. In similar fashion, Excerpt 6.2 shows how well a histogram can depict results in an article.

Histograms are effective because they provide an easily comprehended image of results. However, the image may be distorted by manipulating the spacing of numbers along the vertical dimension of the graph. The intervals between score frequencies can vary, and the size of the units that are used can be changed to give different images. For example, a crafty researcher can make a very small difference appear great by increasing the space between measurement units. Consider the two graphs in Figure 6.2. Each graph has summarized the same data, but the visual result is different.

Frequency Polygons

Another way to illustrate a frequency distribution is to use a **frequency polygon.** A frequency polygon is very similar to a bar graph except that single points rather than bars are graphed and these points are then connected by a line. Figure 6.4 shows our example data in a frequency polygon. Notice that this representation is very similar to Figure 6.3.

Finally, it is also useful to represent the distribution graphically by curving the straight lines of a frequency polygon. The well-known normal curve, discussed later in this chapter, is an example of using this technique.

■ MEASURES OF CENTRAL TENDENCY ■

For most sets of data it is useful to get some idea of the typical or average score or observation in addition to knowing the frequency distribution. While the word *average* has many connotations, in research only the mean refers to the average score. Two other indices, the median and mode, also provide information about typical scores of a group. Together, these three indices are referred to as **measures of central tendency.** Each provides a numerical index of the typical score of a distribution.

The Mean

The **mean** (symbolized by $\overline{X}$ or M) is simply the arithmetical average of all the scores. It is calculated by summing all the scores and then dividing the sum by the number of scores. If, for example, we have a distribution of 5, 8, 9, and 2, the mean is 6 ($5 + 8 + 9 + 2 = 24$; $24 \div 4 = 6$). The mean is the most frequently used measure of central tendency because every score is used in computing it. The weakness of the mean is that when a distribution contains extremely high or low scores, those very untypical of the rest of the distribution, the mean is pulled toward the extreme score. If, for example, a distribution contained scores of 4, 5, 7, and 40, the mean would be 14. Since in this case most of the scores are considera-

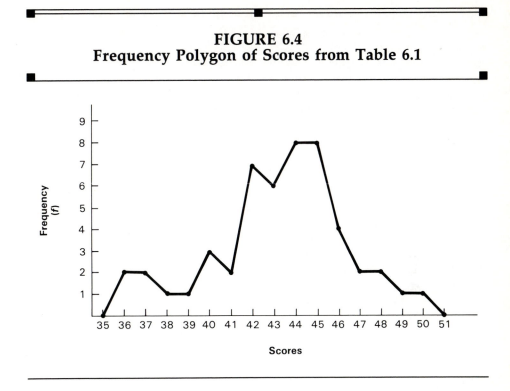

FIGURE 6.4
Frequency Polygon of Scores from Table 6.1

bly lower than 14, the mean is somewhat misleading with respect to central tendency.

The mean is almost always reported in research reports and is essential to the interpretation of results in which groups are compared to each other. Excerpt 6.3 illustrates the use of means in an article.

The Median

The **median** is that point which divides a rank-ordered distribution into halves that have an equal number of scores. Fifty percent of the scores thus lie below the median and fifty percent of the scores above it. The median is unaffected by the actual values of the scores. This is an advantage when a distribution contains atypically large or small scores. The median, for example, of the set of scores 10, 15, 16, 19, and 105 is 16, since half the scores are above 16 and half below. Sixteen would thus be a better indicator of central tendency than the mean, which is 33. If a distribution contains an even number of scores, the median is the midpoint between the two middle scores (for example, for the scores 2, 2, 4, 7, 8, and 12, the median is 5.5).

EXCERPT 6.3
The Mean

The means for the three testing periods are given in Table 3. They show a decrease in the number and percentage of cross-racial friendship choices in the control class from pre- to posttest and an increase over that period in the experimental class.

TABLE 3. Follow-up Sociometric Measures

	Mean number of friendship choices					
	Control[a]			Experimental[b]		
Measure	Pretest	Posttest	Follow-up	Pretest	Posttest	Follow-up
Within-race	5.95	6.37	7.35	4.00	3.77	4.00
Cross-race	2.65	1.58	.80	1.62	2.73	2.44
Percentage	30.8	19.9	9.8	28.8	37.2	37.9

[a]$n = 20$.   [b]$n = 16$.

Source: From "Effects of biracial learning teams on cross-racial friendships" by Robert E. Slavin. *Journal of Educational Psychology*, 71, 1979. Reprinted by permission of the author.

The median is used to describe data that may have extreme scores, such as income level in the United States. Medians also are often employed to divide one group of respondents into two groups of equal numbers. A researcher may, for example, get an indication of perceived degree of success from each respondent on a 7-point scale (extreme success = 7, extreme failure = 1). If the researcher wanted to divide the group of subjects into those with high and low self-perceptions of success, the median could be used. This procedure is called a median-split technique. Excerpt 6.4 shows how the median can be used in reporting research.

The Mode

The **mode** is simply the score that occurs most frequently in a distribution. The mode is a crude index of central tendency and is rarely used in educational research. It is only useful when there is an interest in knowing the most common score or observation or when the data are in nominal form. The word *mode* is used more frequently, perhaps, to describe a distribution by indicating that the distribution is bimodal (two modes) or trimodal (three modes). These terms are used even when, technically, there is only one mode but at least two scores that have definitely higher frequencies than the rest.

EXCERPT 6.4
The Median

One trend in families that has clear implications for educational needs within urban communities is the decrease in financial resources that all families are now experiencing, with an even greater impact in ethnic minority urban families. The latest reported nationwide median income of white families was $18,370, for Hispanics $12,570, and for Blacks $10,880 (ACYF, 1980). While 16% of all children are below the poverty level, a Black child has a 4-times greater chance of being under this level, for 11% of whites and 42% of Blacks live in poverty (Edelman, 1980).

Single mothers had median incomes that were much lower than the total and that earned by two-parent families; Black mothers had a median income that was only 40% that of the two-parent families; Hispanics had 39%, and white mothers had 38% of the two-parent incomes. The lower proportion of white mothers is due to the fact that almost half of white mothers do not work, in spite of the marked increase of white urban employment (see Table 1).

TABLE 1. Median Income and Percentage of Ethnic Groups Unemployed and Below Poverty Line

Year		Black	Hispanic	White
1977	**Husband, wife, family**			
		13,832	13,432	18,756
	Single mothers			
		5,598	5,247	8,799
1978		10,880	12,570	18,370

Source: From McAdoo, H. P., "Youth, school, and the family in transition." *Urban Education*, 16, 261–277. Copyright © 1981 by *Urban Education*. Reprinted by permission of Sage Publications, Inc.

Relationships Among Measures of Central Tendency

As long as a distribution of scores is relatively symmetrical, the mean, median, and mode will be about the same. In what is referred to as a **normal distribution,** these indices are exactly the same. The normal distribution (see Figure 6.8) forms a bell-shaped symmetrical curve. The normal curve is the theoretical distribution that is used to transform data and calculate many statistics. While many educational variables—for example, large numbers of achievement scores—are normally distributed, the data from a single research study may be distributed ab-

FIGURE 6.5
Skewed Distributions

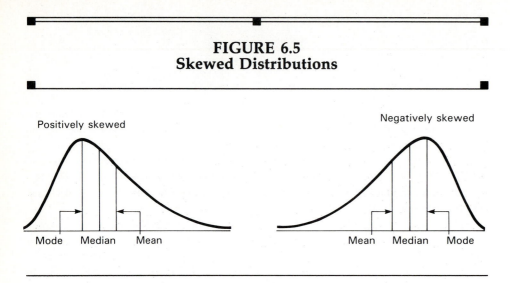

normally; that is, the distributions are unsymmetrical, and the scores tend to bunch up at one end of the distribution or the other. Such abnormal distributions are called **skewed,** and with skewed distributions the choice of measure of central tendency becomes more important. Distributions are called **positively skewed** if most of the scores are at the low end of the distribution, and **negatively skewed** if most scores are located at the high end. To help remember the difference between positive and negative skew, think of the curved shape of the distribution forming an arrow or pointer. If it points in a positive or higher direction the distribution is positively skewed, and if in a negative or lower direction the distribution is negatively skewed. In Figure 6.5, positively and negatively skewed distributions are illustrated with corresponding means, medians, and modes. Notice that the mean in each distribution is further toward the tail of the distribution than the median or mode, and the mode is furthest from the tail.

To further illustrate this relationship, consider the following example. Suppose a teacher wants to report an average reading score for his class. He has a reading score for each of 20 students, ranging from 5 to 90. The distribution of scores is represented in Table 6.4.

If the teacher reports the average as the mean, it would be 22.7. The median is 10, and the mode is 5. Which is correct? Because of a few students who scored very well (80) the distribution is positively skewed, and hence the median is probably the most accurate single indicator. In such cases, however, it is probably best to report the mean for the students who scored between 5 and 15 (8.4) and report the four high scores separately, or to report both the mean and median. Since many distributions in education are at least somewhat skewed, it is often best to report both the mean and median.

TABLE 6.4
Frequency Distribution of Reading Scores

Scores	(f)
5	8
10	4
12	2
15	2
80	4
	n = 20

■ MEASURES OF VARIABILITY ■

Central tendency is only one index used to represent a group of scores. In order to provide a full description, a second statistical measure is also needed. This statistic is referred to as a **measure of variability.** Measures of variability show how spread out the distribution of scores is from the mean of the distribution, or, how much, on the average, scores differ from the mean. Variability measures are also referred to in general terms as measures of dispersion, scatter, or spread.

The need for a measure of dispersion is illustrated in Figure 6.6. This figure shows how two classrooms with the same mean score can actually be very different. In class B the students are rather homogeneous, similar to each other, with few high or low achieving students. In class A, however, the teacher has a great range of achievement, a heterogeneous group of students whose scores spread from 55 to 100.

Or suppose a person is going to bet on Saturday's basketball game between the Bombers and the Dunkers. The sports section of the newspaper lacks the statistics on individual players, but the sports writer reports that both teams have approximately equal height, and the average height is 6'5" and 6'7", respectively, for the Bombers and Dunkers. With only the mean to help decide, the bettor places a bet on the Dunkers. When the bettor sees the program with the heights of the players, he or she discovers a shortcoming of the mean.

Bombers	*Dunkers*
Leary, guard—6'3"	Britt, guard—6'4"
Burns, guard—6'5"	Lambiotte, guard—6'6"
Parker, forward—6'7"	Hambrick, forward—6'8"
Selby, forward—6'7"	Lang, forward—6'8"
Wolf, center—7'3"	Monahan, center—6'9"
$\overline{X}$ = 6'5"	$\overline{X}$ = 6'7"

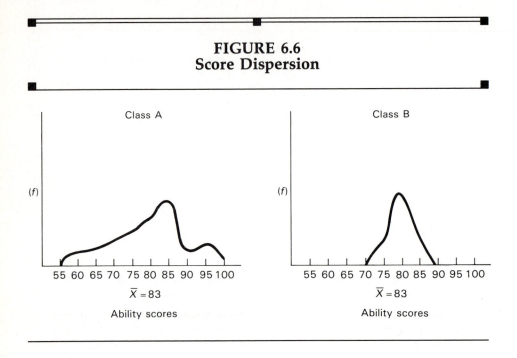

FIGURE 6.6
Score Dispersion

As the Bombers' offensive proceeds to take advantage of Wolf's height over Monahan's to score, the bettor realizes that the mean fails to tell about the characteristics of the distribution. The Dunkers have little variability, while the Bombers have high variability, and so the bettor loses the bet!

Variability, then, tells us about the difference between the scores of the distribution. While we can use such words as *high, low, great, little,* and *much* to describe the degree of variability, it is necessary to have more precise indices. Three common measures of variability are the range, standard deviation, and variance.

The Range

The **range** is the most obvious measure of dispersion. It is simply the difference between the highest and lowest scores in the distribution. If, for example, the lowest of 30 scores on a test was 65 and the highest score 90, the range would be 25 (90 − 65 = 25). Since there are only two scores involved in calculating the range, it is very simple to obtain. It is, however, also a very crude measure of dispersion, and can be misleading if there is an atypical high or low score. The range also fails to indicate anything about the variability of scores around the mean of the distribution.

Standard Deviation

The **standard deviation** is a numerical index that indicates the average variability of the scores. It tells us, in other words, about the distance, on the average, of the scores from the mean. A distribution that has a relatively heterogeneous set of scores that spread out widely from the mean (for example, Class A of Figure 6.6) will have a larger standard deviation than a homogeneous set of scores that cluster around the mean (Class B of Figure 6.5). The first step in calculating the standard deviation (abbreviated *SD*, σ [sigma], or *s*) is to find the distance between each score and the mean, thus determining the amount that each score deviates, or differs, from the mean. In one sense, the standard deviation is simply the average of all the deviation scores.

For any set of scores, then, a standard deviation can be computed that will be unique to the distribution and indicates the amount, on the average, that the set of scores deviates from the mean. (Appendix B reviews the steps for computing the standard deviation. The steps are not complex.) The most common convention in reporting the standard deviation is to indicate that one standard deviation is equal to some number (for example, $SD = 15.0$; $σ = 3.40$). One standard deviation added to and subtracted from the mean has a special meaning; it tells us about the distance that most, but not all, of the scores are from the mean. For example, 68 percent of the scores will fall within the first standard deviation. This property of standard deviation is illustrated in Figure 6.7, where $1\ SD = 5$. Notice that on both sides of the mean (15) there is a line that designates $-1\ SD$ and $+1\ SD$. The negative and positive directions from the mean are equivalent in score units (that is, both $-$ and $+\ 1\ SD = 5$ units) and between -1 and $+1\ SD$ there are about 68 percent of the total number of scores in the distribution. If we assume that the distribution is normal, then 50 percent of the scores are above the mean and 50 percent below the mean. Now since we know there is an equal number of scores on either side of the mean, we know that 34 percent of the scores must be between the mean and $-$ or $+\ 1\ SD$, and if 50 percent of the scores are below the mean and we add 34 percent by going up $+\ 1\ SD$, then we know that about 84 percent of the scores of the distribution are below $+1\ SD$. Similarly, if we subtract 34 from 50, we know that 16 percent of the scores are below $-1\ SD$.

When we indicate that a certain percentage of the scores is at or below a particular score, we are referring to the **percentile rank** of the score. If, for example, a score of 38 is at the 87th percentile, it means that 87 percent of the scores are the same as or lower than 38. In other words, only 13 percent of the scores are higher than 38. With approximately normal distributions $+\ 1\ SD$ is always at the 84th percentile, and $-\ 1\ SD$ is at the 16th percentile.

The interpretation of $1\ SD$ is always the same with regard to the percentage of scores in the distribution. Because the numerical units used to represent scores changes, however, the standard deviation can equal 15 in one distribution and 0.32 in another distribution. Or, in a circumstance with the same numerical units

FIGURE 6.7
Relation of Standard Deviation to Percentile Rank

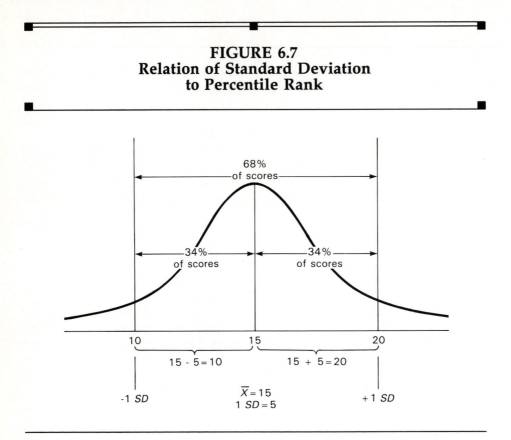

but two different distributions, the standard deviations will be unique to each distribution.

Along with the mean, the standard deviation is an excellent way to indicate the nature of the distribution of a set of scores. Standard deviation is typically reported in research with the mean. A measure of dispersion related to the standard deviation is termed the *variance* of a distribution (noted by $\sigma^2 s^2$; thus the standard deviation is equal to the square root of the variance). The term *variance*, however, is usually used as a general term in regard to dispersion (for example, in stating that the variance is large or small), and is rarely reported as a specific number to indicate variability.

In Excerpts 6.5 and 6.6 there are examples of the way standard deviation can be reported. In Excerpt 6.5 the first line in the table would be read as follows: The mean score of preadolescent male subjects on self-esteem was 13.38, with a standard deviation of 4.13, on the first assessment, and 13.27, with a standard deviation of 5.00, on the second measure. For early adolescent male subjects, the first assessment showed a mean of 13.55, standard deviation 4.76, and the second assessment 14.64 ($SD = 4.91$), and so on.

EXCERPT 6.5
Standard Deviation

Attitude Instrument Means and Standard Deviations by Sex and Group

	Group					
	Preadolescent		Early adolescent		Later adolescent	
Instrument	Time 1	Time 2	Time 1	Time 2	Time 1	Time 2
Male subjects						
Self-esteem						
M	13.38	13.27	13.55	14.64	16.07	15.40
SD	4.13	5.00	4.76	4.91	5.13	5.27
Locus of control						
M	17.49	15.80	15.38	16.38	12.29	12.44
SD	3.55	6.30	4.99	5.36	4.84	5.63
Achievement motivation						
M	97.52	92.36	76.75	85.79	73.17	90.39
SD	12.52	15.40	30.88	11.79	38.49	10.34
Female subjects						
Self-esteem						
M	14.13	13.43	13.73	13.80	15.44	16.34
SD	4.73	4.73	5.10	5.64	5.61	5.78
Locus of control						
M	17.65	15.43	14.30	14.24	10.64	10.87
SD	4.18	5.64	4.52	5.33	5.24	5.74
Achievement motivation						
M	95.55	94.79	88.40	90.42	86.52	92.60
SD	21.52	15.82	15.10	13.42	28.34	13.19

Source: From Prawat, R. S., Jones, H., and Hampton, J. "Longitudinal study of attitude development in pre-, early, and later adolescent samples," *Journal of Educational Psychology*, 71, 363–369. Copyright © 1979 by the American Psychological Association. Reprinted by permission of the publisher and authors.

Standard Scores

You may have observed that it is cumbersome to analyze several distributions if the means and standard deviations are different for each distribution. To alleviate this problem and expedite interpretation, the raw score distributions are often converted to standard scores. **Standard scores** have constant normative or rela-

---

EXCERPT 6.6
Standard Deviation

Table III shows the means and standard deviations of the aptitude and outcome scores of students in all classes. Means and standard deviations of the aptitude scores were similar across the four classes. Students' attitude toward mathematics decreased between pre- and posttest in all four classes. In all classes the average score on the immediate and delayed test was about the same.

TABLE III. Means and Standard Deviations of Aptitudes and Outcomes

	Small-group		Direct	
	1	2	1	2
Class of teacher: Variable	(*N* = 26)	(*N* = 32)	(*N* = 27)	(*N* = 28)
STEP-math computation	40.57	41.44	40.63	41.52
	(8.32)	(8.27)	(9.64)	(7.88)
Raven's Progressive Matrices	37.48	37.69	40.19	38.04
	(9.31)	(9.38)	(8.09)	(8.43)
Attitude toward math pretest	49.83	50.66	45.70	47.93
	(8.59)	(10.73)	(12.14)	(11.21)
Locus of control	69.91	71.25	66.44	71.64
	(8.27)	(10.62)	(12.96)	(8.50)
Preference for learning in small groups	4.04	4.06	3.86	3.96
	(2.25)	(2.20)	(1.98)	(2.17)
Achievement posttest	23.65	23.66	19.85	27.75
	(9.66)	(9.71)	(9.41)	(9.05)
Retention test	23.22	22.44	20.48	26.57
	(9.10)	(9.51)	(10.14)	(9.43)
Attitude toward math posttest	42.52	45.41	42.30	43.86
	(8.84)	(11.06)	(12.06)	(9.72)
Attitude toward teaching approach	20.13	30.03	23.59	30.93
	(8.06)	(5.60)	(6.72)	(5.11)

Note. Numbers in parentheses are standard deviations.

---

tive meaning. They are scores that are obtained from the mean and standard deviation of the raw score distribution, and they are changed in such a way as to represent a normal distribution.

Because, as we have seen, a normal distribution has certain properties that are useful for comparing a person's score with those of others, by converting to standard scores the normal curve properties can be assumed. Thus, raw score

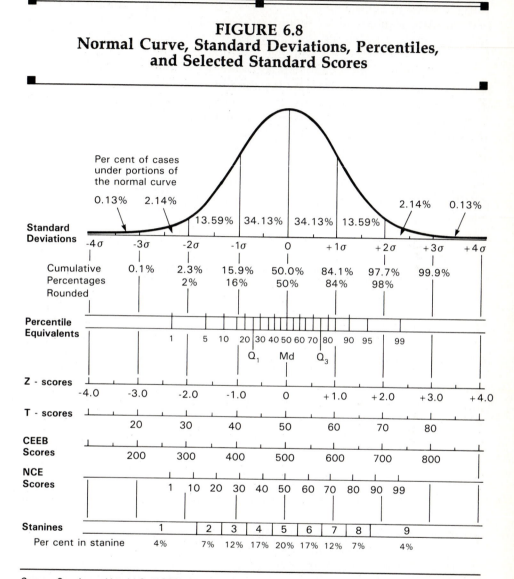

FIGURE 6.8
Normal Curve, Standard Deviations, Percentiles, and Selected Standard Scores

Source: Seashore, Harold G. (1980). Methods of expressing test scores, in *Test Service Notebook 148.* New York: The Psychological Corporation.

distributions that may have different means and standard deviations that are difficult to compare can be transformed to the same standard scores and compared easily. Since standard scores are linear transformations, it is conceivable that a small raw score difference is exaggerated when converted to standard scores. For example, the Scholastic Aptitude Test has a standard score mean of 500 and standard deviation of 100, while the raw scores are much lower. Thus a raw score difference of 2 or 3 questions may result in a standard score difference of 10 to 20 "points." Also, standard scores should only be used when the raw scores approximate a normal distribution. A highly skewed raw score distribution that is converted to standard scores will give misleading results.

The **z-score** is the most basic standard score, with a mean of 0 and a standard deviation of 1. Thus, a z-score of $+1$ is at the 84th percentile, -1 is at the 16th percentile, and -2 is at the 2nd percentile. Other standard scores are linear transformations from the z-score, with arbitrarily selected means and standard deviations. That is, it is possible to choose any mean and any standard deviation. Most IQ tests, for example, use 100 as the mean and from 15 to 16 as the standard deviation. The resultant IQ score is a standard score (the ration IQ, mental age divided by chronological age X 100, is rarely used today). Figure 6.8 shows a normal distribution, standard deviations, percentiles, and some common standard scores.

■　MEASURES OF RELATIONSHIP　■

Up to this point we have been discussing descriptive statistics that are used to summarize or give a picture of groups on one variable at a time. There are, however, many questions of interest that are dependent on the way two or more variables are related to each other within a group of scores. Are brighter students more motivated? If we increase the frequency of reinforcement, will the reinforced or target behavior also increase? Is there a relationship between self-concept and achievement? If students exert more effort in studying, will they feel better about their achievement? In each instance, two variables are measured for each subject in the group.

Scatter Plot

The most fundamental measure of relationship is called a scatter plot or scatter diagram. The **scatter plot** is a graphic representation of the relationship, achieved by forming a visual array of the intersection of each subject's scores on the two variables. As illustrated in Figure 6.9, one variable is rank-ordered on the horizontal axis (age, in this example) and the second variable is rank-ordered on the vertical axis (weight). Each subject's scores are indicated next to the graph and the intersections noted by the number assigned each subject. Together, the intersections form a pattern that provides a general indication of the nature of the relationship. Obviously, as children grow older their weight increases, and in such cases the relationship is said to be positive or direct. Thus, with a **positive relationship,** as the value of one variable increases, it is accompanied by increases in the second variable. Conversely, as the value of one variable decreases, the value of the other variable also decreases.

FIGURE 6.9
Scatter Plot

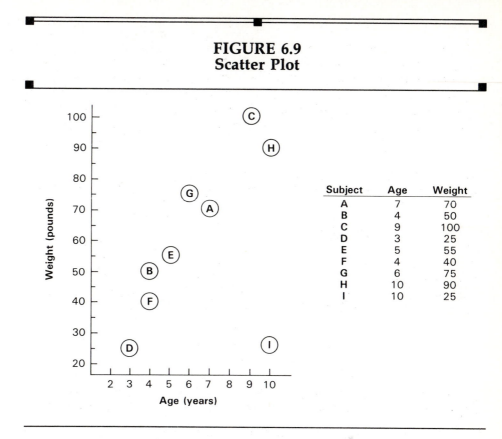

Subject	Age	Weight
A	7	70
B	4	50
C	9	100
D	3	25
E	5	55
F	4	40
G	6	75
H	10	90
I	10	25

Scatter plots are useful in identifying scores that are very atypical (outliers) as compared to the overall pattern. For instance, in Figure 6.9, if a subject who was 10 years old reported a weight of 25 pounds, the intersection would be quite different from what is represented in points A–I. In such cases the researcher might look for errors in scoring, measurement, or recording of data, since the scores represented by the outlier are unlikely. Scatter diagrams also provide a first hint about whether the relationship is linear or curvilinear (see Figure 6.10). (The usual approach in graphing relationships is to use dots, not circles, within the graph at the intersections.)

A number of different types of patterns can emerge in scatter plots. In a case in which one variable decreases as the other increases (for example, the number of miles on a tire and the depth of remaining tread), there is a **negative** or inverse **relationship.** If there is no pattern at all in the graph, there is no relationship. Figure 6.10 illustrates different scatter diagrams. Notice the curvilinear relationship in Figure 6.10(d). Curvilinear relationships are not uncommon but are usually detected only by plotting the scores. An example of a curvilinear relationship might be anxiety level and test performance. Performance could often be low during either high or low anxiety and high for medium level anxiety.

FIGURE 6.10
Scatter Plots of Relationships

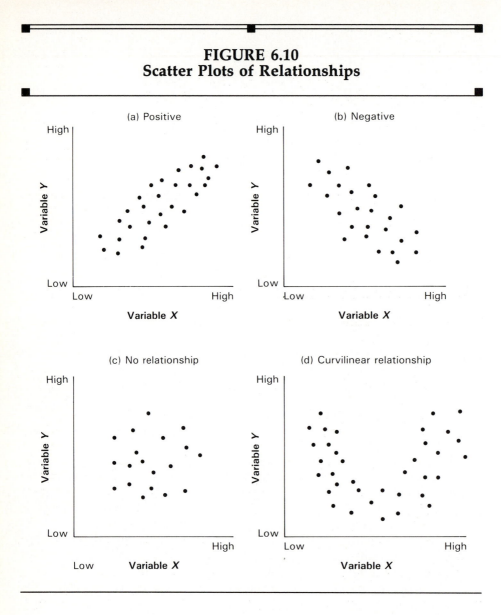

The direction of the pattern in the scatter plot, then, indicates whether there is a relationship and whether the relationship is positive, negative, or curvilinear. If a line is drawn through the plotted dots to minimize the distance of each dot to the line (technically called a regression line), then the degree of clustering around the line indicates the strength of the relationship. Plots that have mostly scattered dots have weak or low relationships, while dots clustered near the line indicate a strong or high relationship. The strength of the relationship is independent of its direction. Dots clustered so tightly as to form a straight line represent a perfect relationship (maximum strength). Correlations thus indicate three things: whether there is any relationship at all; the direction of the relationship; and the strength of the relationship.

Correlation Coefficient[1]

Even though graphs are indispensable tools for evaluating the relationship between two variables, researchers rarely report such graphs in published articles. The typical convention is to calculate a number to represent the relationship, called a **correlation coefficient.** There are many types of correlation coefficients, and the choice of the one to use is determined by the scale used in data collection and the research question. The interpretation of the number used, however, is basically the same. The number that represents the correlation can range from -1.00 to $+1.00$. A high positive value (for example, 0.85, 0.90, 0.90, 0.96) represents a high positive relationship; a low positive value (0.15, 0.20, 0.08) a low positive relationship; a moderate negative value (for example, -0.40, -0.37, -0.52) a moderate negative relationship, a value of 0 denotes no relationship, and so on. Thus the strength of the relationship becomes higher as the correlation approaches either $+1$ or -1 from zero. This is illustrated in Figure 6.11. Note that strength is independent of direction.

The most common correlation technique is the Pearson product-moment coefficient (represented by r), and the correlation is indicated by $r = 0.65$, $r = 0.78$, $r = 0.03$, and so on. (Notice that there is no plus sign before positive values, but there is a negative sign for negative values.) The product-moment correlation is used when both of the variables use continuous scales, such as scores from achievement tests, GPA, self-concept inventories, and age. Since scores can also be reported as dichotomies, in several categories, or ranks, other correlation techniques, depending on the scale for the variables, are used to measure the relationship. Some of these techniques are summarized in Table 6.5.

Excerpts 6.7 and 6.8 show how to report correlational data. In Excerpt 6.7, there is a list of all correlations of interest in the study. In Excerpt 6.8 there is an **intercorrelation matrix,** in which many variables are correlated with each other. The numbers in a row on top of the table correspond to the variables listed vertically on the left. The correlation of sex with itself is thus 1.000 (or perfect) and with marital status is 0.012; the correlation of undergraduate average with curriculum grade is 0.330.

---

[1]This discussion is limited to simple correlation. More advanced correlational procedures, such as multiple correlation, partial correlation, discriminant function analysis, and canonical correlation, are based on these principles to examine the combined relationships of several variables.

TABLE 6.5
Types of Correlation Coefficients

Type of Coefficient	Symbol	Types of Variable
Pearson Product-moment	r	Both continuous
Spearman rho	P	Both rank ordered
Biserial	r_{bis}	One continuous, one an artificial dichotomy
Point-biserial	r_{pbis}	One continuous, one a true dichotomy
Tetrachoric	r^t	Both artificial dichotomies
Phi coefficient	Ø	Both true dichotomies
Contingency coefficients	C	Both 2 or more categories
Correlation ratio, eta	η	Both continuous (used with curvilinear relationships)

FIGURE 6.11
Relationship of Strength and
Direction of Correlations

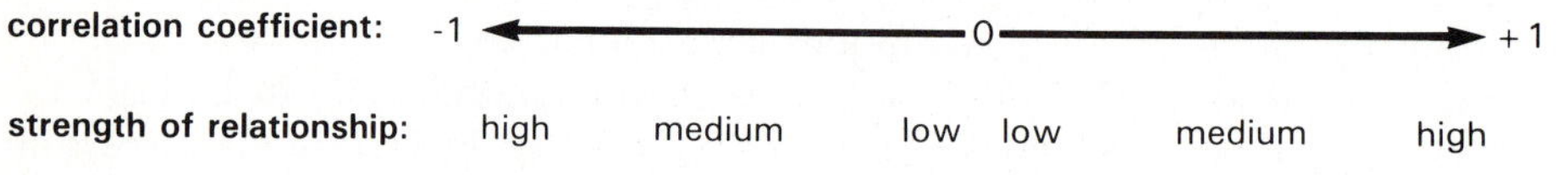

correlation coefficient: -1 ←————————— 0 —————————→ $+1$

strength of relationship: high   medium   low low   medium   high

In Chapter 8 we will discuss important principles of interpretation of correlation coefficients. Note that correlation coefficients are only appropriate for describing linear relationships; other statistics are used for determining the presence of and significance of curvilinear relationships.

EXCERPT 6.7
Pearson Product-Moment Correlation

As presented in Table 3, correlations between the four self-report scales and language score range from .11 to .33 and from .42 to .55 for teacher-ratings. The range for the two sets of correlations for work-study is .08 to .30 and .30 to .48 for self-report and teacher-ratings, respectively. The correlations between self-report scores and the two mathematics scores are almost the same; they range from .08 to .27 and from .07 to .28 respectively. The corresponding correlations for teacher ratings range from .25 to .50 and .22 to .45.

TABLE 3. Correlations of Attitude Measures with Achievement Scores

		Achievement			
Method	**Scale**	**Language**	**Work Study**	**Arithmetic**	**New Math**
Self-report	School	.33	.23	.22	.21
	Teacher	.26	.15	.17	.15
	Self	.33	.30	.27	.28
	Independence	.11	.08	.08	.07
	Multiple R	.41	.35	.31	.32
	N	236			
Teacher-rating	School	.50	.44	.37	.37
	Teacher	.42	.30	.25	.22
	Self	.50	.47	.42	.36
	Independence	.55	.48	.50	.45
	Multiple R	.57	.53	.52	.48
	N	60			
Pictures with explicit instructions	Teacher (1)[a]	−.13	−.14	−.10	−.18
	Teacher (2)	.19	.12	.03	−.05
	School (3)	.21	.16	.03	−.04
	School (4)	.45	.29	.08	.16
	School (5)	.13	.07	−.01	.10
	N	201			
Pictures with implicit instructions	Teacher (1)	−.04	−.02	−.02	−.10
	Teacher (2)	.13	.03	.05	.09
	School (3)	.02	−.05	.06	.04
	School (4)	.32	.24	.38	.29
	School (5)	.26	.21	.19	.21
	N	138			

[a]Item numbers are reported in parentheses.

Source: From Kahn, S. B., "A Comparative Study of Assessing Children's School Related Attitudes," *Journal of Educational Measurement,* 15, 59–66. Copyright © 1978, National Council on Measurement in Education. Reprinted by permission.

EXCERPT 6.8
Intercorrelation Matrix

Table 2 shows the correlations between variables.

   Some interesting relationships were observed among the pre-admission and intraining variables. Females tended to have higher undergraduate averages than males; this may reflect the fact that teaching has traditionally had higher occupational status for females than for males. The students with honors degrees generally had lower undergraduate averages than those with general degrees. Perhaps the more able general degree students seek to become teachers along with the less able honors graduates. As would be expected, undergraduate grades partially predicted grades in teacher education courses. The interview appeared to favor both married students and honors graduates; possibly such students are seen as having greater maturity, self-confidence, or commitment. Curriculum and practice teaching grades are relatively strongly related, as might be expected, many curriculum instructors inevitably being influenced in their grading by their knowledge of their students' success or failure in practice teaching.

TABLE 2. Correlations between Variables

	1	2	3	4	5	6	7	8	9
1	1.000								
2	.012	1.000							
3	−.008	.332**	1.000						
4	.248*	−.034	−.172	1.000					
5	−.135	.220	.148	−.252*	1.000				
6	−.026	.245*	.135	−.002	.279*	1.000			
7	.091	.094	−.030	.330**	−.084	.070	1.000		
8	.071	.203	.045	.132	−.195	.175	.456**	1.000	
9	−.113	.069	−.089	−.092	.268*	.369**	.062	.076	1.000

1　Sex (1M, 2F)	6　Interview score
2　Marital Status (1S, 2M)	7　Curriculum grade
3　Age	8　Practice teaching grade
4　Undergraduate average	9　Survival
5　Degree (1 general, 2 honors)	
	*　significant at .05
	**　significant at .01

Source: From "Predicting Teacher Survival" by David Pratt, *The Journal of Educational Research,* Vol. 71, No. 1, September/October 1977, p. 15. Reprinted by with permission of the Helen Dwight Reid Educational Foundation. Published by Heldref Publications, 4000 Albemarle St., N.W., Washington, DC 20016. Copyright © 1977.

■ SUMMARY ■

This chapter has introduced fundamental principles of descriptive statistics. The statistical procedures are used in one way or another in nearly all quantitative research studies. The major points that are covered are summarized below.

1. Descriptive statistics are indices that summarize or characterize a larger number of observations.
2. Measurement scales (nominal, ordinal, interval, and ratio) and the purpose of the research suggest the descriptive statistics that are appropriate.
3. Frequency distributions in the form of rank order, class intervals, histograms, or frequency polygons provide an overview picture of all the data.
4. Measures of central tendency include the mean, median, and mode. Each measure provides a numerical index of the typical score in the distribution.
5. The mean is the best measure of central tendency for distributions that have no extremely high or low scores; the median is best for highly skewed data. Often, both the mean and the median should be reported.
6. Measures of variability indicate the spread of scores from the mean of the distribution.
7. Standard deviation is a measure of variability peculiar to each distribution that indicates, on the average, how much scores deviate from the mean.
8. Standard scores are converted raw score distributions with common units to indicate the mean and the standard deviation.
9. Scatter plots are used to indicate the general direction and strength of a relationship between two variables in one group or sample.
10. Correlation coefficients are numbers that represent the direction and strength of the relationship between two or more variables.

■ SELF-INSTRUCTIONAL REVIEW EXERCISES ■

Sample answers are in the back of the book.

Test Items

1. Which of the following statements is true (more than one may be true) concerning descriptive statistics?
   a. Descriptive statistics are used to summarize data.
   b. Descriptive statistics are used to infer population characteristics from a sample.
   c. Descriptive statistics are not needed to interpret inferential statistics.
   d. Correlation coefficients are descriptive statistics.
   e. The choice of descriptive statistics depends on the purpose of the research and size of the sample.

2. Scales of measurement that provide categories without order are called
   a. interval.   c. nominal.
   b. nonordinal.   d. ratio.

3. Percentile scores are examples of a scale of measurement called
   a. nominal.   c. ordinal.
   b. interval.   d. ratio.

4. Frequency distributions are represented by all of the following except
   a. histograms.   c. normal curve.
   b. polygons.   d. rank-order grouping.

5. The _____ is the most widely used measure of central tendency.
   a. mean   c. standard deviation
   b. median   d. mode

6. Given the following scores: 4, 7, 7, 8, 10, 12, 12, 12, 18; the mean is
   _____; the median is _____; and the mode is _____.
   a. 8, 12, 10   d. 10, 10, 10
   b. 8, 10, 12   e. 12, 12, 12
   c. 10, 10, 12

7. The average amount of dispersion of a set of scores around the mean is assessed numerically by the
   a. range.   c. percentile ranks.
   b. standard deviation.   d. median.

8. Plus one standard deviation is always at about the _____ percentile in a
   normal distribution.
   a. 60th   c. 90th
   b. 50th   d. 84th

9. Which of the following correlations shows the strongest relationship?
   a. 0.50   c. 0.67
   b. − 0.75   d. − 0.30

10. A good reason to graph correlations is to find
    a. curvilinear relationships.   c. negative relationships.
    b. positive relationships.   d. both a and b.

Application Problems

1. For each case below, choose the most appropriate statistical procedure.
   a. A teacher of a low reading group is interested in what the average score
      is for the group of 25 students.

b. An administration wants to find out if there is a relationship between teacher absences and student achievement.
c. A math teacher wants to know how many ability groups should be formed within a class of 30 students.
d. A student teacher is interested in the number of students who rate his performance as good, excellent, average, or poor.

2. Identify the scale of measurement in each of the following:
   a. attitudes toward school.
   b. grouping students on the basis of hair color.
   c. asking judges to rank order students from most cooperative to least cooperative.

CHAPTER 7

DATA COLLECTION
TECHNIQUES

■ KEY TERMS ■

content-related evidence
criterion-related evidence
concurrent evidence
predictive evidence
construct-related evidence
reliability
stability
test-retest
equivalence
internal consistency
split-half
Kuder-Richardson
Cronbach Alpha
standardized tests
norm-referenced tests
criterion-referenced tests
aptitude test
achievement test
noncognitive instruments
questionnaire
double-barrelled questions
biased
social desirability
closed form

open form
scaled items
Likert scale
Semantic Differential
rank-order
checklist
contingency questions
inter-rater agreement
structured questions
semistructured questions
unstructured questions
leading questions
probing
complete observer
high inference
low inference
duration recording
frequency-count recording
interval recording
continuous observation
time sampling
nonreactive research
unobtrusive measurement

This chapter elaborates on principles of validity and reliability as important considerations of the quality of measures and presents the characteristics of five major techniques for gathering quantitative data: tests, questionnaires, interviews, observation, and unobtrusive measures. The advantages and disadvantages of each type are discussed in relation to the objectives of research problems and procedures employed with each technique. These techniques are used in different types of research, as defined by both purpose and research design. Once the purpose of the research and constraints of the research situation are clear, a particular technique is chosen to fit the research design. No single technique is best, easiest, or most convenient.

■ FUNDAMENTALS OF QUANTITATIVE ■ MEASUREMENT

Quantitative measurement involves using some type of instrument or device to obtain numerical indices that correspond to characteristics of the subjects. The numerical values are then summarized and reported as the results of the study. Consequently, the results depend heavily on the quality of the measurement. If the measure is weak or biased, then so are the results. Conversely, strong measures increase confidence that the findings are accurate. It is imperative, then, to understand what makes measurement "strong" or "weak." Whether you need to choose instruments to conduct a study or evaluate results, it is necessary to understand what affects the quality of the measure. In this section two technical concepts of measurement, validity and reliability, are discussed as important criteria for determining quality.

Validity

As indicated in Chapter 5, validity is the extent to which inferences made on the basis of numerical scores are appropriate, meaningful, and useful. Validity is a judgment of the appropriateness of a measure for specific inferences or decisions that result from the scores generated. In other words, validity is a situation-specific concept: validity is assessed depending on the purpose, population, and environmental characteristics in which measurement takes place. A test can therefore be valid in one situation and invalid in another. Consequently, in order to assure others that the procedures have validity in relation to the research problems, subjects, and setting of the study, it is incumbent on the investigator to describe the validity of the instruments used to collect data.

The new *Standards for Educational and Psychological Testing* (1985) is clear in indicating that an *inference* is valid or invalid not a test. A test by itself is not valid or invalid because it can be used for different purposes. For example, a college entrance test may lead to valid inferences about future performance as an undergraduate, but to invalid inferences about the quality of the high school program (college entrance tests are not built around specific programs). Therefore, it is necessary to gather different types of evidence, depending on the purpose, to support an inference that a test is valid for a certain purpose.

Content-related evidence is the extent to which the content of a test is judged to be representative of some appropriate universe or domain of content. In establishing content-related evidence, expert judges typically examine the test items and indicate whether the items measure predetermined criteria, objectives, or content. Content-related evidence is similar to face validity, but face validity is a less systematic appraisal of the relationship between the criteria and the contents of the text. Face validity is a judgment that the items appear to be relevant, while content validity evidence establishes the relationship more specifically and objectively. Not only is it important to obtain a representative sample of content, it is equally important that there be a correct specification of the universe or domain of content the test is intended to represent. In other words, the test domain should be deemed appropriate, given the proposed use of the test.

It is important to establish content-related evidence for research involving achievement. To use a test to measure whether students know the causes of the American Civil War, therefore, it would be necessary to have a group of judges agree that the test does in fact measure this criterion. To develop a test to assess the knowledge that beginning teachers should demonstrate for certification, it would be necessary to use college and university faculty and public school teachers and administrators for judging the content to make sure it represents what beginning teachers need to know.

Criterion-related evidence addresses the question of the efficacy with which the scores on an instrument predict scores on a well-specified, predetermined criterion. In this type of evidence the specification of the criterion used becomes crucial, and this specification is usually based on professional judgment. The value of criterion-related validity evidence, then, depends on the appropriateness and quality of the criterion, and in establishing criterion-related validity evidence it is best to include a statement of the way the criterion was judged. Within the general definition of criterion-related validity evidence there are two types, concurrent and predictive. **Concurrent evidence** is an empirical procedure that results in a correlation coefficient used to describe the degree of relationship between two measures given at about the same time. A high relationship suggests that the instruments are measuring something similar. This type of evidence is used in the development of new instruments that measure—in a different, perhaps more efficient, way—the same thing as an established instrument. A new test of intelligence, for example, may be correlated with such established instruments as the Wechsler or Stanford-Binet. Of course if a new IQ test is built on a theory of intelligence that is different from the theory used in the Wechsler or Stanford-Binet, the scores may not, indeed should not, be related. In this case the criterion selected (Wechsler or Stanford-Binet) is not appropriate. **Predictive evidence** is similar to concurrent validity evidence. In both procedures an instrument is related to another criterion measure, but with predictive validity one assessment is made at a point in time after a first measure. A correlation coefficient is also reported with predictive validity, but in this case the correlation describes the adequacy with which measures on one instrument will predict later behavior. Thus, if a research problem involves the use of results in a predictive manner (for example, students who attain a certain score on a personality test will be most successful), then the validity of the instruments used to assess the changes across time should have evidence of predictive validity. This is especially important for using research to screen applicants or to make selections on the basis of test scores. In both cases the researcher is assuming that the scores on the instrument will predict future behavior, but this conclusion is acceptable only if predictive validity has been established for the instrument. Good examples of tests that are used in this manner are college entrance examinations such as the Scholastic Aptitude Tests.

Construct-related evidence is an interpretation or meaning that is given to a set of scores. Construct-related evidence is of primary importance with instruments that assess a trait or theory that cannot be measured directly, such as when the purpose of the instrument is to measure an unobservable trait like intelligence, creativity, or anxiety.

Validity is clearly the single most important aspect of an instrument and the findings that result from the data. The quality of the evidence judged by the users of the findings varies a lot in educational research. If standardized tests are used there will be sophisticated evidence; correlations for criterion-related evidence will be .75 or higher (.60–.75 is marginal; less than .60 is weak), while locally developed questionnaires may have little systematic evidence. In either case good researchers always ask: Are the inferences appropriate? What evidence supports my conclusion? The components of test validity are summarized in Table 7.1.

Reliability

Reliability refers to the consistency of measurement, the extent to which the results are similar over different forms of the same instrument or occasions of data collecting. The goal of developing reliable measures is to minimize the influence of chance or other variables unrelated to the intent of the measure. If an instrument is unreliable, the information obtained is ambiguous, inconsistent, and useless. It is therefore important for researchers to select and develop data gathering procedures that will be highly reliable.

Another way to conceptualize reliability is to think of tests taken as a student. The number of questions that were correct, or the raw score, is the result obtained, but a student knows that this score is an imperfect assessment of his or her knowledge of the subject. Many factors contribute to the imperfect nature of measurement. There may have been ambiguous questions, the lighting may have been poor in the room, the student may have been sick, guesses may have been mostly wrong, and so on. If, for example, the student could take a test a second time, the score would probably be different. The score obtained may be thought

TABLE 7.1
Components of Test Validity

Component	Description	Nature of Relationship
Content-related evidence	Logical relationship of the items to predetermined content areas	Between test items and the criteria, objectives, or content
Criterion-related evidence	Empirical relationship between test scores and criterion scores	
Concurrent evidence	A high relationship between scores on an instrument and scores on an existing valid measure	Between two independent measures of the trait taken at about the same time
Predictive evidence	A high relationship between scores on an instrument and on future behavior	Between two independent measures of the trait, one taken in the present and another at a later time
Construct-related evidence	The interpretation and proper use of a set of scores, and the extent to which a test provides a meaningful measure of an unobservable construct	Between an instrument and different methods used to assess the same and different constructs

of as having two components, a *true score,* which represents the actual knowledge or skill level of the individual, and *error,* sources of variability unrelated to the intent of the instrument:

$$\text{obtained score} = \text{true score} + \text{error}$$

Common sources of error are listed in Table 7.2. The objective in selecting or evaluating instruments, then, is to look for evidence that error has been controlled as much as possible. Since educational research is concerned with human traits, there is always some amount of error.

The actual amount of error variance in test scores, or the reliability, is determined empirically through several types of procedures.[1] Each type of reliability is

TABLE 7.2
Sources of Measurement Error

Conditions of Test Administration and Construction	Conditions Associated with the Person Taking the Test
Changes in time limits	Reactions to specific items
Changes in directions	Health
Different scoring procedures	Motivation
Interrupted testing session	Mood
Race of test administrator	Fatigue
Time the test is taken	Luck
Sampling of items	Fluctuation in memory or attention
Ambiguity in wording	Attitudes
Misunderstood directions	Test-taking skills (test wiseness)
Effect of heat, light, ventilation in testing situation	Ability to comprehend instruction
Differences in observers	Anxiety

related to the control of a particular kind of error, and is reported in the form of a reliability coefficient. The reliability coefficient is a correlation statistic comparing two sets of scores from the same individuals. The scale for a reliability coefficient is from 0.00 to 0.99. If the coefficient is near 0.99 the instrument has little error and is highly reliable. The opposite is true for the correlation near 0.00. An acceptable range of reliability for coefficients for most instruments is 0.70 to 0.90.

The four general types of reliability coefficients are stability, equivalence, stability and equivalence, and internal consistency (Table 7.3).

Stability.   A coefficient of **stability** is provided by correlation scores from the same test of a group of individuals on two different occasions. If the responses of the individuals are consistent (that is, if those scoring high the first time also score high the second time, and so on) then the correlation coefficient, and the reliability, are high. This **test-retest** procedure assumes that the characteristic that is

[1]Most of the procedures are based on the assumption that there will be a sufficient dispersion or spread in the scores to calculate correlation coefficients. Some types of tests (such as criterion-referenced) do not provide much score variability, and traditional correlational indicators of reliability may be inappropriate. For such tests researchers examine percentages of test takers who are classified in the same way after taking the test twice or after taking different forms of the same test, rather than the correlation coefficient. The presentation of reliability in this chapter will focus on traditional correlational procedures, since these are the ones you will encounter most frequently in the literature.

TABLE 7.3
Types of Reliability

Type	Description	Procedure	Common Examples[a]
Stability (test-retest)	Consistency of stable characteristics over a period of time	Administer the same test to the same individuals over a period of time	Aptitude tests IQ tests
Equivalence	Comparability of two measures of the same trait given at about the same time	Administer different tests to same individuals at about the same time	Achievement tests
Equivalence and stability	Comparability of two measures of the same trait given over a period of time	Administer different tests to the same individuals over a period of time	Assessments of changes over time. Personality assessment
Internal consistency (split-half; K-R; Cronbach Alpha)	Comparability of halves of a measure to assess a single trait or dimension	Administer one test and correlate the items to each other	Most measures except for speeded tests. Attitude questionnaires

[a]These examples are not meant to suggest that forms of reliability other than those indicated are inappropriate (for example, achievement tests also use test-retest reliability).

measured, such as intelligence, remains constant. Unstable traits, such as mood, should not be expected to yield high stability coefficients. Furthermore, stability usually means that there is a long enough time between measures (often several months) so that the consistency in scores is uninfluenced by a memory or practice effect. In general, as the time gap between measures increases, the correlation between the scores becomes lower.

Equivalence.   When two equivalent or parallel forms of the same instrument are administered to a group at about the same time and the scores are related, the reliability that results is a coefficient of **equivalence.** Even though each form is made up of different items, the score received by an individual would be about the same on both forms. Equivalence is one type of reliability that can be established when the researcher has a relatively large number of items from which to construct equivalent forms. Alternate forms of a test are needed in order to test initially absent subjects who may learn about specific items from the first form, or when an instructor has two or more sections of the same class meeting at different times.

Equivalence and Stability.   When a researcher needs to give a pretest and posttest to assess a change in behavior, a reliability coefficient of equivalence and stability should be established. In this procedure, reliability is attained by administering to the same group of individuals one form of an instrument at one time and a second form at a later date. If an instrument has this type of reliability, the researcher can thus be confident that a change of scores across time reflects an actual difference in the trait being measured. This is the most stringent type of validity and it is especially useful for studies involving gain-scores, or improvement.

Internal Consistency.   **Internal consistency** (or homogeneity) is the most common type of reliability. The procedure for internal consistency is used when there is only one form of the test. There are three common types of internal consistency: split-half, Kuder-Richardson, and Cronbach Alpha method. In **split-half** reliability the items of a test that have been administered to a group are divided into comparable halves, and a correlation coefficient is calculated between the halves. If each student has about the same position in relation to the group on each half, then the correlation is high and the instrument has high reliability. Each test half should be of similar difficulty. The most common approach is to correlate the scores on the odd-numbered items with the scores on the even-numbered items. This method provides a lower reliability than other methods, since the total number in the correlation equation contains only half the items (and experts know that other things being equal, longer tests are more reliable than short tests). (The Spearman-Brown formula is used to increase split-half reliabilities to estimate what the correlation would be for a whole test.) Internal consistency techniques should not be used with speeded tests. This is because not all items are answered by all students, a factor that tends to increase spuriously the intercorrelation of the items.

A second method for investigating the extent of internal consistency is to use a **Kuder-Richardson** (K-R) formula in order to correlate all items on a single test with each other when each item is scored right or wrong. K-R reliability is thus determined from a single administration of an instrument, but without having to split the instrument into equivalent halves. This procedure assumes that all items in an instrument are equivalent to each other, and it is appropriate when the purpose of the test is to measure a single trait. If a test has items of varying difficulty or it measures more than one trait, the K-R estimate would usually be lower than the split-half reliabilities.

The **Cronbach Alpha** also assumes equivalence of all items. It is a much more general form of internal consistency than the K-R, and it is used for items that are not scored right or wrong. The Cronbach Alpha is generally the most appropriate type of reliability for survey research and other questionnaires in which there is a range of possible answers for each item.

Interpretation of Reliability Coefficients.   There are several factors that should be considered in interpreting reliability coefficients:

1. The more heterogeneous a group is on the trait that is measured, the higher the reliability.
2. The more items there are in an instrument, the higher the reliability.
3. The greater the range of scores, the higher the reliability.
4. Achievement tests with a medium difficulty level will result in a higher reliability than either very hard or very easy tests.
5. Reliability, like validity, is usually based on a norming group and, strictly speaking, the reliability is demonstrated only for subjects whose characteristics are similar to those of the norming group.
6. The more that items discriminate between high and low achievers, the greater the reliability.

Researchers often ask how high a correlation should be for it to indicate satisfactory reliability. This question is not answered easily. It depends on the type of instrument (personality questionnaires generally have lower reliability than achievement tests), the purpose of the study (whether it is exploratory research or research that leads to important decisions), and whether groups or individuals are affected by the results (since action affecting individuals requires a higher correlation than action affecting groups).

The remainder of this chapter will consider methods of data collection that are commonly used in quantitative research. While the basic principles of validity and reliability apply to all five types of data collection, note that each data collection technique has unique characteristics that affect the way validity and reliability are established.

■ TESTS ■

The term "test" means that a standard set of questions is presented to each subject that requires completion of cognitive tasks. The responses or answers are summarized to obtain a numerical value that represents a characteristic of the subject. The cognitive task can focus on what the person knows (achievement), is able to learn (ability or aptitude), or chooses or selects (interests, attitudes, or values). Different types of tests, and their uses in research, are summarized briefly in this chapter, but it is important to stress that all tests measure current performance. Tests differ more in their use than in their development or actual test items, particularly when comparing achievement and aptitude tests. In fact, it would be more accurate to say that there are different types of inferences and uses; it is what you do with the test results that creates distinctions such as achievement and aptitude.

Standardized Tests

Standardized tests provide uniform procedures for administering and scoring the instrument. The same questions are asked each time the test is used, with a set of directions that specifies how the test should be administered. This would include information about qualifications of the person administering the test and conditions of administration, such as the time allowed, materials that can be used by subjects, and whether questions can be answered. The scoring of responses is usually objective, and most, but not all, standardized tests have been given to a norming group. The "norm group," as it is called, allows comparison of a score with the performance of a defined group of individuals. This provides important and valuable information, but the researcher should take care in interpreting norm-referenced scores (see norm and criterion-referenced tests below).

Most standardized tests are also prepared commercially by measurement experts. This generally means that there will be careful attention to the nature of the norms, reliability, and validity. This results in instruments that are objective, relatively uninfluenced or distorted by the person who administers the instrument.[2] Because most standardized tests are prepared commercially, they are intended to be used in a wide variety of settings. Consequently, whatever is tested is defined in broad and general terms. This may mean that for some research purposes a standardized test may not be specific enough to provide a sensitive measure of the variable. For instance, if you were conducting a study to investigate the effect of general education at a university on students' knowledge in social science or humanities, a standardized test that you would use would be intended as a measure of social science and humanities outcomes at nearly *all* universities. This means that what is taught at one particular university may not be well represented on the test. This illustrates a trade-off in using standardized tests in research. On the one hand you have a carefully constructed instrument, with established reliability, directions, and scoring procedures. However, the test may not be focused directly on the variable of interest in the study, may have inappropriate norms, or may cost too much. The alternative is to develop your own instrument; it will measure the variable more directly, but it may have questionable technical qualities.

[2]This does not mean that variations in administering the test within the procedures required will not influence the results. A recent review by Fuchs and Fuchs (1986), for example, suggests that the degree of examiner familiarity with the examinee can influence the results. Other variables being equal, examinees who know the examiner may score higher than examinees who are tested by a stranger.

Norm and Criterion-Referenced Tests

A major distinction among tests is whether they are norm or criterion-referenced. The purpose of **norm-referenced** testing is to show how individual scores compare to scores of a well-defined reference or norm group of individuals. The interpretation of results, then, depends entirely on how the subjects compare to others, with little emphasis on the absolute amount of knowledge or skill. That is, what matters most is the comparison group, and the ability of the test or instrument to distinguish between individuals. The goal is to know whether, for example, the subjects know more or less than the norm group, and the score is often reported to indicate specifically where the subject "stands" in relation to others (such as the 67th percentile, or upper quarter).

Researchers need to keep two characteristics of norm-referenced tests in mind. First, because the purpose of the test is to differentiate between individuals, the best distribution of scores is one that shows a high variance. To achieve a high variability of scores the items must discriminate between individuals. To accomplish this, the test items, particularly in standardized norm-referenced tests, are fairly difficult. It is not uncommon for students at the 50th percentile to answer slightly more than half the items correctly. Easy items, ones that most everyone gets correct, are used sparingly (obviously, if all the items are easy, everyone gets a high score, and there is no differentiation between individuals). Thus, important content or skills may not be measured, which will affect the meaning you give to the results. On the positive side, the large variability helps in establishing relationships. The highest correlations are often found with two variables that have large variability.

Second, researchers should attend carefully to the characteristics of the norm or reference group. Perhaps you have had the same experience as we have, being enrolled in a class of bright, hard-working students with an instructor who graded by the curve. You could learn a lot but still get low marks. The interpretation of norm-referenced scores makes sense only when we know what we are being compared against. Many standardized norm-referenced tests indicate that "national" norms are used. Despite the fact that the term "national" is subject to different interpretations, if you are studying gifted students and compare their scores with the national norm, chances are good your students will all score very high and show little variability. This gives you what is called a "ceiling effect" and a restricted range, which in turn would likely lead to nonsignificant results.

In **criterion-referenced** testing an individual's score is interpreted by comparing the score to professionally judged standards of performance.[3] The comparison is between the score and a criterion or standard rather than the scores of others. The result is usually expressed as the percentage of items answered correctly, or as pass/fail in the case of minimum competency testing. There is a focus on "what" the subjects are able to do, with a comparison of that to standards of proficiency. Most criterion-referenced tests result in a highly skewed distribution,

---

[3]See R. A. Berk (1986), A consumer's guide to setting performance standards on criterion-referenced tests, *Review of Educational Research, 56,* 137–172, for a review and discussion of methods for setting standards.

which lessens variability. Despite this limitation, criterion-referenced tests are good to use for diagnosis and for categorizing subjects into pass/fail groups. A related concept, domain-referenced tests, are used to show how much of a specifically defined larger "domain" of knowledge is demonstrated by those being tested. For example, if the domain is knowledge of addition with three-digit numbers, the test will sample this domain, and the researcher will make a professional judgment using the percentage of correctly answered items to judge the "mastery" of the domain.

Aptitude Tests

The purpose of an **aptitude test** is to predict future performance. The results are used to make a prediction about performance on some criterion (like grades, teaching effectiveness, certification, or test scores) prior to instruction, placement, or training. The term "aptitude" refers to the predictive use of the scores from a test, rather than the nature of the test items. Some terms, such as "intelligence" or "ability," are used interchangeably with aptitude. Intelligence tests are used to provide a very general measure, usually reporting a global test score. Because they are general, intelligence tests are useful in predicting a wide variety of tasks. Intelligence is measured by an individual or group test. For most research, group tests of intelligence are adequate and cost much less than individual tests. Most group tests are designed so that researchers need training to administer and score them. Usually these tests produce three scores: a verbal language score, nonverbal or performance score, and a combined score. Since virtually all school children have taken group intelligence tests, the scores are available, with parental and/or school permission, for use in research. The scores are often used to adjust for ability differences in intact groups of subjects. Some of the common individual and group intelligence tests are listed in Table 7.4.

There are a large number of measures that assess multiple aptitudes or specific kinds of aptitudes. Multifactor aptitude tests are used to provide separate scores for each skill or area assessed. Some would argue that this makes more sense than a single score because relative strengths and weaknesses can be identified. Multifactor aptitude tests have become increasingly popular in vocational and educational counseling. However, the usefulness of factor scores in research is more problematic. Because there may be just a few items that measure one factor, the reliability of the scores may be questionable. Total single scores, while more general, are often more stable and reliable. Special aptitude tests are good for research, since the focus is on an accurate indication of ability in one area. Table 7.4 contains examples of both multi- and special aptitude tests.

Achievement Tests

It is not always evident how achievement tests differ from aptitude tests. Often very similar items are used for both types of tests. In general, however, **achievement tests** have a more restricted coverage, are more closely tied to school subjects, and measure more recent learning than aptitude tests. Also, of course,

TABLE 7.4
Examples of Standardized Tests

Aptitude	Achievement
Group Intelligence	**Diagnostic**
Cognitive Abilities Test	Stanford Diagnostic Reading Test
Otis-Lennon School Ability Test	Woodcock Reading Mastery Test
Scholastic Aptitude Test	Key Math Diagnostic Arithmetic Test
	Prescriptive Reading Inventory
Individual Intelligence	**Criterion-referenced**
Stanford-Binet	Objectives-Referenced Bank of
Wechsler Scales	Items and Tests
Kaufman-ABC	Sills Monitoring System
McCarthy Scales of Children's	Writing Skills Test
Abilities	
Multifactor	**Specific Subjects**
Differential Aptitude Test	Metropolitan Readiness Tests
General Aptitude Test Battery	Gates-McGinitie Reading Tests
Armed Services Vocational	Modern Math Understanding Test
Aptitude Battery	
Special	**Batteries**
Minnesota Clerical Test	SRA Assessment Survey
Law School Admissions Test	California Achievement Tests
Medical College Admission Test	Metropolitan Achievement Tests
Bennett Mechanical Comprehension Test	Iowa Test of Basic Skills
Torrance Test of Creative Thinking	Standford Achievement Test
Watson-Glaser Critical Thinking	
Appraisal	

the purpose of achievement tests is to measure what has been learned rather than to predict future performance.

There are hundreds of standardized achievement tests. Some are diagnostic, which isolate specific areas of strength and weakness; some are concerned with measuring achievement in a single content area while others, survey batteries, test different content areas; some are norm-referenced and others are criterion-referenced; some emphasize principles and skills rather than knowledge of specific facts. The choice of achievement test depends on the purpose of the research. If the research is concerned with achievement in a specific school subject, then it would be best to use a test that measures only that subject, rather than using a survey battery. If comparisons between several schools will be made, it is best to use norm-referenced tests.

It is very important to assess the content validity of a standardized achievement test before using it in research. This is because the curriculum in some schools may be different from the content of standardized tests that are designed for use in most schools. The best way to assess evidence for content validity is to examine the items of the test and make professional judgments of the match between what the item tests and the curriculum. Finally, those choosing a test should consider the difficulty level of the test and the abilities of the students. The desired goal is to have a fairly normal distribution of test scores. If results are skewed by a test that is too easy for bright students or too difficult for slow students, it will be difficult to relate the scores to other variables (such as measuring gain in achievement over a year or more with gifted students). Table 7.4 contains examples of some standardized achievement tests.

■ PERSONALITY, ATTITUDE, VALUE, AND ■ INTEREST INVENTORIES

Aptitude and achievement tests are types of cognitive measures. Affective, or **noncognitive instruments** measure traits such as interests, attitudes, self-concept, values, personality, and beliefs. Most agree that these traits are important in school success, but measuring them accurately is more difficult than with cognitive tests. First, noncognitive test results may be adversely affected by response set, which is the tendency of a subject's answer to be influenced by a general "set" when responding to items. There are several types of response sets, including social desirability; responding with all positive or negative answers regardless of the content of the items; guessing; and sacrificing speed for accuracy. Response set is particularly prevalent with ambiguous items or items that use a continuum such as agree-disagree or favorable-unfavorable. Second, noncognitive items are susceptible to faking. While there are some techniques that help reduce faking, such as using forced choice questions, disguising the purpose of the test, and establishing a good rapport with subjects, faking is always conceivable. Third, the reliability of noncognitive tests is generally lower than cognitive tests. Fourth, in most noncognitive tests we are interested in evidence of construct validity, which is difficult to establish. Finally, noncognitive tests do not have "right" answers like cognitive tests. The results are usually interpreted by comparison with other individuals, so the nature of the comparison group is particularly important. Despite these limitations, noncognitive traits are used in research because they are an integral part of the learning process.

Personality tests include a wide range of checklists, projective tests, and general adjustment inventories. Most are self-report instruments containing a structured question-response format, and they require specialized training for interpretation. Because of psychometric weakness in most personality tests the results should be used for groups of subjects rather than individuals. See Table 7.5 for some examples of personality tests.

Attitude and interest inventories are used extensively in educational research. Most are self-report instruments and are subject to faking and response set. Interest inventories measure feelings and beliefs about activities in which an individual can engage. Attitude inventories measure feelings and beliefs about

TABLE 7.5
Examples of Noncognitive Instruments

Personality	Aptitude	Value	Interest
The Adjustment Inventory	Survey of Study Habits and Attitudes	Study of Values	Strong-Campbell Interest Inventory
Minnesota Multiphasic Personality Inventory	Survey of School Attitudes	Rokeach Value Survey	Minnesota Vocational Interest Inventory
California Psychological Inventory	Minnesota School Affect Assessment	Gordon's Survey Values	Kuder Occupational Interest Survey
Personality Inventory for Children	Children's Scale of Social Attitudes	Work Values Inventory	Kuder General Interest Inventory
Omnibus Personality Inventory	Learning Environment Inventory		Vocational Preference Inventory
Rorschach Inkblot Test	Student Attitude Inventory		
Thematic Apperception Test	Revised Math Attitude Scale		
Tennessee Self-Concept Scale			
Piers-Harris Children's Self-Concept Scale			
Coopersmith Self-Esteem Inventory			

something other than an activity, such as an object, a group, or place. Both are concerned with likes and dislikes, preferences, and predispositions. A complete discussion of these types of inventories, such as found in Mehrens and Lehmann (1987), is beyond the scope of this book, although we discuss questionnaires as one way to assess attitudes later in this chapter. Table 7.5 lists a few attitude, interest, and value inventories.

■ QUESTIONNAIRES ■

For many good reasons the questionnaire is the most widely used technique for obtaining information from subjects. A questionnaire is relatively economical, has standardized questions, can assure anonymity, and questions can be written for specific purposes. Questionnaires can use statements or questions, but in all cases the subject is responding to something written. In this section of the chapter, information about questionnaires is presented by following the sequence of steps researchers use in developing questionnaires.

Justification

A questionnaire is one of many ways information can be obtained. The researcher who wants to use one should be sure that, given the constraints of the situation, there are no other more reliable and valid techniques that could be used. This decision is based on knowledge of the strengths and weaknesses of each technique and is addressed later in the chapter by comparing several commonly used techniques. Researchers should give much thought to justification whenever they develop new questionnaires. In many cases existing instruments could be used or adapted for use instead of preparing a new questionnaire. If the researcher can locate an existing questionnaire, he or she will save time and money and may find an instrument with established reliability and validity.

Defining Objectives

The second step in using a questionnaire is to define and list the specific objectives that the information will achieve. The objectives are based on the research problems or questions, and they show how each piece of information will be used. They need not be strict behavioral objectives, but they must be specific enough to indicate how the responses from each item will meet the objectives. By defining objectives the researcher is specifying the information that is needed, and an inability to do this suggests that investigator does not understand the research problem completely. Unfortunately, many researchers include questions that have not been thought through properly, and the results are never used. Time and energy are wasted, and interested audiences are disenchanted.

Writing Questions and Statements

Once the researcher has defined objectives and has ascertained that no existing instruments can be used, he or she begins the task of writing the questions or statements. It is best to write the items by objective and to be aware of the way the results will be analyzed once the data is collected. There are two general considerations in writing the items: comply with rules for writing most types of items and decide which item format is best.

Babbie (1983) suggests the following guidelines for writing effective questions or statements:

1. *Make items clear.* An item achieves clarity when all respondents interpret it in the same way. Never assume that the respondent will read something into the item. Often the perspectives, words, or phrases that make perfect sense to the re-

searcher are unclear to the respondents. The item may also be too general, allowing different interpretations. The question, "What do you think about the new curriculum?" for example, would probably evoke a counter question: "Which curriculum?" Finally, vague and ambiguous words like *a few, sometimes,* and *usually* should be avoided, as should jargon or complex phrases.

2. *Avoid double-barrelled questions.* A question should be limited to a single idea or concept. **Double-barrelled** items contain two or more ideas, and frequently the word *and* is used in the item. Double-barrelled questions and statements are undesirable because the respondent may, if given an opportunity, answer each part differently. If, for instance, a respondent is asked to agree or disagree with the statement, "School counselors spend too much time with recordkeeping and not enough time with counseling of personal problems," it would be possible to agree with the first part (too much recordkeeping) and disagree with the second idea (more time with counseling).

3. *Respondents must be competent to answer.* It is important that the respondents are able to provide reliable information. Some questions that ask teachers to recall specific incidents or reconstruct what they did several weeks ago, for example, are subject to inaccuracy simply because the teachers cannot reliably remember the incidents. Similarly, it would be of little value to ask college professors who teach the historical foundations of education to judge the adequacy of a minimum competency test of reading readiness skills in which prospective teachers should demonstrate knowledge for certification. There are many instances in which the subjects are unable to make a response they can be confident of, and in such circumstances it is best to provide in the response options something like *unsure* or *do not know* in order to give the subjects an opportunity to state their true feelings or beliefs.

4. *Questions should be relevant.* If subjects are asked to respond to questions that are unimportant to them or are about things they have not thought about or care nothing about, it is likely that the subjects will respond carelessly, and the results will be misleading. This may occur, for instance, when teachers are asked their preferences in standardized tests when they rarely if ever use the results of these tests in teaching. Their answers might be based on an expedient response rather than a careful consideration of the tests.

5. *Simple items are best.* Long and complicated items should be avoided because they are more difficult to understand, and respondents may be unwilling to try to understand them. Assume that respondents will read and answer items quickly, and that it is necessary to write items that are simple, easy to understand, and easy to respond to.

6. *Avoid negative items.* Negatively stated items should be avoided because they are easy to misinterpret. Subjects will unconsciously skip or overlook the negative word, so their answers will be the opposite of the intended. If researchers use negative items they should underline or capitalize the negative word (not, or NO).

7. *Avoid biased items or terms.* The way in which items are worded, or the inclusion of certain terms, may encourage particular responses more than others. Such items are termed **biased** and, of course, should be avoided. There are many ways

to bias an item. The identification of a well-known person or agency in the item can create bias. "Do you agree or disagree with the superintendent's recent proposal to . . ." is likely to elicit a response based on an attitude toward the superintendent, not the proposal. Some items provide biased responses because of the social desirability of the answer. **Social desirability** is the tendency to respond to items so that the answer will make the subject look good. If, for example, you ask teachers whether they ever ridicule their students, you can be fairly sure, even if the responses are anonymous, that the answer will be *no* because good teachers do not ridicule students. Student responses to the same question or observations of other teachers might provide different information.

Researchers may also give a hint of what response they are hoping for. This occurs if the respondents want to please the researcher and provide responses they think the researcher wants, or it may occur if the subjects know the consequences of the responses. It has been shown, for example, that student evaluations of college teachers are more favorable if the teacher tells the students before they fill out the forms that the results will have a direct bearing on their (the teachers') tenure and salary raises. The students presumably feel less negative because of the important consequences of the results. Finally, items are ambiguous if the respondent thinks: "Well, sometimes I feel this way, sometimes I feel that way," or "It depends on the situation." Many items fail to specify adequately the situational constraints that should be considered, leading to inaccurate responses. If asked, for instance, to agree or disagree with the statement, "The discovery method of teaching is better than the lecture method," a teacher would likely respond, "It depends on the student."

Given these general guidelines, how do you know if the items are well written? One approach is to ask friends, colleagues, and experts to review the items and look for any problems. Beyond this subjective method, the only way to demonstrate empirically that items are unbiased, unambiguous, and unclear is to construct two equivalent forms of each item and give the items to random groups. If the two groups' responses are nearly the same on each pair of items, then the items are probably good. If not, then the items need to be rewritten.

General Format

The general layout and organization of the questionnaire is very important. If it appears to be carelessly done or confusing, respondents are likely to set it aside and never respond. A well-done format and appearance provides a favorable first impression and will result in cooperation and serious, conscientious responses. The following rules should be adhered to carefully:

1. Carefully check grammar, spelling, punctuation, and other details.
2. Make sure printing is clear and easy to read.
3. Make instructions brief and easy to understand.
4. Avoid cluttering the questionnaire by trying to squeeze many items onto each page. Rather, maximize white space by spreading the items out.

5. Avoid abbreviated items.
6. Keep the questionnaire as short as possible, but keep it short in items and responses, not pages.
7. Provide adequate space for answering open-ended questions.
8. Use a logical sequence, and group related items together.
9. Number the pages and items.
10. Use examples if the items may be difficult to understand.
11. Put important items near the beginning of a long questionnaire.
12. Be aware of the way the positioning and sequence of the questions may affect the responses.

Types of Items

There is a variety of ways in which a question or statement can be worded, and a number of ways in which the response can be made. The type of item should be based on the advantages, uses, and limitations of these options. Below is a summary of the more common approaches to the way questions and statements may be asked and answered.

Open and closed form.   The first consideration is to decide whether the item will have a **closed form,** in which the subject chooses between predetermined responses, or an **open form,** in which the subjects write in any response they want. The choice of form to use depends on the objective of the item and the advantages and disadvantages of each type. Closed form items (also called structured or closed-ended) are best for obtaining demographic information and data that can be categorized easily. Rather than asking "How many hours did you study for the test?" for example, a closed form question would provide categories of hours and ask the respondent to check the appropriate box, as indicated below:

Check the box that indicates the number of hours you spent studying for the test.

☐	0–2
☐	3–5
☐	6–8
☐	9–11
☐	12+

A questionnaire that was used recently for a dissertation illustrates this point further. In the first question, as shown in Excerpt 7.1, the respondent must choose from one of these options; it is a structured item. The researcher could have left the item unstructured, but the range of responses that would have been received (for example, *a lot, sometimes, quite a bit, all the time, occasionally, rarely*) would have made the results much more subjective and less accurate.

Obviously, it will be much easier to score a closed form item, and the subject can answer the items more quickly. It is therefore best to use closed form items with a large number of subjects or a large number of items. It is very time consum-

---

EXCERPT 7.1
Closed Form Item

Set 1 has just one question. Please check in the space after the letter that best answers the question.

1. To what extent are you, or have you been involved, in principal selection?

   1. **a lot** –   reading resumes, interviewing candidates,
            making recommendations, helping to decide.   1. ☐

   2. **some** –   reading resumes, interviewing candidates,
            making recommendations.   2. ☐

   3. **none** –   have little or nothing to do with the
            selection process.   3. ☐

Source: From "The relationship of the social class and personal characteristics of parent association executive board members to the role expectations and personal characteristics which they advocate in the selection of elementary principals in selected American cities," doctoral dissertation by Stanley Cogan. Reprinted by permission of Stanley Cogan.

ing for the researcher to categorize several hundred open-ended responses, not to mention the subjectivity involved.

There are certain disadvantages to using structured items, however. With the question, "How many hours did you study for the test?" for example, if every subject checks a response labelled *3 to 5 hours,* the researcher has lost accuracy and variability (no spread of responses across all response categories) with this factor. In other words, if categories are created that fail to allow the subjects to indicate their feelings or beliefs accurately, the item is not very useful. This occurs with some forced choice items. Another disadvantage is that a structured item cues the respondent with respect to possible answers. If asked, for example, "Why did you do so poorly on the test?" students might, if an open-ended format was used, list two or three factors that were relevant, things that they thought were important. A structured format could, however, list twenty-five factors and have the student check each one that was important (such as *I didn't study hard enough; I was sick; I was unlucky*); the student may check factors that would have been omitted in the open-ended mode. One approach to the case in which both the open and the closed form have advantages is to use open-ended questions first with a small group of subjects in order to generate salient factors, and then use closed-ended items, based on the open-ended responses, with a larger group. Open-ended items exert the least amount of control over the respondent and can capture idiosyncratic differences. If the purpose of the research is to generate specific individual responses, the open-ended format is best; if the purpose is to provide more general group responses, the closed form is best.

Scaled Items.   A scale is a series of graduations, levels, or values that describes various degrees of something. Scales are used extensively in questionnaires because they allow fairly accurate assessments of beliefs or opinions. This is because many of our beliefs and opinions are thought of in terms of graduations. We believe something very strongly or intently, or perhaps we have a positive or negative opinion of something.

The usual format of **scaled items** is a question or statement followed by a scale of potential responses. The subjects check the place on the scale that best reflects their beliefs or opinions about the statement. The most widely used example is the **Likert scale** (pronounced Lick-ert). A Likert scale can be written in two forms, one in which the stem includes a value or direction, in which case the respondent indicates the degree of agreement; and one in which the stem can be neutral, with the direction provided in the response options. Using the first form, for example, a researcher might ask:

Science is very important:

_____	_____	_____	_____	_____
Strongly agree	Agree	Neither agree nor disagree (undecided or neutral)	Disagree	Strongly disagree

The second form might be as follows:

Science is:

_____	_____	_____	_____	_____
Critical	Very important	Important	Somewhat important	Very unimportant

It should be pointed out that while the agree-disagree format is used widely, it can also be misleading. We might, for example, disagree with the statement, "Mrs. Jones is a good teacher" because she is an outstanding teacher.

The Likert scale approach provides great flexibility since the descriptors on the scale can vary to fit the nature of the question or statement. Here are examples:

How often is your teacher well organized?

_____	_____	_____	_____	_____
Always	Most of the time	Sometimes	Rarely	Never

How would you rate Cindy's performance?

_____	_____	_____	_____	_____
Very poor	Poor	Fair	Good	Excellent

Indicate the extent to which your performance was a success or failure.

_____	_____	_____	_____	_____
Extreme success	Success	O.K.	Failure	Extreme failure

Indicate how you feel about your performance:

_____	_____	_____	_____	_____
Immense pride	Some pride	Neither pride nor shame	Some shame	Immense shame

_____	_____	_____	_____	_____
Very happy	Somewhat happy	Neither sad nor happy	Somewhat sad	Very sad

Researchers sometimes wonder whether the undecided or neutral choice should be included in a strongly agree to strongly disagree Likert scale. While both forms are used, it is generally better to include the middle category. If the neutral choice is not included and that is the way the respondent actually feels, then the respondent is forced either to make a choice that is incorrect or not to respond at all. The forced choice format may lead to some frustration by the respondent (Heller & Rife, 1987). However, the argument for deleting the undecided or neutral choice has merit in instances where the respondents have a tendency to cluster responses in that middle category. More information on constructing Likert and other types of scales can be found in most measurement textbooks and in Berdie and Anderson (1974). When the questionnaire items have been written, they should be randomized within each separate section of the questionnaire.

A variation of the Likert scale that is also commonly used is the **Semantic Differential.** This variation uses adjective pairs, with each adjective as an end anchor in a single continuum. On this scale there is no need for a series of descriptors; only one word or phrase is placed at each end. The scale is used to elicit descriptive reactions toward a concept or object. It is an easily constructed scale and can be completed quickly by respondents. The examples that follow illustrate typical uses.

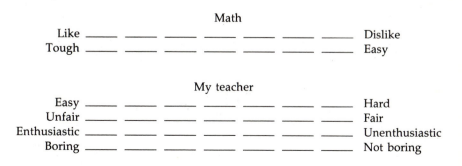

EXCERPT 7.2
Semantic Differential Scale

---

28 Famous plays

important ○ ○ ○ ○ ○ unimportant

pleasant ○ ○ ○ ○ ○ unpleasant

39 Being liked by other students

important ○ ○ ○ ○ ○ unimportant

pleasant ○ ○ ○ ○ ○ unpleasant

---

29 Art

important ○ ○ ○ ○ ○ unimportant

pleasant ○ ○ ○ ○ ○ unpleasant

40 Being liked by teachers

important ○ ○ ○ ○ ○ unimportant

pleasant ○ ○ ○ ○ ○ unpleasant

Source: From *Minnesota School Attitude Survey* by Dr. Andrew Ahlgren. Copyright © 1983 Science Research Associates. Reprinted by permission.

Excerpt 7.2 shows how a Semantic Differential is used to assess responses of students toward various aspects of school. In this instrument, affect is assessed by the scale, anchored by the terms *pleasant-unpleasant*, while value of the activity is measured by *important-unimportant*. In Excerpt 7.3 another type of Semantic Differential is used, one that is obviously oriented toward younger children. The scale is limited but provides a range from *happy* to *sad.*

Ranked Items. One problem with using a Likert scale or a Semantic Differential is that all the answers can be the same, making it difficult to differentiate between each item. If a Likert scale is used to investigate the importance of each of five ways of spending money by a university department, for instance, a respondent can mark *very important* for each one. The result would do little for the researcher's efforts to prioritize expenditure of funds. If, however, the respondents are asked to **rank-order** the five ways in sequential order from most to least important, then the researcher can gather more valuable information on ways to spend the money. A rank-order assessment of the above example might look like this:

Rank-order the following activities with respect to their *importance* as to ways our research fund should be allocated this year. Use 1 = most important; 2 = next most important, and so forth until 5 = least important.

_____ Annual colloquium
_____ Individual research projects
_____ Invited speakers
_____ Computer software
_____ Student assistantships

EXCERPT 7.3
Semantic Differential Scale for Young Children

Black in the nose of the face that shows how YOU feel about what is written in the box.

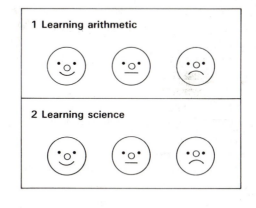

Checklist Items. A **checklist** is simply a method of providing the respondent a number of options from which to choose. The item can require a choice of one of several alternatives (for instance, Check one: The biology topic I most enjoy is ___ecology, ___botany, ___anatomy, ___microbiology, or ___genetics.); or respondents can check as many words as apply:

Check as many as apply. The more enjoyable topics in biology are:
_____ botany
_____ comparative anatomy
_____ genetics
_____ ecology
_____ microbiology
_____ zoology

Checklists can also be used in asking respondents to answer *yes* or *no* to a question, or to check the category to which they belong. For example:

Are you married? ___yes ___no Check the appropriate category:
_____ single, never married
_____ married
_____ separated
_____ divorced
_____ widowed

Note that with categorical responses a respondent can be placed in one category and only one.

Item Format

There are several ways to present items and answers to items. The clearest approach is to write the item on one line and to place the response categories below, not next to, the item. It is also advisable to use boxes, brackets, or parentheses rather than a line to indicate where to place the check mark. For example:

Have you ever cheated?

        [   ] yes
        [   ] no

is better than

Have you ever cheated?   ___yes   ___no

With Likert scales and Semantic Differentials the use of continuous lines or open blanks for check marks is not recommended, since the check mark is often entered between two options.

Sometimes when a researcher asks a series of questions, answering one question in a certain way directs the respondent to other questions. These are called **contingency questions,** and are illustrated below:

Have you used the Mathematics Curriculum Guide?

[   ] yes
[   ] no

> If *yes:* How often have you used the activities
>   suggested?
>
>   [   ] 0–2 times
>   [   ] 3–5 times
>   [   ] 6–10 times
>   [   ] more than 10 times

Did you attend the State Conference on Testing?

    [   ] yes (please answer questions 17–20)
    [   ] no (please skip to question 21)

If several questions will use the same response format, as is typical with Likert scale items, it is often desirable to construct a matrix of items and response categories. An example of a matrix is illustrated in Excerpt 7.4.

Pretesting

It is highly recommended that researchers conduct a pretest of their questionnaires before using them in studies. It is best to locate a sample of subjects with characteristics similar to those that will be used in the study. While the size of the

EXCERPT 7.4
Question Matrix

	Strongly Disagree	Disagree	Agree	Strongly Agree
1. Members of the class do favors for one another.	1	2	3	4
2. The books and equipment students need or want are easily available to them in the classroom.	1	2	3	4
3. There are long periods during which the class does nothing.	1	2	3	4
4. The class has students with many different interests.	1	2	3	4
5. Certain students work only with their close friends.	1	2	3	4

Source: From "Learning environments" by G. Anderson and H. Walberg in *Evaluating Educational Performance*, edited by Herbert J. Walberg. Reprinted by permission of Herbert J. Walberg.

pretest sample should be greater than twenty, it is better to have even ten subjects than no pretest. The administration of the questionnaire should be about the same as that to be used in the study, and the pretest respondents should be given space to write comments about individual items and the questionnaire as a whole. The researcher wants to know if it takes too long to complete, if the directions and items are clear, and so on. If there are enough pretest subjects, an estimate of reliability may be calculated, and some indication will be given of whether there is sufficient variability in the answers to investigate various relationships. There are thus two steps in getting feedback about the questionnaire before it is used in the study: an informal critique of individual items as they are prepared, and a pretest of the full questionnaire.

■ INTERVIEW SCHEDULES ■

Interviews are essentially vocal questionnaires. The major steps in constructing an interview are the same as in preparing a questionnaire—justification, defining objectives, writing questions, deciding general and item format, and pretesting. The obvious difference is that the interview involves direct interaction between individuals, and this interaction has both advantages and disadvantages as compared with the questionnaire. The interview technique is flexible and adaptable.

It can be used with many different problems and types of persons, such as those who are illiterate or too young to read and write, and responses can be probed, followed up, clarified, and elaborated to achieve specific, accurate responses. Nonverbal as well as verbal behavior can be noted in face-to-face interviews, and the interviewer has an opportunity to motivate the respondent. Interviews result in a much higher response rate than questionnaires, especially for topics that concern personal qualities or negative feelings. For obtaining factual, less personal information, questionnaires are preferable.

The primary disadvantages of the interview are its potential for subjectivity and bias and its higher cost and time-consuming nature. Depending on the training and expertise of the interviewer, the respondent may be uncomfortable in the interview and unwilling to report true feelings; the interviewer may ask leading questions to support a particular point of view; or the interviewer's perceptions of what was said may be inaccurate.

To mitigate the disadvantages of interviewing, the interviewer should be thought of as a neutral medium through which information is exchanged. If this goal is attained, then the interviewer's presence will have no effect on the perceptions or answers of the respondent. In other words, if the interview is done correctly, it does not matter who the interviewer is; any number of different interviewers would obtain the same results. This aspect of interviewing is essentially an estimate of reliability. If two or more interviewers agree on the way most of the responses to the questions should be classified, then the process is reliable, as assessed by **inter-rater agreement.** It is also possible to obtain a stability estimate of reliability by correlating the results of an original interview with results obtained a second time by the same interviewer. Another approach that can be used to increase the accuracy of the interview is to allow the respondent an opportunity to check the interviewer's perceptions. This can be accomplished if the interviewers write their perceptions of the answer to each question and send these written perceptions to the respondents. The respondents can then read the answers and make additions and corrections where appropriate. An additional advantage to this approach is that it helps build a positive relationship between the interviewer and respondent. This is helpful if the interviewer will be following up initial interviews or will be involved in a continuing evaluation or study.

Preparing the Interview

Once the researcher makes the decision to use an interview to collect data, he or she constructs an interview schedule. The schedule lists all the questions that will be asked, giving room for the interviewer to write answers. The questions are related directly to the objectives of the study and follow a given sequence that is adhered to in each interview. In most cases, the written questions are exactly what will be asked orally, with appropriate probing questions. The questions are usually in one of three forms: structured, semistructured, or unstructured. **Structured questions** (also called limited response questions) are followed by a set of choices and the respondent selects one of the choices as the answer (for example, "Would you say the program has been highly effective, somewhat effective, or not at all effective?"). **Semistructured questions** have no choices from which the respondent selects an answer. Rather, the question is phrased to allow for individual responses. It is an open-ended question but it is fairly specific in its intent (for example, "What has been the most beneficial aspect of your teacher training program?"). **Unstructured questions** allow the interviewer great latitude in asking broad questions in whatever order seems appropriate. In quantitative educational studies most interviews use a combination of structured and semistructured questions. This provides a high degree of objectivity and uniformity, yet allows for probing and clarification.

After the questions have been written they must be pretested. The pretest is necessary as a check for bias in the procedures, the interviewer, or the questions. During the pretest the procedures should be identical to those that will be implemented in the study. The interviewer should take special note of any cues suggesting that the respondent is uncomfortable or does not fully understand the questions. After the interview the respondent can evaluate the questions for intent, clarity, and so on. The pretest provides a means of assessing the length of the interview and will give the researcher some idea of the ease with which the data can be summarized.

One potential problem that must be addressed before the actual study is conducted is the removal or rephrasing of leading questions. A **leading question** is worded so that the respondent is more aware of one answer than another, or contains information that may bias the response (as summarized earlier for questionnaire items). If, for example, the researcher asks: "Given the expense of adopting a new reading series, should we make the adoption this year?" the wording obviously makes it easy and desirable to answer *no.* Or consider the question: "Do you favor hot lunches in school?" It is more likely to elicit a *yes* than *no* response. As in the case of questionnaires, the best way to avoid leading questions in an interview is to solicit feedback from other experts and to pretest the questions.

A final consideration in preparing the interview is to think about the way personal characteristics of the interviewer may influence the responses. Sax (1979, pp. 243–244) lists the following variables that have been shown to influence responses:

Variable	*Effect on the Interview*
1. Age of interviewer	a. Rapport is high for young interviewers work the middle-aged respondents. Respondent's age is unimportant for older interviewers.
	b. The least inhibition in responding occurs with young persons of same sex.

	c.	Most inhibition in responding occurs with persons of same age but different sex.
	d.	Interviewers between twenty-six and fifty years of age do a better job of interviewing than either younger or older interviewers.

2. College major — Interviewers trained in the behavioral sciences are rated as being more accurate than those in physical sciences; lowest rated are those who majored in fine arts, business, law, and the humanities.

3. Educational level — College graduates are rated higher than noncollege-trained interviewers, but differences are slight.

4. Experience in interviewing — Interviewers' accuracy increases as their experience in interviewing increases.

5. Racial background — Responses of blacks differ depending upon whether they are interviewed by Caucasians or other blacks.

6. Religious background — Negative responses concerning Jews tend to be withheld if the interviewers introduce themselves by Jewish names or if they are "Jewish appearing."

7. Sex of interviewer — Males obtain fewer interview responses than do females.

8. Socioeconomic level — Middle-class interviewers report a greater degree of conservatism among working-class respondents than do working-class interviewers.

Many educational studies use naive or inexperienced interviewers. In this situation not only will the personal characteristics of the interviewer provide possible bias, but there is potential for error simply because the interviewer is unskilled at handling interviews. If novices are used, it is best to provide training and supervision. This can be expensive and time consuming but will increase the validity and reliability of the study. For details on training interviewers, see Babbie (1983), and the *Interviewer's Manual* (1976).

During the Interview

Appearance is very important. It is best for the interviewer to dress according to existing norms or in a fashion similar to the respondents, and not in a way that may lead the respondent to think that the interviewer represents a particular point of view. The interviewer must be friendly, relaxed, and pleasant and must appear interested in the welfare of the respondents. To provide honest answers to questions, the respondent must feel comfortable with the interviewer. Appropriate appearance and demeanor provide a basis for establishing a comfortable relationship and rapport. The interviewer should spend a few minutes with small talk in order to establish a proper relationship.

Before asking specific questions the interviewer should briefly explain the purpose of the interview and ask whether the respondent has any questions or concerns. The questions are then addressed to the respondent in the exact words indicated on the interview schedule. Questions should not be rephrased because wording can be very important to the outcome.

The questions should be read without error or stumbling, in a natural, unforced manner. To accomplish this, the interviewer needs to be very familiar with the questions and should practice asking the questions aloud.

As the subject responds to the questions, the interviewer must record the answers. The recording is usually done in one of two ways, by tape recording or by means of written notes. Taped answers can be analyzed by several judges and used to estimate reliability. Tape recording the answers is generally most useful with open-ended questions. A tape recorder will obviously collect the information more completely and objectively than notes, but the mere presence of a recorder may disrupt the interview and affect the responses, especially if personal questions are asked. If the questions are highly structured there is little need for recorded responses.

The most common method used to record responses is taking notes based on the answers. There are two extremes with note taking. At one extreme the interviewer can try to write the exact response as it is given, and at the other the interviewer waits until the interview is over and then reconstructs the answer to each question. The problem with taking verbatim notes is that it takes much time during the interview; on the other hand much information is lost when interviewers rely solely on their memories to write answers following the interview. Most interviewers compromise between these extremes and during the interview take abbreviated notes that can be expanded upon after the interview is completed.

Probing for further clarification of an answer is a skill that can often lead to incomplete or inaccurate responses. The interviewer must allow sufficient time for the respondent to answer and should avoid anticipating and cuing a potential answer. Probes should also be neutral so as not to affect the nature of the response. If the initial question usually results in probing, then it is useful to list some probes next to the question. This allows time to develop the best probe and standardizes the probes for all interviews.

After all questions have been answered, the interviewer should thank the respondent and allow time for the respondent to make comments or suggestions regarding the topic of the questions or the interview in general. Since the respondent is taking time to cooperate, it is important to end the interview in a positive manner.

Excerpt 7.5 is taken from a study that used interviews as the technique to gather data. The excerpt is the material that was included in the methods section of the article under the subheadings Interviewers and Procedure. The purpose of the

EXCERPT 7.5
Interviewing

INTERVIEWERS

Four interviewers were used to collect the data: two male graduate students in psychology, one female graduate student in psychology, and one female with a Bachelor of Science in psychology. All interviewers were introduced to the children and spent time observing each of the six classrooms from which the subjects were taken.

Interviewers were trained in the use of the Elig-Frieze Coding Scheme (Elig & Frieze, 1975) so that they could recognize responses that were of uncertain codability on one or more of the causal dimensions. When the child's response was unclear for coding purposes, the interviewer probed to clarify the exact meaning of the child's response. The first probe was always a simple repetition of the child's response, in the child's own words. In most cases this would cause the child to elaborate the initial response. However, if the child did not elaborate or if the elaboration still left a dimension uncertain, the interviewer would ask one of a set of prearranged questions. For example, the most common probe involved the clarification of the stability dimension, with a response such as "because he tried." If the repetition probe was ineffective, the interviewer would ask, "Did he always try or just try sometimes?" This always led to clarification. But overall, initial probes were needed in less than 5% of the responses. If during the coding of the transcribed interviews the judges believed that the interviewer's probing had biased the child's response, the judges were instructed to code only that part of the response that preceded the biasing intervention.

PROCEDURE

Interview schedules were determined in advance to incorporate the previously discussed design considerations. Arrangements were made with the school's administration to interview the children in vacant rooms near their classrooms and to audiotape all interviews. Each child was interviewed separately. Interviewers escorted the children from their classroom to the interviewing room. After a period of making the children as comfortable as possible by asking them about their families, what they had heard about the experiment, and by letting them listen to their voice on the tape recorder, the interview began. All interviews began with the interviewer reciting a common introduction.

> I am going to show you pictures that might be used in storybooks to help tell the stories. The stories will be about kids like you. And the stories will be about things that have probably happened to you or someone you know. What I am going to do is show you the pictures and tell you a little bit of the story. Because you know a lot about kids, I would like you to help me make the stories as true as possible.

Using a predetermined randomized order, the four stories with similar outcomes were presented to the child one at a time. Before telling the child the story, the interviewer handed the child a photograph representing the story. When interviewers thought that the child's response was of questionable codability, they probed. When interviewers were satisfied that they understood the child's response, they handed the child the next picture and the process continued. When all four stories were completed, children were escorted back to their classrooms by their interviewers.

Source: From Frieze, I. H., and Snyder, H. M., "Children's beliefs about the causes of success and failure in school settings," *Journal of Educational Psychology*, 72, 186–196, 1980. Copyright © 1980 by the American Psychological Association. Reprinted by permission of the publisher and authors.

Excerpt 7.5 is taken from a study that used interviews as the technique to gather data. The excerpt is the material that was included in the methods section of the article under the subheadings Interviewers and Procedure. The purpose of the study was to assess the causal explanations children use to explain success and failure. The subjects were first, third, and fifth graders, and the second sentence of the excerpt shows that, to establish rapport, the interviewers spent time with the children before the interviews. The second paragraph of the excerpt shows how probes were made, and the Procedure section describes the setting of the interviews. The questions that the subjects responded to were semistructured. The children were to be told the story and then asked, "Why did he get a high grade?" or "Why did he do such a poor job?"

■ OBSERVATION SCHEDULES ■

In a sense, all techniques of gathering data involve observation of some kind. As a general term, then, the word *observation* is used to describe the data that are collected, regardless of the technique employed in the study. Observational research methods also refer, however, to a more specific method of collecting information that is very different from interviews or questionnaires. As a technique for gathering information, the observational method relies on a researcher's seeing and hearing things and recording these observations, rather than relying on subjects' self-report responses to questions or statements.

The role of the observer in most quantitative research is to remain detached from the group or process, and thus act as a **complete observer.** A researcher may, for example, want to study the adjustment of college freshmen to campus life by observing the behavior of freshmen in various settings as an outsider, not participating but simply recording information.

The role of observer also depends on the degree of inference or judgment that is required. At one extreme, the observer makes **high inference** observations, which require the observer to make judgments or inferences based on the observed behaviors. What is recorded with high inference observation is the judgment of the observer. For example, a high inference observation of a teacher would be a rating made by the principal on factors like classroom management and enthusiasm. The principal would observe the class and make a rating of excellent, good, fair, or poor in each of the two areas. **Low inference** observation, on the other hand, requires the observer to record specific behaviors without making judgements in a more global sense. Thus, the principal might record the number of rebukes or cues used by the teacher as information that is used subsequently to judge classroom management. Low inference observation usually is more reliable, but many would argue that it is necessary to make judgments, based on the complexity and multitude of variables in a classroom, for valid observations. An in-between role for the observer is to make judgments (high inference) and then record the specific behaviors and context that led to the inference implied in the judgment.

Justification

The primary advantages of using observational methods are that the researcher does not need to worry about the limitations of self-report bias, social desirability, or response set, and the information is not limited to what can be recalled accurately by the subjects. Behavior can thus be recorded as it occurs naturally. This advantage is very important for research designed to study what occurs in real life as opposed to highly contrived or artificial settings. However, observational research is expensive and difficult to conduct reliably for complex behavior. It is relatively easy and straightforward to record simple behavior objectively, but most studies focus on more complex behavior that is difficult to define and assess through observation. There is also the problem of the way the observer affects the behavior of subjects by being present in the setting.

Defining Observational Units

The first step in developing an observational study is to define in precise terms what will be observed. Beginning with the research problem or question, the variables that need to be observed are ascertained. If the problem or question is general, such as, "How long are students engaged academically?" then the researcher must narrow the purpose to obtain specific, measurable units that can be observed. Since it is impossible to observe everything that occurs, the researcher must decide upon the variables or units of analysis that are most important and then define the behavior so that it can be recorded objectively.

Recording Observations

Once the researcher defines the behavior to be observed, he or she must decide how to record the observations. There are five different recording procedures: duration recording, frequency recording, interval recording, continuous recording, and time sampling.

Duration Recording.   In **duration recording** the observer indicates the length of time a particular kind of behavior lasts. Often a stop watch is used to keep track of the duration of the behavior. The researcher thus simply looks for a type of behavior (for example, *out of seat; talking to other students*) and records the length of time this type of behavior occurs within a given time span.

Frequency-count Recording.   **Frequency-count recording** is used when the observer is interested only in the frequency with which the behavior occurs, not the length of time it may persist. Generally, the observer has a list of several kinds of behavior that will be recorded and keeps a running tally to indicate how often each occurs. Obviously, this type of recording is best when the duration of the behavior is short (from one to five seconds).

Interval Recording.   In **interval recording** a single subject is observed for a given interval of time (usually from ten seconds to one minute) and the behaviors that occur are recorded. The observer could indicate that each kind of behavior either does or does not occur, or he or she may record how many times it occurs within each interval.

Continuous Observation.   In **continuous observation** the observer provides a brief description of the behavior of the subject. The description is written in chronological order and the observer must decide which kind of behavior is important.

Time Sampling.   In **time sampling** the observer selects, at random or on a fixed schedule, the time periods that will be used to observe particular kinds of behavior. This procedure is used in conjunction with each of the four previously mentioned procedures.

If possible, it is best to locate existing observational schedules that have been standardized to some degree. Virtually hundreds of schedules have been developed, and because they have been pilot tested and used in previous studies, they are more likely than new schedules to demonstrate good validity and reliability. Helpful sourcebooks of established schedules are Simon and Boyer (1974) and Borich and Madden (1977).

Training Observers

The most important limitation of complete observation is with the person who records what is seen and heard—the observer. The difficulty lies in obtaining observations that are objective, unbiased, and accurate in the sense that the observer has avoided influencing the behavior of the subjects. The objectivity of the observer is dependent to some degree on the specificity of the behavior. That is, a kind of behavior described as "teasing other students" is much less specific and subject to error in interpretation than something as specific and objective as "raises hand" or "leaves chair."

Bias is a factor in observational research to the extent that the idiosyncratic perceptions and interpretations of the observer, influenced by previous experiences, affect the recording of behavior. While it is next to impossible to eliminate bias, there is a need to control it. One way bias is limited is by carefully choosing observers. Obviously it would be a bad idea to choose, as an observer of the effects of open education, an advocate of that kind of education, just as it would be unfair to choose a known opponent of open education, since their preconceived notions could easily bias their observations. A second approach to controlling bias is to use carefully trained observers, comparing their observations with each other's in similar and different situations. Third, bias is mitigated by using two observers in each setting during the study. As long as the observers agree independently, there is less chance that bias is a confounding factor. A final type of bias that needs to be considered is contamination, which may occur if the observer is knowledgeable about the specifics of the study. In a study of the differences between so-called good and bad teachers, for example, if the observer knows before making the observations which teachers are supposedly good and which bad, this knowledge is likely to bias the observations. It is thus best for the observers to have little or no knowledge of the purpose of the study. Their job is to observe and record in an objective, detached manner.

■ UNOBTRUSIVE MEASURES ■

Questionnaires, interviews, and direct observation are intrusive or reactive in the sense that the participants realize they are being questioned or watched. A major difficulty with subjects' awareness that they are participants is that their behavior may be affected by this knowledge. A type of measurement that is considered to be **nonreactive,** in which subjects are asked or required to do nothing out of the ordinary, is called unobtrusive. **Unobtrusive measures** provide data that are uninfluenced by an awareness of the subjects that they are participants, or by an alteration in the natural course of events. According to Webb et al. (1981), unobtrusive (or nonreactive) measures control four sources of error that may occur because of the respondents' knowledge that they are participating in a study. These sources of error include:

1. The guinea pig effect, in which the subjects behave differently because they feel like guinea pigs. They may try to invalidate the results by being inaccurate, defensive, or dishonest. The feeling they have is one of being used for experiments, and this feeling often leads to antagonism, animosity, or anger.
2. Role selection, in which the subject takes on the behavior that would be expected by a person in that position. The subject takes the perspective: "What kind of a person should I be as I answer these questions or do these tasks?" (Webb et al., 1981, p. 16).
3. Measurement as a change agent, similar to the effect of testing on internal validity.
4. Response sets, the tendency to respond in certain ways because of the nature of the measurement (for example, viewing participation in the study as socially desirable; taking the attitude of acquiescence; finding problems with the wording of the questions).

The major types of unobtrusive measures are as follows:

1. Physical traces. Physical traces are data that can be accumulated by noting the physical changes that occur in something over time. Such a change is

usually either a gain (accretion) or loss (erosion) in physical evidence. Librarians have used the erosion principle for many questions, including the determination of the most popular books by the frequency with which they are checked out or by the wear on the cover and pages.

2. Archives: The running record. Archival running records include public documents that are produced regularly for a particular purpose and are examined at a later date for investigation of a research problem. The level of skills in writing composition and grammar of college students, for example, could be studied by examining copies of student newspapers over a number of years.

3. Archives: The episodic and private record. A second type of archival record is not intended to be public. Rather, these documents are private and produced sporadically. Examples of this type of data include personal letters and diaries, sales records, and industrial and institutional reports. School morale may be studied, for instance, by examining the nature of memos principals send teachers or the minutes from faculty meetings.

4. Simple observation. Simple unobtrusive observation occurs when the observer is unobserved and the situation is unaffected by the observer. The subject is unaware of being researched. At a school assembly, for example, it would be unobtrusive to observe students' behavior without affecting their behavior because the observer could easily blend with the rest of the crowd at the assembly.

5. Contrived observation. Observation that is termed *contrived* involves a deliberate intervention by the researcher in order to make specific observations. It changes naturally occurring events, but the subjects are unaware of being observed and believe the situation has occurred naturally, since it appears uncontrived. Examples of contrived observations include the use of reporting apparatus (microphone or camera), or arranging conditions to deceive the subjects. This type of observation has the potential to be ethically questionable, and any study that uses contrived observations should receive clearance from a review board.

Unobtrusive measures have certain advantages over other types of data collection. Because the techniques are not well known in education, little research has actually involved the use of the techniques. For further information see Webb et al. (1981), and Sechrest (1979). These sources offer many good examples of unobtrusive studies and demonstrate the utility of the techniques for social environments like schools.

■ SUMMARY ■

This chapter has introduced several techniques that are commonly used to collect descriptive, quantitative data. These techniques are used in basic, applied, and evaluation research and can be used in experimental, nonexperimental, or *ex post facto* research. The major points in the chapter are the following:

1. Evidence to establish valid inferences from test scores should be appropriate to the use of the results.
2. Evidence for validity has four components: content-related, concurrent criterion-related, predictive criterion-related, and construct-related.
3. There are four major types of reliability that are used to judge the consistency of measures: stability, equivalence, stability and equivalence, and internal consistency.
4. Standardized tests provide uniform procedures for administration and scoring.
5. Norm-referenced test results are based on comparing a score to the scores of a reference or norming group.
6. Criterion-referenced test results compare a score to an established standard of performance.
7. Aptitude tests predict behavior.
8. Achievement tests measure prior learning.
9. Noncognitive instruments measure personality, attitudes, values, and interests.
10. Written questionnaires are economical, can assure anonymity, and permit use of standardized questions.
11. Existing questionnaires probably have better reliability and validity than questionnaires developed by a researcher.
12. Items in a questionnaire should be based on specific objectives and be clear, relevant, short, and uncluttered. Biased items and terms should be avoided.
13. Items are in a closed or open format, depending on the objectives and nature of the information desired.
14. Scaled items, such as Likert scale and Semantic Differential scale items, use gradations of responses.
15. Questionnaires should be pretested and revised as necessary.
16. Interview schedules provide flexibility and the ability to probe and clarify responses; they note nonverbal as well as verbal behavior. They provide high response rates but are costly and more susceptible to bias.
17. Interview questions are either structured, semistructured, or unstructured. Each type has advantages and disadvantages.
18. Observational procedures can record naturally occurring behavior and avoid some of the disadvantages associated with questionnaires and interviews.
19. Establishing and maintaining reliability and validity in observational research is difficult.
20. Low inference observations stress objective recording of behavior, while high inference observations require greater subjective judgments of observers.
21. Recording procedures in direct observation include duration, frequency, interval, continuous, and time sampling.
22. Unobtrusive measures are nonreactive and can be used to collect data without disruption of a naturally occurring event.

■ SELF-INSTRUCTIONAL ■
REVIEW EXERCISES

Sample answers are in the back of the book.

Test Items

1. Content validity is most appropriate for
   a. predictive tests.
   b. achievement tests.
   c. aptitude tests.
   d. Both b and c are correct.

2. Criterion-related evidence differs from criterion-referenced tests in that
   a. criterion-referenced tests uses norm groups while criterion-related evidence uses criteria.
   b. criterion-related evidence is a type of reliability; criterion-referenced tests uses norm groups.
   c. criterion-related evidence is for validity; criterion-referenced is for reliability.
   d. criterion-referenced uses criteria; criterion-related is for validity.

3. Internal consistency estimates of reliability are widely used because
   a. only one form of a test is needed.
   b. the reliability coefficient is usually very high.
   c. it is the easiest to calculate.
   d. it is more accurate than stability and equivalence estimates.

4. Standardized tests are different from locally devised instruments in that standardized tests
   a. have norms as well as technical support.
   b. have greater flexibility.
   c. are more valid.
   d. have uniform administration and scoring procedures.

5. The purpose of an aptitude test is to
   a. measure intelligence.
   b. predict performance.
   c. measure multiple aspects of potential strengths.
   d. assess achievement.

6. Noncognitive inventories are generally
   a. susceptible to faking.
   b. high in reliability.
   c. high in validity.
   d. socially desirable.

7. Choose the correct sequence for developing a questionnaire.
   a. defining objectives, justification, writing items, pretesting
   b. pretesting, defining objectives, justification, writing items
   c. justification, pretesting, defining objectives, writing items
   d. justification, defining objectives, writing items, pretesting

8. All of the following should be adhered to in writing statements or questions *except* for
   a. avoiding biased items.
   b. avoiding negatively worded items.
   c. using double-barrelled questions.
   d. making items clear.
   e. making items short.

9. Social desirability is a form of
   a. bias.
   b. unreliability.
   c. situational constraint.
   d. Both a and c are correct.

10. The format of a questionnaire should
    a. use every available space on each page.
    b. use abbreviated items to save space.
    c. put important items first on long questionnaires.
    d. be as short as possible in number of pages.

11. Closed-form questions or statements are best used for
    a. easily categorized information.
    b. initial pilot studies.
    c. large scale studies.
    d. Both a and c are correct.

12. Likert scale and Semantic Differential items are similar in that both
    a. use adjective opposites.
    b. are easy to construct.
    c. are difficult to score objectively.
    d. are scales.

13. Questionnaires need to be pretested because
    a. pretesting establishes reliability.
    b. insufficient variation in answers can be noted.
    c. trial data analyses can be noted.
    d. Both a and b are correct.

14. Semistructured questions in interviews are written in a format that allows
    a. free response to a limited question.
    b. forced choice response to a limited question.
    c. free response to a broad question.
    d. forced choice response to a broad question.

15. It is best for interviewers to adapt the specific wording of questions to the individual characteristics of the respondent. True or false?
    a. true   b. false

16. Interviewers should always dress in a businesslike manner (for example, tie, suit, dress). True or false?
    a. true   b. false

17. The most common approach to recording answers in an interview is
    a. audiotape recorder.   c. writing verbatim responses.
    b. videotape recorder.   d. writing notes.

18. The complete observer
    a. tries to become a member of the group of subjects.
    b. is unobtrusive.
    c. is detached from the setting.
    d. is completely informed as to the nature of the study.

19. Observation is most objective when the observer has to check appropriate boxes on a standard, easy to interpret form. True or false?
    a. true   b. false

20. Observer bias can be controlled by all of the following except
    a. choosing observers carefully.
    b. informing the observer of the nature of the study.
    c. carefully training observers.
    d. using two or more observers in each situation.

21. Another word for *unobtrusive* measures would be
    a. biased.   c. nonreactive.
    b. unreliable.   d. unbiased.

Application Problems

1. For each of the following cases indicate whether the questionnaire, interview, or observation technique would be most appropriate, and justify your answer.
    a. Reasons that 1,500 couples believe they have problems in their marriages
    b. The attitudes of seventh-grade students toward mainstreamed children
    c. Knowledge of parents regarding the curriculum in the school
    d. Average age and experience of school principals
    e. Effect of watching violent TV programs on aggressive behavior
    f. College students' perceptions of the effectiveness of residence hall advisors
    g. Attitudes of preschool children toward their parents
    h. Attitudes of teachers toward competence-based instruction

2. Indicate what is wrong with the following questionnaire items:
   a. What do you think about open education?
   b. Rank the statements from most important to least important.
   c. Senior and junior high school teachers need more training in ways to motivate students.

_____	_____	_____	_____
Strongly agree	Agree	Disagree	Strongly disagree

   d. Ms. Jones is a good teacher.

_____	_____	_____	_____
Strongly agree	Agree	Disagree	Strongly disagree

3. It is important for teachers to observe and record indications that their students are studying and trying to learn assigned material. If a third-grade teacher came to you and asked how such observations could be made with the least amount of disruption to the normal routine, what suggestions would you have?

CHAPTER 8

DESCRIPTIVE, CORRELATIONAL, AND SURVEY RESEARCH

■ KEY TERMS ■

descriptive research
developmental studies
longitudinal
cross-sectional
relationship studies
shotgun approach
prediction studies
predictor variable
criterion variable
multiple correlation
multiple regression prediction
   equation

regression coefficient
beta weights
coefficient of multiple
   correlation
spurious correlation
attenuation
restriction in range
coefficient of determination
survey research

This chapter presents the fundamentals of descriptive, correlational, and survey research, the three most common types of research found in education, with an emphasis on the importance of descriptive research. We discuss correlational research as a way to study relationships and predictions, and we summarize cautions in interpreting correlations. Finally, we present survey research as a method of data gathering for many descriptive and correlational studies.

■ DESCRIPTIVE RESEARCH ■

Descriptive research is concerned with the current status of something. This type of research describes existing achievement, attitudes, behaviors, or other characteristics of a group of subjects. A descriptive study asks *what is*; it reports things the way they *are*. Descriptive research is concerned primarily with the present and does not involve manipulation of independent variables. This research is non-experimental, so some use the terms "descriptive" and "non-experimental" interchangeably.

Descriptive research provides very valuable data, particularly when first investigating an area. For example, suppose you want to study how different college environments affect the development of college students. Before you can address this problem directly you must be able to describe accurately "college environments." Thus the first step would be to describe the environments, then relate different environments to student development. Or suppose you want to study the relationship between leadership styles of principals and teacher morale. Again, a first step is to describe principal leadership styles. The appropriate descriptive question might be: what are the leadership styles of principals? Here are some other descriptive research questions:

How much do college students exercise?
What are the attitudes of students toward mainstreamed children?
How often do students cheat?
What do teachers think about merit pay?
How do students spend their time during independent study?
What are the components of the gifted program?

Questions like these are very important because they provide the basis for asking additional questions. Once a phenomena is described adequately, developmental, difference, and relationship questions can be addressed. **Developmental studies** investigate changes of subjects over time. The same group of subjects may be studied over some length of time (**longitudinal**) on factors such as cognitive, social-emotional or physical variables. For example, a longitudinal developmental study of adult development would begin by identifying a group of adults as subjects, measure dependent variables like interests, goal satisfaction, friendship patterns, etc., and then continue to measure these variables for the same subjects every five years. Developmental studies can also be **cross-sectional** in which different groups of subjects (for example, as in our study of adult 20, 25, 30, 35, 40, and 45-year old groups) are studied at the same time.

An obvious advantage of longitudinal research is that the same group is studied over time, which ensures comparability of subjects. Another advantage is that the subjects respond to present circumstances, attitudes, beliefs, etc., rather than trying to recollect the past. A major disadvantage of longitudinal research is that it takes a long time to complete, and it involves significant commitments of the researcher's time, money, and resources. It is also difficult to keep track of subjects and maintain their cooperation for an extended period of time. Researchers involved in cross-sectional studies can study larger groups at less cost, all at the same time. Thus they do not need to wait years to complete the research. The major disadvantage of cross-sectional research is that selection differences between the groups may bias the results. For instance, in cross-sectional research on adult development, it may be difficult to compare today's 25-year-olds to older adults because in recent years young adults have waited somewhat longer to get married, while today's 45- and 50-year-old population married earlier in their lives. Thus, differences between these groups are confounded by marriage.

Difference questions compare the attitudes, behaviors, or characteristics of two or more groups of subjects. Examples of difference questions are:

> Is there a difference in eighth-grade compared to ninth-grade attitudes toward school?
> What is the difference between students attending private schools and students attending public schools?
> How are new teachers different from experienced teachers?
> Is there a difference between second-, third-, and fourth-grade self-concept scores?

In each case, the researcher makes a comparison based on descriptive data.

Relationship studies investigate the degree to which variations in one factor are related to variations in another factor. Relationships can be established either by looking at differences or correlations. Difference relationships can be postulated from difference questions. For example, if you find that the self-concept scores of students increase from second to third and third to fourth grade, then there is a relationship between grade level and self-concept. More commonly, relationship studies are correlational; that is, a correlation coefficient is used to describe the relationship.

Excerpt 8.1 is an example of how descriptive data are reported in journals. This study summarized children's responses to why they succeeded or failed in school. Essentially this is a description of children's responses. Since both success and failure conditions are used to generate the responses, the research also examines differences of success compared to failure conditions.

■ CORRELATIONAL RESEARCH ■

Chapter 6 described the correlation coefficient. In this chapter we use the basic idea of correlation as a way to conceptualize research problems. We first present simple relationship studies, then more complex multifactor prediction research, followed by cautions in interpreting correlations.

Relationship Studies

In a simple relationship study, researchers obtain two scores for each subject and then use the pairs of scores to calculate a correlation coefficient. Each score represents a variable in the study. The variables are selected because theory, research, or experience suggest that the variables may be related. Then they select a sample and collect data from the sample. It is important in correlational research that researchers select the subjects to provide a range of responses on the variables. If the subjects are homogeneous with respect to either variable, a relationship be-

---

EXCERPT 8.1
Descriptive Results

The data in Table I indicate that the children were able to identify the variables that affect their success and failure. Their initial attributions were primarily task attributions (46% to 58% said the words were easy). Their own effort was the next most common cause of their success (40% of the responses). When asked for a second response, the subjects evenly divided their answers among the four types of attributions. From the total responses, when they succeeded in reading a word, they were most likely to attribute their success to their effort (33%) or to task difficulty (37%). When they failed to read a word they were most likely to attribute their failure to task features (40%).

TABLE I. Percentages of Children Who Made Various Attributes in Response to Why They Succeeded (S) or Failed (F)

| | Question Condition | | | | | |
| Types of Attributions | Initial[a] | | Second[b] | | Total | |
	S	F	S	F	S	F
Ability	.10	.02	.22	.05	.16	.03
Effort	.40	.12	.25	.15	.33	.14
Task Difficulty	.46	.58	.28	.22	.37	.40
Luck	.02	.15	.15	.20	.08	.18
Other[c]	.02	.12	.10	.38	.06	.25

[a]*Initial* includes those children who responded spontaneously and those who were given a choice of responses if they did not respond spontaneously.

[b]*Second* is a second attribution the children gave.

[c]Other is composed of "don't know's," "I guessed," and no response.

Note. N = 40.

Source: From Cauley, K. M. and Murray, F. B., "Structure of Children's Reasoning About Attributes of School Success and Failure." *American Educational Research Journal*, 19, 473–480. Copyright © 1982, American Educational Research Association, Washington, DC. Reprinted by permission.

---

tween the variables is unlikely. Similarly, it is important to select instruments that are reliable and will provide a range of responses. Various methods of instrumentation can be used, including tests, questionnaires, interviews, or observations. Regardless of the type of instrumentation it is best to conduct a pilot test or have previous data from similar subjects to assure reliability and variability in responses. For instance, it is often difficult to relate student ratings of professors to other variables because of a ceiling effect in such ratings. Similarly, norm-referenced achievement scores of gifted students are unlikely to correlate with other variables because the scores may have a restricted range (we will discuss restricted range in more detail later in the chapter).

In some relationship studies correlations of several variables may be reported (refer to examples in Chapter 6). In fact, an advantage of correlational research is that it permits the simultaneous study of several variables. However, it is possible for some researchers, without reasonable justification, to measure a large number of variables to find some significant relationships. This is called the **shotgun approach,** and is used inappropriately in the hope that some of the many correlations calculated will indicate significant relationships.

Prediction Studies

There are many situations in education when we need to make predictions. Teachers predict student reactions in making certain assignments. Principals predict teacher behavior on the basis of the criteria used for evaluation of teacher effectiveness. Teachers counsel students to focus on particular majors on the basis of occupational interest or aptitude tests. Students are selected for special programs because teachers predict that they will do better than other students.

We conduct **prediction studies** to provide a more accurate estimation of prediction. Suppose you are the director of admissions at a small, selective college. A large number of students apply to the college each year, many more than can be admitted. How will you decide which students should be admitted? You could draw names from a hat randomly, but then some students will be admitted who may flunk out, while some well-qualified students will be rejected. You decide that it would be best if you could *predict*, on the basis of already established characteristics, which students are most likely to succeed. Since it seems reasonable that prior achievement will predict later achievement, you see if there is a correlation between high school G.P.A. (prior) and college G.P.A. (later achievement). When you discover that these two variables correlate .70, then you have information which can be used to select students. Other things being equal, high school students with high G.P.A.s are more likely to have high college G.P.A.s than high school students with low G.P.A.s.

In this case high school G.P.A. is a **predictor variable,** and college G.P.A. is a **criterion variable.** The predictor variable is measured *before* the criterion variable, whereas in a simple relationship study both variables are measured at about the same time. Thus, in prediction studies, outcomes like grade point average, dropouts, success as a leader or manager, effectiveness of a drug to cure a disease, and the like are related to behaviors that occurred prior to the criterion. To do this it is necessary to have data on the subjects that span some length of time. This can be done retrospectively through records on subjects, or it can be done longitudinally by first collecting predictor variable data, waiting an appropriate amount of time, and then collecting the criterion variable data. Suppose, for example, you need to select the best new teachers for a school division. Essentially you are predicting that the new teachers you choose will be effective. In your state all prospective teachers take the Teacher Examinations (TE), so you are able to study the predictive relationship of the TE to teacher effectiveness (measured by principal and supervisor evaluations). Once you have established the predictive power of the TE with one group of teachers you would test the predictive relationship with another group of new teachers. Once confirmed, the TE could be used to help select future teachers.

In general, short-term predictions are more accurate than long-term predictions. This is because in long-term predictions, like success as a principal, there are more opportunities for additional variables to influence the criterion. Also, we know that the correlation between two factors generally decreases as the amount of time between the variables increases.

Multiple Correlation

Up to this point we have discussed prediction studies that have one predictor variable. It may be obvious to you that in many, perhaps most, situations the prediction would be more accurate if you had additional information to make the prediction. That is, by having several predictor variables you would be able to make a more accurate prediction. Suppose in our example of predicting effective teaching we also had information like college G.P.A., references, results of an interview, and a statement by each applicant in addition to the TE scores. Each subject would receive a score for each variable (the references, results of the interview, and statement would be judged and scored according to a rating system). All of the predictor variables can be combined to form what is called a **multiple regression prediction equation.** This equation adds together the predictive power of several independent variables. Each predictor variable could be represented by X_1, X_2, X_3, etc., and the criterion variable by Y. Thus, in our example:

$$Y = X_1 + X_2 + X_3 + X_4 + X_5$$

where

Y = teaching effectiveness

X_1 = TE score

X_2 = college G.P.A.

X_3 = rating on references

X_4 = rating on interview

X_5 = rating on applicant's statement

To obtain a predicted teacher effectiveness score, values on each of the five predictor variables would be placed in the equation and each would be weighted by a number called a **regression coefficient.** Since the units of each predictor variable are different (ratings might range from 0 to 10, G.P.A. from 0 to 4) the regression coefficients in the equation cannot be compared directly. To compare the predictive power of the variables, the regression coefficients are converted to **beta weights,** which can be compared directly. Thus, in our example the relative contribution of each variable can be compared. If the beta weight for TE is .32 and the beta weight for G.P.A. is .48, then G.P.A. is contributing more than the TE in predicting teaching effectiveness. The combined effect of the independent variables, in terms of predictive power, to the dependent variable is represented by R, the coefficient of multiple correlation. The **coefficient of multiple correlation** can be thought of as a simple correlation of all the independent variables together with the dependent variable.

Excerpt 8.2 provides an example of the use of multiple correlation. In this study teacher burnout was predicted by eleven independent variables. The table summarizes the predictive relationship of the eleven variables to three indices of teacher burnout: emotional exhaustion, depersonalization, and personal accomplishment. Of the eleven independent variables only those that were entered first (sex and age) or added significantly to the overall relationship are included in the table. In multiple regressions some variables can be forced or entered into the equation first to control for certain factors, that is, to remove these factors as influences on the relationship. In this case the researchers wanted to control for the effect of sex and age to see how much other variables could predict.

Interpreting Correlational Research

Correlation coefficients are widely used in research and appear to be simple, straightforward indices of relationship. There are, however, several problems with the use of correlation that need to be understood fully. Most problems concern an overinterpretation—making too much of a measured relationship. In this section we present some important principles that will help you understand the meaning of results of correlational research.

Correlation and Causation.   You may be familiar with the well-known injunction, "never infer causation from correlation." This is a principle that is virtually drilled into the minds of students, and for good reason, since it is probably the most violated principle of measures of relationship.

There are two reasons correlation does not infer causation: first, a relationship between X and Y may be high, but there is no way to know whether X causes Y or Y causes X; and second, there may be unmeasured variables that are affecting the relationship. With respect to the direction of possible causation, consider this example: A researcher finds a high positive correlation between self-concept and achievement. Does this mean that improving self-concept will cause an improvement in achievement? Perhaps, but it would be equally plausible for improved achievement to result in a higher self-concept. If we find that school dropout rates are negatively associated with teacher salaries, should we assume that higher teacher pay will cause fewer dropouts?

Unaccounted-for variables are also important to consider in interpreting correlations. Let us say that there is a positive relationship between attending church-related schools and honesty. Although the schools may help cause greater honesty, there are many other variables, such as family beliefs, parental

Results presented in Table 2 support previous findings that various contributors to burnout have differing effects upon the aspects of emotional exhaustion, depersonalization, and personal accomplishment (Maslach & Jackson, 1981; Schwab & Iwanicki, 1982a). For example, after controlling for sex and age, Role Conflict explained the largest percentage of variance in emotional exhaustion and depersonalization (24% and 12% respectively) while Autonomy does so in personal accomplishment (12%). Five of the hypothesized predictors accounted for significant variance in emotional exhaustion, four in depersonalization and only two in personal accomplishment. The only predictor significantly related to all aspects was Colleague Social Support. As indicated by the beta weights, the relationships between the significant organizational conditions and the aspects of burnout were in the directions hypothesized and had been reported in previous research (Maslach & Jackson, 1981; Schwab & Iwanicki, 1982a).

TABLE 2. Stepwise Multiple Regression Analyses for the Relationship Among Significant Organizational/Personal Variables and Three Aspects of Burnout When Controlling for Age and Sex (N = 339)

				Increase		For R^2
Step	Variable Entered	R	R^2	R^2	Beta	F**
Emotional Exhaustion						
1	Sex and Age[a]	.120	.014	.014		N.S.[b]
2	Role Conflict	.493	.243	.229	.48	35.17
3	Expectations	.537	.288	.059	.26	33.14
4	Colleague Social Support	.553	.306	.018	−.16	28.79
5	Contingent Punishment	.562	.315	.009	.10	24.95
6	Role Ambiguity	.570	.325	.010	−.13	22.27
Depersonalization						
1	Sex and Age[a]	.285	.081	.081		14.56
2	Role Conflict	.352	.124	.043	.21	15.50
3	Participation in Decision Making	.374	.140	.016	−.14	13.26
4	Contingent Punishment	.393	.155	.015	.12	11.92
5	Colleague Social Support	.407	.166	.011	−.12	10.76
Personal Accomplishment						
1	Sex and Age[a]	.192	.037	.037		6.33
2	Autonomy	.349	.122	.045	.29	15.14
3	Colleague Social Support	.366	.134	.012	.12	12.62

---

attitudes, and methods of discipline that would be more plausibly related in a causal way. Or what about the finding that schools that spend more per pupil have higher achievement? It would be a mistake to pump money into poor schools with the expectation that this will cause better achievement since family background, an unmeasured variable, would more likely be a much larger factor in achievement than per pupil expenditure.

These two limitations seem straightforward enough, but correlations are still misinterpreted. We will now convince you that there is a strong positive relationship between body weight and reading achievement. Unbelievable? Examine the explanation that follows (adapted from Halperin, 1978).

1. Plot the body weight and scores of a group of first graders.

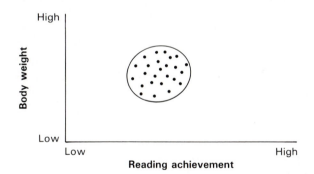

2. Next, add the scores of second graders:

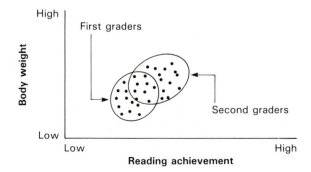

3. Finally, add the scores of pupils in grades three through six:

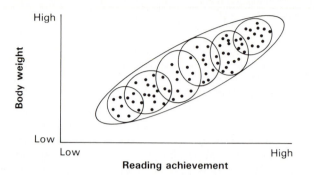

Voilà! We now have a positive relationship between body weight and reading achievement by stringing together a series of near-zero correlations. Why? Because a third variable that was not included, age, happens to be related to body weight, and, obviously, there is a positive relationship between age and reading achievement. If the reader believes that correlation did mean causation, then reading achievement could be improved by fattening up students! (Or improving reading achievement would lead to fatter students.)

Spurious Correlations.   Correlations are called **spurious** if they over- or under-represent the actual relationship. Spurious correlations that overestimate relationships are obtained if there is a common variable that is part of both the independent and the dependent variables. If, for example, a researcher has pretest and posttest data and measures the relationship between posttest scores and the gain scores from pretest to posttest, the correlation would be spuriously high because the posttest score is included in both variables. Obviously, when something is correlated with itself the relationship will be very high. Similarly, if there is a third unmeasured variable that is common to both variables, as with our example of reading achievement and body weight, the correlation will be spuriously high. Such a result would occur when correlating height with weight, since a third factor, age, is common to both.

Correlations obtained from two measures that are imperfectly reliable will result in coefficients lower than the true relationship between the measures. This lowering of the coefficient is referred to as **attenuation,** and occasionally researchers will compute a correction for attenuation to estimate what the correlation might have been if the measures were perfectly reliable. The most common circumstance in which a researcher will use this correlation is with pilot studies in which the measures used have low reliability.

Another situation in which the correlation coefficient is lower than the actual relationship is a case in which the range of scores on one of the variables is confined to a representation of only a part of the total distribution of that variable. This problem is called **restriction in range,** and it results in a lowering of the correlation. Suppose, for example, a researcher wants to investigate the relationship

FIGURE 8.1
Restriction of Range

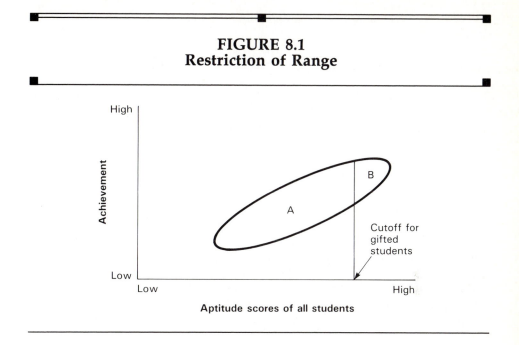

Aptitude scores of all students

between aptitude test scores and achievement of students in a program for the gifted. Figure 8.1 shows why the researcher would probably find only a small positive relationship between these two variables. Note that the figure illustrates the hypothetical aptitude and achievement scores for all students (A and B), along with the sample of students in the gifted program (B).

In this case the range of aptitude scores is thus limited, or restricted, to a small part of the total range of aptitude scores. If the full range of scores is utilized, then the correlation is highly positive. Restriction in range in part explains the usually modest relationship between college admissions tests and achievement in college—the range is restricted to students who have high test scores on the admissions tests. Under certain conditions a correction for restriction in range can be applied in these cases, in order to indicate what the correlation might have been if a large sample had been available.

Another situation that can lead to spurious correlations is one in which the sampling procedures result in a more heterogeneous or more homogeneous sample than is actually present in the population. This sampling bias would lead to either a high spurious correlation, if the sample is more heterogeneous, or a low spurious correlation, for a sample more homogeneous. If, for example, a researcher investigating the relationship between effective teaching behavior and student achievement for all students oversamples high achievers, resulting in a more homogeneous group than the population, the correlation would be spuriously low. If, however, the population had mostly gifted students but the procedures undersampled these gifted students, then the correlation would be spuriously high.

Size of Correlation Coefficients.   It has already been pointed out in Chapter 6 that correlations like 0.86, 0.95, and −0.89 are high; 0.43, −0.35, and 0.57 are moderate, and that 0.07, −0.01, and 0.12 are small, but these words only hint at the magnitude of the relationship. Because correlation coefficients are expressed as decimals, it is easy to confuse the decimal with percentages. The coefficient is a mathematical way of expressing the degree to which the variables covary, not an indication of the degree to which the variables share common properties or characteristics. To obtain an estimate of the proportion of the variance that the two measures share or have in common, the coefficient must be squared. A simple correlation of 0.40, squared, for example, indicates that the variables have 16 percent of their variance in common. In other words, 84 percent is left unexplained or unpredicted by a simple correlation of 0.40. Even for some high correlations, such as 0.70 and 0.80, the square of the correlations thus results in a moderate degree of common variance (49 and 64 percent, respectively, out of a total of 100 percent, which would be a perfect relationship). The index that results from squaring the correlation is called the **coefficient of determination.**

Another consideration with respect to the size of correlations is that many correlations are termed "significant" even though they may be quite low (such as 0.15, 0.08). Researchers use the word *significant* in the context of correlations to indicate that the coefficient is significantly different from zero (no relationship) at a specified level of confidence (Chapter 10 discusses *significance* and *level of confidence* in greater detail). If a study has a very large number of subjects (greater than 1000), then small correlations can be significant, but only in a statistical sense. We know that a simple correlation of 0.30, if significant, accounts for only 9 percent of the common variance, so that our interpretation needs to reflect the 91 percent of the variance that is unaccounted for. For research in which prediction is the primary goal, such low correlations, even though statistically significant, are of little practical significance. Generally, in studies investigating relationships only, correlations as low as 0.30 or 0.40 are useful, but in prediction studies or estimates of reliability and validity, higher correlations are needed. In educational research, if a very high correlation is reported, such as 1.00, 0.99, or 0.98, then the reader should suspect spurious results caused by methodological, design, or calculation inadequacies.

Finally, with respect to interpretation, the usefulness of correlations varies depending on whether the investigation is focusing on groups or on individuals. Generally, a much larger correlation is needed for use with individuals than groups. For correlations below about 0.35, only a small relationship is shown; this is of value in some exploratory research, but has little value in predictions concerning individuals or groups. In the middle range, from 0.35 to 0.75, crude group predictions can be made, and if several moderate correlations can be combined they can be used with individual predictions. Above 0.75 both individual and group predictions are useful with a single measure of correlation.

■ SURVEY RESEARCH ■

In **survey research** the investigator selects a sample of respondents and administers a questionnaire or conducts interviews to collect information on variables of interest. The data that are gathered are used to describe characteristics of a certain population. Surveys are used to learn about people's attitudes, beliefs, values, demographic facts, behavior, opinions, habits, desires, ideas, and other types of information. They are used frequently in business, politics, government, sociology, public health, psychology, and education because accurate information can be obtained for large numbers of people with a small sample. Chances are good, in fact, that you have more than once been part of a survey.

Most surveys describe the incidence, frequency, and distribution of the characteristics of an identified population. In addition to being descriptive, surveys can also be used to explore relationships between variables, or in an explanatory way. Examples of topics in each of the three categories are given below.

Descriptive

What is the average length of time teachers use to prepare lessons?
Describe the science attitudes of fourth-grade students.
What are the most popular counseling techniques used by high school counselors?
What do principals think about mainstreaming emotionally disturbed children?

Exploring a Relationship

Do teachers who favor tenure try innovations less often than teachers who disapprove of tenure?
Is there a relationship between teacher attitudes toward discipline and student satisfaction with the class?
Do marital couples who blame each other for marital problems have more conflict than spouses who blame themselves?

In an Explanatory Way

Why do some principals send regular letters to parents and other principals rarely send letters?
What is the reason some integrated schools are truly integrated while others remain segregated?
Why are the students in one school achieving better than similar students in another school?

Surveys are used in education for a wide variety of purposes. Many doctoral dissertations use surveys; state departments of education use surveys to determine levels of knowledge and to ascertain needs in order to plan programs; schools use surveys to evaluate aspects of the curriculum or administrative procedures; governmental agencies use surveys to form public policy; colleges of education use surveys to evaluate their courses and programs. Much of the use of surveys is for practical purposes and could be classified as evaluation research, although surveys are also used for basic and applied research.

Because surveys are used so frequently and are adaptable to a wide range of uses, some people develop the mistaken opinion that surveys are easy to conduct. Surveys involve much more than simply mailing a set of questions to a group of subjects, however. The reason surveys are so popular is that, if they are done correctly, sound information can be collected from a small sample that can be generalized to a large population. It is thus necessary to employ correct sampling procedures and to design the data collection techniques carefully in order to assure reliability and validity.

In conducting survey research, it is helpful to follow a particular sequence of steps. The sequence is outlined below.

1. *Define purpose and objectives.* The first step is to define the purpose and objectives of the research. This should include a general statement and specific objectives that define in detail the information that needs to be collected. The objectives should be as clear-cut and unambiguous as possible. This is not always as easy as it sounds. An objective like "The purpose of this research is to determine the values of college students" is actually quite vague. What is meant by "values"? Which college students are included? Another way to evaluate the objectives is to ask whether there are specific uses for the results. Often data are collected with the idea that either "it would be nice to know" or "let's see what the results are and then decide how to use the data." Either notion is a weak reason to collect data. The researcher needs to know before the data are collected exactly how the results will be used.

2. *Select resources and target population.* It is necessary to decide upon the total amount of time, money, and personnel available before designing the specific methodology to gather the data. A locally developed questionnaire might be best, for example, but financial constraints may make it necessary to use an instrument that has established reliability and validity. The amount of money available will also affect the size of the sample that should be drawn. The objectives of the study may also need to be modified to reflect the financial constraints. It is better to do a small study well than a large study poorly. It is also important to define the population or target group to which the researcher intends to generalize. The definition is a list of characteristics or boundaries set up so that the external validity is clear and so that the group from which the sampling is done is clear. The definition should consider both design and practicality. If the population is too broad, such as "all teachers," or "all students," then it will be difficult and expensive to obtain a representative sample. If the population is too narrow, such as "male special education teachers with more than five years' teaching experience," then the external validity of the study is weak.

3. *Choose and develop techniques for gathering data.* The questionnaire and personal interview are the most frequently used techniques for collecting data. When used in a survey, the techniques must be standardized, so that information from each respondent is gathered in the same manner. The administration is the same, as is the format and sequence of questions or statements.

4. *Sampling.* The basic principles of sampling were presented in Chapter 5. Most surveys use a form of random sampling in order to assure adequate representation of the population. The random sampling is often stratified on some variables, such as sex, grade level, ability level, and socioeconomic status.

5. *Letter of transmittal.* In the case of mailed questionnaires the nature of the cover letter, or letter of transmittal, is crucial in determining the percentage of subjects who return completed forms. The letter should be brief and establish the credibility of the researcher and the study. This is accomplished by including the following: the names and identifications of the investigators; the purpose and intention of the study without complete details; the importance of the study for the respondent and profession; the importance of the respondent for the study; the protection afforded the respondent by keeping the identities of the respondents confidential; a time limit that is neither too long nor too short (usually a week or less); endorsements for the study by recognized institutions or groups; a brief description of the questionnaire and procedure; mention of an opportunity to obtain results; a request for cooperation and honesty; and thanks to the respondent. Naturally, if the letter is neat, professional in appearance, and without grammatical or spelling errors, the respondent will be more likely to cooperate. Excerpt 8.3 contains a sample letter illustrating these points.

6. *Follow-up.* The initial mailing of the letter of transmittal, questionnaire, and stamped return-addressed envelope will usually result in a response rate of from forty to sixty percent—that is, from forty to sixty percent of the sample will typically return the questionnaires. This rate is higher for short questionnaires of obvious importance and lower for long questionnaires on obscure topics. After a period of from two to four weeks it is a good idea to send follow-up letters to those subjects who have not responded. The follow-up letter should contain another questionnaire, a stamped return-addressed envelope, and a cover letter that again stresses the importance of the study and the importance of the subject's contribution. In the case of surveys that have assured anonymity, it is impossible to know who has or has not returned the questionnaire. In this case researchers can use one of several procedures: They can send a follow-up letter to everyone, indicating that those who did return the questionnaire may ignore the follow-up; the researcher can code the questionnaires without the knowledge of the subjects in order to identify respondents; or the subjects can send a separate postcard when they return the questionnaire. The first follow-up correspondence usually brings ten to twenty percent more returns, and a second follow-up (a postcard, a telegram, or a telephone call) will add another five to ten percent to the return rate. If the researchers can obtain a total return rate of seventy percent or better, they are doing very well. In many studies the return rate is closer to fifty or sixty percent.

7. *Nonrespondents.* In any survey study there will be a percentage of subjects who fail to return the completed questionnaire. These subjects are called nonrespondents, and if the nonrespondents comprise thirty percent or more of the total sample, then the researcher may need to make additional efforts to check whether the inclusion of these subjects would have altered the results. For most surveys that attain a sixty percent return rate or better, the nonrespondents will

EXCERPT 8.3
Letter of Transmittal

Dear Parent Association Executive Board Member,

Your position in education is an important one.

Importance of respondent

Your concern for your children and their school is demonstrated by the position that you hold in the Parent Association. As an executive board member you are a key person in many ways. You listen to the parents and speak for them. You listen and speak to the principal and work with him or her. You are an important link between school and community. Your decisions have great importance for your children and their school.

Importance of study

The elementary principal's position is also important. You are well aware of the serious responsibilities that he or she has. His or her decisions affect your children daily, and may very well affect them for the rest of their lives.

Identify investigator; purpose of study; importance of respondent

I am doing a doctoral study at St. John's University, New York City, that is concerned with Parent Association executive board members and elementary principals. As an executive board member, you, and your executive role, are of particular interest to this study.

This is a nation-wide study. You, and all of the participants, have been randomly selected. Permission has been secured from the superintendent to request your cooperation.

Request cooperation

We share a common interest and concern for the problems under investigation. It is on this basis of a common goal of increased knowledge about education that I am requesting your cooperation in filling out the enclosed questionnaire.

Description of questionnaire

The questionnaire contains three parts. The first two parts are concerned with your perceptions of the principal and the third part requests personal information about you.

Endorsement for the study

The questionnaire has been carefully studied and evaluated by professionals and Parent Association executive board members.

The executive board members were asked to complete the questionnaire. They unanimously reported that it took no more than twenty minutes to fill it out.

Protection afforded respondent

You need not sign the questionnaire and you are assured that your response will remain anonymous and confidential. Your participation is, of course, voluntary.

Description of procedure (time limit vague)

Please answer all of the questions and return the completed questionnaire to me in the enclosed envelope as soon as possible.

Opportunity to
obtain results

{ If you wish a summary of the study, please check the appropriate box at the end of the questionnaire and send your name and address on the enclosed postal card.

Thank respondent

{ Thank you for your cooperation.
Yours truly,

Stanley Cogan, Assistant Principal
New York City Public Schools

Source: From "The relationship of the social class and personal characteristics of parent association executive board members to the role expectations and personal characteristics which they advocate in the selection of elementary principals in selected American cities," doctoral dissertation by Stanley Cogan. Reprinted by permission of Stanley Cogan.

probably not affect the results in an appreciable way. If the results are to be used for important decisions, however, or if the nature of the questions might cause a certain type of subject not to respond, then the nonrespondents should be checked. The suggested approach for investigating the possibility of a biased group of respondents is to somehow obtain a random sample of the nonrespondents. If possible, these individuals are interviewed and their responses are compared to those of the subjects who completed written questionnaires. If the responses are the same, then the researcher is safe in concluding that the obtained written questionnaires represent an unbiased sample. If it is impossible to interview the randomly selected nonrespondents, the next best procedure is to compare them with the subjects who did respond with respect to demographic characteristics. If either the responses or demographic characteristics of the nonrespondents are different, then this difference should be noted in discussing and interpreting the results of the study. Special attention should be focused on studies with a relatively low rate of return (lower than sixty percent) and without an analysis of the way nonrespondents may have changed the results.

Before leaving the topic of survey research we once again want to emphasize that survey research is not simple to prepare and conduct. There are many factors related to item format, positioning of questions, wording, sampling, and other variables that need to be considered. For an excellent review of these problems, see Schuman and Presser (1982), and for additional information on developing and conducting surveys, see Fink and Kosecoff (1985) and Fowler (1984).

■ SUMMARY ■

This chapter has provided a review of descriptive, correlational, and survey research, stressing design principles that affect the quality of the research. The main points in the chapter are:

1. Descriptive research is concerned with the present, with the current status of *what is.*

2. Developmental studies investigate changes of subjects over time and are longitudinal or cross-sectional.
3. Correlational relationship studies use at least two scores that are obtained from each subject.
4. The selection of subjects and instruments in correlational research should assure a range of responses on each variable.
5. In predictive research the criterion variable is predicted by a prior behavior as measured by the independent variable.
6. Multiple correlation allows several independent variables to combine in relating to the dependent or criterion variable.
7. Correlation should never infer causation because of third nonmeasured variables and the inability to assess causal direction between the two variables.
8. Spurious correlations over- or under-represent the actual relationship between two variables.
9. The coefficient of determination is the square of the correlation coefficient, and it estimates the variance that is shared by the variables.
10. Correlation coefficients should be interpreted carefully when they are statistically significant with low relationships and a large number of subjects.
11. Decisions for individuals require higher correlations than decisions for groups.
12. Survey research uses questionnaires or interviews to describe characteristics of populations.
13. Surveys are used for descriptive, relationship, or explanatory purposes.
14. The nature of the letter of transmittal in mail surveys is crucial to obtaining an acceptable response rate of 60 percent or greater.

■ SELF-INSTRUCTIONAL REVIEW EXERCISES ■

Sample answers are in the back of the book.

Test items

1. Descriptive research investigates
   a. difference and causal questions.
   b. dependent variables like achievement.
   c. the current state of affairs.
   d. cause and effect relationships.

2. Longitudinal studies investigate
   a. different subjects over time.
   b. cross-sectional relationships.
   c. different subjects at the same time.
   d. the same subjects over time.

3. Restricted range and homogeneous samples are especially troublesome for
   a. shotgun studies.
   b. relationship studies.
   c. descriptive studies.
   d. longitudinal studies.

4. In a prediction study the measurement of the independent variable
   a. occurs before the measure of the dependent variable.
   b. occurs at the same time as the dependent variable.
   c. should be made directly by the research.
   d. occurs after the measure of the dependent variable.

5. Multiple correlation studies
   a. compare beta weights to regression coefficients.
   b. use many independent variables.
   c. use many dependent variables.
   d. compare R with beta weights.

6. Correlations are spurious if they
   a. are too high.
   b. are interpreted incorrectly.
   c. are too low.
   d. over- or underestimate the true relationship.

7. Correlations should not be used to infer causation because
   a. only two variables are studied.
   b. they are not well controlled.
   c. of third unmeasured variables.
   d. only inferential statistics can be used to infer causation.

8. Survey research employs the following techniques
   a. interviews.
   b. observation.
   c. questionnaires.
   d. Both a and c are correct.
   e. All of the above are correct.

9. Surveys can be used for each of the following purposes *except*
   a. causal.
   b. relationship.
   c. explanatory.
   d. descriptive.

10. Which sequence describes the correct order of steps to be taken in conducting survey research?
   a. define purpose, identify techniques, identify population, sample, mailing, follow-up.
   b. define purpose, sample, identify techniques, mail, follow-up.
   c. define purpose, identify population, sample, identify techniques, mail, follow-up.
   d. define purpose, identify population, identify techniques, sample, mailing, follow-up.

Application Problems

1. In a study of motivation and learning a teacher employed the following research strategy: Students were asked what teaching strategies were most motivating. The teacher then looked back at her test scores to investigate whether the test scores were higher for the more motivating sessions as compared to the less motivating sessions. The teacher found that, indeed, student achievement rose as the teacher used more and more motivating techniques. From this result she decided to use the more motivating techniques all the time. Was her decision to use more motivating techniques correct? Why or why not?

2. Indicate from the description below whether the research is descriptive, relationship, or predictive.
   a. A researcher finds that students who use distributed practice in studying for a test obtain higher grades than students who not use distributed practice.
   b. A researcher finds that students who are more lonely have more permissive parents than students who are less lonely.
   c. The dean of the school of education uses SAT scores to identify students who may have trouble with National Teacher Examinations.
   d. Children in supportive, loving homes have a higher self-concept than children in rejecting homes.
   e. The majority of faculty at U.S.A. university favor abolishing tenure.

CHAPTER 9

EXPERIMENTAL, SINGLE SUBJECT, AND *EX POST FACTO* RESEARCH

■ KEY TERMS ■

experiment
assigned variables
attribute variables
experimental or treatment group
control or comparison group
pre-experimental designs
pretest
one-group posttest-only design
one-group pretest-posttest
   design
posttest-only with nonequivalent
   groups
true experimental designs
pretest-posttest control group
   design

posttest-only control group
   design
quasi-experimental designs
nonequivalent pretest-posttest
   control group design
time series design
control group interrupted time series
   design
single-subject designs
baseline
A-B design
A-B-A design
reversal or withdrawal design
multiple-baseline designs
ex post facto designs

In Chapter 2 the concepts *experiment* and *experimental design* were introduced. In this chapter we consider the conduct of experiments in greater detail. We focus on four major categories of designs that are used to make causal inferences about the relationship between independent and dependent variables. The four categories of design are pre-experimental, true experimental, quasi-experimental, and single-subject.

We summarize the purpose, strengths, and limitations of experimental research in general as well as more specific designs, and we include a discussion of *ex post facto* research, which has some similarities to experimental research. Throughout, we stress the point that in any study in which causation is inferred, the investigator must rule out plausible rival hypotheses that may explain the results. Standards of adequacy for evaluating the designs are suggested at the end of the chapter.

■ AN INTRODUCTION TO ■ EXPERIMENTAL RESEARCH

The term **experiment,** like many other terms, can have different meanings. Defined in a general way, experiments are simply a way of learning something by varying some condition and observing the effect on something else. In other words, we change something and watch for the effect. As humans, we use natural experiments constantly to learn—young children experiment with a host of tactics to see which one will affect Mom or Dad most; teachers try a new approach to discipline to see if it works; and students vary study techniques to see which ones seem to result in the best grades. This simple trial and error behavior is an attempt to show causation, which is the primary purpose of an experiment. The difference between these experiments and highly sophisticated experiments conducted by laboratory scientists is the extent to which the experimenter can be certain that the varied conditions caused the observed effect. It is the interpretation of causation, then, that is a key element in experimental research.

Defined more formally in the context of scientific research, an experiment is a procedure for investigating cause-and-effect relationships by randomly assigning subjects to groups in which one or more independent variables are manipulated. A key element in experimental research is that the investigator deliberately sets up conditions in which different groups of subjects have different experiences.

Characteristics of Experimental Research

Experimental research has six distinguishing characteristics: statistical equivalence of subjects in different groups, usually achieved by random assignment of subjects; comparison of two or more groups or sets of conditions; direct manipulation of at least one independent variable; measurement of each dependent variable; use of inferential statistics; and a design that provides maximum control of extraneous variables. These characteristics are usually present in physical and biological science experimental research, but as we noted in Chapter 2, such conditions can rarely be achieved completely in educational research. This does not, however, diminish the importance of the experimental method for education. Much research in education approximates the characteristics of a pure experiment, and we need to understand the way different methods of conducting research that investigates causal relationships affect the interpretation of the results. This is what Campbell and Stanley (1963) had in mind in writing their classic and influential chapter, "Experimental and Quasi-Experimental Designs for Education." The following quotation leaves little doubt about their perspective:

> This chapter is committed to the experiment: as the only means for settling disputes regarding educational practice, as the only way of verifying educational improvements, and as the only way of establishing a cumulative tradition in which improvements can be introduced without the danger of a faddish discard of old wisdom in favor of inferior novelties (Campbell & Stanley, 1963, p. 2).

We need to distinguish, then, between what can be labeled pure or true experimental research, in which the above six characteristics are completely present, and the experimental method of research more broadly, in which the characteristics are partially present. In this chapter, since we are concerned with research in education, we interpret *experimental* in its more general context.

The first characteristic of experimental research, achieving statistical equivalence of subjects in different groups, is necessary so that the internal validity threat of selection is not a factor in interpreting the results. In other words, the researcher wants to make the groups being compared equivalent so that any differences in their performance cannot be attributed to differences in the groups. Random assignment of subjects is the method used most often to achieve statistical equivalence of the groups. Other methods, such as matching subjects or groups or using subjects as their own controls, are also used for this purpose.

The second characteristic suggests that at least two groups or conditions that can be compared are needed. An experiment cannot be conducted with one group of subjects in one condition at one time. The intent of an experiment is to compare the effect of one condition on one group with the effect a different condition has on a second group, or to compare the effect of different conditions on the same group. At least two groups or conditions are necessary to make such comparisons.

Manipulation of independent variables is perhaps the most distinct feature of experimental research. *Manipulation* in this sense means that the researcher decides upon or controls the group of subjects that will receive a particular treatment or condition. The independent variable is manipulated in that different values or conditions (levels) of the independent variable are assigned to groups by the experimenter. If the conditions cannot be assigned as needed by the researcher, then the study is not a true experiment. Suppose, for example, a research team is interested in investigating whether the order of difficulty of items in a test makes a difference in student achievement. The study might have one independent variable, order of items, with two levels, items ordered from easiest to most difficult, and items ordered from most difficult to easiest. These are the conditions that are manipulated by the researchers, who would probably divide a class into two groups, randomly, and give all students in each group one of two types of item order. The researchers, then, are controlling the choice of group to get each order. It should be pointed out that there are many variables in education that can never be manipulated, such as age, weight, gender, and socioeconomic status. These variables are called **assigned** or **attribute variables** because they cannot be manipulated. Although assigned variables can be included in experimental research, there must be at least one manipulated variable for the research to be classified as a true experiment.

The fourth characteristic of experimental research, measurement of dependent variables, means that experimental research is concerned with things that can be assigned a numerical value. If the outcome of the study cannot be measured and quantified in some way, then the research cannot be experimental.

Another characteristic that involves numbers is the use of inferential statistics. Inferential statistics are used to make probability statements about the results. This is important for two reasons. Because measurement is imperfect in education, and because we often want to generalize the results to similar groups or to the population of subjects, inferential statistics allow us to make such generalizations. (See Chapter 10 for details concerning inferential statistics.)

The final characteristic of experimental research is perhaps most important from a generic point of view because the principle of control of extraneous variables is not unique to experimental research. What is unique to experimental research is that there is a determined effort to make sure no extraneous variables that could be controlled provide plausible rival hypotheses to explain the results. We control extraneous variables by making sure that these variables either have no effect on the dependent variable, or by keeping the effect of the extraneous variable the same for all groups. This chapter places a great degree of emphasis on this characteristic of experimental research.

Strengths and Limitations of Experimental Research

The experimental method is clearly the best approach for determining the causal effect of an isolated, single variable on something. This is primarily because of the high degree of control of extraneous variables and the power of manipulation of variables. The careful control that characterizes good experimental research becomes a liability for the field of education, however. Control is most easily achieved with research on humans only in restrictive and artificial settings. This is a weakness in education for two reasons. Humans react to artificially restricted, manipulated conditions differently from the way they react to naturally occurring conditions, and if the research is conducted under artificial conditions, then the generalizability of the results (external validity) is severely limited.

Here is an example of this dilemma. The problem to be investigated is whether an individualized or a cooperative group discussion is the best method for teaching science concepts to fourth graders. The objective is to find the method of teaching that gives the best results in achievement. An experimental approach is selected because the problem is clearly one of causation, and presumably the method of instruction, the independent variable, could be manipulated easily. To maximize control of extraneous variables the experiment might be arranged as follows: At the beginning of one school day all fourth graders report to a special room, where they are randomly divided into individualized and cooperative groups. To remove any effect the present teachers might have, graduate assistants from the universities act as the teachers. To remove any effect of different rooms, each group of students is taken to similar rooms in different locations. To control possible distractions, these rooms have no windows. To insure that directions are uniform, the teachers read from specially prepared scripts. The science material that is selected has been carefully screened so that it will be new information for all students. After studying the material for an hour, the students are tested on the concepts. The test format, length of time to complete questions, and other procedures are the same for both groups. The results compare the achievement of the groups, and since the design has controlled for most extraneous variables, this difference can be attributed to the independent variable, method of instruction.

What do we do with this knowledge? Because one approach seemed best in this experiment, does it mean that Mr. Jones, in his class, with his style of teaching, in his room, with students that may have particular learning strengths and weaknesses, should use the supposedly proven method? Perhaps, but the difficulty that is illustrated is one of generalizability, a common problem for experiments that are able to exhibit tight control over extraneous variables—that is, internal validity. On the other hand, if we want to maximize external validity, then we need to design the experiment right in Mr. Jones's class, as well as in the classes of other teachers, and somehow design the study to control as many variables as possible without disrupting the natural environment of the class. The researcher would need to select the variables most likely to affect achievement, such as aptitude, time of day, and composition of groups, and control these as well as possible. This approach makes it more difficult to show that one or the other method of teaching is more effective, but the results are more generalizable to normal classrooms. The real challenge is in designing the procedures so that the results obtained can be reasonably generalized to other people and environments—that is, balancing internal and external validity in a design. This task is difficult but not impossible, and one of the objectives of this chapter is to introduce various designs and procedures that allow reasonable cause-and-effect conclusions to be made in the context of natural settings.

We hope the use of the word *reasonable* is not confusing. The simple fact is that we approximate pure experimental design as well as we can because such designs convincingly determine causation. In the final analysis, however, since we are working with human beings in complex situations, we must almost always use professional judgment, or reason, in making conclusions on the basis of observed results. Knowledge of the designs covered in this chapter and threats to internal and external validity help us use this judgment.

Finally, before introducing the designs, it should be pointed out that experimental research is not appropriate for all educational research; it is appropriate only for some investigations seeking knowledge about cause-and-effect relationships. For many educational problems the experimental method would be inappropriate, such as descriptive studies (for example, "What is the attitude or level of achievement?") or studies of relationship (for example, "Is there a relationship between age and self-concept?"). In some situations an ethnographic approach would be more valid for explaining events, and in evaluation studies, experiments are frequently used with other approaches to investigate questions about a single practice.

Planning Experimental Research

While the sequence of steps in experimental research is basically the same as in other types of research, certain procedures and characteristics of planning are unique to the experimental design.

The first step is to define a research problem, search the literature, and state clear research hypotheses. It is essential that experimental research be guided by research hypotheses that state the expected results. The actual results will either support or fail to support the research hypotheses. It is inappropriate to use experimental research with research questions for which the results are not expected to be definitive.

Second, the researcher selects subjects from a defined population, and, depending on the specific design used, assigns subjects to different groups. A simple experimental study involves two groups, one called the **experimental or treatment group** and the other referred to as the **control or comparison group.** Each group is then assigned one level of the independent variable. The control or comparison group is essential in experimental research. Technically, a control group receives no treatment at all (for example, when comparing people who smoke with people who do not), but in most educational research it is unproductive to compare one group receiving a treatment to another group receiving nothing. It would be like comparing children who received extra individual tutoring to children who did not and then concluding on the basis of the results that children need individual tutoring. It is also unrealistic in school settings to expect that a group will be doing nothing while another group receives a special treatment. For these reasons, it is more accurate to conceive of the two groups in experimental research as the treatment and comparison groups, or as one group that receives method A and another group that receives method B, rather than as an experimental and a control group.

In assigning the treatments, as indicated by levels of the independent variable, the researcher chooses the value, forms, or conditions each group receives. This could be a simple assignment, such as lecture versus discussion, loud reprimands versus soft reprimands, or an autocratic versus a participatory leadership style; or there could be more than two levels, with varying degrees of the condition in each level of the independent variable. If, for example, a researcher was interested in the effect of different types of teacher feedback on student attitudes, then feedback, the independent variable, could be represented in four levels: grade only, grade plus one word only, grade plus one sentence, and grade plus three sentences. Hence, the researcher would form four groups and randomly assign subjects to each of the four groups. The researcher would arrange appropriate control so that any difference in attitude could be explained as caused by different types of feedback, or so that no difference in attitude indicates no causative relationship between these types of feedback and attitudes.

One of the difficulties in planning experimental research is knowing that the treatments will be strong enough—that is, if the treatment condition is providing feedback to students, will the feedback make enough of an impact to affect student attitudes? Would feedback given over several consecutive days make a difference? Maybe the feedback has to be given for a month or more. In other words, either the treatment should be tested in advance to ensure that it is powerful enough to make an impact, or sufficient time should be allocated to give the treatment a chance to work. This can be an especially difficult problem in much educational research because there are many influences like achievement, attitudes, motivation, and self-concept that may affect dependent variables, and it is hard to single out a specific independent variable that will have a meaningful, unique effect, given all other influences. Finally, experimental treatments are sometimes insufficiently distinct from treatments given comparison groups for a statistical difference to be possible. In a study of different counseling techniques, for example, if the only difference between the experimental and control conditions was the distance the counselor sat from the clients (say, four feet or six feet), it is unlikely, given all the other influences, that a researcher will obtain a difference in results.

Once treatment conditions have been established, it is necessary to specify the design that will be employed. This chapter summarizes most of the basic designs used in experimental educational research. The designs include the procedures for subject assignment, the number of groups, and the times that treatments are given to each group. The primary concern of the researcher in choosing a design is to maximize internal validity, a concept that is reviewed in the next section.

■ INTERNAL VALIDITY OF ■ EXPERIMENTS

Chapter 5 discussed the concept of internal validity. The internal validity of a study is a judgment that is made concerning the confidence with which plausible rival hypotheses can be ruled out as explanations for the results. It involves a deductive process in which the investigators must systematically examine how each of the threats to internal validity, which constitute rival alternative hypotheses, may have influenced the results. If all the threats can be eliminated reasonably, then the researcher can be confident that an observed relationship is causal, and that the difference in treatment conditions caused the obtained results. Internal validity is rarely an all-or-none decision. Rather, it is assessed as a matter of degree, depending on the plausibility of the explanation. As will be pointed out, some designs are relatively strong with respect to internal validity because most rival hypotheses can be ruled out confidently, while other designs that lend themselves to a host of plausible rival explanations are weak in internal validity. It cannot be stressed too much that, in the final analysis, researchers must be their own best critics and carefully examine all threats that can be imagined. It is important, then, for consumers of research, as well as for those conducting research, to be aware of the common threats to internal validity and of the best ways to control them.

The threats to internal validity discussed in Chapter 5 are summarized in Table 9.1 in order to help you commit each factor to memory. They will be discussed again in the context of each of the designs summarized in the next four sections of the chapter, both in the text and in Tables 9.3 to 9.5, which provide an overview of the threats that are controlled by each design.

TABLE 9.1
Summary of Threats to
Internal Validity

Threat	Description
History	Unplanned or extraneous events that occur during the research and affect the results
Selection	Differences between the subjects in the groups may result in outcomes that are different because of group composition
Statistical regression	A result may be due to respondents' being identified on the basis of extreme high or low scores
Testing	Occurs when the act of taking a test or responding to a questionnaire affects the subjects
Instrumentation	Differences in results due to unreliability, changes in the measuring instrument, or in observers between the pre- and posttest
Mortality	Occurs because of systematic loss of subjects
Maturation	Occurs when an effect is due to maturational or other natural changes in the subjects (for example, being older, wiser, stronger, tired)
Diffusion of treatment	Occurs when subjects in one group learn about treatments or conditions for different groups
Experimenter bias	Deliberate or unintended effects of the researcher on subject responses
Statistical conclusion	Violation of assumptions or misuse of statistical tests

■ EXTERNAL VALIDITY OF EXPERIMENTS ■

External validity is the extent to which the results of an experiment can be generalized to people and environmental conditions outside the context of the experiment. That is, if the same treatment or experimental conditions were replicated with different subjects, in a different setting, would the results be the same? In other words, what are the characteristics of subjects and environmental conditions for which we can expect the same results? We conclude that an experiment has strong external validity if the generalizability is relatively extensive, and has weak external validity if we are unable to generalize very much beyond the actual experiment. Table 9.2 summarizes the sources of threats to external validity (see Chapter 5 for a review of threats to external validity).

TABLE 9.2
Threats to External Validity
of Experiments

Threat	Description
Population	
Selection of subjects	Generalization is limited to the subjects in the sample if subjects are not selected randomly from an identified population.
Characteristics of subjects	Generalization is limited to the characteristics of the sample or population (for example, SES, age, location, ability, race).
Subject-treatment interaction	Generalization may be limited because of the interaction between the subjects and treatment (that is, the effect of the treatment is unique to the subjects).
Ecological	
Description of variables	Generalization is limited to the operational definitions of the independent and dependent variables.
Multiple-treatment interference	In experiments in which subjects receive more than one treatment, generalizability is limited to similar multiple treatment situations because of the effect of the first treatment on subsequent treatments.
Reactive arrangements	Several factors (for example, Hawthorne effect, demand characteristics, evaluation apprehension, social desirability, placebo effect) may be associated with subject awareness of being in a study, and these factors may interact with treatments or effect responses on the dependent variable.
Setting-treatment interaction	Generalization is limited to the setting in which the study is conducted (for example, room, time of day, others present, other surroundings).
Type of measurement—treatment interaction	Results may be limited to the time frame in which they were obtained. Treatments causing immediate effects may not have lasting effects.
Pretest-posttest sensitization	The pretest or posttest may interact with the treatment so that similar results are obtained only when the testing conditions are present.
Novelty or disruption effect	Subjects may respond differently because of a change in routine, and generalization may be limited to situations that involve similar novelty or disruption (for example, an initially effective treatment may become ineffective in time as novelty wears off).
Experimenter effect	Also called Rosenthal effect. Generalization may be limited to the presence of the experimenter who influenced or biased the treatment.

It is difficult to view external validity in the same way we view internal validity because most experiments are not designed specifically to control threats to external validity. Researchers consciously control some threats to internal validity by using a particular design, but most threats to external validity are a consideration regardless of the design. In only a few designs can it be concluded that sources of external validity are controlled. Under the ecological category, for example, such threats as description of variables, reactive arrangements, setting-treatment interaction, time of measurement treatment interaction, and novelty or disruption effect are not controlled with any particular experimental design. These threats are more a function of procedures and definitions than of design, and in most studies the reader decides whether any of the threats are reasonable.

Two of the ecological threats, multiple treatment interference and pretest-posttest sensitization, are present only in particular designs. Multiple treatment interference is a consideration only if more than one treatment is applied in succession. Pretest sensitization is a serious threat when investigating personality, values, attitudes, or opinions, since taking the pretest may sensitize the subject to the treatment. For example, if a study investigating the effect of a workshop on attitudes toward the use of computers in education gave a pretest measure of attitudes, the pretest itself might affect subsequent attitudes regardless of or in interaction with the workshop. Pretest-treatment interaction is minimized in studies conducted over a relatively long period of time, such as several weeks or months, and in studies of small children. Posttest sensitization occurs only if the posttest sensitizes the subject to the treatment and affects the results in a way that would not have occurred without the posttest.

Educational researchers are often confronted with the difficult dilemma that, as internal validity is maximized, external validity may be sacrificed. High internal validity requires strict control of all sources of confounding variables, a type of control that may mean conducting the study under laboratory-like conditions. The more the environment is controlled, however, the less generalizable the results are to other settings. This is a constant dilemma for educators because research that cannot be used with other populations in other settings contributes little to educational practice, but there must be sufficient control for making reasonable causal conclusions. Without internal validity, of course, external validity is a moot question. Most research strives to balance the threats of internal and external validity by using vigor sufficient to make the results scientifically defensible and by conducting the study under conditions that permit generalization to other situations. One good approach to solving the dilemma is to replicate tightly controlled studies with different populations in different settings.

■ PRE-EXPERIMENTAL DESIGNS ■

The three designs summarized in this section are termed **pre-experimental designs** because they are without two or more of the six characteristics of experimental research listed earlier. As a consequence, few threats to internal validity are controlled, and the results are often uninterpretable. This does not mean that these designs are always uninterpretable, nor does it mean that the designs should not be used. There are certain cases in which the threats can be ruled out on the basis of accepted theory, common sense, or other data. Because they fail to rule out most rival hypotheses, however, it is difficult to make reasonable causal inferences from these designs alone. They are best used, perhaps, as a way of generating ideas that can be tested more systematically.

Notation

In presenting the designs in this chapter we will use a notational system to provide information for understanding the designs. The notational system is unique, though similar to the basic notational system used by Campbell and Stanley (1963) and Cook and Campbell (1979). Our notational system is as follows:

R   randomization

O   observation, a measure that records observations of a pre- or posttest

X   treatment conditions (subscripts 1 through n indicating different treatments)

A,B,C,D,E,F   groups of subjects, or, for single-subject designs, baseline or treatment conditions

One-Group Posttest-Only Design

In the **one-group posttest-only design** the researcher gives a treatment and then makes an observation, as is represented in the following diagram.

One-Group Posttest-Only Design

X   O

———————▶

Time

While not all threats to internal validity are applicable to this design, because there is no pretest and no comparison with other treatments, only tentative causal conclusions can, at best, be made. Without a **pretest,** for example, it is difficult to conclude that behavior has changed at all (such as when testing a method of teaching math to students who know the answers to the final exam before receiving any instruction). Without a comparison or control group it is also difficult to know whether other factors occurring at the same time as the treatment were causally related to the dependent variable. Even though only five of the threats to internal validity (see Table 9.3) are relevant to this design, the above weaknesses are so severe that the results of research based on this design alone are usually uninterpretable. The only situation in which this design is reasonable is when the researcher can be fairly certain of the level of knowledge, attitude, or skill of the subjects before the treatment and can be fairly sure that history is not a threat. For example, let's say an instructor in research methods wants to conduct a study of how much students have learned from his or her class. It seems reasonable to conclude that they did not know much of the course content before the course began, and that it is unlikely that they will learn the content in other ways. Consequently, the one-group posttest-only design may provide valid results.

This design should not be confused with what is termed a "case study design." Case study designs are qualitative investigations of one person, group, event, or setting over a single time period. These studies often conduct detailed examinations of complex phenomena and are very useful research designs (see Chapter 11 for further information).

One-Group Pretest-Posttest Design

This common design is distinguished from the one-group posttest-only design by a single difference—the addition of an observation that occurs before the treatment condition is experienced (pretest).

One-Group Pretest-Posttest Design

$$O \longrightarrow X \longrightarrow O$$

$$\longrightarrow$$

Time

In the **one-group pretest-posttest design** a single group of subjects is given a pretest (O), then the treatment (X), and then the posttest (O). The result that is examined is a change from pretest to posttest. (This design is popularized as the so-called **pretest-posttest design**). While the researcher can at least obtain a measure of change with this design, there are still many plausible rival hypotheses that are applicable.

Consider this example. A university professor has received a grant to conduct inservice workshops for teachers on the topic of mainstreaming. One objective of the program is to improve the attitudes of the teachers toward mainstreaming exceptional children. To assess this objective the professor selects a pretest-posttest design, administering an attitude pretest to the teachers before the workshop, then giving the same test again after the workshop. Suppose the posttest scores are higher than the pretest scores. Can the researcher conclude that the cause of the change in scores is the workshop? Perhaps, but there are several threats to internal validity that are plausible, and until these threats can be ruled out the researcher cannot assume that attendance at the workshop was the cause of the change.

The most serious threat is history. Because there is no control or comparison group, the researcher cannot be sure that other events occurring between the pretest and posttest did not cause the change in attitude. Some of these events might occur within the context of the workshop (a teacher gives a moving testimonial about exceptional children in a setting unrelated to the workshop); or they might occur outside the context of the workshop (during the workshop an article about mainstreaming appears in the school paper). Events like these are uncontrolled and may affect the results. It is necessary for the researcher, then, to make a case either that such effects are implausible or that if they are plausible, they did not occur. Data are sometimes used as evidence to rule out some threats, but in many cases it is simply common sense, theory, or experience that is used. However argued, if a plausible threat cannot be ruled out, then the researcher must admit that the effect of the workshop on changing attitudes cannot be determined exactly.

Selection is not a threat to internal validity for this design because only one group is used, but the characteristics of the subjects may well interact with a treatment and affect the external validity of the results.

Statistical regression could be a problem with this design if the subjects are selected on the basis of extreme high or low scores. In our example with the workshop, for instance, suppose the principal of the school wanted only those teachers with the least favorable attitude to attend. The pretest scores would then be very low and, because of regression, would be higher on the posttest regardless of the effect of the workshop.

Testing is often a serious threat to research carried out with this design, especially in research on attitudes because simply taking the pretest can alter the attitudes. The content of the questionnaire might sensitize the subjects to specific problems or might raise the general awareness level of the subjects and cause them to think more about the topic. Instrumentation can also be a threat. If, for example, teachers take the pretest on Friday afternoon and the posttest the next Wednesday morning the responses could be different simply because of the general attitudes that are likely to prevail at each of these times of the day and week.

Mortality can be a problem if, between the pretest and posttest, subjects are lost because of particular reasons. If all the teachers in a school begin a workshop, for example, and those with the most negative attitude toward mainstreaming drop out because they do not want to learn more about it, then the measured attitudes of the remaining subjects will be high. Consider another example. To assess the effect of a schoolwide effort to expand favorable attitudes toward learning, students are pretested as sophomores and posttested as seniors. A plausible argument, at least one that would need to be ruled out, is that improvement in attitudes is demonstrated because the students who have the most negative attitudes as sophomores never make it to be seniors; they drop out. Mortality is especially a problem in cases with transient populations, with a long-term experiment, or with longitudinal research.

Maturation is a threat to internal validity of research based on this design when the dependent variable is unstable because of maturational changes. This threat is more serious as the time period between the pretest and posttest increases. Suppose, for instance, a researcher is investigating self-concept of junior high students. If the time between the pretest and posttest is relatively short (two or three weeks), then maturation is probably not a threat; but if there is a year between the pretest and posttest, changes in self-concept would probably occur regardless of the treatment because of maturation. Maturation includes such threats as being more tired, bored, or hungry at the time of test taking, and these factors might be a problem in some pretest-posttest designs. In the example of the workshop on mainstreaming it is unlikely that maturation is a serious threat, and it would probably be reasonable to rule out these threats as plausible rival hypotheses.

Since there is only one treatment in this design, diffusion of treatment is inapplicable. Experimenter bias and statistical conclusion are threats that may be operating in any study.

From the above discussion it should be obvious that there are many uncontrolled threats to the internal validity of one-group pretest-posttest designs. Consequently, this design should be used only under certain conditions that minimize the plausibility of the threats (use novel variables that are relatively stable, use reliable instruments, use short pretest-posttest time intervals), and when it is impossible to use other designs that will control some of these threats.

Posttest-Only with Nonequivalent Groups

This design is similar to the one-group posttest-only design. The difference is that in a **posttest-only with nonequivalent groups design** a comparison or control group that receives no treatment or a different treatment is added to the one-group posttest-only design. The design is diagramed below.

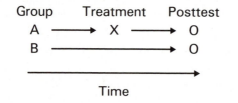

Posttest Only with Nonequivalent Groups Design

Group	Treatment	Posttest
A ⟶	X ⟶	O
B ⟶		O

Time

This design is used frequently after a treatment has been implemented. The procedure is to give the treatment to one group and then assess the dependent variable (via the posttest), and give only the posttest to another group at the same time as the posttest is administered to the first group. The term *nonequivalent groups* is used as the name for the design because selection is the most serious threat to the internal validity of the results. Notice that there is no randomization of subjects to each group. Differences in the groups of subjects may therefore account for any differences in the results of the posttests. The more different the groups are, the more plausible selection thus becomes as a reason for the results. Suppose, for example, the professor conducting the mainstreaming workshop wanted to get a comparison group and located a school willing to help. Even if the posttest scores of the treatment group were better than the scores of the comparison group, it is impossible to conclude that the better scores were due to the workshop. It may be that the teachers in the treatment school had more favorable attitudes to begin with, and that the workshop had little effect on the attitudes of teachers there.

There are also other, less serious threats to the internal validity of research based on this design. These threats occur when the basic design includes alternate treatments, as indicated below.

Alternate Treatment Posttest-Only with Nonequivalent Groups Design

Group	Treatment	Posttest
A $\longrightarrow$	X_1 $\longrightarrow$	O
B $\longrightarrow$	X_2 $\longrightarrow$	O

$\longrightarrow$

Time

This design is used when a researcher wants to compare two or more treatments but cannot give a pretest or randomize the assignment of subjects to each group. In this case internal, or within-group, history is a threat, since what might occur within each group, unrelated to the treatments, could affect the posttest. External history is not usually a threat, unless selection differences expose subjects outside the context of the study to different conditions that affect the results. Regression may be a threat even though only one observation is made. Testing is not a threat because there is no pretest, but instrumentation could be a threat if there are differences in the way the posttest assessments are made for each group (such as an observer's being more alert for one group than the other). Mortality is a threat because subject loss, due either to the initial characteristics of the subjects (selection) or to different treatments, may cause certain subjects to drop out. Maturation may also be a threat, depending on selection characteristics. If the subjects in each group are aware of the treatment given the other group, it is possible for diffusion of treatment to be a threat. Experimenter bias and statistical conclusion threats are also possible.

The posttest-only nonequivalent groups design is relatively weak for testing causation. If the design is used, a researcher should make every effort to get comparable groups in order to decrease the selection threat.

The possible sources of invalidity for research carried out by the three preexperimental designs are summarized in Table 9.3. Since different designs control different factors and also have unique weaknesses, the researcher chooses the best design on the basis of the research conditions. If, for example, the researcher can reasonably argue that two groups are about the same with respect to important variables (socioeconomic status, achievement, age, experience, motivation, and so on), then the strongest design would be the posttest-only with nonequivalent groups. In any event, all these designs are relatively weak for use in testing causal relationships, and usually with sufficient foresight these designs can be modified slightly to permit more reasonable causal inferences.

TABLE 9.3[a]
Threats to Internal Validity of Pre-Experimental Designs

Design	History	Selection	Statistical Regression	Testing	Instrumentation	Mortality	Maturation	Diffusion of Treatment	Experimenter Bias	Statistical Conclusion
1. One-group posttest-only	—	—	—	NA	?	—	—	NA	?	NA
2. One-group pretest-posttest	—	?	—	—	—	—	—	NA	?	?
3. Posttest-only with nonequivalent groups	?	—	?	NA	—	—	?	?	?	?

[a]In this table, and in Tables 9.4 and 9.5, a minus sign means a definite weakness, a plus sign means that the factor is controlled, a question mark means a possible source of invalidity, and NA indicates that the threat is not applicable to this design (and is also, then, not a factor).

■ TRUE EXPERIMENTAL DESIGNS[1] ■

This section presents two designs that have been called **true experimental designs.** Both include procedures for ruling out intersubject differences through randomization of subjects to groups and both include manipulation of the treatment variable. These designs represent what historically has been called experimental in the biological and physical sciences.

Pretest-Posttest Control Group Design

The **pretest-posttest control group design** is an extension of the one-group pretest-posttest design in two ways: a second group is added, called the control or comparison group; and subjects are assigned randomly to each group. This design is represented on the next page.

[1]A third experimental design that is often presented is the Solomon four-group design. The Solomon design seldom appears in the literature but it provides a good illustration of a way to test for the effect of an interaction between the pretest and experimental treatment as well as other threats, and it will be explained later in this chapter.

Pretest-Posttest
Control Group Design

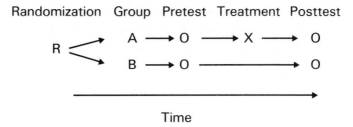

The first step is random assignment of the subjects to the experimental or treatment group and the control group. In studies with a relatively small number of subjects, it is often best to rank-order the subjects on achievement, attitudes, or other factors that may be related to the dependent variable. Then, in the case of a two-group design, pairs of subjects are formed; the researcher randomly assigns one subject from each pair to the treatment and the other subject to the control group. Another procedure is to match subjects on the basis of a variable and then randomly assign members of each matched pair to experimental and control groups. However implemented, the purpose of randomization is to enable the researcher to reasonably rule out any selection differences between the groups that could account for differences found in the results. With a small group of subjects it is thus less likely that all initial differences will be equal. If only ten subjects are randomly assigned to two groups, for example, there is a good chance that even though the assignment is random, there will be important differences between the groups. If two hundred subjects are randomly assigned, however, there is a very small chance that the groups will differ. Generally, educational researchers like to have at least fifteen subjects in each group in order to assume statistical equivalence, and they then have more confidence in the results if there are from twenty to thirty subjects in each group.

The second step is to pretest each group on the dependent variable. The third step is to administer the treatment condition to the experimental group but not to the control group, keeping all other conditions the same for both groups so that the only difference is the manipulation of the independent variable. Each group is then posttested on the dependent variable.

In the diagramed control group design there is no treatment at all for the control group. As indicated previously, it is more common, and usually more desirable, to have what is called "comparison" rather than control groups. A comparison design uses two or more variations of the independent variable and can use two or more groups. Suppose, for example, a teacher wants to compare three methods of teaching spelling. The teacher then randomly assigns each student in the class to one of three groups, administers a pretest, tries the different methods, and gives a posttest. This design would look like this:

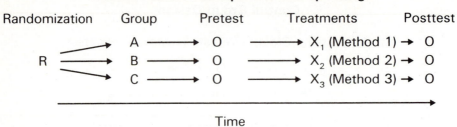

Pretest-Posttest Comparison Group Design

It would also be possible to combine several different treatments with a control group, as shown below.

Pretest-Posttest Control/Comparison Group Design

The pretest-posttest control group design controls four sources of threats to internal validity, as indicated in Table 9.4. Threats related to history are generally controlled insofar as events that are external to the study affect both groups equally. The reason for the question mark in the category, however, is that there is always the possibility that unique events may occur within each group to affect the results. Selection and maturation are controlled because of the random assignment of subjects. Statistical regression and testing are controlled, since any effect of these factors is equal for all groups. Instrumentation is not a problem when standardized self-report procedures are used, but studies that use observers to record data must be careful to avoid observer bias (observers know which students are receiving which treatments, or different observers are used for each group). Mortality is not usually a threat unless a particular treatment causes systematic subject dropout.

Diffusion of treatments may be a source of invalidity in experiments where subjects in one group, because of close physical proximity or communication with subjects in another group, learn about information or treatments not intended for them. Because the conditions that were intended for one group, then, are transmitted to other groups, the effect of the treatment is dispersed and cannot be assessed reasonably. If, for example, a researcher compares two methods of instruction, such as cooperative group instruction and individualized instruction, and conducts the experiment within a single fourth-grade class by randomly assigning half the class to each method, it is likely that students in one group will know what is occurring in the other group. If the students in the individualized

TABLE 9.4
Threats to Internal Validity of True Experimental Designs

Design	History	Selection	Statistical Regression	Testing	Instrumentation	Mortality	Maturation	Diffusion of Treatment	Experimenter Bias	Statistical Conclusion
Pretest-posttest control group	?	+	+	+	?	?	+	?	?	?
Posttest-only control group	?	+	NA	NA	?	?	+	?	?	?

group feel left out, or believe they have a less interesting assignment, they may be resentful and may not perform as well as possible. Diffusion might also occur if students in the cooperative group learn to help others and then assist students in the individualized group.

Experimenter bias is another threat that may be a problem, depending on the procedures of the study. If the individuals who are responsible for implementing the treatments are aware of the purpose and hypotheses of the study, they may act differently toward each group and affect the results. If a teacher is involved in a study to investigate the effect of differential amounts of praise on behavior (more praise, better behavior), and understands what the hypothesized result should be, then the teacher may act more positively toward the students receiving more praise (be closer physically, give more eye contact, offer less criticism) and thus contaminate the intended effect of amount of praise.

Excerpt 9.1 illustrates a pretest–posttest control group design. In this study the investigators administered the same instrument as the pre- and posttest. To assure equal representation of subjects with different pretest scorers in each group, the pretest scores were rank-ordered by score levels, and subjects were randomly assigned from each level to experimental or control groups. The steps in the research, then, are modified somewhat since randomization occurred after the pretest, not before. The design used in Excerpt 9.1 is represented below.

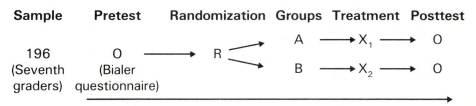

| Sample | Pretest | Randomization | Groups | Treatment | Posttest |

196 (Seventh graders) | O (Bialer questionnaire) | R | A → X_1 → O | B → X_2 → O

Time

EXCERPT 9.1
Pretest-Posttest Control Group Design

The purpose of the present study was to extend the research reported above by considering the effect of individually administered evaluative teacher comments over a period of time on the perception of control among inner-city junior high school students. Limitations of the above studies associated with the use of intact groups were avoided by randomly forming the experimental and control groups. Moreover, the treatments were designed to represent naturalistic interventions to an on-going instructional program rather than a "one-shot" treatment representing rather questionable educational practice.

METHOD

This study was conducted in a large junior high school in Baltimore, Maryland, during the Spring of 1978. The school enrollment for that year was just under 2,500 with more than one-half of the pupils eligible for the federally funded lunch program. Of the slightly more than 700 seventh graders, the 196 enrolled in five regular science classes taught by the second author served as the sample for this study. The sample included 104 females and 94 males with an age range from 11 to 15 years. Thirty-six pupils were repeating the seventh grade. There were 134 black and 62 white pupils.

All 196 pupils were administered the Bialer questionnaire during their regularly scheduled science class. Bialer (1) designed this locus of control scale for use with children. It contains 23 items of the type: "Do you believe a kid can be whatever he wants to be?" to which the child expresses agreement or disagreement with each statement by circling the word yes or no. There are eighteen statements for which a "yes" is scored as an internal response and five items for which "no" is scored as an internal response. The total score is the sum of the number of internal responses marked. The standard directions were used with the exception that the second author read the directions and each item aloud to the students as they read it silently. The directions as well as a complete listing of the items are presented by Lefcourt (6) with only a few exemplar items appearing in the Bialer article cited above. However, neither source presents data regarding the reliability of the scale. The answers were recorded directly on the questionnaire form and were later keypunched for the computer analyses. The pretest questionnaires were arranged by score levels, and within score levels, subjects were assigned at random to either the experimental or control groups.

Five major-subject teachers including the second author cooperated in administering the treatment conditions to the 196 pupils. Each teacher was supplied with the names of students in each treatment condition. The teachers were directed to provide written comments of an encouraging, personalized nature on all papers and tests submitted by all pupils in the experimental groups. The cooperating teachers were given these guidelines: "Comments are to be positive statements regardless of the grade, readily visible to the receiver and contain the pronoun 'you' whenever possible, such as 'you are showing improvement.'" The teachers were directed to write no comments on papers or tests returned to pupils in the control group except for the customary check-mark or grade. Treatment conditions were imposed for a period of six weeks, at which time, the Bialer locus of control instrument was re-administered.

Source: From "Teachers evaluative comments and pupil perception of control" by L. H. Cross and G. M. Cross, *Journal of Experimental Education*, 49, 68–71, 1981. Reprinted with permission of the Helen Dwight Reid Educational Foundation. Published by Heldref Publications, 4000 Albemarle St., N.W., Washington, DC 20016. Copyright © 1981.

Posttest-Only Control Group Design

The purpose of randomization, as indicated previously, is to equalize the experimental and control groups statistically before introducing the independent variable. If the groups are equalized through randomization, is it necessary to give a pretest? While there are certain cases in which it is best to use a pretest with randomization, if the groups have at least fifteen subjects each the pretest is unnecessary—that is, it is not essential to have a pretest in order to conduct a true experimental study. The **posttest-only control group design** is exactly the same as the pretest-posttest control group design except that there are no pretests of the dependent variable. The posttest-only control group design is represented as follows:

Posttest-Only Control Group Design

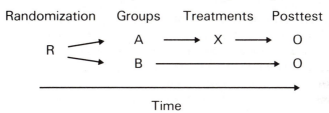

This basic design can be expanded to include several treatments:

The posttest-only control group design is used when it is unfeasible or inconvenient to give a pretest and in situations in which the pretest might have an effect on the treatment. There are four disadvantages to using a posttest-only rather than a pretest-posttest design: if there is any chance that randomization has not controlled for initial group differences, the lack of a pretest makes it difficult either to check whether differences exist or control statistically those differences that may be found; the researcher is unable to form subgroups on the basis of the pretest for investigating effects of the treatment on different subgroups; the researcher is unable to determine whether differential mortality has occurred; and the statistical analysis is less precise and less likely to show a difference between the experimental and control groups as in the pretest-posttest design. If the following conditions exist, the pretest-posttest design may thus be preferable:

1. There are subtle, small differences between treatment conditions.
2. Differential mortality is possible.
3. Subgroup analysis is desirable.
4. Anonymity is unnecessary.
5. Pretesting is a normal part of the subjects' routine.

The advantages of the posttest-only design are that it allows experimental evidence when it is impossible to give a pretest, it avoids the reactive effect of pretesting, and its use makes assuring anonymity easier. This design is especially good, then, for attitude research for two reasons: the use of an attitude questionnaire as the pretest may well affect the treatment, and attitudes are generally reported more honestly if anonymity can be assured.

The posttest-only control group design controls for almost the same sources of invalidity as the pretest-posttest control group design. Table 9.4 summarizes the sources of invalidity.

In Excerpt 9.2 a posttest-only design is used with kindergarten, second-grade, and third-grade children for investigating the effect of various imagery and pictorial strategies on oral prose-learning performance. There were three experimental conditions and a control group, and after listening to a story each subject was asked to respond to questions that constituted the posttest.

Occasionally, a contingency arises in which the researcher needs to rule out the effect of the pretest on the treatment. The design used for this purpose is a combination of the posttest-only control group and pretest-posttest control group design, and is called the Solomon four-group design. Although this design controls for the effects of mortality and pretest-treatment interactions, the design is difficult to carry out in education because it requires twice as many subjects and groups as in other designs.

■ QUASI-EXPERIMENTAL DESIGNS ■

True experimental designs provide the strongest, most convincing arguments of the causal effect of the independent variable because they control for the most sources of internal invalidity. There are, however, many circumstances in educational research for which, while causal inference is desired, it is unfeasible to design true experiments, or in which the need for strong external validity is greater. The most common reasons that experimental designs cannot be employed are that randomization of subjects to experimental and control groups is impossible,

EXCERPT 9.2
Posttest-Only Control Group Design

Design and procedure. Within each age group, subjects were randomly assigned to one of four experimental conditions: control, imagery, partial, and complete. Each subject was tested individually in a small room located within the school buildings. All subjects were told to "listen to the stories carefully because later on I am going to ask you some questions about them." No further instructions were given to control subjects. Subjects in the imagery condition were also instructed to pretend that they were being shown a book with pictures in it that depicted all the objects and events of the story. In the partial condition, subjects were told to look at the pictures and to form an image of the missing objects. Subjects assigned to the complete condition were instructed to look at the pictures because the pictures illustrated everything that was in the story. Before starting, all subjects were provided with a sample one-sentence story and the devices appropriate for their condition.

Source: Guttman, J., Levin, J. R., & Pressley, M. (1977). Pictures, partial pictures, and young children's oral prose learning. *Journal of Educational Psychology. 69*, 473–480.

and that a control or comparison group is unavailable, inconvenient, or too expensive. Fortunately, there are a number of good designs that can be used under either of these circumstances. These designs are termed **quasi-experimental** because, while not true experiments, they provide reasonable control over most sources of invalidity and they are usually stronger than the pre-experimental designs. Although there are a large number of quasi-experimental designs (Cook & Campbell, 1979), we will discuss only the most common ones.

Nonequivalent Pretest-Posttest Control Group Design

This design is very prevalent and useful in education, since it is often impossible to randomize subjects. The researcher uses intact, already established groups of subjects, gives a pretest, administers the treatment condition to one group, and gives the posttest. The only difference between this design, then, and the pretest–posttest control group design is in the lack of randomization of subjects. The design is represented below:

Nonequivalent Pretest-Posttest Control Group Design

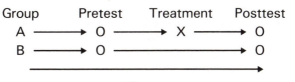

TABLE 9.5
Threats to Internal Validity of
Quasi-Experimental Designs

Design	History	Selection	Statistical Regression	Testing	Instrumentation	Mortality	Maturation	Diffusion of Treatment	Experimenter Bias	Statistical Conclusion
Nonequivalent pretest-posttest control group design	?	—	?	+	?	?	—	?	?	?
Single group interrupted time series	—	?	+	?	?	?	+	NA	+	?
Control group interrupted times series	+	?	+	+	?	?	+	?	?	?

As shown in Table 9.5, the most serious threat to the internal validity of research conducted with this design is selection; that is, because the groups may differ in characteristics that affect the dependent variable, the researcher must address selection and provide reasonable arguments that this threat is not a plausible rival hypothesis. Suppose a researcher is interested in studying the effect of three different methods of changing the attitudes of student teachers toward mainstreamed children. The researcher has three classes of student teachers to work with, and it is impossible to assign students randomly within each class to each of the three methods. The researcher therefore uses each class intact and gives each class a different treatment. The design would be as follows:

Group	Pretest	Method	Posttest
A	O	X_1	O
B	O	X_2	O
B	O	X_3	O

The interpretation of the results will depend largely on whether the groups differed on some characteristic that might reasonably be related to the independent variable. This decision is made by comparing the three groups on such characteristics as gender, time the groups meet, size of groups, achievement, aptitude, socioeconomic status, major, and pretest scores. If, for instance, group A com-

---

EXCERPT 9.3
Quasi-Experimental Design

A quasi-experimental non-equivalent group research design was used for the study (Campbell & Stanley, 1963). Two instructors each taught two classes, one in the morning and one in the afternoon. The assignment of the effort condition was random by class, so that the two levels of the condition for the book and chapter were counterbalanced for teacher and time of day. Each instructor gave a high effort assignment to one class for the book and a low effort assignment for the book to the other class. The opposite assignments were given to each class for the chapter. The second independent variable, high praise or no praise feedback, was administered randomly by student in each of the effort conditions.

Source: McMillan, J. H. (1977). The effect of effort and feedback on the formation of student attitudes. *American Educational Research Journal. 14*, 317–330.

prises all elementary majors and groups B and C secondary majors, and the results showed that group A gained more than B and C, the gain may be attributable to the values and backgrounds of elementary majors as compared to those of secondary majors. On the other hand, if the groups are about the same in most characteristics, then it would be reasonable to assume that selection differences probably would not account for the results. Consequently, if the researcher knows in advance that randomization is impossible, the groups should be selected to be as similar as possible. The pretest scores and other measures on the groups are then used to adjust the groups statistically on the factor that is measured. Another approach to controlling selection when intact groups, such as classrooms, must be used is to use a large number of groups and then randomly assign entire groups to either control or treatment conditions. This procedure then changes the study to a true experimental design. This is, in fact, the preferred approach when diffusion of treatment or local history threats are viable.

The threats of maturation and statistical regression are the only other differences between this design and the pretest-posttest control group design. Regression is a problem if one of the groups happens to have extremely high or low scores. If, for example, a study to assess the impact of a program on gifted children selected gifted children who score low and normal children who score high as comparison groups, then statistical regression will make the results look like a difference in posttest scores when nothing has actually changed. Maturation effects (growing more experienced, tired, bored, and so on) will depend on the specific differences in characteristics between the groups.

In Excerpt 9.3 a nonequivalent group quasi-experimental design is employed by using students in intact classes as subjects. Notice how the researcher anticipates plausible rival hypotheses that may confound the conclusions because of design inadequacies.

Time Series Designs

In the one-group pretest-posttest design a single group of subjects receives one pretest and one posttest. If the group is repeatedly measured before and after the treatment, rather than once before and once after, a different design, called "time series," is created. **Time series designs** are especially useful when there are continuous naturally occurring observations of the dependent variable over time and there is a sudden or distinct treatment during the observations. These designs offer significant improvement over the pretest–posttest design because with a series of pre- and post-observations, patterns of stability and change can be assessed more accurately. There are many different types of time series designs (Cook & Campbell, 1979); we will discuss the most common ones.

Single Group Interrupted Time Series Design.   This design requires one group and multiple observations or assessments before and after the treatment. The observations before the treatment can be thought of as repeated pretests, those after the treatment as repeated posttests. The design can be diagramed as follows:

Single-Group Interrupted Time-Series Design

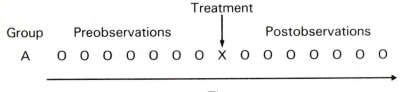

There are several conditions that should be met in employing this design. First, the observations should be made at equal time intervals and should be conducted with the same procedures in order to reduce the threat of instrumentation. Second, the treatment introduced should be a distinctive, abrupt intervention that is clearly new to the existing environment. Third, there should be some evidence that the subjects involved in each observation are either the same subjects (that is, have low mortality) or that the characteristics of the subjects change little. A new curriculum could be assessed well with this design. Student achievement could be plotted for several years with the old curriculum, and then achievement scores could be recorded for several years after the new curriculum is introduced.

Some possible outcomes for the study are indicated in Figure 9.1. If outcome A is achieved, then the researcher may conclude that the curriculum had a positive effect on achievement. Outcome B indicates a steady improvement of scores, so it is difficult to interpret the effect of the curriculum, and outcome C indicates little change over the time span. In interpreting these results, however, the researcher should look for alternate explanations. If there happened to be a change in the

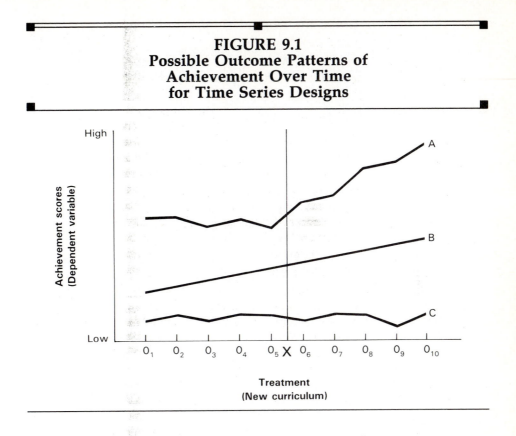

FIGURE 9.1
Possible Outcome Patterns of
Achievement Over Time
for Time Series Designs

student population, such as with migration from the city to suburban schools, then the observations would expect to change. The testing instrument would need to be the same (there should be no change in the norming group). Perhaps the most serious threat to validity is history. It is possible that events other than the treatment, in this case the curriculum, occurred at about the same time and affected the posttest observations; for example, maybe in the same year the curricula were changed, the teachers also changed. Other threats include seasonal variation (self-concept scores may be lower in winter than in spring) and testing (the effect of the pretesting on the treatment).

Control Group Interrupted Time Series Design. In this design a control or comparison group is added to the single group interrupted time series. The addition of a control group strengthens the design considerably, since the major threat of history is eliminated. Instrumentation is also a less likely explanation, and if randomization is included then selection is not a threat to validity. Since a control group is present, however, diffusion of treatment becomes a threat. This design is represented on the next page.

Control-Group Interrupted Time-Series Design

		Treatment	
Group	Preobservations	↓	Postobservations
A	O O O O	X	O O O O
B	O O O O		O O O O

Time

There are many variations of the basic time series design. A treatment can be removed rather than added, for example, and multiple treatments can be compared, either with one group or several groups. Some variations are indicated in the next diagram. In situation 1 three different treatments are compared, using three groups of subjects. In situation 2 only one group of subjects is used and two treatments are compared, and in situation 3 two treatments are compared in two groups at different points in time.

The quasi-experimental designs that have been introduced in this chapter are simple, basic designs that are usually expanded in actual studies, and there are several designs that have not been mentioned. The choice of design will depend on the variables studied, the circumstances of the setting in which the research is conducted, and the plausibility of threats to internal validity. The important point is that there are weaknesses in all research designs, and it is necessary for the investigator and reader of research to search out and analyze plausible rival hypotheses that may explain the results.

	A	O	O	O	O	OX_1O	O	O	O	O			
Situation 1	B	O	O	O	O	OX_2O	O	O	O	O			
	C	O	O	O	O	OX_3O	O	O	O	O			
Situation 2	A	O	O	O	OX_1O	O	O	OX_2O	O	O	O		
Situation 3	A	O	O	OX_1O	O	O	O	O	O	O			
	B	O	O	O	O	O	O	OX_1O	O	O			

■ SINGLE-SUBJECT DESIGNS ■

The pre-experimental, true experimental, and quasi-experimental designs that have been discussed are based on a traditional research notion that behavior is best investigated by using groups of subjects. This is primarily because of the desire to produce results that can be applied to groups, not necessarily to individuals. We are typically interested, for example, in fourth-grade attitudes in general, or whether a particular method of reading is in general best. There are, however, many circumstances in which it is either undesirable or impossible to use groups of subjects, such as when examining instructional strategies to be used with individual students. In these situations **single-subject designs** are often employed to provide rigorous causal inferences for the behavior of an individual. The sample size in single-subject designs is therefore one. The basic approach is to study an individual in a nontreatment condition and then in a treatment condition, with performance on the dependent variable measured continually in both conditions.

Single-subject designs should not be confused with case studies. Both use a sample size of one, but the single-subject design employs several procedures for achieving control of extraneous variables in order to allow reasonable causal inferences. The design characteristics that achieve high internal validity with single-subject designs are somewhat different from those of techniques covered previously in the context of group designs. The most important characteristics of single-subject designs are summarized below:

1. *Reliable measurement.* Single-subject designs usually involve many observations of behavior as the technique for collecting data. It is important that the observation conditions, such as time of day and location, be standardized, that observers be well trained and checked for reliability and bias, and that the observed behavior be defined operationally. Consistency in measurement is especially important as the study moves from one condition to another. Because accurate measurement is crucial to single-subject designs, the researcher typically reports all aspects of data collection so that any threat to validity can be reasonably ruled out.

2. *Repeated measurement.* A distinct characteristic of single-subject designs is that a single aspect of behavior is measured many times, in the same way, throughout the study. This is quite different from measurement in many group studies in which there is a single measure before or after the treatment. Repeated measurement controls for normal variation that would be expected within short time intervals, and provides a clear, reliable description of the behavior.

3. *Description of conditions.* A precise, detailed description of all conditions in which the behavior is observed should be provided. This description allows application of the study to other individuals in order to strengthen both internal and external validity.

4. *Baseline and treatment condition; duration and stability.* The usual procedure is for each condition to last about the same length of time and contain about the same number of observations. If either the length of time or number of observations varies, then time and number of observations become confounding variables that complicate the interpretation of the results and weaken internal validity. It is also important that the behavior be observed long enough for the establishment of a stable pattern. If there is considerable variation in the behavior, then it will be difficult to determine whether observed changes are due to natural variation or to the treatment. During the first phase of single subject research, the target behavior is observed under natural conditions until stability is achieved. This period of time is called the **baseline.** The treatment phase occurs

with a change in conditions by the researcher and also must be long enough to achieve stability.

5. *Single variable rule.* It is important to change only one variable during the treatment phase of single-subject research, and the variable that is changed should be described precisely. If two or more variables are changed simultaneously, the researcher cannot be sure which change, or changes, caused the results.

A-B Designs

In order to distinguish single-subject designs from traditional group designs, a unique notational convention is used for single-subject designs. In it the letters, instead of representing groups of subjects, stand for conditions: *A* stands for the baseline condition and *B* for the treatment condition.

The **A-B design** is the most simple, and least interpretable, single-subject design. The procedure in using it is to observe target behavior until it occurs at a consistent stable rate. This condition is the baseline, or A condition. A treatment is then introduced into the environment in which baseline data has been collected, and this condition is labeled B. The design can be diagramed as follows:

A-B Single Subject Design

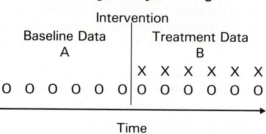

The interpretation of the results is based on the premise that if no treatment were introduced, the behavior would continue as recorded in the baseline. If the behavior does change during the treatment condition, it may be attributable to the intervention introduced by the researcher. Other factors, however, such as testing and history, cannot be ruled out reasonably in this design, so it is relatively weak in internal validity.

A-B-A Designs

A more common design in single-subject research is the **A-B-A design,** also called a **reversal** or **withdrawal design,** in which a second baseline period is added after the treatment. In this design, which is represented below, the researcher establishes a baseline (A), introduces the treatment (B), and then removes the treatment to reestablish the baseline condition (A).

A-B-A Single Subject Design

This design allows strong causal inference if the pattern of behavior changes during the treatment phase and then returns to about the same pattern as observed in the first baseline after the treatment is removed. As a hypothetical example to illustrate this design, suppose a teacher is interested in trying a new reinforcement technique with John, one of the fifth graders, in the hope that the new technique would increase the time John spends actually engaged in study (time on task). The teacher first records the average amount of time on task for each day until a stable pattern is achieved. Then the teacher introduces the reinforcement technique as the intervention, as s/he continues to observe time on task. After a given length of time, the teacher stops using the reinforcement technique to see if the on-task behavior returns to the baseline condition. Figure 9.2 illustrates results of this hypothetical study that provides good evidence of a causal link between the reinforcement technique and greater time on task.

Further evidence of a change in behavior that is caused by the treatment may be obtained if the A-B-A design is extended to reinstitute the treatment, or become A-B-A-B. Not only does the A-B-A-B design provide stronger causal inference than the A-B-A design, it also ends with the treatment condition, which often, for ethical reasons, is more favorable for the subject. If the pattern of results fails to support the effect of the treatment, then the interpretation is less clear. If the behavior is changed during the treatment but fails to return to the baseline condition once the treatment is ended, the researcher does not know whether factors other than the treatment cause the change, or if the treatment was so effective that it could be removed and still have an impact on behavior.

The A-B-A-B design is illustrated in Excerpt 9.4. The purpose of this experiment was to investigate the effects of reprimands given to one student on a second student.

Multiple-Baseline Designs

When it is impossible or undesirable to remove a treatment condition, or when the effects of a treatment condition extend into a second baseline phase, strong causal inference can be made by using **multiple-baseline designs** rather than by using a simple A-B design. Multiple-baseline designs employ the A-B logic but, rather than by using one subject and one kind of target behavior, the researcher

FIGURE 9.2
Results from a Hypothetical Study Using an A-B-A Design

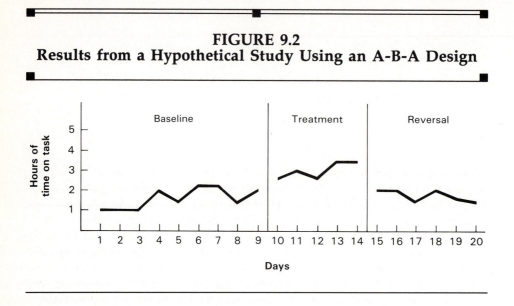

collects data on two or more actions, subjects, or situations, or some combination of actions, situations, and subjects.

Multiple-Baseline Across Behavior. In this design baseline measurements are recorded on two or more discrete, independent behaviors for one subject. After a stable baseline is established for all behaviors the treatment is first applied to one behavior, then, after a constant time interval, it is applied to the second behavior, and so forth until all have received the treatment.

Strong causal inference can be made of the effect of the treatment if performance shows consistent change only after the treatment is introduced for each type of behavior. To provide a meaningful comparison it is necessary to begin the treatments at different times for each one. In this way, behavior remaining at the baseline condition provides control for that receiving the treatment condition. The most troublesome problem with this design is using two or more behaviors that are so similar that the first time the treatment is introduced, it affects both. This problem can be thought of as a threat to internal validity because of diffusion of treatment. Excerpt 9.5 illustrates this design in an experiment that assessed the effect of reinforcement on normal children as tutors of mentally retarded schoolmates for four different types of behavior. Notice that each type of behavior changed significantly whenever the treatment was implemented.

Multiple-Baseline Across Situations. In this design a single type of target behavior of one individual is observed in two or more settings. A teacher might, for example, be interested in investigating whether a student would respond the

EXCERPT 9.4
A-B-A-B Single Subject Design

EXPERIMENTAL DESIGN

A reversal design was used in this experiment. After stable baseline performance was obtained for both Jeanette and Natalie, reprimands were made contingent upon Jeanette's disruptive behavior according to a variable interval 2-min. schedule of punishment. During this condition, Natalie's disruptive behavior was not reprimanded. After a return to baseline conditions, reprimands were again made contingent upon Jeanette's disruptive behavior. The experiment was terminated after this treatment because the school year had come to an end.

Baseline 1. During this condition the teacher was instructed not to praise or reprimand either Jeanette or Natalie and to conduct the class in her usual manner.

Reprimand Jeanette 1. During this condition Jeanette's disruptive behavior was reprimanded by the teacher on a VI 2-min schedule of punishment. The teacher was signaled when to deliver reprimands using the same procedure as in the preceding experiment. As in Experiment 3A, a variety of signals was used.

Baseline 2. This condition was carried out in the same manner as the first baseline condition.

Reprimand Jeanette 2. This condition was carried out in the same manner as the first reprimand Jeanette condition.

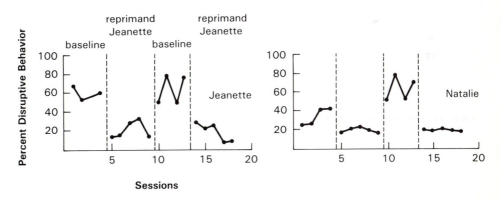

Fig. 6. The percentage of 10-sec intervals during which Jeanette and Natalie were engaged in disruptive behavior during each session of the experiment.

EXPERIMENTAL DESIGN

In order to control for the effectiveness of the first phase of the intervention, a multiple baseline across behaviors design (Baer, Wolf, & Risley, 1968) was used for each participant. That is, baseline and preintervention probing led to the start of intervention on delayed imitation. When this behavior had been at the 80% level or above for 3 consecutive days, 'treatment began on cooperative play. Then, it was extended to the verbalization of "that's good," and finally to the verbalization of "thank you." The second phase of the intervention started simultaneously on all behaviors when the level of the last behavior treated also had been 100% for 3 consecutive days. The end of the second phase was followed by three series of probes which assessed maintenance and generalization.

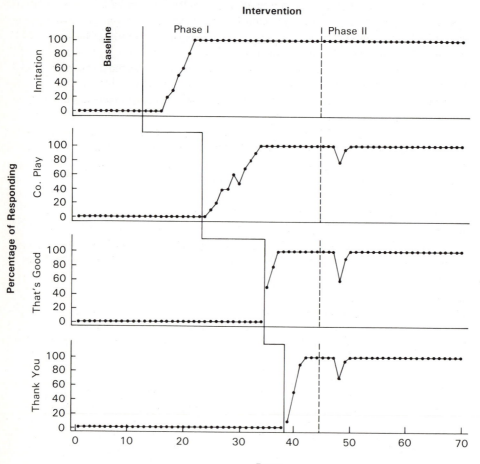

Fig. 1. The data on the acquisition of the target behaviors (Phase I of the Intervention) are the median slopes. That is, for each behavior the graph presents the performance of the subject who needed the median number of days to achieve the 100% level of responding. During baseline as well as from the achievement of the 100% level to end of Phase I, the performance of the subjects was equivalent. The data points presented in the second phase of the Intervention (which was of the same length for all subjects) are means for the three subjects.

Source: From Lancioni, G. E., "Normal Children as Tutors to Teach Social Responses to Withdrawn Mentally Retarded Schoolmates: Training, Maintenance, and Generalization," *Journal of Applied Behavior Analysis*, 15, 17–40, 1982. Copyright © 1982 by the Society for the Experimental Analysis of Behavior, Inc. Reprinted by permission.

same way to individualized feedback in math, science, and English. The basic design is the same as in the multiple-baseline across behaviors design except that situation replaces types of behavior as the condition that is varied (such as learning behavior in both a classroom and grocery store or classroom and cafeteria).

Multiple-Baseline Across Individuals.   This design uses two or more individuals and holds the behavior and the situation constant. After a stable baseline is observed for one subject, the treatment is introduced for that subject only. After a given time interval, the second subject receives the treatment, and so forth. This design is effective as long as the subjects involved are uninfluenced by one another because one of them has received the treatment (for example, with students in the same class or with siblings). This is again an example of diffusion of treatment. A good use of this type of design would be to have a teacher employ the same treatment procedure with individual students in four different classes.

Many variations of the three multiple-baseline designs are possible. A good source for further detail on these designs is Hersen and Barlow (1976). The A-B-A and A-B-A-B formats can be combined with multiple-baseline designs. The designs that involve removal, reversal, or reinstatement of the treatment are generally strongest with respect to internal validity. As might well be suspected, the external validity of single-subject designs is quite limited. The generalizability of results of one study is increased primarily by replication with other subjects and different settings.

■ *EX POST FACTO* DESIGNS ■

In all of the designs we have presented in the chapter, the researcher investigates a problem by observing what *will* happen. In other words, the research approach is to manipulate conditions, observe what happens, and then record the results. There are, however, many situations and research problems that exclude this approach because manipulation of conditions is impossible. Consider the following list of research questions. In each case the implied cause-and-effect relationships rule out experimental manipulation.

— What is the effect of attendance at day care on the social skills of children?
— What is the effect of single parenting on achievement?
— Do teachers who graduate from liberal arts colleges have greater longevity in the teaching field than teachers who graduate from colleges of education?
— What is the relationship between participation in extracurricular activities and self-concept?

Characteristics

It is either simply impossible or unethical to manipulate such variables as single or couple parenting, day care attendance, or choice of college by students, as well as many other variables like race, socioeconomic status, and personality. A researcher would probably have some difficulty assigning children on a random basis to either attend or not attend day care!

This is a situation, then, in which it is desirable to study cause-and-effect relationships, but the circumstances of the research are such that two crucial characteristics of experimental research, manipulation of conditions and random assignment of groups, cannot be carried out. The type of design most frequently used in these situations is called *ex post facto,* or causal-comparative. The purpose of *ex post facto* **research** is to investigate whether one or more pre-existing conditions have possibly caused subsequent differences in the groups of subjects. In other words, the researcher looks to conditions that have already occurred (*ex post facto* is Latin for *after the fact*) and then collects data to investigate the relationship of these varying conditions to subsequent behavior. In *ex post facto* research the investigator attempts to determine whether differences between groups (the independent variable) has resulted in an observed difference on the dependent variable.

Ex post facto designs are easily confused with experimental and quasi-experimental designs because all three types of designs have some common characteristics: a similar purpose, to determine cause-effect relationships; group comparisons; and the use of similar statistical analyses and vocabulary in describing the results. In experimental and quasi-experimental studies, however, the researcher deliberately controls the effect of some condition by manipulation of the independent variable, while in *ex post facto* research there is no manipulation of conditions because the cause has already occurred before the study is initiated. In *ex post facto* designs, therefore, there is usually a treatment and a control group, a factor that can further confuse the research with experimental approaches.

Ex post facto designs are also confused with correlational research, because both involve no manipulation and there are similar limitations in interpreting the results. *Ex post facto* designs, however, attempt to identify causal relationships, while correlational research generally does not. *Ex post facto* designs also usually involve two or more groups that are compared, while correlational studies use one group and two or more observations on each member of the group.

Conducting
Ex Post Facto **Research**

Although in *ex post facto* research the independent variable cannot be manipulated and random assignment of subjects to groups is impossible, there are several procedures that are used in planning *ex post facto* research that enhances control and limits plausible rival hypotheses. The first step is to formulate a research problem that includes possible causes of the dependent variable. The choice of possible causes is based on previous research and on the researcher's interpretation of observations of the phenomena being studied. Suppose, for example, the researcher wants to investigate the effect of class size on achievement, and it is impossible to assign students randomly to different size classes to conduct a true experiment. The researcher's interest may be based on correlational research that shows a negative relationship between class size and achievement and observations that students in smaller classes seem to do better. The research problem, then, is: What is the effect of class size on achievement?

A second step is to identify plausible rival hypotheses that might explain the relationship. The researcher might, for instance, list as possible causes of better achievement in smaller classes several factors like the following: smaller classes have better teachers; higher ability students are in smaller classes; students with higher motivation are in smaller classes; students from high socioeconomic backgrounds attend smaller classes than do students from low socioeconomic backgrounds; and perhaps teachers of smaller classes use a different type of instruction than those of larger classes use. Each of these factors might be related to the reason students in smaller classes achieve more than students in large classes.

The third step is to find and select the groups that will be compared. In our example of class size and achievement, the researcher will first need to define operationally *large* and *small* class size as well as *achievement*. A *small* class could have fewer than fifteen students and a *large* class more than twenty-five. *Achievement* could be defined as the gain in knowledge of the students while in the class. The researcher also needs to indicate whether the study includes all grade levels and locations. Suppose in this case the researcher is interested in elementary grade levels and the accessible population is a single school district. Once the variables are defined, groups must be selected that are as homogeneous as possible in the characteristics that constitute rival hypotheses and that are different with respect to the independent variable. In our example, then, the researcher selects groups that differ with respect to class size but that are similar in such factors as ability, socioeconomic background, teaching methods, quality of teachers, and student motivation. Matching is a good approach to forming groups that will be as homogeneous as possible in factors affecting the dependent variable. For example, in our study of class size, the researcher could match and select students on the basis of initial ability so that only students with about the same level of ability are included in the analysis, even though other students are contained in the classes.

The fourth step is to collect and analyze data on the subjects, including data on factors that may constitute rival hypotheses. Since *ex post facto* research is after the fact, most data that are needed have already been collected, and only the data from appropriate sources need to be gathered. Data analysis is very similar to procedures used for experimental and quasi-experimental studies in that groups are compared on the variables of interest. In our proposed study of class size, for example, all achievement scores in the small class would be averaged and compared to the average achievement in large classes. Data from the extraneous variables are also compared and incorporated into the statistical analyses to help make judgments about plausible rival hypotheses.

It must be stressed, in interpreting the results of *ex post facto* research, that cause-and-effect statements can be made only cautiously. In our example of large and small classes, if a difference in achievement is found between the groups, then the researcher can conclude that there is a relationship between class size and achievement. The results do not mean that being in either small or large classes had a causative effect on achievement. There may be a cause-and-effect relationship, but this depends on the researcher's ability to select comparison groups homogeneous on all important variables except being in small or large classes, and by the confidence with which other plausible rival hypotheses can be ruled out. If, for example, it turned out that all the small classes came from one school and large classes from another, then policies or procedures unique to the schools and unrelated to class size (such as stress on basic skill attainment or a special training program for teachers) may constitute plausible rival hypotheses.

A recent study investigating the effect of same-age and mixed-age preschool classrooms on play is a good example of *ex post facto* research. As pointed out in Excerpt 9.6, modes of play and social interaction of children in four same-age classrooms were compared to children in two mixed-age classrooms. Notice that the researchers summarize in the second paragraph of the excerpt how the same-age and mixed-age classrooms were comparable with respect to physical layout, materials, teacher-child ratio, socioeconomic factors of the children, and the amount of time the children had been in the classroom. Presumably these characteristics were identified before data were collected to rule out these plausible rival hypotheses. Of course there may be other differences between the groups besides the same-age/mixed-age variable that could affect the results. For instance, a difference in instructors could affect play and social interaction.

■ STANDARDS OF ADEQUACY ■

In judging the adequacy of the designs that have been presented in this chapter you should focus your attention on a few key criteria. These criteria are listed below in the form of questions that should be asked for each type of design.

EXCERPT 9.6
Ex Post Facto Research

METHOD

Subjects. The social-cognitive modes of play and peers' responses to them were observed in two classrooms of 3-year-olds ($N = 40$), two classrooms of 4-year-olds ($N = 32$), and two mixed-age classrooms of 3- and 4-year-olds ($N = 36$). The classrooms were considered mixed-age if at least 40% of the children were 3-year-olds and at least 40% of the children were 4-year-olds. Children considered 3-year-olds ranged from 2 years, 9 months to 3 years, 8 months, and 4-year-olds ranged from 3 years, 9 months to 4 years, 8 months at the beginning of the study. To assure equal opportunities for same-sex and cross-sex activities, classrooms were selected in which at least 40% of the children were boys and at least 40% were girls. These criteria for classifying classrooms as mixed-age were similar to those of previous research (e.g., Goldman, 1981; Roopnarine, 1984). These criteria were used because we wanted to study similar age groups of children in order to make comparisons with the findings of previous studies (e.g., Goldman's).

All classrooms assumed a child-centered orientation and were comparable in terms of physical layout, play and instructional materials, and teacher-child ratio (1:9). The children were from middle-income backgrounds as assessed by the Hollingshead Four Factor Index of Social Position (Hollingshead, undated). Preliminary analyses revealed no significant differences in sociodemographic factors between children in same age and mixed-age classrooms. In addition, children in both classroom arrangements were enrolled for approximately the same length of time in the mixed-age classrooms prior to observations (same-age classrooms $\bar{x} = 6$ months; mixed-age classrooms $\bar{x} = 5$ months).

Source: From "Social-Cognitive Play Patterns in Same-Age and Mixed-Age Preschool Classrooms" by N. S. Mounts and J. L. Roopnarine, *American Educational Research Journal*, 24, 463–476. Copyright © 1987 American Educational Research Association, Washington, DC. Reprinted by permission.

True Experimental Designs

1. Was the research design described in sufficient detail to allow for replication of the study?
2. Was it clear how statistical equivalence of the groups was achieved? Was there a full description of the specific manner in which subjects were assigned randomly to groups?
3. Was a true experimental design appropriate for the research problem?
4. Was there manipulation of the independent variable?
5. Was there maximum control over extraneous variables and errors of measurement?

6. Was the treatment condition sufficiently different from the comparison condition for a differential effect on the dependent variable to be expected?
7. Were potential threats to internal validity reasonably ruled out or noted and discussed?
8. Was the time frame of the study described?
9. Did the design avoid being too artificial or restricted for adequate external validity?
10. Was an appropriate balance achieved between control of variables and natural conditions?
11. Were appropriate tests of inferential statistics used?

Quasi-Experimental Designs

1. Was the research design described in sufficient detail to allow for replication of the study?
2. Was a true experiment possible?
3. Was it clear how extraneous variables were controlled or ruled out as plausible rival hypotheses?
4. Were all potential threats to internal validity addressed?
5. Were the explanations ruling out plausible rival hypotheses reasonable?
6. Would a different quasi-design have been better?
7. Did the design approach a true experiment as closely as possible?
8. Was there an appropriate balance between control for internal validity and for external validity?
9. Was every effort made to use groups that were as equivalent as possible?
10. If a time-series design was used, (a) was there an adequate number of observations to suggest a pattern of results? (b) was the treatment intervention introduced distinctly at one point in time? (c) was the measurement of the dependent variable consistent? (d) was it clear, if a comparison group was used, how equivalent the groups were?

Single-Subject Designs

1. Was the sample size one?
2. Was a single-subject design most appropriate, or would a group design have been better?
3. Were the observation conditions standardized?
4. Was the behavior that was observed defined operationally?
5. Was the measurement highly reliable?
6. Were sufficient repeated measures made?
7. Were the conditions in which the study was conducted described fully?
8. Was there stability in the baseline condition before the treatment was introduced?

9. Was there a difference between the length of time or number of observations between the baseline and the treatment conditions?
10. Was only one variable changed during the treatment condition?
11. Were threats to internal and external validity addressed?

Ex Post Facto Designs

1. Was the primary purpose of the study to investigate cause-and-effect relationships?
2. Have the presumed cause-and-effect conditions already occurred?
3. Was there manipulation of the independent variable?
4. Were groups being compared already different with respect to the independent variable?
5. Were potential extraneous variables recognized and considered as plausible rival hypotheses?
6. Were causal statements regarding the results made tenuously?
7. Were threats to external validity addressed in the conclusions?

■ SUMMARY ■

The purpose of this chapter has been to introduce designs that permit investigation of the causal effect of one variable on another. The challenge to most researchers is using the design that, given the conditions of the research, is best suited to their goal. The major points of the chapter are summarized below.

1. Experimental research, as defined in the natural sciences, involves manipulating experimental variables and randomization of subjects to groups in order to investigate cause-and-effect relationships.
2. Classic experimental research is characterized by random assignment of subjects to treatment and control groups, manipulation of independent variables, and tight control of extraneous variables.
3. Strict control of extraneous variables in experimental educational research may lead to limited generalizability of results.
4. Planning experimental research involves the creation of experimental and comparison groups, manipulation of the factor of the group to receive the treatment, and assessment of the effect of the treatment on behavior.
5. The key element in interpreting experimental studies is to rule out plausible rival hypotheses.
6. Pre-experimental designs control for very few threats to internal validity and generally should not be used for making causal inferences.
7. True experimental designs control for most threats to internal validity but some threats, such as local history and diffusion of treatment, may be uncontrolled.

8. Quasi-experimental designs are often employed because of the difficulties in conducting true experiments.

9. Time series designs, in which many observations are made before and after the treatment, are especially useful in cases where periodic testing is a natural part of the environment.

10. Single-subject designs provide techniques for making strong causal inferences about the effect of a treatment on a single individual or group.

11. *Ex post facto* designs are used to study potential causal relationships after a presumed cause has occurred.

12. In *ex post facto* research subjects are selected on the basis of the groups they were in at one time; there is no random assignment of subjects to different groups; and there is no manipulation of the independent variable.

■ SELF-INSTRUCTIONAL REVIEW EXERCISES ■

Sample answers are in the back of the book.

Test Items

1. Classic experimental research, as conducted in the natural sciences, involves
   a. manipulation, randomization, application of results.
   b. randomization, manipulation, control.
   c. control, manipulation, generalizability.
   d. generalizability, control, independence.

2. A disadvantage of experimental research in educational settings is that
   a. it is difficult to make causal inferences.
   b. internal validity is weak.
   c. it is usually expensive to conduct.
   d. generalizability is often limited.

3. The design that has the weakest internal validity is
   a. one-group posttest only.   c. A-B-A-B single-subject design.
   b. one-group pretest-posttest.   d. time-series design.

4. The results of pre-experimental designs usually have many plausible rival hypotheses because of
   a. insufficient planning.   c. lack of generalizability.
   b. lack of randomization.   d. using only one group.

5. True experimental designs control for which of the following sources of internal invalidity?
   a. selection, testing   c. selection, maturation
   b. regression, history   d. diffusion of treatment, selection

6. The most important advantage of using true experiments, with respect to internal validity, is that _____ is controlled.
   a. selection
   b. history
   c. testing
   d. experimenter bias

7. The non-equivalent pretest-posttest design controls for which source of invalidity?
   a. regression
   b. history
   c. testing
   d. selection

8. The distinguishing characteristic of time series designs is that
   a. several treatments are compared.
   b. many pre- and post-observations are made.
   c. history is effectively controlled.
   d. subjects are randomly assigned to groups at different times.

9. The A-B single-subject design is particularly vulnerable to which of the following threats to internal validity?
   a. diffusion of treatment, selection
   b. selection, history
   c. diffusion of treatment, regression
   d. instrumentation, history

10. Which of the following sets of characteristics distinguishes single-subject designs from other experimental designs?
    a. good generalizability, using baseline data
    b. varying only one variable, using multiple methods
    c. using comparison groups, using random assignment
    d. varying only one variable, using random assignment

11. Multiple-baseline designs are especially useful for what type of situation?
    a. when two or more subjects are available
    b. when it is undesirable to use only one baseline
    c. when it is undesirable to remove the treatment
    d. when two or more types of behavior are available for study

12. Two characteristics of *ex post facto* research are
    a. randomization and comparison groups.
    b. nonmanipulation and nonrandomization.
    c. nonrandomization and manipulation of the independent variable.
    d. nonmanipulation and randomization.

13. The selection of appropriate comparison groups is crucial in *ex post facto* research because
    a. the groups must be equal in all respects except the independent variable.

b. the groups must be about the same with respect to the dependent variable.

c. otherwise the groups would not be comparable.

d. if the groups are incorrectly chosen, rival hypotheses may be more plausible.

Application Exercises

For each of the following cases, state the design that is used, and represent it using the notation system discussed in the chapter.

1. A researcher wants to test the effectiveness of three methods of teaching typing to a group of eleventh-grade students. The researcher locates a school willing to cooperate, and a teacher says that the researcher can use three of his classes. The researcher then administers a pretest to all students, each class receives a different method of teaching for two weeks, and then the researcher gives all students a posttest.

2. A teacher is interested in determining the effect of using a point system with students in order to control misbehavior. The teacher decides to record the amount of misbehavior of two students, a boy and a girl who seem to have more problems than other students. For two weeks the teacher records the misbehavior of the students. At the end of the second week the teacher begins using the point system with the boy and at the same time continues to record misbehavior for another two weeks. The girl does not receive the point treatment until the end of the third week.

3. A researcher is interested in whether the order of questions in a multiple-choice test affects the number of items answered correctly. The researcher makes three forms of the test: one with easy items first, difficult last; another with easy items last, difficult first; and a third with no order at all, easiest and difficult mixed together. The test is given to a class of sixty students. The tests are organized into twenty piles, with each pile containing Form 1, 2, and 3. The twenty piles are then put together and the tests are passed out to the students. The researcher then compares the average scores of students taking each form of the test.

CHAPTER 10

INFERENTIAL STATISTICS

■ KEY TERMS ■

probability
null, or statistical, hypothesis
level of significance
alpha level
Type I error
Type II error
statistically significant
t-test
degrees of freedom
independent samples *t*-test
dependent samples *t*-test
correlated samples *t*-test
analysis of variance (ANOVA)

post hoc or multiple comparisons
factorial ANOVA
interaction
analysis of covariance (ANCOVA)
parametric
nonparametric
chi-square
independent samples
  chi-square test
contingency table
phi coefficient
contingency coefficient
multivariate

This is the part of research books that most readers dread. The words *inferential statistics* send waves of anxiety and fear into students already concerned about the so-called more simple descriptive data analysis procedures. Readers base their feelings on the mistaken perception that inferential statistics involves complex and difficult mathematical calculations. It is true that the actual computation associated with inferential statistics is complicated, but students need not learn equations and complete calculations to understand and use the results of these procedures (calculations are presented in Appendix B). Learning the principles of inferential statistics requires study and application, but it is more a matter of understanding logic than calculating mathematics.

In this chapter we will present the logic upon which inferential statistics is based, the principles of hypothesis testing, and a few commonly used statistical procedures. The emphasis throughout is on presenting the concepts so that the student will understand and evaluate the use of these procedures in designing and reading research.

■ THE LOGIC OF INFERENTIAL STATISTICS ■

In some ways it would be very pleasant if we could be certain in predicting the outcomes of events. When we go see a movie, how sure are we that we will enjoy it? When a teacher uses a particular grouping procedure, how sure is he or she that it will work? How confident is a patient that an operation will be successful? Are farmers certain that there will be sufficient rain for their crops? The questions are endless because it is in our nature to try to predict the future, and the degree to which we can be certain about the predictions varies greatly. There are very few things in our world of which we can be absolutely certain, and in the social sciences and education there is always a fair amount of uncertainty. In making statements about investigated phenomena we must therefore use language that reflects the probabilistic nature of the case. The numbers, concepts, and terms used in inferential statistics provide this language. Although there are a great number of inferential statistical procedures, many quite complicated, the purpose is always the same. The goal is to determine in a precise way the probability of something.

Probability

Probability is a scientific way of stating the degree of confidence we have in predicting something. Kerlinger (1979) defines probability theoretically as "the number of 'favorable' cases of the event divided by the total number of (equally possible) cases" (pp. 67–68). (*Favorable* here means favorable to an event whose probability we are assessing.) If the total number of cases is 12, therefore, and the number of favorable cases 6, the probability of the favorable case is 6/12 or 0.50. Dice rolling is a more concrete example. With one die there is a total of six possible cases. If the favorable case is rolling a four, the probability of actually rolling a four would be 1/6, or 0.17; that is, if a die is rolled 100 times, about 17 fours will be rolled. If we have two dice, what is the probability of rolling a seven? Since there is a total of 36 different combinations for throwing two dice (1 and 1; 1 and 2; 1 and 3, and so on) and only six of these equal 7 (1 and 6; 2 and 5; 3 and 4; 6 and 1; 5 and 2; and 4 and 3), the probability of rolling a seven is 6/36, or 0.17. What about throwing boxcars (two sixes)? There is only one combination of numbers that will give you boxcars, so the probability is 1/36, or 0.03.

This logic is applied to more complicated situations in research. How sure, for example, can pollsters be that their predictions are accurate? What is the probability of being right or wrong? As for the Gallup Poll, how certain can we be that the results from a so-called scientific sample accurately reflect the attitudes of the American public? When teachers use positive reinforcement, how sure are they that the desired behavior will increase in frequency? In these situations the number of total cases may be unknown and the assessment of the events is imperfect. We thus make probability statements that are influenced by the amount of error possible in measuring and sampling events.

Error in Sampling and Measurement

Sampling was discussed in Chapter 5 as a technique for studying a portion from the population of all events or observations under consideration. The population is the larger group to which the researcher intends to generalize the results obtained from the sample. As a subgroup of the population, the sample is used to derive data, and then inferential statistics is used to generalize to the population. Let us assume, for example, that a researcher is interested in assessing the self-concept of fourth graders in a school district. The researcher could measure the self-concept of every fourth grader, but that would be time-consuming, expensive, and probably unnecessary. Rather, the researcher takes a *sample* of fourth graders and measures their self-concepts. Then the researcher *infers* what the self-concept of all fourth graders is from the results of the sample chosen. Inferential statistics are used to make such inferences. The group of all fourth graders is the population, and the researcher uses descriptive statistics (mean and standard deviation) from the sample to estimate the characteristics of the population.

Where does probability enter this process? When a sample is drawn, the resulting statistics represent an imperfect estimate of the population. There is error in drawing the sample, and probability relates to our confidence in the fact that the sample accurately represents the population. Even if the researcher uses a random sample, the mean and variance of the particular sample drawn would be slightly different from those of another sample. A third sample would also be different, as would a fourth, a fifth, and so on. The sample descriptive statistics only estimate the population values, so the inferences made must take into account what possible sample statistics could have been generated.

Consider the following example (Figure 10.1). Let us say that a researcher is interested in determining the reading level of ninth graders of a school district. A random sample is selected and the mean of the sample is, let us say, 65, with a standard deviation of 5 (Figure 10.1a). Now let us say the researcher draws another random sample, and this time the mean is 66. Now there are two means (Figure 10.1b). Which one is correct? He or she decides to take five more samples and gets means of 64, 63.5, 64.5, 65.7, and 65.2 (Figure 10.1c). Now which one is correct? The researcher decides to really find out and takes thirty more samples. Surely that will do it! Different sample means are drawn, but when the means are put together they begin to look like something familiar—a normal curve (Figure 10.1d).

In fact, if 100 samples were drawn, the sample means, when put together, would constitute a normal curve, with its own mean and standard deviation. The mean of means, then, and the standard deviation of this new distribution can be calculated, and the researcher can use this information to know not what the population mean is, but the probability of its having a certain value based on the properties of the normal curve: that is, about two-thirds of the means drawn would be within one standard deviation of the mean of means, and 96 percent of the means would be within two standard deviations. The researcher, therefore, can now describe a range of probable means and be fairly certain of the range, even though individual sample means will be slightly different.

FIGURE 10.1
Random Sample with (a) One Mean,
(b) Two Means, (c) Several Means, and
(d) the Means Showing a Normal Curve

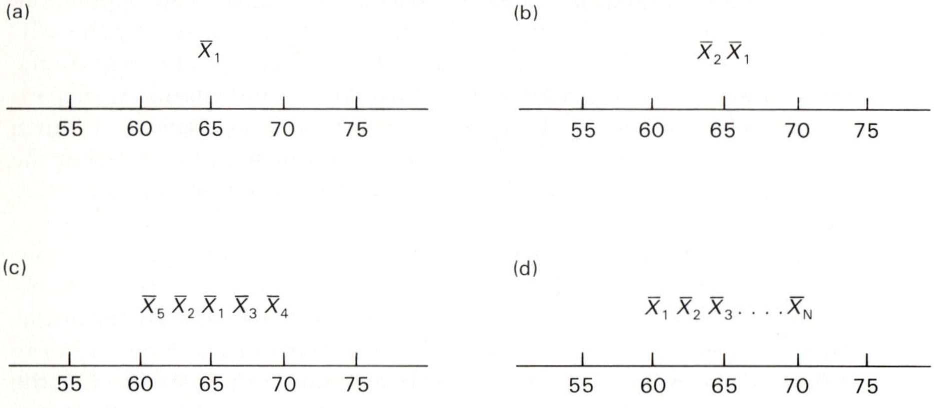

(a)

$\overline{X}_1$

```
  |    |    |    |    |
 55   60   65   70   75
```

(b)

$\overline{X}_2 \overline{X}_1$

```
       |    |    |    |    |
      55   60   65   70   75
```

(c)

$\overline{X}_5 \overline{X}_2 \overline{X}_1 \overline{X}_3 \overline{X}_4$

```
  |    |    |    |    |
 55   60   65   70   75
```

(d)

$\overline{X}_1 \overline{X}_2 \overline{X}_3 \ldots \overline{X}_N$

```
       |    |    |    |    |
      55   60   65   70   75
```

In reality, a researcher rarely takes more than one sample, but from the mean and variance of that sample the range of population means that could be drawn, if possible, can be calculated. Here, then, is where probability is integrated with inferential statistics. Inferential statistics are used to estimate the probability of a population mean's being within a range of possible values. The researcher is able to say, to infer, that 68 times out of 100 the population mean will be within one standard deviation of the mean of means, and that 96 times out of 100 it will be within two standard deviations.

Suppose a researcher is not interested in taking a sample from a population, but rather includes the entire population as the sample. Would this mean that the researcher could ignore the principles of sampling error and inferential statistics in obtaining a result that represents the entire group? While sampling error is not a concern, measurement error is. Recall in Chapter 7 that whenever we assess variables in education the measurement is never perfect—there is always some degree of error, summarized statistically as the standard error of measurement. Thus we *infer* a real or true value on a variable from the imperfect measure. This could be thought of as a type of sampling error in the sense that the one measure obtained is a "sample" estimating the true value. Consequently in all educational research there is definitely measurement error, and in some research there is also sampling error.

This section of the chapter has explained the logic of inferential statistics in estimating population means from sample means. In most research, however, we are interested in much more than estimating populations from samples. We usually want to compare population means with each other or with some established value. The next section discusses how these comparisons are made by incorporating the logic of inferential statistics.

■ NULL HYPOTHESIS ■

Let us assume that a researcher wants to compare the attitudes of sixth graders toward school to those of fourth graders. The researcher randomly selects samples of sixth and fourth graders and finds the means of each group. The means are 30 for fourth graders and 37 for sixth graders. Can the researcher then assume that sixth graders have more positive attitudes than fourth graders? Perhaps, but this conclusion must take into account sampling and measurement error. The population means are thus estimated and compared to find the probability that the possible population means of each group are different. The probabilities are formalized by statements that are tested. These statements are referred to as *hypotheses.* Research hypotheses have already been introduced as the research prediction that is tested (in this example, the research hypothesis might be that sixth graders have more positive attitudes than fourth graders).

When we refer to probability in terms of sampling and measurement error, the statement used is called the **null hypothesis.** The null or **statistical hypothesis,** which is usually implied by the research hypothesis rather than stated explicitly, states that there is no difference between the population means of the two groups. That is, the population means are the same. The researcher employs an inferential statistical test to determine the probability that the null hypothesis is untrue. If the null is false, then there is a high probability that there is a difference between the groups. The null hypothesis in our example would be that attitudes of sixth and fourth graders toward school are the same. If we can show that there is a high probability of being right in rejecting the null, then we have found evidence of a difference in the attitudes.

Theoretically, we know that the population range of means of both groups can be estimated, and if there is little overlap in those ranges then it is likely that the populations are different. This case is diagramed in Figure 10.2. Note that there is virtually no overlap between the two normal curves. This means that we can be confident of being correct in rejecting the null hypothesis.

The reason null hypotheses are used with inferential statistics is that we never prove anything, we only fail to disprove. Failure to disprove is consistent with the reality of probability in our lives. In other words, if we cannot find compelling evidence that they are different, the most plausible conclusion is that they are the same. For conceiving and designing research the research hypothesis is far more important than the null. The null is a technical necessity in using inferential statistics.

It should also be pointed out that failure to reject the null hypothesis does not necessarily mean that the null is true. It is especially difficult to accept null hy-

EXCERPT 10.1
Null Hypothesis

Three major hypotheses were proposed for testing in the present study:

● H_1—There are no statistically significant differences in retention between groups having the original lesson study guide as a review and groups having no review of a previously mastered mathematics lesson.

● H_2—There are no statistically significant differences in retention between groups having a summary audiotape review and groups having no review of a previously mastered mathematics lesson.

● H_3—There are no statistically significant differences in retention between groups having a compressed speech audiotape review and groups having no review of a previously mastered mathematics lesson.

Source: From Smith, H. G., "Investigation of Several Techniques for Reviewing Audio-Tutorial Instruction," *Educational Communication and Technology Journal,* 27(3), 196, Fall 1979. Copyright © 1979 by AECT. Reprinted by permission of the Association for Educational Communication and Technology.

FIGURE 10.2
Range of Population Means of Two Groups

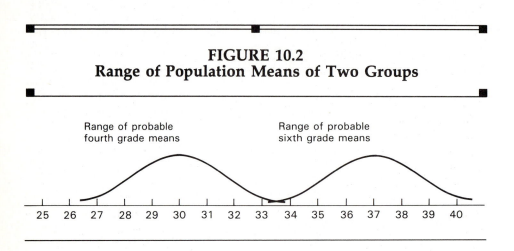

potheses as reality in studies that use a small number of subjects or use instruments with low reliability. The fact that the null hypothesis was not rejected may be because of large sampling or measurement error, or it may be attributable to a number of other factors beyond the scope of this book. In practical terms, be wary of conclusions that are based on unrejected null hypotheses.

Excerpt 10.1 illustrates the use of null hypotheses in a published study, while Excerpt 10.2 shows how alternative research hypotheses can be used.

EXCERPT 10.2
Research Hypothesis

Predictions. Given the persistent findings in many areas attesting to the dramatic impact of perceived control, it was hypothesized that people who attributed their outcome to controllable factors would experience more positive affective reactions than individuals who feel they cannot control the causes of their performance. In addition, although successful students should feel better—in terms of affect—than failing students (e.g., Bailey, Helm, & Gladstone, 1975; McMillan & Sprat, Note 1), the locus of attributed cause should moderate the magnitude of this effect. After success, internal attributions should be associated with more positive affective reactions, whereas negative affective reactions should be related to internal attributions for failure.

Predictions concerning expectancy shifts are less clear-cut. Although such shifts are typically associated with the stability dimension, the more recently suggested controllability factor may again be the more influential factor. The student who fails a test and believes the cause lies in some external, unstable factor—such as the teacher's bad mood—may continue to expect failure because mood, though unstable, is difficult to control. Yet, if students think they can somehow control their teacher's mood, then expectations may become more positive; in other words, the stability of attributed cause is less important when compared to the controllability of the attributed cause. Therefore, all three variables—controllability, performance, and locus of causality—will, in an interactive fashion, be related to expectations. After failure, individuals who attribute their outcomes to external, uncontrollable factors should be the most negative in their expectations. Those who succeed and believe internal, controllable factors were the cause of their success should, in contrast, be the most positive in their expectations of future success.

Sources: Forsyth, D. R., & McMillan, J. H. (1981). Attributions, affect, and expectations: A test of Weiner's three-dimensional model. *Journal of Educational Psychology. 73,* 393–403.

■ LEVEL OF SIGNIFICANCE ■

Since the basis of inferential statistics is the probability of estimation, then accepting or rejecting the null hypothesis is also related to probability or chance; because of error in sampling, that is, we can only give the probability of being correct or incorrect in rejecting or not rejecting the null. Put differently, we can be fairly sure that a certain number of times out of a hundred the means we could draw would not be the same.

We select or state what is called a **level of significance** to indicate what the chance is that we are wrong in rejecting the null. Also called level of probability, *p* level, or α (**alpha**) **level,**[1] it is expressed as a decimal and tells us how many times

---

[1]Technically, the alpha level is set by the researcher before obtaining the results, while the *p* level is what is calculated from the results.

out of a hundred or thousand we would be wrong in rejecting the null (in other words, how often we would expect no real difference even though we rejected the null). The logic of level of significance is that we assume that the null hypothesis is correct, and then see what the probability is that the sample means we have calculated would be different by chance alone. If we find that there is a probability of only one time in a hundred that we would find a particular difference in the means by chance or random fluxations, ($p = 0.01$), then we reject the null because it is quite probable that the null is false. In other words, the level of significance tells us the chance probability of finding differences between the means. The lower the level of significance, therefore, the more confidence we have that we are safe in rejecting the null. After all, for example, if we find a difference of five points between two means that, through our null hypothesis, we assume to be the same, and our statistics tell us there is only one chance in a thousand of finding a five-point difference by chance ($p = 0:001$), then it is only logical to assume that the null hypothesis is false and reject it (or say we are very, very lucky!). We reject the null hypothesis in favor of the research, or alternative, hypothesis. A level of 0.01 is therefore better than 0.05, 0.001 better than 0.01, and 0.05 better than 0.10.

Errors in Hypothesis Testing

The purpose of inferential statistics, null hypotheses, and levels of significance is to make a decision, based on probability, about the nature of populations and real values of variables. It is possible that the decision is wrong. When the decision is to reject the null hypothesis when in fact the null hypothesis is true, the researcher has made what is called a **Type I error.** The probability of making this type of error is equal to the level of significance: that is, with a significance level of 0.05 there is a probability of five times out of 100 that the sample data will lead the researcher to reject the null hypothesis when it is in fact true. A researcher consequently avoids a Type I error to the degree that the level of significance is high (that is, a 0.001 level is better than 0.01 for avoiding Type I errors).

Another type of wrong decision occurs when the null hypothesis is not rejected, when in fact the null hypothesis is actually wrong. This is referred to as a **Type II error.** While there is no direct relationship between the level of significance and the probability of making a Type II error, as the level of significance increases the likelihood of Type II error decreases. A level of significance of 0.10 is thus better for avoiding a Type II error than 0.05 or 0.01.

Interpreting Level of Significance

The interpretation of rejecting or failing to reject a null hypothesis depends on whether the researcher is interested in avoiding a Type I or Type II error, and in whether a predetermined level of significance is set. If a predetermined value is stated, such as 0.05 or 0.01 for a Type I error, then the researcher rejects the null by comparing the computed level of significance with the predetermined level. If the calculated significance is less than the predetermined level (for example, 0.01 < 0.05) then the null hypothesis is rejected.

In many research studies there is no predetermined level of significance. In these studies statisticians use a general rule for rejecting a null hypothesis. If the p value is the same as or less than 0.05, then the null is rejected and the statement is made that there is a **"statistically significant"** difference (though more accurately it is always a difference at some level of confidence). A p value between 0.05 and 0.10 is usually thought of as marginally significant, and anything greater than 0.10 is labeled a nonsignificant difference. We are saying, then, that if there is more than one chance out of ten of being wrong in rejecting the null (one chance in ten that the means are the same) then that is too much risk to take in saying that the means are different. The results may be due more to error than to a treatment or real difference.

It is best to report the p level for each statistical test because the conventions for rejecting the null hypothesis are general rules of thumb. Individual researchers and consumers, depending on the circumstances, may differ with respect to what constitutes a statistically significant difference. A level of 0.05, for example, generally agreed to be statistically significant, would probably be unacceptable if the test concerned usage of a drug that might cause death (five times out of a hundred, the researcher is wrong in saying no death will occur). In such a situation a level of 0.000001 may be more appropriately considered statistically significant.

Another important point in interpreting p levels and corresponding conclusions is that while it is common for researchers to fail to reject the null (e.g., $p = .20$), the failure to find a statistically significant difference or relationship does not necessarily mean that in *reality* there is no difference or relationship. Only when the circumstances of the research warrant (in which there is what is called adequate power in the test) is a nonsignificant finding taken as evidence that there is no relationship. The reason a nonsignificant finding is uninterpretable is that many factors, such as low reliability, diffusion of treatment, insufficient number of subjects, and so forth, can cause the nonsignificance. We thus tend to believe a significant finding as indicating that a real relationship exists, but the opposite is not necessarily true. Especially in cases with a small sample size (which makes it more difficult to find a significant difference) a nonsignificant finding should be interpreted to mean that further research is necessary, not that there is no relationship.

One of the most important issues that create confusion in interpreting statistics is the decision as to whether the results are meaningful. That is, how much will the results make a difference in the real world? Are the results educationally significant, not just statistically significant? The statistical test tells only that there is a difference, but the worth of a finding must also be judged. When a finding is reported to be statistically significant, the reader should examine the reported means to see how different they are. Meaningfulness must also be related to the specifics of a situation. There may, for example, be a statistically significant difference in reading achievement among first graders who use curriculum X as

---

EXCERPT 10.3
Levels of Significance

Adjusted means and standard deviations for the mentions and accuracy scores are presented in Tables 3 and 4. The analysis of mentions scores indicated that across passages (initial and transfer), there is a significant main effect of test-taking training $F(1,68) = 5.32$, $p = .02$. Groups who received test-taking training cooperatively recalled more than those who received individual test-taking training. The main effect of cooperative versus individual study training approached significance, $F(1,68) = 3.31$, $p = .07$. There were no significant interactions.

The analysis of accuracy scores revealed that across passages, the main effect of cooperative vs. individual study training was significant, $F(1,68) = 4.70$, $p = .03$. The study–training by passage interaction was also significant, $F(1,70) = 5.89$, $p = .01$. Post hoc comparisons revealed that groups who studied Passage 1 cooperatively recalled significantly more accurate information than groups who studied Passage 1 individually ($p < .05$). No other differences between group means were significant.

Source: From "Cooperative learning and test taking: Transfer of skills" by J.G. Lambiotte, et al., *Contemporary Educational Psychology*, Vol. 12, No. 1, January 1987. Reprinted by permission of Academic Press, Inc.

---

opposed to curriculum Y, but that does not mean curriculum X should be purchased. It is possible that the difference represents only one percentile point and that curriculum X costs several thousand dollars more than curriculum Y. Only the reader can judge what is meaningful. Many researchers tend to assume automatically that statistical significance means educational significance, but that is simply untrue.

Excerpts 10.3 and 10.4 give levels of significance to show which of the results are statistically significant. Remember that various conventions can be used in reporting the level of significance, such as level of significance, p level, and alpha, α. Some researchers may report that the probability (p) is less than ($<$) a specific value (for example, $p < 0.05$ or $p < 0.001$) rather than reporting the actual level of significance.

■ COMPARING TWO MEANS: THE *t*-TEST ■

There are many research situations in which a mean from one group is compared to a mean from another group to determine the probability that the corresponding population means are different.

The most common statistical procedure for determining the level of significance when two means are compared is the ***t*-test.** The *t*-test is a formula that

---

EXCERPT 10.4
Levels of Significance

Table I also presents the mean values for the ability attribution data by grade level. The results of a four-way ANOVA indicates two significant main effects: Outcome, $F(1,154) = 637.00$, $p < .001$ and Effort, $F(1,154) = 29.00$, $p < .001$. A significant Effort $\times$ Grade interaction, $F(6,154) = 20.56$, $p < .001$, indicates a grade-wise trend that moderates the main effect of Effort as reflected in Figure 1.

Source: Harari, O., & Covington, M. V. (1981). Reactions to achievement behavior from a teacher and student perspective: A developmental analysis. *American Educational Research Journal.* Spring. *18*, 15–18.

generates a number, and this number is used to determine the probability level (*p* level) of rejecting the null hypothesis.

What happens is that the sample means, standard deviations, and size of the samples are used in the *t*-test equation to give a *t* value (sometimes called *t* statistic). The formula for calculating the *t* value is

$$ t = \frac{\overline{X}_1 - \overline{X}_2}{s_{\overline{x}1 - \overline{x}2}} $$

where

$$ \begin{aligned} \overline{X}_1 &= \text{mean of group 1,} \\ \overline{X}_2 &= \text{mean of group 2,} \\ s_{\overline{x}1 - \overline{x}2} &= \text{standard error of the} \\ &\quad\ \text{difference between the means.} \end{aligned} $$

The standard error of the difference between the means can be conceived of as a measure of the amount of error in estimating the population mean from a sample mean. As the distance between $\overline{X}_1$ and $\overline{X}_2$ gets larger, then, and as the error involved in estimating the means gets smaller, the *t* statistic is greater. The calculated *t* value is a three- or four-digit number with two decimal places, rarely greater than 15.00 (such as 2.30; 3.16; 8.72; 0.85). To determine the level of significance, the researcher compares this number to theoretical *t* values in a table. The table is called distribution of *t*, or critical values for the *t*-test, and is found in Table 10.1. The researcher uses the table by locating two numbers: the **degrees of freedom** (*df*), and the level of significance desired. The term *degrees of freedom* is a mathematical concept that denotes the number of independent observations that are free to vary. For each statistical test there is a corresponding number of degrees of freedom that is calculated, and then this number is used to estimate the statistical significance of the test. In the distribution of a *t*-table, the number at the

TABLE 10.1
t Distribution

	Level of significance for a one-tail test				
	.05	.025	.01	.005	.0005
	Level of significance for a two-tail test				
df	.10	.05	.02	.01	.001
1	6.314	12.706	31.821	63.657	636.619
2	2.920	4.303	6.965	9.925	31.598
3	2.353	3.182	4.541	5.841	12.924
4	2.132	2.776	3.747	4.604	8.610
5	2.015	2.571	3.365	4.032	6.869
6	1.943	2.447	3.143	3.707	5.959
7	1.895	2.365	2.998	3.499	5.408
8	1.860	2.306	2.896	3.355	5.041
9	1.833	2.262	2.821	3.250	4.781
10	1.812	2.228	2.764	3.169	4.587
11	1.796	2.201	2.718	3.106	4.437
12	1.782	2.179	2.681	3.055	4.318
13	1.771	2.160	2.650	3.012	4.221
14	1.761	2.145	2.624	2.977	4.140
15	1.753	2.131	2.602	2.947	4.073
16	1.746	2.120	2.583	2.921	4.015
17	1.740	2.110	2.567	2.898	3.965
18	1.734	2.101	2.552	2.878	3.922
19	1.729	2.093	2.539	2.861	3.883
20	1.725	2.086	2.528	2.845	3.850
21	1.721	2.080	2.518	2.831	3.819
22	1.717	2.074	2.508	2.819	3.792
23	1.714	2.069	2.500	2.807	3.767
24	1.711	2.064	2.492	2.797	3.745
25	1.708	2.060	2.485	2.787	3.725
26	1.706	2.056	2.479	2.779	3.707
27	1.703	2.052	2.473	2.771	3.690
28	1.701	2.048	2.467	2.763	3.674
29	1.699	2.045	2.462	2.756	3.659
30	1.697	2.042	2.457	2.750	3.646
40	1.684	2.021	2.423	2.704	3.551
60	1.671	2.000	2.390	2.660	3.460
120	1.658	1.980	2.358	2.617	3.373
∞	1.645	1.960	2.326	2.576	3.291

Source: Taken from Table III of Fisher and Yates': *Statistical Tables for Biological, Agricultural and Medical Research* (6th Edition 1974) published by Longman Group UK Ltd. London (previously published by Oliver and Boyd Ltd. Edinburg) and are reprinted by permission of the authors and publishers.

intersection of the degrees of freedom row and the level of significance column is the relevant theoretical value of *t*. If this critical *t* is less than the *t* value calculated by the *t*-test equation, it means that the observed difference in means is greater than could have been expected under the null hypothesis, so the hypothesis can be rejected at that level of significance.

The calculated *t*-statistic and corresponding *p* level are reported in most studies. In Excerpt 10.5 the results section of a research study is reproduced to show how *t*-tests are summarized. The number in parentheses following the *t* is the degrees of freedom.

There are two different forms of the equation used in the *t*-test, one for independent samples and one for samples that are paired, or dependent. Independent samples are groups of subjects that have no relationship to each other; the two samples have different subjects in each group, and the subjects are usually either assigned randomly from a common population or drawn from two different populations. If a researcher, therefore, is testing the difference between an experimental group and a control group mean, the **independent samples *t*-test** would be appropriate. Comparing attitudes of fourth and sixth graders would also utilize an independent samples *t*-test.

The second form of the *t*-test can be referred to by several different names, including paired, dependent, correlated, or matched *t*-test. This *t*-test is used in situations in which the subjects from the two groups are paired or matched in some way. A common example of this case is the same group of subjects tested twice, as in a pretest-posttest study. Whether the same or different subjects are in each group, as long as there is a systematic relationship between the groups it is necessary to use the **dependent samples *t*-test** to calculate the probability of rejecting the null hypothesis.

Although the formulas and degrees of freedom are different for each form of the *t*-test the interpretation and reporting of the results is the same (the *df* for the dependent *t*-test is the number of pairs minus one). A reader of research thus need not worry about the correct formula to use since the researcher already has used it. An example of the way to report a **correlated samples *t*-test** is in Excerpt 10.6.

It should be pointed out that the *t*-test can be used for purposes other than comparing the means of two samples. The *t*-test is used when a researcher wants to show that a correlation coefficient is significantly different from 0 (no correlation). The mean of a group can be compared to a number rather than another mean, and it is possible to compare variances rather than means. Because there are so many uses for the *t*-test it is frequently encountered in reading research.

A more concrete explanation of using the *t*-test is the following example. Suppose a researcher is interested in finding out whether there is a significant difference between blue-eyed and brown-eyed sixth graders with respect to reading achievement. The research question would be: Is there a difference in the reading achievement (the dependent variable) of blue-eyed fourth graders as compared to brown-eyed fourth graders (the independent variable)? The null hypothesis would be: There is no difference between blue-eyed and brown-eyed fourth graders in reading achievement. To test this hypothesis the researcher would randomly select a sample of brown- and blue-eyed fourth graders from

EXCERPT 10.5
Independent Samples *t*-Test

Then, *t* tests were performed to detect the presence of significant differences between the means of the high- and low-scoring infants for each of the maternal, infant, and dyadic measures. Neither sex nor parity was systematically related to any of the dependent measures.

A significant relationship was found between our measure of maternal sensitivity during feeding and subsequent infant performance on the cognitive task, $t(16) = 2.48$, $p < .05$. Mothers of high-scoring infants were more sensitive to the infant behaviors than were mothers of low-scoring infants. The total number of maternal signals did not differentiate mothers of high- and low-scoring infants, $t(16) = .38$, nor did the infants differ in terms of the frequency of gaze, toward, or away behaviors during feeding or in the relative time spent in each of the three categories.

Source: From "Early Cognitive Development and its Relation to Maternal Physiologic and Behavioral Responsiveness" by W. L. Donovan and L. A. Leavitt, *Child Development*, 1978, 49, 1251–1254. Copyright © 1978 by the Society for Research in Child Development, Inc. Reprinted by permission of The University of Chicago Press.

the population of all fourth-grade students. Let us say that the sample mean of blue-eyed students' reading achievement is 54, and the sample mean for brown-eyed fourth graders is 48. Since we assume the null hypothesis—that the population means are equal—we use the *t*-test to show how often the difference of scores in the samples would occur if the population means are equal. If our degrees of freedom (total sample size minus 1) is 60 and the calculated *t* value 2.00, we can see by referring to Table 10.1 that the probability of attaining this difference in the sample means is 0.05, or five times out of a hundred. Since it is unlikely, then, for us to have found such a difference, we reject the null hypothesis and say that there is a statistically significant difference between the reading achievement of blue-eyed and brown-eyed fourth graders.

■ COMPARING TWO OR MORE MEANS: ■
ANALYSIS OF VARIANCE

One-Way Analysis of Variance

If a study is done in which two or more sample means are compared on one independent variable, then to test the null hypothesis the researcher would employ a procedure called one-way analysis of variance (abbreviated ANOVA). ANOVA is simply an extension of the *t*-test. Rather than the researcher's using multiple *t*-

---

EXCERPT 10.6
Correlated Samples *t*-test

For the matched groups' *t* tests the mean differences showed relatively greater GPA achievement for the high extrinsic motivation–low intrinsic motivation group, mean differences being: most challenging, .04; least challenging, .30. The *t* test for correlated samples yielded a *t* of 2.19, $p < .05$, for the least challenging difference, establishing a statistically significant superiority of extrinsic motivation over intrinsic motivation subjects on GPA in least challenging courses.

Source: Kahoe, R. D., & McFarland, R. E. (1975). Interactions of task challenge and intrinsic and extrinsic motivations in college achievement. *Journal of Educational Psychology. 67*, 432–438.

tests to compare all possible pairs of means in a study of two or more groups, ANOVA allows the researcher to test the differences between all groups and make more accurate probability statements than when using a series of separate *t*-tests. It is called **analysis of variance** because the statistical formula uses the variances of the groups and not the means to calculate a value that reflects the degree of differences in the means. Instead of a *t* statistic, ANOVA calculates an *F* statistic (or *F* ratio). The *F* is analogous to the *t*. It is a three- or four-digit number that is used in a distribution of *F* table with the degrees of freedom to find the level of significance that the researcher uses to reject or not reject the null. There are two distinct degrees of freedom that are used. The first is the number of groups in the study minus one, and the second is the total number of subjects in each group minus the number of groups. These numbers follow the *F* in reporting the results of ANOVA (for example, $F(4, 80) = 7.80$).

ANOVA addresses the question: Is there a significant difference between any two population means? If the *F* value that is calculated is large enough, then the null hypothesis (meaning there is no difference among the groups) can be rejected with confidence that the researcher is correct in concluding that at least two means are different. Let us assume, for example, that a researcher is comparing the locus of control of three groups—high, medium, and low achievement students. The researcher selects a random sample from each group, administers a locus of control instrument, and calculates the means and variances of each group. Let us further assume that the sample group means are A (low achievement) = 18, B (medium achievement) = 20, and C (high achievement) = 25. The null hypothesis that is tested, then, is that the population means of 18, 20, and 25 are equal, or, more correctly, that these are different only by sampling and measurement error: If the *F* was 5.12, and $p < 0.01$, then the researcher can conclude that at least two of the means are different and that this conclusion will be right 99 times out of 100.

The number of trials each subject required to reach criterion was used to calculate the mean number of trials for each training group. A one-way analysis of variance was performed that revealed a statistically significant effect for Group, $F(2,21) = 5.97$, $p < .01$. Group means and standard deviations are presented in Table 2. To determine the order of acquisition of each of the concepts. Duncan's multiple range test was performed. The results of this analysis indicated that the ICT and ECT training groups were significantly different from each other, as were the ICT and TIT groups ($p < .05$). The only comparison that failed to reach significance was between ECT and TIT.

TABLE 2. Means and Standard Deviations of Trials to Criterion

	Trials	
	M	**SD**
Identity	12.50	6.88
Equivalence	6.75	4.39
Transitive inference	4.00	3.38

Source: From "Induction, emergence, and generalization of logical operations in retarded children: A training-to-criterion procedure" by M. Abramson, J. Cooney, and L. Vincent, *Journal of Special Education,* Vol. 14, No. 21, 1980, pp. 190–198. Reprinted by permission.

The results of a one-way ANOVA are usually reported by indicating in the results section the groups that are different. A table of means and standard deviations will accompany the written information. Excerpt 10.7 is an example of reporting the one-way ANOVA.

In reporting results, occasionally the researcher will write two numbers in front of the ANOVA. This will be a number 1, a multiplication sign, and then another single digit number (for example, 1×3; 1×5; 1×2). This means that there is one independent variable (1) that has the number of groups or levels indicated by the second number. A 1×4 ANOVA is thus a one-way ANOVA that is comparing four group means.

Multiple Comparison Procedures

When a researcher uses ANOVA to test the null hypothesis that three means are the same, the resulting F ratio and level of significance tells the researcher only that some combination of the means is different. It fails to indicate which groups are different. The researcher needs to employ further statistical tests that will indicate those means that are different from each other. These tests are called **post hoc comparisons** or **multiple comparisons.** They are designed to test each possible pair of means.

There are five common multiple comparison tests: Fisher's LSD: Duncan's new multiple range test, the Newman-Keuls, Tukey's HSD, and Scheffé's test. Each test is used in the same way, but they differ in the ease with which a significant difference is obtained: for some tests, that is, the means need to be farther apart than for other tests for the difference to be statistically significant. Tests that require a greater difference between the means are said to be conservative, while those that permit less difference are said to be liberal. The listing of the tests above is sequential, with Fisher's test considered most liberal and Scheffé test most conservative. The two most common tests are Tukey (pronounced too-key) and Scheffé, but different conclusions can be reached in a study depending on the multiple comparison technique employed. Hopkins and Anderson (1973) discuss in some detail the merits of different procedures, and this article should be reviewed for a more thorough understanding of ways to interpret and use various multiple comparison techniques.

The reader may be wondering why a researcher does not use separate *t*-tests as a follow-up to the significant *F* ratio. The answer is that if multiple *t*-tests were used, the researcher would increase the likelihood of finding a significant difference where none exists. If for example, the research involves computing 100 *t*-tests and the level of significance is 0.05, the researcher can expect that 5 out of 100 *t*-tests would be significant by chance alone. The post hoc tests control this problem by taking into account the number of comparisons being made. In some studies there are no post hoc tests employed even though the *F* ratio is significant. This occurs because a visual examination of the group means obviously shows which means are different. If, for example, three group means are 15, 20, and 20.5, and the *F* ratio is significant with a *p* level of 0.01, it is rather obvious where the differences exist, and there is no need for post hoc tests. A related point should be emphasized here: it is impossible to interpret a *t*-test or analysis of variance without examining the group means; for the inferential statistics to have meaning, it is essential to look at the sample means.

Excerpt 10.8 is an example of using one-way ANOVA and a post hoc test.

Factorial Analysis of Variance

One-way ANOVA has been introduced as a procedure that is used with one independent variable and two or more groups identified by this variable. It is common, however, to have more than one independent variable in a study. In fact, it is often desirable to have several independent variables because with more than one the analysis will provide more information. If, for example, a group of researchers investigates the relative effectiveness of three reading curricula, they would probably use a 1 × 3 ANOVA to test the null hypothesis that there is no

EXCERPT 10.8
ANOVA and Post Hoc Tests

Sex, $F(1, 878) = 4.10$, $p < .05$, and grade, $F(2,878) = 11.56$, $p < .01$, were both significant factors as far as performance on the locus of control measure was concerned. Females were significantly more internal than males at all grade levels. Tukey's test for comparisons involving unequal *n*s revealed that the mean locus of control score for both males and females increased significantly from sixth to seventh ($p < .01$) and from seventh to eighth grade ($p < .01$).

Source: From "Mapping the affective domain in young adolescents" by Richard S. Prawat, *Journal of Educational Psychology*, 68. Copyright © 1976 by the American Psychological Association. Reprinted by permission of the author.

difference in achievement between any of the three groups (that is, $\bar{X}_1 = \bar{X}_2 = \bar{X}_3$). If the researchers were also interested in whether males or females achieved differently, gender would become a second independent variable. Now there are six groups, since for each reading group males and females are analyzed separately. If X is the reading curriculum and M/F is sex, then the six groups are: X_1, M; X_1, F; X_2 M; X_2F; X_3M; and X_3F. This situation is diagramed below.

First independent variable: Reading curriculum groups

Second independent variable: Sex

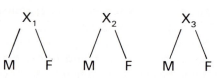

Another way to illustrate the study is to put each independent variable on one side of a rectangle, as follows:

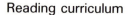
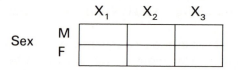

In this hypothetical situation, then, there are two independent variables analyzed simultaneously and one dependent variable (achievement). The statistical procedure that would be used to analyze the results would be a two-way ANOVA (*two-way* because of two independent variables). Since *factor* is another word for independent variable, *factorial* means more than one independent variable. **Factorial ANOVA,** then, is a generic term that means that two or more independent variables are analyzed together. The more specific term, such as *two-way* or *three-way* ANOVA, tells the exact number of independent variables. Researchers can be even more precise in indicating what the analysis is by including the levels of each independent variable. As pointed out earlier, *levels* refers to the subgroups or categories of each independent variable. In the example cited above, *reading curriculum* has three levels and *gender* two levels. The levels can be shown by numbers that precede the ANOVA abbreviation. In our reading example, it is a 2 × 3 ANOVA. (For a three-way ANOVA there would need to be three numbers, such as 2 × 2 × 3 ANOVA. This means that there are two levels in two of the variables and three levels in one variable.) Using this notation, a researcher can communicate concisely a lot of information. The number of factors is usually two, three, or four, and the number of levels can be any number greater than one (though rarely above 10). In the hypothetical example above, if there were four reading curriculums and the researcher was interested in the way each curriculum affected high, low, and medium achievers, then the resulting analysis would be a 3 × 4 ANOVA. It is still a two-way ANOVA, but the number of levels is different. This situation can be illustrated with the following diagram:

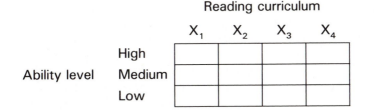

Excerpt 10.9 is an example of the way researchers refer to two-way factorial designs.

To clarify the tests of significance that result from a two-way ANOVA, we present another hypothetical example. A teacher is interested in whether specific techniques to aid retention are effective in improving the achievement of high-anxiety and low-anxiety students. The teacher has developed two techniques, one with mnemonics and the other with distributed practice in memorizing the material. The teacher also has a control group. There are thus two independent variables, one with two levels (anxiety: high and low) the other with three levels (treatment techniques: mnemonics, distributed practice, and control group). This would constitute a 2 × 3 ANOVA design and is illustrated in Table 10.2.

Within each square in the diagram is a mean for that group. These squares are called cells. The number 50 in the upper right hand cell ($\overline{X}_5$) thus refers to the mean of highly anxious subjects who served as the control group. The 2 × 3 ANOVA to tests three null hypotheses: that there is no difference between high-

---

EXCERPT 10.9
Factorial ANOVA

Results and Discussion

A 2 × 2 analysis of variance, which took into account reward condition and sex, yielded no significant IQ difference due to reward, $F(1, 88) < 1$, and no significant interaction between reward and sex, $F(1, 88) < 1$. However, there was a significant IQ difference between boys and girls, with boys making higher scores, $F(1, 88) = 17.19, p < .01$. Table 1 presents the means and standard deviations for all groups.

Source: Quay, L. C. (1975). Reinforcement and Binet performance in disadvantaged children. *Journal of Educational Psychology. 67* (1), 132–135.

---

and low-anxiety students; that there is no difference between the treatment groups; and that there is no interaction between the two factors (interaction is defined in the next paragraph). The first two hypotheses are similar in interpretation to one-way ANOVAs. They tell the researcher whether any differences occur for each of the factors independent of each other. These are termed *main* or *simple effects* in a factorial ANOVA. There is a main (not necessarily significant) effect for anxiety and another main effect for treatment technique. In computing the 2 × 3 ANOVA there will be a separate F ratios for each main effect, with corresponding levels of significance. In our example the main effect for anxiety is tested by comparing $\overline{X}_7$ with $\overline{X}_8$. These row means disregard the influence of the techniques and address anxiety only. Since $\overline{X}_7$ and $\overline{X}_8$ both equal 54, the null hypothesis that $\overline{X}_7 = \overline{X}_8$ would not be rejected; examining anxiety alone, that is, there is no difference in achievement between high- and low-anxiety students. For the main effect of technique, $\overline{X}_9$, $\overline{X}_{10}$ and $\overline{X}_{11}$ are compared. Again, it appears that there is no difference in achievement between the three technique groups. The first two null hypotheses could have been tested by using separate one-way ANOVAs, but the 2 × 3 ANOVA is more accurate, more powerful in detecting differences, and more parsimonious than using two one-way ANOVAs. In addition, the 2 × 3 ANOVA allows the researcher to test the third null hypothesis. This hypothesis is concerned with what is called an interaction between the independent variables.

An **interaction** is the effect of the independent variables together: that is, the impact of one variable on the dependent measure varies with the level of a second variable. Stated differently, it is the joint effect of the independent variables on the dependent variable. An interaction is evident if the differences between levels of one independent variable are inconsistent from one level to another of the other independent variable. In other words, an interaction exists if the effect of one variable differs across different levels of the second variable. In our example, if we look at the difference between $\overline{X}_1$ and $\overline{X}_2$ (62 − 44 = 18) and compare that

TABLE 10.2
Hypothetical 2 × 3 ANOVA

Treatment techniques

		Mnemonics	Distributed practice	Control	
Anxiety	**High**	$\overline{X}_1 = 62$	$\overline{X}_3 = 50$	$\overline{X}_5 = 50$	$\overline{X}_7 = 54$
	Low	$\overline{X}_2 = 44$	$\overline{X}_4 = 59$	$\overline{X}_6 = 59$	$\overline{X}_8 = 54$
		$\overline{X}_9 \cong 53$	$\overline{X}_{10} \cong 55$	$\overline{X}_{11} \cong 55$	

difference with $\overline{X}_3 - \overline{X}_4 (-9)$ and $\overline{X}_5 - \overline{X}_6 (-9)$, we find that there is a large difference between high and low anxiety as we move across each of the treatment techniques. This is visual evidence of an interaction. Statistically, an F ratio is reported for the interaction with a corresponding level of significance. This statistical test is called the interaction effect.

Now it is clear how a factorial ANOVA can provide more information than one-way ANOVAs. In our example it is evident that treatment techniques do make a difference for high- or low-anxiety students. High-anxiety students do better with mnemonics than distributed practice or with no treatment, while low-anxiety students do better with distributed practice or with no treatment than they do with mnemonics. This finding would be statistically significant even though neither of the main effects by themselves was significant. In Excerpt 10.10 the authors report a significant interaction

It is common to present a graph of an interaction that is significant. The graph shows the nature of the interaction more clearly than cell means do. The graph is constructed by placing values for the dependent variable along the vertical axis (ordinate) and the levels of one independent variable on the horizontal axis (abscissa); all the cell means are located within the graph and identified with the second independent variable. For our hypothetical example the interaction is illustrated in Figure 10.3. In the figure, lines are used to connect the cells means. If the lines are parallel, then there is no interaction. If the lines cross, the interaction is said to be disordinal.

Analysis of Covariance

Analysis of covariance (ANCOVA) is a statistical procedure used in cases similar to ones in which a one-way or factorial ANOVA is used. ANCOVA has two major purposes: to adjust initial group differences statistically on one or more variables

EXCERPT 10.10
ANOVA Interaction

Results and Discussion

Cell means are reported in Table 2. The mean proportion (reported as a percentage) of a word needed by third-grade subjects to achieve identification was 65.19%; for first graders, 72.75%. This difference was significant at the .01 level, $F(1, 70) = 13.2, p < .01$. The mean for high-frequency words was 51.38%; for low-frequency words, 86.56%. the difference was significant beyond the .001 level, $F(1, 70) = 319.25, p > .001$. However, the significant interaction between frequency and grade, $F(1, 70) = 5.40, p < .025$, indicated that the difference between third and first graders was more pronounced for high-frequency words than it was for low-frequency words (see Figure 1).

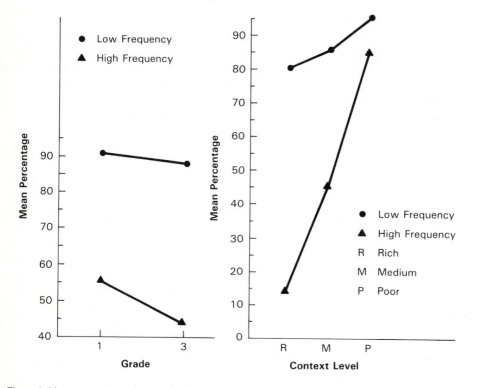

Figure 1. Mean percentage of word needed for identification for the Frequency × Grade interaction.
Figure 2. Mean percentage of word needed for identification for the Frequency × Context interaction.

Context proved to have a significant effect, $F(2, 140) = 138.19, p < .01$, with levels ranking from rich context ($\overline{X} = 49.13\%$) to moderate ($\overline{X} = 68.51\%$) to poor context ($\overline{X} = 89.27\%$).

This effect of context differs across frequency levels, as is indicated by the interaction between frequency and context, $F(2, 140) = 91.49$, $p < .01$. The interaction graph (see Figure 2) indicates that while the context levels are ranked in the same order in both levels of frequency, the differences among context levels for high frequency words were much greater than they were for low-frequency words.

Source: Pearson, P. D., & Studt, A. (1975). "Effects of word frequency and contextual richness on children's word identification abilities. *Journal of Educational Psychology*, 67, 1975, pp. 89–95. Copyright © 1975 by the American Psychological Association. Reprinted by permission of the publisher and author.

FIGURE 10.3
Interaction for Hypothetical Study

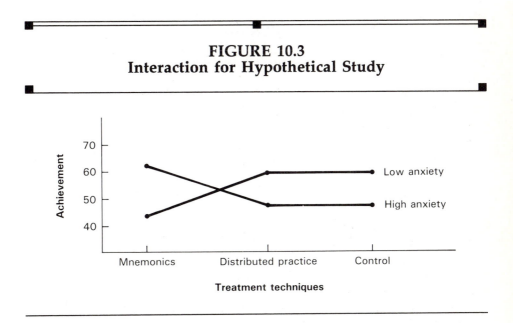

that are related to the dependent variable but uncontrolled, and to increase the likelihood of finding a significant difference between group means.

For the first purpose, consider the following example. A researcher uses two classes to investigate whether cooperative or individualized instruction is most effective. On the basis of a pretest the researcher knows that one class has greater knowledge of the dependent variable (achievement in mathematics) than the other group (for example, the cooperative group pretest mean is 12 and the individualized group pretest mean is 10). If a posttest is given and it is found that the cooperative group mean is 24 and the individualized group mean 20, the researcher might be tempted to conclude that the cooperative group achieved more than the individualized. This would be likely to happen if the pretest scores were ignored. An alternative approach would be to look at pretest-posttest gain scores and use a *t*-test to determine whether the gain scores are significantly different. This approach would result in comparing 12 (24–12) to 10 (20–10). While this approach is theoretically better than not using the pretest scores, for reasons beyond the scope of this book there are technical problems with comparing gain scores. The best method of analyzing the data in this circumstance is by using ANCOVA. ANCOVA would statistically adjust the posttest scores by the differences that existed between the groups on the pretest. In this example the posttest score of the cooperative group would be lowered by one point, since this group's mean was higher by one point than the mean of both groups on the pretest. Similarly, because the individualized group pretest mean is one point lower than the mean of the two pretests, the posttest score of 20 would be raised by one point to 21. Instead of comparing 20 to 24, ANCOVA would thus compare 21 to 23.

The variable that is used in ANCOVA to adjust the scores (in the above example the pretest) is called the *covariate* or *concomitant variable*. Covariates are often pretest scores or results from achievement, attitude, or aptitude tests that would be related to the dependent variable. IQ scores and scores on prior standardized achievement tests, for instance, are commonly used as covariates. The covariate hence represents a source of error that is related to the dependent variable but is uncontrolled by the design of the research.

The second purpose of covariance analysis is to increase what is called the power of the statistical test to find differences between groups. A full explanation of the concept of power is beyond the scope of this book but, briefly, it is useful to increase power when the sample size is low or when the researcher has reason to believe that the differences between the groups will be small.

ANCOVA can be used in several situations: with two groups and one independent variable in place of a *t*-test; with one independent variable that has more than two groups in place of one-way ANOVA; and with factorial analysis of variance. Studies can also use more than one covariate in a single ANCOVA procedure. The reporting of ANCOVA is very similar to the reporting of ANOVA. Excerpt 10.11 shows how covariance analysis was used in an actual study to adjust initial group differences.

Since ANCOVA is used frequently with intact groups, without randomization, it should be noted that the interpretation of results should weigh the possibility that other uncontrolled and unmeasured variables are also related to the dependent variable and hence may affect the dependent variable. In other words, while statistical adjustment of the effect of the covariate can be achieved, the researcher cannot conclude that the groups are equal in the sense of randomization.

■ NONPARAMETRIC TESTS ■

In our discussion of statistical tests so far we have been concerned with procedures that are parametric. **Parametric** statistics are used with data that the researcher assumes have a population that is normally distributed and have vari-

EXCERPT 10.11
ANCOVA

A Sex $\times$ Attention analysis of covariance of these scores, using reading readiness as the covariate, found the following: a significant main effect for attention ($F = 8.46$, $df = 3/79$, $p < .001$) and a significant main effect for sex ($F = 3.96$, $df = 1/79$, $p < .05$). The Sex $\times$ Attention interaction was not significant ($F < 1$).

Newman-Keuls tests were computed to determine which of the word recognition scores were significantly different from each other for each of the four attention categories. The following was found: All comparisons were significantly different from each other ($p < .05$) with the exception of Q_2 and Q_3.

Source: Samuels, S. J., & Turnure, J. E. (1974). Attention and reading achievement in first-grade boys and girls. *Journal of Educational Psychology.* *66* (1), 29–32.

ances within groups that are the same (homogeneity of variance). A final assumption is that the data are interval or ratio in scale.

As long as the assumptions upon which parametric statistics are based are, for the most part, met, the researcher uses a *t*-test, ANOVA, ANCOVA, or some other parametric procedure. If these assumptions are not met—that is, if the data are not interval or ratio or are distributed abnormally—the researcher should consider using a **nonparametric** analog to the parametric test. For most parametric procedures there is a corresponding nonparametric test that can be used. The interpretation of the results is the same with both kinds of tests. What differs is the computational equation and tables for determining the significance level of the results. Both procedures test a hypothesis and report a level of significance for rejecting the null. The parametric tests, however, are generally more powerful in detecting significant differences and are used frequently even when all assumptions cannot be met.

Table 10.3 gives the names of nonparametric tests that are analogous to parametric tests we have already discussed.

Chi-square (pronounced kī square) is another nonparametric procedure. It is used when the data are in nominal form. This test is a means of answering questions about association or relationship based on frequencies of observations in categories. The frequencies can be in most any form—people, objects, votes—and are simply counted in each category. The researcher thus forms the categories and then counts the frequency of observations or occurrences in each category. In the single sample chi-square test the researcher has one independent variable that is divided into two or more categories. A college administrator may, for example, be interested in the number of freshmen, sophomore, junior, and senior students who attended the counseling center, or, in other words, the relationship between year in college and use of counseling services. The independent variable

TABLE 10.3
Parametric and Nonparametric Procedures[a]

Parametric	Nonparametric
Independent samples *t*-test	Median test
	Mann-Whitney *U* test
Dependent samples *t*-test	Sign test
	Wilcoxon matched-pairs signed-ranks test
One-way ANOVA	Median test
	Kruskal-Wallis one-way ANOVA of ranks

[a]For further information on nonparametric tests, see Siegel (1956) and Marascuilo and McSweeney (1977).

TABLE 10.4
Hypothetical Single Sample Chi-Square

	Freshmen	Sophomores	Juniors	Seniors
Observed	30	25	15	30
Expected	25	25	25	25

is year in college, with four categories. The researcher might select a random sample of fifty students from each category and record the number of students in each category who attended the counseling center. The statistical test compares the reported, or observed, frequencies with some theoretical or expected frequencies. In our example the college administrator might expect that the frequencies in each category would be the same. Then the null hypothesis that is tested is that there is no difference in the number of students attending the counseling center among the four categories. Table 10.4 illustrates this example.

To obtain the level of significance the researcher computes a formula to obtain a chi-square value (χ^2), uses the appropriate degrees of freedom, and refers to a chi-square table (see Appendix B) in order to determine the level of significance in rejecting the null. In our example it appears that the test would be significant,

EXCERPT 10.12
Chi-Square[a]

Results

For the question on their general opinion of grade repetition, parents, teachers, and principals were asked to mark one of the following terms: "never," "rarely," "occasionally,"
"usually," or "always" in response to the question, "Children should _____ be retained if they do not meet the requirements of the grade." When responses of parents,
teachers, and principals were examined by *chi*-square analysis, the contrasts attained the
.0001 level of significance. As shown in Table 1, the most obvious difference was in the tendency for parents to mark the extreme answers of "never" and "always" more frequently than
teachers or principals.

All three groups were also asked to check from the following reasons, (a) chronic
nonattendance, (b) parent request, (c) emotional immaturity, (d) academic failure due to
reasons other than lack of basic skills, and (e) lack of basic skills, those which the respondent
felt were singularly valid grounds for retention. As shown in Table 1, the views of parents,
teachers, and principals were significantly different on excessive absences ($p < .0001$),
emotional maturity ($p < .0001$), academic failure due to reasons other than lack of basic
skills ($p < .0006$), and lack of basic skills ($p < .0001$).
The last question common to all three questionnaires asked parents, teachers, and principals
who should have the final say on whether a child is retained. A significant difference ($p <
.0001$) in opinion was evidenced (see Table 1).

Table 1. Comparisons Among Parents, Teachers, and Principals

	Opinions Representative of Their Views					
	To Be Retained					**N**
	Never	**Rarely**	**Occasionally**	**Usually**	**Always**	
Parents	3.6%	13.0	23.9	37.0	22.6	1,063
Teachers	.7	9.7	24.8	52.4	12.4	145
Principals	.0	8.6	17.1	71.4	2.9	35

($X^2 = 35.474$; $p < .0001$)

	Appropriate Reasons for Retention					
	Excessive Absences		**Parental Request**		**Emotional Immaturity**	
	Yes	**No**	**Yes**	**No**	**Yes**	**No**
Parents	13.6%	86.3	15.2	84.8	18.6	81.4
Teachers	39.3	60.7	15.9	84.1	53.1	46.9
Principals	68.6	31.4	20.0	80.0	54.3	45.7

($X^2 = 119.109$; $p < .0001$)   ($X^2 = 103.933$; $p < .0001$)

	Academic Failure		Lack of Basic Skills		Other Reasons	
	Yes	No	Yes	No	Yes	No
Parents	29.6%	70.3	62.6	37.4	5.9	94.1
Teachers	36.6	63.4	85.4	13.9	—	—
Principals	57.1	42.9	94.3	5.7	—	—

$(X^2 = 14.271; p < .006)$ $(X^2 = 51.451; p < .0001)$

	The Final Say on Retention Decision								
	(T) Teacher	(PR) Principal	(P) Parent	(C) Child	T & PR	T,P, & PR	T & P	PR & P	All Others
Parents	47.8%	14.6	19.6	.4	3.0	3.2	9.2	1.5	.7
Teachers	66.2	11.7	3.4	.0	13.1	3.4	.7	.0	1.4
Principals	22.9	54.3	2.9	.0	11.4	5.7	.0	.0	2.9

$(X^2 = 128.481; p < .0001)$

Source: From "Views on grade repetition" by D. Byrnes and K. Yamamoto, *Journal of Research and Development in Education*, Fall 1986. Reprinted by permission.
[a]There were 1063 parents, 145 teachers, and 35 principals in the sample.

showing that freshmen and seniors attend the counseling center more than sophomores and juniors and that juniors attend less than any other class.

If the researcher has more than one independent variable, the **independent samples chi-square test,** or **contingency table,** can be used to analyze the data. In our example above, if the administrator was also interested in differences between males and females at each class level, then the analysis is like a factorial ANOVA. In this case it would be a 2×4 contingency table.

There are many uses for the chi-square test, and it is a popular statistical procedure. It can be used in attitude research if the researcher categorizes responses to favorable and unfavorable; with high, low, and medium ability students displaying on-task behavior; in special education research with frequencies of appropriate behavior; and many other problems. Researchers may report a generic measure of relationship with the chi-square results. These measures would be termed **phi coefficient** or **contingency coefficient** and would be interpreted in about the same way as a Pearson product-moment correlation coefficient. Excerpts 10.12 and 10.13 are examples of ways chi-square test results are reported in actual studies.

■ MULTIVARIATE ANALYSES ■

Our discussion of inferential statistics would be incomplete if we did not introduce multivariate analyses. Social scientists have realized for many years that human behavior can be understood best by examining many variables at the

EXCERPT 10.13
Chi-Square

As can be seen in Table 1, Type A subjects showed a greater preference than did Type B subjects for waiting with others while filling out the questionnaire. A 2×2 chi-square analysis of affiliative preference by Type A-B revealed that while 76% of Type A preferred to wait with others, only 44% of the Type B subjects did so, $x^2(1) = 4.08$, $p < .05$. Similar chi-square analyses carried out separately for the high- and low-threat conditions suggested that the Type A subjects were slightly more affiliative under the high threat condition (Table 1), but this difference was not statistically significant. A chi-square test of the effect of threat on waiting preference pooled across the A-B dimension suggested an overall tendency for high threat to increase the tendency to wait with others, but this effect was not statistically significant.

Source: Dembroski, T. M., & MacDougall, J. M. (1978). Stress effects on affiliation preferences among subjects possessing the type A coronary prone behavior pattern. *Journal of Personality and Social Psychology. 36*, 23–33.

same time, not by dealing with one variable in one study, another variable in a second study, and so forth. It is only recently, however, that we have had the technical capacity for carrying out this approach. Before computers became available, all statistical calculations had to be done by hand or with the aid of a calculator. This was an arduous task, but not impossible as long as the equations were not too complex. This limitation forced researchers to restrict their analyses to *t*-tests, one- and two-way ANOVA, chi-square, correlations, and other relatively simple procedures. But these procedures have failed to reflect our current emphasis on the multiplicity of factors in human behavior. For simple experimental studies investigating the effect of one variable on another the *t*-test is adequate, but in the reality of complex social situations the researcher needs to examine many variables simultaneously. The statistical procedures for analyzing many variables at the same time have been available for many years, but it has only been since the computer age that researchers have been able to utilize these procedures. There is thus a lag in training of researchers that has militated against the use of these more sophisticated procedures. They are in evidence more each year in journals, however, and it is necessary to introduce the terminology and principles of the procedures.

The term **multivariate** means more than one independent and more than one dependent variable, although the term is also used in a more generic sense for any study with many variables. (Some researchers will refer to multiple regression as multivariate.) All of the statistical procedures discussed to this point have had only one dependent variable. Yet there are many instances in which the researcher is interested in more than one dependent variable. If, for example, a researcher is studying attitudes toward science, many aspects of a general attitude toward

---

EXCERPT 10.14
Multivariate ANOVA

RESULTS

Means and variances for the fifteen variables by school are presented in Table 4. The nine achievement scores from the Stanford Achievement Test are preported in grade equivalency form based on national averages. Formal Operational Thought was scored on the basis of number of correct responses out of a possible maximum of 25 items. Locus of Control was scored on the basis of the number of internal locus responses out of a maximum of thirty. The Coopersmith Self-Esteem Inventory was scored for positive self-esteem on a scale with a maximum of fifty. The Phillips' School Anxiety Questionnaire was scored for high anxiety responses on a scale with a maximum anxiety score of 23.

Pupil outcome differences as a result of the two educational approaches were assessed by two 2×2 (school by sex) multivariate analyses of variance procedures. Sex was included as a second independent variable in these analyses to account for a possible systematic sex by educational environment interaction. The nine achievement test scores were used as dependent measures in the first analysis. The multivariate F ration for overall achievement differences between the two schools was significant ($F = 2.56$, $df = 9$; 88, $p < .01$). Six of the nine univariate F ratios for these variables were significantly different for the two school samples. These variables include the measures of: Word Meaning, Paragraph Meaning, Arithmetic Concepts, Arithmetic Application, Social Studies, and Science. An examination of the achievement means by school indicated that achievement was higher in all nine areas for the traditional school students.

The multivariate test for a main effect by sex was also significant ($F = 3.87$, $df = 9$; 88, $p < .001$). None of the univariate tests reached significance. The test for a multivariate interaction of sex by school was not significant.

The second multivariate analysis included six pupil outcome variables as the dependent measures. These included: Formal Operations, Locus of Control, Self Esteem, School Anxiety, Verbal Creativity and Figural Creativity. Table 6 presents the results of this analysis. The multivariate F ratio for overall differences on these six variables was not significant ($F = 1.07$, $df = 9$; 88). The only univariate difference to reach significance on this vector was School Anxiety. An examination of the direction of this difference indicates that students of the open school have higher levels of school anxiety.

A significant multivariate main effect by sex was found ($F = 3.94$, $df = 6$; 91, $p < .002$). Four significant univariate F tests for this main effect indicate that girls tend to have higher levels of creativity and school anxiety, and lower levels of self esteem than boys. The multivariate test for an interaction between school type and sex was not significant.

Source: From Wright, R. J., "The Affective and Cognitive Consequences of an Open Education Elementary School." *American Educational Research Journal*, 12, 449–468. Copyright © 1975, American Educational Research Association, Washington, DC. Reprinted by permission.

TABLE 10.5
Multivariate Analogs

Univariate Test	Multivariate Test
t-test	Hotelling's T^2
ANOVA	MANOVA (Multivariate analysis of variance)
ANCOVA	MANCOVA

science would be of interest, such as enjoying science as well as valuing science, for chemistry as well as biology, for dissection as well as field trips, and so on. In fact, most attitude instruments have subscales that more specifically and accurately reflect feelings and beliefs than one general score can. The researcher could combine all these different aspects and consider the attitude as a general disposition, but it is better to look at each aspect separately. The reader may be wondering why researchers do not use a separate univariate analysis for each dependent variable. That is, why not compute as many ANOVAs or *t*-tests as there are dependent variables? The reason is that as long as the dependent variables are correlated, the use of separate univariate analysis will increase the probability of finding a difference simply because so many tests are employed. It is similar to the reason that in ANOVA we use post hoc tests rather than many *t*-tests. Multivariate analyses are also more parsimonious, that is, more direct, quicker, with fewer calculations.

Although the computation and interpretation of multivariate tests are quite complex, the basic principle of rejecting null hypotheses at some level of significance is the same as for all inferential statistics. The difference is that all the dependent variables are considered together in one analysis. For most of the procedures previously discussed that have one dependent variable, a multivariate analog can be used when there is the same independent variable or variables but more than one dependent variable. Table 10.5 summarizes the multivariate tests that correspond to procedures used with one dependent variable.

Excerpt 10.14 is an illustration of the way a researcher used a multivariate procedure, MANOVA, to analyze the data.

■ SUMMARY ■

This chapter has introduced the logic of inferential statistics and described some of the more common statistical procedures researchers use to analyze data. The following points summarize the concepts presented.

1. Inferential statistics are used to make inferences based on measured aspects of a sample about the characteristics of a population.
2. In conducting research, probability is a concern because of the error involved in sampling and measurement.
3. Sample statistics represent imperfect estimates of the population.
4. Inferential statistics estimate the probability of population characteristics' being within a certain range of values.
5. The null hypothesis is used to test the assumption that there is no difference between population values.
6. Researchers attempt to reject the null hypothesis by using inferential statistics to indicate the probability of being wrong in rejecting the null.
7. The level of significance of the statistical test tells the researcher the probability of making a Type I error in rejecting the null hypothesis.
8. Most researchers use a p level of 0.05 or less (< 0.05) to indicate statistical significance.
9. The t-test is used to compare two means, and, depending on the nature of the research, it uses an independent samples equation or a dependent samples equation to calculate the t value.
10. Analysis of variance is used to compare two or more means, and it reports F statistics with corresponding p levels.
11. One-way ANOVA tests the difference between levels of one independent variable, while factorial ANOVA examines more than one independent variable.
12. Multiple comparison procedures (such as Tukey and Scheffé) are post hoc tests designed to locate significant differences among pairs of means in ANOVA.
13. An interaction is examined in factorial ANOVA as the unique effect of the independent variables acting together to affect the dependent variable results.
14. Parametric tests assume ratio, interval, or ordinal data, homogeneity of variance, and a normal distribution. Nonparametric tests can be used in cases in which the assumptions are violated and the test is not robust for that violation.
15. Analysis of covariance is used to adjust differences between groups on a covariate variable that is related to the dependent variable.
16. Chi-square is a frequently encountered nonparametric test that is used when the researcher is examining frequencies of occurrences.
17. Multivariate analyses are used in cases in which there are several related independent or dependent variables.

■ SELF-INSTRUCTIONAL REVIEW EXERCISES ■

Sample answers are in the back of the book.

Test Items

1. Probability statements are made in research because
   a. the total number of expected cases is rarely known.
   b. error exists in sampling.

    c. of the reliability and validity of measurement.
    d. Both b and c are correct.

2. The null hypothesis is a statement that is
    a. the same as the expected result.
    b. necessary because we can only disprove, not prove.
    c. stated in the negative to correspond to statistical tests.
    d. necessary in reporting research.

3. All of the following are used to indicate level of significance except for
    a. p.   c. t.
    b. α.   d. alpha.

4. Check all of the following statements that are true about level of significance.
    a. $0.05 < 0.01$.
    b. 0.05 is better than 0.01.
    c. 0.001 is better than 0.01.
    d. $0.05 < 0.10$.
    e. 0.20 is marginally significant.
    f. 0.01 is statistically significant.
    g. 0.03 means being wrong in rejecting the null 3 times out of 100.

5. The t-test is used to compare
    a. two or more means.
    b. one mean with an established value of interest.
    c. two means.
    d. Both b and c are correct.

6. Another name for the dependent samples t-test is
    a. related pairs.   c. nondependent.
    b. matched pairs.   d. independent.

7. In one-way analysis of variance the researcher would report
    a. one F statistic.   c. results for all independent
    b. three F statistics.   variables.
                                  d. results for all dependent variables.

8. Factorial ANOVA is used when
    a. there are two or more independent variables.
    b. there are two or more dependent variables.
    c. t-tests are unfeasible.
    d. Both a and c are correct.

9. Multiple comparison procedures are used because
    a. it is more convenient.
    b. it reduces the chance of making an error in drawing conclusions.

    c. it is the only way to test for all group differences.

    d. other procedures are too conservative.

10. An interaction occurs when
    a. the results of each variable are different.
    b. the effect of each variable is different.
    c. two or more variables combine to result in unique effects.
    d. two or more people talk with each other.

11. A 2 × 4 ANOVA means
    a. two independent variables and one dependent variable.
    b. one independent variable with two levels and one dependent variable with four levels.
    c. eight independent variables.
    d. one independent variable with two levels and another independent variable with four levels.

12. Examples of nonparametric statistical procedures include
    a. chi-square, ANOVA, MANOVA.
    b. MANOVA, ANCOVA.
    c. chi-square, *t*-test.
    d. chi-square, median test.

13. Multivariate procedures are used when
    a. there are several variables.
    b. there is more than one related dependent variable.
    c. independent variables have more than two levels.
    d. there are multiple tests to be done.

Application Problems

In each of the examples below select a statistical procedure that would best analyze the data.

1. This researcher was interested in the way three different approaches to discipline work with fifth graders. Student teachers were assigned randomly to one of three groups. Each group received instruction in a different approach to handling discipline problems. Each student teacher was then observed over a three-week period, and the frequency and duration of discipline problems was recorded.

2. A teacher is interested in whether her sixth graders' attitudes toward sex will change following a four-week sex education course. To assess the impact of the program, the teacher measures the students' attitudes before and after the course.

3. The teacher in problem 2 now decides to test her program more thoroughly and is able to assign her students randomly to one group that receives a control condition. The teacher also analyzes the effects on boys and girls.

4. A counselor wants to know if there is a relationship between self-esteem of eleventh graders and frequency of visits to the counseling center.

5. A doctoral student is interested in studying the attitude differences between high- and low-achieving students who receive different kinds of teacher feedback following performance on tests. Four types of teacher feedback are designed for the study, and there are eight attitudes, such as attitude toward teacher, toward the subject studied, toward learning, and so on.

PART III

QUALITATIVE RESEARCH DESIGNS AND METHODS

Qualitative research designs and methods include both interactive and non-interactive strategies in an emergent design. Educators frequently ask: When does one employ an interactive strategy such as participant-observation or ethnographic interviews? When do researchers rely primarily on documents and how does one locate relevant documents? Should one combine different data collection strategies in a single study? What kind of data analysis is done in qualitative research? How do qualitative researchers handle issues of reliability and those of internal and external validity of design? How does one present non-statistical findings? How does a reader judge the validity of the findings in a qualitative study?

In Part III, we discuss strategies to collect and analyze qualitative data. Interactive data collection strategies are primarily used in the study of current social happenings, social scenes, and processes. Non-interactive data collection strategies are primarily used in the study of the past. Inductive analysis builds from descriptive data of people's meanings derived from or ascribed to particular events and processes. Qualitative research suggests tentative causal explanations which can extend our understanding of educational phenomenon or propose grounded theories.

CHAPTER 11

ETHNOGRAPHIC RESEARCH

■ KEY TERMS ■

field research
naturalistic inquiry
phenomenology
grounded theory
educational ethnography
social construction
foreshadowed problems
theoretical and conceptual
  frameworks
case study design
site selection
research role
holistic emphasis
mapping the field
purposeful sampling
multimethod
participant observation
field residence
field notes

summary observations
ethnographic interview
informal conversational interview
interview guide approach
standardized open-ended interview
key-informant interview
career and life history interview
interview probes
artifact collections
archival and demographic record
  collection
physical trace collections
inductive analysis
categorizing and ordering data
constant comparison
data trustworthiness
triangulation
data displays
context

Most initial research questions begin with an observation that generates puzzlement or wonderment. This leads to further observation, reading, thinking, discussions, and perhaps writing. Observation can be the preliminary step in forming problems and selecting a methodology. Many studies that focus on pupil learning styles, instructional models, and organizational climates begin with observation even though the formal study uses another methodology. In addition, observations during quantitative research provide insights for data interpretation. In a broad sense, observation is the basis for all empirical research.

A form of observation is also the primary data collection strategy in a research methodology called *ethnography*. Ethnography is *interactive* research which requires extensive time in the field to observe, interview, and record processes as they occur naturally in a selected site. Ethnography has been called educational anthropology, participant-observation, field research, and naturalistic inquiry. Although there is no specific set of research procedures, as in statistical analysis, there are common methodological strategies which distinguish it from other types of inquiry: participant observation, ethnographic interviews, and archival collection. Most ethnographic studies are exploratory or discovery-oriented research to understand people's views of their world and to develop new theories. Ethnographies frequently identify areas of inquiry which prior research had not considered important or even recognized. This chapter describes ethnographic research design, interactive research strategies, inductive data analysis, the importance of ethnography in educational research, and standards for appraising an ethnographic study.

■ QUALITATIVE RESEARCH TRADITIONS ■ AND EDUCATIONAL ETHNOGRAPHY

Alternatives to traditional experimental and correlational research are usually viewed as a single methodology—often called the "qualitative" approach.[1] Qualitative research is derived from subfields of the disciplines of anthropology, sociology, and psychology. Even within anthropology, for example, there are different approaches to providing cultural description and interpretation (Chilcott, 1987).[2] In education, as in the original disciplines, adaptations, extensions, and new syntheses abound. As L. M. Smith noted in the *Encyclopedia of Educational Research* (1982), the most fundamental assessment of ethnography as used in education is that it is "evolving and changing rapidly" (p. 588). Accompanying the explosion of qualitative research is a proliferation of terms for over thirty variants of ethnography!

There are, in fact, a variety of qualitative approaches in educational research which may be clarified by using the concept of research tradition. A research tradition is "a group of scholars who agree among themselves on the nature of the universe they are examining, on legitimate questions and problems to study, and on legitimate techniques to seek solutions" (Jacob, 1987, pp. 1–2). American qualitative research traditions are ecological psychology, holistic ethnography, ethnography of communication, cognitive anthropology, and symbolic interactionalism. Except for ecological psychology, these qualitative traditions

---

[1]Methodological literature in ethnographic research is more extensive than was available for our first edition; however, the research strategies and appropriate methodological language are still developing as researchers make explicit the qualitative processes. Historical and legal research which focus on the recorded past are not associated with current definitions of "qualitative" research.

[2]J. H. Chilcott (1987) identifies seven fields within cultural anthropology: functionalism, symbolic interactionism, structuralism, psychological anthropology, cognitive anthropology, sociolinguistics, and cultural ecology. Each sub-field is associated with one or combinations of twelve different data collection strategies.

emphasize cultural standards for behavior as influencing a group's patterns of face-to-face social interactions and the "meanings" developed to guide their collective and individual actions. Other commonalities are an emergent research design, field research in either the preliminary phase or the entire research process, frequent use of multiple sources, and primarily qualitative analysis.

Differences among these qualitative research traditions lie in the relative importance of the researcher's subjective experiences to acquire insights and focus the research specifically. Most anthropological traditions seek to report participants' cultures accurately by recording verbatim statements of individuals' views of the world. Symbolic interactionalism considers the researcher's own subjective experiences as an important source of data. Each qualitative tradition (Jacob, 1987) tends to focus on such different research problems as:

1. linguistic and nonverbal features of teacher and student discourse and behavior in a classroom (ethnography of communication);
2. how various parts of the educational system form a systematic whole, such as how student culture relates to teacher culture, or how the school, district, and community influence the classroom, or how the larger culture (legislative mandates, parental values, economic factors) contribute to educational processes (holistic ethnography);
3. the mentalistic culture of groups in an institution with similar circumstances, such as how principals and teachers classify students or how different student groups define success in school (cognitive anthropology); and
4. the process by which a group who shares the same position in an organization develops "meanings" to guide their actions, such as how students deal with the cultural patterns, like "rules" of teachers to achieve their own goals (symbolic interactionalism).

Characteristics of
Ethnographic Research in Education

General distinctions between qualitative and quantitative research were summarized in Chapters 1 through 5. The major characteristics of ethnographic research are presented here briefly.

1. *Assumptions about the world.* Ethnographic research is based on a naturalistic-phenomenological philosophy which assumes *multiple realities* are socially constructed through individual and collective definitions of the situation. Most descriptions and situational meanings are portrayed with words rather than numbers, although numerical data may be used to elaborate the different realities identified in a qualitative analysis.

2. *Purpose.* Ethnographic research is concerned with *understanding* the social phenomenon from the participants' perspective through participation in a research role in the life of those actors. Understanding is acquired by analyzing the many contexts of the participants and by narrating the "stories" of the partici-

pants. For example, learning to read occurs in the contexts of social settings, of human and institutional purposes, and of prior learning and instruction with material and physical elements, and it involves personal and interpersonal histories.

3. *Research process and methods.* There is a flexibility in the research strategies with various combinations of participant-observation, in-depth interviews, and artifact collection. Most ethnographers employ an *emergent design* and make decisions about data collection strategies during the study. The multiple realities are viewed as so complex that one cannot decide *a priori* on a single methodology. Careful ethnographers describe their methods in detail with justifications of the strategies chosen, their assumptions and limitations.

4. *Research role.* Ethnographers become "immersed" in the situation and the phenomenon studied. Researchers assume interactive social roles in which they record observations and interactions with participants in a range of contexts. Scholars emphasize the importance of data collected by a skilled, prepared *person.* Qualitative research is marked by "disciplined subjectivity" (Erickson, 1973), self-examination and criticism of the quality of the data obtained, and the problems encountered.

5. *Context sensitivity.* Other features of ethnographic research derive from the beliefs that human actions are strongly influenced by the settings in which they occur. Thus, ethnographic research develops *context-bound generalizations.* Because the researcher collects data in the setting over a prolonged time, ethnography is viewed as **field research.** Ethnography is **naturalistic inquiry,** the use of noninterfering data collection techniques to describe the natural flow of events and actions.

6. *Concept analysis.* Most ethnographic studies provide an inductive analysis of a single concept such as a "whole language" classroom (Edelsky, Draper, & Smith, 1983), a literacy-related speech event (Gilmore, 1983), mental retardation (Taylor & Bogdan, 1984), student seatwork (Anderson, Brubaker, Alleman-Brooks, & Duffy, 1985), and career in elementary schoolteaching (Biklen, 1985). Ethnographic research generally is classified as primarily phenomenological (Bruyn, 1966) or grounded theory (Glaser & Strauss, 1967). **Phenomenology** provides an understanding of a concept from the participants' views of their social realities. **Grounded theory,** a more sophisticated analysis, links participants' perceptions to social science and suggests new concepts or mini-theories about humans in general rather than linking the findings to educational events or processes. The concepts are "grounded theory" because these abstractions are built from observations rather than deduced from prior theories.

7. *Exploratory and discovery research.* Most ethnographic studies focus on relatively "new" research questions or attempt to discover the important questions to investigate about new educational phenomena. Some ethnographic studies spawn a new research direction in the study of the phenomenon. Thus, the research is viewed as an exploratory or discovery-oriented study. Although ethnographic research provides context-bounded generalizations, the understandings or grounded theories are intended to be *extended* in subsequent research with additional case studies or more structured designs.

B. Malinowski, an eminent anthropologist, captured the essence of qualitative research when he wrote in 1922:

> . . . the final goal, which an Ethnographer should never lose sight . . . is briefly, to grasp the native's [peoples of the south sea islands] point of view, his relation to life, to realize *his* vision of *his* world . . . . To study the institutions, customs, and codes or to study the behavior and mentality without the subjective desire of feeling by what these people live, of realizing the substance of their happiness—is, in my opinion, to miss the greatest reward which we can hope to obtain from the study of man (1922 [Reprint 1961], p. 25).

Educational Ethnography

Educational ethnography is defined several ways. First, **educational ethnography** is an analytical description of social scenes and groups which recreate for the reader the "shared beliefs, practices, artifacts, folk knowledge, and behaviors" of those people in an educational activity (Goetz & LeCompte, 1984, pp. 2–3). Ethnographers believe that reality is a **social construction,** that individuals or groups derive or ascribe meanings to specific entities such as events, persons, or objects. Individuals form constructions in order to make sense of these entities and organize or reorganize these constructions as viewpoints, perceptions, and belief systems. These viewpoints, perceptions, and belief systems are "constructed realities" of individuals or groups. In other words, the "data are, so to speak, the *constructions* offered by or in the sources; data analysis leads to a *reconstruction* of those constructions" (Lincoln & Guba, 1985, p. 332).

Second, educational ethnography is also a process, a way of studying human life as it relates to education. Data collection strategies are conducive to obtaining people's perceptions in social settings. The process is inductive which builds abstractions from the particular social constructions (data) that have been gathered (see Chapters 3 and 5).

To demonstrate how an ethnographer searches for meaning from observations and perspectives, let us look at an example and contrast it with traditional research (Wilson, 1977). Let us assume that a traditional researcher wants to see whether a relationship exists between some teacher behavior and the variable of interstudent aggression. To determine the frequency of different kinds of aggression, the researcher sets up an observation schedule that categorizes types of aggression and trains the observers to be reliable.

In our hypothetical situation, one of these categories of aggression is *student hits other student.* Experienced observers or coders in the classrooms are aware intuitively that not all *student hits other student* occurrences are exactly alike. Quantitative researchers, in their training and orientation, put these reservations aside and report the so-called facts—that is, the number of times students hit other students.

The ethnographer is unwilling to do this. The qualitative researcher believes that understanding the subtle differences between similar hitting events is important, and much of the research tries to get this information. The ethnographer believes that coding, classifying, and categorizing behavior early in the research may cause the neglect of important findings related to the qualitative interest.

The ethnographer systematically works at deriving meanings of events. In our hypothetical example, the researcher would be aware of the whole situation and the perspectives of the participants and thus be able to select the relevant details to determine the meaning of one student's hitting another student. The ethnographer would be able to answer the following questions:

1. What was occurring in the classroom at the time the incident happened, such as teacher actions and actions of other students?
2. What happened immediately preceding and following the incident?
3. How do the various participants (hitter, person being hit, other students, teacher) perceive the incident?
4. Do they even see it as aggression?
5. Do the hitter and the person being hit concur on the meaning?

The ethnographer does *not* immediately decide the meaning of one student's hitting another. The observations, along with knowledge and experience, generate working hunches that will be checked out in subsequent data collection. The incident may not even be an act of aggression, it could be:

1. An act of affection, as in a game of exchange
2. Part of acceptable behavior in a subculture norm, such as a show of male strength
3. An attempt to get the teacher's attention or to disrupt a class rather than an act directed at the person being hit

Even if the incident is aggression, there are many critical distinctions among the incidents that are important to understand:

1. The incident could be an initial act, or it could be the final blow of a series of aggressive actions between the two persons.
2. The incident could be a powerful overreaction to some imagined similarity to previous actions unlinked in time, location, or even kind.
3. The incident could be a part of the personal relationship between two persons involved in or part of a larger social system of cliques or gangs.

Finally, remember that the research orientation of the ethnographer differs from that of the quantitative researcher. Ethnographic research is based on a naturalistic-phenomenological philosophy of human behavior. An ethnographer seeks to understand people's constructions—their thoughts and meanings, feelings, beliefs, and actions as they occur in their natural context. As an observer of the entire context, the researcher is in a unique position to understand those elements that influence behavior, to articulate them, and to interpret them—to reconstruct these multiple constructed realities.

■ DESIGNING ETHNOGRAPHIC RESEARCH ■

Ethnographic studies vary in the extent of their formal design, however, any interactive inquiry is guided systematically by the cannons of research methods, logical reasoning, and conceptual frameworks shared by scholars. Designing a participant-observation study requires planning and decisions which need to be explicit. Research phases involving related tasks, seldom accomplished in a step-by-step progression, develop an emergent design. Below is a brief overview of the research phases.

1. Stating the initial focus, purpose, and questions to be investigated
2. Selecting a research design and the site
3. Developing a research role in the field
4. Choosing the participants, contexts, and activities after preliminary mapping of the field (purposeful sampling)
5. Choosing data collection strategies before and during data collection
6. Selecting data analysis techniques during and after data collection
7. Selecting forms of data display and developing interpretations

Foreshadowed Problems: Research Purpose and Questions

Educational ethnography provides detailed descriptions about the contexts, activities, and beliefs of selected participants in educational activities. Usually the researcher is at the site for a lengthy time period and the research foci are described within the total context. Ethnographic studies are conducted to understand a phenomenon and to develop theory. These different research purposes affect the statement of the problem.

The ethnographer begins with **foreshadowed problems**—anticipated research problems which will be reformulated in the field during data collection. Foreshadowed problems are typically broadly phrased research questions about the setting (participants, time, place, events), what happens, why it happens, and how it happens. Such problems can focus on the structure and the processes operating in a site and different social scenes. Below is an example.

> In order to describe the personnel task of the principal, it is necessary to describe and analyze three sub-topics. First, what were the types of teacher behaviors that principals identified as unsatisfactory? Second, having identified the unsatisfactory behaviors, what actions were then taken by the principals in an attempt to resolve the problems? Third, what are the factors which influenced the principals' decision-making during the identification-resolution process? (Luck, 1985, p. 4)

Ethnographic research problems derive from several possible sources: common, recurring everyday events in education or personal experiences, ideologies and philosophies, theories, prior research, and problems and ideas identified by others in the setting. In other words, empirical problems lie all around in varying forms and for the most part need only to be recognized for their possibilities. There is almost an intuitive feel for the problems in the form of such questions as, "I wonder what will happen now that . . . ," "What does this event really mean to the participants?," or "How are they going to manage to do that?" in the origin of an ethnographic research problem.

Recognizing a possible research problem is an ethnographic skill. Ethnographers have their curiosity aroused or are puzzled about the whys and hows of what they observe or experience. Ethnographers study theory and previous research as much as other researchers do, but they purposely put aside this knowledge until their experience in the field suggests its relevance. The statement of foreshadowed problems indicates that the researcher has tentatively decided the research purpose, the role of theory, and the focus of the data collection strategies. Most foreshadowed problems reflect the naturalistic discovery-orientation and the initial conceptual frameworks.

Naturalistic Discovery. In a naturalistic discovery-orientation, the ethnographer seeks to discover the multiple participant "meanings" of events and processes in the field and does not deliberately manipulate or attempt to control the situation. Foreshadowed problems, therefore, are *not* preconceived ideas but a working knowledge of facts, issues, concepts, and theories which guide the decisions for an emergent design. Discovering participant "meanings" necessitates problem reformulation in the field. Malinowski, a noted anthropologist, emphasized the essential ability of the researcher to recast initial ideas during field work by stating:

> If a man sets out on an expedition, determined to prove certain hypotheses, if he is incapable of changing his views constantly and casting them off ungrudgingly under the pressure of evidence, needless to say his work will be worthless. But the more problems he brings with him into the field, the more he is in the habit of . . . seeing facts in their bearing upon theory, the better he is equipped for the work. . . . (1922 [Reprint, 1961], pp. 8–9)

In an exploratory study (Schumacher, 1975) of a planned curriculum diffusion (widespread usage) in one state, for example, the foreshadowed problems were phrased in terms of sequential events planned to result in local school district adoptions of the curriculum. Despite drastic modification of the plans and scheduled events during the year, diffusion of the curriculum occurred. Rational planning models and decision-making theories failed to explain the diffusion, however, political concepts of cost-benefit, negotiation, and compromise between the state department of education and the local school systems could explain diffusion.

Theoretical and Conceptual Frameworks. Ethnographic studies have an eclectic approach toward the role of theories in the research. In general, theories influence the development of foreshadowed problems in one of three ways.

EXCERPT 11.1
Theoretical Orientation

The purpose of the principal investigator was twofold. He wanted to look at the "real world" and describe it carefully and in considerable detail. Then he wanted to back away and conceptualize this "real world" in broader, more abstract terms that would be applicable to any classroom. This latter process is what is meant by developing a model of the classroom. The investigator was interested in learning more about how a middle-class teacher copes with a group of lower-class children. It was his conviction that no one had a very clear idea about how this is done. . . .

Substantively, the personality theory of McClelland, the social theory of Homans, and the learning theory of Skinner had been his concern as he thought through problems of educational psychology. Most certainly, these ideas guided the selection of events that he noted.

Source: From Smith, L. M. and Geoffrey, W., *The Complexities of the Urban Classroom: An Analysis Toward a General Theory of Teaching* (New York: Holt, Rinehart and Winston, 1968). Reprinted by permission of Louis M. Smith.

1. *Generate research questions.* Researchers may state questions which extend or refine established theories. *The Invisible Children: School Integration in American Society* (Rist, 1978) focused on what happened to students when a school integrated, but the ethnographer first had to conceptualize the question, "what do we mean by integration?" from the literature (pp. 4–20). For this study, integration could mean racial assimilation, racial pluralism, class assimilation, and class pluralism. The ethnographer generated the study's questions from theories of assimilation.

2. *Provide conceptual frameworks in phrasing questions.* Scholars trained in certain disciplines and their dominant traditions commonly formulate questions which reflect the concepts and assumptions in that discipline. Structural functionalism and acculturalism in anthropology, behavioralism and social learning theories in psychology, and social systems and social roles in sociology may influence the phrasing of the foreshadowed problems. In Excerpt 11.2, for example, the more specific foreshadowed problems were phrased in sociological terms.

3. *Reformulate research questions.* Initial foreshadowed questions are reformulated in the field for more appropriate explanations and concepts to provide latent meanings of the observations. In Excerpt 11.1 L. M. Smith and W. Geoffrey (1968) originally wanted to describe the "real world" of how a middle-class teacher copes with a group of lower-class children. His observations and interviews of Geoffrey, the teacher, lead to the reformulation of the foreshadowed problems in terms of personality theory, social theory, and learning theory.

Whether one enters the field with a sociological, psychological, anthropological, or policy perspective, it is important that this be made explicit. In essence, the

---

EXCERPT 11.2
Foreshadowed Problems

THE RESEARCH PROBLEM

The Initial Proposal. However, our study did not begin as an investigation of teacher turnover nor of administrative succession. It began as we suggested in our research proposal.

The problem[5] to be studied in this investigation contains several components. In its most general aspect, we are trying to capitalize on a rather unusual naturalistic event, the building of a new and uniquely designed elementary school building. Figure 1.2 contains the floor plan and design.

Although in a general sense, the question, What happens in such a novel situation?, is the focus of the research, the more specific problems to be analyzed are: (1) the development of the faculty social system; (2) the principal's role vis-à-vis the faculty social system; (3) the teachers' innovations in instruction; (4) the development of the school-wide pupil social system.

Source: From L. M. Smith and P. Keith, *Anatomy of Educational Innovation.* Copyright © 1971 by John Wiley & Sons, Inc. Reprinted by permission.

---

ethnographer who enters the field with several **theoretical and conceptual frameworks,** such as concepts and assumptions among scholars in certain disciplines and their dominant traditions, is able to recognize more easily the events to expand the conceptual aspects of the settings.

Focus of Data Collection Strategies.   The foreshadowed problems indicate the focus for data collection. This is particularly important for the selection of the site and of participants and contexts to observe. Foreshadowed problems do *not*, however, restrict observations, because more research questions evolve during the lengthy field work. Excerpt 11.2 illustrates the selection of a site—the first year of an innovative elementary school with new faculty and administrators, a new curriculum, a new leadership style, and a new building without the traditional classroom walls. The original focus of the data collection strategies was the development of the faculty social system, the principal's role, the instructional innovations, and the schoolwide pupil social system. Data collection strategies yielded findings for these initial questions and later yielded additional findings, reformulating research questions about high teacher turnover and administrative succession.[3]

---

[3]Fifteen years after the opening of the innovative school, a second qualitative study was conducted by L. M. Smith, P. L. Kleine, J. P. Prunty, & D. C. Dwyer in a trilogy of studies: *Educational Innovators: Then and Now, The Fate of an Innovative School,* and *Innovation and Change* (1987).

Case Study Design:
Site Selection and the Research Role

Traditional ethnographic studies are a case study design, conducted at a single site composed of a number of participants, settings, processes, and activities. **Case study design** refers to the one phenomenon the researcher selects to understand in-depth regardless of the number of settings, social scenes, or participants in the study. The "case" relates to the research foci and influences what the researcher can state empirically upon completion of the study. **Site selection** is the specification of site criteria implied in the foreshadowed problems and obtaining a suitable and feasible research site. The site selected should offer the likelihood that the phenomenon and processes stated in the foreshadowed problems are present and can be studied. In the negotiations to obtain formal permission to conduct an ethnographic study at a site, the researcher also makes explicit the research role to be assumed for data collection.

Site Selection.   Choosing a site is a negotiation process to obtain freedom of access to a site which is *suitable* for the foreshadowed problems and *feasible* for the ethnographer's resources of time, mobility, skills, and the like. The field researcher usually obtains information in advance through informal channels such as the identities and the power alignments of the principal actors—what they do (their immediate interests and concerns) and a general history of the site, the routines, and the social structure—and the activities. Information regarding the site and its potential suitability is obtained from a variety of sources: documents, present and prior associates, and public information. Much depends on the researcher's good judgment, timing, and tact in gathering information informally.

After the ethnographer identifies a possible site, contact is made with a person who can grant research permission. Some researchers make a formal contact after informal confirmation that the research proposal will be reviewed positively. Most ethnographers prepare a brief written statement which specifies the site, the participants and activities, the length of time for the entire study, and the research role. The statement also provides information about the researcher, the sponsor of organizational affiliation, and the general uses of the data, including the protection of the rights of human subjects. Access to the site and the people are crucial at this time. Schatzman and Strauss suggest that "any restrictions initially accepted by the researcher should be regarded as renegotiable at later, more propitious times" (1973, p. 29). Formal authorization is essential for research ethics and for proceeding to enter the field and establish a research role. Once authorization has been granted, the researcher disengages himself from the leadership of the site to establish a research role, map the field, and conduct purposeful sampling.

Research Role.   The ethnographer chooses a **research role**—the relationships acquired by and ascribed to the ethnographer in interactive data collection—that is appropriate for the purpose of the study. Four possible roles are: observer,

observer-participant, participant-observer, and participant. These roles vary in terms of the way the ethnographer's presence affects the social system under study. The role of pure observer is that of one who is essentially physically and psychologically absent. An example is that of an observer looking through a one-way window. The role of pure participant is similar to that of living through an experience, recalling the experience and writing personal insights. Because neither of these roles are interactive, they are inappropriate for ethnographic research, but they may be used in other forms of qualitative research.

The roles of observer-participant or participant-observer are appropriate ethnographic roles. In observer-participant, the role would not be established except for the study. The ethnographer receives permission to create the role for the sole purpose of data collection. L. M. Smith (Smith & Geoffrey, 1968), in his study of an inner city classroom, was an observer-participant. Smith made every effort not to impinge on the classroom's social system and resisted attempts by the school system to involve him in other roles. The participant-observer is a person who has a role in the site in which he or she intends to study. The role (that is, superintendent, counselor, teacher) exists whether or not the study is conducted.[4] In school ethnographies conducted by participant-observers, however, the possibility exists that the findings could be distorted by observer-setting interaction effects which limit the external validity of the study. The traditional ethnographic role is that of the outsider and observer-participant.

A research role is really many roles as the ethnographer acquires language fluency with the participants, is interactive to obtain data, establishes social relationships and moves from role sets appropriate in one group to different role sets for other groups.[5] The ethnographer is a sensitive observer and records phenomena as faithfully as possible. Unlike mechanical recording devices, however, ethnographers are able to raise additional questions, check out hunches, and move deeper into analysis of the phenomenon.

Valid data results when the events unfold naturally and the participants act in typical fashion in the ethnographer's presence. Because the research role affects data collection, the role is stated in the study. Excerpt 11.3 demonstrates the assumed role for a study of a principal. Wolcott (1973), in the role of the observer-participant, was jokingly called the "principal's shadow." This meant observing and recording the principal's behavior and conversations in formal and informal settings and in school and out of school settings, talking with many individuals, and reviewing the principal's notes, records, and files.

---

[4]Some studies on highly sensitive problems probably could not be done by an outside investigator. Lutz and Iannaccone (1969) suggest that the study of politics and power by a participant in a school system would yield more valid data than one conducted by an outside observer.

[5]Goetz and LeCompte (1984) delineate three types of role relationships: 1) external to the study as a scholar within an academic discipline, 2) internal to the study as a participant in a culture, and 3) interface roles between the internal and external roles after sufficient time in the field when the ethnographer can be considered as a legitimate spokesperson for the social group examined.

EXCERPT 11.3
The Ethnographer's Research Role

During the period in which I was looking for a subject, the principals whom I met volunteered a number of descriptive titles for my role, such as "anthropologist in residence," "assistant without portfolio," "lap dog," and "shadow." Ultimately the last term became my nickname, perhaps because it simultaneously provided a capsule description of my role, a nickname for people who could not remember my real name or were uncertain how to address me, and an entrée into a joking relationship where no other pattern for behavior existed: "Hey Shadow, how come you're here on a dark day like this?"

Before extending my invitation to Ed to participate in the study, I reviewed the kinds of activities I intended to pursue with him as his "shadow": maintaining a constant written record of what I observed in behavior and conversation; attending formal and informal meetings and conferences; accompanying him on school business away from the building as well as occasionally accompanying him in nonschool settings; interviewing "everybody"; and, with his permission, sifting through notes, records, and files.

Source: Harry F. Wolcott, *The Man in the Principal's Office: An Ethnography.* Orlando, Florida: Holt, Rinehart and Winston, Inc., 1973.

Mapping and Purposeful Sampling

Ethnographic research, unlike hypotheses-testing or survey research, describes and interprets any subset of context-bound data within the larger context of the site. This characteristic is often referred to as a **holistic emphasis;** subcases of data are related to the total context of the phenomenon studied. For example, the findings reported on the development of a faculty social system and school-wide pupil social system in Excerpt 11.2 were related to the larger context of the establishment of an innovative elementary school. Although all that occurs within a setting is a potential source of data, ethnographers *cannot and do not need to observe everything,* but they can obtain sufficient data for a holistic emphasis. By using mapping strategies, the ethnographer gains a sense of the "totality" and is in a better position to do purposeful sampling of information-rich cases.

Mapping the Field.   Gaining entry into the field requires establishing good relations with all individuals at the research site. Research permission comes without a guarantee that the participants will behave naturally before an outsider who takes field notes or that the participants will share their perceptions, thoughts, and feelings with the observer. The ethnographer's skill is reflected in whether the participants see the researcher as an interested, respectful, nonjudgmental observer who maintains confidentiality, or whether they view the researcher as a rude, disruptive, critical observer who cannot be trusted. The ethnographer must attend to maintaining the trust and confidentiality of the participants constantly throughout the entire data collection period (Schumacher, 1984a). The participants at any time may decline to share their perceptions, feelings, and thoughts with the ethnographer.

As ethnographers assume a research role, they also begin **mapping the field,** acquiring data of the social, spatial, and temporal relationships in the site to gain a sense of the total context. A social map notes the numbers and kinds of people, the organizational structure, and the activities people engage in. A spatial map notes the locations, the facilities, and the specialized services provided. A temporal map describes the rhythm of organizational life, the schedules, and the unwritten routines.

Once ethnographers have initially mapped the field, they selectively choose those persons, situations, and events most likely to yield fruitful data about the evolving foreshadowed problems. As new questions emerge during data collection, ethnographers change, through purposeful sampling, the observation times and locations in order to collect valid data. Excerpt 11.4 illustrates the relationship between problem statement, site selection, research design, and mapping the field in a study of the admission process of developmentally delayed children for institutionalization consideration.

Purposeful Sampling.   Initially the researcher searches for information-rich informants, groups, places or events from which to select subunits for more in-depth study. In other words, **purposeful sampling** is a strategy to choose small groups or individuals likely to be knowledgeable and informative about the phenomenon of interest. Below is a review of purposeful sampling strategies discussed in Chapter 5.

The primary purposeful sampling strategies are: comprehensive selection, maximum variation sampling, and network or snowball sampling. After ethnographers have mapped the field, they may combine these strategies with the selection of extreme-cases, typical-cases, unique-cases, reputation-cases, and critical-cases. Each strategy is an example of the possible ways ethnographers select information-rich cases for the evolving research focus. They are called *strategies* rather than procedures, because each requires preliminary information acquired through mapping the field and are continually refined throughout the entire data collection process. Furthermore, most ethnographers do not know in advance if potentially information-rich cases will yield data about extreme-case, typical-case, and so on until formal data analysis is completed. Thus, at the beginning, usually comprehensive sampling is planned for an ethnographic study, and network selection is planned for an ethnographic interview study.

1. *Comprehensive selection* is the ideal type in which every participant, group, setting, event, and other relevant information is examined because the subunit is manageable in size and is so heterogeneous that one does not want to lose possible variation. See Excerpts 2.5, 3.6, 5.5, 5.6, 5.7, 5.8, 5.9, and all excerpts in this chapter except 11.2 and 11.3.

EXCERPT 11.4
Problem Statement, Site Selection, Research Design, Mapping the Field

---

I wanted to learn how the people directly affected by and involved in the process of institutional commitment thought about and defined their experience. I used qualitative research techniques, including participant observation and open-ended interviews, to gather information. These techniques are usually associated with the theoretical approaches of symbolic interaction and ethnography (Bogdan and Taylor, 1975; Spradley, 1979). Both symbolic interaction and ethnography are concerned with the ways in which people interpret their experiences and make sense of their world. Thus, they were ideally suited to my purpose[1].

The design of the project was to follow those persons who were admitted to the Weston Center and/or applied for admission or readmission to the Center between January 1 and December 31, 1981. During this period sixteen applications were filed, of which twelve were admitted and four were turned down. A seventeenth person whose application was approved prior to January 1 was admitted to the Center in March, 1981.

Of the total of seventeen, thirteen are included here. One was not included because the family could not be reached for permission. Two others were not included because the families were unwilling to participate. The fourth was not included because by the time the parent was contacted and had agreed to join the project, the collection of data had been completed. . . .

GAINING ACCESS TO THE WESTON CENTER

I approached the Weston Center in December, 1980. During January and February, 1981, their Research Committee reviewed my proposal and developed the guidelines according to which I was to conduct my research. Parents and staff were required to sign "informed consent" forms before I could include them in the study. I was given complete access to the Center and allowed to attend all meetings which I deemed relevant to my project.

Even with this "carte blanche" from the administration, I realized that my entry into the field was dependent on acceptance by staff at all levels of the organization[2]. Consequently, I spent several weeks introducing myself to staff, discussing the project with them, and answering their questions.

Occasionally, ideas brought out at these meetings would prove instrumental to the later success of the study. For example, it was suggested that I be introduced to parents personally by the social worker in charge of the case rather than making my request over the phone or by mail. While there is no way to compare this approach with what would have happened without a personal introduction, it is significant that only two out of sixteen families contacted refused to participate in the study. In addition, no staff person refused me an interview.

Source: From *The Politics of Caring* by Susan Bannerman Foster (London: Falmer Press Ltd., 1987). Reprinted by permission of Falmer Press Ltd. and the author.

2. *Maximum variation sampling* or *quota selection* is a strategy to "represent" subunits of the major unit of analysis (the research problem). See Excerpt 2.8.

3. *Network selection* or *snowball sampling* is a strategy in which each successive participant or group is named by a preceding individual or group as "fitting" the profile of traits or attributes identified by the researcher (especially useful in ethnographic interviews of persons who do not form a naturally bounded group but are scattered throughout the subunits or population). See Excerpt 3.5.

4. *Extreme-case selection* requires first the identification of typical or average cases and then the selection of the extreme cases. See Excerpt 3.7.

5. *Typical-case selection* requires the researcher to develop a profile of characteristics of an average case and then find examples of the case. See Excerpt 11.3.

6. *Unique-case selection* focuses on the unusual or rare case of some dimension which natural historical events frequently provide. See Excerpts 5.9 and 11.2.

7. *Reputational-case selection* occurs when knowledgeable experts recommend individuals or groups based on the attributes sought by the ethnographer.

8. *Critical-case selection* requires the identification of critical cases, those which can make points quite dramatically or are, for some reason, considered particularly important such as the "ideal or typical" case, the "real test" case, or the politically sensitive case.

Ethnographers view selection and sampling strategies as dynamic and *ad hoc* rather than static or *a priori* parameters of populations for a research design. Thus, purposeful sampling is a process conducted simultaneously as one collects data. The specification of the site selection criteria and the purposeful sampling strategies chosen are reported in a study to reduce threats to design validity. In addition, the person or groups who actually participated in the study are reported in a manner to protect confidentiality of data.

■ DATA COLLECTION STRATEGIES ■

A major characteristic of ethnography is the incorporation of strategies during data collection to meet canons of research credibility. Appropriate definitions of reliability and validity, both internal and external, were explained in Chapter 5. Data collection and analysis strategies attempt to minimize threats to qualitative reliability and validity and to report those effects which limit the usefulness of the study. Because traditional ethnography is done by one or two researchers, reliability can be a problem unless the study is exploratory research. Validity is the major strength of ethnographic research in discovery inquiry.

Choosing Data Collection Strategies

Ethnography is associated with particular data collection strategies: interactive observation, interviewing, and artifact collection. Each of these can be subdivided into more specific techniques. Typically, the ethnographer uses

---

EXCERPT 11.5
Multiple Data Collection Strategies

COLLECTING DATA

Archival records

As soon as the project was approved, I began data collection. First, I reviewed the clinical histories of the people included in the study as it was described in their case files, as well as general official documents describing the Weston Center and its activities. Records represent a particular understanding of the individuals concerned, embodied in formal identification and description (Biklen, 1978). The purpose of the review of records was to get at this perspective.

Observation

Second, I spent time as an observer at the Weston Center. I sat in on meetings which were relevant to the intake, evaluation, and placement process at the Center. In several cases, these observations extended to living units and classrooms at the Center. Field

Field notes

notes were written at the end of each observation describing in detail the setting and activities of subjects.

Conducting observations at meetings was relatively easy. Since many of the participants were taking notes and observing the conversation of others, I could do the same without attracting

Other observations

attention. However, it was not possible to record field notes while conducting observations in other kinds of settings, such as institution living units and department offices. In order to assure the

Summary observations

accuracy and detail of these notes, I had to allow several hours for recording notes after leaving the field.

Drawings in field notes

Drawings were an important element of the field notes. For example, I always sketched the seating arrangement at meetings as a way of recalling and describing, in shorthand, conversations and interactions. Similarly, drawings of hospital rooms and institutional living units were useful ways of summarizing an environment, often capturing details which would be difficult to describe in words.

Informal conversation interviews

In addition to these observations, I interviewed participants in the institutionalization process, including staff from the Center and other social service agencies, and members of the client's family. These interviews were often more like a conversation than a formal interview and took place in a variety of settings, including offices, living rooms, cars, and hallways. The purpose of these interviews was to allow those involved in the institutionalization process to describe in detail their perceptions and interpretations of the experience.

Interview guide approach; taping and elaborations

I brought a tape recorder on scheduled interviews and, with the respondent's permission, recorded our conversation. However, observational field notes were also recorded for every interview, describing the setting in which the interview took place, the people, and activities. Often these details would prove as important as the interview itself. For example, one mother stood up and paced back and forth while describing the accident which rendered her child comatose. As she walked from one room to the other, pointing to the spot where the accident occurred and to where she had been standing, it became clear that she had relived this moment many times. In another instance, the parent showed me pictures of her children. As we looked at the pictures together, the story about life with the disabled child unfolded.

Other conversations

Sometimes, conversations at the beginning or end of meetings yielded very rich data. Once, a social worker whose client had been denied admission stopped me in the hall afterwards to offer her interpretation of the politics involved in the decision. In cases like this, I would usually take the time to write down notes in my car before driving home in order to insure an accurate and detailed recording of the conversation.

Source: From *The Politics of Caring* by Susan Bannerman Foster (London: Falmer Press Ltd., 1987). Reprinted by permission of Falmer Press Ltd. and the author.

multimethods—multiple strategies to corroborate the data obtained from any single strategy and/or ways to confirm data within a single strategy of data collection. Ethnographers assume any data can be corroborated during data collection. A study of elementary classrooms could confirm observations with interviews of teachers and students. A study of a school system's politics and bureaucracy would corroborate data with interviews, observations of meetings and hearings, press coverage of events, newsletters of interest groups, and Board of Education studies. Ethnographers generally rely on observation, interviewing, and artifact analysis or some combination of these. Excerpt 11.5 illustrates multimethods.

Decisions regarding data collection strategies are usually made after site selection, entry into the field, and initial mapping of the field. Initial plans are reviewed and refined. Information originally planned to be obtained by observation may only be available through interviewing; preliminary findings from interview data may have to be substantiated through researcher-constructed questionnaires or artifact analysis. Analysis of documents or unexpected events may suggest new directions for observing or interviewing. Choosing data collection strategies is a process of deciding among available alternatives for collection and corroboration of data and of modifying one's decisions to capture the "reality" of the phenomena.

EXCERPT 11.6
On-Site Observation

THE METHODOLOGY

The investigation was a formulative or model-building study, and the principal method of data collection was participant observation. This was supplemented by informal interviews, intensive analysis of records, and verbatim accounts of meetings. Access to all documents had been given; this included faculty and parent school-council bulletins, committee reports, and district-wide curriculum materials. Observations were made of classroom interaction, the use of facilities, the total faculty meetings, the team meetings, the curriculum committee meetings, and the parent school-council meetings.

These varied observations enabled us to follow the development of the organization through three main periods of time. The first block was a four-week workshop prior to the beginning of school. In the months of September to December, the school's three academic divisions—the Independent Study Division (ISD), Transition Division, and Basic Skills Division—were temporarily housed in three widely separated facilities. From December to June, the divisions were located in the building designed for the program. . . .

[7]Although we were not there at "all" times, we did approximate this situation. In the summer workshop and through the first few weeks of September, Paul F. Kleine worked full time on the project. Smith and Keith (who was on a fellowship at the time) devoted almost full time to the project. During the study, school was in session 177 days from September to June. The workshop had involved four weeks in August. The observers have field notes from 153 *different* days at the school or in the district and 247 total entries. The latter indicates the overlap when both of us were in the field. Although it is possible to speak of 247 man-days of observation, this is faulty in the sense that some of the entries reflect part days and some reflect early morning to midnight days. One of our colleagues phrased it colloquially but cogently when he commented. "You were all over that school." The intensity of involvement is a key issue in the validity of the data.

Participant Observation

Participant observation is the primary data collection technique in ethnographic studies. As much as possible, ethnographers live the daily activities of the participants, recording in the field notes the perceptions of individuals as they interact with each other and with the researcher.

On-Site Observation.   The most elementary requirement of the methodology is **field residence,** in which the researcher is present in the field or site for an extensive time. Field work is, in general, a labor intensive mode of inquiry. Many ethnographic studies focus on processes over time and note change. Excerpt 11.6 demonstrates procedures for on-site observation in the study of the innovative elementary school. The ethnographers observed the four-week workshop prior to school opening and for 153 of the 177 days from September to June, as the school program was moved from temporary housing to a new building. Observations were supplemented with other types of data.

Prolonged Data Collection. Data collection continues until the logical termination of the naturalistic event or when the situation changes so dramatically that the site is not relevant for the research focus. The natural boundary for data collection may be the entire three-week period of a state-sponsored summer school arts program. The natural boundary for a study of psychiatric nursing clinical instruction is the length of the rotation, ten weeks. When the examined situation is no longer relevant to the research foci, the field residence terminates. Data collection might end with the unexpected promotion or resignation of a key actor, which, of course, would remove him or her from the site.

Participants' Constructed Realities. Participant observation enables the researcher to obtain people's perceptions of reality expressed in their actions and expressed as feelings, thoughts, and beliefs. People's perceptions are really constructs of their world, or constructed realities. It is crucial that the ethnographer acquire the particular linguistic patterns and language variations of the individuals observed because language conveys these social constructions. Observation is an active process which includes muted cues—facial expressions, gestures, tone of voice, and other unverbalized social interactions which suggest the subtle meanings of language.

Ethnographers record detailed descriptive, not vague or judgmental, field notes. Below are hypothetical examples of vague notes contrasted to the actual field notes in a study of adult beginning readers (Boraks & Schumacher, 1981, pp. 76, 86).

Vague Notes	Descriptive Notes
1. Bea misreads *wood* for *would*.	"(OBS: Intensity of Bea is demonstrated by her heavy breathing, even swearing during the reading. There is little doubt she is trying hard.) Sometimes she cues herself, when reading: 'Would you believe I would not do it again,' Bea read *would* as *wood*. The tutor says *would*. Bea tries again to reread, then says 'Oh, I missed the point, *would he.*'"
2. June retells few parts of a story and only the parts which relate to herself. She elaborates on these parts.	"June is a tall, thin, talkative woman. A staff member said she was referred by a treatment center and was considered mentally retarded and emotionally disturbed. When asked to tell a story from the text cue, she had to be prompted. For example, her story about an accident:

> June: 'My hair caught on fire.'
>
> Tutor: 'How did your hair catch fire? Can you tell me more?'
>
> June: 'I was smoking a cigarette and my lighter went up. I had the lighter close to my ear and it caught and carried to my hair and my whole head was in flames.'
>
> Tutor: 'Can you tell me anything more?'
>
> June: 'And they told me I looked like a Christmas tree all lit up.'"

Participants' stories, anecdotes, and myths—such as found in the daily gossip in the teacher's lounge or among student groups in hallways—indicate the content of their world and how they construct the different realities of their lives.

Listening is also a demanding task; ethnographers listen with all their senses. Listening involves being able to take on the role of the other person, to see the world as the participant does. The ethnographer listens especially for the *ises* and *becauses*. The *is* reveals perceptions of things, people, events, and processes that appear real or factual to a person. The *because* reveals the *whys* and *wherefores*, the beliefs, thoughts, feelings, and values—in essence, the logic about the content of a person's constructions. To listen intently requires the ethnographer to put aside his or her own perceptions and seek first those of the participants.

Corroborating Field Observations.   Although the researcher is noninterfering, he or she actively seeks different views of events from different participants for accuracy and for confirmation. By observing for a long time different participants in many contexts, the ethnographer elicits data that is "nearly impossible with other approaches, and he has access to some unique kinds of information" (Wilson, 1977, p. 256). Ethnographers can, for example, corroborate what a participant says in response to a comment or question, to other people, in different situations, or at different times; what the participant actually does; what the participant implies with nonverbal communication, such as tone of voice and body movements; and what he or she perceives others are feeling, saying, or doing about an activity.

The essence of seeking and corroborating different perceptions lies in obtaining data from multiple data sources—different persons in different contexts at various times. Multiple data sources can best be illustrated in a study by listing the strategies, participants, situations, or organizations. Table 11.1 illustrates the multiple data sources in a study of interagency curriculum development. Data was collected by observation, casual conversations, interview guides, and artifacts from more than fifty participants in the state department of education, a school system, a university, and other organizations in a variety of contexts during one year.

TABLE 11.1
Multiple Data Sources

Multiple methods	Observation
	Casual conversations
	Focused interviews
	Documents: project proposals, social studies policy statements, state survey, unit outlines, PERT planning charts, director's journal
Multiple participants	State department officials
	School division central office personnel
	Curriculum specialist
	Director
	Principal and teachers
	Visiting monitoring team
Multiple situations	Project planning council meetings
	Summer workshop
	Teacher writing team meetings
	University curriculum resource center
	State department conferences

Source: Schumacher, S. (1979). *Ethnographic inquiry: Theory and application in educational research and evaluation.* Richmond, VA: Virginia Commonwealth University. (ERIC Document Reproduction Service No. ED 184 108), p. 11.

Ethnographers, in seeking to corroborate data, frequently discover discrepancies between what people say and what people do in their observed actions. Participant observation allows the ethnographer to corroborate what individuals think they are doing or the researcher thinks they are doing. Ethnographic studies have documented how the implementations of innovations differ from the plans of innovations and the discrepancies between the purposes of education reform and the available resources.[6]

[6]Traditionally, participant observation is nonjudgmental in describing social groups and cultural scenes. It is frequently used in educational evaluation research to describe, interpret, and assess. A variety of data collection strategies often identifies discrepancies between goal-orientations, objectives and implementation, program developers and decision-makers, patterns in social interaction, conflicting authority jurisdictions, and methods of conflict resolution among program participants. See Center for the New Schools, 1972, 1976; Herriott, 1977; Schumacher, 1972, 1974, 1975, 1984b; Schumacher, Esham, & Bauer, 1985; and Schumacher & Rommel-Esham, 1986.

Salient Observations.   Because the interactive social scene is too complex and too subtle to observe or record everything, the researcher does *not* seek to capture everything that happens. Ethnographers rely on the prolonged field residences to develop skills in deciding what should be included and what can be excluded. Ethnographers observe and record the phenomena salient to the foreshadowed problems, their broader conceptual frameworks and the contextual features of the interactions. These elements explain the diversity of field notes cited in ethnographies despite the commonalities on the methodology.

What do ethnographers observe? Most ethnographers record descriptive details about who, what, where, when, how, and why an activity or social scene occurred. This information then can be used to obtain more subtle information. A general outline is presented below.

1. *Who* is in the group or scene? How many people are present; what are their kinds or identities? How is membership in the group or scene acquired?

2. *What* is happening here? What are the people in the group or scene doing and saying to one another?

    a.   What behaviors are repetitive and irregular? In what events, activities, or routines are people engaged? How are activities organized, labeled, explained, and justified?

    b.   How do the people in the group behave toward one another? How do the people organize themselves, connect, or relate to one another? What statuses and roles are evident? Who makes what decisions for whom?

    c.   What is the content of their conversations? What topics are common and rare? What languages do they use for verbal and nonverbal communication? What beliefs do the content of their conversations illustrate? What formats and processes do the conversations follow? Who talks and who listens?

3.   *Where* is the group or scene located? What physical settings form their contexts? What natural resources and technologies are created or used? How does the group allocate and use space and physical objects? What sights, sounds, smells, tastes, and feelings are found in the group contexts?

4.   *When* does the group meet and interact? How often and how long are these meetings? How does the group conceptualize, use, and distribute time? How do participants view their past and future?

5.   *How* do the identified elements connect or interrelate—from either the participants' viewpoint or the researcher's perspective? How is stability maintained? How does change originate, and how is it managed? What rules, norms, or mores govern this social organization? How is this group related to other groups, organizations, or institutions?

6.   *Why* does the group operate as it does? What meanings do participants attribute to what they do? What symbols, traditions, values, and world views can be found in the group?

Although no ethnographer addresses all these questions at once in studying a group scene, the framework does indicate major areas of participant observation foci.[7]

[7]See observation grids of Goetz & LeCompte, 1984; Hall, 1959; and Spradley, 1979.

Recording Observations.   Data are recorded as **field notes,** observations of what occurs while the ethnographer is in the field. Field notes are dated and the context is identified. The notes are often filled with idiosyncratic abbreviations and are difficult for others to read without editing. **Summary observations,** written immediately after leaving the site, synthesize the main interactions and scenes observed and, more important, suggest questions and tentative interpretations. In both the field notes and summary observations, the tentative interpretations, called "interpretative asides" or "observer's comments," are separated from the actual observations. Sometimes these insights have the quality of free associations: they may cite analogies, use metaphors and similes, or note theories and literature that may be useful in subsequent data analysis.

Both field notes and summary observations are presented as data in a study. Excerpt 11.7 illustrates presentation of data. Field notes record the difficulty of moving to a new school building in December. Two days later, the summary observation tries to make sense out of the move by referring to theories of intergroup conflict and cooperation to provide insights on faculty competition, the priority of goals, and the principal's leadership role.

Ethnographic Interviews

Ethnographic interviews, which are open-response questions to obtain data of *participant meanings,* may be the primary data collection strategy or a natural outgrowth of observation strategies. *Participant meanings* refer to how individuals in social scenes conceive of their world and how they explain or "make sense" of the important events in their lives. Ethnographic interviews vary in formats, specialized applications, question content, question sequence, and the logistics of conducting and recording interviews.

Types of Interviews and Specialized Applications.   Qualitative interviews may take several forms: the informal conversational interview, the interview guide approach, and the standardized open-ended interview. Each of these forms vary in their degree of structure and planning and the comparability of responses in data analysis. In the **informal conversational interview,** the questions emerge from the immediate context and are asked in the natural course of events; there is no predetermination of question topics or phrasing. Informal conversations are an integral part of participant observation. In the **interview guide approach,** topics are selected in advance but the researcher decides the sequence and wording of the questions during the interview. Both the informal conversational and the interview guide approach are relatively conversational and situational. In the **standardized open-ended interview,** participants are asked the same questions in the same order, thus reducing interviewer effects and bias, however, standardized wording of questions may constrain and limit the naturalness and relevancy of the response.

Selection of the interview strategy depends on the context and purpose: 1) to obtain the present perceptions of activities, roles, feelings, motivations, concerns,

---

EXCERPT 11.7
Summary Observations

(Note: The building is a new school. Eugene is the new principal.)

Later in the same day, the observers had just finished a brief visit to the building and they commented on the potential consequences of the move.

The building is so far from being ready that it is going to create a good many problems in implementing the program. The issue that keeps coming back to me again and again is that they are getting involved, once again, in situations that are not ready or are not prepared for them. And what should be a beautiful and happy move to a crystallized physical setting that can implement the kind of program they want seems very likely to degenerate into a move to another "almost ready" kind of temporary setting that must be lived with for the moment. This will take some of the edge and some of the excitement and some of the novelty off of the new building. And what could be a real plus in terms of having them get on top of the world again will probably be a minus (12/3).

Further aspects of the strategy of moving arose in the observer's speculations two days later, early on Saturday morning.

This morning I am trying to make sense out of some of the odds and ends left over from the images of the move in the last two days. For some reason the image that gets aroused is that of Sherif's book on the robber's cave experiment, *Intergroup Conflict and Cooperation.* The genesis of the ISD inter-team hostility was on grounds other than the competitiveness introduced by an outsider or by a leader. In a sense, however, the North and the South teams were fighting over the scarce resources. Or better, they soon came to be fighting over that whereas, initially, the problems arose in difficulty in points of view, in ends and means, and in holding to commitments. A very interesting problem would be to try to conceptualize superordinate goals that would, in effect, eliminate this. Perhaps, Eugene missed a very great opportunity. You have a "naturally defined" starting all over again that could have been generalized to a whole series of other things. As far as I know, this has not occurred and the opportunity if it is not taken this morning or this afternoon will be gone forever. This poses an interesting problem for the leader's role in that it puts him in the position of being able to perceive the problem, perceive the alternatives open to the solution of the problem, some of which could be derived from theories such as Sherif's, and then begin to implement them in some kind of fashion where he has legitimate power and authority. It becomes even more interesting, since Eugene has given away most of that legitimate power and authority. Seemingly, he has lost credits not only because he gave them away, but because the handling of many of the routine administrative chores has been so troublesome (12/5).

---

thoughts; 2) to obtain future expectations or anticipated experiences; 3) to verify and extend information obtained from other sources; and 4) to verify or extend hunches and ideas developed by the participants or ethnographer.

Specialized applications of the interview strategy are key-informant interviews, career and life-history interviews, and surveys. **Key-informant interviews** are in-depth interviews of individuals who have special knowledge, status, or communication skills who are willing to share that knowledge and skill with the researcher. They are usually chosen because they have access to observations unavailable to the ethnographer. They are often atypical individuals and must be selected carefully from among possible key informants.[8]

Career and life history interviews, which elicit life narratives of individuals, are used by anthropologists to obtain data about a culture. Educational ethnographers use this interview technique for career histories or narratives of professional lives. For example, when an examination of female elementary school teachers' notion of career differed from the prior research of men's careers, the ethnographer suggested that the concept of career should be extended to encompass professional women (Biklen, 1985). Career and life history research of educators frequently requires two- to seven-hour interviews and may take considerable time to locate the informants if the shared social experience occurred years ago. *Survey instruments*, usually used to verify other data, may take the form of confirmation-surveys, participant-constructed instruments, and even projective techniques with photographs, drawings, and games. Data of a preservice teacher induction activities, obtained through nine months of participant observation, for example, could be corroborated with a closed- and opened-response questionnaire administered to principals and participant-constructed instruments administered during planning retreats and workshops (Schumacher & Rommel-Esham, 1986). Key-informant interviews, career history interviews, and confirmation-surveys are typically used in conjunction with other data collection strategies.

Qualitative Questions.   Question content varies because of different research purposes and problems, theoretical frameworks, and the selection of research sites, participants, and contexts. Adopting questions from prior research will probably not produce valid interview data, however, the examination of different alternatives is essential in interview script construction.[9] A classification of questions is summarized below as an illustration (Patton, 1980, pp. 207–208).

1. *Experience/behavior questions* elicit what a person does or has done—descriptions of experiences, behaviors, actions, activities during the ethnographer's absence. In other words, if I had been here that day, what experiences would I see you having?

2. *Opinion/value questions* elicit what the person thinks about their experiences which can reveal a person's intentions, goals, and values—what would you like to see happen or what do you believe about . . . ?

3. *Feeling questions* elicit how the persons react emotionally to their experiences—do you feel anxious, happy, afraid, intimidated, confident about . . . ?

4. *Knowledge questions* elicit factual information the person has or what the person considers as factual—tell me what you know about . . . .

[8]See J. P. Spradley, *The Ethnographic Interview* (1979), for a detailed discussion of key-informant interviews.

[9]See Denzin, 1978; Lofland, 1984; Patton, 1980; Pelto and Pelto, 1978; Schatzman & Strauss, 1973; Spradley, 1979.

5. *Sensory questions* elicit the person's descriptions of what and how they see, hear, touch, taste, and smell in the world around them—what does the counselor ask you when you walk into her office? How does she actually greet you?

6. *Background/demographic questions* elicit the person's descriptions of themselves to aid the researcher in identifying and locating the persons in relation to other people—routine information on age, education, occupation, residence/mobility questions.

Each of the above six types of questions can be phrased in a present, past, or future time frame.

Qualitative interviewing requires asking truly open-ended questions. Novice researchers often begin with what data, usually referring to which answer, they want to obtain and phrase questions in a manner that interviewees can infer the desired responses. These are *dichotomous response questions* which elicit a yes/no or short phrases as a response. When these occur, the interview assumes an interrogative rather than a conversational interactive tone.

Several techniques to assure qualitative questions are: interview script critiques by experienced interviewers, interview guide field-testing, and revision of initial question phraseology for final phraseology to reveal the respondents' views of their world. Below are examples of initial phrasing with the field-test responses and the final phrasing of an interview guide (Schumacher, Esham, & Bauer, 1985, pp. 150–153).

Initial Dichotomous Response Questions	Final Qualitative Questions
Q: Did teachers have difficulty in the seminars? R: Yes.	Q: What did you expect teachers to have difficulties with in the seminar?
Q: Did teachers change? R: Some of them did.	Q: How did participation in the seminar affect the teachers?
Q: Did you learn anything in teaching the seminars? R: Yes.	Q: What did you learn about the teaching strategies you presented to this group?
Q: Did you identify any problems the Planning Committee should address? R: Yes.	Q: What would you like to see the Planning Committee do?

Although the above is an extreme example of responses to initial dichotomous response questions, it is obvious that the qualitative questions would (and did) generate different data, revealing multiple meanings of the seminars.

Dichotomous response questions can be *leading questions* which imply a preferred response. Leading questions may frame a "devil's advocate" or a *presupposition question*, a query that implies a deliberate assumption designed to provoke a complex or elaborate response. Examples in the left column are dichotomous response lead-in questions which were rephrased as presupposition lead-in questions in the right column from a study of the development of a collaborative teacher education program (Schumacher, 1984, pp. 75-82).

Dichotomous Response Lead-in Questions	*Presupposition Lead-in Questions*
Were inservice teachers enthusiastic about taking a class after school hours?	"What were the most difficult aspects [of the program] to implement?" (Presupposition: many difficulties.)
Did you expect the teachers to be different from having participated in the seminars?	"How did you expect the teachers to be different from having participated in the seminars?" (Presupposition: there was an immediate change.)
Do you know of any unexpected results or spill-over effects?	"How did the Planning Committee handle unanticipated opportunities?" (Presupposition: there were unexpected opportunities.)

Some interviewers emphasize the general ineffectiveness of questions preceded with the interrogative *why*. *Why* questions are usually assumptive, frequently ambiguous, and often too abstract to elicit concrete data. In some situations, however, beginning with the interrogative *why* enables the researcher to elicit cause-and-effect processses or relationships which are potentially informative by revealing assumptions about the world in which these persons live.

Question Sequence.   Effective interviewing depends on efficient probing and sequencing of questions. Guidelines are suggested below.

1. *Interview probes* elicit elaboration of detail, further explanations, and clarification of responses. Well-designed interview scripts are field tested to identify the placement and wording of probes necessary to adjust topics to the variation in individuals' responses. Researchers should talk less than the respondent; the cues respondents need can usually be reduced to a few words.

2. *Statements of the researcher's purpose and focus* are usually made at the onset. Assurances of protection of the person's identity and an overview of the possible discussion topics are given at this time. The information communicated is that the data are important, the reasons for that importance, and the willingness of the interviewer to explain the purpose of the interview in respect for the interviewee. Researchers provide explanations or shifts in the interview focus for informants to adopt their thinking along new areas.

3. *Order of questions* varies, although most ethnographers make choices to enable them to obtain adequate data for each question and use the informant efficiently. Rigid sequencing may assure comprehensiveness but it may also produce both informant and interviewer fatigue and boredom. Generally questions are grouped by topic, but in many instances, interviewers ignore the script sequence as people voluntarily elaborate on earlier replies.

4. *Demographic questions* may be spread throughout the interview or presented in the concluding remarks. Some researchers prefer to obtain this data at the beginning of the interview to establish rapport and focus attention.

5. *Complex, controversial, or difficult questions* are usually reserved for the middle or later periods in the interview when the informant's interest has been aroused. Some ethnographers prefer to begin interviews with descriptive, present-oriented questions and move to more complex issues of beliefs and explanations.

Interview Logistics.   Ethnographers choose interview topics and questions while planning the general logistics that influence an interview session. Five contingencies that affect an interview session are: 1) *duration,* or length of session; 2) *number,* or how many separate interviews are required to obtain the data; 3) *setting* or location of the interview; 4) *identity of the individuals* involved and the number present in the session;[10] and 5) *informant styles,* or communication mores of the interviewees. Some research designs plan for periodically scheduled interviews and other designs require interviewing only after important events.

Interviewers vary their interactive styles. Interactive modes can be adversarial, emotionally neutral but cognitively sophisticated, or empathetic. Specific techniques can be used for pacing, keeping control of the interview and appropriate usage of support and recognition. Most qualitative interviewers prefer a conversational tone to indicate empathy and understanding while conveying acceptance to encourage elaboration of subtle and valid data.

A variation of the ethnographic interview is the *focused group interview* (FGI), a strategy for obtaining a better understanding of a problem or an assessment of a problem, concerns, a new product, program, or idea by interviewing a purposefully sampled group of people rather than each person individually. By creating a social environment in which individual group members are stimulated by the perceptions, opinions and ideas of each other, one can increase the quality and richness of data through a more efficient strategy than one-on-one interviewing.[11]

Interview Records, Transcripts, and Elaborations.   The primary data of qualitative interviews are verbatim accounts of what transpires in the interview session. Tape recording the interview assures completeness of the verbal interaction and provides material for reliability checks, transcription, and playback with a record of nonverbal cues to search for deeper meanings. These advantages are offset with possible respondent distrust and mechanical failure. The use of a tape

---

[10]The number of interviewers at one session rarely exceeds two to maintain rapport with respondents. Schumacher and Rommel-Esham (1986) interviewed co-directors from two organizations to stimulate appropriate probes for questions.

[11]FGIs are used primarily in educational evaluation, however, sociologists originally developed the approach (Lofland 1984; Schatzman & Strauss, 1973). FGI is frequently done in marketing research, and to some extent in health care services and policy research (Hambrick, 1987). Hambrick (1987) suggests guidelines for FGIs.

recorder does not eliminate the need for taking notes to help reformulate questions and probes and to record nonverbal communication which facilitates data analysis. In many situations, handwritten notes may be the best method of recording. Interviewer-recording forces the interviewer to be attentive, can help control the pacing of the interview, and legitimizes the writing of researcher insights (beginning data analysis) during the interview. Neither notetaking nor tape recording, however, should interfere with the researcher's full attention on the person.

Immediately following the interview, the researcher completes and types the handwritten records, or transcribes the tape. Typed drafts will need to be edited for transcriber/typist error and put into final form. The final record contains accurate verbatim data and the interviewer's notation of nonverbal communication with initial insights and comments to enhance the search for meaning in subsequent data analysis. Interviewer notations and comments are usually identified by the interviewer's initials. The final form also includes the date, place, and informant identity. Excerpt 11.8 illustrates data obtained from ethnographic interviews.

Interviewers write *elaborations* of each interview session—self-reflections on his or her role and rapport, interviewee's reactions, additional information, and extensions of interview meanings. This activity is a critical time for reflection and elaboration to establish quality control for valid data. Many initial ideas developed at this time are subsequently checked out through other data collection activities. As a rule of thumb, for every hour of interviewing, a researcher usually allows four hours of further work to obtain the final record or transcript and the additional elaborations.

Artifact Collection

Artifact collection is a noninteractive strategy for obtaining ethnographic data with little or no reciprocity between the researcher and the participant. Artifact collection is less reactive than interactive strategies in that the researcher does not extract the evidence. During field residence in school settings, for example, ethnographers must interact with individuals even if only nonverbally—and become, to some degree, participants. This is *not* an impediment if the researcher notes the consequences of this interactive role. In contrast, artifact collection strategies are noninteractive[12] but may require imaginative fieldwork to locate relevant data.

Artifact collections, which are tangible manifestations of the beliefs and behaviors that form a culture, describe peoples' experience, knowledge, and

---

[12]Another noninteractive strategy is that of *nonparticipant observation.* Adaptations of this strategy commonly used by qualitative researchers are: 1) stream-of-behavior chronicles (see ecological psychology research tradition), 2) analysis of proxemics (details of bodily movement) and kinesics (interpersonal symbolic use of space; see E. T. Hall, 1959, 1966, 1974) and 3) interaction analysis protocols using Flander-like observation rating systems (see Medley & Mitzel, 1963).

EXCERPT 11.8
Ethnographic Interview

Mother: Playing with the other children in the street she'd pinch or something, like if she wanted to swing and they were on it she'd pinch them and then the kid would start crying and the mother would call me up and then she'd send Sally home. It was the same thing almost every day. There was just no peace. I mean, she couldn't play with the other children like the other ones did. She had no friends like the other ones did.

If the child was non-ambulatory and needed total care, parents described the later years as a time of utter exhaustion. Routines and activities of daily care such as bathing and feeding the child became less endurable as it became increasingly clear that these responsibilities would never be diminished, let alone ended completely. One father said he began to feel as if nobody else could understand the strain of caring for a completely disabled child day after day:

Father: A lot of these people (professionals), they say these things but they never really had to deal with Bobby. You know, we could show people Bobby for an hour and have them take care of Bobby—well, they would think Bobby was nothing. But you take care of him all day, it was a different thing. Trying to feed him . . . anybody could take care of anybody for an hour or so, it would be no problem, handicap or no handicap. But when they have to deal with him all day, that was a different story. Plus trying to take care of the other children besides.

Source: From *The Politics of Caring* by Susan Bannerman Foster (London: Falmer Press Ltd., 1987). Reprinted by permission of Falmer Press Ltd. and the author.

---

behaviors and connote their values, feelings, and perceptions. Educational ethnographers studying current groups have adopted the techniques of historians who analyze documents (see Chapter 12) and of archaeologists who examine objects created by ancient peoples.

Types of Artifacts.   Artifacts of present-day educational groups frequently take two forms: archival and demographic records collection, and physical trace collection.

1. *Archival and demographic record collections* are written and symbolic records kept by or on the participants in a social group. These usually take the form of official educational documents—memos, minutes of meetings, student papers, enrollment records, lesson plans, student personnel records, or government documents. Existing archival and demographic collections may be located while mapping the field and during field residence. School board minutes from 1915 to 1980, for example, were an important source in the study of an innovative school fifteen years after an ethnographic study and the original job applications of the school staff provided demographic clues to locate these persons for ethnographic interviews (L. M. Smith, Kleine, Prunty, & Dwyer, 1987). Records of planning meetings, for example, were used to infer the extent of collaboration between two

institutions (Schumacher, Esham, & Bauer, 1985). In the same study, a symbolic record was a newly created logo which combined parts of the emblems of the university and of the school system to represent a new relationship between the two organizations. Interactive data revealed the difficulties surmounted to obtain official approval to use institutional emblems in a new form. The data obtained the following year described the use of the new logo. Archival collections may also be researcher-stimulated such as teacher diaries, logs, and written recollections.

2. **Physical trace collections** are *erosion measures* where the degree of selective wear on some material yields the measure and *accretion measures* where the research evidence consists of natural objects produced or used by a group. Examples of erosion measures are the pathways students make across outside school grounds or the wear of vinyl tiles in specific hallways as suggestive of frequency of use and possible social gatherings. Although erosion is the measure, the interpretation of the erosion rate derives from a check with the records of ground and building maintenance for grass reseeding and tile replacement during the last five years.

Natural objects or accretion measures are remnants of recent activity accumulated without researcher interaction. Anthropologists have used people's garbage to discover from wasted foodstuffs the differences in dietary patterns related to social class. Qualitative evaluators may investigate the teacher-value of students' work by periodically checking bulletin board displays in elementary classrooms. An evaluator can then corroborate this finding with other ethnographic data. For example, photographing art objects as students created their shapes and forms in a study of creativity in gifted students could be analyzed if students usually took their final art products home to parents. Content analysis of a jointly produced slidetape of two institutions, for example, suggests the value and definition of the nature of collaboration in a teacher education program (Schumacher & Rommel-Esham, 1986).

Analysis and Interpretation of Artifact Collections.   Collection and analysis of artifacts requires five strategies:

1. *Location of artifacts* begins with mapping the field and continues during field residence. Ethnographers anticipate the artifacts and proceed to locate and obtain documents and objects.

2. *Identification of artifacts* requires placing the artifact in retrievable form and cataloguing for access. Documents are xeroxed; objects are photographed, filmed, or taped. Identifications are made by noting the category of artifacts, a brief description of the artifact, a history of its use and owners/successors, and data on frequency and representativeness.

3. *Analysis of artifacts* requires descriptive data about the production or acquisition of the artifact by the group. Important questions are who uses it, how is it used, where is it used, and the purpose of its use.

4. *Criticism of artifacts* is the determination of its authenticity and accuracy (see Chapter 12) to identify the meanings of the artifact in the social setting.

5. *Interpretation of artifact meanings* must then be corroborated with observation and interview data. Artifact interpretation for subtle meanings depends upon the social context and other data.

■ QUALITATIVE DATA ANALYSIS ■
AND PRESENTATION

Data analysis is an ongoing cyclical process integrated into all phases of qualitative research. (See Figure 5.4 in Chapter 5.) Data analysis leads initially to a narrative or "story" about the people examined and their social world. Data analysis is *not* data reduction, a quantitative approach, nor is it dependent upon computer data storage-retrieval systems and word processing programs. Because the analysis appears less exact than statistical procedures, readers often view the techniques as less rigorous. Qualitative analysis, however, is a systematic process of selecting, categorizing, comparing, synthesizing, and interpreting to provide explanations of the single phenomenon of interest. Throughout the process, the ethnographer qualitatively assesses the trustworthiness of the data but does *not* conduct formal verification for universal propositions. Qualitative data analysis varies widely because of the different research foci, purposes, and data collection strategies.

Data analysis entails several cyclical phases which are:

1) continuous discovery, especially in the field but also throughout the entire study, so as to identify tentative themes and develop concepts and mini-theories;

2) categorizing and ordering of data, typically after data collection, so as to *refine* one's understanding of patterns and themes;

3) qualitatively assessing the trustworthiness of the data, so as to *refine* one's understanding of the setting and social scenes.[13]

Most ethnographers have learned that 1) there is no set of standard procedures for data analysis and for keeping track of data analysis strategies for the methodology presentation; 2) although the data analysis is inductive, a deductive mode of thinking at appropriate times is used—moving back and forth between analyzing raw data and recasting tentative analyses at each phase of building to more abstract levels of synthesis; and 3) "making sense" of the data depends largely on their *intellectual rigor* and a tolerance for tentativeness of interpretation until the entire analysis is completed.

Ethnographers rarely make explicit their data analysis strategies in a manner which satisfies quantitative researchers. Excerpt 11.9 provides two examples of statements of qualitative data analysis. Ethnographers are not trying to be magical or mysterious; inductive data analysis is more difficult to express briefly than statistical analysis. This discussion illustrates the systematic approach a researcher uses without limiting one's subjective analytical processes or "forcing" the data into predispositions.

---

[13]These strategies are called "discounting data" (Taylor & Bogdan, 1984, pp. 140–142), "validation and verification" (Patton, 1980, pp. 326–339), "trustworthiness criteria" (Lincoln & Guba, 1985, pp. 301–316); "negative-case and discrepant-case selection" (Goetz & LeCompte, 1984, pp. 174–176); and "tactics for testing or confirming findings" (Miles & Huberman, 1984, pp. 230–242).

> ## EXCERPT 11.9
> ### Inductive Analysis

11.9A

The analytical process that we fell into years ago was simple: 1) read along; 2) stop after each item—sentence, paragraph, or longer more involved episode; 3) ask oneself what does it mean; 4) figure out a tentative label or heading; 5) write a paragraph or few pages quickly to exhaust the immediate meaning; 6) build a little sketch or tentative model of any larger conceptualization (miniature theory?) of which it might be a part; 7) do it while it's hot rather than reading on for full significance of meaning, figuring that will come anyway; 8) accumulate lots of the little pieces; 9) gradually seek order and integration into larger patterns.

11.9B

Data Analysis. Although I completed some analysis of data while in the field—for example, developing analytic questions and concepts which serve to focus data collection, trying out themes on subjects—most of the analysis was done after leaving the field. In general, I followed the suggestions for data analysis outlined by Bogdan and Biklen (1982). I read through all the data, jotting down ideas, words, and phrases, and patterns of behavior. These notes later formed the basis for 'coding', a process by which the data are sorted into topic categories. Once I developed the list of coding categories, I went through the data again, organizing them according to my codes.

At the end of this procedure, I had thirty-five folders, each holding all the data relative to the particular code. Examples of codes include 'descriptions of the Weston Center', 'parents' perceptions of the admissions process', and 'cooling parents out'. These thirty-five codes, in combination with my memos and the literature I had been reading throughout the study, formed the foundation for the final report.

11.9A *Source:* From "Educational Innovation: A Life History Research Perspective" by Louis M. Smith and Paul F. Kline. Presented at the conference, *Teachers' Careers and Life Histories*, St. Hilda's College, Oxford University, September 1983. Reprinted by permission of Louis M. Smith.
11.9B *Source:* From *The Politics of Caring* by Susan Bannerman Foster (London: Falmer Press Ltd., 1987). Reprinted by permission of Falmer Press Ltd. and the author.

Inductive Analysis

Inductive analysis means the patterns, themes, and categories of analysis emerge from the data rather than being imposed on data prior to data collection and analysis as done in verification research.[14] Inductive analysis is the process of 1) discovery analysis in the field, 2) preliminary analysis of the data, 3) categori-

---

[14]Inductive analysis should not be confused with analytical induction. Taylor and Bogan (1984, pp. 125–142) discuss two approaches in data analysis: grounded theory approach and analytic induction procedures which qualitatively develop *and* verify or test universal propositions and causal laws.

zation and ordering data to identify emerging patterns and themes, 4) descriptive-analytical synthesis, and 5) may extend the analysis to integrate major findings to propose grounded concepts and mini-theories. The strategies below can only serve as a guideline to qualitative analysis.

Discovery Analysis in the Field.   Because ethnographers, unlike soothsayers, do not know what exactly will unfold in the field, they sequentially select the final foci of a study. Some approaches which facilitate the sequential selection of the research foci are: the selection of foreshadowed problems, the choice of conceptual and theoretical frameworks, the data collection strategies actually used in the study including purposeful sampling in the field, and preliminary data analysis in the field. Ethnographers may find that initial theoretical frameworks are inadequate for illumination of the deeper meanings of people's social "reality" and may either narrow, broaden, or change the theoretical thrust during data collection and formal data analysis. Choosing data collection strategies in the field and assessing the validity of the data as it is collected aids in focusing the research. No ethnographer reports all the data; focusing the study before, during, and even after data collection is necessary.

Below are some discovery analysis strategies which experienced ethnographers use to develop tentative and preliminary ideas.

- Write many "observer comments" and "elaborations" in the field notes to identify themes, hunches, interpretations, questions.
- Write summary-observations and memos to synthesize and focus the study.
- Construct exploratory data displays from data as it is collected.
- Play with ideas, an intuitive process, to develop themes and concepts.
- Begin exploring the literature while in the field and write how it helps or contrasts to observations.
- Play with metaphors and analogies, not to label, but to flush out ideas or capture the essence of what is observed and the dynamics of social situations.
- Try out emerging ideas and themes on the participants to clarify ideas.

Ethnographers learn to balance speculation and divergent thinking with accurate recording. The facts and details are a means, not an end, to generate ideas, themes, and concepts. The detailed findings are soon forgotten in social science, but not the concepts and ideas.

Preliminary Data Analysis.   Preliminary data analysis is the first step in making sense out of mounds of data—recognizing patterns that emerge in the data. *Looking for patterns means examining the data in as many ways as possible.* Ethnographers with prolonged field residences are often surprised at the ideas generated in the field and recorded in their notes. Identifying regularities, configurations, and clusters of meaning suggests patterns.

Strategies some ethnographers use are:

1. Organizing the data. All pages of field notes, transcripts, and artifacts collections are numbered sequentially to help locate the data. Because working with

data means extensive rearrangement of it either manually or by computer, several copies are made and one is retained as a permanent copy.

2. Scanning all data for possible categories and the topics the data contain. By the time intensive categorization and ordering data is done (next phase), the researcher "knows" the data.

3. Looking for themes, patterns, and ideas. Themes come from conversations, topics, language in the social settings, recurring activities, feelings, folk sayings and the ethnographer's "interpretative asides," elaborations, and memos. Some patterns are obvious; others are discovered only through later analysis.

4. Writing memos about the regularities and clusters of meaning.

5. Reading the literature for what has been done in the topic and for useful concepts, models, or theories to help understand the data. Frequently the researcher finds useful literature in a totally different substantive area. The ethnographer does not force the data into *a priori* framework but instead *explores* different ways of looking at the data.

6. Refocusing the inquiry for *this* particular data analysis and study. Most ethnographic data can be used for several studies. Once again, the researcher narrows the focus for the intensive data analysis.

Categorizing and Ordering Data.   **Categorizing and ordering data** *are inductive processes of divergent thinking and logical analysis to refine the researcher's understanding of the emerging patterns and themes.* Although this process appears mechanical with the use of codes, it requires cognitive flexibility. The time required depends partially on the amount of data, resources for working with data, and purposes. By categorizing and ordering data, the researcher is inductively identifying "chunks of meaning" (Marshall, 1981). "Chunks" are potentially meaningful data; they relate to the research foci and purpose. The purpose of the research influences the generation of categories: some foreshadowed problems and evaluation concerns generate obvious categories; grounded theory-oriented studies may emphasize other categories.

Ethnographers have found the following strategies useful in categorizing, sorting and ordering data. Listing the strategies does *not* imply these are discrete, step-by-step processes.

1. *Categorize* by **constant comparison** (Glaser & Strauss, 1967), noting the similarities and differences. For example, all possible incidents of production of art forms by gifted children in the program was a category in a study of creativity (Loomer, 1982). This category was sorted into instances of creativity and noncreativity by students.

2. *Sort* each instance several ways (sometimes called "coding") to identify patterns. In a study of principals and unsatisfactory teachers, the category of unsatisfactory teachers was sorted first by types of unsatisfactory teachers and then by types of resolutions (Luck, 1985). Each category was rearranged to see if there was a pattern between type of unsatisfactory teacher and type of resolution. When no pattern was found, another category was created—methods of identification of unsatisfactory teachers. This category led to an emerging pattern.

3. *Identify* the attributes of each potential category and state a *tentative name* for the category which captures its essence, the "chunk of meaning". The *preferred name is one which comes from the data.* For example, one instructor described the conference room as the "hub" in every clinical location of the psychiatric nursing rotation (Rosenthal, 1987), or Geoffrey described one of his teaching roles as "ringmaster" (Smith & Geoffrey, 1968). These *indigenous categories* form a classification system which divides some aspect of the world into parts from the participants' constructions. A provisional name may be developed by the researcher from general knowledge which captures the essence and is meaningful to the participants, yet was not heard in the site.

4. *Order* the categories. Ordering the categories is enlarging, combining, subsuming and creating new categories that make empirical and logical sense—they "go together" in meaning. Through divergent thinking, patterns and themes are refined. Categories may be expanded to include other data, subsumed into other categories, or created for a miscellaneous category, such as data which is meaningful but fits no category. Some miscellaneous incidents now appear clearly irrelevant to the research focus and others are incomplete categories which need further analysis.

Gauging the Trustworthiness of the Data.   At each phase of the data analysis, ethnographers qualitatively assess **data trustworthiness,** which is the extent to which emerging categories, patterns, and themes reflect valid and reliable data. Ethnographers vary in how explicit they make this process and its integration with data analyses. Estimating the quality of the data and one's understanding of it takes many forms; three major analysis strategies are searching for negative evidence, using triangulation, and constructing data displays.

1. *Look for negative evidence,* which refutes a construction such as an exceptional or discrepant instance. Because most ethnographers use comprehensive selection (collecting all possible instances from many participants, not knowing in advance what is categorized later as an extreme-case, unique-case, or critical-case), these exceptions to a pattern are usually present in the data. Exceptions yield insights to enable the ethnographer to modify the emerging patterns and themes.

2. *Use* **triangulation** (Denzin, 1978), which is the cross-validation among data sources, data collection strategies, time periods, and theoretical schemes (see Figure 11.1). The ethnographer "weighs" the evidence or selects trustworthy evidence, that evidence which suggests a regularity or pattern by sifting through evidence and qualitatively assessing solicited versus unsolicited data, observer's influences on the social scene, subtle influences among the people present in the setting, specific versus vague statements about a theme, the contextual accuracy of the sources (an observant person? a thoughtful person? an emotional person? a biased person?) and the ethnographer's assumptions, predispositions, and self-reflections. A theme of "institutional collaboration," for example, could be cross-checked by comparing data found in artifact collections (minutes, memos, official brochures, letters), informants (project co-directors, teachers, principals), and ethnographic observation. When insufficient data exist for some instances, events, or processes, such incidents may not be part of a pattern or may be sub-

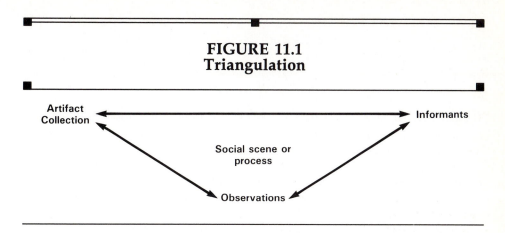

FIGURE 11.1
Triangulation

sumed into a larger pattern. Ethnographers know, however, that even though they only observed and recorded one instance, for some purposes a single incident is meaningful.

3. *Construct* **data displays,** an organized assembly of information, such as figures, matrices, and flow charts, which assist in the analysis. There are many forms of data displays. One example is the chart in Excerpt 11.11. Many ethnographers using a discovery approach are cautious not to reach hasty closure in building data displays. Descriptive contextual data must accompany data displays, an abstraction which limits the types of interpretations which can be drawn. Data displays are devices to assist in a more abstract analysis and are not "reality" per se. The ethnographer attempts to balance a respect for the complexity of reality with the need to simplify for analytical and communication purposes.

Presentation of Findings: Levels of Abstraction

A hallmark of ethnographic studies is the lengthy narrative presentation and the lack of statistical tables. Data are presented in descriptive language citing field notes and quotations from participants with data displays. For most ethnographic studies the data are overwhelming—files of field notes, bookcases of documents, and notebooks of summary observations. Not all observations are reported in a single study. Selection of the final and major focus on the study is based on the complexities of the naturalistic event and the level of abstraction desired for presenting the results (the purpose of the research).

Ethnographic studies describe the **context** of the naturalistic event, the site and the selected settings and social scenes, the participants, and the entire data collection time period. All proper names are coded for confidentiality. Smith and Keith (1971), for example, describe in detail the new school building, the new staff members, and the faculty mandate for the academic year. The description of the setting is so vivid that if readers had been there they would recognize the school building, identify the principal and team leaders at Kensington, and sense the ex-

EXCERPT 11.10
Presentation of Findings: An Analytical Interpretation

The parents in this study had learned ways of thinking about parenting and disabled people before their child was born. Later they learned about life with a disabled child. In adapting to their new and unanticipated situation, they adjusted their expectations for themselves and their child. Informed by others as well as their own experience, they met the challenges of raising a disabled child as best as they could. Professionals, family, friends, television, and popular literature were all influential. Attempts to explain their decisions and behaviors must take all these influences into account.

The perspectives of the parents included in this study changed over time. These changes illustrate their efforts to redefine themselves and their child, in light of their experiences and expectations.

There are four major areas in which the parents' perspectives changed dramatically over time. The first is 'hope to despair'. After the initial shock of discovery, parents were hopeful about their child's potential for development. Later they lost this hope. The second is 'energy to exhaustion'. Parents tackled their child's problems with energy in early years. Later they talked more about the strain and burden the child had become. Third, parents shifted from a sense of 'self-confidence to reliance on experts'. Parents felt capable of caring for their handicapped child when the child was young. As the child got older, they said they couldn't handle the child and deferred to others as experts. The fourth area of change is 'parents in control to others in control'. Parents' descriptions of the early years were full of references to their 'responsibility as parents'. In deciding to institutionalize the child, parents said they were 'giving their child away' and that others are now responsible for the child.

These parents were confronted by an unexpected and unwanted situation with the news of their child's disabilities. In response, they were forced to reappraise their most basic understandings of such concepts as handicap, family, and the limits of parental responsibility. Within this new framework, the decision to institutionalize the disabled child became a necessary, and acceptable action.

By listening to parents and taking them seriously, the decision to institutionalize can be understood as part of a history of experiences, rather than an isolated incident. Although institutionalization was not an inevitable outcome of their experiences, it was at least an understandable decision, deeply rooted in the history of the family. The decision was not made capriciously, nor will it easily be reversed.

Source: From *The Politics of Caring* by Susan Bannerman Foster (London: Falmer Press Ltd., 1987). Reprinted by permission of Falmer Press Ltd. and the author.

citement, the frustrations, the joys, and the problems of the opening of the new school building. By placing the setting in the context of educational organizations and processes, a reader can note aspects that appear particular to the setting and those that seem similar to the broader array of educational phenomena.

The presentation of results depends on the intended level of abstraction. Levels of abstraction used in presenting the results may classify the study as a descriptive narration, an analytical interpretation, or a theoretical exploration. Each of these kinds of studies make different contributions to social science and applied research.

Descriptive Narration.   In a descriptive narration, the focus is usually on groups and their activities that changed over time. The narration, in lay language, is a story of the events, based on the common sense explanations of the participants, that synthesizes the reasons the events occurred as they did. A descriptive narration closely resembles that of investigative reporting. The study contributes to knowledge by preserving a record of a past event made by a trained observer. This description may be used in subsequent research.

Descriptive-analytical Interpretation.   A second level of abstraction is one of description, analysis, and interpretation. The ethnographer selectively analyzes aspects of human actions and events to provide explanations. The complexity and the interrelationships of the events and in human lives are emphasized. The study contributes to knowledge by providing an understanding of the phenomena studied. This type of study also enables others to anticipate, but not predict, what may occur in similar situations. A reader of Wolcott (1973), for example, would gain an understanding of the difficulties of the principal's role and could anticipate that other principals might have complex roles. Excerpt 11.10 illustrates the presentation of an analytical interpretation.

Grounded Theoretical Research.   Other studies go beyond descriptive analysis to add a theoretical dimension. Miniature or middle-range theories seem appropriate for ethnographic studies. Concepts induced from observations are derived from the data and therefore, are called "grounded" theory. Grounded theory differs from quantitative research where theoretical constructs are deduced from theory identified in the literature review. Examples of concepts developed in ethnographic studies are "conceptual clarity" by Smith and Schumacher (1972) and "realistic opportunism" by Schumacher (1979). The relationships between two or more concepts are the bases for hypotheses and theories. Ethnographic studies have developed miniature theories of pupil roles (Smith & Geoffrey, 1968), of individualized instruction (Smith & Keith, 1971), and of involuntary superintendent turnover (Iannaccone & Lutz, 1970) to name a few. Excerpt 11.11 demonstrates a method of presenting theoretical findings with a data display of the intended and unintended consequences of the "alternative of grandeur" strategy of innovation in the Kensington study (Smith & Keith, 1971) and contrasts it with another strategy, "gradualism" in the literature.[15]

[15]Research phases can move a descriptive-analytical study to a grounded theoretical exploration as Schumacher did with 1970–71 data in 1972, 1975, and 1976 (*cf.* Goetz & LeCompte, pp. 195–205). Theoretical emphases augment the significance of the study but usually require more of a commitment to inference-making, divergent thinking, and time than doctoral students are willing to make. The use of metaphors and analogies and an interdisciplinary knowledge of theories are essential.

EXCERPT 11.11
Presentation of Findings: A Theoretical Model

THE ALTERNATIVE OF GRANDEUR: A STRATEGY OF INNOVATION

The Rationale and the Realities. When one begins to change a society, an institution, or a school, the system interlinkages present an ever-increasing multiplicity of items open for change. This poses the decision of the degree of change to be attempted. Our observations of Kensington suggest that they chose what we have called "the alternative of grandeur": the change was to be pervasive. This decision had a number of important consequences. As we have stated several times, the strategies of educational innovation were not high in our initial research priorities, although we were intrigued from the start with some of the specific innovative procedures, . . .

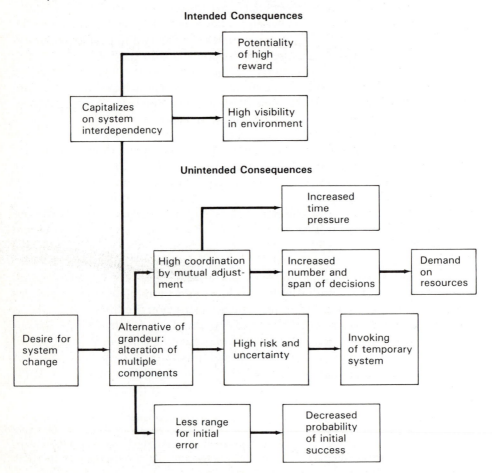

At this point, our theoretical analysis suggests that the concepts of unanticipated consequences, unintended outcomes, and the magnitude of resources are vital to anyone contemplating change. A more pervasive change is accompanied by more unanticipated events. The more outcomes that are unanticipated, the greater becomes the need for additional resources both to implement the program and to respond to the increased variety introduced by the unintended events. A step-by-step gradual shift would seem to temper this chain of events. . .In short, the simultaneous change in persons, interactions, programs, and structures illustrates the strengths and weaknesses of the high degree of interdependency implicit in the alternative of grandeur. . . .

Gradualism: An Alternative Strategy. After we had phrased the Kensington strategy of innovation as "the alternative of grandeur," we became acquainted with Etzioni's (1966) essay, "A gradualist strategy at work." Our reading of this case-study essay of the European Economic Community, EEC, suggests the broader theoretical significance of the kind of analysis we have been attempting. He contrasts a revolutionary strategy, our alternative of grandeur, with a strategy of gradualism. His broad generalization, "aim high, score low: aim low, score high," supports the gradualist position. In his analysis, a strong negative correlation exists between the level of ambition and the degree of success. The mediating mechanisms underlying these results are several, and they contrast with the dynamics observed at Kensington.

■ THE IMPORTANCE OF ETHNOGRAPHIC ■ METHODOLOGY IN RESEARCH

Ethnographic strategies, because of their flexibility and adoptability to a range of contexts, processes, people and foci, are some of the most useful methods available in educational research. The impact of ethnographic research on educational inquiry is a dynamic one—for the methodology allows researchers to discover what *are* the important questions to ask of a topic and what *are* the important topics in education to pursue through empirical methods. Without the continual stimulation of new ideas, educational research could become stagnant and filled with rhetorical abstractions.

Ethnographic methodology is used in basic, applied, and evaluation research. Ethnographic studies examine questions to develop social science and educational theories, provide descriptive-analytical interpretations of educational phenomena, and assess the worth of a practice. Ethnographic research contributes in several ways to the development of research-based knowledge.

Theoretical Contributions.   Ethnography is an appropriate methodology in exploratory and discovery-oriented research. *Exploratory studies,* which examine a topic in which there has been little previous research, are designed to lead to

FIGURE 11.2
Ethnographic Inquiry and Education Research

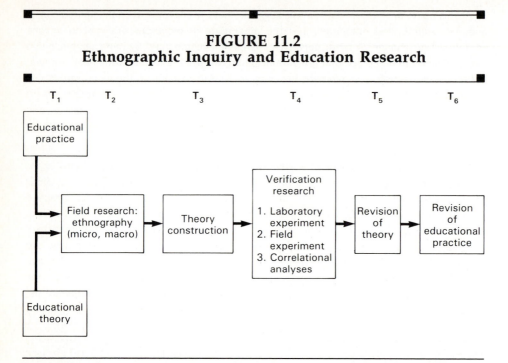

Source: From Smith, L. M. and Geoffrey, W., *The Complexities of the Urban Classroom: An Analysis Toward a General Theory of Teaching* (New York: Holt, Rinehart and Winston, 1968). Reprinted by permission of Louis M. Smith.

further inquiry. The focus may be educational events or processes. Ethnography is an alternative methodology when measurement problems in a research area limit data validity. Figure 11.2 demonstrates the function of ethnographic studies in the scientific process and its relation to educational theories and practices.

Contribution of Preponderance of Evidence. A series of ethnographies with similar research foci, conducted *independently* by different researchers in different settings over a *span of years,* may contribute to educational knowledge through the preponderance of evidence accumulated. Specific areas of education for which quantitative designs were inadequate have begun to accumulate case-study evidence. One example is a model of pedagogical reasoning developed from case studies of "expert" professional secondary teachers (Shulman, 1987). The increase in informed readers and trained ethnographic researchers augments this potential contribution of case study research similar to that found in medical and legal research.[16] Until quantitative design difficulties can be resolved, knowledge based on preponderance of evidence cannot be ignored easily.

[16]Traditional training is through apprenticeship and colleagueship. Learning field work is only part of the larger process of becoming a social scientist. Ethnographers who continue to develop their skills are curiosity-seekers, puzzle-solvers, and careful recorders (Junker, 1960). More recently, as many as four methodology courses may be required in doctoral training for ethnographic research.

Contribution in Large-scale Research Projects.   Ethnography is appropriate in large-scale research projects that involve a number of research specialists. Campbell stated that qualitative case study designs that "regularly contradict the prior expectations . . . are convincing and informative," have "a probing and testing power," and "validly pick up unanticipated effects missed by more structural approaches" (1974, pp. 24–25). He suggests that in large-scale projects where specialists produce partial knowledge, "a project anthropologist, sociologist, or historian, assigned to the task of common-sense acquaintance with the overall context including the social interactions producing the measures, could often fill this gap" (p. 25). Ethnography addresses the processes and interrelationships among substudies that may aid in the interpretation of more narrowly focused studies.

Contributions in Evaluation Research.   Ethnography is appropriate in evaluation studies when the program or innovation must be studied systematically before more structured designs can be developed. Multiple data collection strategies are especially useful in formative evaluation (see Chapter 13). Ethnographic methodologies can be used when the evaluation is responsive to many audiences representing different values that are internal and external to the educational program; when evaluation findings need to be communicated in nontechnical language; when the context of the events is important and self-evaluation by the participants is desired; when the scope of the program evaluation is broad, including strengths, weaknesses, and side effects anticipated and unanticipated; when process evaluation is desired and when the focus is evaluation of individualized outcomes with case studies.

Precursor to Quantitative Research.   Researchers using more structured designs and statistical analysis sometimes conduct a preliminary ethnographic study. Before using a structured observation schedule, researchers may observe social scenes and collect a stream-of-behavior chronicle or participant-observation data. Ethnographic interviews of a few individuals can aid in the selection of question content and phrasing for questionnaire construction.

■ THE STANDARDS OF ADEQUACY ■
FOR ETHNOGRAPHIC STUDIES

Standards for assessing the quality of ethnographic studies differ from those applied to quantitative studies. Most ethnographic studies are published as books rather than as journal articles. The number of chapters in an ethnographic study may vary from five to nine. The literature may be presented in a separate chapter or may be woven into the substance of the findings. In the last chapter, most studies contrast the results with previous research. Those studies published in journals are highly synthesized or only one of many findings is reported to fit the journal format. The typical journal article may also reduce the methodological procedures that should be explicit in the full study.

A reader appraises the quality of an ethnographic study in four aspects: the focus and purpose of the study, the research design and methodology, the presentation of the findings and conclusions, and the contribution to educational research and knowledge. Questions that aid a reader in judging the adequacy of a study in each of these aspects are listed below.

Focus and Purpose of the Study.   The following questions help a reader ascertain and evaluate the focus and purpose of a study.

1. Is the focus or topic of the study clearly stated?
2. Are the foreshadowed problems to be addressed in the findings presented?
3. Is the context of the study noted—time period, people, event, site characteristics—such as in a study of the *first* year of school integration in a *metropolitan* district?
4. Are the conceptual and theoretical frameworks chosen for the study stated—that is, organizational, sociological, psychological, political?
5. Does the researcher convey a knowledge of previous research and literature on the topic?
6. Is the purpose of the study stated, such as: to provide a descriptive narration of a naturalistic event, to analyze and interpret an event, or to discover new concepts and theories for verification research?

Research Design and Methodology.   The research design and methodology may be found in an introductory chapter or in a separate chapter. Sufficient information should be presented for the reader to judge the adequacy of the data collection methods, including the limitations. A reader also indirectly assesses the ability of the ethnographer to move beyond his or her own perspective. The following questions will aid a reader:

1. How long was the field residence? What social scenes were observed and which participants were interviewed?
2. What was the research role assumed by the ethnographer and how did this role affect data collection?
3. Did the ethnographer actively seek different perspectives? Were multiple data collection strategies employed?
4. What was the training, background, and previous field work experience of the ethnographer?
5. Does the evidence presented, such as the use of participants' language, indicate an inductive analysis?
6. Are the limitations of the study, in both design and data collection strategies, recognized?

Presentation of Findings.   The major body of an ethnographic study is the presentation of the findings and conclusions. A reader assesses the adequacy of the presentation by asking:

1. Are the social scenes described, enabling a reader to recognize the mundane and gain a sense of the totality?
2. Are the descriptions of the participants, actions, and processes so vivid and detailed that a reader feels as if he or she was there?
3. Is the level of abstraction appropriate for the stated purpose of the study—that is, description, analytical-interpretation, theoretical?
4. Are multiple perspectives presented, corroborated, and synthesized, with negative evidence cited?
5. Are the interpretations and explanations reasonable and logically derived from the findings presented?
6. Are personal feelings and insights clearly separated from data, that is, quoting "interpretative asides" or writing an epilogue as distinct from research findings?

Contributions to Knowledge and Further Research.   It is the responsibility of the ethnographer to state how the study makes its contributions. The following questions aid in assessing this aspect:

1. Does the study contribute to knowledge by preserving a historical record of a naturalistic event?
2. Does the study further understanding by detailed analytical-interpretation of a previously studied problem? How do the findings contrast or extend previous research?
3. Does the study suggest further research by the discovery of new concepts or mini-theories that could be verified in later research?
4. Does the study identify new research questions to be investigated in subsequent research?
5. Is there a logical relationship between the stated purpose and how the findings contribute to knowledge and further research?

Readers often criticize ethnographic studies on inappropriate grounds. A reader may wish the ethnographer had asked another question or reported some interesting but irrelevant details. Only the ethnographer can judge the quality of the data and decide the focus and specific research questions. A second inappropriate criticism is that of preferring a different conceptualization, such as psychological analysis rather than a political analysis. The choice of an analytical framework is the ethnographer's, but it should be stated clearly.

Ethnographic studies can be read at different levels of understanding. Persons familiar with research but uninformed in ethnography would note whether the elements of any empirical study—problem statement, conceptual and theoretical framework, literature review, methodology, findings, and conclusions—are present. In other words, they would note whether the study was done systematically and carefully. Trained and experienced ethnographers not only note these elements, but also make judgments about the quality of the study. The quality of the study is determined by the logical relationship among the purpose, methodology, findings, and contributions to educational research and knowledge.

■ SUMMARY ■

The following statements summarize the major characteristics of ethnographic research:

1. Qualitative approaches, derived from sub-fields of anthropology, sociology, and psychology, vary in educational research.
2. Qualitative research differs from quantitative research in its assumptions about the world, purpose, research methods and process, researcher role, context sensitivity, concept analysis, and the discovery-orientation of the research.
3. Educational ethnographies are analytical descriptions of social scenes and groups which recreate for the reader the shared actions, thinking, and beliefs of those people in an educational activity.
4. Foreshadowed problems emphasize naturalistic discovery, state the initial focus and conceptual frameworks, and guide the field work, but do not limit observations, because other research foci may develop at the site.
5. Most ethnographic research is a case study design to examine one phenomenon in-depth at a selected site, regardless of the number of participants, settings, processes, and activities.
6. Site selection is guided by the criteria implied in the foreshadowed problems and concerns of suitability and feasibility.
7. The ethnographer assumes an interactive research role to collect valid data for the research purpose and foci.
8. The ethnographer first maps the field—temporal, spacial, and social mapping—to obtain a sense of the total context and for purposeful sampling, therefore gaining a selection of information-rich informants and social scenes.
9. Data collection strategies use multimethods, such as participant observation, ethnographic interviews, and artifact collection.
10. Participant observation strategy is a prolonged field residence to obtain and corroborate salient observations of different perspectives, that is, multiple constructed realities recorded in field notes and summary observations.
11. Ethnographic interviews vary in the kinds of questions posed, question sequence, interview logistics, and interview records to obtain participant meanings of their world.
12. Artifact collections are archival and demographic records and physical traces which must be corroborated with other evidence.
13. Inductive analysis uses strategies for: a) discovery analysis in the field, b) preliminary data analysis, c) categorization and ordering data, and d) appraising data trustworthiness with negative evidence, triangulation, and data displays.
14. Data can be presented in one of three possible levels of abstraction: a descriptive narration, a descriptive-analytical interpretation, or as a grounded-theoretical study.

15. Ethnographic methodology contributes to research-based knowledge by a) proposing grounded theory, b) accumulating a preponderance of evidence in case-studies, c) providing contextual and holistic data in large-scale research projects, d) facilitating specific forms of evaluation research and e) serving as a precursor to quantitative research.

16. Readers appraise the quality of an ethnographic study in four aspects: a) focus and purpose of the study, b) research design and methodology, c) presentation of findings, and d) the contribution to educational knowledge and research.

■ SELF-INSTRUCTIONAL REVIEW EXERCISES ■

Sample answers are in the back of the book.

Test Items

1. Which statement connotes qualitative research?
   a. There is a single reality which is separate from individual and collective definitions of the situation.
   b. The researcher seeks to understand social phenomena from the participants' perspective through interactive data collection strategies.
   c. The ideal researcher role is one of detachment.
   d. The study ignores the context of the social scenes and the setting.

2. The origins of the research problem in ethnography is primarily from
   a. an extensive review of the literature.
   b. the ethnographer's prior personal experience.
   c. deductions from previous experimental studies.
   d. the ethnographer's experience in the setting.

3. The ethnographic research problem begins with
   a. a relatively general research question and foreshadowed problems.
   b. a research hypothesis.
   c. a list of variables.
   d. a statistical hypothesis.

4. A statement of foreshadowed problems indicates that the ethnographer will
   a. adhere rigidly to these preconceived ideas.
   b. observe only those problems anticipated.
   c. reformulate these problems in the field during data collection.
   d. test theories for verification studies.

5. Case study design refers to
   a. the size and representativeness of the sample.
   b. the comparison of two groups, experimental, and control.

    c. clinical and medical case histories.

    d. the one phenomenon which the researcher seeks to understand in-depth regardless of the number of social scenes, settings, and participants.

6. Purposeful sampling refers to
    a. sampling procedures designed before data collection.
    b. strategies to find information-rich cases simultaneously while one collects data.
    c. the least desirable strategy, comprehensive sampling.
    d. probability sampling.

7. Data collection strategies are
    a. participant observation.
    b. ethnographic interviews.
    c. artifact collection.
    d. multimethod, or a combination of several of the above strategies.

8. Inductive analysis refers to
    a. qualitative procedures to develop and verify or test universal propositions and causal laws.
    b. the patterns, themes, and categories of analysis emerging from the data.
    c. generalizing from theories to specifics.
    d. ignoring participant meanings, especially verbatim statements and phrases.

9. On which of the following levels of abstraction can findings of qualitative research be presented?
    a. a descriptive narration of events or processes similar to journalistic reporting
    b. an analytical interpretation to provide an understanding of the phenomenon
    c. discovery of concepts or mini-theories, or grounded theory
    d. All of the above are possible.

10. Ethnographic contributions to research include all of the following *except:*
    a. exploratory or discovery-oriented research.
    b. preponderance of evidence of many case studies.
    c. generalizability to different settings and populations.
    d. evaluation research, especially formative evaluation.

11. In appraising an ethnographic study, one would look for:
    a. the conceptual frameworks and research questions for the study.
    b. prolonged field residence or an appropriate number of ethnographic interviews.

c. the research role assumed and how the role affected data collection.

d. All of the above stated explicitly.

Application Problems

Answer the questions for each methodological problem.

1. A superintendent asked an ethnographer to observe how one elementary school implemented a new science curriculum to decide whether other schools should use the curriculum. The ethnographer easily established rapport with the science supervisor and the principal and observed the teaching of five of the six teachers. The sixth teacher, who seemed to oppose the innovation, only related her experiences with the new curriculum. This teacher skillfully managed to avoid teaching the curriculum when the investigator was present. What should the ethnographer do?

2. An ethnographer is living in a student dormitory in order to study how high school students attending a state summer school program develop creativity through photography. Although the ethnographer originally thought observation of the photography classes and the evening program would be sufficient, she found that student social activities during free time and extracurricular activities on the weekends influenced students' photographic productions. Should the ethnographer observe and record these informal happenings? Would student products—photographs—be a source of data?

3. During data collection, an adult education program director overhears the negative remarks made by some adults and sees the ethnographer recording these remarks. The director explains to the ethnographer that such remarks, if made public, could create a poor image for the program. The director asks the ethnographer to destroy those particular field notes. How should the ethnographer handle this situation?

4. Below is part of a problem statement for a proposed study.
   There are many studies of the impact of desegregated schools on minority students that focus on the social-psychological dimensions (self-esteem, motivation, racial attitudes, and so on) and on the academic achievement dimensions (grades, standardized achievement test scores, retention and graduation rates, and so on). Most studies, however, have focused on the assessment of quantitative outcomes of either segregated or desegregated schools and not on the qualitative processes in daily schooling. There is a lack of knowledge about classroom processes and the milieu of the school and community in which these processes occur regarding the patterns and dynamics of socialization within desegregated schools. Does the focus of the study seem appropriate for ethnography? Justify your answer.

5. Rephrase the following interview guide questions for qualitative questions and place the questions in an appropriate sequence to elicit teachers' perceptions regarding evaluation by their building principal.

1. Do you think teachers as professionals should be evaluated by their principals?
2. Did your principal visit your classroom several times before he did your annual evaluation?
3. Does your principal hold a conference with you after each visit?
4. Is the principal's evaluation of your teaching fair?

CHAPTER 12

ANALYTICAL RESEARCH: HISTORICAL, LEGAL, AND POLICY STUDIES

■ KEY TERMS ■

documents
oral testimonies/oral
   history
relics
generalization
causal explanations
conceptual analysis
primary source
secondary source

external criticism
internal criticism
facts
reporters
commentaries
digests

One way to understand current educational practices is to know how these practices developed and to clarify the issues concerning them. How often have educators and noneducators made statements or justified decisions on the basis of what they assumed happened in the past? Explanations of past educational ideas or concepts, events, legal principles, and policy-making suggest insights about current educational events.

Analytical research describes and interprets the past from selected sources. With this methodology the researcher does not directly observe, measure, or experiment with current educational phenomena, nor are the findings tested statistically. Instead, researchers use logical induction to analyze qualitatively traces of the past, usually documents preserved in collections. Rigorous techniques of criticism are applied to the documents. The validity of an analytical study lies in the procedures inherent in the methodology, which includes the search for and criticism of sources, and the interpretation of facts for causal explanations.

■ GENERAL CHARACTERISTICS OF ■ ANALYTICAL RESEARCH

Underlying the varieties of analytical research are common methodological characteristics that distinguish analytical studies from other kinds of educational research. These methodological characteristics include a research topic related to past events, primary sources for data, techniques of criticism used in searching for facts, interpretative explanations, and types of analyses. Because these characteristics are general, they may be applied in different ways within a particular study.

Topics of Analysis

Analytical research includes many topics, such as philosophy, linguistics, comparative education, and international education. The general characteristics and more specific methodological procedures described later in this chapter are limited to examples drawn from American educational historical, legal, and policy events. Many of these studies require the analysis of educational concepts—that is, the meaning of the language used.

Historical research may focus on biographies of educators (John Dewey, Phillis Wheatley); movements (progressive education, lifelong learning); institutions (public education, kindergarten); and concepts (schooling, the child, literacy, professionalism). The past may be interpreted to mean a time as recent as the previous year or those decades in which the historian has no personal experience. Recent studies have focused on the educational aspects of the family; the church; professional associations; the urban environment; special institutions such as reform schools, orphanages, and juvenile courts; regionalism in American education; minority groups; and aspects of popular culture, such as television, songs, and literature (S. Cohen, 1976, pp. 313–325). Examples of historical studies are Cremin (1961), *The Transformation of the School: Progressivism in American Education, 1876–1957*; Tyack (1974), *The One Best System: A History of American Urban Education;* Katz (1975), *Class, Bureaucracy and Schools: The Illusion of Educational Change in America;* and Ravitch (1974), *The Great School Wars: New York City, 1805–1973.*

Legal research focuses on legal issues and analyzes relevant laws and court decisions in order to understand the law. Legal studies identify legal principles from an analysis of past judicial interpretations of the "law" and constitutions at local, state, and national levels (Hudgins & Vacca, rev. ed., 1985). Legal studies may also review judicial interpretations of constitutions and statutes as they apply to specific court cases. When a series of cases on a legal issue is analyzed, the resulting study identifies the principles by which state and federal judges have interpreted the law. Recent studies have centered on the legal aspects of desegregation, religion in the public schools, teacher incompetence, and student rights. Legal commentaries are found typically in law reviews published by law schools. Specialized journals on school law are the *Journal of Law and Education, West's Ed-*

ucational Law Reporter, and *Education Law Specialty Digest.* Organizations like the National Organization on Legal Problems of Education (NOLPE), conduct research projects and publish monographs and yearbooks of educational law.

Policy research is directed toward past and contemporary policy-making of the legislative, judicial, and executive branches of educational government (such as school boards) and general government (such as state legislatures) as they relate to education. A policy prescribes a course of action, and the process includes both policy formulation and implementation. A policy may be developed at different government levels (local, state, national) and be binding for only that level or for other levels (Miller, 1981). Policy research interprets educational policy formation and implementation as a means to achieve public goals.

Public policy goals are equality, liberty, and efficiency, which are considered just and right in the American cultural and legal heritage. It is almost impossible to implement these goals to their fullest degree because the exclusive pursuit of one restricts the others (Guthrie, 1980). The balance among these three goals at any one time is the result of compromises in the political and economic system. Recent studies have analyzed the policy aspects of racial desegregation, school finance, school efficiency, school district consolidation, specialized programs and issues, collective bargaining, and the role of state and federal power in education. Studies may focus on governance, as in Salisbury (1980), *Citizen Participation in the Public Schools;* Mann (1976), *The Politics of Administrative Representation;* and Finn (1977), *Education and the Presidency;* or on specialized issues, as in Goldstein (1978), *Changing the American Schoolbook: Politics, Law, and Technology;* Colton and Graber (1982), *Teacher Strikes and the Courts;* and Fishel and Pottker (1977), *National Politics and Sex Discrimination in Education.* These studies analyze complex events in their historical context and clarify current policy issues.

Policy research is a broader field than the qualitative analysis of educational policy-making processes and issues presented in this chapter.[1] Policy analysis is carried out by a policy analyst specialist rather than by a political scientist or an educational researcher and consists of cost analysis, impact assessment, forecasting and future analysis, evaluation, and social indicator analysis. These studies are designed to provide "a perspective" to facilitate political choices of alternative policies (Carley, 1980, p. 34). The techniques, some of which have been used in educational evaluation, are beyond the scope of an introductory educational research book.[2]

Analytical studies provide knowledge and understanding about past educational historical, legal, and policy events. Major ideas and concepts are clarified for meaning. Research questions focus on events (who, what, when, where), how

---

[1]Policy studies in education have historically been economic analysis of educational fiscal policies, such as C. Benson (1978), *The economics of education,* and J. S. Berke (1974), *Answers to inequity: An analysis of new school finance.*

[2]S. S. Nagel (1980), *The policy-studies handbook* provides an overview of the field of policy analysis. Research methods are described in M. Carley (1980), *Rational techniques in policy analysis;* F. P. Scioli, and T. S. Cook (1980), *Methodologies for analyzing public policies;* and R. Zeckhauser and E. Stokey (1978), *A primer for policy analysis.* Also see *Policy Studies Review Annual,* Volumes 1–9.

an event occurred (descriptive), and why the event happened (interpretative). This contrasts with quantitative studies, which test hypotheses and ask "Is there a relationship between variable x and variable y?" or "Is there a statistically significant difference between the scores of the experimental and control group?"

Types of Sources

The data for these studies are written sources, many of which have been preserved in archives, manuscript collection repositories, or libraries. Sources are documents, oral testimonies, and relics. All of these sources are generally classified as documents. A study may require one or several types of sources.

Documents are records of past events. They are written or printed materials that may be official or unofficial, public or private, published or unpublished, prepared intentionally to preserve an historical record or prepared to serve an immediate practical purpose. **Documents** may be letters, diaries, wills, receipts, maps, autobiographies, journals, newspapers, court records, official minutes, proclamations, regulations, laws, and the like.

A special type of document is quantitative records, which may include enrollment records, staff employment records, membership lists, census records, tax lists, voting records, budgets, test score data, and any compilation of numerical data. The condensation of data, when it is clearly legitimate, makes the information easier to describe and analyze. The difficulty of using quantitative records usually increases with the remoteness of the period studied. As Aydelotte (1966, p. 14) noted, "formal statistical presentations are feasible only for a limited range of historical problems"; however, some political, economic, and demographic data have been handled quantitatively with success.[3]

A second type of source is records of the spoken word called **oral testimonies** *or* **oral history.** In these records, oral testimonies of persons who have witnessed events of educational significance are taped and verbatim transcripts made. Oral testimonies are autobiographical or extended interviews that differ from structured interview schedules. Such testimonies may be recorded by participants in or witnesses of the establishment of a new institution, a legal hearing, the passage of an educational law, or the implementation of a policy.

Relics, a third type of source, are any objects that provide information about the past. Although relics may not be intended to convey information directly about the past, the visual and physical properties of the objects can provide evidence of the past. **Relics** may be textbooks, buildings, equipment, charts, examinations, the physical evidence presented in a court case, or the physical objects in policy-making. Table 12.1 illustrates types of sources for historical, legal, and policy-making research.

---

[3]An example is M. Katz (1968), *The irony of early school reform.* Methodological procedures are described in C. M. Dollar and R. J. Jensen (1971), *Historian's guide to statistics: Quantitative analysis and historical research;* W. O. Aydelotte, A. G. Bogue and R. W. Fogel (1972), *The dimensions of quantitative research in history;* and R. Floud (1979), *An introduction to quantitative methods for historians.*

TABLE 12.1
Illustrative Types of Sources for Analytical Research

Source	Historical Research	Legal Research	Policy-making Research

Documents	Letters
	Diaries
	Bills and receipts
	Autobiographies
	Newspapers
	Journals, magazines
	Bulletins
	Catalogues
	Films
	Recordings
	Personal records
	Institutional records
	Budgets
	Enrollment records
	Graduation records
		Court decisions
		Majority and dissenting
		  opinions of judges
		Laws (statutes)
		Constitutions
		Administrative
		  law decisions
		Copies of
		  pleadings
		  filed with
		  the Court
			Official and unofficial
			  federal, state, local, and
			  school government
			  records:
			    Legislative hearings,
			      debates, reports,
			      publications
			    Committee prints,
			      minutes, reports
			    Agency reports
			    Statistical data,
			      budgets
			    Regulations, directives
			    Laws
			    Voting records
			Speeches of government
			  officials
			Proclamations

Oral
Testimonies/
Oral
History
	Participants in an
	  historical event
		Transcripts of
		  participants in a
		  court case: defendant,
		  plaintiff, attorneys,
		  witnesses
			Participants in
			  policy-making processes:
			  administrators, school
			  board members, government
			  officials, professional
			  staff, special interest
			  groups, professional
			  associations

Relics	Textbooks
	Buildings
	Maps
	Equipment
	Samples of
	  student work
	Furniture
	Teaching materials
		Physical evidence
		  presented in a court
		  case
			Physical objects presented
			  in legislative hearings or
			  other policy-making
			  processes: charts,
			  diagrams, historical
			  relics

The Search for Facts

The analytical researcher approaches a research problem differently from the way quantitative researchers approach it. The search for facts begins with the location of sources. While quantitative researchers typically create the data, usually by administering instruments to a sample or population, the analyst is dependent on those sources that were preserved. As Gottschalk notes (1969), the "whole past" can only be known to the researcher "through the surviving record of it . . . , and most of history-as-record is only the surviving part of the recorded part of the remembered part of the observed part of the whole" (pp. 45–46).

The search for facts requires locating both primary and secondary sources. Primary sources are those documents or testimonies of eyewitnesses to an event. Secondary sources are those documents or testimonies of individuals who did not actually observe or participate in the event and thus speak from hearsay evidence. Eyewitness accounts are valued more than secondary sources, but both types of sources are subjected to techniques of criticism.

Techniques of criticism are used to assess the authenticity and trustworthiness of the source. Authenticity determines whether the source is a genuine document, forged document, or variant of the original document. Trustworthiness of the source refers to the accuracy of the statements found in the source. The researcher locates the most authentic and trustworthy sources and, from these sources, ascertains the most accurate parts of the description—the facts. Interpretations of an event are based on facts.

Analytical Generalizations and Explanations

Analytical studies suggest **generalizations,** which are interpretations of facts. When inductive logic is applied to a series of generalizations about an event or a legal principle, a **causal explanation** is suggested for the specific event or legal principle. Such terms as *cause, because, since, on account of,* and *for the reason that* connote causal explanations. Causal explanations are implied with such statements as "under the circumstances, it is not surprising that. . . ," "naturally at this point, he. . . ," "it was inevitable that. . ." Causal explanations are suggested with such nouns as *impossibility, necessity, influence, impulse, development, consequence,* and *motives,* and such verbs as *lead to, result in, bring about, stimulate, force,* and *compile* (Gardiner, 1952).

The validity of analytical explanations differ from statistical explanations and common-sense explanations in the following ways.

1. *An analytical generalization summarizes separate facts which assert that an event took place.* The researcher is interested in the particular circumstances under which an event occurred and recognizes that these circumstances may never be repeated again. Analytical explanations differ from common-sense explanations because they require critical judgment using specialized knowledge about the era in which the event occurred and the connecting circumstances.

2. *Explanations suggest multiple causes for any single event.* Explanations are interpretations of the connections between the generalizations, that is, the causes. Cause and effect are not treated in an absolute manner. The more complex the events and the wider their spread in time and space, the greater the need for the analyst's interpretation. Usually, an event of any degree of magnitude and complexity needs many generalizations to explain it.

3. *When analytical explanations are justified or supported by the facts stated in the study, the explanations are considered valid.* Analysts will say, "If you do not believe my explanation, take a closer look at the facts." The specification of details—the who, what, when, where and how—is precisely the feature of the explanation that differentiates it from statistical explanations (Gardiner, 1952). Analysts seldom claim, however, that they have all of the facts. Instead, a study contains "that group of associated facts and ideas which, when clearly presented in a prescribed amount of space, leave no questions unanswered *within* the presentation, even though many questions could be asked *outside* it" (Barzun & Graff, 1985, p. 19).

4. *Analytical explanations are made from different points of view.* For example, a question about the reasons for World War I is answerable from the point of view of individual human purposes, desires, weaknesses, and abilities; national policies, traditions of diplomacy, and plans; political alignments, treaties, and the international structure of Europe in 1914; and economic trends, social organization, political doctrines, and ideology. Each point of view is at a higher level of abstraction.

It appears that there are no absolute causes waiting to be discovered and offered as explanations by the analytical researcher. Instead, analysts write at different levels of abstraction, at different chronological distances from the past event, for different purposes, in different contexts, and from different points of view. Not surprisingly, different studies suggest apparently contradictory but valid explanations of the past.

Kinds of Analyses

The type of analysis indicates the research purpose. A study may be an analysis of an educational concept, an edition or compilation of documents, a descriptive narration of an event, a comparative analysis of several events or periods, or a universal theory or philosophy. Each type of study differs in scope and level of generalization (Gottschalk, 1963). Table 12.2 illustrates the types of analyses in historical, legal, and policy research.

1. *Conceptual analysis.* Educational concepts are clarified by describing the essential or generic meaning of the concept, specifying the different meanings of the concept, or describing the appropriate usage for the concept in a variety of instances. The analysis of an educational concept like *professionalism* may be the focus of an entire study.

2. *Edition or compilation.* An edition or compilation of documents preserves and publishes documents placed in chronological order. For a compilation, the editor restores the document to its original text, with annotations for contextual meanings.

3. *Descriptive narration.* A descriptive narration of an event tells the story from the beginning to end in chronological order. Limited generalizations are intended to be confined strictly to the subject matter under study.

4. *Interpretative analysis.* An interpretative analysis relates the educational event to other events of the period. The analysis includes economic, social, and

TABLE 12.2
Types of Analysis in Historical, Legal, and Policy-making Research

Analysis	Historical Research	Legal Research	Policy-making Research
Analysis of educational concepts	Schooling	Due process in education	Equality in education
Edition-compilation	Restores an original document; compiles documents on a historical topic, period, person	Compiles and classifies cases on an educational legal issue, period, or a justice's term of office	Compiles and classifies documents on an educational policy, i.e., a law, directive, rule
Descriptive narrative	Narrates a single historical educational event, i.e., establishment of an institution, biography	Narrates an educational court case(s)	Narrates an educational policy-making process
Interpretative analysis	Interprets the event in the context of the period	Interprets a case(s) by legal principles, rules of evidence, etc. of the times	Interprets a policy-making process in the context of other policies or political events of the times
Comparative analysis	Compares the event to other events or previous eras	Compares a case(s) to other cases of previous courts	Compares the policy to other educational policies of previous political periods
Universal analysis	Develops a theory or philosophy of educational history	Analyzes educational legal philosophy of previous courts	Analyzes educational public policy goals or political philosophy of previous eras

political events that occurred simultaneously. The event is studied not in isolation but rather in its broader context.

5. *Comparative analysis.* The comparative analysis qualitatively compares similarities and differences in educational events to those of other historical periods. The analysis may indicate a consistent trend, a series of unique situations, or the beginning of a new direction.

6. *Universal analysis.* A theoretical or philosophical analysis presents universal interpretations. In it, historical parallels, regularities or past trends, and sequences of events suggest propositions that explain the course of educational events, past and future. Philosophies of cyclical progression and the linear progression of education are examples of universal generalizations.

Each type of analysis is useful in educational research. Analysis of educational concepts specify implied meanings and connotations of a concept. An edition or compilation of documents preserves the documents for future research. Descriptive narrations may be secondary sources for subsequent interpretative or comparative analyses. Interpretative and comparative studies state causal explanations to further understanding of the past. Other interpretations by revisionists are often suggested, especially as new sources become available or different social science concepts are applied to the sources. Similarly, a philosophy or theory is usually modified or at least questioned by subsequent studies.

The next sections of this chapter describe the methodology used in analytical research. We will describe techniques of conceptual analysis, procedures for studying past historical and policy events, and techniques for legal research.

■ ANALYSIS OF EDUCATIONAL CONCEPTS ■

A **conceptual analysis** is a study that clarifies the meaning of a concept by describing the essential or generic meaning, the different meanings and the appropriate usage for the concept. By presenting an analysis of the concept, the study helps us understand the way people think about education.[4] The focus is on the meaning of the concept, not on the researcher's personal values or on factual information. For example, the question, "What are the aims of education?" is not answered by collecting data to show that educators have aims or do not have aims, or by making a value statement that educators should have aims. Instead, the analyst begins by asking, "Is having an aim an integral and necessary part of our concept of being an educator?" or "Can a person be an educator without having an aim?" (Soltis, 1978, p. 15). Asking such questions allows the analyst to get at the meaning of education by carefully examining some ideas attached to the concept of aims as an aspect of education. The analyst assumes a neutral position while analyzing a concept before taking a value position or collecting factual information.

Three strategies may be used to analyze such concepts as *education, literacy, knowledge, teaching, learning, equal opportunity,* and *due process.* Soltis (1978) illustrates generic, differential, and conditions analyses. Each of these strategies begins with a different prior question and applies specific techniques to clarify the concept.

1. *A generic analysis identifies the essential meaning of a concept.* The analysis isolates those elements that distinguish the concept from other words. To clarify the concept *academic discipline*, one might, therefore, compare history, mathematics, and physics as clear standard examples with home economics, animal husbandry, and water-skiing as counterexamples in order to arrive at the generic meaning of *academic discipline.*

[4]We gratefully acknowledge the assistance of S. Craver, Virginia Commonwealth University, in concept analysis and historical research for this section.

2. *A differential analysis distinguishes among the basic meanings of the concept and provides a clearer idea of the logical domain covered by the concept.* Differential analysis is used when a concept seems to have more than one standard meaning and the basis for differentiating between meanings is unclear. The prior question is, "What are the basic (different) meanings of the concept?" One could, for example, ask the question, "What are the different meanings of subject matter?" and analyze the concept of *subject matter* by intuitively classifying the typical uses with concrete examples, such as *Silas Marner*, solar system, school subjects, knowledge, and skills. The distinguishing characteristics of each type of subject matter is ascertained to clearly separate the types, and a typology is developed. An example of differential analysis is the distinction between basic, applied, and evaluation research made in Chapter 1, which is intended to provide a clearer understanding of the concept *research.*

3. *A conditions analysis identifies the conditions necessary for proper use of the concept.* The prior question is "Under what context conditions would it be true that the concept is present?" Conditions analysis begins by providing an example that meets the necessary conditions of the concept but can easily be made a noninstance by changing the context. This forces either revision or rejection of the condition and leads to additional conditions with other examples and counterexamples. The purpose of the conditions analysis "is to produce a set of necessary and sufficient conditions for the proper application of a concept to any of its many and varied instances" (Soltis, 1978, p. 65).

Critical to the analysis of educational concepts is the selection of the typical uses of the concept and counterexamples. The analyst uses *purposeful sampling* by choosing examples which demonstrate implicit meanings in the language which are then analyzed logically. Examples may be drawn from generally accepted common uses of the concepts. Because different sets of examples are used frequently, the analysis of educational concepts may lead to reanalysis and further conceptual clarity.

Analysis of educational concepts is applied in the study of educational concepts and in historical, legal, and policy-making research. A study of the public school movement, due process in education, or groups that influence the passage of a law must first determine the meaning of *public school, due process,* and *influential groups.*

■ ANALYSIS OF EDUCATIONAL HISTORICAL ■
AND POLICY-MAKING EVENTS

Analytical research requires systematic application of methodological procedures to phrase an analytical problem, locate and criticize sources, and interpret facts for causal explanations. Specialized training is necessary in order to conduct historical and policy-making research. The analyst proceeds in a circular fashion because of the interrelationship of the research problem, sources, criticism, analysis, and explanations.

The Topic and Problem Statement

The analyst begins with an initial subject, such as a historical period, person, idea, practice, institution, or a policy. As the analyst obtains background knowledge, the topic is defined more exactly. Simultaneously, the analyst notes possible primary sources relevant to the topic. Statement of the problem delimits and focuses the research study. The problem must be narrow enough to examine the event in detail but broad enough to identify patterns for the interpretation.

In order to phrase the research topic, the analyst initially reads widely in secondary sources for background knowledge. Background knowledge suggests the breadth of the subject, previous research on the problem, gaps in knowledge, and possible sources. Background knowledge is obtained from textbooks, monographs, encyclopedias and other reference works, dissertations, and specialized journals. General bibliographies cite secondary sources. Some bibliographies specifically for the historian are *A Guide to Historical Literature* (1961), the *Historian's Handbook: A Descriptive Guide to Reference Works* (1972), and *A Bibliography of American Educational History* (1975). Secondary sources for policy research are located with general historical bibliographies and such specialized bibliographies as *The Study of Politics and Education: A Bibliographic Guide to Research Literature* (1981).

Limiting and phrasing a topic is a continuing effort. The problem statement is expressed most succinctly and clearly at the end of the research when the sources have been collected, analyzed, and interpreted. Considerations in limiting a topic are the availability and accessibility of primary sources; the analyst's interests, specialized knowledge, and time to complete the study; and the type of analysis to be done.

The statement of an analytical problem indicates the particular event, person, institution, or policy. Problems are delimited by the time period, geographic location, and viewpoint of the analysis. Excerpt 12.1 illustrates stating a historical problem by contrasting the study to previous research and by stating the historical period (1825 to 1930s), the institution (the Chicago school system), the educational level (secondary schools), the focus (integration-segregation dilemma), and the viewpoint (student and society).

Location and Criticism of Sources

Primary sources are essential for analytical research, but secondary sources are used selectively when necessary. Both primary and secondary sources are subjected to techniques of criticism. The sources for a study are cited in the bibliography and frequently footnoted in a study. Criticism of sources may be in the study or in a methodological appendix.

Classification of Sources.   A **primary source** is the written or oral testimony of an eyewitness, a participant, or a record made by some mechanical device present at the event, such as a tape recorder, a transcript, or a photograph. Primary sourc-

---

EXCERPT 12.1
Problem Statement

In recent years scholars representing various academic disciplines have carried on government sponsored research to determine the impact of integration on black and white students. These scholars have produced such nationally influential and widely adopted studies as the first "Coleman Report." (1) Nevertheless, the research has made little reference to the history of integration and has therefore called into question whether such practices are best for every school system. Moreover, the studies have had broad foci, rarely concentrating on specific school grades or areas of student growth and development. Using the secondary schools of Chicago, both high schools and junior high schools, this essay will examine the historical integration-segregation dilemma from the passage of the first Illinois school law in 1825 to the solidification of the segregation era in the 1930s.

Source: From "A History of Discrimination Against Black Students In Chicago Secondary Schools" by Philip T. K. Daniel, *History of Education Quarterly*, Vol. 20, No. 2, Summer 1980. Reprinted by permission of the author.

es for a historical biography are the person's personal and public papers and the relics of his or her life. Primary sources for policy-making research are records of government action and the oral testimonies of eyewitnesses. A primary source is original in the sense that it contains underived or firsthand eyewitness accounts of the events.

A **secondary source** is the record or testimony of anyone not an eyewitness to or participant in the event. A secondary source obtains the information from someone else, who may or may not have witnessed the event. Secondary sources contain historical and policy-making research that interprets other primary and secondary sources. These sources provide insights and possibly facts for analysis.

The classification of sources as primary or secondary depends on the research problem. Some sources may be primary in one study and secondary in another. The number of primary sources necessary for a study varies with the topic. To obtain primary sources, the analyst thinks of the sources that would yield information on the topic and then investigates whether the records were preserved and are accessible. A single study may use different kinds of sources, but it is essential that primary sources serve as the basis for documentation. Documentation is the process of proof based upon any kind of source, whether written, oral, or an object.

Location of Sources. The quality of an analytical study is determined partly by the selected primary sources. The problem statement and limitations point to the necessary primary sources. A study of admissions policies of a university would be seriously flawed without institutional records. A biography of G. Stanley Hall would be questioned if his private papers and writings were ignored. The bibliography cites only those sources actually used for the study.

Documents.   The historian locates primary sources through specialized guides, catalogues, indexes, and bibliographies or through archival research centers. Examples of specialized reference works are *A Catalogue of Rare and Valuable Early Schoolbooks* (1932), *Educational Periodicals During the Nineteenth Century* (1919), *Selective and Critical Bibliography of Horace Mann* (1973), and guides to national archives and private manuscript collections. *A Guide to Manuscripts and Archives in the United States* (1961) describes the holdings of 1,300 repositories and the *Guide to the National Archives of the United States* (1974) indexes educational records of government agencies. The *National Union Catalogue of Manuscript Collections*, published annually by the Library of Congress, cites the increasing number of educational collections made available to scholars. Archival research centers devoted to particular historical subjects often contain educational records.[5]

Studies of educational policy-making use government documents and oral testimonies. Federal government documents are indexed in the *Monthly Catalog of United States Government*, the *Publication Reference File (PRF)*, the *Congressional Information Service/Index (CIS)*, the *American Statistical Index (ASI)*, the *Index to Government Documents*, and agencies' publication lists. The *Legislative Research Checklist*, issued monthly by the Council of State Governments, often abstracts the published reports of commissioners or councils that recommend and draft new legislation. Because research tools for state legislative history vary widely from state to state, state law libraries or legislative reference librarians are consulted. Local government documents are not centrally indexed and must be obtained from the agency.

Oral Testimonies or Oral History.   To investigate a research problem, the analyst may also use oral testimonies or oral history. The researcher decides which individuals are knowledgeable about the topic, locates these individuals, and collects data through interviews.[6] The selection of informants for oral testimonies is done with purposeful sampling procedures such as snowball sampling or reputational-case selection (see Chapter 5). A panel of experts, for example, nom-

---

[5]The archives of Labor History and Urban Affairs at Wayne State University is perhaps the oldest collection. Other topical centers that have documents relevant to education history are the Urban Archives Center at Temple University, the Archives of the Industrial Society at the University of Pittsburgh, the Archives of the History of American Psychology at the University of Akron, the Ohio History of Education Project at the Ohio Historical Society, and the Social Welfare Archives at the University of Minnesota.

[6]See W. W. Cutler (1971), Oral history: Its nature and uses for educational history. *History of Education Quarterly, 11*, 184–194; R. Jensen (1981), Oral history, quantification and the new social history. *Oral History Review, 9*, 13–27; and D. Lance (1980), Oral history archives: Perceptions and practices. *Oral History, 8*(2), 59–63.

inates individuals on the basis of criteria from the problem statement. Additional considerations are accessibility to the individuals and feasibility, such as time, finances, number of investigators, and so on. The analyst states the selection criteria.

Oral history is the collection of data through an interview guide approach, similar to certain ethnographic interviews, rather than a standardized interview schedule. (See Chapter 11). The analyst desires information on the research problem and any other information that may further an understanding of the topic. Oral testimonies are time-consuming to obtain and result in extensive transcripts. The transcripts are subjected to internal and external criticism, as are other documentary sources. Excerpt 12.2 illustrates the creation of sources by obtaining oral testimonies. This study investigated the impact of social science on legislative policy-making. One hundred and sixty "key legislative policy influentials" in Arizona, California, and Oregon were tape-recorded for from twenty minutes to an hour and a half. The selection criteria are not stated in this brief article, but they would be in the full report. It is inferred that the "influentials" were nominated and selected by position since respondents were members of the educational and fiscal committees, elected legislative leaders, staff consultants, lobbyists, and professional staff (see paragraph three). The testimony centered on five broad questions (see paragraph two). The excerpt illustrates the relationship between the primary sources and the problem statement.

Criticism of Sources.   Techniques of internal and external criticism are applied to all kinds of sources, such as documents, oral testimonies, and relics. Even sources that are official publications or preserved in archives are subjected to criticism. **External criticism** determines the authenticity of the source. **Internal criticism** determines the credibility of the facts stated by the source. Although external and internal criticism ask different questions about the source, the techniques are applied simultaneously. The criticism of sources may be covered in a methodological discussion or in an appendix to a study.

External Criticism.   **External criticism** determines whether the source is the original document, a forged document, or a variant of the original document. Typical questions are: "Who wrote the document?" and "When, where, and what was the intention?" The more specialized knowledge the analyst has, the easier it is to determine whether a document is genuine. The analyst needs knowledge of the way people in the era that produced the document lived and behaved, the things they believed, and the way they managed their institutions. The educational analyst is less likely to deal with forged documents than is a social scientist who studies controversial political, religious, or social movements. Claims to a title or the date of an institution can, however, be forged. Sometimes it is impossible to determine the contribution of an individual for government reports or speeches if there are multiple authors.

The date and place of writing or publication can be established by means of the citation on the document, the date of the manuscript collection, or the contents of

EXCERPT 12.2
Selection of Oral Testimonies

In 1976, in an effort to develop a clearer understanding of the impact of social science on policy making and to focus much needed attention on the role of state legislatures in formulating basic educational policies, the National Institute of Education funded a study of social science utilization among state legislatures.[1] This paper summarizes several key findings from that study.

THE STUDY

Data for the study were collected from 160 key legislative policy influentials in the states of Arizona, California and Oregon. Tape recorded interviews with the respondents (lasting 20 minutes to 1½ hours) covered the development of six educational policy issues: basic skills, personnel (including collective bargaining), finance, special education, governance reform, and categorical aid programs. Each respondent was asked to: (1) describe recent legislation in one or more of the six issue areas, (2) identify the key actors who formulate and influence these legislative decisions, (3) discuss how the legislature is influenced by these key actors, (4) define "the issues" being resolved as legislation is enacted, and (5) identify the resources utilized to control or influence the decision-making process.

Respondents included members of education and fiscal committees, elected legislative leaders; personal, committee or chamber staff consultants; lobbyists representing educational interest groups; and professional staff members from state departments of education and the governor's executive staff.

Verbatim transcripts were produced from approximately one-third of the tape recorded interviews and were subjected to content analysis. As a general framework for interpretation was developed from the transcribed interviews, it was checked against the remaining interview tapes for consistency and elaboration.

Source: From "Social Science Impact on Legislative Decision Making: Process & Substance" by Douglas E. Mitchell, *Educational Researcher*, November 1980. Copyright © 1980 American Educational Research Association. Reprinted by permission.

the document. However, working papers internal to an institution, or drafts made by an individual may contain no dates or be insufficient for use if only the year is stated.

What the educational analyst is more likely to find is variant sources. Variant sources are two or more texts of the same document, or two or more testimonies to the same event. For example, a newspaper account of the results of a state educational testing program may differ from the actual statistical report published by the State Department of Education, and both may differ from the separate drafts of the report. In this situation, the newspaper account, the official report, and the separate drafts are all authentic sources of different texts. Oral testimonies by different individuals may be authentic but variant sources.

Internal Criticism.   Internal criticism determines the accuracy and trustworthiness of the statements in the source. The analyst asks: "Are the statements accurate and the witnesses trustworthy?" Accuracy is related to a witness's chronological and geographical proximity to the event, the competence of the witness, and the witness's attention to the event. All witnesses equally close to the event are obviously not equally competent observers and recorders. Competence depends on expertness, state of mental and physical health, educational level, memory, narrative skill, and the like. It is well known that eyewitnesses under traumatic or stressful conditions remember selective parts of an event, yet they are convinced that because they were present, their accounts are accurate. Even though a witness may be competent, he or she may be an interested party or biased. Bias or preconceived prejudice causes a witness to habitually distort, ignore, or overemphasize incidents. The conditions in which the statements were made may influence accuracy. The literary style, the laws of libel, the conventions of good taste, or a desire to please may lead to exaggerated politeness or expressions of esteem.

Several techniques estimate the accuracy and dependability of a statement. Statements by a witness made as a matter of indifference, those injurious to the person stating them, or those contrary to the personal desires of the person stating them are less likely to be biased than others. Statements considered common knowledge or incidental are less likely to be in error. Other credible sources can confirm, modify, or reject statements. In a qualitative analysis, however, the simple agreement of statements from independent witnesses can be misleading since the research depends only on preserved sources. Agreement with other known facts or circumstantial evidence increases the credibility of a statement. An analyst may cite the source by referring to it: "according to the judge's opinion," "Horace Mann says," or "the Speaker of the House is our authority for the statement that. . . ."

Internal and external criticism requires knowledge about the individuals, events, and behavior of the period under study. "The ability to put oneself in the place of the individuals . . . to interpret documents, events, and personalities with their eyes, standards, sympathies (without necessarily surrendering one's own standards) has sometimes been called *historical mindedness*" (Gottschalk, 1969, pp. 136–137). Throughout the whole process, the analyst is skeptical and critical of the sources and statements. An analyst is not easily satisfied or convinced that the sources have yielded evidence as close to actual events as possible.

Criticism of Sources.   Criticism of sources is treated in several ways within a study. The most obvious citations are the footnotes and the items labeled *Notes, References,* or *Bibliography* following the study. The list is usually extensive. There are, for example, eighty-three footnotes for the twelve-page journal article, "A History of Discrimination Against Black Students in Chicago Secondary Schools" (Daniel, 1980); they include official reports of the U.S. Department of Health, Ed-

> ## EXCERPT 12.3
> ## Analytical Criticism
>
> A handful of Troy pupils left some record of what they thought the long-term influence of the institution and its founder upon them had been. A number who replied to the questionnaires sent out in the 1890's responded with long letters, and others, even in brief answers, threw some light on how they recalled the experience. Still others, simply by describing their lives, inadvertently bore witness to the kind of strength of character which Troy reinforced. What stands out in most of these records is the great importance of Willard's own personality in providing her pupils with a new image of what woman could be. . . .
>
> Of course such evidence must be interpreted with care. Obviously, a woman who felt very much attached to Troy would be likely to write a detailed response to the questionnaire; children who remembered such attachment would be likely to take the trouble to reply. There was certainly a process of self-selection on the part of the women who chose to go to Troy. These fragments do bear witness, however, to the beginning of a new personality type, the educated woman who was not ashamed of learning and who would inevitably have a wider notion of what the world had to offer than her sisters who had not been encouraged to read widely or to think for themselves. (35)
>
> ---
>
> *Source:* From "The Ever Widening Circle: The Diffusion of Feminist Values from the Troy Female Seminary, 1822–1872" by Anne Firor Scott, *History of Education Quarterly*, Vol. 19, Spring 1979. Reprinted by permission of the author.

ucation, and Welfare and other federal departments and agencies, *Laws of Illinois, Board of Education Annual Reports,* the *Census of the United States,* articles from *The Chicago Tribune* and *Chicago Defender,* the *Municipal Code of Chicago,* interviews with participants, reports of the Chicago Commission on Race Relations, the Vice Commission of Chicago, and the Chicago Real Estate Board, and secondary sources.

In methodological discussions in the study or in an appendix, the analyst also refers to criticism. Excerpt 12.2 merely cited the sources. The author of Excerpt 12.3 criticized the sources by noting that the long letters, the brief answers on the questionnaires of the 1890s, and the pupil records at Troy must "be interpreted with care." The researcher noted the possible bias of the documents because of the self-selection of those who attended Troy and because those who maintained contact with Troy probably had favorable experiences at the seminary and developed feminist values.

Methodological appendices are written because the study uses sources that are newly collected and analyzed. An appendix, rather than the study *per se,* allows the analyst to expand on the methodological problems of the sources and comment on their scholarly value. Excerpt 12.4 illustrates a reference to

---

EXCERPT 12.4
Analytical Criticism

A major research task was to locate and monitor teacher strikes which occurred during 1978–79. We needed to identify all strike sites so that we could conduct a mailed survey of affected districts, and we needed to locate sites where field studies could be conducted. As it turned out, the task of monitoring strikes was extraordinarily difficult. There is no central national agency which has a reliable system for quickly identifying strike sites. Information gathered by state and national professional associations, and by state and national government agencies, contains serious discrepancies. Some are traceable to differing definitions of what constitutes a strike. Some are traceable to gaps in information sources. The basis for our own calculation that there were 158 strikes is set forth in a technical appendix. . . .

Source: Colton, D. L., and Graber, E. E. (1980). *Enjoining teacher strikes: The irreparable harm standard.* Grant No. NIE-G-78-0149, 26. Washington, DC: National Institute of Education.

---

methodological problems and the need for a methodological appendix. This study required the identification of all teacher strikes that occurred in 1978–79. Information gathered by state and national government agencies and by state and national professional associations contained "serious discrepancies" that were due to different definitions of a strike and to information gaps in sources. The method of identifying the 158 strikes was presented in an appendix. The method was made available to other researchers.

Facts, Generalizations, and Causal Explanations

Facts are the basis for generalizations which may be interpreted as causal explanations. The process is not this simple, however. Criticism of sources may lead to rephrasing the problem and a further search for sources and facts.

1. *Facts describe the who, what, when, and where of an event.* Most analysts, however, go beyond obtaining descriptive facts and ask the interpretative questions of the ways a historical event occurred and the reasons for it. The analyst thus moves from identifying facts to stating generalizations to inferring causal explanations. The questions asked of the sources are crucial to the entire process.

The analyst's skill in questioning is similar to that of a detective in search of evidence and that of a scientist systematically testing that evidence. Questions may be very specific, such as, "When did Henry Barnard die?" or may be abstract, such as, "How did the scientific movement influence school administration practices?" Methodological training and experience, both general and specialized knowledge, disciplined intuition, and logic influence the analysis. The analyst operates primarily in an inductive mode of reasoning, going from the specific facts to generalizations. The more questions asked of the sources about the topic, the more comprehensive and complex the analysis is.

When statements and facts conflict, additional information is sought to resolve the apparent differences. Eventually, though, the analyst must decide. Even the sentence, "The Troy Female Seminary, officially opened in 1821 but tracing its roots to 1814, was the first permanent institution offering American women a curriculum similar to that of the contemporary men's colleges" (Scott, 1979, p. 3) required *"decisive* evidence"—evidence that confirms one view and denies alternative views. The decision to accept a statement as fact *"rests not on possibility nor on plausibility but on probability"* (Barzun & Graff, 1970, p. 155). Qualitative probability means that given a set of facts, it is reasonable to assume that the event happened in a certain way, or did not even occur. Facts are weighed and judged by consistency, the accumulation of evidence, and other techniques.

2. *Interpretations of the relationships between facts are generalizations.* As D. M. Potter notes, "generalization in history is inescapable and . . . the historian cannot avoid it by making limited statements about limited data. For a microcosm is just as cosmic as a macrocosm. Moreover, relationships between the factors in a microcosm are just as subtle and the generalizations involved in stating these relationships are just as broad as the generalizations concerning the relationships between factors in a situation of larger scale" (Potter, 1963, p. 191). Each generalization is subjected to analysis and is usually modified or qualified. Elements that often appear as facts in a study are frequently generalizations of facts for which there is no space for presentation in the study. Excerpt 12.5, for example, taken from the text of a historical study, contains facts (Miss Strachan was president of the Interborough Association of Women Teachers, 1906–1912), generalizations ("when the struggle was over," "chief spokeswoman," "most irritating of gadflies"), and causes of an event (a leader, an organization, unequal pay scales between men and women), and it also implies two theories of change: accident (an individual with certain qualities "happens to be at the right place at the right time") and the "great leader" ("right proportions of character, leadership qualities, ambition, and moral fervor").

3. *Causal explanations are abstract syntheses of generalizations, usually stated as conclusions.* Generalizations presented throughout the study are reanalyzed for context, internal consistency, documentation, accumulation of evidence, and logical induction. The process is cyclic, one of constantly returning to the facts and, if necessary, to the documents to derive meaning. A causal explanation stated as an overview in an introduction does not mean the analyst began with this interpretation and set out to prove personal notions. The introductory overview was probably the last section of the study to be written, because the logic of the study must flow from it and the criteria for judging the quality of the study is derived from it.

Conclusions synthesize generalizations and concepts previously documented in the study. In other words, conclusions are an interpretative summary of the generalizations. Conclusions may be stated in narrative form or as a brief list, fol-

---

EXCERPT 12.5
Example of Generalizations

Perhaps the most important reason why the equal pay movement began in New York City can be found in one of those happy accidents of history where a single individual, equipped with the right proportions of character, leadership qualities, ambition, and moral fervor just happens to be at the right place at the right time. Clearly one cannot study the history of the equal pay movement without concluding that it would have been much different, and probably much less effective had not Grace Strachan emerged as its leader and its chief spokeswoman, as well as the most irritating of gadflies to the educational and political establishment. A product of the Buffalo Normal School, Miss Strachan came to the New York City schools as a classroom teacher, probably sometime in the late 1880s. At the time the equal pay movement was at its greatest intensity she was serving as District Superintendent of Districts 33 and 35, containing upwards of 32,000 school children. One of the organizers of the Interborough Association of Women Teachers in 1906, Miss Strachan became its president in 1907 and held that post until 1912 when for all practical purposes the struggle was over.

Source: From "Tempest on the Hudson: The Struggle for 'Equal Pay for Equal Work' in the New York City Schools, 1907–1911" by Robert E. Doherty, *History of Education Quarterly*, Vol. 19, Winter 1979. Reprinted by permission of the author.

---

lowed by statements about the status of knowledge on the topic, identification of policy issues, or suggestions for further research. Excerpt 12.6 illustrates a conclusion that contains three causal explanations (paragraph 1) on ways social science is used in legislative policy-making, reasons it is used, and the effects of its usage. Two policy recommendations (paragraph 2) are made from these findings.

■ ANALYSIS OF EDUCATIONAL CASE LAW ■

Educational law influences curriculum, finance, personnel, student assignment, and many other day-to-day operations of schools.[7] Historically, each state government has the legal responsibility and complete authority to provide public education for its children restricted by the provisions of the United States Constitution and by the acts of the state legislature. The courts of law have a particularly important role in a legal system dependent upon precedent cases. Constitutional provisions, federal and state statutes, and city ordinances are generally legal abstractions without practical meaning until they are interpreted by a court of law

---

[7]We gratefully acknowledge the assistance of R. S. Vacca, Virginia Commonwealth University, and H. C. Hudgins, University of North Carolina at Greensboro, in legal research for this section.

EXCERPT 12.6
Analytical Conclusions and Implications

CONCLUSION

The data analyzed here supports three basic conclusions regarding social science utilization within state legislatures: (1) social science is only one of four distinct types of expert authority influencing legislative decisions. The other types of expertise (legal, political and technical) are more prevalent and therefore more frequently utilized. However, social science is frequently utilized by full-time legislators and by fully professional staff consultants. (2) The utilization of social science contributes to both intellectual and social aspects of the decision-making process. Intellectually, scientific expertise orients policy makers to certain aspects of the decisions which they must make. Socially, science utilization alters the processes of collaboration and conflict that control decision outcomes. (3) The contributions of social science shift significantly as legislative proposals move through the four phases of decision making: articulation, aggregation, allocation and oversight. During the earliest phase, science may have both powerful and largely noncontroversial impacts. As legislative issues become more clearly defined and the specifics of who will benefit and who will pay for a proposed policy become identified, social science utilization becomes more partisan and more controversial as it is transformed into a tool or weapon of political conflict.

These findings suggest that social scientists, state legislatures, and science-sponsoring agencies would all be well served if: (a) the development of scientific advocacy for various policy solutions were recognized as a *political* process, requiring the talents of frankly partisan as well as scientifically sophisticated professionals, and (b) systematic efforts were made to bring scientific analysis to bear *earlier* in the legislative process. That is, science utilization should be seen as the mobilization of scientific expertise in support of specific political interests of state legislators who are required to make political rather than scientific decisions. Science utilization serves best to refine and criticize—not to replace—other, more fundamental mechanisms for defining and resolving public policy issues.

Note

[1]National Institute of Education Grant No. NIE-G-76-0104 entitled, "Improving Social Science Utilization in Legislative Policy Making for Basic Skills Education." This grant to the University of California, Riverside (Douglas E. Mitchell, principal investigator) was funded in October, 1976.

Source: From "Social Science Impact on Legislative Decision Making: Process & Substance" by Douglas E. Mitchell, *Educational Researcher*, November 1980. Copyright © 1980 American Educational Research Association. Reprinted by permission.

---

and are made to apply in a given situation. As H. C. Hudgins and R. S. Vacca (1985) note, "Even though statutes control all situations legally contested, the interpretations of statutes by judges in courts of law are what give meaning and force to written legislative pronouncements" (p. 3).

The Topic and Legal Issue

The purpose of legal research is to locate and analyze "authoritative statements of the law which would be considered binding or highly persuasive to the court or other body which must make the ultimate decision on the particular matter in issue" (Peterson, Rossmiller, & Volz, p. 496). In other words, most legal research is to discover what *is* the law in a specific situation. Although federal, state and local governments affect educational practices, the law of one may not be binding in the jurisdiction of another. It is axiomatic, however, that law stemming from a superior government is authoritative upon lesser governments and its citizens. Thus, the law of the United States is considered the supreme law of the land and supersedes any contrary state or local law. Similarly the law of a state, except for an overriding federal law, is supreme throughout the state, including its counties and cities. Traditionally, education has been a state function except when the federal law is made applicable to an educational practice.

Legal issues may be divided into substantive and procedural ones. *Procedural issues* address the various rules of form in legal proceedings such as due process. *Substantive issues* are concerned with legal rights and principles such as tort liability of school boards and employees, collective negotiations, the legal status of professional employees, academic freedom, student control and punishment, use of school property, and others. Even though educational issues generally contain both procedural and substantive questions, procedural questions are usually of greater interest to attorneys than to educators.[8]

In selecting a problem for legal research, it is helpful to analyze a problem in terms of the specific legal issue or issues to be researched. A problem may be broken down in terms of 1) the parties or party, 2) the subject matter or property involved, 3) the nature of the claim, and 4) the object or remedy sought.

1. The *parties* may be important because one or more may belong to a class governed by special rules, to a particular occupation (teaching), or because a special relationship may exist between them (parent and child, teacher and student).

2. The *subject matter* or *property* refers to the essential things and places involved in the problem (a teacher's contract, a school bus, a playground).

3. The *nature of the claim or issue* could be an act of commission (assault and battery, libel and slander, embezzlement or conversion of school funds), an act of omission (failure to inspect the condition of playground equipment or to employ a competent bus driver), or a violation of a statutory provision (disregarding a teacher's tenure rights).

4. The *object* or *remedy sought* in a civil case may be money damages, an injunction (to prevent a strike), specific performance of a contract, a declaration of rights, and so on.

---

[8]Beginning researchers should consult methodological writings, such as L. J. Peterson, R. A. Rossmiller, & M. M. Volz (2nd ed., 1978), *The law and public school operation;* M. W. LaMorte (1982), *School law and concepts;* H. C. Hudgins & R. S. Vacca (rev. ed., 1985), *Law and education;* M. Cohen (1978), *Legal research in a nutshell.*

Frequently, both the problem and the limitations are stated. In the example below, the problem is stated (judicial definition of teacher incompetence) and the limitations noted by stating the period (1958–1981), the jurisdiction (state appellate and federal courts), and the cases (tenured public school teachers who were charged by school officials with incompetence and who were found to be incompetent).

> The problem of this study was to examine and analyze legal grounds upheld by federal and state courts in cases involving the dismissal of tenured public school teachers for alleged incompetence during the period beginning with the Supreme Court decision in *Beilan v. Board of Education* and ending with cases reported in 1981 in an effort to determine teacher incompetence. ....
>
> The study was limited to court cases which were adjudicated from *Beilan* (1958) to the cases reported in 1981. Cases during that period which reached the state appellate courts and the federal courts involving the dismissal of tenured public school teachers were used. Another limitation included litigation involving only tenured public school teachers who were charged by school officials with incompetence. In addition, only those cases where the federal and state courts have upheld the charges of incompetence were included (Shackelford, 1982, pp. 5, 7).

Notice that in the above legal problem the parties are tenured public school teachers and school boards; the property is a teaching contract; the legal issue is alleged incompetence; and the remedy sought is termination of the contract (dismissal of a tenured teacher). After analyzing the legal problem the researcher can frame the question to be searched in sources of law.

Sources for Researching Educational Law

Sources of law, including educational law, are commonly classified as primary sources, secondary sources and search aids to locate primary sources of law. *Primary sources of law* are highly persuasive. State and federal statutes and constitutional provisions, along with the court decisions interpreting them, are important primary sources of law. *Secondary sources in legal research* include legal periodicals, legal encyclopedias and yearbooks, monographs and dissertations, and others. *Search aids* include digests of case law, citators, and various indexes (LaMorte, 1982). We will discuss each of these briefly.

Primary Sources of Law.   Primary sources for legal research consist of two broad categories: 1) federal, state, and local statutes (codes), and 2) court decisions. Many primary sources have both official compilations and unofficial annotated editions. Constitutions, government rules and regulations, and federal and state statutes are examples of official compilations. Annotated versions of the official records include supplemental historical notes, editorial comments, and a digest of interpretative material. One may locate federal and state codes by the *de-*

scriptive word method, the *topic method,* or the *popular name method.*[9] Federal statutes may be located through the publications of the codes or the codes annotated. State codes may be located through state compilations and for all fifty states through *Martindale-Hubbell Law Directory* or *The Lawyers Directory. Shepard's Citations* indicates if a statute has been amended or repealed and references state and federal court decisions which cite the statute.

Court decisions state authoritative interpretations of statutory and constitutional provisions by resolving disputes between parties. Lawsuits are initiated in trial courts whose decisions generally may be appealed to higher courts. An appellate court reviews lower courts' decisions and affirms, reverses, vacates, or modifies the judgment of the lower court, or it orders that the case be tried again. Most trial court decisions are not reported by general distribution and are obtained from the court issuing the decision. Decisions of most appellate courts and certain trial courts of record are available in official and unofficial reporters. **Reporters** are a series of bound volumes and looseleaf services which contain the text of court decisions.

Board of Education policies and regulations at state and local level are also published by state and local agencies. A state's attorney general's opinions, although only advisory, are considered authoritative until superceded by a code or court decision and are published as *Opinions of the Attorney General.* Examples of primary sources in legal research are illustrated in Table 12.3.

Legal citation refers to a standard shorthand method of reference for all legal sources in both briefs and law reviews. Citations of constitutions, statutes, legislative materials, periodicals, works not formally printed and even books of legal material use this standard form. *A Uniform System of Citation,* periodically updated by the Harvard Law Review Association, is a reference for rules of legal citation for both primary and secondary sources.

Secondary Sources for Legal Research.   Secondary sources include 1) periodical literature, 2) encyclopedias and yearbooks, 3) monographs, casebooks, and dissertations, and 4) other secondary sources.

1. *Legal periodicals* are primarily law reviews published by law schools. Specialized journals are also available to researchers such as *The Journal of Law and Education* and *West's Education Law Reporter;* however, commentaries may also be found in the *Education Law Specialty Digest.* Both law review and legal periodicals publish **commentaries,** extensive articles which analyze and interpret specialized educational law subjects and provide extensive case citations in the footnotes. The *Index to Legal Periodicals* provides a table of contents, an index, and a table of cases. A bound copy appears every three years with monthly and annual cumulative indexes. The *Current Index to Journals in Education* and *Educational Administrative Abstracts* also index legal educational articles.

---

[9]The *descriptive word method* is similar to using an index in a book; the *topic method* is similar to using the contents page of a book. The *popular name method* allows the researcher to find the official name and citation of a law when the statute is known by its popular name.

TABLE 12.3
Examples of Primary Sources in Legal Research

Constitutions	U.S. Constitution: *U.S. Code Annotated* U.S. Constitution and states constitutions: annotated volumes of state statutes
Government rules and regulations	*Federal Register* *Code of Federal Regulations* Publications of regulations by state agencies Compilations of regulations by local agencies
U.S. statutes	*Statutes at Large* *U.S. Code; U.S. Code Annotated* *Federal Rules and Decisions* *Federal Code Annotated Popular Name Table for* *Acts of Congress*
State statutes	Publications by state agencies Annotated publications by private publishers; such as *Vernon's Annotated Missouri Statues*
Court decisions	U.S. Supreme Court: *Supreme Court Reporter* Federal Circuit Court of Appeals: *The Federal Reporter* U.S. district courts: *Federal Supplement* State courts: publications by state agencies; nine regional reports of National Reporter System Educational decisions: *West's Educational Law Reporter*
Books of index	American Digest System *Shepard's Citations*

2. *Legal encyclopedias and yearbooks* provide an overview of a legal issue by an expert with case citations. The *Corpus Juris Secundum* gives a narrative discussion of a wide variety of legal topics including "school" and "school districts." Each volume contains a word index for each topic. Cumulative supplements—cumulative pocket parts which keep the citations up-to-date—should also be searched. Although legal principles are stated, the researcher should read the actual court opinion. The *American Jurisprudence,* unlike *Corpus Juris Secundum,* is based on selected rather than all court cases in its 82 volumes. The *American Jurisprudence* contains the topic "schools" and has volume and cumulative indexes. Similar encyclopedias are published by several states for state laws. *The American Law Reports* (A. L. R.) is a series of volumes that contain commentary and annotations on selected decisions and topics by legal authorities. The topics are selected for

their general interest and cases are those in which there was a difference of judicial opinion. Each subject is treated by authorities who present balanced arguments on a legal issue.[10] The *Yearbook of School Law 1986* is one of a series of annual yearbooks published since 1982 which contain a table of cases decided by courts of record for that year. Each yearbook has a review and analysis of education law decisions for the previous year written by authorities in the field.

3. *Monographs, casebooks, and dissertations* may be in-depth treatise on a legal subject or an analysis and interpretations of selected legal topics. Monographs on educational legal issues are useful interpretations of a specific topic, such as drug and alcohol abuse (James, Hastings, & Lewis, 1987), teacher evaluation (Frels, Cooper, & Reagan, 1984), discrimination in public employment (McCarthy, 1983). Casebooks, similar to textbooks, contain a broader range of selected legal topics which are analyzed and interpreted. A legal dissertation is a comprehensive treatment of a particular topic or case.

4. *Other secondary sources* are conference papers and legal dictionaries. *The School Law Update,* issued annually since 1981, is a series of compilations of papers presented at the annual convention of NOLPE by national experts in school law. Legal dictionaries give the legal meaning of terms which often have other connotations in nonlegal situations, such as expulsion. The most comprehensive legal dictionary is *Words and Phrases* which includes any word or phrase which has been defined in any case in the American courts since 1658. It cites those cases from which the definition was derived. Other general dictionaries are *Ballentine, The Self-Pronouncing Law Dictionary, Black's Law Dictionary,* and *Bouvier's Law Dictionary and Concise Encyclopedia.*

Finding Aids.   Various methods, similar to the procedures described in Chapter 4, are used to locate primary legal sources—both statutes and court decisions. The researcher will probably have to use several methods in reviewing existing case law. Finding aids include 1) case digests, 2) looseleaf services, 3) citators, and 4) computer searches.

1. *Case **digests*** are indexes to case law, the law growing out of court decisions. To locate a case, a researcher may use the *descriptive word method,* the *topic method,* the *table of cases method* or any combination of these methods.[11] A table of cases will provide parallel citations in the American Digest System, the National Reporter System, the State Reports and the Annotated Reports and other pertinent information.

---

[10]The first A. R. L. covered reports from 1919 to 1948 in 175 volumes; the A. R. L. 2d covered from 1948 to 1965; the A. R. L. 3rd covered from 1965 to 1980. The A. R. L. 4th has been published to cover reports since 1980.

[11]The *descriptive word method* is similar to using an ERIC index by searching for cases with the descriptive word. The *topic method* is similar to using the *ERIC Thesaurus* by checking the cross-references to topics and their scope notes. The *table of cases method* requires the researcher to know the name of the case from which other citations appropriate for the topic can be located.

The American Digest System, the most comprehensive and most used of the digests, is a multi-volume index to the National Reporter System.[12] The National Reporter System (see Table 12.3) is a series of hundreds of volumes organized by regions (Atlantic, Pacific, South Eastern, and so on) and contains all cases from all courts of record. It gives the actual court opinion in each case. The National Reporter System also reports other kinds of decisions such as those found in the Federal Rules Decisions. Digests are available for Supreme Court decisions, for other federal court decisions, and for all courts of record of a given state.

West's Educational Law Reporter, beginning in 1982, cites decisions of both federal and state courts of record solely for the field of education. The *Reporter* provides the full court opinion, identical to that published in the National Reporter System. Further, the *Reporter* contains commentaries on significant court decisions which analyze the court opinion and provides guidelines for administrators and educators.

2. *Looseleaf services* aid the researcher in locating both pertinent and the most recent statutes and court decisions. The *United States Law Week* publishes text of important legislation. The *Congressional Index* gives current references to pending and new legislation. Several services provide rapid access to the most recent court decisions. The *NOLPE School Law Reporter*, issued monthly, contains all educational law decisions of state and federal courts of record. *NOLPE Notes*, issued monthly, highlights current developments in educational law and reports selected court opinions. A more general service is that of *United States Law Week*, which provides information on both Congressional legislation and the Supreme Court. The General Law Section summarizes significant weekly developments in the legislative and administrative action at both federal and state level. This section also produces *verbatim* Congressional laws that are of general interest, such as "slip laws". The Supreme Court Section reports the proceedings of the Court and contains "slip decisions".[13]

3. *Shepard's Citations* is an up-to-date authority to ascertain whether a court decision has been affirmed, reversed, overruled, vacated, distinguished, or otherwise modified by a subsequent court action. In addition, it functions as a citations index similar to the *Social Science Citations Index*. By "shepardizing" statutes, one can determine the current status of constitutional and statutory provisions. In conducting legal research, it is essential that the researcher identify the most current applicable law.

4. *Computer searches* enable a researcher to lessen the time in developing a comprehensive bibliography of sources. Two of the best known computer legal

---

[12]Each digest is published in 10-year periods as Decennial Digests with the exception of the *Century Digest* for cases from 1658 to 1896. After 1976, a series called the *Ninth Decennial Digest* provides digests of court decisions from 1976 to 1981.

[13]Because "slip decisions" (official text in pamphlet form) are mailed within a day of their being announced, subscribers such as libraries have access to the actual court decision within a week. These "slip decisions" are later paginated and compiled into advanced sheets.

retrieval systems are LEXIS and WESTLAW. WESTLAW allows a researcher to shepardize a case, browse through a case at the display terminal, and to search for other citations by key terms.

Techniques for Researching the Law

The purpose of a study of educational law is to become knowledgeable about "what the law actually is" as it applies to education. The research design is similar to that used in most law schools: a case study. This usually means an analysis of relevant court cases, augmented with an analysis of statutory law where applicable, to derive legal principles. The objective is to understand the law at the point in time. Because a court decision today may be overturned tomorrow and statutes may be passed, modified, or repealed, the law is never static.

One begins by framing a problem as a legal issue. In the process of limiting a topic, one decides if it has national or local implications. Once these preliminary steps are taken, the researcher locates primary sources of statutes and court decisions and supplements them with secondary sources.

To study a legal issue, the researcher first analyzes the statutes that may be controlling and, if appropriate, federal and state constitutions. After obtaining the relevant statutes, a bibliography of court cases is made. Each court decision is read and analyzed. Using an analytical scheme allows the researcher to proceed systematically in the case-by-case analysis and later in the synthesis of all cases selected. One analytical scheme is provided below.[14]

The facts. Who is suing whom? What situation precipitated a suit? What is the plaintiff's case based on—constitutional or statutory law, or something else? What is the defendant's response to the plaintiff's charge? What remedy is the plaintiff seeking?

The question. What is the court asked to decide, in its simplest form?

The decision and rationale. What is the court's actual decision? What are its reasons for this decision? Were there concurring and/or dissenting opinions? What was the reasoning of these judges?

Implications. Does the decision have general or local applicability? Is it consistent with prior rulings on the same subject or does it set a precedent? What effect will it probably have on a school system?

After one has analyzed the relevant statutes and court decisions, the researcher examines secondary sources. After synthesizing both primary and secondary sources, the analyst should be able to state a definitive position on the given legal issue.

---

[14]Hudgins & Vacca, *op. cit.*, pp. 51–52.

EXCERPT 12.7
Legal Commentary: "Landmark" Case

On January 20, 1988, the United States Supreme Court issued its decision in *Honig v. Doe*.[1] The Court held that the Education of the Handicapped Act (EHA)[2] precludes school officials from unilaterally excluding special needs students who become disruptive; however, authorities still have several options when they are faced with disruptive conduct: They may follow the usual discipline guidelines for regular education children; seek another placement pursuant to EHA's placement procedures; or, negotiate an interim placement with parents until another educational program is finalized.[3] . . .

CONCLUSION

At the very least, the Supreme Court has resolved a longstanding controversy regarding discipline of handicapped children. School authorities must show that the child's current educational placement is not appropriate because it will result in injury to himself, his classmates, or teachers. According to the Court, the purpose of the statute was inclusion. Yet, questions remain: How will disruptive handicapped students be treated in light of this decision? Will they by excluded, however briefly, in increasing numbers because school administrators will find it more expeditious to exclude, rather than to develop alternatives to inappropriate placements?[36]

Moreover, this case has been decided at a critical time for EHA. There is increasing empirical evidence that EHA may not be working as intended. This developing line of research indicates that the adversarial model created by Congress is not well received either by school officials, or the parents the law was intended to include.[37] *Honig* may be well-received by advocates for disabled children, but past experience with implementation suggests that its holding may be rejected by school administrators.[38] . . .

Source: From "Discipline, Disability, and Disruptive Students: Honing v. Doe" by Steven S. Goldberg, *West's Education Law Reporter*, October 15, 1987. Copyright © 1987 by West Publishing Company. Reprinted by permission.

Legal commentaries in educational law journals may discuss a single "landmark" case or a series of cases dealing with a legal issue. Commentaries on a single case, as in Excerpt 12.7, analyze the statutory law and the case, including the facts and judicial history of the case. The discussion links the case with prior cases and presents implications for policy-makers and school administrators.

Commentaries on a legal issue involving a series of cases follow a similar method of analysis. Researchers frequently identify the legal principles induced from their analysis of the cases. In Excerpt 12.8, four types of legal causes were accepted in termination of faculty tenure in the 44 cases decided from 1982–1987.

EXCERPT 12.8
Legal Commentary: Legal Principles

The case law reviewed in this paper will clarify the specific requirements institutions must meet to guarantee due process to tenured faculty and to avoid the infringement of constitutional rights of faculty at public institutions. The discussion will begin with cases challenging the existence of a tenure contract followed by case law clarifying due process procedures for termination of tenured faculty for cause. The next section will review the constitutional rights litigated by tenured faculty removed for cause and the final section will outline the types of cause used in removal of tenured faculty. Forty-one cases involving removal of tenured faculty for cause decided since 1982 provide substantial case law for this review. . . .

CONCLUSIONS

This review of the case law reveals the nature of the procedures to be followed in termination of tenured faculty for cause. The review also points out areas where courts have failed to clarify specifics of due process requirements.

- The causes reviewed above will be accepted by the courts but must be substantiated at the hearing.
- The specific charges must be clearly stated in the letter of notification to the tenured faculty member. The letter should also advise the faculty member of his or her rights under the due process procedures as outlined in institutional policy.
- The question of the right to legal counsel is yet unsettled. Although the court may hold that institutions could not deny counsel the right to attend the hearing, the institution may be able to limit counsel's participation in the proceedings. . . .

Source: From "Removing Tenured Faculty for Cause" by Robert M. Hendrickson, *West's Education Law Reporter*, October 15, 1987. Copyright © 1987 by West Publishing Company. Reprinted by permission.

Conclusions in this commentary identified the procedures to be followed in termination of tenured faculty for cause and areas of due process which the courts had failed to clarify.

■   ANALYTICAL RESEARCH IN PERSPECTIVE   ■

Analytical studies of educational topics aid in the development of knowledge and the improvement of practices. By comprehending educational concepts and events of the past, one can understand better the educational policies, trends, and practices of the present. Below are a few of the uses of analytical research.

1. *The analysis of educational concepts can aid in the selection of research problems, designs, and methodology.* The analysis of the concept of teaching as different types of teaching acts, for example, could suggest research questions and aid in designing research on teaching (Soltis, 1978). A conceptual map of the logical domain of teaching might give a clearer view of the focus of previous research and suggest topics of needed research. An analysis of a concept can provide insights for the selection of a design. Such concepts as *behavioral objectives, alternative schooling,* and *problem-solving* are not merely words but part of a language system that constructs a framework for organizing ideas in the researcher's mind. Ascertaining the meaning of the concept before data collection enables the researcher to select more appropriate variables and measures for investigating the concept.

2. *Analytical research provides knowledge about the so-called roots of educational ideas, institutions, leaders, and practices.* Knowledge of the past informs educational professionals, policy-makers, and the general society about education and its role in American society. Such knowledge often questions educational fables. By examining the fate of past solutions to enduring problems, decision-makers may become more realistic and moderate in their claims and more informed in their choices.

3. *Analytical research can clarify present legal and policy discussions by interpreting the past with disciplined detachment and reasoned historical judgment.* Analytical studies interpret the complexity of past collective educational, social, economic, legal, and political relationships. F. M. Wirt (1980) suggests that such research is useful because it is "through the process of removing the unsupportable from discussion of public life that public policy is enriched" (p. 17). Analytical research, however, never claims that it predicts future legal and policy actions.

4. *Analytical research, in a broader and perhaps more philosophical sense, can create a sense of common purpose.* Historical research may demythologize idealized notions about past events, but these interpretations also reflect a fundamental belief that public education in America has served and can serve a common good. Legal research reminds readers of basic principles reflected in constitutions and laws and interpreted by the courts. Policy-making research analyzes the implementation of these laws and decisions as they are put into practice. Common goals of education and the role of education in the American society are often neglected in fragmented empirical research. Implicit in the purpose of analytical research is a concern that the goals of education and educational practices benefit both the individual and American society.

5. *Analytical research is a dynamic area of educational inquiry because each generation reinterprets its past.* Analytical philosophers focus on the changing meanings of educational concepts. Educational historians, especially the revisionists (Cohen, 1976; Sloan, 1973; and Warren, 1978), ask new questions, use a greater variety of sources, analyze the past with a wide range of social science concepts, and apply quantitative procedures when appropriate. Often the conclusions of legal and policy-making studies are revised. A recent court case or a new policy may indicate a basic shift in previous legal principles, policy-making, or collective educational goals.

■ STANDARDS OF ADEQUACY FOR ■
ANALYTICAL RESEARCH

Analytical research requires methodological procedures to phrase an analytical topic, locate and critique primary sources, establish facts, and form generalizations for causal explanations or principles. These research processes suggest criteria for judging a historical, legal, or policy-making study as adequate research. Criteria for judging the adequacy of historical studies is followed by criteria for evaluating legal research.

Historical and Policy-Making Research

The reader judges a study in terms of the logical relationship among the problem statement, sources, generalizations, and causal explanations. The logic for the entire study flows from the problem statement. Implicit in the evaluation of a study is the question, "Did the analyst accomplish the stated purpose?" If all the elements of the research are not made explicit, the study can be criticized as biased or containing unjustifiable conclusions.

Problem Statement.   The problem statement is in the introduction to a study.

1. Is the topic appropriate for analytical research—that is, does it focus on the past or recent past?
2. Does the problem statement indicate clearly the information that will be included in the study and the information that is excluded from the study?
3. Is the analytical framework or viewpoint stated?

Selection and Criticism of Sources.   The sources are listed in the bibliography, and the criticism of the sources may be discussed in the study, the footnotes, or in a methodological appendix.

1. Does the study use primary sources relevant to the topic?
2. Are the criteria for selection of primary sources stated?
3. Were authentic sources used for documentation?
4. Does the analyst indicate criticism of sources?

Facts and Generalizations.   A reader assesses the findings or the text of the study by asking the following questions:

1. Does the study indicate the application of external criticism to ascertain the facts? If conflicting facts are presented, is a reasonable explanation offered?
2. Are the generalizations reasonable and related logically to the facts?

3. Are the generalizations appropriate for the type of analysis? One would, for example, expect minimal generalization in a study that restores a series of documents to their original text or puts a series of policy statements into chronological order. One would expect some synthesis in a descriptive or comparative analysis.
4. Are the generalizations qualified or stated in a tentative manner?

Causal Explanations.   In an analytical study, causal explanations are presented as conclusions.

1. Are the causal explanations reasonable and logically related to the facts and generalizations presented in the study?
2. Do the explanations suggest multiple causes for complex human events?
3. Does the study address all the questions stated in the introduction—that is, does it fulfill the purpose of the study?

Legal Research

Because commentaries in legal research do not follow the formats of other analytical research, the criteria for judging a study as adequate differ somewhat. A reader first notes the reputation of the institution or organization which sponsors the journal and the reputation of the author(s).

1. Is the legal issue or topic clearly stated with the scope and limitations of the problem explained?
2. Is the commentary organized logically for the analysis?
3. How were the sources selected and are they appropriate for the problem? The reader needs to scrutinize the bibliography and footnotes.
4. Is the topic or issue treated logically in an unbiased manner?
5. Do the conclusions relate logically to the analysis?

■ SUMMARY ■

The following statements summarize the major characteristics of analytical methodology and its application in educational conceptual, historical, policy-making and legal studies.

1. Analytical research, in contrast to experimental research, describes and interprets the past or recent past from selected sources.
2. Sources are written documents, oral testimonies, and relics.
3. Primary sources are documents or eyewitness testimonies of an event. Secondary sources are those documents or testimonies of individuals who did not actually observe the event.

4. Analytical studies suggest generalizations, or syntheses of facts (who, what, where, and when), about an event and state explanations, or interpretations of generalizations, which suggest multiple causes for any single event.

5. Kinds of analyses include: conceptual analysis, an edition or compilation of documents, a descriptive narration of a single event, an interpretative analysis, a comparative analysis, and a universal analysis.

6. A conceptual analysis focuses on the meanings of the language of education by describing the generic meaning, the different meanings and the appropriate usage of the concept.

7. An analysis of educational historical events focuses on biographies, movements, institutions, and practices. Policy-making studies focus on the decision-making processes of legislative, judicial, and executive branches of educational and general government.

8. A historical problem is delimited by the time period, the geographic location, the specific event studied, and the viewpoint of the analysis.

9. Specialized bibliographies and indexes locate the primary sources necessary for historical analytical research.

10. Oral testimonies, called oral history, are in-depth interviews of informants to study past events.

11. External criticism determines whether the source is the original document, a forged document, or a variant of the original document. Internal criticism determines the accuracy and trustworthiness of the statements in the source.

12. Legal studies focus on legal issues and analyze the principles derived from judicial interpretations of the law when applied to a specific court case or series of cases.

13. Important primary sources of law are state and federal statutes and constitutional provisions, and the court decisions interpreting them.

14. Secondary legal sources are legal periodicals, encyclopedias and yearbooks, monographs, casebooks, dissertations, conference papers, and others.

15. Legal sources may be found through case digests, looseleaf services, *Shepard's Citations,* and computer searches.

16. Analytical research provides knowledge and explanations of the past, clarifies present legal and policy discussions by interpreting the past with disciplined detachment, and can create a sense of common purpose about education in the American society.

17. Analytical studies are not intended to predict to future events in an exact manner.

18. Standards of adequacy for historical research emphasize the logical relationship between the problem statement, selection and criticism of sources, and the facts, generalizations, and causal explanations. Standards of adequacy for legal commentaries emphasize the reputation of the journal and the author, the scope of the legal issue, the appropriateness of the legal sources and the logical treatment of the issue and conclusions.

■ SELF-INSTRUCTIONAL REVIEW EXERCISES ■

Sample answers are in the back of the book.

Test Items

1. Analytical research differs from experimental research in that it
   a. uses primarily preserved documents.
   b. focuses on past events of the recent past.
   c. uses logical induction to interpret facts.
   d. All of the above are correct.

2. Analytical explanations
   a. are usually biased interpretations of so-called facts.
   b. suggest single causes for educational events.
   c. are abstract syntheses of generalizations that summarize collaborated facts.
   d. are seldom revised in subsequent studies.

3. A conceptual analysis of an educational concept is done to identify
   a. only the essential meaning of a concept.
   b. by random sampling of the examples and counterexamples of the typical uses of the concept.
   c. focuses on nonstandard meanings of a concept.
   d. the generic meaning, the different meanings and the appropriate usage for the concept.

4. Which of the following is an example of an analytical question?
   a. Is there a relationship between variable x and variable y?
   b. Is there a statistically significant difference between the scores of the experimental and control group?
   c. How did schools become bureaucracies during the 1920s?
   d. What is the cognitive developmental stage of students in an accelerated fifth-grade math program?

5. List in order the following items for the general research process for an analytical researcher.
   a. identifies facts and obtains collaboration
   b. applies techniques of criticism to sources
   c. uses specialized bibliographies and indexes to locate sources
   d. acquires background knowledge for the problem statements
   e. selects a research topic

6. Criticism of sources requires
   a. questioning the accuracy of each statement in a source.
   b. questioning each source as authentic.

    c. use of specialized knowledge about the way people lived and behaved in the era.

    d. All of the above are correct.

Match the following studies with the appropriate types of analytical research:

  7. a study of a school board's   a. legal research
     decision-making processes   b. historical research
  8. a biography of the National Ed-   c. policy-making research
     ucation Association founder   d. analysis of an educational concept
  9. an analysis of interpretations of
     progressive education
10. a study of the judicial interpre-
     tation of student rights

11. A legal problem does *not* involve which of the following?
    a. the parties involved
    b. the property or subject matter involved in the dispute
    c. the nature of the claim or issue in the dispute
    d. arbitrary definitions of legal terms
    e. the remedy sought in a dispute

12. Analytical studies serve several functions in educational research. Which functions are analytical studies *least* able to serve?
    a. clarify collective meanings of education that operated in the past and perhaps in present policy discussions
    b. provide knowledge and interpretations of past educational historical, legal, and policy-making events
    c. predict in an exact manner future events
    d. identify a sense of a common heritage and common purpose in American education

Application Problems

Answer the following questions for each methodological problem.

  1. A policy analyst wants to study the decision-making of a local school board.
    a. How could this topic be narrowed and delimited?
    b. List the types of possible sources and examples of sources for this topic.

  2. An analyst wants to study student discipline.
    a. How could this research problem be stated if it were a historical study? a legal study? a policy study? an analysis of a concept?
    b. State at least one specialized bibliography or index for each type of study.

3. An analyst is studying the life of Dr. Henry Daniel, who served as the chief state school officer from 1959 to 1979. The following article appeared in a newspaper reporting the remarks of various speakers given at a dinner to honor Dr. Daniel after twenty years of service as the state superintendent of education.

   More than one hundred educational leaders throughout the state honored Dr. Henry Daniel last evening at the Hotel Johnson in the state capital. Following the remarks of several officials, an engraved plaque was presented to Dr. Daniel in recognition of his outstanding educational leadership to the state.

   The governor of the state noted that because of the efforts of Dr. Daniel alone, the state established a junior college system which has rapidly grown to meet important state needs in technical-vocational education for the state's industry, provided the only institutions of higher education in rural regions, and given a better general education to freshman and sophomores than four-year colleges and universities.

   The president of the state teachers' organization praised Dr. Daniel for his efforts to raise public school teachers' salaries and to maintain professionalism by expanding the requirements for certification of teachers. However, the president noted that salaries for public school teachers still remained below the national average.

   The president of the state association for curriculum development and supervision stated that the efforts of Dr. Daniel alone established the state minimum competency testing program. This innovation has raised standards for all high school subjects and proved to the public that the high school diploma represented a high level of "educational competency."

   a. Why would the analyst question the accuracy of the statements reported in this document?
   b. How could the analyst corroborate the document's statements?

PART IV

EVALUATION RESEARCH DESIGNS AND METHODS

Most educators recognize the increasing emphasis on formal evaluation research. Educators frequently ask how evaluation research can help decision-makers and various policy-making groups improve our schools and make wise educational policies. Which designs and methods are most appropriate? Can evaluation research also yield more general educational knowledge about specific practices which are common to many schools?

In this part we describe a variety of approaches that are used in the evaluation of educational practices. Different approaches emphasize different questions regarding a specific practice. Some evaluation approaches are primarily quantitative; some approaches are primarily qualitative; and some approaches may combine both quantitative and qualitative methods.

CHAPTER 13

EVALUATION RESEARCH

■ KEY TERMS ■

merit

worth

formative evaluation

summative evaluation

objectives-oriented evaluation

target group

behavioral objectives

unit of analysis

management systems analysis

cost analysis modes

cost-benefit analysis

cost-effectiveness analysis

cost-utility analysis

cost-feasibility analysis

decision-oriented evaluation

naturalistic and participant-

   oriented evaluation

responsive evaluation

audiences

evaluation focus

memorandum of agreement

evaluation design

This chapter draws on the previous chapters concerning design, data collection, and data analysis. Evaluators need a breadth of research knowledge sufficient to make informed decisions throughout the evaluation process and educators need sufficient research knowledge to commission and interpret an evaluation report.

Evaluation is the application of research skills to determine the worth of an educational practice. Evaluation research aids in decision-making at a given site(s) and adds to the research-based knowledge about a specific practice which may or may not be relevant to more general audiences. Decisions are those which plan and improve a practice or which justify (or do not justify) widespread adoption of a practice. Evaluation skills include abilities to analyze the practice to be evaluated, acquire a knowledge of the site context and the values operating in the site, work cooperatively with diverse evaluation audiences, and communicate technical data in nontechnical language. An evaluator is both a researcher and a concerned educator whose work is essential in the overall functioning of educational organizations.

This chapter summarizes the purposes of evaluation research, presents an overview of evaluation approaches, and discusses four approaches: objectives-oriented, systems and cost-oriented, decision-oriented, and naturalistic and participant-oriented. Evaluation research is illustrated with sample studies and criteria for adequacy of evaluation proposals and studies. The potential uses and limitations of evaluation research are cited.

■ PURPOSES AND DEFINITION OF ■ EVALUATION RESEARCH

Evaluation activities have always been an integral part of education. Frequently, professional judgments have been made about the placement of students in special programs, the extent of student learning, the selection of materials, and the modification of programs. In the past, these activities were often done unsystematically and informally. The need for formal evaluation increased as society allocated greater responsibilities and resources to education, especially with the passage of the Elementary and Secondary Educational Act (ESEA) of 1965.[1] The accountability movement of the 1970s placed heavy emphasis on formal evaluation studies, particularly when educational agencies used federal monies. Presently, evaluation studies are used to determine the allocation of scarce resources and the effectiveness of alternative educational programs and to make and justify value decisions in many aspects of education.

Purposes and Roles of Evaluation

A brief definition of evaluation research is the determination of the *worth* of an educational program, product, procedure, or objective, or of the potential utility of alternative approaches to attain specific goals. Many authors have tried to categorize the purposes for which evaluations are conducted. For example, three major reasons for conducting evaluation research are *planning, improving,* and *justifying* (or not justifying) procedures, programs, and/or products.

Most educators recognize that evaluation can serve a formative purpose (such as helping to improve a curriculum) or a summative purpose (such as deciding whether that curriculum should be continued). Anderson and Ball (1978) further specify the purposes of evaluation as applied to formal programs. Evaluation can:

1. Aid decision-making processes in the installation of a program
2. Aid decision-making processes about program modification
3. Aid decision-making processes about program continuation, expansion, or certification

---

[1]See R. M. W. Travers (1983), *How research has changed American schools,* and H. Talmage (1982), Evaluation of programs, in H. E. Mitzel (Ed.), *Encyclopedia of educational research* (5th ed.).

4. Obtain evidence to rally support or opposition to a program
5. Contribute to the understanding of psychological, social, and political processes within the program and external influences on the program

H. Talmage in the *Encyclopedia of Educational Research* (1982) suggests "three purposes [which] appear most frequently in definitions of evaluation are: 1) to render judgments on the worth of a program; 2) to assist decision-makers responsible for deciding policy; and 3) to serve a political function" (p. 594). Talmage also notes that, while these purposes are not mutually exclusive, they receive different emphases in different evaluation studies, thus negating the possibility of any single comprehensive evaluation approach.

Evaluation Research Defined

Evaluation, defined from a research orientation, requires a formal evaluation design and procedures in order to collect and analyze data systematically for determining the value of a specific educational practice or anticipated practice. As Lincoln and Guba (1980) note, "the root of the term *evaluate* suggests that the function of evaluation is to place a value on the thing being appraised" (p. 61). In our discussion, educational practice refers to a program, a curriculum, a policy or administrative regulation, an organizational structure, or a product. Most examples will, however, be drawn from curriculum and program evaluation.

Merit and worth are two different attributes of value of a practice (Lincoln & Guba, 1980). **Merit** refers to those valued characteristics intrinsic to the practice for which there is relatively consistent agreement among professional peers and groups. Most educators would, for example, judge a curriculum as having merit if it worked—that is, if student objectives were achieved. A social studies curriculum has merit if students learn basic social studies skills, obtain knowledge, and develop attitudes, including that of good citizenship. A language arts curriculum would lack merit if students learned the vocabulary but failed to comprehend paragraphs and disliked reading. These criteria relate to specific characteristics of the curriculum.

The **worth** of a practice is considered in adoption decisions and requires extensive knowledge of the potential adopting site, for it is there that the values, standards, and practical constraints by which worth is judged are found. Typical evaluation questions are, "Should we use this curriculum?", "Do we need this program?", and "Can we implement this practice without unusual costs?" Worth is determined by an assessment of local needs conducted by normative methods. If the site is changed for a practice, the worth of the practice changes. A sex education program might, for example, be judged as meritorious, but its worth will vary with the values and needs of groups at different sites. Thus, one school system might have a sex education program while another thirty miles away might reject it because new personnel would be necessary and because parents and some vocal groups believe that sex education should be taught by the family and the church.

Formative and Summative Evaluation

The distinction between formative and summative evaluation, first made by Scriven (1967), has been widely accepted. In **formative evaluation,** researchers collect data to modify or revise a curriculum in a development stage. Typical questions are, "How can we teach this better?", "Is the sequence of skills and knowledge effective for student learning?", and "Is the curriculum achieving its objectives?" The evaluation results may lead to a decision to revise the curriculum, to extend the field testing to gather more data, or to abort further development in order not to waste resources on a program that ultimately may be ineffective.

Summative evaluation can be conducted once the program is fully developed—that is, when it functions well or does what the curriculum intended with few detrimental side effects. **Summative evaluation** determines the effectiveness of a program, especially in comparison with other competing programs. A typical question may be, "Which of several programs achieves these objectives most effectively and efficiently?" Summative evaluation can aid educators who make purchase or adoption decisions concerning new programs, products, or procedures.

Note that the audiences and uses for formative and summative evaluation are very different. In formative evaluation, the audience is program personnel; in summative evaluation, the audience is potential users (teachers and professionals at other sites), funding agencies, supervisors and other educational officials, as well as program personnel. Both formative and summative are essential because decisions are needed during the developmental stages of a program to improve it and again, when it is stabilized, to judge its final worth or determine its future. Unfortunately, far too many educational agencies conduct only summative evaluation (Worthen & Sanders, 1987).

Two important factors which influence the usefulness of formative evaluation are *control* and *timing*. Formative evaluation should collect data on variables over which program administrators have some control. Information which reaches administrators too late for use in program improvement is obviously useless. Table 13.1 summarizes the distinctions between formative and summative evaluation research.

The distinctions between formative and summative evaluation aid in the selection of an evaluation design. Other considerations in choosing an evaluation strategy are what "insiders" and "outsiders" want to know and the feasibility of alternative strategies. Some formative studies planned for insiders' use may yield information of interest to broader external groups[2] just as most summative evaluation studies are intended to do.

The formative-summative distinction traditionally has been used to indicate the locus of the evaluation. Formative studies are typically conducted by an inter-

---

[2]Because the level of discourse and generalizability differs between basic, applied, and evaluation research, an evaluation study which produces findings of general interest must be subsequently rewritten with appropriate literature for more general audiences. Compare Smith & Schumacher (1972) with Schumacher (1976) or Schumacher, Esham, & Bauer, 1985, 1987, 1988.

TABLE 13.1
Differences in Formative and Summative Evaluation

	Formative Evaluation	Summative Evaluation
Purpose:	To improve program	To certify program utility
Audience:	Program administrators and staff	Potential consumer or funding agency
Who Should Do It:	Internal evaluator	External evaluator
Major Characteristic:	Timely	Convincing
Measures:	Often informal	Valid/reliable
Frequency of Data Collection:	Frequent	Limited
Sample Size:	Often small	Usually large
Questions Asked:	What is working? What needs to be improved? How can it be improved?	What results occur? With whom? Under what condition? With what training? At what cost?
Design Constraints:	What information is needed? When?	What claims do you wish to make?

Source: From *Educational Evaluation: Alternative Approaches and Practical Guidelines* by R. Worthen and James R. Sanders. Copyright © 1987 Longman Inc. All rights reserved. Reprinted by permission.

nal evaluator; summative studies are typically conducted by an external evaluator. Although educational evaluators disagree about the best locus of the evaluation, wisdom suggests the use of an external evaluator in both formative and summative evaluations for credibility, a fresh outside perspective, and a neutral attitude toward worth of the practice.[3]

Standards for Judging the Quality of Evaluation Research

The publication of the *Standards for Evaluations of Educational Programs, Projects and Materials* (1981) indicates the growing professionalization and specialization of this type of research. The Joint Committee on Standards for Educational Evaluation, under the direction of Daniel Stufflebeam, represented many important educational organizations: American Association of School Administrators,

[3]Compare Anderson & Ball, 1978; Campbell, 1984; Cronbach, 1982; Scriven, 1972.

American Educational Research Association, American Federation of Teachers, American Personnel and Guidance Association, American Psychological Association, Association for Supervision and Curriculum Development, Council for American Private Education, Education Commission of the States, National Association of Elementary School Principals, National Council on Measurement in Education, National Education Association, National School Boards Association and the like. The standards were developed because of concerns about the quality of some evaluation studies, the insensitivity of some studies to the practice being evaluated, and lack of agreed-upon criteria to improve the professionalization of this type of research. The thirty standards, similar to the *Standards for Educational and Psychological Tests,* were developed to provide a common language, a conceptual framework for evaluation, and a basis for self-regulation by professional evaluators.

The Joint Committee developed four criteria which a good evaluation study satisfies: utility, feasibility, propriety, and accuracy. Each criterion is described further with specific standards. These are summarized below.[4]

1. *Utility Standards* are to ensure that an evaluation will serve the practical and timely information needs of given audiences. These eight standards are: audience identification, evaluator credibility, information scope and selection, valuation interpretation, report clarity, report dissemination, report timeliness, and evaluation impact.

2. *Feasibility Standards* are to ensure that an evaluation will be realistic, frugal, and diplomatic. These three standards are: practical procedures, political viability, and cost-effectiveness.

3. *Propriety Standards* are to ensure that an evaluation will be conducted legally, ethically, and with due regard for the welfare of those involved in the evaluation and those affected by its findings. These standards are: formal obligation, conflict of interest, full and frank disclosure, public's right to know, rights of human subjects, human interactions, balanced reporting, and fiscal responsibility.

4. *Accuracy Standards* are to ensure that an evaluation will state and convey technically adequate information about the features of the practice studied that determine its value. These eleven standards are: object identification, context analysis, described purposes and procedures, defensible information sources, valid and reliable measurement, systematic data control, analysis of quantitative information, analysis of qualitative information, justified conclusions, and objective reporting.

The standards are not a cookbook of steps to follow, but, rather, a compilation of commonly agreed-upon characteristics of good evaluation practice. In any specific formal evaluation situation, choices and trade-offs relating to each standard are within the province of the evaluator. Further, the standards serve as a guide as an evaluator proceeds from deciding whether to do a study, clarifying and assessing purposes, data collection, data analysis, and reporting findings.[5]

[4]See Joint Committee on Standards for Educational Evaluation (1981), *Standards for evaluations of educational programs, projects, and materials,* New York: McGraw-Hill.

[5]See Analysis of the Relative Importance of Thirty Standards in Performing Ten Tasks in Evaluation, in B. R. Worthen & J. R. Sanders, *op cit.,* (1987, p. 377).

■ SELECTED APPROACHES ■
TO EVALUATION

Many types of studies are called evaluation research. Evaluation studies are responses to recognized needs by educators and various policy groups. A broad array of educational entities are evaluated. These include:

1. Curriculum materials (textbooks, films, microcomputers, hand calculators, educational television)
2. Programs (Head Start, language arts program, talented and gifted programs, preventive dropout programs)
3. Instructional methods (discussions, lectures, language experience in reading, discovery)
4. Educators (administrators, preservice teachers, volunteer tutors, inservice teachers)
5. Students (learning disabilities students, elementary students, college students, advanced placement students)
6. Organizations (alternative schools, high schools, vocational-technical schools, higher education)
7. Management, resource utilization, and costs

Crucial to evaluation is the decision on the entity to be evaluated: a group, a product, a method, an organization, or a management system. Careful delineation of the entity and all of its components helps the evaluator decide which aspects or components are the most important for evaluation.

Models are relatively explicit procedures, but no model provides such specific directions that, even if followed carefully, a satisfactory evaluation will result. More important, no one model is sufficient for even a simple evaluation. We thus prefer to call these approaches to evaluation rather than models.

Despite the diversity, commonalities do exist among evaluation approaches. Because evaluation is multifaceted and it can be conducted in different phases of a program's development, the same evaluation model can be classified in diverse ways, depending on the emphasis. A number of evaluators have published schema, grouping the "models" as approaches. Each approach has prominent theorists, explicit rationales, discussions in the literature, a group of practitioners, actual evaluation studies, and critics. Major evaluation approaches are classified in the list below.

1. *Objectives-oriented approaches,* where the focus is on specifying goals and objectives and determining the extent to which they have been attained.
2. *Systems and cost-oriented approaches,* where the central concern is that of identifying and meeting the informational needs of government funding agencies and policy-makers.
3. *Consumer-oriented approaches,* where the central issue is developing evaluative information on educational "products," broadly defined, for

use by educational consumers in choosing among competing curricula, instructional products, and the like.[6]

4. *Expertise-oriented approaches,* which depend primarily on the direct application of professional expertise to judge the quality of educational endeavors, especially the resources and the processes.[7]

5. *Decision-oriented approaches,* where the emphasis is describing and assessing an educational change process and resulting outcomes to provide information to a decision-maker.

6. *Adversary-oriented approaches,* where planned opposition in points of view of different evaluators (pro and con) is the focus of the evaluation.[8]

7. *Naturalistic and participant-oriented approaches,* where naturalistic inquiry and involvement of participants (stakeholders in the practice which is evaluated) are central in determining the values, criteria, needs, and data for the evaluation.

Four approaches most frequently used are discussed in this chapter. The approaches illustrate the diversity of evaluation research: objectives-oriented evaluation, systems and cost-oriented analysis, decision-oriented evaluation, and naturalistic and participant-oriented evaluation. These approaches contain diverse orientations to evaluation, especially in the source of the evaluation questions. The source of the evaluation questions determines the evaluation focus, which in turn influences the evaluation design and the usefulness of the evaluation report. The source of questions in an objectives-based study is the curriculum or instructional objectives. In management and cost analysis the source of questions is typically the government agency funding the project or the policy-maker. The source of questions in the decision-making study is the decision-maker, whereas in naturalistic evaluation the source of the questions is the different audiences (that is, stakeholders, including the participants, affected by the practice).

Objectives-Oriented Evaluation

Objectives-oriented evaluation determines the degree to which the objectives of a practice are attained by the target group. In other words, the evaluation measures the outcomes of the practice.[9] The discrepancy between the stated

[6]See M. Scriven (1974), Standards for the evaluation of educational programs and products in G. D. Borich (Ed.), *Evaluating educational programs and products* and G. D. Tallmadge (1977), *Ideabook: JDRD.* An analogy to the consumer-oriented approach is product ratings by the Consumers Union.

[7]Examples are 1) accreditation and informal professional review systems, 2) ad hoc panel reviews such as those by funding agencies or blue-ribbon panels (such as the National Commission on Excellence in Education), and 3) educational connoisseurship and criticism (see E. Eisner, 1979).

[8]See Levine (1982), Stenzel (1982), and Wolf (1979). An analogy is one of a jury trial with teams of prosecutors and defenders operating under rules of evidence.

[9]R. W. Tyler (1942, 1950) is credited with conceptualizing and popularizing this approach in education. Tyler's approach included general goals to establish purposes, rather than premature formation of behavioral objectives. General goals, however, eventually require operational definitions to select instruments and groups.

TABLE 13.2
Steps in Conducting
Objectives-Based Evaluation

Step 1	Step 2	Step 3	Step 4	Step 5
Selection of measurable objectives	Selection of instrument(s)	Selection of evaluation design	Data collection and analysis	Interpretation of results

objectives and the outcomes is the measure of success of the practice.[10] The practice may be a curriculum, in-service training, an in-school suspension program, parent education, or the like. The **target group,** the group whose behavior is expected to change, may be students, parents, teachers, or others. We will illustrate the steps (see Table 13.2) with curriculum evaluation. Although the approach appears simple, a reader should be aware of the research decisions that affect the usefulness of the results.

Selection of Measurable Objectives.   An evaluation study measures objectives, not abstract goals, of the practice. Curriculum goals are usually broad, general statements, representing values in the society. Objectives are specific statements which are related logically to the goals and attainable through instruction. A typical social studies goal is that students will become law-abiding citizens. "Law-abiding citizen" refers to an informed adult who pays taxes, votes in elections, serves on juries, and participates in a democracy. This behavior occurs outside the instructional process and is difficult to relate to a specific curriculum. Students can, however, be evaluated on their knowledge of a citizen's duties and rights, their participation in mock elections, and their skills in analyzing current issues.

Only student outcomes stated as **behavioral objectives** are evaluated. Behavioral objective is synonymous with performance or measured objective. Behavioral objectives are either the terminal student behaviors or student products (a research paper, clay figurine, oral presentation, and so on), but *not* the process leading to the terminal behavior. The criteria for achievement of the objective may or may not be stated in the objective. Four examples of behavioral objectives that differ in level of generality are:

---

[10]Other models are Mitfessel and Michael's (1967) evaluation paradigm, Hammond's (1973) evaluation approach, and Provus's (1971) discrepancy evaluation model.

A student, on request, will be able to spell and capitalize his or her name correctly.

A student will be able to compute correctly the answer to any division problems chosen randomly from the review exercises.

A student will produce a drawing that is judged by three raters as creative by the criteria of originality, flexibility, and elaboration developed by the raters.

At least 90 percent of the students will be able to pass 70 percent of a competence test in mathematics.

The last example is a performance objective that states the minimal group performance of 90 percent and the minimal individual student performance.[11] An analysis of the curriculum content coverage and emphasis will suggest those objectives that are the most important (Walker & Schaffarzick, 1974).

If the objectives are stated in other than behavioral terms, the evaluator has three choices: reword the objectives in behavioral terms without changing the intent, ignore the nonbehavioral objectives, or communicate to the client the fact that nonbehavioral objectives will not be measured, but that these objectives could be described or appraised with other procedures.

Selection of Instruments and Design. Instruments may be tests, questionnaires and self-report devices, rating scales, observation systems, and interview schedules. The typical instrument is a standardized norm-referenced achievement test. Evaluators frequently use data from a routine testing program. Existing test data should be valid for the evaluation. *Content validity* evidence can be determined by a panel of local experts logically comparing the curriculum content with the test items to determine the goodness-of-fit. The validity and reliability of a subtest may be considerably lower than for the entire test and should be checked in *Mental Measurements Yearbooks*. Other considerations are the appropriateness of the norms for the target group and the type of information sought. Most standardized norm-referenced tests provide only general information about students as compared to those in the norm group.

Criterion-referenced instruments may be used to assess student outcomes. Criterion-referenced instruments compare performance to predetermined criteria, standards, or a well-defined behavioral domain: that is, the test developers state the objectives and then develop test items. Criterion-referenced instruments assess both group and individual students. Scores may range from low to high achievement because the reference is to a criterion, not a norm group whose scores are distributed as a normal curve.

---

[11]For further discussion of objectives, see W. J. Popham (1975), *Educational evaluation*, pp. 50–51, 86–87. Taxonomies of cognitive, affective, and psychomotor domains provide a continuum of difficulty level of objectives in each domain. See B. S. Bloom, et al. (1956), *Taxonomy of educational objectives, handbook I: Cognitive domain;* D. R. Krathwohl, et al. (1964), *Taxonomy of educational objectives, handbook II: Affective domain;* E. J. Simpson (1966), *The classification of educational objectives: Psychomotor domain.*

Criterion-referenced instruments must meet the requirements of any measurement procedure. If an evaluator or a local school system plans to develop a criterion-referenced instrument, knowledge of measurement and instrument development is necessary. The instrument should be valid and reliable for the evaluation purposes, although the type of validity and reliability may differ from that associated with norm-referenced tests.[12] Field testing is essential. There is controversy over the use of criterion-referenced tests. Some contend that criterion-referenced tests are superior, while others claim that they are questionable and invalid (Popham & Ebel, 1978).

The most useful design in an objectives-based evaluation is a randomized or matched groups design; however, it may not be feasible. Quasi-experimental designs, such as the one-group pretest and posttest, time series, or counterbalanced designs are used. Because most programs have both cognitive and affective objectives, a comprehensive evaluation would measure different types of objectives if valid and reliable instruments were available or could be developed. Factors in selecting a design are the nature and number of objectives, the target groups, internal and external validity, and the unit of analysis. The **unit of analysis** is the smallest independent unit of data: a group or an individual.

An evaluation report states the validity and reliability of the instrument, which is the only source of data for determining achievement of objectives. Previous validity and reliability studies may be cited. The report also gives a description of the developmental process and field testing results for locally developed instruments. Factors relating to internal and external validity of the design with their possible effects on the results are noted.

Interpretation of Results.   The evaluation assesses the percentage of the target group that achieved the predetermined objectives, or it assesses which program, compared to others with similar objectives, is more successful in achieving the objectives. When the evaluator looks more closely at the objectives, he or she often finds that they are stated at different levels of specificity and that not all objectives can be evaluated. The means for selecting the objectives for formal evaluation are often inconsistent. Because only terminal outcomes are actually assessed, process evaluation is omitted. The results may suggest modifications of a practice but provide no specific directions for intervention to improve a practice, nor do the results provide complete information necessary for adopting a practice at other sites.

Objectives-based evaluation, however, is probably the most frequently used approach for several reasons. Most educators would agree that successful attainment of objectives does indicate both the merit and worth of a practice. Educators can demonstrate accountability and the productive use of public funds when objectives are attained. Another advantage of the objectives-based approach is its

---

[12]For a minimal competency test required for, say, high school graduation, *curricular validity* is important. It seems unfair to withhold a diploma from someone who did not learn a competency because it was not in the curriculum. The problems of obtaining evidence of curricular validity and *instructional validity*, a more restrictive term, are myriad. See W. A. Mehrens and I. J. Lehmann (1987), *Measurement and evaluation in education and psychology* (4th ed.).

highly definable methodology. The procedures for this approach have been worked out in great detail, a fact that appeals to a number of novice evaluators who must conduct annual evaluations. No other approach has such an elaborate technology and scientific basis. Furthermore, the nonattainment of objectives or of some objectives can lead to questioning programmatic components and a closer scrutiny of the practice.

Systems and Cost-Oriented Analysis

A systems analysis approach to evaluation answers such questions as: Is the program reaching the target group? Is it being implemented as planned? Is it effective? How much does it cost, and what are the costs relative to its effectiveness? The evaluation provides information about program planning, program monitoring, impact assessment, and economic efficiency. Cost-benefit analysis is the hallmark of the approach, which is mandated by federal funding agencies; however, components of the approach are applicable to a number of educational situations.

Management Systems Analysis.   The history of the evaluations of Title I of the Elementary and Secondary Education Act, which provided funds for economically disadvantaged children, is that of an attempt to use the systems analysis approach. The Office of Education mandated such an approach in all 30,000 Title I projects serving more than five million children. These mandated evaluations use test scores as the only measure of success, although other management data are reported. The evaluations are concerned with maximizing and aggregating rather than with distribution. All results are reported as a specially developed normal-curve equivalent and are aggregated at the state and national level. Presumably, one score can represent the state or the nation.

In **management systems analysis** a consensus on goals is assumed, and the problem is to document the implementation of government programs and to measure outcomes. Experimental design is necessary to establish cause-and-effect relationships between programs and outcomes. After outcomes have been measured in psychological, sociological, or economic terms, programs can be compared on costs to determine the outcome that can be produced for the least money. Social science methodology is essential in this evaluation approach.

Cost Analysis.   Modes of cost analysis have recently been developed that are more widely applied than federal programs evaluation. Levin (1981) delineates four **cost analysis** modes to aid in policy choices: cost-benefit, cost-effectiveness, cost-utility, and cost-feasibility. Cost-benefit and cost-effectiveness, as summative evaluation, are most frequently found in evaluation reports and publications, but cost-utility and cost-feasibility may be carried out as part of formative evaluation.

Cost-effectiveness analysis illustrates the evaluation approach. Cost-effectiveness determines whether the most effective programs are also the most cost-effective. For example, a study compared the effects of computer-assisted instruction (CAI) and teacher instruction and found that seven minutes a day of drill and practice on a computer terminal provided gains in arithmetic scores equivalent to twenty-five minutes a day of teacher instruction. When a cost factor is included in the analysis, however, one finds that seven minutes a day of CAI would have required at least an additional twenty percent of the instructional budget, while additional classroom drill and practice with similar student gains would have required only an additional five percent (Levin, 1975).

Cost analysis is based on the assumption that policy choices should take into account the resource demands of alternatives as well as their outcomes. "Only those alternatives which provide the best results for a given level of resource use or impose the least cost for a given level of results will enable us to maximize the overall effectiveness of programs" (Levin, 1981, p. 17). The modes of analysis—cost-benefit, cost-effectiveness, cost-utility, and cost-feasibility—differ in distinguishing features, strengths, and weaknesses, as noted in Table 13.3.

Cost-benefit analysis (CB) evaluates decision alternatives by comparing the costs and benefits to society. Both costs and benefits are measured in monetary values. The alternative that produced the highest benefits relative to costs should thus be selected. The advantage of CB is that a range of comparisons can be made among alternatives within education (different instructional programs) and among service types (education, health, and transportation). Benefits from three adult literacy programs, for example, could be expressed as improvements in productivity, earnings, and self-provided services in society or could directly assess the changes in earnings, occupational attainments, and self-provided services among the three treatment groups. The advantages of CB in policy-making are apparent, but all benefits and costs must be expressed in pecuniary terms. Because of the difficulty of converting some educational benefits, such as affective outcomes of learning, to monetary value, CB would be inadequate if those benefits are important. Other modes of cost analysis could be used, however.

Cost-effectiveness analysis (CE) compares program outcomes (effectiveness) with the costs of alternative programs when the objectives of different programs are similar and when common measures of effectiveness are used. Effectiveness could be measured by standardized achievement tests, psychological tests, or physical tests. A study might, for example, indicate that it costs less to produce similar gains in mathematics achievement with peer tutoring than with computer-assisted instruction or small group instruction. Outcome measures need not be converted to monetary values, and the analysis is replicable.

Cost-utility analysis (CU) and cost-feasibility analysis (CF) are carried out when administrators must choose between possible alternatives and they lack the resources for a formal evaluation. A **cost-utility analysis** yields the alternatives that, according to professional judgments, are most likely to produce the most desired outcomes at the lowest cost. A **cost-feasibility analysis** estimates the costs to ascertain whether or not the alternative is realistic, given an existing budget.

Cost analysis evaluations enable educators and policy-makers to consider the impact of costs on different alternatives in order to make feasibility decisions, to estimate the probability of several desired outcomes relative to costs, and to compare cost-effectiveness and cost-benefits of alternative programs. However, CB

TABLE 13.3
Modes of Cost Analysis

Type of Analysis	Distinguishing Feature	Strengths	Weaknesses
Cost-benefit (CB)	Outcomes measured in monetary values	Compares alternative within service Compares across services Results expressed as internal rate of return, net benefits, or cost-benefit ratios Replicable	Difficulty of converting all outcomes to monetary values
Cost-effective (CE)	Outcomes measured in units of effects	Outcomes can be measured as psychological or physical changes Replicable	Unit of effectiveness must be same among programs with same goals
Cost-utility (CU)	Outcomes measured by subjective judgments	Can integrate multiple outcomes into a single value	Measures are subjective Not replicable
Cost-feasibility (CF)	Estimate possibility of cost within fiscal constraint	Indicates if further consideration of alternative is feasible	Not deal with outcomes of alternative

Source: From "Cost Analysis" by Henry M. Levin, cited in *New Techniques for Evaluation,* edited by Nick L. Smith (Beverly Hills, California: Sage Publications, 1981). Reprinted by permission of Henry M. Levin.

and CE evaluations fail to provide automatic policy choices between alternatives because nonquantifiable outcomes and constraints are not part of the analysis, and small differences between CB and CE ratios among alternatives are not meaningful in decision-making. Expertise in cost analysis requires formal mastery of the underlying tools of both economic analysis and evaluation.[13]

[13]For further explanation of these approaches, see P. H. Rossi & H. E. Freeman (1982), *Evaluation: A systematic approach* (2nd ed.); J. Rothenberg (1975), Cost-benefit analysis: A methodological exposition, in M. Guttentag & E. L. Struening (Eds.), *Handbook of evaluation research II;* H. M. Levin (1981), Cost analysis, in N. Smith (Ed.), *New techniques for evaluation;* and M. S. Thompson (1980), *Benefit-cost analysis for program evaluation.*

Decision-Oriented Evaluation

Decision-oriented evaluation has a broader scope than the objectives-based and systems approaches and implies a theory of educational change. In this approach, "evaluation is the process of determining the kinds of decisions that have to be made; selecting, collecting, and analyzing the information needed in making these decisions; and reporting this information to appropriate decision-makers" (Alkin, 1969, p. 2). Decision alternatives are identified by the evaluator and the decision-maker, who determines merit and worth. Decision alternatives can be routine maintenance decisions (staff policies) or incremental decisions leading to system-wide change requiring major resource allocation. **Decision-oriented evaluation** studies may thus be done at any point in a change process: needs assessment, program planning, implementation, or process and outcome evaluation. The types of evaluation studies with their subsequent decisions are summarized in Table 13.4 and below.

1. *Needs assessment* compares the current status and values of an educational system to desired outcomes. The evaluation identifies the *context*, provides baseline data on accomplishments of the site, and identifies unmet needs. Needs can be stated by students, the community, other groups, or the society as a whole in relation to the system. The summary data are primarily historical, descriptive, and comparative. Needs assessment leads to selection of a program to achieve specific objectives.

2. *Program planning and input evaluation* examines alternative strategies, such as adoption of an available program or development of a new program, to achieve the new objectives. Researchers study existing programs for practicality, cost, and the ease of reproducing components to achieve the objectives. They also examine the feasibility of local development of a program. Input evaluation provides information for deciding how to use the resources to meet desired program objectives. The purpose is to assess one or more strategies in terms of how each strategy might affect staffing, time, and budget as well as their potential for meeting the objectives. Program planning evaluation leads to the selection of a plan, including procedures, materials, facilities, equipment, schedule, staffing, and budgets for program development or implementation.

3. *Implementation evaluation* assesses the extent to which a program is developed or implemented as planned, and it identifies any defects in the program. It also provides information with which to anticipate changes necessary for continued program development and implementation. Implementation evaluation monitors and records what happened in program development. The record is useful in retrospective analysis of decisions, strengths, and weaknesses in the plans.

4. *Process evaluation* provides information on the relative success of the various components of a program and the extent to which the enroute objectives and products are achieved. The evaluator is in the role of a so-called "interventionist," collecting data that will lead to immediate program improvement. Data collection requires testing procedures and other methods. This kind of evaluation could also focus on the impact of a program on other processes or programs. Process evaluation results in program modification.

TABLE 13.4
Decision-Oriented Evaluation[a]

Needs Assessment

Evaluation   Current status contrasted with desired status—educational need

Decision   Problem selection

Program Planning and Input Evaluation

Evaluation   Kinds of programs that fit objectives derived from needs assessment and possible strategies

Decision   Program plan

Implementation Evaluation

Evaluation   Degree to which the program is implemented as planned

Decision   Program modification

Process Evaluation

Evaluation   Extant program achieves its objectives and enroute products

Decision   Program modification and improvement

Outcome or Product Evaluation

Evaluation   Worth of program as reflected by process and outcomes

Decision   Program certification and adoption

---

[a] Based on Stufflebeam, D. L., et al. (1971). *Educational evaluation and decision-making*, pp. 215–239; Alkin, M.C. (1969). Evaluation theory development. *Evaluation comment*, 2, 2–7; and Popham, W. J. (1975). *Educational evaluation*, pp. 37–38.

5. *Outcome or product evaluation* assesses the extent to which objectives were achieved. The data obtained include objectives-based evaluation and other information from earlier evaluations. Previous information explains why the objectives were or were not achieved, and it helps the decision-maker to eliminate, modify, retain, or expand the program for wider use. The general worth of the program is determined by the way the outcomes it produces relate to the objectives selected from the needs assessment. Outcome evaluation leads to decisions regarding program certification and adoption.

Finally, the decision-oriented approach to evaluation focuses on gathering information by a variety of methods to aid in the decisions made for program development and adoption or for its wider use. Educational change is a logical, rational activity, and evaluation is an extension of this rationality. Possible difficulties in using it lie in conflicting values and goal dissension in a complex educational system and between the educational organization and its constituencies (Schumacher, 1979). The decision-oriented approach assumes that the decision-maker is sensitive to possible problems in bringing about educational change and is willing to obtain information regarding these realities. Collaboration rather than cooperation between the evaluator and decision-maker could, however, result in biased data. Furthermore, decisions are not usually expressed as clear alternatives and often change meaning dramatically over time. In other words, with this approach it is more difficult to specify and anticipate decisions to be served than it would first appear. Because the evaluator works closely with the decision-maker, the impact of the evaluation effort is dependent as much on the skills of the evaluator as it is on the leadership of the decision-maker.

Despite these difficulties, the decision-oriented approach allows for educational and methodological soundness in evaluation. Program evaluation is *not* based on an isolated outcome since context, input, plans, process, and outcome data are collected and the strengths, weaknesses, and side effects are assessed. The degree of program implementation is addressed before student outcomes are assessed. Participant involvement in evaluation and in communication of useful information is emphasized. The evaluation may affect educational practices informally through the evaluation process or formally through the final evaluation study.[14] The approach is flexible—it may be used for a formative purpose to guide decision-making throughout an educational change process; it may be used for a summative purpose to demonstrate accountability with a record of prior decisions and the bases for those decisions and a record of the actual process, attainments, and recycling decisions.

Naturalistic and Participant-Oriented Evaluation

Since 1967, a number of evaluation theorists and users have reacted to what they consider to be the dominance of mechanistic and insensitive approaches to evaluation in education. Concerns expressed were: 1) technically sophisticated instruments and reports often distracted from what was really happening in education; 2) many large-scale evaluations were conducted without evaluators even once visiting some classrooms; and 3) report recommendations did not reflect an understanding of the phenomena behind the numbers, charts, and tables. Educators further argued that the human element, which was found in the complexities of every day reality and the different perspectives of those engaged in education, was missing from most evaluation studies. Hence, these approaches are called naturalistic and participant-oriented by some authors.[15]

Naturalistic and participant-oriented evaluation is a holistic approach using multiplicity of data to provide an understanding of the divergent values of a practice from the participants' perspectives. The literature and actual evaluation studies illustrate some commonalities of naturalistic and participant-oriented evaluation which are:

[14]See D. L. Stufflebeam et. al. (1971), *Educational evaluation and decision-making;* D. L. Stufflebeam (1983), The CIPP model for program evaluation, in G. F. Madaus, M. Scriven & D. L. Stufflebeam (Eds.), *Evaluation models;* and D. L. Stufflebeam & A. J. Shinkfield (1985), *Systematic evaluation.* Also see M. Q. Patton (1987), *Utilization-focused evaluation* (2nd ed.).

[15]Robert Stake (1967, 1975a, 1975b, 1978) provided an impetus and the principles which guided the evolution of this approach.

1. Uses a *holistic approach* which sees education as a complex human endeavor.
2. Accommodates and protects *value pluralism* by presenting or summarizing disparate preferences about the practice evaluated.
3. Reports *"portrayals"*—as they have come to be called—of a person, classroom, school, district, project, or program which is placed in the broader context in which it functions.
4. Depends on *inductive reasoning* which emerges from grassroots observation and discovery.
5. Uses *multiplicity of data* from a number of different sources, usually within a qualitative methodology or combining qualitative and quantitative data.
6. Uses an *emergent design* to give an understanding of one specific practice with its contextual influences, process variations, and life histories.
7. Records *multiple realities* rather than a single reality.

Ethnographic methodology has been adopted for evaluation purposes.

Robert Stake noted that many evaluation studies are not used because the report is irrelevant, that is, unresponsive to the client's needs. According to Stake, "an educational evaluation is responsive evaluation if it orients more directly to program activities than to program intents; responds to audience requirements for information; and if the different value-perspectives present are referred to in reporting the success and failure of the programs" (1975a, p. 14). **Responsive evaluation** is an old alternative based on what people do naturally when they evaluate things: they observe and react. "The responsive evaluation approach tries to respond to the *natural* ways in which people assimilate information and arrive at *understanding*" (Stake, 1973, p. 3). The evaluation design emerges from the issues and concerns expressed at the site.

Prominent Events: Informal Strategies.   Responsive evaluation, in contrast with research procedures, includes events that recur. To Stake, "any event can follow any event, many events occur simultaneously, and the evaluator returns to each event many times before the evaluation is finished" (1975b, p. 18). In Figure 13.1 the prominent events are presented as the face of a clock, thus emphasizing the cyclic nature of the approach.

The events in responsive evaluation can be expressed as research phases. In phase 1 (noon to 4 o'clock, Figure 13.1) the evaluator talks with clients, program staff, and **audiences**—anyone directly or indirectly connected with the program— to get a sense of the different perspectives and values of the program. The evaluator observes the program in operation. From these activities, the evaluator discovers the meaning of the purposes of the program and conceptualizes the issues and problems. In phase 2 (4 to 7 o'clock, Figure 13.1) the evaluator ascertains the data needs and selects data collection methods. Although Stake expects observers and judges to be the primary method of data collection, instruments may be appropriate. The data are organized as antecedents, transactions, and outcomes, including both intended and unintended outcomes. In phase 3 (8 to 11 o'clock, Figure 13.1) the evaluator is concerned with communicating the findings in natural ways. Por-

FIGURE 13.1
Prominent Events in Naturalistic and Participant-Oriented Evaluation

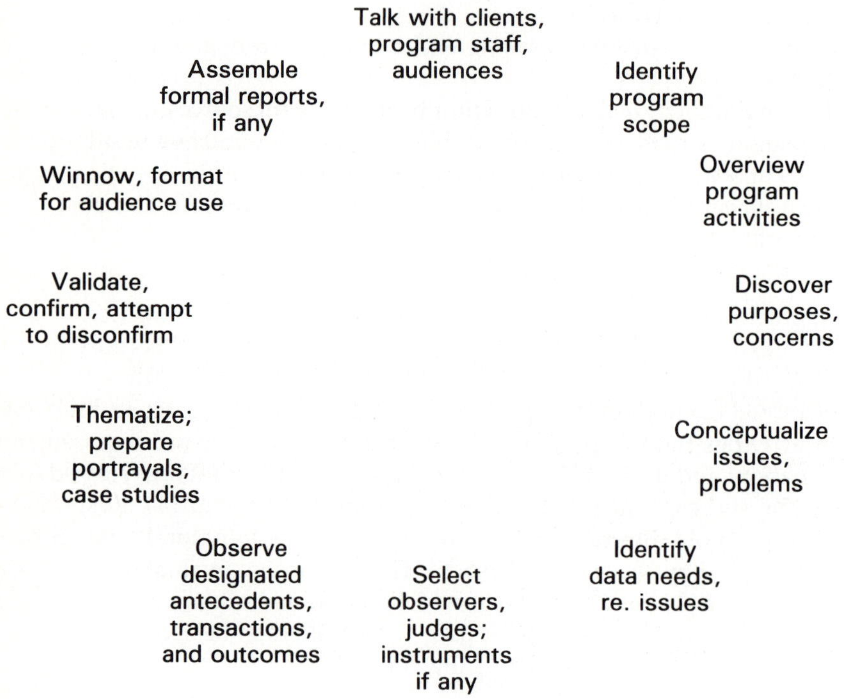

Talk with clients,
program staff,
audiences

Assemble
formal reports,
if any

Identify
program
scope

Winnow, format
for audience use

Overview
program
activities

Validate,
confirm, attempt
to disconfirm

Discover
purposes,
concerns

Thematize;
prepare
portrayals,
case studies

Conceptualize
issues,
problems

Observe
designated
antecedents,
transactions,
and outcomes

Select
observers,
judges;
instruments
if any

Identify
data needs,
re. issues

Source: From *Evaluating the Arts in Education: A Responsive Approach* by Robert E. Stake (Columbus, Ohio: Charles E. Merrill, 1975). Reprinted by permission of the author.

trayals can be embodied in the conventional research report, but they usually will take the form of descriptive case studies, artifacts, round table discussions, newspaper articles, graphics, or videotapes, depending on the audience. Only the primary concerns of each audience are reported to that audience. Last, the evaluator assembles formal reports, if any.

Evaluator's Role.   Two aspects of responsive evaluation, the evaluator's role and continuous feedback, distinguish this approach from the prior approaches discussed. The evaluator responds to audience concerns as these change throughout program development and stimulates ideas by trying out data-based insights and findings on the respondents. Guba and Lincoln suggest that the "evaluator is drawn into the activity as a full partner, no longer objective and aloof but *interactive*" (1981, p. 31). Negotiation and interaction are part of the method of insuring accuracy and communication. Communication is a two-stage process in which findings are tried out on different audiences. This may lead to the evaluator's returning to the field for additional data or altering the way findings are stated in order to communicate more effectively. The results presented in the final report should not surprise any audience, because its content has been thoroughly criticized before release.

In summary, the naturalistic evaluator recognizes that the concerns of different audiences about a program represent different values and data needs. The evaluator must select those concerns and issues that, within the limits of time and resources, are important, legitimate, and relevant. The discovery of pluralistic values surrounding a program is made by the evaluator and is independent of the perception of any single decision-maker. The source for the evaluation focus and questions is thus the various audiences. A variety of methodologies and designs can be used. The flexibility of responsive evaluation assures that the evaluation will be serviceable to the audiences.[16]

Naturalistic and participant-oriented evaluation is usually a case study, and as with other subjective approaches there is some difficulty in establishing its credibility in a predominantly scientific community.[17] Although most case studies differ in matters of emphasis rather than in matters of truth or falsity, different observers emphasize different events. Methodological consistency remains a problem with this approach, as does the representation of diverse interests. Some believe that evaluators should balance the interests according to their own sense of justice; other evaluators take a disinterested and neutral position, providing descriptions and analysis but not recommendations. In addition, writing portrayals or case studies requires skill, training, and an ability to handle confidential data. Despite these difficulties, a well-constructed case study is a powerful evaluation, with the potential for being coherent, fair to holders of diverse views in complex situations, and accurate, especially on the inner workings of a program.

■ SAMPLE EVALUATION STUDIES ■

Evaluation approaches are theoretical models which guide the designing of an evaluation of a practice in a particular context. As previously noted, evaluation approaches are typically combined or one aspect of an approach emphasized in a single study. Determining the information needs and the potential use of that information is crucial. Two examples are presented for illustration: an objectives-setting study with multivariate statistics and an implementation-outcome study using qualitative and quantitative data.

---

[16]See R. E. Stake (ed.), (1975a), *Evaluating the arts in education: A responsive approach* and (1975b), *Program evaluation, particularly responsive evaluation*; E. G. Guba (1978), *Naturalistic inquiry*; E. G. Guba and Y. S. Lincoln (1981), *Effective evaluation*; M. Q. Patton (1980), *Qualitative evaluation*.

[17]Advances in naturalistic and participant-oriented approaches have largely neutralized the concerns regarding credibility (external validity), applicability (external validity), consistency (reliability), and the neutrality of the evaluator. See D. D. Williams (Ed.), (1986), *Naturalistic evaluation*, *New Directions for Program Evaluation, No. 30* and M. M. Mark & R. L. Shotland (Eds.) (1987), *Multiple methods in program evaluation, New Directions for Program Evaluation, No. 35.*

Objectives-Setting Study

This study was conducted after an informal planning group of school principals and elementary-education university professors completed the feasibility planning for a collaborative teacher-education program by an urban university and a metropolitan school system. This planning group envisioned that school personnel—including principals and supervising teachers of student teachers—and university professors would be involved in the planning and development of the collaborative teacher education program. The co-directors were concerned that although all participants agreed on the goals of preservice teacher education, there were no clearly articulated objectives regarding professional knowledge expectations for those preservice elementary education students who entered the program. One of the first studies done in the three-year project was an objectives-setting study. Excerpt 13.1 reports the results.

Design.   A professional education knowledge and beliefs inventory, developed and used for five years at another College of Education, was made available to program personnel. The Professional Knowledge section of the inventory contained five topics of pedagogical knowledge: Students (twelve items), Social Context of Schooling (thirteen items), Curriculum (twelve items), Teachers (eight items), and Teaching Strategies (fifteen items). For the items which described specific topics of professional knowledge, respondents were asked to indicate "How important is it for participants in this program to acquire a substantial working knowledge of. . ." on a scale of *crucial, very important, important, somewhat important*, and *not important*. Examples of knowledge items were: cognitive development (like Piaget's stages), the influence of communities on schools and vice versa, procedures for analyzing/evaluating curriculum materials, and the like. Respondents also could indicate that their interpretation of the programmatic goals did not provide sufficient information to respond and could add other possible objectives.

Several tests of statistical significance were used in the data reduction and analyses. Multivariate profile analysis was used to compare the patterns of responses which identified crucial knowledge objectives. Analysis of variance and chi-square techniques were used to determine whether significant differences existed between the university and school respondents in the importance of the five pedagogical topics and each item which composed the knowledge inventory.

The respondents were twenty-eight elementary-education university professors and thirty-six school personnel. The school personnel were teachers from three elementary schools and the program planning committee (central office personnel, principals, and teachers).

Commentary.   Because program personnel needed to set priorities among possible objectives, a second analysis with descriptive statistics was done to determine the "collaborative preservice professional knowledge objectives," those objectives which were common to both groups of teacher educators. In this

---

EXCERPT 13.1
Objectives-Setting Study

PROFILES OF CRUCIAL PROFESSIONAL KNOWLEDGE OBJECTIVES

The mean percent of knowledge items rated *crucial* for each of the five topics representative of professional knowledge provides a comparison of school and university teacher educators' profiles of crucial professional knowledge for preservice teachers. The profiles of crucial professional knowledge objectives of the two groups of teacher educators differ significantly ($p = .055$). As summarized in Table 1, the grand mean percent of items judged as crucial by university educators is 27.4% and by school educators is 30.0%. The profiles of crucial knowledge portrayed in Figure 1 indicate which pedagogical topics are more crucial to each group of teacher educators. University educators consider knowledge about social context of schooling and curriculum as crucial slightly more than do school educators. School educators consider knowledge about students, teachers and especially about teaching strategies as crucial more than do university educators. The largest difference is the mean percent of crucial items relating to teaching strategies. University educators rate crucial 36.7% of the items and school educators rate crucial 48.1% of the items.

It is interesting to note that of the 60 items representative of professional knowledge, the two groups of teacher educators differ significantly ($p < .05$) on only 12 items. Thus, the patterns of responses for the remaining items are similar for school and university teacher educators. There appears to be high concensus regarding professional knowledge objectives for elementary preservice teachers.

TABLE 1. Mean Percent of Professional Knowledge Items Rated as "Crucial"

Pedagogical Topic	University Educators	School Educators
Students	28.0	28.4
Social Context	19.0	17.7
Curriculum	31.8	27.0
Teachers	16.5	22.6
Teaching Strategies	36.7	48.1
Grand Mean	27.4%	30.0%

Profile Analysis: F = 2.46, df = 4,60, $p = .055$.

Source: S. Schumacher, K. Esham, & D. Bauer (1985), *Evaluation of a collaborative teacher education program: Planning, developing and implementation, phase III,* pp. 101–103. Richmond: Virginia Commonwealth University, School of Education. (ERIC Document Reproduction Service No. ED 268 119).

analysis thirty-six statements were collaborative objectives (over 50 percent of both groups considered the objective *crucial* or *very important*); ten items were discrepancy statements, and fourteen statements were *not important* as preservice teacher objectives but might be important in the subsequent development of a professional career teacher. Neither the discrepancy statements nor the statements identified as *not important* were considered as priority objectives for guiding program development. The findings were presented to several groups of program participants and to other interested audiences (Schumacher, Esham, & Bauer, 1985, 1987, 1988).

Implementation-Outcome Study

The context is a small rural school system implementing a comprehensive Arts Program in a three-year federal project. The evaluation focus is the Arts Program, which has four goals that, when analyzed, contained three processes or enabling objectives that were the project components: a comprehensive Arts Education program, enrichment activities in general education classes, and an Arts Performance Series. If these objectives were attained, then terminal objectives for four target groups—grades 1–12 students, arts students, general education teachers, and parents and patrons—could be assessed. The evaluation purpose was to assess the implementation processes and students' products as indicators of creativity in the arts.

Design.   The methodological section of Excerpt 13.2 indicates that data were collected for each objective, but it fails to specify clearly the rationale for the procedures chosen. The lack of valid and reliable instruments in visual arts knowledge, art attitudes, and art creativity presented in the first-year evaluation report was the rationale for developing a Creativity Rating Scale for student products. (Appropriate methods to establish the validity and reliability of the scale [inter-rater reliability was 0.89] were reported in Chapter 3.) Further, the design was a time-series design, but inconsistent administration of the "inspiration" for the art drawings made the data invalid. The design thus became a one-group pretest-posttest design. The limitation for the study on self-esteem was not the instrument but the design: an art achievement variable could not be operationalized, and the skewed distribution of the sample influenced the non-significant statistical results. The other evaluation questions were clearly local concerns, which required site participants for developing the instrument, supplying the documents, or the evaluator observing and conducting informal interviews.

Commentary.   The results indicated that a comprehensive Arts Education program was implemented with required courses, elective courses, and system-wide Arts Performance Series. The analysis of the sample of student arts products indicated non-significant changes in student creativity, partially because of a skewed distribution on the Creativity Rating Scale. Although tenth graders achieved the largest increase in pre-post means of self-esteem, the other grade-level mean

---

EXCERPT 13.2
Implementation-Outcome Study

CHAPTER I—INTRODUCTION: THE ARTS PROGRAM AND EVALUATION DESIGN

Evaluation Focus and Design. The first year evaluation report primarily focused on program development. The importance of assessing the degree of program implementation before evaluating project outcomes has been noted in the decision-making models of evaluation. The second year evaluation design focused on program implementation and outcomes. The conceptual frameworks for the evaluation were: (1) responsive evaluation (Stake, 1975), (2) decision-making evaluation (Stufflebeam et al., 1974), and (3) educational criticism and connoisseurship (Eisner, 1975).

Focus. The second year evaluation design focused on five evaluation questions. Below are listed the five questions.

1. To what extent were the planned arts curriculum and enrichment activities implemented? To what extent did students become aware of the arts and develop a general appreciation for the arts (Grades 1–12)?
2. To what extent did students in art classes (Grades 6–12) increase in creativity?
3. To what extent did students in art classes (Grades 6–12) increase in positive self-esteem?
4. To what extent did teachers (Grades K-12) use arts activities and perceive the importance of the arts in general education?
5. Did parents/patrons increase their participation in school arts activities?

Methodology. Qualitative and quantitative data were collected from students, teachers, and administrators. Data were collected by ethnographic observations, structured interviews, division records and publications, a questionnaire, and two measurement instruments. The External Evaluator collected extensive field notes from observations and informal interviews, averaging one visit to the school division per month. During each visit she observed classes and talked to several arts teachers, principals, and the Project Director. The Project Director periodically informed the External Evaluator of events and observations between visits. The teacher questionnaire was developed by the project staff and the External Evaluator to assess teachers' perceptions of the importance of the arts. The Evaluator interviewed all administrators in May.

Changes in student creativity and self-esteem were assessed in two quasi-experimental designs. Student creativity was measured with a Creativity Rating Scale developed by the project staff and refined by the University Art Education Department. The Creativity Rating Scale measured flexibility, originality, and elaboration (J. P. Guilford, 1957, and E. P. Torrance, 1965). The stimulus or "inspiration" used for drawings done in art classes on February 4, 1980, and April 15, 1980, was Carl Sandburg's poem "Chicago." A random sample of 30 drawings, stratified by school level and proportional by sex for pretest and posttest was drawn and a t-test computed.

Self-esteem of the junior high school art student sample (30 subjects) and high school art student sample (60 subjects) was measured with Coopersmith's Self-Esteem Inventory. The Inventory was field-tested at the sites and considered reliable. S. Coopersmith (1967) reports the total score test-retest reliability coefficient of 0.88 for a five week interval and 0.77 for a three-year period. The pretest-posttest results were analyzed with a t-test. In addition, a regression analysis was performed across grades with post-esteem as the dependent variable and pre-esteem and standardized achievement scores as independent variables. Other variables such as socio-economic status and special education status were not possible because of the skewed distribution of the population. It was not feasible to operationalize an art achievement variable.

Source: Adapted from Schumacher, S., with Linder, F. (1980). *Arts program: A qualitative and quantitative evaluation of program development and implementation, 1979–80.* Richmond: Virginia Commonwealth University, School of Education (ERIC Document Reproduction Service No. ED 209 302), pp. 1–5.

scores (both pre- and post-) were positively skewed or well above the mid-point of the scale. Teachers attributed to the Arts Program, in rank order, an increase in their appreciation of student arts activities (84 percent), knowledge of the community resources in the arts (72 percent), and knowledge about the arts (61 percent). Teachers also rated those activities most important for the program, participated in at least one arts activity (54 percent), and used arts activities in the classroom instruction (44 percent). Parents and patrons increased their participation in the Arts Program from the previous year (Schumacher with Linder, 1980, pp. 75–80).

Perhaps the superintendent captured best the impact of the program from the school system's perspective when he said in an interview the second year:

> It's been great! The project really took off. This is the first year in the history of our county that we have had art in the high school. The musical performances are probably the best we have ever done. Next year our county adds two of the teachers to our budget. The community is aware of the program and participates. There was such a need! We now have our community participation back up to where it was before. . . . (5/22) (Schumacher with Linder, 1980, pp. 80–81).

Two years later, the school board voted to build a new elementary school to replace two buildings and included appropriately designed classrooms for the art and music classes.

■ ADEQUACY OF EVALUATION ■
PROPOSALS AND REPORTS

Evaluation proposals containing the evaluation focus and design are reviewed critically by the intended users at the site and by funding agencies. Developing a proposed evaluation design requires critical preliminary work which affects the subsequent evaluation report and the use of it.

Evaluation Proposal Development

Developing an evaluation design is a two-step process. The first step is preparation of a memorandum of agreement between the evaluator and the sponsor, or decision-maker, whom we will call the client. The evaluator may be either external to the organization or internal—having an official position in the project, program, or organization. The memorandum represents a written understanding about the **evaluation focus** (what is to be evaluated) and some technical aspects.

More specifically, the **memorandum of agreement** specifies the client, the practice to be evaluated, the purpose of the evaluation, the audiences, the reporting procedures, the time frame for the evaluation, and some technical aspects of evaluation (Guba & Lincoln, 1981). The memorandum states access to records, the confidentiality of data, and activities necessary to propose a design. The client is informed of the emergent design: to gather useful information as the evaluation needs change and to keep the client informed throughout the process.

The memorandum of agreement legitimizes the next set of activities necessary to propose a design. The evaluation design is developed from the concerns and questions about the practice expressed by the stakeholding audiences for the evaluation report. Sources of concerns and questions are interviews with key informed personnel, observation of participant-activities including planning sessions and documents such as project proposals, prior needs assessment studies, and the like.

The evaluation questions and data needs are developed from the list of concerns of the stakeholding audiences. For each evaluation question the **evaluation design** specifies the procedure: the type of data to be collected, the persons who will collect the data, the time when the data will be collected, the population or the event to be observed, the ways the data will be analyzed, and the date the information will be available. A simplified method of presenting an overview of an evaluation design is with a matrix, which is further explained in the proposal submitted to the client.

After presentation, the proposed evaluation design is negotiated with the client by the evaluator. Clarification and adjustments in the design may be necessary. Once these are agreed upon, the evaluation design represents an understanding of the specific expectations and responsibilities of the evaluator and the client. Both parties have a legal and ethical obligation to conduct the evaluation effort according to this design in a professional manner or to renegotiate the design.

Adequacy of Evaluation Proposals

Evaluation proposals are judged by the focus and design and by other considerations. The following questions illustrate typical criteria.[18]

1. Is the practice to be evaluated clearly identified?
2. Does the description of the practice include the objectives and expected

---

[18]See Sanders and Nafziger (1975), *A basis for determining the adequacy of evaluation designs.*

outcomes? Are the components or scope of the practice briefly and comprehensively described?

3. Are the general purposes of the evaluation effort specified?
4. Are all relevant audiences for the evaluation effort specified?
5. Are the selected evaluation questions relevant to the audiences for judging merit, worth, or both, of the educational practice?
6. Are data collection procedures proposed for each evaluation question? Does the design allow for emergent evaluation questions to be addressed?
7. Are the selected measurement techniques valid and reliable for this evaluation?
8. Does the design call for different kinds of data from different sources to provide a comprehensive and accurate evaluation?
9. Are data collection and analysis feasible for informal feedback and formal reports?

Other elements are considered in accepting an evaluation proposal. Although they may not all be stated in the plan, the evaluator and client need a mutual understanding about them. The questions below illustrate other considerations.

1. Is the release of scheduled reports timely so that audiences can best use the information?
2. Are the method and process of reporting (written, oral, or audiovisual) specified? Does the evaluation plan state editorial control and name the person who will release intermediate and final reports? Are executive reports of the full evaluation report for various audiences specified?
3. Are the rights of human subjects protected?
4. Is the evaluation plan cost-effective? Are fiscal accountability procedures designated?
5. Is the evaluation effort politically feasible for collecting data and presenting a balanced report to all audiences?

Adequacy of Evaluation Reports

A full evaluation is typically long, with several chapters. The report consists of an introduction (focus and design), findings organized by evaluation questions or components of the practice, and a summary with recommendations. Criteria for judging the adequacy of an evaluation report emphasize two aspects of the report: the evaluation focus and design, and the findings, conclusions, and recommendations. The following questions illustrate typical criteria.

1. Is the evaluation focus stated, along with the context, objectives, and description of the practice, the general purposes of the evaluation, and the evaluation approaches used?
2. Are the evaluation questions stated, with the data collection and analysis procedures specified? Are the procedures defensible?

3. Are the results reported in a balanced manner, with full and frank disclosure, including the limitations of the evaluation?
4. Is the reporting objective to the extent that the findings are based on verified facts and free from distortion by personal feelings and biases?
5. Are the conclusions and recommendations justified, with sufficient information presented to determine whether these conclusions and recommendations are warranted? Are plausible alternative explanations presented, when appropriate, for findings?

■ EDUCATIONAL EVALUATION: ■ POTENTIAL AND LIMITATIONS

Evaluation research offers many potential benefits to education, although it is not a panacea for all the "ills" of education. Education is a complex activity within a larger, changing interdependent social and political society. In this context, evaluation research offers a rational and empirical perspective on educational practices.

Potential Benefits

The list of potential benefits increases as more educators gain experience in conducting and using evaluation studies. The most frequently mentioned potential benefits of evaluation research are listed below.

1. *Plan and implement improvements on a systematic basis.* Identifying needs, selecting the best strategies from known alternatives, monitoring the changes as they occur, and measuring the impact of the changes minimizes the chance of misdirected changes and justifies expenditures. In a similar manner, systematic evaluation can avoid faddism, overreaction to political pressure, and lack of effort for letting the public know what is happening in schools or in new programs.

2. *Conduct cost-benefit analysis of programs and practices that require large expenditures.* Accountability and the best use of scarce resources can be demonstrated.[19]

3. *Test a number of popular myths about the effects of education on student development.* Professional experience usually dictates most teaching and educational management practices. Systematic and often subtle information to supplant or confirm casual observations generates evaluation studies.

---

[19]H. M. Levin (1987) notes that cost-benefit and cost-effectiveness analyses are not done extensively and suggests that until these analyses can address multiple educational outcomes within a single design, the approach will be limited in its usefulness.

4. *Demonstrate professional responsibility by appraising the quality of educational programs.* Educators continually seek ways to improve the quality of programs and evaluation can play a vital role.

5. *Reduce uncertainty about educational practices when experience is limited.* Unanticipated side effects or possible detrimental effects can be identified early.

6. *Satisfy external agencies' requirements for reports to legitimize decisions and improve public images.* Through credible, data-based decision-making, images of schooling may become more realistic. As evaluation activities increase, more accreditation groups and agencies expect, if not demand, some form of evaluation research.

Limitations of Evaluation

Listed below are the two limitations of evaluation most often cited.

1. *Failure of many evaluation studies to improve educational practices and educational policy formulation.* The inadequacies of the conceptualization and the conduct of many evaluation studies partly explains this occurrence. Studies are conducted frequently without understanding factors which affect the use of evaluation information even when the studies are well done.[20]

2. *Lack of appreciation that evaluation is only one of many influences on educational policies, practices, and decisions.* Evaluation cannot *correct* a problem, but it can identify strengths and weaknesses, highlight the accomplishments, and expose the faults. Correcting a problem is a separate step from using evaluation findings.

■ SUMMARY ■

1. Evaluation research requires a formal design and procedures to determine the merit and worth of a practice. Evaluation research is used to plan, improve, and justify (or not justify) educational procedures, programs, and/or products.
2. Merit refers to those valued characteristics intrinsic to a practice for which there is relatively consistent agreement.
3. Worth is related to the usefulness of a practice and depends on the context, needs, and values operating at a given site.
4. Formative evaluation helps modify or revise a practice in a developmental cycle.
5. Summative evaluation is conducted when a practice is well developed, and it determines the effectiveness of a practice compared to other competing practices.
6. A good evaluation study satisfies the standards of utility, feasibility, propriety, and accuracy.

[20]See E. Chelimsky (1987), The politics of program evaluation, in D. S. Cordray, H. S. Bloom & R. J. Light (Eds.), *Evaluation practice in review, New Directions for Program Evaluation, No. 34,* San Francisco: Jossey-Bass, for the "lessons" learned in the use of evaluation research for federal policy formulation.

7. Major evaluation models include objectives-based, systems and cost-analysis, consumer-oriented, expertise, decision-making, adversary, and naturalistic and participant-oriented approaches.

8. Objectives-oriented evaluation focuses on the terminal or outcome objectives: the extent to which measurable objectives of a practice are attained by the target group.

9. Systems and cost analyses provide evaluation information about program management, impact assessment, and cost-effectiveness.

10. Decision-oriented evaluation, such as needs assessment, program planning, implementation, and process and outcome assessment, provides information to decision-makers who determine the merit and worth of a practice.

11. Naturalistic and participant-oriented evaluation gathers information about the different concerns and values of various groups through a holistic approach. Multiplicity of data, inductive reasoning, and writing portrayals or a series of case studies characterize the approach.

12. Developing an evaluation design is a two-step process whereby the written evaluation focus is first agreed upon. A memorandum of agreement names the client, the practice to be evaluated, the purpose, the audiences, the reporting procedures, the time frame, and some technical aspects.

13. Evaluation planning requires a detailed description of the practice and the concerns regarding the practice.

14. For each question the evaluation design specifies the procedure: the type of data collected, the data collector, the time of data collection, the population or events to be observed, data analysis, and when the information will be available.

15. Collecting multiple kinds of data from different groups provides comprehensive, accurate, and verified information. Both quantitative and qualitative data are useful.

16. An evaluator, client, and users can judge the adequacy of an evaluation proposal or report by using a checklist of criteria.

17. Potential benefits of evaluation research are a systematic implementation of improvements, a cost-analyses of large expenditures, an assessment of educational effects on students, an appraisal of the quality of education, a reduction of uncertainty in innovative practices, and a legitimization of decisions.

■ SELF-INSTRUCTIONAL REVIEW EXERCISES ■

Sample answers are in the back of the book.

Test Items

1. Evaluation research
   a. tests theories to develop knowledge in the social sciences.
   b. discovers scientific laws that are generalizable.

    c. determines the value of a specific practice.

    d. lacks a design and procedures to collect information.

2. Merit, in contrast with worth, of a practice
   a. indicates the practice has intrinsic characteristics for which there is a relatively consistent agreement.
   b. may be investigated only as summative evaluation.
   c. requires less rigorous methodologies.
   d. depends on the context, needs, and values, which differ in local sites.

3. The major distinction between formative and summative evaluation is that
   a. formative evaluation is more time-consuming than summative evaluation.
   b. formative evaluation more often uses social science methodologies than summative evaluation.
   c. the evaluations are conducted at different stages of program development.
   d. formative evaluations are more concerned about the validity and reliability of assessment measures.

4. Which is an *incorrect* description of objectives-oriented evaluation?
   a. determines which objectives are attained by the target group
   b. evaluates only measurable objectives
   c. requires valid and reliable instruments
   d. provides process evaluation

5. A cost analysis approach to evaluation
   a. assumes that choices of decision alternatives should consider the resource use or cost in relation to the outcome level.
   b. assesses benefits only in terms of society—that is, productivity or earnings.
   c. requires that all inputs and outputs be stated as monetary values.
   d. does not require formal mastery of economic analysis and evaluation.

6. A decision-oriented evaluation
   a. determines the effectiveness of a practice by assessing one outcome.
   b. can focus on needs, program planning, implementation, and process/outcome or a combination.
   c. focuses only on decisions to improve a practice.
   d. is inflexible—that is, it focuses only on system-wide changes.

7. In a naturalistic and participant-oriented evaluation, an evaluator would
   a. collect data specified by the decision-maker or client.
   b. use only one data collection method.

    c. prefer inductive reasoning from grass-roots observation and discovery with an emergent design.

    d. assume a single reality rather than multiple participants' perspectives or realities.

8. Evaluation questions are derived from
    a. data available from existing testing programs.
    b. a review of the research and other published literature.
    c. concerns and information needs expressed by the stakeholding audiences.
    d. the evaluator's interests and methodological preferences.

9. To develop an evaluation design, an evaluator would
    a. rely on documents for a description of the practice.
    b. identify data needs from the evaluation questions.
    c. assume the client agrees with the evaluation focus.
    d. ignore local resources for developing data collection methods.

10. A potential benefit of evaluation research is that it
    a. plans and implements improvements on a systematic basis.
    b. tests popular myths about the effects of education on student development.
    c. satisfies external agencies' requirements for reports and improvement of public images.
    d. All of the above are potential benefits of evaluation research.

11. An evaluation report would be judged adequate if the report
    a. was accurate but the description of the practice was ambiguous.
    b. was clearly written but biased toward the viewpoint of the decision-maker.
    c. presented justified conclusions but the information sources were indefensible and instruments were invalid.
    d. presented full disclosure of relevant and valid information with limitations cited.

Application Problems

Analyze the following evaluation situations by identifying the problem and suggesting alternative procedures.[21]

1. A supervisor of instruction wanted an evaluation in order to compare a new independent study approach with the regular instructional approach in high school mathematics. A written formal agreement with the district evaluation staff stated that:

---

[21]Adapted from the Joint Committee on Standards for Educational Evaluation (1981), *Standards for evaluations of educational programs, projects, and materials*, New York: McGraw-Hill, pp. 42–43, 109–111, 118–119, 132–134, 136–137.

a. The evaluation was to help the high school mathematics department chairpersons decide whether to adopt the independent study approach district-wide.
b. The procedures were to conduct a district-wide comparison of the two approaches, involving twenty percent of the high school's mathematics teachers selected randomly and all their students.
c. Mathematics achievement, student attitude, and teacher enthusiasm would be assessed.
d. Teachers would be selected randomly and assigned to the two different approaches.

The supervisor later decided that the evaluation should provide feedback to improve the new approach rather than decide adoption. She changed the procedure for assigning teachers and students to the project, a change that resulted in their not being assigned randomly.

The evaluation staff, assuming that the evaluation focus and design, once agreed upon, would remain the same, collected and analyzed data as originally planned. The evaluators found that student attitudes toward both approaches were similar, but student achievement and teacher enthusiasm were significantly greater for the independent study approach. The report judged this approach as superior and recommended it for adoption.

The supervisor was disappointed that the report did not help improve the independent study approach. The department chairpersons complained that the findings were undependable because many teachers assigned to the independent study approach were biased in favor of it before the study began, and the students in independent study classes were generally high achievers prior to entering the program.

2. Two members of a school district's evaluation office were assigned to the superintendent to help her staff analyze qualitative data on a special crime prevention project. The evaluation data needs were as follows: The superintendent wanted a description of the project activities as they changed for a progress report to the funding agency, a report due in three months. The funding agency wanted to know if the contacts between the youngsters in the project and various law enforcement agencies—the police, the courts, and the juvenile officers—had been reduced during the first year.

The evaluators spent more than a month reading the information that had been collected: staff daily logs, hearings records, newspaper articles, school cumulative files for each enrolled youngster, and official records of police court and juvenile probation officers. The evaluators developed a classification scheme in which every entry could be categorized. They also did a frequency count of the number of times each enrolled youngster had contact with a law enforcement agency during the first project year and in the preceding year. Two things were quickly evident: only a small proportion of the categorized data yielded any insights into the nature of the project activities and the way they changed during the year, and the number of law enforcement agency contacts was almost identical in each of the two years analyzed.

The evaluators, running out of time, provided only sketchy accounts of activities and informed the superintendent that the project had proved unsuccessful in reducing law enforcement agency contacts. When the superintendent reported these findings to the funding agency, support was withdrawn and the project was ended.

The project staff was stunned, especially because the number of contacts weighed so heavily in the decision. Its members pointed out that during the preproject year these contacts were arrests and court trial appearances, while during the first project year these contacts were supervisory and counseling sessions with juvenile officers. The juvenile officers said they were pleased with the changes seen in the enrolled youngsters' attitudes and behavior.

3. Units on ecology were introduced in all grades in a middle school. The school's curriculum committee requested that the school district's evaluation department evaluate the effectiveness of these units. Specifically, the committee wanted to know if students increased their knowledge about environmental issues (preservation of endangered species and conservation of scarce resources) and decreased their practice of littering the school grounds.

The evaluators used a pretest-posttest design with a test and a questionnaire. The test was the science subtest of a national standardized achievement test, including hygiene, biology, and earth science. The questionnaire was a self-report instrument by which students rated themselves and their classmates on school citizenship (respect for other students, respect for teachers, and respect for school property). The analysis of the data showed there was no change in the pretest-posttest scores on the subtest or on the citizenship questionnaire. The curriculum committee was disappointed in the evaluation and pointed out that it did not really answer their questions.

4. A faculty committee and the principal of a middle school developed materials for role-playing activities to improve school discipline. The materials were then tried out in half the school's social studies classes. After a year of use, the faculty committee requested that the central office's evaluation staff evaluate the materials. The faculty committee wanted to know whether the materials needed revision and whether they should be used in all social studies classes in the school.

The evaluator interviewed the teachers and students who had used the materials. The evaluator also surveyed the entire faculty with a questionnaire to see whether the teachers believed there had been any changes in school discipline. The evaluator prepared a report that was very favorable to the materials, suggesting few changes in the materials and recommending their use the next year in all social studies classes. The evaluator discussed the report and its findings with the building principal.

When word got out, two groups strongly protested: the faculty committee responsible for the materials, and the social studies teachers who taught the materials. The committee disavowed the report because it had had no input into the evaluation. The social studies teachers who had used the materials believed they should have been the first to receive the report, since they had used the materials and provided much of the data for the findings.

PART V

COMMUNICATION OF EDUCATIONAL RESEARCH

Educators are frequently puzzled by the variety of ways in which research is communicated to diverse audiences and readers. How does writing research differ from creative or literary writing? Why is there so much variation among the formats and styles in different research journals, proposals, and reports? How does the nature of the research problem and selected methodology—quantitative or qualitative—influence the format of research communication? How does the audience or the reader affect research communication? How are quantitative and qualitative research proposals written? These questions are addressed in Chapter 14.

CHAPTER 14

GUIDELINES FOR RESEARCH PROPOSALS

■ **KEY TERMS** ■

refereed journals
research writing style
references

bibliography
format
style

In the first chapter of this book we defined research as scientific and disciplined inquiry using quantitative and qualitative approaches for knowledge development and educational improvement. Research employs systematic methods to collect and analyze data and embraces a probing, open attitude in examining research critically. Subsequent chapters presented principles of designing and assessing different types of research. The ultimate purpose of all types of research is to describe or measure phenomena with objective evidence as accurately as possible.

This chapter describes both the various forms by which research is communicated and three types of arguments used in research. Communication of research involves a choice of what to include, use of a research writing style, and a choice of format. The formats for quantitative and qualitative research proposals are described. Although many of the elements of a proposal are similar for quantitative and qualitative research, there are methodological variations. This chapter also explains the preparation and typical criticisms of research proposals.

■ COMMUNICATION IN RESEARCH ■

Research is communicated in different forms to various professional groups. Some forms of research communication are proposals, theses and dissertations, journal articles, evaluation and technical reports, and papers presented at professional meetings. Two general groups read and use research: the community of scholars, scientists, and educational researchers who conduct research studies, and the community of professional educators who use research results in practical situations such as in school systems, universities, state and federal educational organizations, funding agencies, professional associations, and the like.

Forms of Research Communication

Each form of research communication is distinctive and made available to scholarly and professional communities through various means. Listed below are the major research communication forms.

1. *Research proposal*—a carefully delineated problem statement with the design and significance of the proposed study.
2. *Thesis or dissertation*—an original completed study which investigates a narrowly defined problem to develop new knowledge and is available through Dissertation Microfilm Service, the university, or the researcher.
3. *Journal articles*—a published abbreviated presentation of a completed study or part of a larger study.
4. *Evaluation and technical reports*—an original completed study which is usually available through ERIC Reproduction Services, the professional association or agency which sponsored the study, or the author.
5. *Paper presentations at professional meetings*—conceptual or theoretical analyses, research-in-progress, and completed studies presented in abbreviated form and made available by the presenter or through ERIC Reproduction Services. These are frequently revised and published.

Each of these forms of research communication have various groups which guide the thinking, the activities, and the communication of the researcher. A research proposal can be guided by a professor of a course, a thesis or dissertation committee, or a funding agency review committee. Original research such as theses or dissertations, research studies and evaluation reports are guided by selected committees and the researcher's colleagues. Journal articles and paper presentations are reviewed by selected "blind reviewers." These various groups provide appropriate guidance and criticism to encourage important, valid research which communicates to several audiences.

Thinking in Research

The most difficult aspect of research is not learning how to draw a sample of subjects, write a research problem, obtain access to a site or an archival collection, conduct statistical analyses, or set up data tables. Like the physicist or chemist, a researcher in education can learn about these techniques by referring to appropriate sources. The difficult thing about research is that it requires *thinking*. As noted in Part I, to make the best use of research the consumer and the researcher must be able to reason and think analytically.

TABLE 14.1
Arguments for Factual Accuracy and Generality

Type of Argument	Strength of Argument If Used Alone	Main Location of Argument in Journal Article	Readers Should Judge the Argument by . . .
Reasoning—what the researcher said	Weak	In introduction and discussion sections	—asking how good was the reasoning given —inventing own reasons —using own knowledge of subject matter
Methods—what the researcher did	Stronger	In procedures section	—asking how good were the methods used —inventing own reasons —using own knowledge of subject matter
Replication/ extension—what other researchers said or did	Strongest	In literature review section	—asking how good and encompassing were the studies reported —inventing own reasons —using own knowledge of subject matter
Some combination of reasoning, methods, and replication/ extension	Depends	In all of the above sections	—all of the above

---

Source: From *Evaluating Information*, Second Edition, by Jeffrey Katzer, Kenneth Cook and Wayne C. Crouch. Copyright © 1982 Random House, Inc. Reprinted by permission.

There are two aspects that are most fundamental to this thinking process: internal validity, the accuracy of reported results; and external validity, the generalizability or extension of the results. These two aspects are assessed by examining the research interpretations, conclusions, and qualitative generalizations. Katzer, Cook, and Crouch (1982) give three types of arguments that are used to make a case for internal and external validity. These arguments are summarized in Table 14.1. The weakest argument is based only on what the researchers say, not what they do or show. This type of argument is often used in explaining why particular threats to internal validity do not constitute plausible rival hypotheses. With this type of argument communication of ideas and *reasoning* is very important. A stronger argument is made when it can be demonstrated that certain *methods* and techniques were used to control threats to internal validity, and still stronger arguments are made when the findings can be used to further knowledge development. *Replications* of prior research verify the results in quantitative research. *Extensions* of prior research allow ethnographers and historians to compare and contrast logically their findings to previous research at other sites or with other archival collections. The strongest type of argument is made when reasoning, methods, and replications/extensions are compared.

In reading and interpreting research the reader of research should be aware of the types of arguments that are being made and the relative strength of each. This chapter illustrates in more detail the manner in which these arguments are presented in a research proposal.

■ COMMUNICATION OF RESEARCH ■

Educational research is shared and communicated to others. Communication is a process that requires both a sender and a receiver, and problems related to communication originate from both these sources. Depending on what researchers choose to include in a proposal, an article or report, how the material is written, and the way the reader interprets the information, the importance of the research can vary greatly. Effective communication is thus the responsibility of both the researcher and the consumer.

Choosing What to Include

With the possible exception of some doctoral dissertations, virtually all research reports do not include everything that was done in the study. There are pragmatic and research reasons why researchers do not report everything that happened in a study. From a pragmatic point of view, most journals prefer to publish short articles, and many consumers avoid reading reports that are long and appear full of tedious detail. A more defensible reason for omitting some information is that if details that are clearly unrelated to the findings are included, time is wasted by reading the unnecessary details, and the significance of the study may be left unclear. Researchers are thus constantly deciding what should be left out of a report, and the quality of these judgments depends on the experience and expertise of the researcher, the reviewers, and the community of scholars and users who may ultimately read the report. Competent researchers consciously decide what to omit, but novice researchers, because they are unaware of the information that might be important, unconsciously make omissions. There is, hence, something to be said for the high quality of articles that appear in **refereed journals** (journals that use a blind review by accomplished researchers of submitted manuscripts) and of articles written by researchers who have attained credibility in their field. Of course, some research that is published in refereed journals still omits important information, but at least with the contributions of reviewers and an editor, the consumer can have greater assurance that important information has probably not been omitted.

The amount of detail that is included also depends on the type of journal or report in which the study is published. The format of most academic journals (those concerned only with research within a particular discipline or applied field) usually consists of an introduction, a review of literature, a methodology section, a section on results or findings, a discussion and an interpretation, as presented in Chapter 2. These components help other researchers understand and analyze important aspects of the study. The detail is usually sufficient to allow other researchers to replicate or extend the study. It should be stressed that research which is reported in these journals is intended for other researchers who have the skills to read and understand all aspects of the study. In education, this means that a large segment of our profession, and that includes most public school teachers and administrators, needs to have some research knowledge to read the research reported in these journals.

In some applied journals (*Instructor, Educational Leadership, Phi Delta Kappan, Psychology Today*) generalized accounts of research may omit the technical details of the research. Often the review of literature, methodology, and analysis sections are left out and only the research problem, results, and conclusions are included. Since these journals are meant for nonresearchers, it seems reasonable to omit technical details that probably would be of no interest. Because information is omitted, however, there is a likelihood that important sources of error and bias will be overlooked. In effect, because of lack of information the consumer of these journals must place a great amount of confidence in the editor and authors.

Research Writing Style

Because of the precise nature of research, the way ideas are stated can make a great difference for the reader. Perhaps the most difficult skill in writing research reports is making a transition from a literary style of writing to scientific and scholarly **research writing,** a style that reflects precise thinking. Effective writing of research requires an objective, clear, concise style of communicating an unambiguous description. The researcher is reporting something, and should not write in the style of a position paper or of creative writing.[1] Of course, mastery of gram-

---

[1] Some forms of qualitative research writing may appear literary with the narrative flow of description when contrasted to more technical styles of reporting research.

mar is essential, but a good research report also incorporates clear thinking, logically developed and sequenced ideas, and a smoothness so that the reader is encouraged to continue reading.

The *Publication Manual of the American Psychological Association, Third Edition* (1983) (APA style manual), and *The Chicago Manual of Style: Thirteenth Edition, Revised and Expanded* (1982) (CMS manual), lists a few guidelines that will help researchers communicate effectively through clear writing.[2] These guidelines are sufficiently general for both quantitative and qualitative research:

1. *Use of the precise word.* It is important to use words in such a way that the meaning of the word will be uniform and will communicate exactly what the researcher intends. Some common trouble makers are prefixes (*disinterested* means impartial; *uninterested* means apathetic) and qualifiers (*almost always, some, very few*). Some words are used incorrectly (*feel* when *think* is meant, or *data is* rather than *data are*). Colloquial expressions, such as *put in* for *insert* or *write up* for *report*, should also be avoided.

2. *Avoiding ambiguity.* Ambiguity often results because the researcher is so familiar with the study that he or she overlooks unclear sentences. The researchers understand the meaning, but only because they are intimately involved in the project. Some of the more common ambiguity problems are in the use of referents (*which, this, that, these,* and *those*), because often the referent is left out and the reader needs to search through prior material to find it. Another common weakness is to use a long string of modifiers before the noun modified. "An old performance test of verbal skills used in high school" is better, for example, than "an old verbal skills performance high school test." Finally, using numbers or letters to identify groups in the text of a manuscript can be very confusing. Instead, it is best to use a key word to designate each group.

3. *Orderly presentation of ideas.* It is important that thought units, concepts, and sequences are ordered coherently to provide a reasonable progression from paragraph to paragraph. Transitions inform the reader as the logic moves from one idea to the next. It is common to find topics, especially in the literature review, introduced abruptly and arguments or development of a theme abandoned suddenly.

4. *Economy of expression.* Wordiness and redundancy are characteristic of many research reports. Long, involved sentences are difficult to read and understand. Without being choppy, it is better to use shorter sentences. Short, simple words are better than long words. Long terms should be used only for precision or when one long word expresses an idea better than several short words. Long paragraphs should also be avoided.[3]

5. *Smoothness of expression.* Good writing requires smooth expression. There are several principles of writing that can help assure a smooth presentation. These include avoiding shifts in tense and subject-verb agreement. Within each

[2]Also see K. L. Turabian (1987), *A manual for writers of term papers, theses, and dissertations* (5th ed.) and L. F. Locke, W. W. Spirduso, & S. J. Silverman (1987) *Proposals that work: A guide for planning dissertations and grant proposals* (2nd ed.).

[3]See H. Becker (1986), *Writing for social scientists;* W. Strunk & E. B. White (1959), *The elements of style;* W. Zinsser (1980), *On writing well: An informal guide to writing nonfiction;* and J. M. Williams (1981), *Style: Ten lessons in clarity and grace.*

paragraph the tense should be consistent. Although different tenses may be used throughout the manuscript, there are occasions when verb tense should be used in a specific way:

    a. Past tense or present perfect tense is appropriate for the literature review and the description of the procedures if the discussion is of past events. Stay with the chosen tense.

    b. Past tense is used to present the findings of a study.

    c. Present tense is appropriate to discuss the results and to present research conclusions and interpretations. The present tense is used as a dialogue between author and reader in presenting and discussing results.

    d. Future tense, except in proposals, is rarely used.

    6. *Consideration of the reader.* It is best to write research reports so that the reader can concentrate on the information that is read, and not be distracted by alliterations, embellishments, accidental rhymes, poetic expressions, and cliches. Traditionally, research has been written in the third person with passive voice. Recently, a more personal style of writing with judicial employment of the active voice and first person has been used by experienced researchers and scholars for a more concise, accurate statement.

    7. *Guidelines for non-sexist language.* The generic use of male or female nouns and pronouns should also be avoided by using such alternatives as plurals ("researchers investigate their problems" rather than "the researcher investigates his problem"). Other guidelines exist to avoid stereotyping such as *Jane Smith* for *Mrs. John Smith, men and women* for *men and girls,* and the like.

    8. *Criticism, assistance, and improvement.* It is advisable to seek advice, criticism, and recommendations from others (preferably outside the academic discipline of the report or at least one's immediate peers and colleagues) to receive needed feedback concerning the style of writing. It is often difficult to ask others to review a manuscript, but for researchers interested in effective communication of their ideas, it is a necessary step.

The Interpretation of the Reader

As suggested previously, communication is a two-way process between the writer and the reader. It is obvious that each individual has a unique background and brings to communication particular experiences, prejudices, skills, knowledge, and reasons for reading. These idiosyncracies act as a screen through which the written word is filtered. The challenge of the writer, then, is to communicate the same meaning despite these interindividual differences, but each individual should be aware of the way his or her particular perspective may affect the meaning of the information. Many readers of research compound this problem by failing to read the entire research report. Instead, these readers skim the material and consequently miss some information, making misinterpretation more likely.

Some readers are affected by their beliefs about a particular author, journal, or topic. Their beliefs act like a halo effect. If the reader has a positive predisposition about an author or journal, then the research that is reported in it is viewed as more credible. Such attributes of a journal or report as size and type of print, the association publishing the journal, attractiveness of the paper, type of illustrations, and number of references at the end of an article can affect the overall judgment of the information. The mere fact that certain statistical procedures are used can likewise bring about a halo effect.

The approach readers take in reading research can also affect the information they obtain from it. If readers are looking for a particular point of view, or for errors that would invalidate the research, they will be unable to understand the information accurately. In other words, the reader's motivation in reading the research is important, and it is best to be open-minded, with the attitude of reading the research to be better informed.

■ QUANTITATIVE RESEARCH PROPOSALS ■

Writing a research proposal can be the most difficult yet exciting step in the research process. In this phase, the entire project synthesizes into a specific form. In a proposal, researchers demonstrate that they know what they are seeking, how they will seek and recognize it, and explain why the research is worthwhile. Quantitative proposals reflect a deductive approach to educational research. The format may be a relatively informal outline offered by a professor to satisfy a course requirement, a formal thesis or dissertation proposal presented to a committee, or a structured funding proposal requested by a foundation or government agency.

General Format

Quantitative research proposals generally follow the format presented below. The outline contains all the steps necessary for formulating and proposing a quantitative research study.

I. Introduction
    A. General Statement of the Problem
    B. Review of the Literature
    C. Specific Research Questions and/or Hypotheses
    D. Significance of the Proposed Study

II. Design and Methodology
    A. Subjects
    B. Instrumentation

      C. Procedures

      D. Data Analyses and Presentation

      E. Limitations of the Design

  III. References

  IV. Appendices

Guidelines for Quantitative Research Proposals

I. Introduction. The *general problem statement* is a clear, precise statement of the research problem which helps the reader recognize the importance of the problem and the area of education in which it lies. The problem statement is then linked to the related literature, to the specific research questions and/or hypotheses, and finally to the significance of the proposed study. A concise and direct statement of the problem is made very early in the introduction, ideally in the first paragraph, followed by a description of the background of the problem. It is crucial to phrase the problem in intelligible terms for someone who is generally sophisticated but who may be relatively uninformed in the area of the problem.

    The *literature review* presents what is known about the problem from theoretical discussions and prior research to date, thus providing the background and need for the study. Chapter 4 contains suggestions for organizing and logically presenting a literature review. The literature review concludes with a discussion of the knowledge to date on the problem and the researcher's insights such as criticisms of designs of prior research and identification of gaps in the literature. The review of the literature, although thorough at this time, frequently is extended as the research progresses.

    Specific research questions and/or hypotheses are stated, followed by definitions of key terms and variables. Question format is appropriate for survey research. Question or hypothesis format is appropriate for correlation studies, experimental, and quasi-experimental design studies. The statement of the specific questions and/or hypotheses should clearly indicate the empirical nature of the investigation, such as a specific type of research design. Definitions—preferably operational definitions—of variables follow the statement of specific research questions and/or hypotheses. (See Chapter 3.)

    The *potential significance of the proposed study* notes the importance of the study in terms of 1) the development of knowledge and 2) implications of further research and educational practices. The researcher discusses how the results of the study could add to theory and knowledge in the area identified in the general problem statement. Implications for further research are stated. Finally, the researcher tentatively states potential implications for educational practices. Implications for educational practices are not recommendations for specific problems but general statements for educational practitioners. Typical criteria for the significance of a selected problem are stated in Chapter 3.

Some researchers prefer and some formats require that the significance of the proposed study be placed after the research design is described. Most researchers write and rewrite this part of a proposal because it is a major criterion in obtaining proposal approval.

II. Design and Methodology. The design and methodology in quantitative research includes the subjects, instrumentation, procedures for obtaining the data, data analysis and presentation, and design limitations.

The researcher identifies the type of design to be used—survey, correlational, experimental, quasi-experimental, and the like. This orients the reader to expect certain design components to be discussed in the proposal.

The *subjects* are identified by describing the population of interest— elementary school principals, fourth-grade reading students, and so forth—and how the probability sample will be drawn from this population. (See Chapter 5.) The sample size is stated. A rationale for the sampling procedure and the sample size is given. A careful description of the subjects helps the reader to determine if the results of the study can be generalized to the extent desired.

The *instrumentation* for the proposed study identifies the instrument(s) to be used and explains why the instrument(s) was selected as the most appropriate operational definition of the variable(s) in research question(s) and/or hypotheses. If the instrument is already established, the reported evidence of its reliability and also its validity for the purpose of the study is given. (See Chapter 5 and Chapter 7.) If the instrument(s) must be developed, then the steps to obtain validity and reliability data for the instrument are outlined. The more technical details of these procedures are often discussed in a separate appendix to the proposal.

The *procedures* describe the way in which the study will be conducted so that the relationships between variables can be investigated. In survey research this includes preparing the questionnaire or interview schedule, training the interviewer or providing directions for those who administer questionnaires or tests, and the like. In experimental and quasi-experimental research, the procedures may be more complex—identification of the groups, specification of the experimental treatment, and procedures to minimize confounding variables. Procedures for replacement of subjects are noted.

The *data analysis and presentation* states the statistical techniques to be used in data analysis and specifies how the data will be presented. The researcher states the statistical test for *each* research question and/or hypothesis and, if necessary, the rationale for the choice of the test. The rationale may be in terms of purpose of the study, sample size, and type of scales used in the instrument—categorical, nominal, or interval. A statistical technique is selected on the basis of appropriateness for investigating the research question and/or hypothesis; nothing is gained by using a complicated technique when a simple one will suffice.

A researcher often states the forms of data presentation—the kinds of tables, figures, and charts to be used to organize and summarize each set of data. Those forms selected are usually linked to each research question and/or hypotheses. Guidelines to the expression of numbers and statistical symbols and for tables and figures are presented in the *Publications Manual of the American Psychological Association* (3rd ed).

The *limitations of the design* section cites those limitations which the researcher can identify at this time: scope of the study, the design, and/or the methodology. The researcher recognizes that the proposed study focuses on only one delineated aspect of a larger research problem, such as the effects of labeling elementary school exceptional children rather than the effects of labeling all students. Stating the design limitations illustrates the researcher's knowledge of the threats to internal and external validity in the proposed design. (See Chapter 5 and Chapter 9.) It is better for the researcher to recognize the limitations rather than claim he or she has a "perfect" design. Methodological limitations relate specifically to validity and reliability of the proposed instrumentation or the instrument(s) which have been developed. Limitations are tempered with reasonableness and should not be so extensive that the study is unimportant. Sometimes researchers prefer to state research assumptions made in order to conduct the study rather than pointing out the limitations. The specification of limitations or assumptions aids later in the interpretation of the results.

III. References. The **references** list the sources which the researcher actually used to develop the proposal *and* are cited in the text of the proposal. References are those cited primarily in the literature review, but any sources cited in the general problem statement, significance of the study, and in some instances, in the methodological section, are also listed. Every source cited in the proposal *must* be included in the references and every entry listed in the references *must* appear in the proposal.

An ethical researcher does not cite abstracts of dissertations or journal articles as references. Part of a study which is quoted in another source is not cited, but the source containing that quotation is cited if it is properly cited in the proposal. The *Publication Manual of the American Psychological Association* (3rd. ed.) provides guidelines for quotations, reference citations, and reference lists.

IV. Appendices. The appendices provides supplementary materials for clarity and economical presentation and are keyed to appropriate references in the text. When placed in the appendices, these materials become options available to the reader as needed, rather than distractions to the logical flow of a proposal. Included in the appendices may be such items as the following:

a. instructions to subjects
b. informed subject consent forms
c. letters of permission to conduct the study in an educational agency or organization
d. pilot studies
e. copies of instruments-questionnaires, interview schedules, observation schedules
f. instructions and training of data collectors
g. credentials of experts, judges, or other specialized personnel to be used in the study
h. diagrammatic models of research design or statistical analysis
i. chapter outline for the final report
j. proposed time schedule for completing the study

■ QUALITATIVE RESEARCH PROPOSALS   ■

Writing a qualitative research proposal, similar to quantitative research, can be the most difficult yet exciting step in the research process. Unlike quantitative research proposals, however, proposals for qualitative research are more tentative and open-ended for an emergent design. Qualitative research proposals reflect an inductive approach to research.[4] Qualitative researchers and scholars recognize that the degree of specificity in a written proposal *depends on the extent of preliminary work* in either site selection and mapping the field in ethnographic research or in locating and previewing archival collections of historical and legal documents. A proposal, however, can be sufficiently specific to indicate systematic research to yield valid data without being so specific that the initial focus and design cannot be reformulated as the data are collected. Guidelines for ethnographic proposals are presented first, followed by guidelines for historical and legal proposals.

Ethnographic Research Proposals

General Format.   The general format for an ethnographic research proposal loosely resembles a quantitative research proposal with methodological variations for an interactive mode of data collection. The outline below contains the elements of an ethnographic proposal.

I. Introduction
   A. General Problem Statement
   B. Preliminary Literature Review
   C. Foreshadowed Problems
   D. Significance of Proposed Study

II. Design and Methodology
   A. Site Selection
   B. Research Role
   C. Purposeful Sampling Strategies
   D. Data Collection Strategies
   E. Inductive Data Analysis
   F. Limitations of the Design

III. References or Bibliography

IV. Appendices

The general format varies somewhat for the particular ethnographic research.

---

[4]See J. Van Maanen (1988), *Tales of the field: On writing ethnography.*

Guidelines for Ethnographic Research Proposals.   *I. Introduction.* The introduction consists of the general problem statement, literature review, foreshadowed problems, and the potential significance of the proposed study. Each of these are briefly explained below.

The *general problem statement* is a clear, succinct statement of the research problem which enables the reader to recognize the importance of the problem and the area of education in which it lies. A direct statement of the problem is made very early in the introduction followed by a description of the background of the problem. Typically the general problem statement is phrased as "to describe and analyze" an on-going event or a process in a discovery orientation.

The *preliminary literature review* presents the *possible* conceptual frameworks used in phrasing foreshadowed problems/questions and a need for the study by identifying gaps in our knowledge or prior research. The literature review frequently cites broad areas of scholarly thinking—sociological, psychological, anthropological, or political—with representative scholars, and it illustrates why certain concepts may become relevant in data collection and analysis. The literature review is *not* exhaustive, but it is a preliminary review which makes explicit the initial conceptual frameworks on which the ethnographer enters the field to focus the beginning observations and interviewing. The literature review clearly justifies the need for an in-depth descriptive study using an ethnographic approach. For example, prior studies did not examine the phenomena in depth or as a process; related research was conducted with quantitative procedures.

The *foreshadowed problems* are stated as broad, anticipated research questions to be reformulated in the field. To state the foreshadowed problems, ethnographers have usually selected the site and obtained tentative or formal permission to conduct the study at the site in an assumed researcher role. In other words, the researcher already has preliminary information about what is likely to occur at the site and where and when the phenomena may be observed initially.

The *potential significance of the study* describes how the ethnographic study can add to 1) the development of knowledge and 2) implications for further research and educational practices. Ethnographic studies frequently add to our knowledge by providing detailed descriptions of a naturalistic event which has not been described fully in the literature. Ethnographic studies also may develop concepts or a theoretical explanation for what was observed. Most ethnographic proposals in a discovery orientation state the intent to suggest further research with similar designs to extend the findings or with other designs and methodologies to verify the findings. The intent to state implications for educational practices based on the findings are noted very generally.

II. Design and Methodology. The design and methodology in an ethnographic research proposal includes the site selection, the research role, purposeful sampling strategies, data collection strategies, inductive data analysis and modes of data display, and design limitations.

The researcher identifies the proposal as a *case study design* using ethnographic methodology. This orients the reader to expect certain design components to be discussed in the proposal.

The *site selected* is described in terms which illustrate that the site is suitable to investigate the phenomena and processes stated in the foreshadowed problems. For example, if the foreshadowed problems focus on instructional processes, then the site should contain courses or classes—social scenes—which have instructional processes. A description of the site characteristics is essential—public or private school, type of educational agency, and its purpose or role in society, typical activities and processes, the kinds of participants, and the like. The description helps identify typicality to allow for extension of findings.

The researcher states the *research role* to be assumed for data collection. The researcher, at this time, can describe the role only in general terms, as in observer-participant, participant-observer, or primarily an interviewer. Because the research role affects the relationships in interactive data collection, the role must be delineated as much as is possible in terms of the expected social relationships and role sets during data collection. Further, the research role must be appropriate for the foreshadowed problems.

The intent to use *purposeful sampling strategies* and examples of *possible* strategies are stated in a proposal. The researcher recognizes that strategies will be selected in the field as the research progresses. Purposeful sampling strategies are easier to describe after the researcher has "mapped the field," yet proposals are sometimes written with little preliminary work. The intent of purposeful sampling is to obtain small samples of information-rich cases of individuals, social scenes, or processes. Some examples often specified in a proposal are comprehensive selection, maximum variation sampling, network selection and reputational-case selection. Others, such as extreme-case, typical-case, unique-case, and critical-case, are usually selected in the field to match the evolving research foci.

Possible *data collection strategies* are stated. Although specific data collection strategies will emerge in the field, the intent to use multiple methods should be explicit to enable corroboration of the data. The researcher specifies which strategies will be used: participant observations, the form(s) of ethnographic interview, and expected artifacts to be collected in the field. Some ethnographers specify certain data collection strategies for each research focus in the foreshadowed problems (Dobbert, 1982). The researcher also states the expected *length of the field residence,* the natural boundary of the event to be observed, such as a semester, the entire program, and the like. Ethnographers usually state the forms which the data will take, such as field notes, summary observation, and interview records, transcripts, and elaborations. Because the collected data can become "mounds" of information, ethnographers sometimes state how they will catalogue, store, and retrieve data either manually or with a micro-computer. Although data collection strategies in a proposal are written as possible or tentative strategies, they do indicate that the researcher is aware of possible strategies and the need to make choices in the field to obtain valid data as the foreshadowed problems are reformulated.

The description of *inductive data analysis* includes strategies to facilitate discovery in the field, preliminary data analyses, categorizing and ordering the data, and gauging the trustworthiness of the data (see Chapter 11). The mode of presentation of results or level of abstraction is typically stated as a descriptive narration, a descriptive-analytical interpretation, or as grounded theoretical research (see Chapter 11). The level of abstraction selected is related logically to the problem statement.

The *limitations of the design,* similar to quantitative research, cites those limitations which the researcher can identify at this time: the scope of the study, the design and/or the methodology. The limitation of scope relates to the problem statement. The foreshadowed problems usually focus on one aspect of possible research foci at the selected site, such as to describe instructional processes but not to evaluate the teacher or the effectiveness of these processes for student learning. Sometimes design limitations are an advantage in ethnographic research (see Chapter 5). Findings from a case study design are not generalizable, but without a case study design, other research purposes could not be achieved. The methodological limitations refer to possible difficulties in assuming the research role, purposeful sampling, and naturalistic events which the ethnographer cannot interrupt legitimately.

III. References or Bibliography. References for an ethnographic study are similar to that for a quantitative study if one uses the APA style manual. Some ethnographers prefer to use the CMS style manual with its bibliographic format.

IV. Appendices. The appendices in an ethnographic proposal provide supplementary materials for economical presentation as in quantitative proposals. The items in the appendices, however, are appropriate for the proposal. Included in the appendices for an ethnographic proposal may be such items as the following:

a. letters of permission granting access to the site
b. agreements of informed rights of human subjects from key participants
c. brief hypothetical examples of field notes and summary observations, interview records, and transcripts
d. proposed time schedule for completing the study

Historical and Legal Research Proposals

General Format.   The general format for a historical or legal research proposal resembles other proposals with some methodological variations for a focus on past events using documents in archival collections.[5] The outline below contains the elements of a historical or legal research proposal.

I. Introduction
   A. General Problem Statement
   B. Preliminary Literature Review
   C. Specific Research Historical Questions or Legal Issue
   D. Significance of the Proposed Study

---

[5]See J. Barzun (1985), *On writing editing, and publishing: Essays explicative and hortatory* (2nd ed.).

II. Design and Methodology
   A. Case Study Design
   B. Sources: Search, Selection and Criticism
   C. Inductive Data Analysis
   D. Limitations of Design

III. References or Bibliography

IV. Appendices

As in other discovery-oriented approaches to research, there is a tentative and open-ended quality to the proposal. The more preliminary work the researcher has done, the more detailed the proposal is. A proposal, however, reflects the initial planning for study because many of the methodological decisions are made during data collection.

Guidelines for a Historical or Legal Research Proposal.   *I. Introduction.* The introduction consists of a general problem statement, literature review, the specific historical or legal question, and the potential significance of the study.

The *general problem statement* is a clear, precise statement of the research problem which enables the reader to recognize the importance of the problem and the area of education in which it lies. A direct statement of the problem is made early in the introduction followed by a description of the background of the problem. Historical research problem statements usually identify the time period (Colonial Period, Civil War era, post World War II, and the like), the place (such as United States, a state or region, city or county), the person, movement, or organization (John Dewey, Horace Mann, desegregation movement, female equity, or opinions of Circuit Court judges). Legal research also identifies the time, the legal issue to be examined, and the area of education law, such as academic freedom in a science curriculum or tort liability of school boards in sports. Legal research problems also may identify a legal principle to be investigated as it was applied to selected cases. Problem statements reflect a discovery-orientation about past phenomena.

The *preliminary literature review* presents what is known in general about the problem to date and provides a rationale for the study. Because of the discovery-orientation of the research, the literature review may not be extensive. Prior research on other topics during the same historical period, on a similar problem but in another period, or on a similar problem but using other archival collections or legal cases provide a rationale for a historical or legal proposal. The literature review may also discuss the historical roots of a legal principle or a movement. Literature for a legal study may include the importance of understanding "the law" or the legal principle for current educational practices. For example, the growth of sports-related injuries suggests the importance of understanding school board tort liability in sports.

If known at proposal time, the *specific research historical question* or *legal issue* is stated, followed by definitions of key concepts or terms. A typical legal issue is clarified by noting the parties, the subject matter or property, the nature of the claim or issue and the object or remedy sought (see Chapter 12). Historical questions often are phrased with concepts which are further defined. Sometimes only a problem statement is made in a proposal and the specific research question or legal issue emerges from the documents analyzed.

The *potential significance of the proposed study* notes the importance of the study in terms of 1) the development of knowledge and 2) implications of further research and educational practices. The researcher discusses how the results of the analysis could add to our *understanding* of "the law" or of the historical period, person, or organization. Implications for educational practices are stated in general terms, citing how an understanding of the past could inform educational practitioners and policy-makers. References are frequently made to recent or current events, such as the growth of unionization among educational professionals, increase in legal suits against school boards for negligence, and the like, which indicate the need for an understanding.

II. Design and Methodology. The design and methodology in historical and legal research include the search, selection, and criticism of sources, inductive data analysis and presentation of facts and generalizations, and design limitations.

Because historical and legal scholars are knowledgeable about the methodology, the *case study design* may be only *implied* in the problem statement, the specific historical question or legal issue and design limitations. Beginning researchers often provide a rationale for a case study design.

The description of the planned *search, selection, and criticism of sources* is crucial in the methodology for a proposal. At proposal time, however, often only a framework for the search and selection of sources is stated. Both the historian and legal researcher use reference aids to locate primary sources. The historian uses appropriate general historical bibliographies and specialized bibliographies to locate archival collections of newspapers, government documents, organizational records, and personal documents such as a president's papers or an individual's diary. If the researcher has already searched these bibliographies, then the key index or topic words used in the search are identified and the period searched. If the researcher has previewed an archival collection, then more specific descriptions of the content of the archival collection can be made. A legal researcher states which search aids such as specific digests of case law, reporters, citators, and various indexes will be used to obtain relevant statutes, court decisions, and other legal documents. The methods of search—the descriptive word method, topic method, or popular name method—are also stated. If the researcher has completed the search by proposal time, frequently the primary sources are listed. Because the search for primary documents continues during the research process, proposal reviewers expect additional sources will be added.

Not all primary sources will yield data relevant to the problem, thus a clear statement of the specific historical question or legal issue implies how relevant primary sources will be selected. Some researchers prefer to make this selection process more explicit in a proposal. Other researchers prefer to make these decisions explicit as they do the study and then describe the selection process in the actual report.

Most historical researchers can anticipate how they will use techniques of internal and external criticism of sources (see Chapter 12) to obtain *both* relevant sources and valid factual data from these sources. Legal researchers, because of the nature of official records, usually do not state techniques of internal and external criticism of sources in a proposal.

A proposal states the use of *inductive analysis* and presentation to derive facts and present generalizations and may state causal explanations. Because an inductive analysis builds on the initial analysis of the documents and is a cyclic process, the researcher cannot be very specific in a proposal. The researcher, however, can state tentatively the general type of analysis planned. The general type of analysis envisioned relates to the research purpose, such as making a compilation of original sources, providing a descriptive narration, doing an interpretative analysis, and, for more advanced researchers, doing a comparative or universal analysis (see Chapter 12). Data are usually presented in narrative style but, when appropriate, simple tabulation of numerical data in charts and use of figures may be legitimate. *The Chicago Manual of Style* (13th ed.) presents guidelines for use of quotations, abbreviations, names and terms, and the distinctive treatment of words, numbers, tables, and mathematics in type.

The researcher either notes the *limitations of the design* or implies these limitations in the problem statement and selection of sources. If limitations of the design are explicit, the researcher cites those which can be identified at this time: the scope of the study, the design, and/or the methodology. The specific historical questions or legal issues, if well stated, imply the scope limitations. The design, although a case study, is viewed, not as a limitation, but as a necessity in order to investigate a carefully delineated problem thoroughly. The methodology, however, may be a limitation if the researcher does not use appropriate search techniques, cannot obtain access to relevant archival collections, or cannot locate relevant sources known to have been created. These limitations, however, are usually not known at proposal time and are reported in the actual study.

III. References or Bibliography. A **bibliography** lists all the sources which the researcher actually used to develop the proposal: primary, secondary, and sources which provided background material. Unlike references which follow the APA style manual, as this book does, the secondary sources which provided background information for the problem are cited in a bibliography in the CMS style. Although the APA style manual provides citation guidelines for historical and legal sources, most scholars prefer *The Chicago Manual of Style* (13th ed.) or the current edition of *A Uniform System of Citation* published by the Harvard Review Association.

IV. Appendices. The appendices in a historical or legal proposal provide supplementary materials which can be referred to by a reader without interrupting the logical flow of the proposal. The items in the appendices, however, are appropriate for the particular proposal. Items which may be included in appendices are:

a. letters of permission to use an archival collection
b. descriptions of the content of an archival collection
c. list of constitutions, statutes, and legal cases already located through a legal search process
d. proposed time schedule for completing the study

■ PREPARATION AND CRITICISM ■
OF A PROPOSAL

Preparation of a proposal involves two additional tasks: conforming to the format and style required for the proposal and obtaining criticisms of a draft proposal before it is typed in finished form.

Preparation of a Proposal

Most colleges and universities either have developed their own format and style manual or selected a style manual to be followed such as the *Publication Manual of the American Psychological Association* (3rd ed.) or *The Chicago Manual of Style* (13th ed.). **Format** refers to the general pattern of organization and arrangement of the proposal. **Style** refers to the rules of spelling, capitalization, punctuation, and typing followed in preparing a proposal. Although neither manual refers specifically to research proposals, many universities and colleges follow a general format and the style adopted from one of these authoritative manuals. Reference or bibliographic style and format, the headings and sections, and the writing style differ in each manual. Whereas APA style practically eliminates the use of footnotes, the CMS style provides for extensive use of explanatory footnotes to cite specific sources for facts presented, methodological insights, comments, and additional information for a greater understanding of the text.

Correct spelling, grammar construction, and punctuation are expected in a research proposal, and use of abbreviations and contractions is generally discouraged. Experienced researchers know that "to write means to rewrite, and rewrite and rewrite and. . . ." Personal pronouns such as *I, my, we,* and *our* should be avoided by beginning researchers. If the first word of a sentence is a number, or if the number is nine or less, numbers are usually expressed as words. Otherwise, numbers are usually expressed as arabic numerals.

Format also includes the preliminary pages. In a proposal this usually refers to the title page and perhaps a table of contents if the proposal is over fifteen pages. The title page contains the titles of the proposal, the author's name and date for a course required proposal. The title page for a thesis or dissertation proposal may include the title, the author's name, the degree requirement being fulfilled, the name and location of the college or university awarding the degree, the date of submission, and space for the signatures of the committee. The title should be brief (fifteen words or less) yet descriptive of the purpose of the proposal study. The Table of Contents is basically the outline of the proposal with the page number of each major section, the references or bibliography, and any appendices.

All proposals are typed and the same standards of scholarship are applied to the typing of the proposal as to the writing of the proposal. The final typing should be proofread carefully by the author. Word processing software has greatly facilitated scholarly writing. Common features include automatic page numbering and heading centering; the ability to edit "on-screen" words, sentences, and paragraphs; spelling checkers; outlining features; and automatic footnotes or endnotes. Proofreading is essential because spell checkers do not proof for grammar.

Criticism of a Proposal

After completing a draft of a proposal, authors read it critically in terms of research criteria appropriate for the purpose and design of the study. Many of these criteria were suggested in prior chapters. In addition to self-criticism, researchers give a draft to colleagues for feedback. Below are some common weaknesses of proposals.

1. *The problem is trivial.* Problems which are of only peripheral interest to educators or show little likelihood of adding to knowledge in education are seldom approved enthusiastically. The problem should be related to one of the mainstreams of educational knowledge, scholarly thinking, research, and educational practices.

2. *The problem is not delimited.* A problem must be focused for both research and practical reasons. Designs cannot yield valid data for every possible variable nor can qualitative researchers encompass extremely broad questions in a single study. Experienced researchers know how time-consuming research processes are from the initial conceptualization of an idea through the final report. Researchers rationally, but reluctantly, delimit the problem. The specific research questions and/or hypothesis or the qualitative foreshadowed problems are stated in such a way so the delineation of the focus is apparent.

3. *The objectives of the proposal are too general.* Sometimes hypotheses are stated in such broad, general terms that only the research design really conveys what the study is about. If the research design does not logically match the specific research questions and/or hypothesis or the qualitative research questions, then the planned study is not capable of meeting proposal objectives. Failure to consider extraneous or confounding variables is a serious error in a quantitative proposal. Qualitative proposals are also focused. Although generally the phrasing of research questions is in broader terms, the particular viewpoint narrows the focus.

4. *The methodology is lacking in detail appropriate for the proposed study.* Quantitative proposals should be detailed sufficiently in subjects, instrumentation, and data analysis to allow for replication. Qualitative proposals, by their inductive nature, are less specific in certain aspects. A qualitative proposal, however, can be sufficiently specific to connote *possible* purposeful sampling, data collection, and data analysis strategies. This specification assures a review committee that the researcher is aware of subsequent decisions to be made.

■ SUMMARY ■

1. Some forms of research communication are proposals, theses and dissertations, journal articles, evaluation and technical reports, and papers presented at professional meetings.
2. Both the researcher and the consumer of research must be able to reason analytically, especially regarding internal validity and the generalizability or extension of the research.
3. Three types of arguments that are used for internal and external validity are reasoning, methods, and replications or extensions of the research.
4. Communication of research involves choices of what to include, a research writing style, and the interpretations of the reader.
5. Quantitative research proposals can be more specific than qualitative research proposals. Quantitative research proposals reflect a deductive approach to research; qualitative research proposals reflect an inductive approach to research.
6. Research proposals specify the general statement of the problem, the review of the literature, the specific research questions and/or hypotheses and the significance of the proposed study.
7. Quantitative research proposals usually specify for the design and methodology: subjects, instrumentation, procedures, data analysis and presentation, and design limitations.
8. Ethnographic research proposals specify for the case study design, the site selection, research role, purposeful sampling procedures, data collection strategies, inductive analysis, and design limitations. The degree of specification depends on the extent of the researcher's preliminary work.
9. Historical and legal research proposals specify for the case study design: the initial search, selection and criticism of sources, inductive data analysis, and design limitations. The degree of specification depends on the extent of the researcher's preliminary work.
10. Preparation of a proposal requires following a format and style for the title page, the proposal text, references or bibliography, and appendices.
11. Proposals are frequently criticized because the problem is trivial and not delimited, the objectives of the study are too general, and the methodology is lacking in detail appropriate for the study.
12. Experienced researchers self-criticize a proposal and obtain criticism from peers and colleagues before completing a proposal.

■ SELF-INSTRUCTIONAL REVIEW EXERCISES ■

Sample answers are in the back of the book.

Test Items

1. Which of the following arguments is the strongest in communication of research?
   a. logical reasoning

    b. methods of research utilized in a study

    c. replications and extensions are possible from the research

    d. All of the above are combined.

2. Communication in research involves

    a. choices of what to include.

    b. use of a creative writing style.

    c. violations of rules for a research writing style.

    d. use of cliches and embellishments.

3. Which of the following would be *inappropriate* in the communication of research?

    a. transitions for orderly presentation of ideas

    b. non-sexist language

    c. ambiguous words or referents

    d. the use of past tense in literature review

4. Both qualitative and quantitative research proposals

    a. are idiosyncratic for the particular study.

    b. have a format of introduction, design and methodology, references or bibliography, and appendices when appropriate.

    c. contain similar types of literature reviews.

    d. contain similar types of design and methodological sections.

5. Qualitative and quantitative research proposals differ in

    a. degree of specificity in the research design.

    b. the nature of the literature review.

    c. data analysis section.

    d. All of the above are correct.

6. Qualitative and quantitative research proposals should reflect

    a. a deductive approach or logical reasoning.

    b. an inductive approach or logical reasoning.

    c. the appropriate mode of reasoning for the study proposal.

    d. a non-rational, intuitive mode of reasoning.

7. Preparation of a proposal involves

    a. using a unique format and style.

    b. letting the typist decide the format and edit for style.

    c. using the first person voice in writing.

    d. carefully following the required format and style.

8. The APA style requires

    a. entries in the reference list match citations in the text.

    b. extensive explanatory footnotes.

    c. references to cite all background sources used but not cited in the text.

    d. no headings or sections.

9. A typical weakness in a proposal is
    a. the problem is delimited.
    b. the problem is too broad for the proposed research design.
    c. the proposed study shows potential for contributing to knowledge development.
    d. the methodology is sufficiently detailed for the proposed study.

APPENDIX A

Glossary

A-B design: A single-subject design that compares frequency of behavior during the baseline (A) to treatment (B) conditions.

A-B-A design: A single-subject design that compares the baseline (A) to treatment (B) and then baseline (A).

abstract: A brief summary of a study or article, located at the beginning of the article.

achievement test: A test that measures knowledge, skills, or behavior.

alpha level: *See* level of significance.

analysis of covariance (ANCOVA): An inferential statistical test that is used to control statistically the effect of an independent variable that is related to the dependent variable.

analysis of variance (ANOVA): An inferential statistical procedure for determining the level of probability of rejecting the null hypothesis with two or more means.

analytical: Describes and interprets the past from selected sources—historical, legal, policy, and philosophical studies.

applied research: Research that is conducted in a field of common practice and is concerned with the application and development of research-based knowledge.

aptitude test: A test that is used to predict behavior.

archival and demographic record collections: Written or symbolic records kept by or on the participants in a social group.

artifact collections: Tangible manifestations of beliefs and behaviors that form a culture, describe peoples' experience, knowledge, and behaviors, and can connote their values, feelings, and perceptions.

assessment: The act of determining the standing of an object on some variable—for example, testing students and reporting raw scores.

assigned variables: *See* attribute variables.

attenuation: The lowering of a measure of relationship between two variables because of the unreliability of the measures.

attribute variables: *Also* assigned variables. Independent variables that cannot be manipulated.

audiences (in evaluation research): Those persons who will be guided by the evaluation in making decisions; anyone directly or indirectly connected to the program.

availability sampling: Using subjects who are not drawn from a large population.

baseline: The first phase of single-subject research in which behavior is recorded before any changes are introduced.

basic research: Research that tests or refines theory; not designed to be applied immediately to practice.

behavioral objectives: Objectives of a practice stated in terms of observable terminal performances that can be measured; also called performance objectives, measured objectives.

beta weight: Standardized regression coefficient.

biased: A term that refers to the influence of a particular perspective, desire, or point of view on something.

bibliography: A list of all the sources which the researcher actually used to develop a proposal, manuscript, or article: primary, secondary, and sources which provided background material.

career and life history interviews: Interviews which elicit life narratives of individuals or career histories of professional lives.

case: A particular situation selected by the researcher in which some phenomena will be described by participants' meanings of events and processes.

case study design: The one phenomenon the researcher selects to understand in-depth regardless of the number of settings, social scenes, or participants in a study; an analysis whose results are not generalizable.

categorical variable: A variable used to categorize subjects, objects, or entities into two or more categories.

categorizing and ordering data: Inductive logical processes for refining the researcher's understanding of the emerging patterns and themes.

causal explanation: In analytic research, abstract syntheses of generalizations using inductive logic, usually stated as conclusions in a study.

checklist: A type of questionnaire item in which subjects check appropriate responses that are provided.

chi-square: *Also* goodness of fit. A nonparametric statistical procedure that is used with nominal data to test relationships between frequency of observations in categories of independent variables.

closed form: A type of questionnaire item in which the subject chooses between or among predetermined responses.

cluster sampling: A form of sampling in which subjects are first grouped according to naturally occurring units.

coefficient of determination: Squared correlation coefficient that indicates the percentage of variance accounted for in a relationship.

coefficient of multiple correlation: An indicator of the combined relationship of several variables to another variable.

commentaries: Extensive articles which analyze and interpret specialized educational law topics and provide extensive case citations in the footnotes.

comparability: In qualitative research, the degree to which the research site(s), participant characteristics, documents used, unit of analysis, and the concepts generated are adequately described so researchers may use the study to extend understandings in subsequent research.

comparison group: One of the groups whose performance in behavior is compared in an experiment.

complete observer: An observer who remains completely detached from the group or process of interest.

comprehensive sampling: The ideal type of sampling in qualitative research in which every participant, group, setting, event or other information is examined.

concept: An abstraction from observed phenomena. A word that states the commonalities among those observed events and situations and distinguishes the phenomena from other events and situations.

conceptual analysis: A study that clarifies the meaning of a concept by describing the essential or generic meaning, the different meanings, and the appropriate usage for the concept.

concurrent evidence: A type of validity evidence in which test scores are correlated with scores from an existing instrument given at about the same time.

constant comparison: A technique for developing major categories in order to analyze qualitative data by noting similarities and differences.

construct: A complex abstraction that is not directly observable, such as anxiety, intelligence, self-concept; a meaningful combination of concepts.

construct validity: A type of external validity that refers to the extent to which the study represents the underlying construct.

construct-related evidence: A type of evidence for test validity in which scores represent an underlying meaning, interpretation, trait, or theory.

contamination: In quantitative research, a type of observer bias that results from observer knowledge of the study.

content-related evidence: A type of evidence for test validity in which the content of a test is judged to be representative of a larger domain of content.

context (in ethnography): The site and selected settings, social scenes, and participants observed during the entire data collection period.

contingency coefficient: *Also* phi coefficient. A single index that shows the degree of relationship in a contingency table.

contingency questions: Questions that when answered in a certain way provide directions to subsequent questions.

contingency table: *Also* independent samples chi-square test. A chi-square test with two or more independent variables.

continuous observation: An observational data-gathering technique in which the observer records all important behaviors.

continuous variable: *Also* measured variable. A variable in which the property or attribute of an object, subject, or entity is measured numerically and can assume an infinite number of values within a range.

control: Efforts to remove or otherwise take account of factors or variables other than the independent variable that might affect the dependent variable.

control group: The subjects in an experiment who receive no treatment.

control group interrupted time series design: A quasi-experimental time series study that compares the treatment group to a control group.

correlated samples t-test: *See* dependent samples t-test.

correlation: A measure of relationship that uses a correlation coefficient.

correlation coefficient: A number that is calculated to indicate the size and direction of the degree of relationship between two variables.

correlational design: Research in which information on at least two variables is collected for each subject in order to investigate the relationship between the variables.

cost analysis modes: An analysis that compares the costs with the benefits, effectiveness, or utility or the feasibility of alternative practices.

cost-benefit analysis: Evaluates decision alternatives by comparing the costs and benefits to society.

cost-effectiveness analysis: Compares the outcomes of similar practices in relation to their costs, when the different programs have the same objectives and measures.

cost-feasibility analysis: Estimates the cost of a practice to determine whether the practice is a realistic consideration within an existing budget.

cost-utility analysis: Compares alternative practices to determine the practice that is most likely to produce the most desired outcomes at least cost.

credibility: In qualitative studies, the use of appropriate definitions of research criteria for internal and external validity.

criterion variable: In a prediction study, the variable that is predicted.

criterion-referenced tests: Instruments whose scores are interpreted by referral to specific criteria or standards rather than to the performance of others.

criterion-related evidence: A type of evidence for test validity in which the test scores are correlated with scores from a meaningful criterion.

Cronbach alpha: A type of internal consistency reliability for items with scaled responses.

cross-sectional: A research strategy in which several different groups of subjects are assessed at the same time.

data: Results obtained by research from which interpretations and conclusions are drawn.

data collection and analyses strategies: In qualitative research, techniques which are flexible and dependent on each prior strategy and the data obtained from that strategy.

data displays: An organized assembly of information such as figures, matrices, and flow charts which assist in qualitative analysis.

data trustworthiness: The extent to which emerging categories, patterns, and themes reflect valid and reliable data.

database (in computer searches): Sources which are indexed by a particular reference service.

decision-oriented evaluation: An evaluation that supplies information for prespecified decisions, such as needs assessment, program planning, program implementation, or outcomes.

deductive reasoning: A reasoning which assumes that if the premises are correct, the conclusion is automatically correct.

degrees of freedom: A mathematical concept that indicates the number of observations that are free to vary.

dependent samples t-test: *Also* correlated samples t-test. An inferential statistical procedure for determining the probability level of rejecting the null hypothesis with two samples of subjects that are matched or related.

dependent variable: A measured variable that is the consequence of or is dependent upon antecedent variables.

descriptive design: Research that describes an existing or past phenomenon quantitatively.

descriptive questions: Research questions that infer that the purpose is to describe *what is*—that is, a status study, survey research—or *what was*— that is, analytical research.

descriptive research: Research that describes the current status of something.

descriptive statistics: Statistical procedures that describe something.

developmental studies: Research that investigates change of subjects over time.

digests: Indexes to case law, the law growing out of court decisions.

diffusion of treatment: A threat to internal validity in which subjects are aware of other conditions of the independent variable.

disciplined inquiry: Research conducted in such a way that the argument can be examined painstakingly.

documents: In analytical research, records of past events; synonymous with *sources* and usually preserved in collections.

domain-referenced tests: *See* criterion-referenced tests.

double-barrelled questions: Single questions that contain two or more ideas to which the subject must make one response.

duration recording: A type of observer recording procedure in which the duration of behavior is recorded.

ecological external validity: Refers to the extent to which results of research can be generalized to other conditions or situations.

educational ethnographies: analytical descriptions of social scenes and groups which recreate for the reader the shared beliefs, practices, folk knowledge, and behaviors.

emergent design: A plan in which each step depends on the results of the previous steps.

empiricism: Guided by evidence, data, or sources.

empirico-inductive approach: A research approach typical of qualitative studies in which abstractions or generalizations are built from elements or particulars.

equivalence: A type of test reliability in which scores from equivalent or parallel forms of the same instrument, given at about the same time, are correlated.

ethnographic interview: A data collection strategy which uses in-depth interviews with open-response questions to obtain data of participant meanings.

ethnographic observation: Participant-observation of phenomena in naturally occurring situations over an extended period of time to obtain descriptive field notes.

ethnographic study: *See* educational ethnographies.

evaluation design: Determines the way an evaluation will be conducted; for example, the questions to be addressed, the data to be collected and analyzed, the management plan, the report schedule. Designs may be predetermined or emergent.

evaluation focus: The practice to be evaluated, including its components.

evaluation research: Designed to aid and assess the merit and worth of a specific practice in terms of the values operating at the site(s).

ex post facto **design:** Research that investigates events that have already occurred and implies cause-and-effect relationships from the results.

exhaustive literature search: A literature search on a narrowly focused problem for ten or more years using the most relevant reference services.

experimental design: Research in which the independent variable is manipulated to investigate cause-and-effect relationships between the independent and dependent variable.

experimental group: The subjects who receive the condition that the experimenter hypothesizes will change behavior.

experimental research: *See* experimental design.

experimental variable: The variable in experimental or quasi-experimental design that is manipulated or changed by the researcher to see the effect on (relationship to) the dependent variable.

experimenter bias: *Also* experimenter contamination. A threat to internal validity in which the researcher's differential treatment of subjects affects results.

explanation: A theory or analytical generalization that states cause-and-effect relationships in simple statements.

extension of understandings: Detailed descriptions of the events and people studied which enable others to understand similar situations and extend these understandings in subsequent research.

external criticism: Analytical procedures carried out to determine the authenticity of the source, i.e., if the source is the original document, a forged document, or a variant of the original document.

external validity: Refers to the extent to which results of a study can be generalized to other subjects, conditions, or situations.

factorial analysis of variance: An analysis of variance statistical procedure with two or more independent variables that permits testing each independent variable and the interaction of the variables.

facts: In analytical research, descriptions of who, what, when, and where an event occurred, obtained from decisive evidence.

field notes: Data that are obtained by direct observation in the setting while the ethnographer is in the field.

field research: Research that views the setting as a natural situation in which the researcher collects data over a prolonged time.

field residence (in ethnography): Being present in the field or site for an extensive time to collect data.

field test: A study of a program or materials, or a test in a setting like those where it is to be used; field tests may range from preliminary studies to full-scale evaluations.

foreshadowed problems: Anticipated research problems which will be reformulated during data collection.

format: The general pattern of organization and arrangement of the proposal, manuscript, or article.

formative evaluation: Evaluation designed and used to improve a practice, especially when it is still being developed.

frequency-count recording: A type of observer recording procedure in which the frequency of behavior is recorded.

frequency distribution: A display of a set of scores by means of a list of the number of times each score was attained.

frequency polygon: A graphic representation of a frequency distribution formed by connecting in a line the highest frequency of each score.

generalizability: The extent to which the findings of one study can be used as knowledge about other populations and situations.

generalization: In analytical research, interpretation of facts that focus on the way or the reason an event occurred.

grounded theory: A sophisticated analysis which links participant perceptions to more general social science theories and suggests new concepts and mini-theories.

Hawthorne effect: Refers to the tendency of people to act differently because they realize they are subjects in a study.

histogram: Graphic illustration of a frequency distribution, using bars to represent the frequency of each score.

historical analysis: Application of analytical methodology to the study of the past, as in biographies and studies of movements, institutions, and concepts.

history: A threat to internal validity in which incidents or events that occur during the research affect results.

holistic emphasis (in ethnography): Sub-cases of data are related to the total context of the phenomenon studied.

hypothesis: A statement of the expected relationship between two or more variables.

hypothetic-deductive approach: A research typical of quantitative experimental studies which investigate hypotheses deduced from theories.

independent samples chi-square test: *See* contingency table.

independent samples *t*-test: An inferential statistical procedure for determining the probability level of rejecting the null hypothesis with two samples of subjects that have no relation to each other.

independent variable: A variable antecedent to or preceding the dependent variable; also called, in experimental design and quasi-experimental design, the experimental or manipulated variable.

inductive analysis: Patterns, themes, and categories of analysis emerge from the data rather than being imposed on the data prior to data collection.

inductive reasoning: A reasoning by which observation of particular cases are generalized to the whole class.

inferential statistics: Procedures that indicate probabilities associated with saying something about populations based on data from samples.

informal conversational interview: Questions that emerge from the immediate context and are asked in the natural course of events; there is no predetermination of question topics or phrasing.

informed consent: Obtaining permission from individuals to participate in research before the research begins.

instrumentation: A threat to internal validity in which changes in the instruments affect the results.

interaction: The unique effect of different levels of independent variables on the dependent variable.

interactive techniques: Ethnographic observation (participant-observation) or ethnographic interview as a data collection strategy.

intercorrelation matrix: A table that presents intercorrelations among many variables.

internal consistency: A type of test reliability in which the homogeneity of the items of an instrument is assessed after one administration of the instrument.

internal criticism: Analytical procedures to determine the credibility of the statements in a source; the accuracy and trustworthiness of the facts.

internal validity: The degree to which extraneous variables are controlled in concluding or interpreting observed relationships.

interobserver reliability: In qualitative research, the agreement on the description or composition of events rather than on the frequency of occurrence of events.

inter-rater agreement: A type of reliability calculated by the correlation of several raters.

interval recording: A type of observer recording procedure in which behavior that occurs during a given time interval is recorded.

interval scale: A type of measurement scale in which numbers are rank-ordered with equal intervals between ranks.

interview guide approach: Topics are selected in advance but the researcher decides the sequence and wording of the questions during the interview.

interview probes: Brief questions or phrases which elicit elaboration of detail, further explanations, and clarifications of responses.

interview schedule: *See* standardized interviews.

ipsative: A type of measurement response format in which answers to one question or category determine what the answers can be in remaining questions or categories.

key-informant interview: In-depth interview of an individual who has special knowledge, status, or communication skills.

Kuder-Richardson: A type of internal-consistency reliability for items scored right or wrong.

leading question: In qualitative interviews, a question in which the wording encourages certain responses.

legal analysis: Application of analytical methodology to the study of legal issues in order to understand the law or identify legal principles.

level of significance: *Also* level of probability, level of confidence. A value that is selected to indicate the chance that it is wrong to reject the null hypothesis.

Likert scale: A type of scale in which subjects express degrees of agreement or disagreement with a statement.

literature review: A compressed critique of the status of knowledge on a carefully defined educational topic; a section of a study or proposal that provides the rationale for the research problem.

longitudinal: A research strategy in which quantitative data are collected on one group of subjects over a period of time.

management systems analysis: An evaluation that provides information on systems planning, monitoring, impact, and economic efficiency.

manipulated variable: The independent variable in experiments that is determined by the researcher.

mapping the field: In ethnographic research, acquiring data of the social, spatial, and temporal relationships in the site to gain a sense of the total context.

maturation: A threat to internal validity in which maturational changes in subjects such as growing older or more tired, or becoming hungry, affect the results in quantitative research.

mean: A measure of central tendency, the arithmetical average of the scores.

measured variable: *See* continuous variable.

measurement scale: Properties that describe the relationships between numbers.

measures of central tendency: Summary indices of a set of scores that represent the typical score in a distribution.

measures of variability: Numerical indices that indicate the degree of dispersion of scores from the mean.

median: A measure of central tendency, the point or score in a distribution that is the midpoint.

memorandum of agreement (in evaluation): A statement between the evaluator and the client that specifies the practice to be evaluated, the purpose and audiences of the evaluation, the reporting procedures, and the like; a mutual understanding of expectations and responsibilities of both parties.

merit: The valued characteristics intrinsic to the practice for which there is relatively consistent agreement.

meta-analysis: A research procedure which uses statistical techniques to synthesize the results of prior independently conducted studies.

methodology: The methods used to collect information.

mode: A measure of central tendency; the most frequently occurring score.

mortality: A threat to internal validity in which loss of subjects affects the results in quantitative research.

multimethods: The use of multiple strategies to corroborate the data obtained from any single strategy and/or ways to confirm data within a single strategy of data collection.

multiple-baseline designs: A type of single-subject design that uses several subjects, types of behavior, or situations simultaneously.

multiple comparisons: *See* post hoc comparison.

multiple correlation: A statistical procedure for indicating the degree of relationship between one dependent variable and two or more independent variables.

multiple regression prediction equation: A statistical procedure for using several variables to predict something.

multivariate: A family of statistics used when there are more than one independent variable, more than one dependent variable, or both.

naturalistic and participant-oriented evaluation: A holistic evaluation using multi-methods to provide an understanding of the divergent values of a practice from the participants' perspectives.

naturalistic inquiry or observation: Field research using noninterfering data collection techniques to describe the natural flow of events and actions.

negative relationship: A relationship in which increases of one variable correspond to decreases of another variable.

negatively skewed: A distribution of scores that has a disproportionately large number of high scores.

network selection (snowball sampling): A qualitative strategy in which each successive participant or group is named by a preceding group or individual.

nominal scale: A type of measurement scale in which objects or people are named, classified, or numbered.

noncognitive instruments: Areas other than mental processes, such as affect and emotions.

nonequivalent pretest-posttest control group design: A quasi-experimental design in which groups that have not been randomly assigned to treatments are compared.

nonexperimental design: Research that is primarily descriptive but may suggest causal explanations through designs that require no direct manipulation of variables, such as correlational research.

non-interactive techniques: Qualitative data collection strategy which uses documents as data.

nonparametric: Types of statistical procedures used when the assumptions necessary to use parametric procedures are violated.

non-proportional sampling: Stratified sampling in which the number of subjects selected from each stratum is not based on the percentage of the population represented by each stratum.

nonreactive research: *See* unobtrusive measures.

norm-referenced tests: A standardized test in which a score or group of scores is compared to the typical performance of a given (norm) group.

normal distribution: A symmetrical bell-shaped distribution of scores with the same mean, median, and mode.

null hypothesis: *Also* statistical hypothesis. A formal statistical statement that usually is a statement of no relationship between two or more variables.

objectives-oriented evaluation: An evaluation that determines the degree to which the objectives of a practice are attained by a target group.

objectivity: Data collection and analysis procedures from which only one meaning or interpretation can be made.

observation schedule: *See* structured observations.

observational research: Field research in which data are collected in a participant-observation role through noninterfering procedures.

one group posttest-only design: A pre-experimental design in which a single group of subjects receives a treatment and a posttest.

one group pretest-posttest design: A pre-experimental design in which a single group of subjects receives a pretest, a treatment, and then a posttest.

open form: A type of questionnaire item in which subjects write in a response to a question.

operational definition: A definition of a variable achieved by assigning meaning to a variable by specifying the activities or operations necessary to measure, categorize, or manipulate the variable.

oral testimonies or oral history: Records or interview transcripts of witnesses of or participants in the event studied.

ordinal scale: A type of measurement scale in which objects or persons are rank-ordered from lowest to highest.

parametric: Types of statistical procedures that assume normality in the population distributions, homogeneity of variance, and interval or ratio scale data.

participant-observation: The primary data collection strategy of ethnographers who live, as much as possible, the daily activities of participants and record their observations and interactions.

percentile rank: The point in a distribution at or below which a given percentage of scores is found.

phenomenology: An analysis of qualitative data to provide an understanding of a concept from the participants' perspectives and views of social realities.

phi coefficient: *See* contingency coefficient.

physical trace collections: Erosion measures of wear on material and accretion measures of natural objects produced or used by a group.

plausible rival hypotheses: Possible explanations, other than the effect of the independent variable, for cause-and-effect relationships.

policy research (analytical): Application of analytical methodology to the study of past and contemporary policy-making in educational and general government.

population: A group of individuals or events from which a sample is drawn.

population external validity: Refers to the extent to which the results of research can be generalized to other people.

positive relationship: A relationship in which increases of scores of one variable correspond to increases of scores of another variable.

positively skewed: A distribution of scores that has a disproportionately large number of low scores.

post hoc comparison: *Also* multiple comparison, a posteriori test. Statistical tests that are used with pairs of means, usually conducted after a test of all means together.

posttest-only control group design: A true experimental design in which one or more randomly assigned groups of subjects receives a treatment and a posttest, and one randomly assigned group of subjects receives only a posttest.

posttest-only with nonequivalent groups: A pre-experimental design in which one or more groups of subjects, not randomly assigned, receives a treatment and a posttest, and one group of subjects receives only a posttest.

prediction studies: Research in which behaviors or skills are predicted by one or several variables.

predictive evidence: A type of evidence for test validity in which scores from a test are correlated with future behavior.

predictor variable: The antecedent variable in a prediction study.

pre-experimental designs: A type of experimental design that generally has weak internal validity.

preliminary literature search: A search limited by use of one or two reference services, number of years to be reviewed, or number of sources desired; usually to select a research problem.

pretest: An assessment of performance given before a treatment is administered.

pretest-posttest control group design: A true experimental design in which one or more randomly assigned groups of subjects receives a pretest, a treatment, and a posttest, and one randomly assigned group of subjects receives only the pretest and posttest.

primary source: In a literature review, an original research study or writing by a researcher or theorist; in analytical research—a document or testimony of an eyewitness to an event.

probability: A scientific way of stating the degree of confidence in predicting something.

probability sampling: Subjects drawn from a population in known probabilities.

probing: *See* interview probes.

proportional sampling: A type of stratified sampling in which the number of subjects selected from each stratum is based on the percentage of subjects in the population of each stratum.

purposeful sampling: A strategy to choose small groups or individuals likely to be knowledgeable and informative about the phenomenon of interest; selection of cases without needing or desiring to generalize to all such cases.

purposes (of an evaluation study): The objectives of an evaluation (such as, to judge the relative merits of alternative textbooks, or to monitor and report the effectiveness with which a plan is implemented) and the intended use of its reports (such as to help teachers choose a textbook, or to help a school district carry out a project).

qualitative descriptions: Detailed narrations of people, incidents, and processes.

qualitative design: A design in which data collection strategies are identified during the research rather than predetermined ahead of time.

qualitative observations: Observations obtained over a lengthy time and recorded as field notes of ethnographic observation, transcripts of ethnographic interviews, or researcher notes of historical documents.

qualitative research: Research which presents facts in a narration with words.

qualitative techniques: Data collection strategies which acquire data in the form of words rather than numbers.

quantitative research: Research which presents results with numbers.

quantitative techniques: Data collection techniques that use numbers to describe or measure the results.

quasi-experimental: Research that has no random assignment of subjects or complete control of extraneous variables, but investigates cause-and-effect relationships by manipulating the independent variable.

questionnaire: A written set of questions or statements that assesses attitudes, opinions, beliefs, and biographical information.

questionnaire research: Research in which information is collected by subjects' responses to written questions.

random assignment: A procedure used to assign subjects to different groups so that every subject being assigned has an equal chance of being in every group.

random sampling: Selecting subjects from a population in such a way that every member of the population has an equal chance of being selected.

range: A measure of variability; the difference between the highest and lowest scores in a distribution.

rank-order: A procedure requiring subjects to arrange items in order of magnitude.

ratio scale: A type of measurement scale in which numbers are expressed meaningfully as ratios.

refereed journals: Journals that use a blind review of submitted manuscripts by accomplished researchers.

references: A list of sources which the researcher actually used and are cited in the text of a proposal or manuscript.

regression coefficient: A factor used in multiple regression to weight the contribution of each variable in the equation.

related literature: Literature that is obviously relevant to the problem or is related in some essential way to the problem.

relationship questions: Research questions that imply that the purpose is to determine whether, and to what degree, a relationship exists between two or more quantifiable variables.

relationship studies: Research that investigates the relationship of two or more variables.

reliability: The extent to which measures from a test are consistent.

relics: In analytical research, any object that provides information about the past.

replication: A study which duplicates a prior study but uses different settings or techniques.

report literature: Documents other than journals that are in the ERIC Document Microfiche Collection and indexed by *Resources in Education;* that is, presentations, final reports of projects, or evaluation studies.

reporters: A series of bound volumes and looseleaf services which contain the text of court decisions.

research: A systematic process of collecting and logically analyzing data for some purpose.

research design: The plan that describes the conditions and procedures for collecting information.

research methods: Procedures used to collect and analyze data.

research problem: A formal statement of purpose, question, or hypothesis that implies empirical investigation.

research role (in ethnography): The relationships acquired by and ascribed to the ethnographer in interactive data collection, appropriate for the purpose of the study; typical role is observer-participant.

research synthesis: A research procedure which systematically evaluates and statistically summarizes comparable studies.

research writing style: A style that reflects precise thinking.

responsive evaluation: An evaluation designed to supply information about the issues and concerns of the audiences; uses an emerging design to provide an understanding of the program.

restriction in range: A set of scores that represents only a part of the total distribution.

reversal designs: *Also* withdrawal designs. In single-subject research, refers to ending a treatment condition and reinstituting the baseline condition.

sample: The group of subjects from which data are collected; often represents a population.

scaled items: Questionnaire items that consist of gradations, levels, or values describing various degrees of something.

scatter plot: A graphic representation of relationship made by forming a visual array of the intersections of subjects' scores on two variables.

science: The generation and verification of theory through research.

scientific inquiry: The search for knowledge by using recognized procedures in data collection, analysis, and interpretation.

scientific law: A statement that has a theoretical base and considerable empirical support for generalizability.

scientific method: A sequential research process of defining a problem, stating a hypothesis, collecting and analyzing data, and interpreting results.

secondary sources: In analytical research, documents or testimonies of individuals who did not actually observe or participate in the event, so are dependent on hearsay evidence.

secondary sources (in literature review): A synthesis of previous literature, theoretical or empirical or both.

selection: A threat to internal validity in which differences between groups of subjects affect results.

semantic differential: A type of scale in which subjects make a response between adjective pairs in relation to a concept or object.

semistructured questions: A type of interview question that allows individual, open-ended responses to questions that are fairly specific.

shotgun approach: A relationship study that investigates many correlations to find some that are significant.

significance level: *Also* alpha level. *See* level of significance.

significance of the problem: The rationale for a problem or importance of a study as it relates to developing educational theory, knowledge, and/or practice.

simple random sampling: *See* random sampling.

single-subject design: Research done with individual subjects in order to study the changes in behavior associated with the intervention or removal of a treatment.

site selection: The specification of site criteria implied in the foreshadowed problems and for obtaining a suitable and feasible research site.

skewed: *See* positively skewed *or* negatively skewed.

social construction: The view that reality consists of the meanings which individuals or groups derived from or ascribed to specific entities such as events, persons, or objects.

social desirability: The tendency of subjects to respond to items in a manner that will appear desirable to others.

split-half: A type of internal-consistency reliability in which equal halves of a test are correlated.

spurious correlation: A correlation that over- or underrepresents the true relationship.

stability: A type of test reliability in which scores from the same instrument taken on two occasions are correlated.

standard: A principle commonly agreed to by experts.

standard deviation: A measure of variability; a numerical index that indicates average dispersion or spread of scores around the mean.

standard scores: Converted numbers from raw distributions with constant means and standard deviations.

standardized interviews: Systematic interviews that employ the same questions and response categories.

standardized open-ended interview: A form of ethnographic interview in which participants are asked the same questions in the same order to obtain data of participant meanings.

standardized tests: Tests that are administered and scored according to highly structured, prescribed directions.

statistical conclusion: A threat to the internal validity of a study because of inappropriate uses of statistical procedures.

statistical hypothesis: *See* null hypothesis.

statistical regression: The tendency for extreme scores to become closer to the mean score on a second testing.

statistically significant: A term used in evaluating results of inferential statistics that indicates that the differences noted are very probably not due to chance.

statistics: Procedures for organizing and analyzing quantitative data.

stratified random sampling: A form of random sampling in which a population is first divided into subgroups or strata and subjects are selected from each subgroup.

structured observations: Systematic observations of behavior according to specific categories.

structured questions: *Also* limited response questions. A type of interview question that is followed by a predetermined set of responses.

style: The rules of spelling, capitalization, punctuation, and typing followed in preparing a proposal, manuscript, or article.

subjects: The person or persons from whom data are collected in a study.

summary observations (in ethnography): A synthesis of the main interactions and scenes observed written immediately after leaving the site; also suggest questions and tentative interpretations.

summative evaluation: Evaluation designed to determine the merit, the worth, or both of a developed practice and to make recommendations regarding its adoption and widespread use.

survey research: The assessment of the current status of opinions, beliefs, and attitudes by questionnaires or interviews from a known population.

systematic sampling: A form of sampling in which subjects are selected from a continuous list by choosing every *n*th subject.

T-scores: A type of standard score with a mean of fifty and a standard deviation of ten.

***t*-test:** An inferential statistical procedure for determining the probability level of rejecting the null hypothesis that two means are the same.

target group: The group whose behavior is expected to change as a result of a practice.

test reliability: An indication of the consistency of measurement.

test research: Research in which test scores of subjects are used as data.

test-retest: *See* stability.

test validity: The extent to which inferences made on the basis of test scores are appropriate.

testing: A threat to internal validity in which taking a test can affect the results.

tests: Instruments that have a structured set of questions that measure cognitive knowledge and skills.

theoretical and conceptual framework: The major concepts and assumptions among scholars in certain disciplines that guide ethnographic observations and data analysis.

theory: The prediction and explanation of natural phenomena.

thesaurus: A publication that lists and cross-references key terms or descriptors used in an index for a reference service (database) such as ERIC or *Psychological Abstracts*.

time sampling: A type of observer recording procedure in which specific time periods are used in order to observe behavior.

time series designs: Research designs in which one group of subjects is measured repeatedly before and after a treatment.

translatability: In qualitative research, the degree to which the researcher uses theoretical frameworks and research strategies that are understood by other researchers and thus the meaning of the findings can be extended.

treatment group: *See* experimental group.

triangulation: Qualitative cross-validation among multiple data sources, data collection strategies, time periods, and theoretical schemes.

true experimental design: Research in which subjects are randomly assigned to groups, at least one independent variable is manipulated, and extraneous variables are controlled to investigate the cause of one or more independent variables on the dependent variable or variables.

Type I error: Rejecting a null hypothesis when it is in fact true.

Type II error: Failing to reject a null hypothesis when it is in fact false.

unit of analysis: The smallest independent unit of data: a group or individual.

unobtrusive measurement: *Also* nonreactive. Use of methods to collect information so that the subject is unaware of being a participant in the research.

unstructured questions: A type of interview question that is broad and allows open-ended responses.

variability: *See* measures of variability.

variable: An event, category, behavior, or an attribute that expresses a construct and has different values, depending on how it is used in a study.

variance: The degree of dispersion or spread of scores.

verification: Research results that can be or are confirmed or modified in subsequent research.

withdrawal design: *See* reversal design.

worth: The value of a practice in relationship to the values, standards, and practical constraints of a potential adopting site.

z-score: A type of standard score with a mean of zero and a standard deviation of one.

CALCULATIONS FOR SELECTED DESCRIPTIVE AND INFERENTIAL STATISTICS

In this appendix we will present a step-by-step guide for performing calculations for several simple statistical procedures.[1] Our intent is not to derive formulas, but to show how the statistics are calculated. We believe that being able to apply these formulas assists greatly in understanding the meaning of the statistics.

■ MEASURES OF CENTRAL TENDENCY ■

Measures of central tendency are descriptive statistics that measure the central location or value of sets of scores. They are used widely to summarize and simplify large quantities of data.

The Mean

The mean is the arithmetical average of a set of scores. It is obtained by adding all the scores in a distribution and dividing the sum by the number of scores. The formula for calculating the mean is

$$\overline{X} = \frac{\Sigma X}{n},$$

where

$\overline{X}$ is the mean score,
ΣX is the sum of the Xs—i.e., $X_1 + X_2 + X_3 \ldots X_n$,
n is the total number of scores.

[1]Statistical tables are located at the end of the appendix.

Example: Calculation of Mean. If we have obtained the sample of eight scores—17, 14, 14, 13, 10, 8, 7, 7—the mean of this set of scores is calculated as:

$$\Sigma X = 17 + 14 + 14 + \ldots + 7 = 90,$$
$$n = 8.$$

Therefore,

$$\overline{X} = \frac{90}{8} = 11.25.$$

The Median

The median is the score in a distribution below which half the scores fall. In other words, half the scores are above the median and half are below the median. The median is at the 50th percentile.

To calculate the median, the scores are rank-ordered from highest to lowest; then one simply counts, from one end, one half the scores. In distributions with an odd number of scores the median is the middle score, as illustrated below:

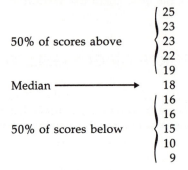

If the distribution has an even number of scores, the median is the average of the two middle scores. In this case the median is a new score or point in the distribution, as shown below:

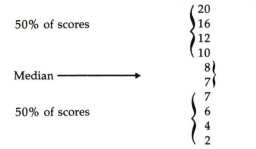

Thus, the median in this example is:

$$\frac{7 + 8}{2} = \frac{15}{2} = 7.5.$$

The median is relatively easy to find in studies with a small number of subjects. As the number of scores increases, the calculation is done either by a formula or by placing the scores into intervals of scores and using the interval to make the calculations. The computer is able to apply these more complicated calculations easily, quickly, and reliably.

The Mode

The mode is simply the most frequently occurring score in a distribution, and it is found by counting the number of times each score was received. The mode in the distribution below, for example, is 22.

$$23$$
$$22$$
$$22$$
$$22$$
$$20$$
$$18$$
$$18$$
$$17$$
$$16$$

■ MEASURES OF VARIABILITY ■

Measures of variability are used to show the differences among the scores in a distribution. We use the terms *variability* or *dispersion* because the statistics provide an indication of how different, or dispersed, the scores are from one another. We will discuss three measures of variability: range, variance, and standard deviation.

The Range

The range is the simplest, but also least useful, measure of variability. The range is defined as the distance between the smallest and the largest scores, and is calculated by simply subtracting the bottom, or lowest, score from the top, or highest, score:

$$\text{Range} = X_H - X_L,$$

where

X_H is the highest score, and
X_L is the lowest score

For the following scores, then, the range is $26 - 6 = 20$.

$$6 \quad 8 \quad 10 \quad 11 \quad 15 \quad 20 \quad 26$$

The range is a crude measure of variability and is unstable. Because the range can be biased, it is rarely used as the only measure of variability.

Variance

The variance (s^2 or σ^2) is a measure of dispersion that indicates the degree to which scores cluster around the mean. The variance provides the researcher with one number to indicate, in a sense, the average dispersion of scores from the mean. Computationally, the variance is the sum of the squared deviation scores about the mean divided by the total number of scores.

$$s^2 = \frac{\Sigma\,(X - \overline{X})^2}{N},$$

where

s^2 is the variance,
$\Sigma\,(X - \overline{X})^2$ is the sum of the squared deviation scores,
$(X - \overline{X})$ is the deviation score, and
N is the total number of scores.

For any distribution of scores the variance can be determined by following five steps:

1. Calculate the mean: $(\Sigma\,X/N)$.
2. Calculate the deviation scores: $(X - \overline{X})$.
3. Square each deviation score: $(X - \overline{X})^2$.
4. sum all the deviation scores: $\Sigma\,(X - \overline{X})^2$.
5. Divide the sum by N: $\Sigma\,(X - \overline{X})^2/N$.

These steps are illustrated with actual numbers as follows:

(1) Raw scores	(2) $(X - \overline{X})$	(3) $(X - \overline{X})^2$	(4)	(5)
20	7	49		
15	2	4		
15	2	4		
14	1	1		
14	1	1	$\Sigma\,(X - \overline{X})^2 = 120$	$\dfrac{\Sigma\,(X - \overline{X})^2}{N} = 12$
14	1	1		
12	−1	1		
10	−3	9		
8	−5	25		
8	−5	25		

$\Sigma\,X = 130$
$N = 10$
$\overline{X} = 13$

Substituting directly in the formula:

$$s^2 = \frac{120}{10} = 12.$$

Another formula that can be used to calculate the variance, which is computationally more simple, is

$$s^2 = \frac{\Sigma\, X^2 - N\, \overline{X}^2}{N}$$

Because the variance is expressed as the square of the raw scores, not the original units, it is not usually reported in research. To return to units that are consistent with the raw score distribution, we need to take the square root of the variance. Taking the square root of the variance yields the standard deviation.

Standard Deviation

The standard deviation (s, σ, or SD) is the square root of the variance. It is a measure of dispersion that uses deviation scores expressed in standard units about the mean; hence the name standard deviation. The standard deviation is equal to the square root of the sum of the squared deviation scores about the mean divided by the total number of scores. The formula is

$$s = \sqrt{\frac{\Sigma\, (X - \overline{X})^2}{N}},$$

where

s is the standard deviation,
$\sqrt{}$ is the square root,
$\Sigma\, (X - \overline{X})^2$ is the sum of the squared deviation scores,
$X - \overline{X})$ is the deviation score, and
N is the total number of scores.

To calculate the standard deviation, simply add one step to the formula for variance; take the square root. In our example for variance, for instance, the standard deviation would be

$$s = \sqrt{\frac{\Sigma\, (X - \overline{X})^2}{N}} \;=\; \sqrt{\frac{120}{10}} \;=\; \sqrt{12} \;=\; 3.46.$$

The standard deviation is commonly reported in research and, with the mean, is the most important statistic in research. It tells the number of scores (that is, the percentage of scores) that are within given units of the standard deviation around the mean. This property of standard deviation is explained in the section called "Normal Distribution," which follows.

■ STANDARD SCORES ■

Standard scores are numbers that are transformed from raw scores to provide consistent information about the location of a score within a total distribution. They are numbers that are related to the normal distribution.

FIGURE B.1
Graph of the Standard
Normal Distribution or Normal Curve

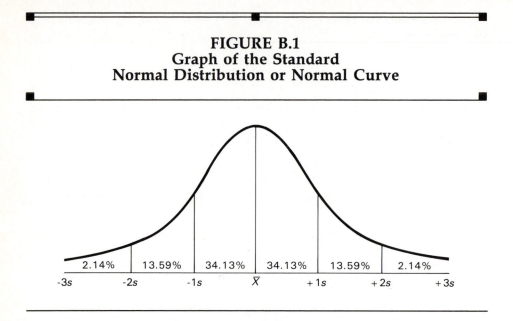

| 2.14% | 13.59% | 34.13% | 34.13% | 13.59% | 2.14% |

-3s   -2s   -1s $\overline{X}$ + 1s   + 2s   + 3s

Normal Distribution

The normal distribution is a set of scores that, when plotted in a frequency distribution, result in a symmetrical, bell-shaped curve with precise mathematical properties. The mathematical properties provide the basis for making standardized interpretations. These properties include: possessing one mode, a mean, and median that are the same; having a mean that divides the curve into two identical halves; and having measures of standard deviation that fall at predictable places on the normal curve, with the same percentage of scores between the mean and points equidistant from the mean. This third characteristic is very important. We know, for example, that at +1 s, we will always be at about the 84th percentile in the distribution (percentile score is the percentage of scores at or below the designated score). This is because the median is at the 50th percentile, and +1 s contains an additional 34 percent of the scores (50 + 34 = 84). Similarly, the percentage of scores between +1 s and +2 s is about 14 percent, which means that + 2 s is at the 98th percentile. These characteristics are illustrated in Figure B.1, the graph of the standard normal distribution.

The pleasing aspect of this property is that, for any raw score distribution with unique units, such as 1 or 2 as s, the interpretation is always the same. If one distribution has a mean of 10, therefore, and a standard deviation of 3, and a second distribution a mean of 50 and a standard deviation of 7, a score of 4 in the first case is at about the same percentile (the second) as a score of 36 on the second distribution.

z-Scores

The most basic standard score is called a z-score, and it is expressed as a deviation from the mean in standard deviation units. A z-score of 1 is thus at one standard deviation, − 1 is at minus one standard deviation, + 2 at two standard deviations, and so forth.

After the mean and standard deviation are calculated for a set of scores, it is easy to convert each raw score to a z-score, which then indicates exactly where each score lies in the normal distribution.

The formula for calculating a z-score is

$$z = \frac{X - \overline{X}}{s},$$

where

z is the z-score value,
X is any particular score,
$\overline{X}$ is the arithmetic mean of a distribution of scores, and
s is the standard deviation of that same distribution.

Taking the scores used in order to illustrate variance and standard deviation, the z-scores would be found as follows:

For the raw score of 20: $z = \dfrac{20 - 13}{3.46} = 2.02.$

For the raw score of 14: $z = \dfrac{14 - 13}{3.46} = 0.29.$

For the raw score of 10: $z = \dfrac{10 - 13}{3.46} = -0.87.$

Once the z-score has been calculated, it is easy to refer to conversion tables to find the percentile rank corresponding to each z-score.

T-Scores

One limitation of using z-scores is the necessity for being careful with the negative sign and with the decimal point. To avoid these problems, other standard scores are used by converting the z-scores algebraically to other units. The general formula for converting z-scores is

$$A = \overline{X}_A + s_A(z),$$

where

A is the new standard score equivalent to z,
X_A is the mean for the new standard-score scale,
s_A is the standard deviation for the new standard-score scale, and
z is the z-score for any observation.

For T-scores, which are very common, $\overline{X}_A = 50$ and $s_A = 10$. The equation for converting z-scores to T-scores is thus

$$T = 50 + 10 \ (z).$$

For example, the *T*-scores for our earlier illustration would be as follows:

For the raw score of 20: $T = 50 + 10 \ (2.02) = 70.2$.
For the raw score of 14: $T = 50 + 10 \ (0.29) = 52.9$.
For the raw score of 10: $T = 50 + 10 \ (- 0.87) = 41.3$.

Other Standard Scores

Other common standard scores include the following:

1. Normal Curve Equivalent (NCE) has a mean of 50 and *s* of 21.06. Thus NCE = 50 + 21.06 (*z*-score).
2. IQ score has a mean of 100 and *s* of 15 or 16. Thus IQ = 100 + 15 (*z*-score).
3. College Entrance Examination Boards (CEEB, such as SAT) uses a mean of 500 and an *s* of 100. Thus CEEB = 500 + 100 (*z*-score).
4. ACT (American College Testing Program) uses a mean of 20 and an *s* of 5. Thus, ACT = 20 + 5 (*z*-score).
5. Stanine. The stanine is also commonly reported. Stanines are standardized on a mean of 5 and *s* of 2, but unlike other standard scores, the numbers refer to intervals rather than to specific points on the normal distribution. Stanine 5 is located in the center of the distribution and includes the middle 20 percent of scores; stanines 4 and 6 include 17 percent of the scores; 3 and 7, 12 percent; 2 and 8, 7 percent; and 1 and 9, 4 percent. Stanines are illustrated in Figure 6.7, the normal curve.

The important thing to remember is that all standard scores are based on the normal distribution. Consequently, if a set of raw scores is distributed abnormally, conversion to standard scores may bias the results or be misleading.

■ MEASURES OF RELATIONSHIP ■

Measures of relationship are used to indicate the degree to which two sets of scores are related, or covary. We intuitively seek relationships by such statements as: "If high scores on variable X tend to be associated with high scores on variable Y, then the variables are related," or "If high scores on variable X tend to be associated with low scores on variable Y, then the variables are related." As we have indicated in Chapter 6, the relationship can be either positive or negative and either strong or weak.

We use correlation coefficients as a statistical summary of the nature of the relationship between two variables. They provide us with an estimate of the quantitative degree of relationship. The numbers are almost always between $- 1.00$ and $+ 1.00$. We will show how to calculate two common correlation coefficients, the Pearson product-moment and the Spearman rho correlations.

Pearson Product-Moment (Pearson *r*)

The Pearson product-moment correlation coefficient is the most widely used measure of relationship. The Pearson *r* is calculated to show the linear relationship between two variables. To compute the Pearson *r*, two measures on each subject are needed. Suppose, for example, we have a group of ten subjects, and for each subject we have measures of self-concept and achievement. We can then calculate the Pearson *r* between self-concept and achievement for these ten subjects, using the following formula:

$$\text{Pearson } r = \frac{N \, \Sigma \, X \, Y - (\Sigma \, X)(\Sigma \, Y)}{\sqrt{N \, \Sigma \, X^2 - (\Sigma \, X)^2} \, \bullet \, \sqrt{N \, \Sigma \, Y^2 - (\Sigma \, Y)^2}}$$

where

$\Sigma \, X \, Y$ is the sum of the $X \, Y$ cross products,
$\Sigma \, X$ is the sum of the X scores,
$\Sigma \, Y$ is the sum of the Y scores,
$\Sigma \, X^2$ is the sum of the squared X scores,
$\Sigma \, Y^2$ is the sum of the squared Y scores, and
N is the number of pairs of scores.

This formula may appear complex but is actually quite easy to calculate. The scores can be listed in a table, as shown below; to use it, one simply finds the values for each summation in the formula, substitutes where appropriate, and performs the math indicated.

Subject	Self-concept Score X	X^2	Achievement Score Y	Y^2	$X \bullet Y$
1	25	625	85	7225	2125
2	20	400	90	8100	1800
3	21	441	80	6400	1680
4	18	324	70	4900	1260
5	15	225	75	5625	1125
6	17	289	80	6400	1360
7	14	196	75	5625	1050
8	15	225	70	4900	1050
9	12	144	75	5625	900
10	13	169	60	3600	780

$\Sigma \, X = 170 \qquad \Sigma \, X^2 = 3038 \qquad \Sigma \, Y = 760 \qquad \Sigma \, Y^2 = 58400 \qquad \Sigma \, X \bullet Y = 13130$
$(\Sigma \, X)^2 = 28900 \qquad\qquad\qquad (\Sigma \, Y)^2 = 577600$

Step 1: Pair each set of scores; one set becomes X, the other Y.
Step 2: Calculate $\Sigma \, X$ and $\Sigma \, Y$.
Step 3: Calculate X^2 and Y^2.
Step 4: Calculate $\Sigma \, X^2$ and $\Sigma \, Y^2$.
Step 5: Calculate $(\Sigma \, X)^2$ and $(\Sigma \, Y)^2$.
Step 6: Calculate $X \bullet Y$.
Step 7: Calculate $\Sigma \, X \bullet Y$.
Step 8: Substitute calculated values into formula.

$$\text{Pearson } r = \frac{10\,(13130) - (170)\,(760)}{\sqrt{10\,(3038) - 28900} \cdot \sqrt{10\,(58400) - 577600}}$$

$$= \frac{131300 - 129200}{\sqrt{30380 - 28900} \cdot \sqrt{584000 - 577600}}$$

$$= \frac{2100}{\sqrt{1480} \cdot \sqrt{6400}}$$

$$= \frac{2100}{(38.47) \cdot (80)}$$

$$= \frac{2100}{3078}$$

$$= 0.68.$$

The value of 0.68 shows a moderate positive relationship between self-concept and achievement for this set of scores. The level of significance of correlation coefficients is indicated in Table B.2 at the end of this appendix.

Spearman Rank
(*r* ranks or Spearman rho)

The Spearman rho is used when ranks are available on each of two variables for all subjects. Ranks are simply listings of scores from highest to lowest. The Spearman rho correlation shows the degree to which subjects maintain the same relative position on two measures. In other words, the Spearman rho indicates how much agreement there is between the ranks of each variable.

The calculation of the Spearman ranks is more simple than calculating the Pearson *r*. The necessary steps are

Step 1: Rank the *X*s and *Y*s.
Step 2: Pair the ranked *X*s and *Y*s.
Step 3: Calculate the difference in ranks for each pair.
Step 4: Square each difference.
Step 5: Sum the squared differences.
Step 6: Substitute calculated values into formula.

The formula is

$$\text{Spearman rho} = 1 - \frac{6 \, \Sigma \, D^2}{n(n^2 - 1)}.$$

For the data used in calculating the Pearson *r*, the Spearman rho would be found as follows:

Subjects	Self-concept Rank X	Achievement Rank Y	Difference D	D²
1	1	2	−1	1
2	3	1	2	4
3	2	3.5	−1.5	2.25
4	4	5.5	−1.5	2.25
5	6.5	8	−1.5	2.25
6	5	3.5	1.5	2.25
7	8	8	0	0
8	6.5	5.5	1	1
9	10	8	2	4
10	9	10	−1	1
				$\Sigma D^2 = 20$

Note: When ties in the ranking occur, all scores that are tied receive the average of the ranks involved.

$$r \text{ ranks } = 1 - \frac{6\,(20)}{10\,(100 - 1)},$$

$$= 1 - \frac{120}{990},$$

$$= 1 - 0.12,$$

$$= 0.88.$$

In most data sets with more than fifty subjects, the Pearson *r* and Spearman rank will give almost identical correlations. In the example used here the Spearman is higher because of the low *n* and the manner in which the ties in rankings resulted in low difference scores.

■ CHI-SQUARE ■

Chi-square (χ^2) is a statistical procedure that is used as an inferential statistic with nominal data, such as frequency counts, and ordinal data, such as percentages and proportions. In the simplest case, the data are organized into two categories, such as yes and no, high and low, for and against. If, for example, a researcher is interested in the opinions of college professors about tenure and asks the question, "Should tenure be abolished?" then all responses could be categorized as either *yes* or *no*. The total frequency in each category (observed frequencies) is then compared to the expected frequency, which in most cases is chance. This means that with two categories, half the responses should be *yes* and half *no*. Assume the following results:

Should tenure be abolished?

	Yes	*No*
Observed	40	60
Expected	50	50

These values are then used in the following formula to calculate the chi-square statistic:

$$\chi^2 = \Sigma \frac{(f_o - f_e)^2}{f_e},$$

where

χ^2 is the chi-square statistic,
Σ is the sum of,
f_o is the observed frequency, and
f_e is the expected frequency.

Inserting the values from the table, the result is:

$$\chi^2 = \frac{(40 - 50)^2}{50} + \frac{(60 - 50)^2}{50},$$

$$= \frac{100}{50} + \frac{100}{50},$$

$$= 2 + 2,$$

$$= 4.0.$$

The obtained value, in this case 4, is then used with the degrees of freedom in the problem ($df = k - 1$, where k equals the number of categories; in our example $df = 2 - 1$, or 1) to find the value of the chi-square in the critical values of chi-square table (Table B.3 at the end of this appendix) to determine the level of significance of the results. By referring to the table and locating 4.00 within the table with 1 df, the result is significant at just less than a p value of 0.05. Consequently, it would be appropriate to say that there is a significant difference in the number of professors responding *yes* as compared to the number responding *no*.

Suppose the researcher wanted to go a step further with this problem and learn whether administrators and professors differ in their responses to the question about abolishing tenure. The researcher would then have what is called a contingency table, which is a cross-tabulation of the frequencies for the combinations of categories of the two variables.

A hypothetical contingency table is shown below for administrators and professors. Should tenure be abolished?

	Professors	Administrators	Raw Totals
Yes	40 ($p = 0.40$)	40 ($p = 0.80$)	80 ($p_e = 0.53$)
No	60 ($p = 0.60$)	10 ($p = 0.20$)	70 ($p_e = 0.47$)
	$n = 100$	$n = 50$	$n = 150$

Notice in the table that the proportion of responses in each response category (*yes* and *no*) is shown for both professors and administrators, and the total proportions are shown in the last column. These proportions are used in the following equation:

$$\chi^2 = \Sigma n \, \frac{(P - P_e)^2}{P_e},$$

where

χ^2 is the chi-square statistic,
Σ is the sum of all cells in the problem (in our example there are four cells),
n is the number of total observations in each column,
P is the proportion of observed frequencies in each cell, and
P_e is the expected proportion for each row.

For our example, therefore, the result would be:

$$\chi^2 = 100 \, \frac{(0.4 - 0.53)^2}{0.53} + 100 \, \frac{(0.60 - 0.47)^2}{0.47}$$

$$+ \, 50 \, \frac{(0.80 - 0.53)^2}{0.53} \quad + \, 50 \, \frac{(0.20 - 0.47)}{0.47}$$

$$= \, 100 \, \frac{0.02}{0.53} + 100 \, \frac{0.02}{0.47} + 50 \, \frac{0.07}{0.53} + 50 \, \frac{0.07}{0.47}$$

$$= \, 3.77 + 4.26 + 6.60 + 7.45$$

$$= \, 22.08$$

In contingency tables the degrees of freedom are equal to $(r - 1)(c - 1)$ where r is the number of rows and c is the number of columns. In our example the $df = (2 - 1)(2 - 1) = 1$. By locating 22.08 with 1 degree of freedom in the critical values of chi-square table (Table B.3) we note that the result is highly significant, $p < 0.001$. This result indicates that there is a significant association or relationship between the two variables (professors and administrators, and yes and no).

■ *t*-TEST ■

The *t*-test is used to indicate the probability that the means of two groups are different. We will present two common forms of the *t*-test, one used with independent samples, the other with dependent samples.

Independent Samples *t*-test

The independent samples *t*-test, or *t*-test for independent groups, is used to determine whether the mean values of a variable on one group of subjects is different from a mean value on the same variable with a different group of subjects. It is important to meet three statistical assumptions: that the frequency distributions of scores for both the populations of each group are normal; that the variances in each population are equal; and that the observation of scores in one group is independent from the other group. If the sample size is greater than 30, violating the assumption of normality is not serious; and as long as the sample sizes are equal, violation of the assumption of homogeneity is not a problem. It is crucial, however, that the observations for each group are independent.

The formula for calculating the *t*-test statistic is:

$$t = \frac{\overline{X}_1 - \overline{X}_2}{s_{\overline{x}_1 - \overline{x}_2}},$$

where

t is the *t*-test statistic,
$\overline{X}_1$ is the mean of one group,
$\overline{X}_2$ is the mean of the second group, and
$s_{\overline{x}_1 - \overline{x}_2}$ is the standard error of the difference in means.

The standard error of the difference in means ($s_{\overline{x}_1 - \overline{x}_2}$) is estimated from the variances of each distribution. This part of the formula is calculated by pooling the variances of each distribution to result in s. This is done by the following formula:

$$s = \sqrt{\frac{\Sigma \, x_1^2 + \Sigma \, x_2^2}{df_1 + df_2}} \, x.$$

Then,

$$s_{\overline{x}_1 - \overline{x}_2} = s \sqrt{\frac{1}{n_1} + \frac{1}{n_2}} \, .$$

As an example, consider the data we have presented below:

Group x_1	Group x_2
$\overline{X}_1 = 18$	$\overline{X}_2 = 25$
$n_1 = 20$	$n_2 = 20$
$\Sigma x_1^2 = 348$	$\Sigma x_2^2 = 425$

From this point we can calculate the *t*-test statistic in the following steps:

1. Calculate *s:*

$$s = \sqrt{\frac{348 + 425}{19 + 19}}$$

$$= \sqrt{20.34}$$

$$= 4.51.$$

2. Calculate $s_{\overline{x}_1 - \overline{x}_2}$:

$$= 4.51 \sqrt{\frac{1}{20} + \frac{1}{20}}$$

$$= 4.51 \sqrt{\frac{1}{10}}$$

$$= (4.51)(0.32)$$

$$= 1.44.$$

3. Substitute into *t*-test formula:

$$t = \frac{18 - 25}{1.44}$$

$$= \frac{7}{1.44}$$

$$= 4.86.$$

Once the *t*-test statistic is calculated, it is found in the critical values for *t*-table (Table 10.1) with corresponding degrees of freedom (which for the independent samples *t*-test is $n_1 + n_2 - 2$, or in our example $20 + 20 - 2 = 38$) to determine the significance level of the results. In this example the *t*-test statistic of 4.86, with 38 *df*, is significant at $p < 0.001$.

Here is another example of a computation with the *t*-test, beginning with raw data:

	Group 1			Group 2	
x_1	x_1^2		x_2	x_2^2	
8	64		7	49	
8	64		7	49	
7	49		8	64	
6	36		6	36	
5	25		6	36	
5	25		4	16	
6	36		4	16	
6	36		3	9	
9	81		5	25	
8	64		5	25	

$$\Sigma x_1 = 68 \quad \Sigma x_1^2 = 480 \qquad \Sigma x_2 = 55 \quad \Sigma x_2^2 = 325$$
$$n = 10 \qquad n = 10$$
$$\overline{X}_1 = 6.8 \qquad \overline{X}_2 = 5.5$$

Step 1: $s = \sqrt{\dfrac{480 + 325}{9 + 9}} = \sqrt{44.72} = 6.69.$

Step 2: $s_{\overline{x}_1 - \overline{x}_2} = 6.69 \sqrt{\dfrac{1}{10} + \dfrac{1}{10}} = 6.69 \sqrt{\tfrac{1}{5}} = (6.69)(0.45) = 2.99.$

Step 3: $t = \dfrac{6.8 - 5.5}{2.99} = \dfrac{1.3}{2.99} = 0.43.$

In this case the *t*-test statistic of 0.43, with 18 *df*, is not statistically significant. Even though the means for the groups are different, therefore, there is a good possibility that they could be different by chance alone.

Dependent Samples *t*-test

When two groups that have been matched are being compared, as in a pretest-posttest design, the *t*-test formula must take into account the interrelationship between the groups: that is, the groups are not independent; rather, they are related. The formula for this type of *t*-test is easier to calculate than for the independent samples *t*-test:

$$t = \dfrac{\overline{D}}{\sqrt{\dfrac{\Sigma D^2 - \dfrac{(\Sigma D)^2}{N}}{N(N-1)}}}$$

where $\quad\quad\quad\quad\quad\bar{D}$ is the mean difference for all pairs of scores,
$\quad\quad\quad\quad\Sigma\,D^2$ is the sum of the squares of the differences,
$\quad\quad\quad\quad(\Sigma\,D)^2$ is the square of the sum of the differences,
$\quad\quad\quad\quad\quad N$ is the number of pairs of scores, and
$\quad\quad\quad\quad N-1$ is the degrees of freedom (one less than the number of pairs
$\quad\quad\quad\quad\quad\quad$ of scores).

Consider the following example and steps:

Subjects	Posttest scores x_1	Pretest scores x_2	D	D^2
1	22	15	7	49
2	21	16	5	25
3	20	17	7	49
4	23	16	7	49
5	19	14	5	25
6	21	15	6	36
7	18	12	6	36
8	22	18	4	16
			$\Sigma D = 47$	$\Sigma D^2 = 285$

Step 1: $\bar{D} = \dfrac{\Sigma\,D}{N} = \dfrac{47}{8} = 5.9.$ $\quad\quad\quad$ Step 2: $(\Sigma\,D)^2 = 47^2 = 2209.$

Step 3: Substitute into formula $\quad t = \dfrac{5.9}{\sqrt{\dfrac{285 - \dfrac{2209}{8}}{8\,(8-1)}}}$

$$= \dfrac{5.9}{\sqrt{\dfrac{285 - 276}{56}}}$$

$$= \dfrac{5.9}{\sqrt{\dfrac{9}{56}}}$$

$$= \dfrac{5.9}{0.40}$$

$$= 14.75$$

The calculated t-test statistic (14.75) is located in the critical values of t table, with the degrees of freedom ($N-1$, or in this example $8-1=7$). The result from the table is that the group means are clearly different from each other, statistically significant at $p < 0.001$.

TABLE B.1
Random Numbers

03 47 43 73 86	36 96 47 36 61	46 98 63 71 62	33 26 16 80 45	60 11 14 10 95
97 74 24 67 62	42 81 14 57 20	42 53 32 37 32	27 07 36 07 51	24 51 79 89 73
16 76 62 27 66	56 50 26 71 07	32 90 79 78 53	13 55 38 58 59	88 97 54 14 10
12 56 85 99 26	96 96 68 27 31	05 03 72 93 15	57 12 10 14 21	88 26 49 81 76
55 59 56 35 64	38 54 82 46 22	31 62 43 09 90	06 18 44 32 53	23 83 01 30 30
16 22 77 94 39	49 54 43 54 82	17 37 93 23 78	87 35 20 96 43	84 26 34 91 64
84 42 17 53 31	57 24 55 06 88	77 04 74 47 67	21 76 33 50 25	83 92 12 06 76
63 01 63 78 59	16 95 55 67 19	98 10 50 71 75	12 86 73 58 07	44 39 52 38 79
33 21 12 34 29	78 64 56 07 82	52 42 07 44 38	15 51 00 13 42	99 66 02 79 54
57 60 86 32 44	09 47 27 96 54	49 17 46 09 62	90 52 84 77 27	08 02 73 43 28
18 18 07 92 46	44 17 16 58 09	79 83 86 19 62	06 76 50 03 10	55 23 64 05 05
26 62 38 97 75	84 16 07 44 99	83 11 46 32 24	20 14 85 88 45	10 93 72 88 71
23 42 40 64 74	82 97 77 77 81	07 45 32 14 08	32 98 94 07 72	93 85 79 10 75
52 36 28 19 95	50 92 26 11 97	00 56 76 31 38	80 22 02 53 53	86 60 42 04 53
37 85 94 35 12	83 39 50 08 30	42 34 07 96 88	54 42 06 87 98	35 85 29 48 39
70 29 17 12 13	40 33 20 38 26	13 89 51 03 74	17 76 37 13 04	07 74 21 19 30
56 62 18 37 35	96 83 50 87 75	97 12 25 93 47	70 33 24 03 54	97 77 46 44 80
99 49 57 22 77	88 42 95 45 72	16 64 36 16 00	04 43 18 66 79	94 77 24 21 90
16 08 15 04 72	33 27 14 34 09	45 59 34 68 49	12 72 07 34 45	99 27 72 95 14
31 16 93 32 43	50 27 89 87 19	20 15 37 00 49	52 85 66 60 44	38 68 88 11 80
68 34 30 13 70	55 74 30 77 40	44 22 78 84 26	04 33 46 09 52	68 07 97 06 57
74 57 25 65 76	59 29 97 68 60	71 91 38 67 54	13 58 18 24 76	15 54 55 95 52
27 42 37 86 53	48 55 90 65 72	96 57 69 36 10	96 46 92 42 45	97 60 49 04 91
00 39 68 29 61	66 37 32 20 30	77 84 57 03 29	10 45 65 04 26	11 04 96 67 24
29 94 98 94 24	68 49 69 10 82	53 75 91 93 30	34 25 20 57 27	40 48 73 51 92
16 90 82 66 59	83 62 64 11 12	67 19 00 71 74	60 47 21 29 68	02 02 37 03 31
11 27 94 75 06	06 09 19 74 66	02 94 37 34 02	76 70 90 30 86	38 45 94 30 38
35 24 10 16 20	33 32 51 26 38	79 78 45 04 91	16 92 53 56 16	02 75 50 95 98
38 23 16 86 38	42 38 97 01 50	87 75 66 81 41	40 01 74 91 62	48 51 84 08 32
31 96 25 91 47	96 44 33 49 13	34 86 82 53 91	00 52 43 48 85	27 55 26 89 62
66 67 40 67 14	64 05 71 95 86	11 05 65 09 68	76 83 20 37 90	57 16 00 11 66
14 90 84 45 11	75 73 88 05 90	52 27 41 14 86	22 98 12 22 08	07 52 74 95 80
68 05 51 18 00	33 96 02 75 19	07 60 62 93 55	59 33 82 43 90	49 37 38 44 59
20 46 78 73 90	97 51 40 14 02	04 02 33 31 08	39 54 16 49 36	47 95 93 13 30
64 19 58 97 79	15 06 15 93 20	01 90 10 75 06	40 78 78 89 62	02 67 74 17 33
05 26 93 70 60	22 35 85 15 13	92 03 51 59 77	59 56 78 06 83	52 91 05 70 74
07 97 10 88 23	09 98 42 99 64	61 71 62 99 15	06 51 29 16 93	58 05 77 09 51
68 71 86 85 85	54 87 66 47 54	73 32 08 11 12	44 95 92 63 16	29 56 24 29 48
26 99 61 65 53	58 37 78 80 70	42 10 50 67 42	32 17 55 85 74	94 44 67 16 94
14 65 52 68 75	87 59 36 22 41	26 78 63 06 55	13 08 27 01 50	15 29 39 39 43
17 53 77 58 71	71 41 61 50 72	12 41 94 96 26	44 95 27 36 99	02 96 74 30 83
90 26 59 21 19	23 52 23 33 12	96 93 02 18 39	07 02 18 36 07	25 99 32 70 23
41 23 52 55 99	31 04 49 69 96	10 47 48 45 88	13 41 43 89 20	97 17 14 49 17
60 20 50 81 69	31 99 73 68 68	35 81 33 03 76	24 30 12 48 60	18 99 10 72 34
91 25 38 05 90	94 58 28 41 36	45 37 59 03 09	90 35 57 29 12	82 62 54 65 60
34 50 57 74 37	98 80 33 00 91	09 77 93 19 82	74 94 80 04 04	45 07 31 66 49
85 22 04 39 43	73 81 53 94 79	33 62 46 86 28	08 31 54 46 31	53 94 13 38 47
09 79 13 77 48	73 82 97 22 21	05 03 27 24 83	72 89 44 05 60	35 80 39 94 88
88 75 80 18 14	22 95 75 42 49	39 32 82 22 49	02 48 07 70 37	16 04 61 67 87
90 96 23 70 00	39 00 03 06 90	55 85 78 38 36	94 37 30 69 32	90 89 00 76 33

Source: Taken from Table XXXII of Fisher and Yates': *Statistical Tables for Biological, Agricultural and Medical Research* (6th Edition 1974) published by Longman Group UK Ltd. London (previously published by Oliver and Boyd Ltd, Edinburg) and is reprinted by permission of the authors and publishers.

TABLE B.2
Critical Values for the Pearson Correlation Coefficient

df	Level of significance for a one-tail test				
	.05	.025	.01	.005	.0005
	Level of significance for a two-tail test				
	.10	.05	.02	.01	.001
1	.9877	.9969	.9995	.9999	1.0000
2	.9000	.9500	.9800	.9900	.9990
3	.8054	.8783	.9343	.9587	.9912
4	.7293	.8114	.8822	.9172	.9741
5	.6694	.7545	.8329	.8745	.9507
6	.6215	.7067	.7887	.8343	.9249
7	.5822	.6664	.7498	.7977	.8982
8	.5494	.6319	.7155	.7646	.8721
9	.5214	.6021	.6851	.7348	.8471
10	.4973	.5760	.6581	.7079	.8233
11	.4762	.5529	.6339	.6835	.8010
12	.4575	.5324	.6120	.6614	.7800
13	.4409	.5139	.5923	.6411	.7603
14	.4259	.4973	.5742	.6226	.7420
15	.4124	.4821	.5577	.6055	.7246
16	.4000	.4683	.5425	.5897	.7084
17	.3887	.4555	.5285	.5751	.6932
18	.3783	.4438	.5155	.5614	.6787
19	.3687	.4329	.5034	.5487	.6652
20	.3598	.4227	.4921	.5368	.6524
25	.3223	.3809	.4451	.4869	.5974
30	.2960	.3494	.4093	.4487	.5541
35	.2746	.3246	.3810	.4182	.5189
40	.2573	.3044	.3578	.3932	.4896
45	.2428	.2875	.3384	.3721	.4648
50	.2306	.2732	.3218	.3541	.4433
60	.2108	.2500	.2948	.3248	.4078
70	.1954	.2319	.2737	.3017	.3799
80	.1829	.2172	.2565	.2830	.3568
90	.1726	.2050	.2422	.2673	.3375
100	.1638	.1946	.2301	.2540	.3211

Source: Taken from Table VII of Fisher and Yates': *Statistical Tables for Biological, Agricultural and Medical Research* (6th Edition 1974) published by Longman Group UK Ltd. London (previously published by Oliver and Boyd Ltd, Edinburg) and is reprinted by permission of the authors and publishers.

TABLE B.3
Critical Values of Chi-Square

df	.99	.98	.95	.90	.80	.70	.50	.30	.20	.10	.05	.02	.01	.001
1	.0002	.0006	.0039	.016	.064	.15	.46	1.07	1.64	2.71	3.84	5.41	6.64	10.83
2	.02	.04	.10	.21	.45	.71	1.39	1.41	3.22	4.60	5.99	7.82	9.21	13.82
3	.12	.18	.35	.58	1.00	1.42	2.37	3.66	4.64	6.25	7.82	9.84	11.34	16.27
4	.30	.43	.71	1.06	1.65	2.20	3.36	4.88	5.99	7.78	9.49	11.67	13.28	18.47
5	.55	.75	1.14	1.61	2.34	3.00	4.35	6.06	7.29	9.24	11.07	13.39	15.09	20.52
6	.87	1.13	1.64	2.20	3.07	3.83	5.35	7.23	8.56	10.64	12.59	15.03	16.81	22.46
7	1.24	1.56	2.17	2.83	3.82	4.67	6.35	8.38	9.80	12.02	14.07	16.62	18.48	24.32
8	1.65	2.03	2.73	3.49	4.59	5.53	7.34	9.52	11.03	13.36	15.51	18.17	20.09	26.12
9	2.09	2.53	3.32	4.17	5.38	6.39	8.34	10.66	12.24	14.68	16.92	19.68	21.67	27.88
10	2.56	3.06	3.94	4.86	6.18	7.27	9.34	11.78	13.44	15.99	18.31	21.16	23.21	29.59
11	3.05	3.61	4.58	5.58	6.99	8.15	10.34	12.90	14.63	17.28	19.68	22.62	24.72	31.26
12	3.57	4.18	5.23	6.30	7.81	9.03	11.34	14.01	15.81	18.55	21.03	24.05	26.22	32.91
13	4.11	4.76	5.89	7.04	8.63	9.93	12.34	15.12	16.98	19.81	22.36	25.47	27.69	34.53
14	4.66	5.37	6.57	7.79	9.47	10.82	13.34	16.22	18.15	21.06	23.68	26.87	29.14	36.12
15	5.23	5.98	7.26	8.55	10.31	11.72	14.34	17.32	19.31	22.31	25.00	28.26	30.58	37.70
16	5.81	6.61	7.96	9.31	11.15	12.62	15.34	18.42	20.46	23.54	26.30	29.63	32.00	39.25
17	6.41	7.26	8.67	10.08	12.00	13.53	16.34	19.51	22.62	24.77	27.59	31.00	33.41	40.79
18	7.02	7.91	9.39	10.86	12.86	14.44	17.34	20.60	22.76	25.99	28.87	32.35	34.80	42.31
19	7.63	8.57	10.12	11.65	13.72	15.35	18.34	21.69	23.90	27.20	30.14	33.69	36.19	43.82
20	8.26	9.24	10.85	12.44	14.58	16.27	19.34	22.78	25.04	28.41	31.41	35.02	37.57	45.32
21	8.90	9.92	11.59	13.24	15.44	17.18	20.34	23.86	26.17	29.62	32.67	36.34	38.93	46.80
22	9.54	10.60	12.34	14.04	16.31	18.10	21.34	24.94	27.30	30.81	33.92	37.66	40.29	48.27
23	10.20	11.29	13.09	14.85	17.19	19.02	22.34	26.02	28.43	32.01	35.17	38.97	41.64	49.73
24	10.86	11.99	13.85	15.66	18.06	19.94	23.34	27.10	29.55	33.20	36.42	40.27	42.98	51.18
25	11.52	12.70	14.61	16.47	18.94	20.87	24.34	28.17	30.68	34.38	37.65	41.57	44.31	52.62
26	12.20	13.41	15.38	17.29	19.82	21.79	25.34	29.25	31.80	35.56	38.88	42.86	45.64	54.05
27	12.88	14.12	16.15	18.11	20.70	22.72	26.34	30.32	32.91	36.74	40.11	44.14	46.96	55.48
28	13.56	14.85	16.93	18.94	21.59	23.65	27.34	31.39	34.03	37.92	41.34	45.42	48.28	56.89
29	14.26	15.57	17.71	19.77	22.48	24.58	28.34	32.46	35.14	39.09	42.56	46.69	49.59	58.30
30	14.95	16.31	18.49	20.60	23.36	25.51	29.34	33.53	36.25	40.26	43.77	47.96	50.89	59.70

Source: Taken from Table IV of Fisher and Yates': *Statistical Tables for Biological, Agricultural and Medical Research* (6th Edition 1974) published by Longman Group UK Ltd. London (previously published by Oliver and Boyd Ltd, Edinburg) and is reprinted by permission of the authors and publishers.

SAMPLE ANSWERS TO SELF-INSTRUCTIONAL REVIEW EXERCISES

■ CHAPTER 1 ■

Sample Answers for Test Items

1b, 2a, 3a, 4d, 5a, 6c, 7b, 8b, 9a, 10a-b-c, 11c, 12d, 13b

Sample Answers for Application Problems

1. A. The teacher is more aware that classroom misbehavior might be related to the home environment.
2. C. A new research question might concern whether the reading comprehension test is also valid for grades 3 and 4.
3. C. A new research problem would be to study the organization of schools since the 1954 Supreme Court rulings.
4. B. The principal decides to send an information letter to parents which explains the new report card and grading system.
5. B. The curriculum developer decides to revise the module to reflect the suggestion from the field-testing of the pilot module.
6. C. The professor proposes a new study to investigate the degree and type of autonomous behavior of superintendents, principals, and teachers.

■ CHAPTER 2 ■

Sample Answers for Test Items

1c, 2d, 3c, 4c, 5d, 6d, 7c, 8b, 9c, 10b, 11b, 12b

Sample Answers for Application Problems

1. a. non-experimental
   b. experimental or *ex post facto*
   c. non-experimental or qualitative
   d. experimental
   e. non-experimental
   f. *ex post facto*
   g. *ex post facto*
   h. experimental
   i. qualitative

■ CHAPTER 3 ■

Sample Answers for Test Items

1d, 2d, 3d, 4d, 5b, 6d, 7c, 8c, 9d, 10c, 11b, 12d, 13c

Sample Answers for Application Problems

1. a. Need to specify population, "different ways of learning," and "effects." Example: Is there a difference between the SRA social studies achievement scores of eighth graders who had an inquiry approach and those who had a lecture approach?
   b. Need to specify population and measures of two variables. Example: Do the attitudes toward learning of middle school students differ between those in cooperative instruction and those in competitive instruction?
   c. Need to specify which educational opinions of which parents (population). Example: What are the opinions of parents of Fox School pupils toward the proposed athletic eligibility regulations?
   d. Need to specify which family characteristics are to be measured or categorized and measurement for school attendance. Example: Is there a relationship between educational level of parents and number of siblings and their average daily school attendance?
   e. Need to specify type of validity sought, population, and criterion for validity. Example: Is there a relationship between the scores of the WISC and the CAT among primary grade minority children?

2. Directional Hypothesis: Low-achieving students reinforced with tangible rewards will demonstrate greater achievement in basic skills than low-achieving students reinforced with intangible rewards. Independent variable is type of reward (categorical) and dependent variable is achievement (continuous or measured).

3. a. High school students in an individualized curriculum will score higher on a social studies test than students in a structured curriculum.
   b. Teacher positive task introduction compared to teacher neutral task introduction statements will produce sustained student engagement in those tasks.
   c. Students who are retained have higher scores on a measure of personal adjustment than comparable students who are promoted.
   d. Comparable middle school children produce more narrative text in a cognitive-development teacher's class than in an academic teacher's class.
   e. There is a significant difference in the scores of a teacher burnout inventory among teachers of mildly retarded, moderately retarded, and nonretarded children, or, the degree of teacher burnout increases as the students' level of intellectual ability decreases.

4. a. Independent variable: liberal grading
      Dependent variables: faculty evaluations,
                                              student performance
   b. Variable: classroom behavior
   c. Independent variable: teacher cognitive styles
      Dependent variable: academic achievement gains

    d. no variables

    e. Independent variable: contextual aids

        Dependent variable: inter-sentence interference

    f. Independent variable: two school-based intervention
                                           programs

        Dependent variable: depressive symptoms

5. b and f

6. a. female faculty members of an urban university

    b. the School Board discussions of a suburban school system, 1900 to 1960

    c. Miss Sue's first year as a teacher in an elementary school

    d. court cases which define academic freedom for public school personnel, 1950 to 1985

    e. a faculty implementing an innovative middle school program

■ CHAPTER 4 ■

Sample Answers for Test Items

1c, 2c, 3e, 4a, 5b, 6e, 7d, 8e, 9c, 10b, 11c, 12a, 13e, 14d, 15c, 16b, 17a, 18a, 19c

Sample Answers for Application Problems

1. Search *RIE* by type of document: curriculum guidelines and evaluation studies for Title I ESEA Act mathematics programs and by years desired. By using connecting identifiers with key terms, Chapter I (new terminology) can be located.

2. a. For a narrow search:
       A and E and H and J

    b. For a more thorough search:
       Search 1: (A or B) and (E or F) and (H or I) and J
       Search 2: (A or B) and (E or F) and (H or I) and (J or K)
       Search 3: (A or B or C or D) and (E or F or G) and (H or I) and J
       Search 4: (A or B or C or D) and (E or F or G) and (H or I) and (J or K)

3. The order of priority for presenting sources in a literature review is from the least related or most general to the most related literature. The sources would thus be organized as (d) theories, (e) studies on animal behavior, (b) program descriptions, (a) evaluations of instruction, and (c) evaluations of students.

■ CHAPTER 5 ■

Sample Answers for Test Items

1b, 2c, 3d, 4a, 5d, 6a, 7b, 8a, 9c, 10b, 11b, 12a, 13a, 14a, 15c, 16a, 17d, 18b, 19c, 20a, 21d, 22b, 23b

Sample Answers for Application Problems

1. a. Evidently the instructor knew about the study, and his or her bias could affect the results. Subjects choose the section they will be in; hence selection is a

major threat. The time of day of the sections may affect selection, and is itself a threat to internal validity. There is no assurance that the instructor will treat each section the same. Diffusion of treatment may be a problem if students from different sections interact. Some students may purposely score low on the pretest in order to show significant improvement in the course (instrumentation—the results may be inaccurate). History may also be a threat, depending on the nature of the class groups. The generalizability is limited to the students taking the course in this particular college, the course itself (tennis), the instructor, and the methods used in the class.

b. Instrumentation is a potential threat, since details about the nature of the observations are lacking. Test validity could also be considered, since measuring prosocial behavior in a playground may not reflect the benefits of day care attendance. Compensatory rivalry or resentment might be a factor, because mothers who were chosen as a control group might arrange other experiences for their children that would enhance prosocial behavior. External validity is limited because of the volunteer nature of the sample and the specific programs of the day care institutions utilized. If there are many different day care organizations represented, it would be difficult to generalize about the cause of the difference. Each case would have to be examined individually.

c. The question here is whether the population that votes is the same as the population from which the sample is drawn; after all, those who rent can also vote, so depending on the percentage of renters in the district, sampling property owners alone may be misleading. In addition, not all property owners have children going to school, and only a portion of the population ever votes. The generalizability of the results thus would be suspect. Depending on the nature of the issue at hand, some respondents may provide less than honest information. They may also change their minds within the two weeks before voting.

d. The major threat is selection, since only sixty percent of the population returned questionnaires, and teachers could withhold information if they wanted to. Instrumentation may be a threat, depending on the way the questionnaire was designed (validity and reliability, and the standardization of the way it is administered—that is, its directions). There is a chance for scoring error, since each instructor does his or her own scoring. Mortality might be a problem. Since the questionnaire was given only once, students who were absent would be excluded. The generalizability of the results would be limited by the nature of the sample that returned questionnaires and the time of year the study was done.

■ CHAPTER 6 ■

Sample Answers for Test Items

1a and d, 2c, 3c, 4d, 5a, 6c, 7b, 8d, 9b, 10a

Sample Answers for Application Problems

1. a. mean
   b. Pearson Product-moment correlation
   c. standard deviation (the wider the dispersion, the greater the number of groups)
   d. frequencies and percentages

2. a. interval or ordinal
    b. nominal
    c. ordinal

■ **CHAPTER 7** ■

Sample Answers for Test Items

1b, 2d, 3a, 4d, 5b, 6a, 7d, 8c, 9a, 10c, 11d, 12d, 13d, 14a, 15b, 16b, 17d, 18c, 19a, 20b, 21c

Sample Answers for Application Problems

1. a. questionnaire, to enhance confidentiality of sensitive topics and keep expenses low
    b. observation, since self-report measures would be susceptible to social desirability
    c. phone interview, to assure representative responses
    d. questionnaire, because the information is simple and easily obtained
    e. observational, to keep the situation as natural as possible
    f. interview, since there would be a need to probe
    g. interview; most small children are honest and are unable to respond to questionnaires
    h. questionnaires or interviews, depending on the specificity of the information needed. With problems that begin general, an interview is useful for generating specific items that can then be used on a questionnaire.

2. a. ambiguity of the term *open education*
    b. no information about how to rank; is 1 or 10 most important?
    c. use of both senior and junior high teachers creates ambiguity; should ask about either senior or junior high teachers but not both
    d. ambiguity permitting a respondent who thinks "she's not just good, she's great" to answer "strongly disagree"

3. a. alternate individual work sessions and group activities and observe during individual work sessions
    b. teach students to observe themselves (that is, record time taken to complete assignments)
    c. use unobtrusive measures, such as number of requests from students for help, pencil shavings in pencil sharpener, detail and care in assignments, and amount of eraser that is used

■ **CHAPTER 8** ■

Sample Answers for Test Items

1c, 2d, 3b, 4a, 5b, 6d, 7c, 8e, 9a, 10d

Sample Answers for Application Problems

1. Her decision may have been correct, but her inference that the techniques caused the achievement is incorrect because it is possible that other events occurred at the same time as the techniques did to cause greater achievement. This is an example of inferring causation from correlation.

2. a. relationship
   b. relationship
   c. predictive
   d. relationship
   e. descriptive

■ CHAPTER 9 ■

Sample Answers for Test Items

1b, 2d, 3a, 4b, 5c, 6a, 7c, 8b, 9d, 10b, 11c, 12b, 13d

Sample Answers for Application Problems

1. Quasi-experimental pretest-posttest design

   $$A \longrightarrow O \longrightarrow X_1 \longrightarrow O$$

   $$B \longrightarrow O \longrightarrow X_2 \longrightarrow O$$

   $$C \longrightarrow O \longrightarrow X_3 \longrightarrow O$$

2. Multiple Baseline Across Subjects Design

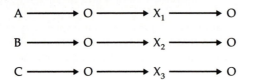

```
                              X X X X X X X X X X
        Boy    OOOOO  OOOOO  OOOOOOOOOO
        Girl   OOOOO  OOOOO  OOOOOX X X X X
                                      OOOOO
```

3. Posttest-Only Control Group Design

Randomization	Groups	Treatment	Posttest
60 students	A	X_1	O
	B	X_2	O
	C	X_3	O

■ CHAPTER 10 ■

Sample Answers for Test Items

1d, 2b, 3c, 4c-d-f-g, 5d, 6b, 7a, 8a, 9b, 10c, 11d, 12d, 13b

Sample Answers for Application Problems

1. There are three groups in this study. The researcher would hence use one-way ANOVA or an appropriate nonparametric analog, depending on the nature of the dependent variables. Most likely, means would be reported for the groups, and the parametric procedure would be acceptable, followed by post hoc comparisons if necessary.

2. Since the same group of students is assessed twice, a dependent samples *t*-test is the statistical procedure. If there were more than one dependent variable (that is, several facets to sex education), then the teacher should employ a multivariate test.

3. The teacher should now use a 2 x 2 ANOVA (group *x* gender). The analysis will provide a test for each main effect and a test for the interaction between group and gender.

4. There would be two ways to analyze this data: first, a correlation could be computed between self-esteem and frequency of visits and tested by a *t*-test to see whether the correlation is significantly different from zero; or, second, groups of students could be identified (for example, high, low, medium self-esteem), and a 1 x 3 ANOVA computed on the mean frequencies of each group.

5. There are two independent variables and eight related dependent variables, resulting in the need for a 2 x 4 MANOVA, with appropriate post hoc tests if necessary.

■ CHAPTER 11 ■

Sample Answers for Test Items

 1b, 2d, 3a, 4c, 5d, 6b, 7d, 8b, 9d, 10c, 11d

Sample Answers for Application Problems

1. The ethnographer can collect data by observations and casual conversations with other teachers and school personnel. Rapport is maintained with the sixth teacher by indicating interest without demanding the teacher to use the curriculum in the researcher's presence. Sufficient data about the curriculum can be obtained from other sources. Further, the ethnographer, for confidentiality of the data, should not tell other district officials of the teacher's reluctance.

2. An ethnographer tries to observe all the happenings, formal and informal, in the setting although the major foci may be on the processes within the photography class and the evening programs. Thus, social activities, meals, and extracurricula activities are potential sources of data. Student photographs are sources of data. Field notes of all observations and conversations are made because the ethnographer does not know what is important at the time of the occurrence.

3. The ethnographer can remind the director of the agreement established at entry into the field—all data is confidential and all names and places will be coded. Second, the ethnographer does not know what the remarks mean nor if the remarks will be reported in the findings which reflect only patterns established through cross-checking with other sources. Third, the ethnographer could use the occasion to encourage the director to talk more about these adults so the researcher could assess the trustworthiness of the adult testimony. The ethnographer could also use the occasion to have the director talk about her concerns regarding the public image of the adult education program.

4. Yes. The proposed study focuses on the dynamic processes of socialization in desegregated schools. Other justifications for the use of ethnography are (1) an interest in the school and community milieu in which the classroom dynamics occur, (2) previous studies have not addressed this research question, and (3) previous research has not used on-site observation as a methodology.

5. A sample qualitative interview guide is:
   a. How do you feel when your principal visits your class?
      Probe: Could you tell me why?
   b. Principals usually have a conference with the teacher after observing their instruction. Can you tell me what these conferences are like?
   c. Do you think that your principal's evaluation of your teaching is fair?
      Probe: Why fair or unfair?
   d. How do you think evaluation relates to your idea of being a professional teacher?

■ CHAPTER 12 ■

Sample Answers for Test Items

1a, 2c, 3d, 4c, 5e-d-c-b-a, 6d, 7c, 8b, 9d, 10a, 11d, 12c

Sample Answers for Application Problems

1. a. This topic could be delimited by which local school board, the years to be included in the study, and by the type of decision—personnel, fiscal, curriculum decisions.
   b. Sources for the study could be (1) documents, (2) oral testimonies, and (3) relics. Documents may be the official board minutes, reports submitted to the school board and released by the school board, budgets, local newspapers, and newsletters by the school system. Oral testimonies include extended interviews with the incumbents and past members of the school board, the incumbent and past superintendent, the incumbent and past president of the teachers organization, and other living witnesses who appeared before the school board. Examples of relics are charts and diagrams used in presentations before the school board.

2. a. The research problem could be stated as follows:
    1) for a historical study: The research problem is to analyze the concept of the student in the last fifty years with references to moral development.
    2) for a legal study: The research problem is to analyze selected federal and state court decisions on student discipline and control from 1960 to 1980 to determine legal indicators of disruption.
    3) for a policy study: The research problem is to analyze the implementation of the legislative mandate that "each school division shall develop standards of student conduct and attendance and shall have implemented a plan conducive to learning and good citizenship in an atmosphere free of disruption."
    4) for an analysis of a concept: The research problem is to identify the essential meaning of "student discipline," the different meanings of "student discipline," and the necessary conditions for the appropriate usage of the concept "student discipline."
  b. Specialized bibliographies for history include *The Historian's Handbook: A Descriptive Guide to Reference Works* and *A Bibliography of American Educational History*. Specialized digests for legal research are the National Reporter System and the American Digest System. Because the policy study focuses on the implementation of a state mandate, the researcher will probably have to obtain assistance from the state law library or legislative reference library and reports from state agencies.

3. a. An analyst questions the accuracy of statements made at a testimonial dinner. Considerations of good taste probably influenced statements that (1) "due solely to," (2) the junior college system meets state needs and provides a better general education, (3) "alone established" minimum competency testing, and (4) the innovation raised standards and proved to the public. . . .
  b. Other documents about the junior college system, teacher salaries and certification requirements, and the minimum competency testing program from 1959–1979 would confirm, reject, or modify the newspaper account. The private oral testimonies of the dinner speakers and members of the educational agencies and associations might vary from the public statements.

■ CHAPTER 13 ■

Sample Answers for Test Items

1c, 2a, 3c, 4d, 5a, 6b, 7c, 8c, 9b, 10d, 11d

Sample Answers for Application Problems

1. The evaluators should have monitored and noted the changes in purpose and procedures as they occurred. The evaluators could have met periodically with the supervisor to review purposes or data needs and check on those procedures which

were not directly under their control. Near the end of the evaluation, the evaluation staff could have met with the supervisor and department chairpersons to consider the changed purpose and procedures in preparation for forming recommendations.

2. Two errors were made by the evaluators. First, they failed to recognize the need to plan their evaluation in terms of evaluation questions and the time frame for the evaluation. Qualitative analysis must be focused around questions, just as quantitative analysis. Secondly, they allowed frequency counts to substitute for an adequate analysis of the nature of the contacts between enrolled youngsters and law enforcement agencies. The evaluators should have entered only those records most likely to furnish the information they sought, such as staff logs. The evaluators should have been less hasty to convert contact records to numbers which failed to reflect differences in kinds of contacts. Even cursory thought about the kinds of contact being recorded should have led the evaluators to question the data and eventually question the project staff. Had they done this, they could have drawn a different conclusion about the project's effectiveness.

3. The evaluators should have chosen or developed instruments and procedures that focused directly on the curriculum committee's questions. The evaluators could have (1) checked the validity of these instruments against the content and objectives of the ecology units, and/or (2) asked the curriculum committee and the middle school teachers to judge the validity of the instruments for their questions. The evaluators could have observed the ecology units in operation and the students in and out of the classroom to discover unintended effects of the units on their behavior. The evaluators could have used unobtrusive measures to collect data on the amount of wastepaper, bottles, and cans found in specific locations around the school, the extent to which students used both sides of the notebook paper, and so on.

4. The evaluator erred in not meeting earlier (when planning the evaluation) with the faculty committee and principal to develop a dissemination plan and to identify all of the audiences for the report. When the report was completed, he should have discussed the findings with the principal and given copies of the report to the committee. He should have provided an executive summary of the report for the entire faculty. He should have at least suggested to the principal that the report and its findings be discussed with those social studies teachers who had used the materials.

■ CHAPTER 14 ■

Sample Answers for Test Items

1d, 2a, 3c, 4b, 5d, 6c, 7d, 8a, 9b

REFERENCES

Agar, M. (1980). *The professional stranger: An informal introduction to ethnography.* New York: Academic Press, Inc.

Allen, J. D. (1986). Classroom management: Students' perceptions, goals, and strategies. *American Educational Research Journal, 23*(3), 437–459.

Allender, J. S. (1986). Educational research: A personal & social process. *Review of Educational Research, 56*(2), 173–193.

Alkin, M. C. (1969). Evaluation theory development. *Evaluation Comment, 2,* 2–7.

American Psychological Association. (1983). *Publication manual of the American Psychological Association* (3rd ed.). Washington, DC: Author.

American Psychological Association. (1985). *Standards for educational and psychological tests.* Washington, DC: Author.

Anderson, S. B., & Ball, S. (1978). *The profession and practice of program evaluation.* San Francisco: Jossey-Bass, Inc., Publishers.

Aydelotte, W. O. (1966). Quantification in history. *American Historical Review, 71,* 803–825.

Aydelotte, W. O., Bogue, A. G., & Fogel, R. W. (1972). *The dimensions of quantitative research in history.* Princeton: Princeton University Press.

Babbie, E. R. (1973). *Survey research methods.* Belmont, CA: Wadsworth, Inc.

Babbie, E. R. (1983). *The practice of social research* (3rd ed.). Belmont, CA: Wadsworth, Inc.

Barzun, J. (1985). *On writing, editing and publishing: Essays explicative and hortatory* (2nd ed.). Chicago: The University of Chicago Press.

Barzun, J., & Graff, H. G. (1970). *The modern researcher* (rev. ed.). New York: Harcourt Brace & World.

Barzun, J., & Graff, H. G. (1985). *The modern researcher* (4th ed.). New York: Harcourt Brace & World.

Becker, H. (1986). *Writing for social scientists.* Chicago: The University of Chicago Press.

Becker, H. S. (1958). Problems of inference and proof in participant observation. *American Sociological Review, 28,* 652–660.

Becker, H. S., Geer, B., Hughes, E. C., & Strauss, A. (1961). *Boys in white: Student culture in medical school.* Chicago: The University of Chicago Press.

Becker, H. S., Geer, B., & Hughes, E. C. (1968). *Making the grade: The academic side of college life.* New York: John Wiley & Sons, Inc.

Bednarz, D. (1985). Quantity and quality in evaluation research: A divergent view. *Evaluation and Program Planning, 8,* 289–306.

Benson, C. (1978). *The economics of public education* (3rd ed.). Boston: Houghton Mifflin Co.

Berdie, P. R., & Anderson, J. F. (1974). *Questionnaires: Design and use.* Metuchen, NJ: Scarecrow Press, Inc.

Berk, R. A. (1986). A consumer's guide to setting performance standards on criterion referenced tests. *Review of Educational Research, 56*(1), 137–172.

Berke, J. S. (1974). *Answers to inequity: An analysis of new school finance.* Berkeley, CA: McCutchan Publishing Corp.

Biklen, S. K. (1985). Can elementary school teaching be a career?: A search for new ways of understanding women's work. *Issues in Education, 3*(3), 215–231.

Bloom, B. S., et al. (1956). *Taxonomy of educational objectives. Handbook I: Cognitive domain.* New York: David McKay Co., Inc.

Bogdan, R., & Bilken, S. K. (1982). *Qualitative research for education.* Boston: Allyn & Bacon, Inc.

Boraks, N., & Schumacher, S. (1981). *Ethnographic research on word recognition strategies of adult beginning readers: Technical Report.* Richmond: Virginia Commonwealth University, School of Education. (ERIC Document Reproduction Services ED No. 207 007)

Borich, G. D., & Madden, S. K. (1977). *Evaluating classroom instruction: A sourcebook of instruments.* Reading, MA: Addison-Wesley Publishing Co., Inc.

Boruch, R. F., & Cecil, J. S. (1979). *Assuring the confidentiality of social research data.* Philadelphia: University of Pennsylvania Press.

Bruyn, S. T. (1966). *The human perspective in sociology: The methodology of participant observation.* Englewood Cliffs, NJ: Prentice-Hall, Inc.

Buros, O. K. (Ed.). (1974). *Tests in print II.* Highland Park, NJ: Gryphon.

Buros, O. K. (Ed.). (1978). *The eighth mental measurement yearbook* (2 Vols.). Highland Park, NJ: Gryphon.

Campbell, D. T. (1974, September). *Qualitative knowing in action research.* Kurt Lewis Award Address presented at the meeting of the Society for the Psychological Study of Social Issues. Meeting with the American Psychological Association, New Orleans.

Campbell, D. T. (1982, March). *Can we be scientific about policy research?* AERA Award Address, American Educational Research Association Annual Meeting, New York.

Campbell, D. T. (1984). Can we be scientific in applied social science? In R. F. Conner, D. G. Altman, & C. Jackson (Eds.), *Evaluation studies review annual* (Vol. 9). Beverly Hills, CA: Sage Publications, Inc.

Campbell, D. T., & Stanley, J. C. (1963). *Experimental and quasi-experimental designs for research.* Chicago: Rand, McNally & Co.

Carley, M. (1980). *Rational techniques in policy analysis.* London: Heinemann Educational Books, Inc.

Cassell, J., & Wax, M. (Eds.). (1980). Ethical problems in fieldwork. Special issue of *Social Problems, 27.*

Center for New Schools (1972). Strengthening alternative high schools. *Harvard Educational Review, 42,* 313–350.

Center for New Schools (1976). Ethnographic evaluation in education. *Journal of Research and Development in Education, 9*(4), 3–11.

Chelimsky, E. (1987). The politics of program evaluation in D. S. Cordray, H. S. Bloom & R. J. Light (Eds.), *Evaluation Practice in Review, New Directions for Program Evaluation, No. 34.* San Francisco: Jossey-Bass, Inc., Publishers.

Chicago manual of style: Thirteenth edition, revised and expanded. (1982). Chicago: The University of Chicago Press.

Chilcott, J. H. (1987). Where are you coming from and where are you going? The reporting of ethnographic research. *American Educational Research Journal, 24*(2), 199–218.

Chun, K. T., Cobb, S., & French, J. R. P., Jr. (1975). *Measures for psychological assessment: A guide to 3,000 original sources and their applications.* Ann Arbor: Institute for Social Research, University of Michigan.

Clifford, G. J. (1973). A history of the impact of research on teaching. In R. Travers (Ed.), *Second handbook of research on teaching.* Chicago: Rand, McNally & Co.

Cohen, M. (1978). *Legal research in a nutshell.* St. Paul, MN: West Publishing Co.

Cohen, S. (1976). The history of the history of American education, 1900–1976: The uses of the past. *Harvard Educational Review, 46*(3), 298–330.

Colton, D. L., & Graber, E. E. (1982). *Teacher strikes and the courts.* Lexington, MA: D. C. Heath & Co.

Committee on Scientific and Professional Ethics and Conduct (1977). Ethical standards of psychologists, *APA Monitor, 8,* 22–23.

Comrey, A. L., Backer, T. E., & Glaser, E. M. (1973). *A sourcebook for mental health measures.* Los Angeles: Human Interaction Research Institute.

Cook, T. D., & Campbell, D. T. (1979). *Quasi-experimentation: Design and analysis issues for field settings.* Chicago: Rand, McNally & Co.

Cooper, H. (1984). *The integrative research review: A systematic approach.* Beverly Hills: Sage Publications, Inc.

Cousins, J. B., & Leithwood, K. A. (1986). Current empirical research on evaluation utilization. *Review of Educational Research, 56*(3), 331–364.

Cremin, L. A. (1961). *The transformation of the school: Progressivism in American Education, 1876–1957.* New York: Vintage.

Cronbach, L. J. (1975). Beyond the two disciplines of scientific psychology. *American Psychologist, 30,* 116–127.

Cronbach, L. J. (1982). *Designing evaluations of educational and social programs.* San Francisco: Jossey-Bass, Inc., Publishers.

Cronbach, L. J. & Suppes, P. (Eds.). (1969). *Research for tomorrow's schools: Disciplined inquiry for education.* New York: Macmillan Publishing Co.

Cusick, P. A. (1973). *Inside high school: The student's world.* New York: Holt, Rinehart & Winston.

Cutler, W. W. (1971). Oral history: Its nature and uses for educational history. *History of Education Quarterly, 11,* 184–194.

Denzin, N. K. (1978). *The research act: A theoretical introduction to sociological methods* (2nd ed.). Chicago: Aldine.

Dobbert, M. L. (1982). *Ethnographic research: Theory and application for modern schools and societies.* New York: Praeger Publishers.

Dollar, C. M., & Jensen, R. J. (1971). *Historian's guide to statistics: Quantitative analysis and historical research.* New York: Holt, Rinehart & Winston.

Ebmeier, H., & Good, T. L. (1979). The effects of instructing teachers about good teaching on the mathematics achievement of fourth grade students. *American Educational Research Journal, 16*(1), 1–16.

Eisner, E. (1979). *The educational imagination: On the design and evaluation of school programs.* New York: Macmillan Publishing Co.

Erickson, F. (1973). What makes school ethnography "ethnographic?" *Anthropology and Education Quarterly, 9,* 58–69.

Fink, A., & Kosecoff, J. (1985). *How to conduct surveys: A step by step guide.* Beverly Hills: Sage Publications, Inc.

Finn, C. E. (1977). *Education and the presidency.* Lexington, MA: D. C. Heath & Co.

Firestone, W. A. (1987). Meaning in method: The rhetoric of quantitative and qualitative research. *Educational Researcher, 16*(7), 16–21.

Fishel, A., & Pottker, J. (1977). *National politics and sex discrimination in education.* Lexington, MA: D. C. Heath & Co.

Floud, R. (1979). *An introduction to quantitative methods for historians.* London: Methuen, Inc.

Fowler, F. J. (1984). *Survey research methods.* Beverly Hills: Sage Publications, Inc.

Frels, K., Cooper, T., & Reagan, J. (1984). *Practical aspects of teacher evaluation.* Topeka, KS: NOLPE.

Fuchs, D., & Fuchs, L. S. (1986). Test procedure bias: A meta-analysis of examiner familiarity effects. *Review of Educational Research. 56*(2), 243–262.

Gardiner, P. (1952). *The nature of historical explanation.* London: Oxford University Press.

Geer, B. (1964). First days in the field. In P. Hammond (Ed.), *Sociologists at work* (pp. 322–344). NY: Basic Books, Inc.

Giesbrecht, M. L., & Routh, D. K. (1979). The influence of categories of cumulative folder information on teacher referrals of low-achieving children for special education services. *American Educational Research Journal, 16*(2), 181–187.

Gilmore, P. (1983). Spelling "Mississippi:" Recontextualizing a literacy-related speech event. *Anthropology and Education Quarterly, 14*(4), 235–255.

Glaser, B. G., & Strauss, L. L. (1967). *The discovery of grounded theory: Strategies for qualitative research.* Chicago: Aldine.

Glass, G. V. (1976). Primary, secondary, and meta-analysis of research. *Educational Researcher, 5*(10), 3–8.

Glass, G. V., McGaw, F., & Smith, M. L. (1981). *Meta-analysis in social research.* Beverly Hills, CA: Sage Publications, Inc.

Goetz, J. P., & LeCompte, M. D. (1984). *Ethnography and qualitative design in educational research.* Orlando, FL: D. C. Heath & Co.

Goldstein, P. (1978). *Changing the American schoolbook: Politics, law and technology.* Lexington, MA: D. C. Heath & Co.

Goodwin, W. L., & Driscoll, L. A. (1980). *Handbook for measurement and evaluation in early childhood education.* San Francisco: Jossey-Bass, Inc., Publishers.

Gottschalk, L. (1963). Categories of historical generalization. In L. Gottschalk (Ed.), *Generalizations in the writing of history.* Chicago: The University of Chicago Press.

Gottschalk, L. (1969). *Understanding history: A primer of historical method* (2nd ed.). New York: Alfred A. Knopf, Inc.

Groobman, D. G., Forward, J. R., & Peterson, C. (1976). Attitudes, self-esteem, and learning in formal and informal schools. *Journal of Educational Psychology, 68*(1), 32–33.

Guba, E. G. (1978). *Toward a methodology of naturalistic inquiry in educational research. CSE Monograph Series in Evaluation.* 8. Los Angeles: Center for the Study of Evaluation, UCLA Graduate School of Education.

Guba, E. G., & Lincoln, Y. S. (1981). *Effective evaluation.* San Francisco: Jossey-Bass, Inc., Publishers.

Guthrie, J. W. (1980). An assessment of educational policy research. *Educational Evaluation and Policy Analysis, 2*(5), 41–55.

Gutowski, T. W. (1988). Student initiative and the origins of the high school extracurriculum: Chicago, 1880–1915. *History of Education Quarterly, 28*(1), 49–72.

Hall, E. T. (1959). *The silent language.* New York: Doubleday & Co.

Hall, E. T. (1966). *The hidden dimension.* New York: Doubleday & Co.

Hall, E. T. (1974). *Handbook for proxemic research.* Washington, DC: Society for the Anthropology of Visual Communication.

Halperin, S. (1978, March). *Teaching the limitations of the correlation coefficient.* Paper presented at the annual meeting of the American Educational Research Association, Toronto.

Hambrick, R. S. (1987). *Analysis for decision-making: Using non-quantitative group methods. Commonwealth papers, 1987.* Richmond: Virginia Commonwealth University, Center for Public Affairs.

Hammon, R. L. (1973). Evaluation at the local level. In B. R. Worthen & J. R. Sanders, *Educational evaluation: Theory and practice.* Belmont, CA: Wadsworth, Inc.

Harvard Law Review Association. (1980). *A uniform system of citation* (13th ed.). Cambridge, MA: Author.

Haslett, N. R., Bolding, D. D., Harris, J. A., Taylor, A. L., Simon, P. M., & Schedgick, R. (1977). The attachment of a retarded child to an inanimate object: Translation into clinical utility. *Child Psychiatry and Human Development, 8*(1), 55–60.

Hedges, L. V., & Olkin, I. (1985). *Statistical methods for meta-analysis.* New York: Academic Press, Inc.

Hedges, L. V. & Olkin, I. (1986). Meta-analysis: A review and a new view. *Educational Researcher, 15*(8), 14–21.

Heller, E. S., & Rife, F. N. (1987). *Questionnaire response scales: Design factors that influence respondent satisfaction.* Paper presented at the annual meeting of the American Educational Research Association, Washington, DC.

Herriott, R. E. (1977). Ethnographic case studies in federally funded multidisciplinary policy research: Some designs and implementation issues. *Anthropology and Education Quarterly, 8,* 106–115.

Herriott, R. E., & Firestone, W. A. (1983). Multisite qualitative policy research: Optimizing description and generalizability. *Educational Researcher, 12*(2), 14–19.

Hersen, M., & Barlow, D. (1976). *Single case experimental designs.* New York: Pergamon Press, Inc.

Hoepfner, R., et al. (Eds.) (1972). *CSE-RBS test evaluation: Tests of higher order cognitive, affective, and interpersonal skills.* Los Angeles: Center for the Study of Evaluation, UCLA Graduate School of Education.

Homans, G. C. (1967). *The nature of social science.* New York: Harcourt Brace, and World.

Hopkins, K. D., & Anderson, B. L. (1973). Multiple comparisons guide. *Journal of Special Education, 7,* 319–328.

Hopkins, K. D., & Glass, G. V. (1978). *Basic statistics for the behavioral sciences.* Englewood Cliffs, NJ: Prentice-Hall, Inc.

Hopkins, K. D., & Stanley, J. C. (1981). *Educational and Psychological Measurement* (6th ed.). Englewood, NJ: Prentice-Hall, Inc.

House, E. R. (1980). *Evaluating with validity.* Beverly Hills: Sage Publications, Inc.

Hudgins, H. C., & Vacca, R. S. (1985). *Law and education* (rev. ed.). Charlottesville, VA: Mitchie.

Hunter, J. E., Schmidt, F. L., & Jackson, G. B. (1982). *Meta-analysis: Cumulating research findings across studies.* Beverly Hills: Sage Publications, Inc.

Iannaccone, L., & Lutz, F. W. (1970). *Politics, power and policy: The governing of local school districts.* Columbus, OH: Charles E. Merrill.

Jackson, G. B. (1980). Methods for integrative reviews. *Review of Educational Research, 9*(3), 438–460.

Jacob, E. (1987). Qualitative research traditions: A review. *Review of Educational Research, 57*(1), 1–50.

James, R. J., Hastings, S. C., & Lewis, J. F. (1987). *Drug and alcohol abuse in the schools.* Topeka, KS: NOLPE.

Jensen, R. (1981). Oral history, quantification, and the new social history. *Oral History Review, 9*, 13–27.

Johnson, O. G. (1976). *Tests and measurements in child development: Handbook II.* San Francisco: Jossey-Bass, Inc., Publishers.

Joint Committee on Standards for Educational Evaluation. (1981). *Standards for evaluations of educational programs, projects, and materials.* New York: McGraw-Hill Publishers, Inc.

Joyce, B. (1987). A rigorous yet delicate touch: A response to Slavin's proposal for "best-evidence" reviews. *Educational Researcher, 16*(4), 12–16.

Junker, B. H. (1960). *Field work: An introduction to the social sciences.* Chicago: The University of Chicago Press.

Katz, M. B. (1968). *The irony of early school reform: Educational innovation in mid-nineteenth century Massachusetts.* Cambridge, MA: Harvard University Press.

Katz, M. B. (1975). *Class, bureaucracy, and schools: The illusion of educational change in America.* New York: Praeger Publishers.

Katzer, J., Cook, K. H., & Crouch, W. W. (1982). *Evaluating information: A guide for users of social science research* (2nd ed.). Reading, MA: Addison-Wesley Publishing Co.

Kerlinger, F. N. (1979). *Behavioral research: A conceptual approach.* New York: Holt, Rinehart & Winston.

Kerlinger, F. N. (1986). *Foundations of behavioral research* (3rd ed.). New York: Holt, Rinehart & Winston.

Krathwohl, D. R., et al. (1964). *Taxonomy of educational objectives: Handbook II: Affective domain.* New York: David McKay Co., Inc.

LaMorte, M. W. (1982). *School law and concepts.* Englewood Cliffs, NJ: Prentice-Hall, Inc.

Lance, D. (1980). Oral history archives: Perceptions and practices. *Oral history, 8*(2), 59–63.

Lesko, N. (1986). Individualism and community: Ritual discourse in a parochial high school. *Anthropology and Education Quarterly, 17*(1), 25–39.

Levin, H. M. (1975). Cost-effectiveness analysis in evaluation research. In M. Guttentag & E. L. Struening (Eds.), *Handbook of evaluation research* (Vol. II). Beverly Hills, CA: Sage Publications, Inc.

Levin, H. M. (1981). Cost analysis. In N. Smith (Ed.), *New techniques for evaluation.* Beverly Hills, CA: Sage Publications, Inc.

Levin, H. M. (1987). Cost-benefit and cost-effectiveness analysis. In D. S. Cordray, H. S. Bloom, & R. J. Light (Eds.), *Evaluation Practice in Review: New Directions for Program Evaluation, No. 34.* San Francisco: Jossey-Bass, Inc., Publishers.

Levine, M. (1982). Adversary hearings. In N. L. Smith (Ed.), *Communication strategies in evaluation.* Beverly Hills, CA: Sage Publications, Inc.

Lewis, O. (1951). *Life in a Mexican village: Tepoztlan restudied.* Urbana: University of Illinois Press.

Light, R. J., & Pillemer, D. B. (1984). *Summing up: The science of reviewing research.* Cambridge, MA: Harvard University Press.

Lincoln, Y. S., & Guba, E. G. (1980). The distinction between merit and worth in evaluation. *Educational Evaluation and Policy Analysis, 2*(4), 61–72.

Lincoln, Y. S., & Guba, E. G. (1985). *Naturalistic inquiry.* Beverly Hills: Sage Publications, Inc.

Locke, L. F., Spirduso, W. W., & Silverman, J. J. (1987). *Proposals that work: A guide for planning dissertations and grant proposals* (2nd ed.). Beverly Hills: Sage Publications, Inc.

Lofland, J. & Lofland, L. H. (1984). *Analyzing social settings: A guide to qualitative observation and analysis* (2nd ed.). Belmont, CA: Wadsworth, Inc.

Loomer, S. (1982). *A campus microcosm: Creativity and noncreativity of gifted students in art settings and social situations.* Unpublished doctoral dissertation. Virginia Polytechnic Institute and State University, Blackburg, VA.

Luck, J. S. (1985). *The principal and the unsatisfactory teacher: A field study.* Unpublished doctoral dissertation. Virginia Polytechnic Institute and State University, Blacksburg, VA.

Lutz, F. W., & Iannaccone, L. (1969). *Understanding educational organizations: A field study approach.* Columbus, OH: Charles E. Merrill.

Malinowski, B. (1922). *Argonauts of the western Pacific.* New York: E. P. Dutton. (Reprint, 1961).

Mann, D. (1976). *The politics of administrative representation.* Lexington, MA: D. C. Heath & Co.

Marascuilo, L. A., & McSweeney, M. (1977). *Nonparametric and distribution-free methods for the social sciences.* Monterey, CA: Brooks/Cole Publishing Co.

Mark, M. M., & Shotland, R. L. (Eds.). (1987). *Multiple methods in program evaluation: New Directions for Program Evaluation, No. 35.* San Francisco: Jossey-Bass, Inc., Publishers.

Marshall, J. (1981). Making sense as a personal process. In P. Reason & J. Rowan (Eds), *Human inquiry: A sourcebook of new paradigm research.* New York: John Wiley & Sons, Inc.

Maslow, A. H. (1966). *The psychology of science: A reconnaissance.* New York: Harper and Row, Publishers, Inc.

McCarthy, M. M. (1983). *Discrimination in public employment.* Topeka, KS: NOLPE.

Medley, D. M., & Mitzel, H. E. (1963). Measuring classroom behavior by systematic observation. In N. L. Gage (Ed.). *Handbook of research on teaching* (2nd ed.) (pp. 247–328). Chicago: Rand, McNally & Co.

Mehrens, W. A., & Lehmann, I. J. (1987). *Measurement and evaluation in education and psychology* (4th ed.). New York: Holt, Rinehart & Winston.

Mehrens, W. A., & Lehmann, I. J. (1987). *Using standardized tests in education.* (4th ed.). New York: Longman, Inc.

Miles, B. M., & Huberman, A. M. (1984). *Qualitative data analysis: A sourcebook of new methods.* Beverly Hills, CA: Sage Publications, Inc.

Miller, S. I. (1981). Defining educational policy studies as a field. *Educational Studies.* 12(2), 119–124.

Miskel, C., & Cosgrove, D. (1985). Leader succession in school settings. *Review of Educational Research, 55*(1), 87–105.

Mitchell, J. V. (Ed.) (1983). *Tests in print III.* Lincoln, NE: University of Nebraska Press.

Mitchell, J. V. (Ed.) (1985) *The Ninth Mental Measurements Yearbook.* Highland Park, NJ: Gryphon.

Mitfessel, N. S., & Michael, W. B. (1967). A paradigm involving multiple criterion measures for the evaluation of school programs. *Educational and Psychological Measurement, 27,* 931–943.

Mitroff, I. I., & Kilmann, R. H. (1978). *Methodological approaches to social sciences.* San Francisco: Jossey-Bass, Inc., Publishers.

Nagel, S. S. (1980). *The policy-studies handbook.* Lexington, MA: D. C. Heath & Co.

Parker, W. C., & Gehrke, N. J. (1986). Learning activities and teachers' decision-making: Some grounded hypotheses. *American Educational Research Journal, 23*(2), 227–242.

Patton, M. Q. (1980). *Qualitative evaluation methods.* Beverly Hills, CA: Sage Publications, Inc.

Patton, M. Q. (1986). *Utilization-focused evaluation* (2nd ed.). Beverly Hills, CA: Sage Publications, Inc.

Patton, M. Q. (1987). *How to use qualitative methods in evaluation.* Newbury Park, CA: Sage Publications, Inc.

Pelto, P. J., & Pelto, G. H. (1978). *Anthropological research: The structure of inquiry* (2nd ed.). Cambridge, England: Cambridge University Press.

Peterson, L. J., Rossmiller, R. A., & Volz, M. M. (1978). *The laws and public school operation* (2nd ed.). New York: Harper and Row, Publishers, Inc.

Popham, W. J. (1975). *Educational evaluation.* Englewood Cliffs, NJ: Prentice-Hall, Inc.

Popham, W. J. (1981). *Modern educational measurement.* Englewood Cliffs, NJ: Prentice-Hall, Inc.

Popham, W. J., & Ebel, R. L. (1978). Annual meeting presidential debate. *Educational Researcher. 7*(11), 3.

Popper, K. R. (1959). *The logic of scientific discovery.* New York: Basic Books, Inc., Publishers.

Potter, D. M. (1963). Explicit data and implicit assumptions in historical study. In L. Gottschalk (Ed.), *Generalizations in the writing of history.* Chicago: The University of Chicago Press.

Provus, M. (1971). *Discrepancy evaluation.* Berkeley, CA: McCutchan Publishing Corp.

Quantz, R. A. (1985). The complex visions of female teachers and the failure of unionization in the 1930s: An oral history. *History of Education Quarterly, 25*(4), 439–458.

Rafferty, J. (1988). Missing the mark: Intelligence testing in Los Angeles Public Schools, 1922–32. *History of Education Quarterly, 28*(1), 73–93.

Ravitch, D. (1974). *The great school wars: New York City, 1805–1973.* New York: Basic Books, Inc.

Redfield, R. (1930). *Tepoztlan—a Mexican village: A study of folklife.* Chicago: The University of Chicago Press.

Reynolds, P. (1982). *Ethnics and social research.* Englewood Cliffs, NJ: Prentice-Hall, Inc.

Riemer, J. W. (1977). Varieties of opportunistic research. *Urban Life, 5,* 467–477.

Rist, R. C. (1977). On the relations among educational research paradigms: From disdain to detente. *Anthropology and Education Quarterly, 8,* 42–49.

Rist, R. C. (1978). *The invisible children: School integration in American society.* Cambridge, MA: Harvard University Press.

Robinson, J. P., & Shaver, P. (1973). *Measures of social psychological attitudes* (rev. ed.). Ann Arbor: University of Michigan.

Rosenthal, R. (1984). *Meta-analytic procedures for social science research.* Beverly Hills: Sage Publications, Inc.

Rosenthal, R., & Rosnow, R. L. (1975). *The volunteer subject.* New York: John Wiley & Sons, Inc.

Rosenthal, R., & Jacobson, L. (1968). *Pygmalion in the classroom: Teacher expectation and pupil's intellectual development.* New York: Holt, Rinehart & Winston.

Rosenthal, T. (1987). *An ethnographic study of clinical instruction in associate degree psychiatric nursing education.* Unpublished doctoral dissertation, Virginia Commonwealth University, Richmond, VA.

Rossi, P. H., & Freeman, H. E. (1982). *Evaluation: A systematic approach* (2nd ed.). Beverly Hills, CA: Sage Publications, Inc.

Rothenberg, J. (1975). Cost-benefit analysis: A methodological exposition. In M. Guttentag and E. L. Struening (Eds.), *Handbook of evaluation research* (Vol. II). Beverly Hills, CA: Sage Publications, Inc.

Rowntree, J. S. (1941). *Poverty and progress: A second social survey of York.* London: Longman, Green.

Salisbury, R. H. (1980). *Citizen participation in the public schools.* Lexington, MA: D. C. Heath & Co.

Samson, G. E., Trykowski, B., Weinstein, T., & Walberg, H. J. (1987). The effects of teacher questioning levels on student achievement: A quantitative synthesis. *Journal of Educational Research, 80*(5), 290–295.

Sanders, J. R., & Nafziger, D. H. (1975). *A basic for determining the adequacy of evaluation designs.* Occasional Paper Series, No. 6. Kalamazoo, MI: Evaluation Center, Western Michigan University.

Sax, G. (1979). *Foundations of educational research.* Englewood Cliffs, NJ: Prentice-Hall, Inc.

Sax, G. (1980). *Principles of educational and psychological measurement and evaluation* (2nd ed.). Belmont, CA: Wadsworth, Inc.

Schatzman, L., & Strauss, A. L. (1973). *Field research: Strategies for a natural sociology.* Englewood Cliffs, NJ: Prentice-Hall, Inc.

Schumacher, S. (1972). *Limitations of a research, development and diffusion strategy in diffusion: A case study of nine local implementations of a state-adopted curriculum.* Paper presented at the Annual Meeting of the National Council for the Social Studies, Boston. (ERIC Document Reproduction Service No. S0 005 632)

Schumacher, S. (1974). *ESEA interagency policy-making as "realistic opportunism": A case study of a national laboratory's curriculum diffusion project.* Paper presented at the annual meeting of the American Educational Research Association, Chicago. (ERIC Document Reproduction Services No. ED 114 981)

Schumacher, S. (1975). *Political processes for an interagency project renewal policy: A case study of a federal agency's negotiations to influence state and local policies.* Paper presented at the AERA Annual Meeting, Washington, DC. (ERIC Document Reproduction Service No. 111 024)

Schumacher, S. (1979). *Ethnographic inquiry: Theory and application in educational research and evaluation.* Paper presented at the College Reading Association Annual Meeting, Boston. (ERIC Document Reproduction Services No. ED 246 272)

Schumacher, S. (1984a). *Ethnographic methodology in a study of word recognition strategies of adult beginning readers.* Paper presented at the Adult Education Research Conference, Raleigh, NC. (ERIC Document Reproduction Services No. ED 246 272)

Schumacher, S. (1984b). *Evaluation of CoTEEP field-testing of workshop-seminar series and principles for summative evaluation.* Richmond: Virginia Commonwealth University, School of Education (ERIC Document Reproduction Service No. ED 252 499)

Schumacher, S. with Linder, F. (1980). *Arts program: A qualitative and quantitative evaluation of program development and implementation, 1979–1980.* Richmond: Virginia Commonwealth University, School of Education. (ERIC Document Reproduction Services No. ED 209 302)

Schumacher, S., & Boraks, N. (1981). *1980 cultural shock: Evolving ethnographic procedures to study adult learning-to-read behaviors.* Paper presented at the Second

Annual Ethnography in Education Research Forum, University of Pennsylvania. (ERIC Document Reproduction Service No. ED 207 007)

Schumacher, S., Esham, K., & Bauer, D. (1985). *Evaluation of a collaborative teacher education program: Planning, development and implementation, Phase III.* Richmond: Virginia Commonwealth University, School of Education. (ERIC Document Reproduction Services No. ED 278 659)

Schumacher, S., & Rommel-Esham, K. (1986). *Evaluation of a collaborative planning and development of school-based preservice and inservice education, Phase IV.* Richmond: Virginia Commonwealth University, School of Education. (ERIC Document Reproduction Services No. ED 278 659)

Schumacher, S., Rommel-Esham, K., & Bauer, D. (1987). *Professional knowledge objectives for preservice teachers as determined by school and university educators.* Paper presented at the American Educational Research Association Annual Meeting. Richmond: Virginia Commonwealth University. (ERIC Document Reproduction Service No. ED 288 822)

Schumacher, S., Rommel-Esham, K., & Bauer, D. (1988). *Professional knowledge objectives for preservice elementary teachers as selected by school and university educators: Implications for program development and evaluation.* Paper presented at the American Association of Colleges of Teacher Education Annual Meeting, New Orleans.

Schuman, H. & Presser, S. (1982). *Questions and answers: Experiments in the form, wording and context of survey questions.* New York: Academic Press, Inc.

Scioli, F. P., Jr., & Cook, T. S. (1980). *Methodologies for analyzing public policies.* Lexington, MA: D. C. Heath & Co.

Scriven, M. (1967). The methodology of evaluation. In R. E. Stake (Ed.), *Curriculum evaluation. AERA Monograph Series on Curriculum Evaluation, No. 1.* Chicago: Rand, McNally & Co.

Scriven, M. (1972). Objectivity and subjectivity in educational research. In L. G. Thomas (Ed.), *Philosophical redirection of educational research.* (71st Yearbook, Part I). Chicago: National Society for the Study of Education, The University of Chicago Press.

Scriven, M. (1972). Pros and cons about goal-free evaluation. *Educational Comment, 3,* 1–4.

Scriven, M. (1973). Goal-free evaluation. In E. R. House (Ed.), *School evaluation.* Berkeley, CA: McCutchan Publishing Corp.

Scriven, M. (1974). Standards for the evaluation of educational programs and products. In G. D. Borich (Ed.), *Evaluating education programs and products.* Englewood Cliffs, NJ: Educational Technology Publishers.

Sechrest, L. (Ed.). (1979). *Unobtrusive measurement today.* San Francisco: Jossey-Bass, Inc., Publishers.

Shackelford, P. L. (1982). Teacher incompetence: A compilation of the legal grounds used in federal and state cases involving the dismissal of tenured public school teachers. *Dissertation Abstracts International, 43*(5), Section A (University Microfilms No. 82–23, 941).

Shulman, L. S. (1981). Disciplines of inquiry in education: An overview. *Educational Researcher, 10*(6), 5–23.

Shulman, L. S. (1986). Paradigms and research programs in the study of teaching: A contemporary perspective. In M. Wittrock (Ed.), *Handbook of research on teaching, Third edition* (pp. 3–36). New York: Macmillan Publishing Co.

Shulman, L. S. (1987). Knowledge and teaching: Foundations of a new reform. *Harvard Educational Review, 57*(1), 1–22.

Siegel, S. (1956). *Nonparametric statistics for the behavioral sciences.* New York: McGraw-Hill Publishing Co.

Simon, A., & Boyer, E. G. (Eds.). (1974). *Mirrors for behavior: An anthology of classroom observation instruments.* Philadelphia: Research for Better Schools.

Simpson, E. J. (1966). *The classification of educational objectives: Psychomotor domain.* Urbana, IL: University of Illinois Press.

Slavin, R. E. (1984). Meta-analysis in education: How has it been used? *Educational Researcher, 13*(8), 6–15.

Slavin, R. E. (1986). Best-evidence synthesis: An alternative to meta-analytic and traditional reviews. *Educational Researcher, 15*(9), 5–11.

Sloan, D. (1973). Historiography and the history of education. In F. N. Kerlinger (Ed.), *Review of Research in Education* (Vol 1). Itasca, IL: F. E. Peacock.

Smith, H. G. (1979). Investigation of several techniques for reviewing audio-tutorial instruction. *Educational Communication and Technology Journal, 27*(3), 195–204.

Smith, J. L. (1983). Quantitative versus qualitative research: An attempt to clarify the issue. *Educational Researcher, 12*(3), 6–13.

Smith, J. L., & Heshusius, L. (1986). Closing down the conversation: The end of the quantitative-qualitative debate among educational inquirers. *Educational Researcher, 15*(1), 4–11.

Smith, L. M. (1979). An evolving logic of participant observation. In L. S. Shulman (Ed.), *Review of research in Education.* Vol. 6 (pp. 316–377). Itasca, IL: F. E. Peacock.

Smith, L. M. (1982). Ethnography. In *Encyclopedia of educational research* (5th ed.) (pp. 587–592). New York: The Free Press.

Smith, L. M., & Geoffrey, W. (1968). *The complexities of an urban classroom.* New York: Holt, Rinehart & Winston.

Smith, L. M., & Kleine, P. F. (1986). Qualitative research and evaluation: Triangulation and multimethods reconsidered. In D. D. Williams, (Ed.), *Naturalistic Evaluation. New Directions for Program Evaluation, No. 30.* San Francisco: Jossey-Bass, Inc., Publishers.

Smith, L. M., & Kleine, P. F. (1983). *Educational innovation: A life history research perspective.* St. Louis: Washington University. Paper presented at the conference: Teachers' Careers and Life Histories, St. Hilds's College, Oxford University: England.

Smith, L. M., Kleine, P. F., Prunty, J. J., & Dwyer, D. C. (1987). *Educational innovators: Then and now.* Philadelphia: Taylor & Francis.

Smith, L. M., Prunty, J. J., Dwyer, D. C., & Kleine, P. F. (1987). *The fate of an innovative school.* Philadelphia: Taylor & Francis.

Smith, L. M., & Keith, P. (1971). *Anatomy of educational innovation.* New York: John Wiley & Sons, Inc.

Smith, L. M., & Schumacher, S. (1972). *Extended pilot trials of the Aesthetic Education Program: A qualitative description, analysis, and evaluation.* St. Louis, MO: CEMREL, Inc.

Smith, N. (Ed.). (1981). *New techniques for evaluation.* Beverly Hills, CA: Sage Publications, Inc.

Soltis, J. F. (1978). *An introduction to the analysis of educational concepts.* (2nd ed.). Reading, MA: Addison-Wesley Publishers, Inc.

Spradley, J. P. (1979). *The ethnographic interview.* New York: Holt, Rinehart & Winston.

Spradley, J. P. (1980). *Participant observation.* New York: Holt, Rinehart & Winston.

Stake, R. E. (1967). The countenance of educational evaluation. *Teachers College Record, 68,* 523–540.

Stake, R. E. (Ed.). (1975a). *Evaluating the arts in education: A responsive approach.* Columbus, OH: Charles E. Merrill.

Stake, R. E. (1975b). *Program evaluation, particularly responsive evaluation.* Occasional Paper Series, No. 5. Kalamazoo, MI: Evaluation Center, Western Michigan University.

Stake, R. E. (1978). The case study method of social inquiry. *Educational Researcher, 7*(2), 5–8.

Stake, R. E., & Easley, J. A. (Eds.). (1978). *Case Studies in Science Education.* (Vols 1–2). National Science Foundation, Washington, DC: U.S. Government Printing Office. (ERIC Document Reproduction Service Nos. ED 166 058 and ED 166 059)

Stenzel, N. (1982). Committee hearings as an evaluation format. In N. L. Smith (Eds.), *Field assessments of innovative evaluation methods. New Directions for Program Evaluation, No. 13.* San Francisco: Jossey-Bass, Inc., Publishers.

Stock, W. A., Okun, M. A., Haring, M. J., Miller, W., Kenney, C., & Ceurvorst, R. W. (1982). Rigor in data synthesis: A case study of reliability in meta-analysis. *Educational Researcher, 11*(6), 10–14.

Strunk, W., & White, E. B. (1959). *The elements of style.* New York: Macmillan Publishing Co.

Stufflebeam, D. L. (1983). The CIPP model for program evaluation. In G. F. Madaus, M. Scriven, & D. L. Stufflebeam (Eds.), *Evaluation models: Viewpoints on educational and human services evaluation.* Boston: Kluwer-Nijhoff.

Stufflebeam, D. L., Foley, W. J., Gepart, W. J., Guba, E. E., Hammond, R. L., Merriman, H. O., & Provus, M. (1971). *Educational evaluation and decision-making.* Itasca, IL: F. E. Peacock.

Stufflebeam, D. L., & Shinkfield, A. J. (1985). *Systematic evaluation.* Boston: Kluwer-Nijhoff.

Tallmadge, G. K. (1977). *Ideabook: JDRP* (ERIC DL 48329). Washington, DC: U. S. Government Printing Office.

Talmage, H. (1982). Evaluation of programs. In H. E. Mitzel (Ed.), *Encyclopedia of educational research* (5th ed.). (pp. 595–610). New York: John Wiley & Sons, Inc.

Taylor, S. J., & Bogdan, R. C. (1984). *Qualitative research methods: The search for meanings* (2nd ed.). New York: John Wiley & Sons, Inc.

Thompson, M. S. (1980). *Benefit-cost analysis for program evaluation.* Cambridge, MA: Harvard University Press.

Travers, R. M. W. (1983). *How research has changed American schools.* Kalamazoo, MI: Mythos Press.

Turabian, K. L. (1987). *A manual for writers of term papers, theses, and dissertations* (5th ed.). Chicago: The University of Chicago Press.

Tyack, D. B. (1974). *The one best system: A history of American urban education.* Cambridge, MA: Harvard University Press.

Tyack, D. B. (1979). The high school as a social service agency: Historical perspectives of current policy issues. *Educational Evaluation and Policy Analysis, 1*(5), 45–57.

Tyler, R. W. (1942). General statement on evaluation. *Journal of Educational Research, 35,* 492–501.

Tyler, R. W. (1950). *Basic principles of curriculum and instruction.* Chicago: The University of Chicago Press.

Van Maanen, J. (1988). *Tales of the field: On writing ethnography.* Chicago: The University of Chicago Press.

Walberg, H. J. (1986). Synthesis of research on teaching. In M. Wittrock (Ed.). *Handbook of research on teaching. Third edition* (pp. 214–229). New York: Macmillan.

Walberg, H. J., Schiller, D., & Haertel, G. D. (1979). The quiet revolution in educational research. *Phi Delta Kappan, 61*(3), 179–183.

Walker, D. F., & Schaffarzick, J. (1974). Comparing curricula. *Review of Educational Research. 44*(1), 83–111.

Walker, D. K. (1973). *Socioemotional measures for preschool and kindergarten children.* San Francisco: Jossey-Bass, Inc., Publishers.

Warren, D. R. (1978). A past for the present. In D. R. Warren (Ed.), *History, education, public policy.* Berkeley, CA: McCutchan Publishers.

Wax, R. H. (1971). *Doing fieldwork: Warnings and advice.* Chicago: The University of Chicago Press.

Webb, E. J., Campbell, D. T., Schwartz, R. D., Sechrest, L., & Grove, J. B. (1981). *Nonreactive measures in the social sciences* (2nd ed.). Boston: Houghton Mifflin Co.

Whyte, W. F. (1955). *Street corner society: The social structure of an Italian slum* (2nd ed.). Chicago: The University of Chicago Press.

Wiersma, W. (1986). *Research methods in education: An introduction* (4th ed.) Boston: Allyn & Bacon, Inc.

Williams, D. D. (Ed.). (1986). *Naturalistic evaluation. New Directions for Program Evaluation, No. 30.* San Francisco: Jossey-Bass, Inc., Publishers.

Williams, J. M. (1981). *Style: Ten lessons in clarity and grace.* Glenview, IL: Scott, Foresman & Co.

Wilson, S. (1977). The use of ethnographic techniques in educational research. *Review of Educational Research, 47*, 245–265.

Wirt, F. M. (1980). Neoconservatism and national school policy. *Educational Evaluation and Policy Analysis, 2*(6), 5–18.

Wolcott, H. F. (1973). *The man in the principal's office: An ethnography.* New York: Holt, Rinehart & Winston.

Wolf, R. L. (1979). The use of judicial evaluation methods in the formulation of educational policy. *Educational Evaluation and Policy Analysis, 1*(3), 19–28.

Worthen, B. R., & Sanders, J. R. (1973). *Educational evaluation: Theory and practice.* Belmont, CA: Wadsworth, Inc.

Worthen, B. R., & Sanders, J. R. (1987). *Educational evaluation: Alternative approaches and practical guidelines.* New York: Longman, Inc.

Zeckhauser, R., & Stokey, E. (1978). *A primer for policy analysis.* New York: W. W. Norton.

Zinsser, W. (1980). *On writing well: An informal guide to writing nonfiction.* New York: Harper and Row, Publishers, Inc.

AUTHOR INDEX

SUBJECT INDEX

A-B-A-B single subject designs, 331, 335
  sample of, 333
A-B-A single subject designs, 330–31,
  332, 335
A-B single subject designs, 330, 331
Abstracting services *see* Reference
  services
Abstraction levels, in ethnographic
  data, 421, 427
Abstracts, 44, 47, 122–27, 131, 137
*Abstracts of Instructional and Research
  Materials in Vocational and
  Technical Education* (AIM/ARM),
  125–26
Accretion measures, 413
Accuracy, as standard for evaluation
  research, 477
Achievement tests, 251–52
Adequacy standards
  in analytical research, 464–65
  in ethnography, 425–27
  in evaluation research, 497–99
  in *ex post facto* designs, 341
  in literature reviews, 151–52
  in quasi-experimental designs, 340
  in single subject designs, 340–41
  in true experimental designs, 339–40
Adversary-oriented approaches, to
  evaluation research, 479
Affective instruments, 253–54
Alpha level, 351, 354; *see also* Level of
  significance
Alternate treatment posttest-only with
  nonequivalent group designs, 315
Ambiguity, in questionnaires, 257
American Digest System, 458, 459
American Jurisprudence, 457
American Law Reports (ALR), 457
American Statistical Index (ASI), 126, 445
Analyses, in analytical research, 439–41
Analysis of covariance (ANCOVA),
  365–68, 369
Analysis of variance (ANOVA),
  358–60, 361, 362, 369
Analytical explanations, 438–39
Analytical induction, 415

Analytical premises, of qualitative
  research, 189
Analytical research, 36, 39, 433–69
ANCOVA *see* Analysis of covariance
Annual Reviews of Psychology, 122
Anonymity, in research design, 322
ANOVA *see* Analysis of variance
Antecedent variables, 83
APA style manual, 513, 517, 518, 522,
  525, 526
Appendices, format of, 518, 522, 525
Applied research, 16, 19–20, 21, 25–26,
  275
Aptitude tests, 251
Archival collections, 275, 412–13
Artifact collections, 397, 411–13
Assigned variables, 303
Attenuation, 290
Attitude inventories, 253–54
Attitude research, 322
Attribute variables, 303
Availability sampling, 161

Background questions, in interviews, 408
Baseline conditions, 329, 330, 331–35
Basic research, 16, 18–19, 21, 25, 26, 275
Behavioral objectives, in evaluation
  research, 480–81
Beta weights, 286–87
Bias
  in analytical sources, 448
  control of, 42, 172
  in interviews, 266, 268
  in questionnaires, 256–57
  in research design, 158–59
  of researcher, 15, 176, 193, 194,
    273–74; *see also* Contamination
Bibliographies, citation of, 525
*A Bibliography of American Educational
  History*, 443
Black's Law Dictionary, 458
Boards of Education, guides to policies
  of, 456
Books in Print, 122
*Bouvier's Law Dictionary and Concise
  Encyclopedia*, 458